Frommer's®

SO-AYC-071

New York State
3rd Edition

by Neil E. Schlecht, Rich Beattie
& Brian Silverman

Here's what the critics say about Frommer's:

"Amazingly easy to use. Very portable, very complete."
—*Booklist*

"Detailed, accurate, and easy-to-read information for all price ranges."
—*Glamour Magazine*

"Hotel information is close to encyclopedic."
—*Des Moines Sunday Register*

"Frommer's Guides have a way of giving you a real feel for a place."
—*Knight Ridder Newspapers*

Wiley Publishing, Inc.

Published by: DEC 2 7 2007.

Wiley Publishing, Inc.

111 River St.
Hoboken, NJ 07030-5774

ISBN: 978-0-470-18182-9

Editor: Shelley W. Bance
Production Editor: Lindsay Conner
Cartographer: Nick Trotter
Photo Editor: Richard Fox
Production by Wiley Indianapolis Composition Services

Front cover photo: Heart Lake of the Adirondacks
Back cover photo: Niagara Falls; American Falls: Cave of the Winds tour; tourists in yellow slickers

For information on our other products and services or to obtain technical support, please contact our Customer Care Department within the U.S. at 800/762-2974, outside the U.S. at 317/572-3993 or fax 317/572-4002.

Wiley also publishes its books in a variety of electronic formats. Some content that appears in print may not be available in electronic formats.

Manufactured in the United States of America

5 4 3 2 1

3 9082 10775 1193

Contents

12 The North Country 363

by Rich Beattie

13 Western New York 391

by Rich Beattie

Index 422

List of Maps

An Invitation to the Reader

In researching this book, we discovered many wonderful places—hotels, restaurants, shops, and more. We're sure you'll find others. Please tell us about them, so we can share the information with your fellow travelers in upcoming editions. If you were disappointed with a recommendation, we'd love to know that, too. Please write to:

Frommer's New York State, 3rd Edition
Wiley Publishing, Inc. • 111 River St. • Hoboken, NJ 07030-5774

An Additional Note

Please be advised that travel information is subject to change at any time—and this is especially true of prices. We therefore suggest that you write or call ahead for confirmation when making your travel plans. The authors, editors, and publisher cannot be held responsible for the experiences of readers while traveling. Your safety is important to us, however, so we encourage you to stay alert and be aware of your surroundings. Keep a close eye on cameras, purses, and wallets, all favorite targets of thieves and pickpockets.

About the Authors

Neil E. Schlecht is a writer and photographer who travels frequently along the Hudson between an old farmhouse in northwestern Connecticut and New York City. He is the author of a dozen travel guides—including *Spain For Dummies* and Frommer's guides to Texas, Cuba, and Peru—as well as art catalogue essays and articles on art and culture.

Rich Beattie is a freelance writer who lives in New York City. Formerly the Managing Editor of *Travel Holiday Magazine* and Executive Editor of the adventure-travel site GORP.com, he now writes for *Travel + Leisure,* the *New York Times, Four Seasons Hotel Magazine, Boating Magazine,* and *Modern Bride,* among others.

Brian Silverman, author of *Frommer's New York City, Frommer's New York City from $90 a Day,* and *Portable New York City,* has written about travel, food, sports, and music for publications such as *Saveur, Caribbean Travel & Life, Islands, American Way,* the *New Yorker,* and the *New York Times.* He is the author of several books including *Going, Going, Gone: The History, Lore, and Mystique of the Home Run* (HarperCollins), and co-editor of *The Twentieth Century Treasury of Sports* (Viking Books). Brian lives in New York, New York, with his wife and son.

Other Great Guides for Your Trip:

Wonderful Weekends from New York City
Frommer's New York City
Frommer's Memorable Walks in New York City
Frommer's Irreverent Guide to New York City

Frommer's Star Ratings, Icons & Abbreviations

Every hotel, restaurant, and attraction listing in this guide has been ranked for quality, value, service, amenities, and special features using a **star-rating system.** In country, state, and regional guides, we also rate towns and regions to help you narrow down your choices and budget your time accordingly. Hotels and restaurants are rated on a scale of zero (recommended) to three stars (exceptional). Attractions, shopping, nightlife, towns, and regions are rated according to the following scale: zero stars (recommended), one star (highly recommended), two stars (very highly recommended), and three stars (must-see).

In addition to the star-rating system, we also use **seven feature icons** that point you to the great deals, in-the-know advice, and unique experiences that separate travelers from tourists. Throughout the book, look for:

Finds	Special finds—those places only insiders know about
Fun Fact	Fun facts—details that make travelers more informed and their trips more fun
Kids	Best bets for kids and advice for the whole family
Moments	Special moments—those experiences that memories are made of
Overrated	Places or experiences not worth your time or money
Tips	Insider tips—great ways to save time and money
Value	Great values—where to get the best deals

The following **abbreviations** are used for credit cards:

AE	American Express	DISC	Discover	V	Visa
DC	Diners Club	MC	MasterCard		

Frommers.com

Now that you have the guidebook to a great trip, visit our website at **www.frommers.com** for travel information on more than 3,600 destinations. With features updated regularly, we give you instant access to the most current trip-planning information available. At Frommers.com, you'll also find the best prices on airfares, accommodations, and car rentals—and you can even book travel online through our travel booking partners. At Frommers.com, you'll also find the following:

- Online updates to our most popular guidebooks
- Vacation sweepstakes and contest giveaways
- Newsletter highlighting the hottest travel trends
- Online travel message boards with featured travel discussions

What's New in New York State

Travel rates to New York State are up, and the area's many hot destinations continue to evolve and grow. Here are some highlights of the new developments.

PLANNING YOUR TRIP   Calendar of Events   A couple of major golf championships are frequently played in New York, and in June 2009 the **U.S. Open Golf Championship** (© 908/234-2300; www.usopen.com) will return, this time to **Bethpage State Park (Black Course)** in Farmingdale. See p. 29.

NEW YORK CITY   See chapter 5 for complete details. New York City continues to be the most visited city in the United States. A record 44 million visitors came to New York City in 2006 and the forecast is for 45.5 million in 2007.

Attractions   The beloved **Intrepid Sea, Air & Space Museum** was towed away for much-needed renovations in late 2006. The World War II vessel will be refurbished over the next year and areas of the ship that were hidden will be open to the public. While it's in dry dock, the outside of the ship will be repainted in classic battleship gray, and many of the military aircraft on its flight deck will be restored. Pier 86 will be entirely rebuilt as well. The ship should return and reopen by fall of 2008.

In the Bronx, a new **Yankee Stadium** is being built adjacent to the historic "House That Ruth Built." Will this one be the "House That Jeter Built?" Whatever it will be known as, the new stadium is scheduled to open for the 2009 season.

Not to be outdone by the Yankees, the Mets also broke ground on their own new stadium in Flushing, Queens, next to the crumbling **Shea Stadium** that it will replace. It should also be ready for the 2009 season. A name for the stadium has yet to be determined.

Where to Stay   To accommodate the influx of tourists, new hotels are sprouting all over the city. Many will be in areas not known for hotels, including NoHo, where **The Bowery Hotel,** 355 Bowery (© 212/505-9100; www.thebowery hotel.com), had a soft opening in mid-2007. With the same owners as The Maritime Hotel, The Bowery features loft-style rooms and modern conveniences such as flatscreen HDTVs, along with old-world European ambience.

Despite numerous delays, TriBeCa will finally get its signature hotel when actor Robert DeNiro's $43-million, 83-room **Downtown Hotel** in his beloved TriBeCa opens late in 2007.

After more than 2 years of renovations, **The Plaza** (© 212/546-5380) is scheduled to reopen in late 2007, albeit a bit smaller, with 350 rooms and 150 new residential units.

Where to Dine   New Yorkers crave red meat, or so one would assume with the opening of countless new steakhouses including **Kobe Steak, Quality Meats, Benjamin Steakhouse, Harry's Steaks,** and **Porter House New York.**

New York has also welcomed the arrival of two renowned European chefs. The notorious superchef Gordon Ramsay from London opened his restaurant **Gordon Ramsay at The London** in **The London NYC** hotel, 151 W. 54th St. (© **212/468-8888;** www.gordonramsay.com), and quickly earned two stars from the *New York Times.* Joel Robuchon from Paris opened **L'Atelier de Joel Robuchon** in the **Four Seasons Hotel** 57 E. 57th St. (© **212/350-6658**) and earned three *New York Times* stars.

LONG ISLAND & THE HAMPTONS
See chapter 6 for complete details.

Where to Stay The small **Jedediah Hawkins Inn,** 400 S. Jamesport Ave., Jamesport (© **631/722-2900**), claimed the title of best place to stay on the North Fork when it opened in 2006. Its six rooms, set in a historic house, are luxurious and exquisitely decorated.

Where to Dine The inn has crafted an excellent restaurant, **Jedediah's,** serving up rich, complex dishes in its formal dining room. In fact, the North Fork is really coming alive from a culinary point of view. Also new and exceptional is the **North Fork Table and Inn,** 57225 Main Rd., Southold (© **631/765-0177**), with chef Gerard Hayden brought in from New York City's Aureole to create dishes like a miso-glazed Montauk tilefish and a thyme-basted Long Island duck in a country inn setting. See p. 164.

HUDSON RIVER VALLEY See chapter 7 for complete details.

Where to Stay **Madalin Hotel** (© 845/757-2100; www.madalinhotel.com), a reincarnated 1909 hotel on the main drag in Tivoli, which is fast becoming a Hudson Valley destination, has opened to rave reviews.

Where to Dine An excellent new restaurant, **Madalin's Table** (© 845/757-2100), is connected to the new, albeit historic, Madalin Hotel in Tivoli. Broadway in tiny Tivoli has quickly become the restaurant row of the Upper Hudson Valley. See p. 222.

What to See & Do Staatsburgh (Mills Mansion) (© 845/889-8851; www.hvnet.com/houses/mills), one of the most notable Hudson River estates, is undergoing an extensive exterior and interior restoration expected to last several years; limited visits are by guided tour only. See p. 205. **Montgomery Place Historic Estate** (© 914/758-5461; www.hudsonvalley.org), another great Hudson estate, is currently closed for restoration but should reopen in 2008; until then, only self-guided tours of the grounds, on weekends, are possible. See p. 205.

CATSKILL MOUNTAIN REGION See chapter 8 for complete details. The Catskill region, particularly Sullivan and Delaware counties, was devastated by heavy rains and flooding in 2006 and 2007—totaling four catastrophic floods to hit the region in the past 3 years. FEMA declared three counties federal disaster areas. A number of local businesses, in addition to homes and roads, were severely damaged and forced to close, so some additional planning may be required in advance of a trip to the region. Each of the most damaging flood incidents was registered in June.

Plans for a $600-million **St. Regis Mohawk Casino** to be built at the Monticello Raceway in Sullivan County were approved by Governor Eliot Spitzer in February 2007, though a coalition of environmental and other groups, led by the Natural Resources Defense Council, filed a lawsuit demanding a comprehensive review of the full environmental impact of such a development in the sensitive Catskill Mountain region. It will likely be 2008 before a determination by the U.S. Secretary of the Interior is made. In 2001, New York State authorized the building of three Indian-administered casinos in Sullivan and/or Ulster counties, but only the Monticello project has progressed to the point of being awarded state approval.

Where to Stay   One of the most elegant hotels in upstate New York, the swanky **Emerson Resort & Spa,** (© 877/688-2828; www.emersonresort.com) in Mount Tremper, has reopened for business after being completely gutted by fire in 2005. The new incarnation was rebuilt across the street, next to Emerson Place and the Lodge, under the same ownership.

What to See & Do   The **Bethel Woods Center for the Arts,** 200 Hurd Rd., Bethel (© 866/781-2922; www.bethel woodslive.org), is on the grounds of the 1969 Woodstock concert and plays hosts to a wide range of mainstream rock, pop, jazz, and classical concerts, from Bob Dylan to the Boston Pops. By 2008, a **museum and interpretive center** that places Woodstock in its historical context should be finished, drawing nostalgic baby boomers from across the country.

SARATOGA SPRINGS   See chapter 9 for complete details.

Where to Stay   The **Saratoga Hotel & Conference Center** (© 866/937-7746; www.thesaratogahotel.com) is a new and large, handsomely styled, modern luxury hotel (actually it's a renovation of a previously existing hotel in downtown Saratoga, but with such a dramatic improvement it's as good as new).

Where to Dine   The French eatery **Chez Sophie** (© 518/583-3538) moved from its retro-styled diner outside town to stylish new modern digs at The Saratoga Hotel in downtown Saratoga. Though some of its oddball charm is gone, the restaurant remains one of the best upstate.

ALBANY   See chapter 9 for complete details.

Where to Dine   Longtime favorite **Yono's,** an unusual purveyor of upscale Indonesian cuisine, has found a new home at the Hampton Inn & Suites in downtown Albany, 25 Chapel St. (© 518/436-7747). See p. 283.

CENTRAL NEW YORK   See chapter 10 for complete details.

Where to Stay   This area finally has a world-class spa, with the opening of the Skaná Spa at **Turning Stone Resort,** 5218 Patrick Rd., Verona (© 800/771-7711). It has an authentic sweat lodge built by Native Americans, along with fresh herbal spa treatments.

THE FINGER LAKES REGION   See chapter 11 for complete details.

Getting There   The long-awaited Rochester–Toronto high-speed ferry remains mired in controversy and debt, and the dream of connecting the two cities by ferry remains exactly that.

What to See & Do   The beautiful **New York Wine & Culinary Center** (© 585/394-7070; www.nywcc.com) was inaugurated in 2006 on the north shore of Canandaigua Lake. The stunning complex contains a wine tasting room, New York Lounge restaurant and bar, and swanky instruction kitchen for cooking classes. The center's mission is to promote the agriculture, food, and wine of New York State, and it appears to be succeeding admirably. Finger Lakes wineries now number nearly 100, and one of the newest and most interesting is the tiny **Damiani Wine Cellars** (© 607/546-5557; www.damianiwinecellars.com), in Hector on the east side of Seneca Lake. The family-owned winery produced its first vintage in 2004, and the cabernet franc and meritage are quite notable for its young age. This is one to watch. Or drink.

Where to Stay   Two small inns that opened in 2007 near Keuka and Canandaigua lakes, in the western section of the Finger Lakes, are among the finest B&Bs in the state. **The Chalet of**

Canandaigua (© 585/394-9080; www. chaletbandb.com), with just three massive, tricked-out rooms, is like a secluded Alpine-style luxury cottage. The **Black Sheep Inn** (© 607/569-3767; www.stay blacksheepinn.com), in Hammondsport, is one of the few remaining octagon houses from the mid–19th century; it has five very stylish rooms and a chef and owner dedicated to organic and green practices. Even more curious is the new inn by the founders and erstwhile owners of the ceramics maker MacKenzie-Childs; their B&B, **Home Again** (© 315/364-8615; www.stayhomeagain.blogspot.com), in King Ferry, on the east side of Cayuga Lake, has all the oddball flavor and decor you would expect. Another fine new B&B to open in the past couple of years is **The Fox and the Grapes** (© 607/582-7528; www.thefoxandthegrapes.com), in Lodi on the east bank of Seneca Lake, near some of the region's best wineries and restaurants. See p. 319.

Where to Dine   The **Simply Red Bistro** (© 607/532-9401), a creative little restaurant, has moved from its bohemian digs in Trumansburg and set up shop, now larger and more "uptown," at the Sheldrake Point Winery, in Ovid, on the west bank of Cayuga Lake. One of the region's most distinguished new restaurants is **Dano's Heuriger** (© 607/582-7555), a modern take on a Viennese wine tavern, overlooking Seneca Lake. See p. 321.

BUFFALO & NIAGARA FALLS   See chapter 13 for complete details. Buffalo is still trying to turn its fortunes around, which will certainly be helped by new developments downtown.

Where to Dine   Buffalo has seen the opening of an excellent new restaurant, **Tempo,** 581 Delaware Ave. (© 716/885-1594).

Where to Stay   Nearby in Niagara Falls, the building frenzy—started by the opening of Canadian casinos a few years ago—continues today. The newish **Embassy Suites,** 6700 Fallsview Blvd. (© 800/420-6980), is currently the tallest hotel, at 42 floors (with the kind of dramatic views you'd expect), and the new Hilton that's under construction is slated to go even higher. But the biggest news is from the American side, with the full opening of the **Seneca Niagara Casino & Hotel,** 310 Fourth St. (© 877/873-6322). The most luxurious hotel on this side of the falls, it gives any area hotel a run for its money. What it lacks in a full-on view of the falls it makes up for with dramatic decor, comfortable accommodations, a spa, and several great restaurants (in addition to the gambling, of course). See p. 417.

1

The Best of New York State

Visitors to New York State who venture both downstate and upstate have an array of options unequaled elsewhere in the country. Besides the urban allure, culture, and shopping of Manhattan, much of New York State is still, in many ways, waiting to be discovered on a grand scale. The state is endowed with outstanding beauty and diversity of scenery from one end to the other. Although New Yorkers have long vacationed in the Catskill and Adirondack mountains, and at Long Island beaches, most have seen too little of the state between its tourist bookends, New York City and Niagara Falls. The historic Hudson Valley, a majestic river lined with elegant estates, is finally positioning itself as a destination, not just a day trip from the city. The great wilderness of the Adirondack and Catskill mountains is magnificent for outdoors and sporting vacations, but those spots are also home to the easygoing charms of small towns. The pristine glacial-lake beauty and outstanding wineries of the Finger Lakes make it one of the state's most spectacular, yet lesser-known destinations. And Long Island is home to splendid sandy Atlantic Ocean beaches, but also the gulf of New York economic extremes, ranging from blue-collar immigrant enclaves to palatial summer homes in the Hamptons.

Planning a trip to a state as large and diverse as New York involves a lot of decision making, so in this chapter we've tried to give some direction. Below we've chosen what we feel is the very best the state has to offer—the places and experiences you won't want to miss. Although sites and activities listed here are written up in more detail elsewhere in this book, this chapter should give you an overview of New York State's highlights and get you started planning your trip.

—*Neil E. Schlecht*

1 The Best Hotels

- The **Ritz-Carlton New York, Central Park,** 50 Central Park South (© **212/308-9100**): The combination of a great location across from Central Park, large well-outfitted rooms, and excellent Ritz-Carlton service is as good as it gets. See p. 96.
- **Casablanca Hotel,** 147 W. 43rd St. (© **888/922-7225**): In the Theater District, the Casablanca not only offers clean, well-outfitted rooms at value rates, but also includes extras like complimentary breakfast, bottled water,

free high-speed Internet access, and a lovely roof deck perfect for a cocktail on a balmy evening. See p. 98.
- **Seatuck Cove House** (Eastport; © 631/325-3300): On the edge of the Hamptons, this enormous Victorian home sits right out on the water with gorgeous views. Because the inn has only five rooms, you'll feel like you own the place. The rooms are painted white and decorated with an appropriately beachy decor. Four of the five are also large enough to comfortably

New York State

Legend:
- **86** Interstate
- **90** Toll Highway
- **62** US Highway
- State Road
- ⚝ State/Province Capital
- ✪ National Capital

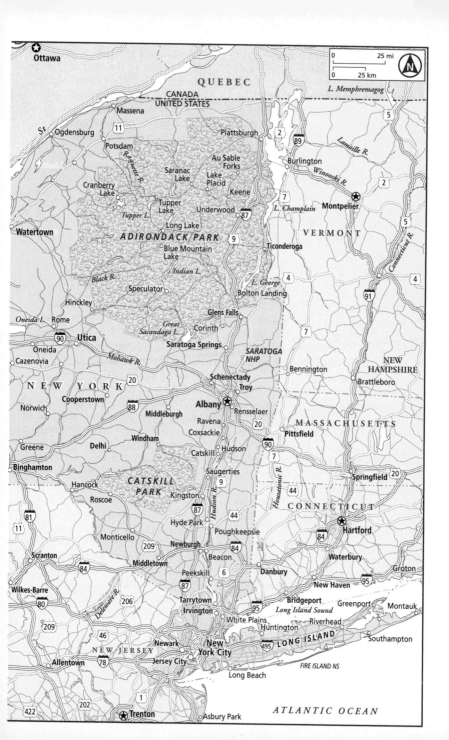

accommodate a separate sitting area. Take a walk along the waterfront or a dip in the pool, then grab one of the best B&B breakfasts on Long Island. See p. 175.

- **Mohonk Mountain House** (Lake Mohonk; © 800/772-6646): A legendary Victorian castle perched on a ridge overlooking the Catskill region's Shawangunk Mountains, the Mohonk Mountain House is more than a hotel; it's a destination unto itself. Still in the hands of the original family, the whimsical lodge lives up to its exalted reputation, earned over the past 130 years. In the midst of the 6,400-acre Mohonk Forest Preserve, its setting is beyond compare and outdoor activities include something for everyone. Rooms are decorated in Edwardian, Victorian, or Arts and Crafts style, and the massive place is loaded with fireplaces and pretty nooks. See p. 232.

- **Emerson Resort & Spa** (Mt. Tremper; © 877/688-2828): Rebuilt after a devastating fire, this chic inn and spa hotel lost some of its exoticism but none of its sleek elegance, which remains a rarity in the Catskill Mountains. Its sybaritic spa and restaurant are unequaled in the region, making this a perfect place for big-city types who want to be in the country, but not in rustic lodgings. See p. 232.

- **The Saratoga Hotel & Conference Center** (Saratoga Springs; © 866/937-7746): Saratoga is loaded with charming Victorian B&Bs, but until recently it didn't have anything approaching a modern luxury hotel. This large and chic, newly remodeled business hotel, right on the main drag, fills that niche nicely, and it has one of upstate's best restaurants to boot: the relocated Chez Sophie bistro. See p. 269.

- **The Otesaga** (Cooperstown; © 800/348-6222): The grande dame of central New York, dating from 1909, sits grandly on the shores of Lake Otsego. While renovations have brought bathrooms and air-conditioning into the 21st century, the hotel is firmly rooted in the past, maintaining its historic feel with high ceilings, heavy wooden doors, and formal furniture. Still, with a plethora of patios and balconies, along with a renowned golf course and plenty of watersports, this seasonal hotel is focused on the equally gorgeous outdoors that surround it. See p. 291.

- **Aurora Inn** (Aurora; © 866/364-8808): A mid-19th-century inn saved from demolition and given a glorious new life, this small boutique hotel is the centerpiece of a sweet little town on the east bank of Cayuga Lake. Although small, the inn has the superb service and style of a luxury hotel, as well as stunning water views, rooms that are models of graceful interior design, and one of the most elegant restaurants in the Finger Lakes. See p. 312.

- **Sherwood Inn** (Skaneateles; © 800/3-SHERWOOD): Occupying a prime position in the most delightful town in the Finger Lakes, this longtime small hotel—a stagecoach stop from the early 19th century—looks out onto Skaneateles Lake and exudes a relaxed, genteel feel. The old staircase, wide-plank floorboards, and colorfully designed rooms may seem old-world and old-money, but travelers can stay for moderate prices. It also features a very nice restaurant and tavern, both of which look out onto the lake. See p. 357.

- **The Point** (Saranac Lake; © 800/255-3530): A former Rockefeller Great Camp, this exclusive, secluded retreat overlooking Saranac Lake is today the ultimate in wilderness indulgence. Huge rooms are decked out with touches like enormous stone fireplaces, but it's the all-inclusive, satisfy-any-request character of this 11-room camp that really makes it a special experience. Have a gourmet lunch aboard their boat or at a remote cabin, go water-skiing, watch the chefs at work, enjoy the open bar, trade tales around the nightly bonfire, or just hide out in the rustic ambience of your room. See p. 377.

- **Lake Placid Lodge** (Lake Placid; © 877/523-2700): Awash in rustic luxury, the lodge is the quintessential Adirondacks experience. Sitting on the shores of secluded Lake Placid, this exclusive getaway features meticulous and personalized service, along with rooms filled with one-of-a-kind pieces of furniture, many built by local artists from birch or cedar (and for sale!). With lots of quiet nooks and a gorgeous stone patio, you can grab your own corner of the 'dacks and feel like you have the place to yourself. See p. 376.

- **The Sagamore** (Lake George; © 800/358-3585): One of the last grand Adirondack lodges still standing, this 1883 hotel sits on its own island in Lake George and comes with a stellar restaurant, a great spa, a terrific golf course, a wonderful waterfront, and loads of amenities. While a conference area keeps it open in the winter, this is mostly a summertime resort, where you'll have your pick of room styles, restaurants (there are six), and activities—and you can always just grab an Adirondack chair and sit out on the patio overlooking the lake. See p. 369.

- **The Mansion on Delaware** (Buffalo; © 716/886-3300): This renovated mansion on Millionaire's Row blends in so well with the gorgeous private homes around it that you'd never even guess it was a hotel. Inside, you'll find ultramodern (but comfy) furniture, luxurious (and huge) bathrooms, and ultrapersonalized service. Rooms have been styled around the existing mansion, creating unique spaces in the city's most unique property. See p. 398.

2 The Best Inns & B&Bs

- **Buttermilk Falls Inn & Spa** (Milton-on-Hudson; © 877/746-6772): Secluded among 70 acres along the Hudson River, this soothing boutique hotel is an excellent choice to get away from it all or to use as a base for exploring the Hudson Valley or the eastern edges of the Catskills. Part historic inn (the main house is a 1764 Colonial), part posh day spa, and part rustic retreat—with wooded trails, waterfalls and ponds, gardens, and separate cottage houses—there's something for almost everyone. Rooms are elegant without being fussy. See p. 210.

- **The Inn at Lake Joseph** (Forestburgh; © 845/791-9506): A first-class country estate in the southeastern quadrant of the Catskill region, this secluded Victorian inn is elegant and peaceful. It has manor house rooms in a 19th-century summer getaway, as well as splurge-friendly carriage and cottage houses that are more like princely private apartments. See p. 254.

- **The Morgan State House** (Albany; © 888/427-6063): One doesn't ordinarily expect elegance and luxury from the gritty state capital, which has few decent hotels, but this small inn goes against conventional wisdom. A lovely 1888 town house on "Mansion Row," it features spacious rooms that are as luxuriously appointed as any five-star hotel. But it's much more intimate and has more flair, with beautiful 19th-century period details, antiques, and extraordinary linens and bedding.

While sipping coffee in the serene interior garden courtyard, you'll never realize how many trench-coated bureaucrats and lobbyists hover just down the street. See p. 282.

- **Hillcrest Manor** (Corning; © 607/936-4548): A refined B&B in a gateway town to the Finger Lakes, this gorgeous 1890 Greek Revival mansion is just minutes from the world-renowned Corning Museum of Glass in a peaceful residential neighborhood. The opulent inn, owned by two art collectors, has tasteful parlors and very spacious bedrooms. Few inns can match this level of sophistication and luxury, and fewer still match the relatively affordable prices you'll find here. See p. 324.

- **Hobbit Hollow Farm B&B** (Skaneateles; © 315/685-2791): Overlooking graceful Skaneateles Lake, this sumptuous and intimate small inn gives you a chance to make believe that you're a privileged country gentleman or -woman relaxing on your horse farm. The century-old Colonial Revival, ensconced on 400 acres with panoramic lake views, is as luxurious and attentive to detail as they come. Rooms are charmingly elegant; for those on a budget, the smaller rooms are a decent value and you can still imagine yourself the prince of Skaneateles. See p. 357.

- **The Mansion Inn of Saratoga** (Rock City Falls/Saratoga Springs; © 888/996-9977): This sophisticated 1866 Victorian inn sits on 4 acres just outside Saratoga Springs and is replete with luxurious details, both in common rooms and in the spacious accommodations. The owners are serious about high-end pampering, making it an ideal weekend getaway. See p. 269.

- **Black Sheep Inn** (Hammondsport; (© 607/569-3767): A new arrival to the Finger Lakes is this inn occupying a rare 1859 octagon house, immaculately restored and converted by the young owners, one of whom is a chef devoted to organic cooking and the other an interior designer. The house is lavishly outfitted, but not at all fussy. The location, in a pretty, small town near beautiful Keuka Lake, is a bonus. See p. 332.

- **The Chalet of Canandaigua** (Canandaigua; © 585/394-9080): This tiny luxury inn has enormous rooms of immense style, a surprise within the walls of a unique log cabin. Equipped to the nines, it's a perfect blend of rusticity and stylish warmth, with no detail overlooked. Whatever the season, this chalet makes a dignified retreat. See p. 336.

3 The Best Restaurants

- **Aquavit** (New York City; © 212/307-7311): The Scandinavian seafood dishes here will frequent your daydreams. The restaurant moved from its intimate town house setting, but the food and service are just as spectacular, if not better. Enjoy the herring plate with a glass of Aquavit (distilled liquors not unlike vodka, flavored with fruit and spices) and a frosty Carlsberg beer. See p. 115.

- **Peter Luger** (Great Neck; © 516/487-8800): Hands down, this is one of the best steakhouses in the country. People flock here for one thing and one thing only: porterhouse. In fact, if you try to order anything else (or even ask for a menu), you'll likely get a quizzical stare from your waiter. The dry-aged meat comes brushed with a tasty glaze and is tender enough to make vegetarians reconsider. See p. 156.

- **Culinary Institute of America (CIA)** (Hyde Park; © 845/471-6608): The most elite training ground in the country for chefs has not one, but four on-campus restaurants run by students—but they're a far cry from what college students typically eat. Choose the sophisticated Escoffier Restaurant (French), Ristorante Caterina de Medici (Italian), American Bounty Restaurant (regional American), or St. Andrew's Café (casual). You'll be impressed and unsurprised that so many of America's finest restaurants have CIA chefs at the helm. Plan ahead, though, because reservations are about as tough to come by as admission to the school. See p. 212.

- **The Valley Restaurant at The Garrison** (Garrison; © 845/424-2339): Ensconced within the gently rolling grounds of a golf course high above the Hudson Valley, this understated but quietly creative restaurant has quickly become one of the finest in the valley. Its seasonal American menu features the best from local Hudson Valley farms, and its wine cellar is peerless in the region. While golfers munch on simple fare next door at World's End Bar, the dining room draws foodies from New York City and around the region who are anxious to check out this buzz restaurant. See p. 198.

- **Terrapin Restaurant** (Rhinebeck; © 845/876-3330): Chef/owner Josh Kroner ambitiously adds creative Mexican and Asian accents to American cuisine in this popular restaurant that inhabits a 19th-century church in the quaint village of Rhinebeck. There's fine dining in the evenings on one side, and a casual bistro on the other, and the well-thought-out wine list is as good as they come in the Hudson Valley. See p. 212.

- **Depuy Canal House** (High Falls; © 845/687-7700): A fabulously creative restaurant in a lovely, rambling 200-year-old stone tavern in the Catskills, Depuy Canal House is the longtime standard-bearer in this part of upstate New York. It draws foodies from New York City and around the state for elegant and surprising selections served in a perfectly elegant but rustic setting. If you've brought an empty stomach and full wallet, check out the four- or seven-course prix-fixe dinners; otherwise, drop in to the more casual downstairs bistro in the wine cellar. See p. 237.

- **Chez Sophie** (Saratoga Springs; © 518/583-3538): Having made the leap from a 1950s stainless steel diner outside of town to a large luxury hotel downtown, Sophie's hasn't suffered. It remains a charming French bistro and one of the best restaurants upstate. The original Sophie became something of a local culinary legend, and her son is now the chef, continuing his mom's simple but refined approach. One of the best bargains around is the "pink plate special," a three-course meal for just $30. See p. 271.

- **Alex & Ika** (Cooperstown; © 607/547-4070): This couple recently took the plunge, moving their tiny restaurant into Cooperstown from nearby Cherry Valley and expanding the space and hours. Fortunately, the food has lost none of its punch—it's still packed with so many flavor combinations that you'll be talking about your dinner long after you leave. With a menu that changes weekly, it's hard to believe they can hit a home run with every dish, but somehow they do. See p. 292.

- **Suzanne Fine Regional Cuisine** (Hector; © 607/582-7545): Suzanne's looks like a harbinger of the future in the Finger Lakes—fine dining to accompany the region's swiftly improving wines. Meticulously crafted American food, using the finest local ingredients, is the calling card at this sophisticated but relaxed country-elegant spot, in an old farmhouse with swoon-worthy views of Seneca Lake. Locals consider it *the* place for a special dinner. See p. 320.

- **The Dining Room at Mirbeau Inn & Spa** (Skaneateles; © 877/MIRBEAU): Though part of a stylish and swanky spa boutique hotel in Skaneateles, this restaurant manages to shine in its own right. The romantic grounds evoke the Provence countryside, and the dining room wouldn't be out of place in that region of sophisticated eaters. The prix-fixe menus are calibrated to show off the young chef's creativity and artfully prepared dishes. See p. 358.

- **The Bistro at Red Newt Cellars** (Hector; © 607/546-4100): At the forefront of the movement to focus on the bounty of local farms, this terrific and creative bistro restaurant is also keen on matching food with local wines. And why not, since the restaurant is intrinsically connected to one of the Finger Lakes' better wineries (which not coincidentally is run by the chef's husband). Try a wine flight and some imaginative dishes from Debra: Red Newt is the perfect place to explore all that's great

about Finger Lakes gastronomy. See p. 320.

- **Dano's Heuriger** (Lodi; © 607/582-7555): A radical departure from what one might expect to find along the shore of one of the Finger Lakes, this Austrian restaurant, a modern version of a Viennese wine garden, is nonetheless perfectly at home. The menu encourages diners to sample small plates and unique tastes, which pair perfectly with the local wines (or Austrian varietals, such as Grüner Veltliner). As at nearby Red Newt, the proprietors are a husband-wife team. See p. 321.

- **Tempo** (Buffalo; © 716/885-1594): This newcomer has quickly risen to the top of the city's dining scene with a creative Italian menu and a modern, romantic setting. The inventive food is dramatically presented, but dig in and you'll see that Tempo will be no flash in the pan. See p. 399.

- **The View** (Mirror Lake Inn, Lake Placid; © 518/523-2544): This top-notch inn has always served up some of the best dishes in the Adirondacks, and with its change from black tie to casually clad servers, it fits in better with the area's laid-back atmosphere. Meals are consistently excellent, so whether you order meat or fish, you won't be disappointed. Best of all, they come with a gorgeous view out over Mirror Lake. See p. 379.

4 The Best Places for Antiques Hounds

- **Greenport:** This bustling hub out on Long Island's North Fork attracts all kinds of visitors, but antiques hunters will be especially satisfied. Here is one of the best selections of antiques reflecting the old seafaring world on the North Fork. See chapter 6.

- **Jamesport:** You may miss tiny Jamesport, on Long Island's North Fork, if you blink, but keep your eyes open

long enough and you'll see a Main Street lined with antiques shops. There's the usual assortment of furniture and books, and a selection of nautical items to remind you of the area's history as a fishing community. See chapter 6.

- **Locust Valley:** Most antiques hunters head to Port Jefferson, farther east on Long Island's north shore. And that's exactly why you should hit this tiny town that's not even on many maps—the goods are less picked over and the antiques are of excellent quality. See chapter 6.

- **Hudson:** This formerly run-down town along the Upper Hudson has exploded with high-end and eclectic antiques shops, making it *the* antiquing destination of the Hudson River Valley (indeed of any place in the state north of Manhattan). Almost all the dealers are confined to the long stretch of Warren Street, making it ideal for window-shopping. See chapter 7.
- **Bloomfield Antique Country Mile:** Just west of Canandaigua, this mile-long cluster of antiques dealers along

routes 5 and 20 in Bloomfield is one of the best concentrations for antiquing in the Finger Lakes, with several multidealer shops lined up back-to-back. See chapter 11.

- **East Aurora:** This town outside Buffalo hosts a wealth of craftspeople, not technically sellers of antiques, who make furniture in the 100-year-old style of famed builder Elbert Hubbard. His movement of Roycrofters created some of the sturdiest and most beautiful pieces of wooden furniture anywhere, and while it's possible to find originals, you'll more likely find work from the expert builders who follow Hubbard's style. See chapter 13.

5 The Best Hikes

- **Mashomack Preserve, Shelter Island:** With more than 2,000 pristine acres in the southeastern part of the island, this preserve, run by the Nature Conservancy, is about as remote as you can get on Long Island. There are 11 miles of easy hiking trails that run through the oak woodlands, marshes, ponds, and creeks. Keep an eye out for osprey, ibis, foxes, harbor seals, and terrapins. See chapter 6.
- **Hudson River Valley:** Though the Hudson Valley is more hilly than mountainous, tucked in the southern highlands are several excellent spots for day hikes. Hudson Highlands State Park near Cold Spring has a number of great day trails, as do Bear Mountain and Harriman state parks, some following a section of the Appalachian Trail. Many are surprisingly challenging. See chapter 7.
- **Catskill Region:** Some of the most scenic hiking in New York State is through the dense forests and along the stony ridges lacing the Catskills,

where there are nearly three dozen peaks above 3,500 feet. The 6,000-acre Mohonk Preserve, part of the Shawangunk Mountains, has 60 miles of trails. Nearby Minnewaska State Park Preserve offers another 12,000 acres perfect for hiking and mountain biking, with 30 miles of footpaths and carriageways. See chapter 8.

- **Southern Adirondacks:** How adventuresome are you feeling? Head to Lake George for a crazy steep climb up Black Mountain, an 8.5-mile round-trip with a 1,100-foot vertical rise and some amazing views of the lake and mountains. If you want a great view without so much work, Bald Mountain, east of Old Forge, is also steep but much shorter (2 miles round-trip). For a hike back in the woods, check out Cascade Lake, just north of Eagle Bay. It's an easy 5-mile walk to the lake that takes you past a gorgeous waterfall. See chapter 12.
- **Northern Adirondacks:** New York State's highest peak is Mount Marcy,

at 5,344 feet. It's not the easiest climb, but for anyone with aspirations to nab the state's highest spot, it's a must. Just watch out for crowds: Most people hike to the peak from the north, but take the Range Trail and you'll find fewer people and better views along the way. For an easier hike, check out High Falls Gorge, which offers a great and easy stroll along the Ausable River and past waterfalls. See chapter 12.

- **Letchworth State Park:** This western New York park is home to a stunning 400-foot-deep gorge, with all sorts of hiking trails taking you past views of the deep chasm that's cut by the Genesee River. There, trails go either deep into the forest or along the rim of the canyon; the Gorge Trail hits the most scenic spots. It's a 7-mile trail one-way, and moderately difficult, but, of course, you can turn around at any time. Take the kids along the Pond Trail, an easy .75-mile walk that leads you to a small pond stocked with fish. See chapter 13.

6 The Best Family Vacation Spots

- **Shelter Island:** Hardly the raging party scene that exists in the nearby Hamptons, Shelter Island makes for a quiet family retreat on the eastern end of Long Island. Hike, boat, or just relax. And since it's an island, there are very few ways to escape, meaning that—for better or worse— on this family vacation, you'll always be together. See chapter 6.

- **Mount Tremper & Phoenicia:** This spot in the southeastern Catskills— two small towns bunched together off the main road—serves up a surprising roster of activities for families. In Mount Tremper, at Catskill Corners, the Kaatskill Kaleidoscope Theatre is the world's largest kaleidoscope, occupying an old barn silo. In Phoenicia, just a couple of miles up the road, families can rent inner tubes and float down Esopus Creek, which slices the valley between towering mountains. The Catskill Mountain Railroad runs along Esopus Creek from the Mount Pleasant depot to Phoenicia's 1910 station. See chapter 8.

- **Healing Waters Farm/Delaware & Ulster Railride:** A fantastic farm in Walton, in the northeastern Catskills, Healing Waters overflows with cool things for kids. Its petting zoo, Little Boy Blue Animal Land, has an amazing array of gregarious animals, including camels, llamas, emus, and baby goats, and the farm holds all kinds of special events as well as hayrides. In Arkville, the Delaware & Ulster Railride transports visitors through the Catskill Mountains in a historic train that departs from the old depot. Kids will especially love the special "Great Train Robbery" train, where costumed actors playfully hijack and "rob" the train. See chapter 8.

- **Saratoga Springs:** This genteel resort town welcomes families with its plenitude of parks, the Saratoga Children's Museum, and Saratoga Spa State Park, a huge and lovely urban park with miles of hiking trails, swimming pools, and a skating rink. But surely the most entertaining feature for kids is the Saratoga Race Course and the opportunity to attend a thoroughbred horse race. Kids can take a walking tour of the stables, learn how horses and jockeys prepare for races, and even dress up like a jockey. See chapter 9.

- **Rochester:** As the northeastern gateway to the Finger Lakes, this amiable upstate city overflows with fine family activities. With Lake Ontario beaches, a 96-foot urban waterfall in the High Falls Historic District, and proximity to watersports at any of the Finger Lakes, it has plenty of good outdoor pastimes. But it also has three indoor spots with huge appeal to families, including the Strong Museum, one of the top children's museums in the country; the George Eastman House, a museum of photography in the home belonging to the founder of Kodak; and Genesee Country Village & Museum, a re-creation of a 19th-century village staffed by interpreters in period costume. See chapter 11.
- **Skaneateles:** This charming village at the north shore of the Finger Lake of the same name has tons of shops, restaurants, and inns that parents will love, but also plenty of activities for the entire family. In summer, children are sure to love the nostalgic long pier that extends over the water, as well as swimming and boating in one of the state's most beautiful lakes.

But best of all are the winter holidays, when Skaneateles comes alive with a Dickens Christmas celebration, with costumed Dickens characters taking over the streets, singing Christmas carols. A good excursion from Skaneateles is the easy drive into Syracuse to visit the Museum of Science & Technology (MOST), whose excellent interactive exhibits and IMAX theater are huge hits with kids. See chapter 11.
- **Lake George:** This southern Adirondacks town is hardly a calm getaway in the summer, but it boasts distractions galore for kids, including amusement parks, haunted houses, family restaurants, and all the lake swimming you can handle. See chapter 12.
- **Niagara Falls:** It isn't just for honeymooners anymore—it's also jammed with families. The famous cascading water appeals to people of all ages, and you can see it from high above, behind, or way down below on the ever-popular *Maid of the Mist.* But over on the Canadian side in the Clifton Hill area is where your kids will really want to go: There you'll find haunted houses, rides, and fun museums. See chapter 13.

7 The Best Places for Watersports

- **North Fork:** The protected waters of Long Island Sound (to the north of the fork) and Peconic Bay (to the south) make for the perfect place to head out with a boat. Whether it's a canoe, kayak, jet ski, or powerboat, you'll cruise around on relatively calm waters while keeping an eye out for herons, osprey, hawks, fish, and turtles. See chapter 6.
- **Hudson River:** One of the best ways to see the Hudson River, America's first highway and one of the great rivers in the nation, is from the middle of it: on a boat. You can board a sightseeing cruise at Rondout Landing in

Kingston on the *Rip Van Winkle,* or in Newburgh on *The Pride of the Hudson,* or take a sunset cruise aboard *Doxie,* a 31-foot sloop, or a traditional-style yacht. See chapter 7.
- **Delaware River:** The western Catskills are one of North America's top fishing destinations, drawing serious anglers from around the world. Fly-fishing is legendary along the Delaware River and nearby Beaverkill and Willowemoc trout streams. The junction pool at Hancock, where the east and west branches join to form the main stem of the Delaware River, has long been celebrated for its preponderance of

massive brown and rainbow trout. Pepacton Reservoir, also in the western Catskills, is perfect for open-water brown trout fishing. See chapter 8.

- **Finger Lakes & Erie Canal:** The gorgeous Finger Lakes are incredibly scenic spots for boating, water-skiing, and sailing. Seneca Lake has a picture-perfect port where you can hire a yacht or sailboat, including a vintage 1930 schooner yacht. At Keuka Lake, considered by many locals to be the prettiest of the Finger Lakes, there are boat cruises aboard the *Keuka Maid.* At several Finger Lakes, you can also rent kayaks and canoes if you're looking for an even more intimate experience on the water. Skaneateles Lake has one of the longest cruise boat traditions in the region, and the lake is perfect for relaxed sightseeing and dinner cruises. See chapter 11.

- **Alexandria Bay, Thousand Islands:** The miles-wide St. Lawrence River, dotted with somewhere between 1,000 and 1,800 islands, comes tailor-made for watersports. Tool around in a powerboat, canoe, or kayak and check out the castles and mansions that some of America's wealthiest families have built. Just watch out for tankers and other big ships—this is one of America's busiest shipping lanes! See chapter 12.

- **Lake George:** Peppered with islands small and large, 32-mile-long Lake George offers endless exploration, whether you're in a canoe, kayak, powerboat, or paddle-wheel tour boat. Get out and experience the thrill of water-skiing, or just kick back and paddle quietly along the shores. Rent boats in the town of Lake George or in Bolton Landing. See chapter 12.

- **Mirror Lake, Lake Placid:** This lake, surrounded by the gorgeous peaks of the Adirondacks, comes to life in the summer with all kinds of boats plying the waters. The only drawback is that while it's superconvenient (Lake Placid sits right above it), it can get a little too crowded. See chapter 12.

8 The Best One-of-a-Kind Experiences

- **Walking the Brooklyn Bridge:** One of the great New York activities of all time. The skyline view heading toward Manhattan from Brooklyn is unparalleled. The walk takes 20 to 40 minutes, depending on your pace, and every minute on this 19th-century architectural marvel is exhilarating. See chapter 5.

- **Sleeping in a Historic Lighthouse:** Several hotels tout their proximity to the Hudson River, but in the Upper Hudson Valley, you can sleep at the 1869 Saugerties Lighthouse (© 845/ 247-0656), which functions as a B&B and is perched at water's edge. The only way to get to it is by walking a mile-long trail through woods and wetlands. See chapter 8.

- **Reliving America's Glory Days:** Vintage "base ball," a nostalgic sport played by old-school traditionalists partial to the 19th-century rules and uniforms of America's classic sport, is played in several parts of New York. In Roxbury, in the northwest Catskill region, locals take it especially seriously. The best time to see a game is on Labor Day, when the Roxbury Nine hosts a home game and the town celebrates "Turn of the Century Day." Locals turn out in period costume, and the opposing team arrives by vintage train. See chapter 8.

- **Attending a Baseball Hall of Fame Induction Ceremony:** Every July, a new generation of players is transformed from mortal to legendary as inductees take their place alongside Babe Ruth, Lou Gehrig, and the other greats in Cooperstown's Hall of Fame. See chapter 10.

- **Gorging on Grape Pie in Naples, Finger Lakes Region:** There's a reason why grape pie hasn't earned a spot alongside apple, cherry, and peach in the pie pantheon: It's just too laborious to peel the grapes. But every year on the last weekend in September, the attractive little village of Naples near Keuka Lake becomes the grape-pie capital of the world; nearly everyone seems to be selling, buying, and eating them. Grape fanatics and pie pilgrims come from all over to attend the Naples Grape Festival and stuff themselves silly with grape pie. See chapter 11.

- **Soaring the Friendly Skies:** The Finger Lakes are gorgeous from any angle, but a bird's-eye perspective—in a vintage warplane or a silent glider plane—is one of the most unique experiences to be had in New York State. At the National Warplane Museum, near Elmira, you can take to the sky in a PT-17 or even a B-17 bomber. And at the nearby National Soaring Museum, visitors can climb aboard sailplanes for peaceful, quiet rides that soar above the valleys around Corning. See chapter 11.

- **Ice-Skating on the Olympic Rink, Lake Placid:** Slip on your silver skates and take to the same rink where Eric Heiden won his gold medals in the 1980 Olympics. It's a public rink, so there's no pressure to race, just glide at your leisure while taking in the majesty of the surrounding Adirondacks. See chapter 12.

- **Eating Chicken Wings in the Place They Were Invented:** It was a snowy night back in the '60s when the owners of Buffalo's Anchor Bar dumped some chicken parts into a deep fryer and served them with blue cheese and celery. The rest, as they say, is history. You can still sample the original recipe in the divey bar where they became an American staple. See p. 400.

- **Watching Fireworks over Niagara Falls:** On the Canadian side of the falls every Friday and Sunday from May to September, there's a concert from 8 to 10pm, followed by an amazing show as the sky lights up with fireworks and colored lights shine on the cascading water. Not going during the summer? No worries: You can see the falls lit up every night of the year. Walk along the railing of the Canadian side for the best view. See chapter 13.

9 The Best Historic Places

- **Grand Central Terminal.** Despite all the steel-and-glass skyscrapers in New York, there are still many historic marvels standing, and the best is this Beaux Arts gem. This railroad station, built in 1913, was restored in the 1990s to recapture its brilliance. Even if you don't have to catch a train, make sure you visit. See chapter 5.

- **Sagamore Hill, Oyster Bay:** Theodore Roosevelt's summer White House still stands out on his beloved stretch of earth overlooking Long Island Sound. The decor of this 23-room Victorian estate reflects the president's travels with the Rough Riders; it's jammed with animal skins, heads, and exotic treasures from East Africa to the Amazon. See chapter 6.

- **Hudson Valley's Great Estates:** American history was made up and down the Hudson River, and not just at Revolutionary War battle sites. The grand estates of important literary figures, railroad magnates, and finance barons—including Washington Irving's Sleepy Hollow, the Lyndhurst Estate, the Rockefeller Family's Kykuit Estate, and the Vanderbilt Mansion—are lasting portraits of a young country's great expansion and riches at the height of the Industrial Age. History lessons that go to the core of the country's development are sensitively presented at the Philipsburg Manor, an 18th-century farm that serves as a living-history museum about slavery in the North, while the FDR Presidential Library and Home and Eleanor Roosevelt's Val-Kill Cottage in Hyde Park document another crucial period in the country's more recent history. See chapter 7.

- **Huguenot Street Stone Houses, New Paltz:** Founded in 1678, New Paltz is built around one of the oldest streets of surviving stone houses in North America. Along Huguenot Street are a half-dozen original Colonial-era stone houses built by French religious refugees, the Protestant Huguenots. The earliest was built in 1692, and all have been restored with period furnishings and heirlooms and operate as house museums (but guided tours of the houses are conducted in summer months only). See chapter 8.

- **Seneca Falls:** The small town of Seneca Falls is where the women's and civil rights movements got their start in the mid–19th century. The first Women's Rights Convention was held here in 1848, and today the Women's Rights National Historical Park has a museum erected next to the chapel where brave activists like Elizabeth Cady Stanton, Lucretia Mott, and Frederick Douglass formalized the women's rights and abolitionist movements that would ultimately redefine the concept of individual liberty. Other important historic sites in the area, such as the Elizabeth Cady Stanton House, are part of a "Women's Rights Trail." See chapter 11.

- **Great Camp Sagamore:** Back when wealthy industrialists were exploring the concept of leisure travel, they discovered the Adirondacks. Of course, "roughing it" to the Vanderbilts wasn't exactly sleeping in a lean-to. This camp, 4 miles south of Raquette Lake, is a 27-building "Great Camp" filled with rustic luxury—there's even a bowling alley. Today, you can check out what this camp in the woods was all about. See chapter 12.

- **Downtown Buffalo:** It's hard to believe that 100 years ago, this area was home to more millionaires per capita than anywhere else in the U.S. Fortunately, those wealthy industrialists left behind a wonderful architectural legacy, and buildings designed by the likes of E. B. Green and H. H. Richardson still grace the city's skyline. From City Hall to the amazing Ellicott Square building, it's worth walking around downtown and checking out the sites. See chapter 13.

10 The Best Places to Commune with Nature

- **Fire Island, Long Island:** This slender island protecting the mainland is replete with trees, wilderness, and one entire side of gorgeous golden-sand beach. Best of all, cars aren't allowed, meaning bikes and little red wagons are the only things that can run you over. And because the island is 32 miles long but just a half-mile wide, you're never more than a short walk from the ocean's waves and beach. For a truly remote wilderness experience, head to the eastern end, where it'll likely just be you and the deer in the gorgeous environment. See chapter 6.

- **Mashomack Preserve:** With more than 2,000 pristine acres in the southeastern part of Shelter Island, this preserve, run by the Nature Conservancy, is about as remote as you can get on Long Island. There are 11 miles of easy hiking trails that run through the oak woodlands, marshes, ponds, and creeks. Keep an eye out for osprey, ibis, foxes, harbor seals, and terrapins. See chapter 6.

- **Kaaterskill Falls:** The Catskill Mountains are all about the great outdoors, providing lots of invitations to hike, bike, ski, boat, and fish. But one of those unique spots where everyone is sure to feel just a little closer to nature is Kaaterskill Falls, the highest waterfall in New York State. It's not nearly as powerful and massive as Niagara Falls, though it is indeed higher. An easy but beautiful walk, wending along a flowing creek, takes you to the bottom of the falls. See chapter 8.

- **Montezuma National Wildlife Refuge, Finger Lakes Region:** Smack in the middle of the Atlantic Migratory Flyway, at the north end of Cayuga Lake, this 7,000-acre wetlands nature park, established in 1938, is superb for birding and a spectacular nature experience for families. The marshes draw thousands of Canada geese, blue herons, egrets, wood ducks, and other water birds on their sojourns from nesting areas in Canada, reaching temporary populations as great as two million birds during the fall and spring migrations. You can drive, cycle, or walk along a road that takes you up close and personal with birds and other creatures. See chapter 11.

- **Watkins Glen State Park:** There are too many great nature spots in the Finger Lakes to even discuss or hope to visit on a single trip, starting with the sinewy lakes themselves, but this 776-acre park is surely at the top of any list. Its centerpiece is an amazing slate gorge carved out of the earth at the end of the last ice age, gradually shaped by the waters of Glen Creek. Along the beautiful walking trails are 19 waterfalls. See chapter 11.

- **St. Regis Canoe Wilderness:** It's not easy these days to find a single body of water expressly reserved for non-motorized boats, and it's even harder to find several bodies of water for the canoer/kayaker. But this remote area, tucked deep in the heart of the Adirondacks, is just that. Take your boat out on these waters and it'll likely just be you and the birds as you cruise quietly through this amazing backcountry. See chapter 12.

11 The Best Leaf-Peeping

- **Hudson River Valley:** Fall is one of the best times to visit the Hudson Valley. Temperatures are perfect and the great estates, many of them set among large old trees and gardens with gorgeous views of the Hudson, are splendid for aesthetic visits. The light is always great on the Hudson, but it's really special during the fall. See chapter 7.

- **Catskill Region:** Pick a county and go on a hike. Or kayak down the Delaware River. This extremely rural region is ideal for fall leaf-peeping. It's full of dairy farms and farmers' markets, emboldened by mountains and laced with lakes. The dense Catskill Forest Preserve is a kaleidoscope of color in autumn. See chapter 8.

- **Finger Lakes Region:** Autumn in the Finger Lakes region is impossibly scenic, with the golden hues of vineyards gracing the banks of deep-blue lakes, all set off against autumnal colors. It's a perfect time to visit the excellent wineries, take a boat cruise, or bike around the lakes. See chapter 11.
- **Warrensburg to Indian Lake:** This drive north nets you some amazing scenery and even more amazing fall colors. From I-87, take Route 73 through Keene Valley and Keene and you'll head straight into the Adirondack High Peaks area, one of the most scenic in the state, even without fall colors. You'll see mountains ablaze with oranges and reds; once you hit Lake Placid, go north on Route 86 and you'll be driving along the west branch of the Ausable River, also bright with color. See chapter 12.
- **Letchworth State Park:** Long and slender, the park's central feature is a 400-foot-deep cavern; the water from the Genesee River feeds tons of deciduous trees that absolutely light up with color during the fall. Go on a hike deep in the woods or see it all from above in a balloon. See chapter 13.

12 The Best Four-Season Towns

- **Saratoga Springs:** Although summer is the star season in Saratoga, this small city is also an excellent year-round destination. In warm months, the one-time "Queen of the Spas" sees thoroughbred racing at the famed Race Course, where the season lasts from the end of July to Labor Day; open-air concerts in the park; the New York City Ballet and Philadelphia Orchestra in residence; and boating and fishing on Saratoga Lake. However, Saratoga is eminently enjoyable in spring, fall, and even winter, when visitors can enjoy cross-country skiing and ice-skating. See chapter 9.
- **Ithaca:** This college town is a great place to visit no matter what season, with its varied menu of sports and culture available year-round. The great hikes along Cayuga Lake and to nearby gorges are perfect ways to enjoy spring, summer, and fall. Cornell University's attractions, including the Herbert F. Johnson Museum of Art and Cornell Plantations' botanical garden, wildflower garden, and arboretum can easily be enjoyed at any time of year. The nearby wineries of the Cayuga Wine Trail make great visits in any season (though they're perhaps best in fall during harvest). In winter, there's nearby downhill skiing and lots of cross-country skiing. See chapter 11.
- **Lake Placid:** In the summer, go boating on Mirror Lake, hike the many trails just outside town, or canoe along your own quiet stretch of lake. In winter, things really swing: The home of two Olympic Games, Lake Placid offers the opportunity to ski Whiteface Mountain, ice-skate, try the bobsled run, or go dog-sledding on Mirror Lake. See chapter 12.
- **Buffalo:** Okay, it might be a little crazy to visit Buffalo in the depths of snowy winter, but things never shut down here. At any time of year, you can walk (or drive) downtown to check out the city's gorgeous architecture, stroll through its amazing Albright-Knox Art Gallery, take in a professional football or hockey game (in the right season, of course), and finish off the day with an order of chicken wings in the bar where they were invented. See chapter 13.

13 The Most Adorable Towns

- **Greenport:** This is the cutest town on Long Island's North Fork. Filled with Colonial buildings, inns, homes, and shops, the town sits right on the protected waters of Peconic Bay. There's a strong sense of the town's history as a fishing village, with the smell of salt in the air, but there are also nice galleries and restaurants that line Main Street. See chapter 6.

- **Cold Spring:** Perhaps the most visitor-friendly small town on the Hudson, warm and inviting Cold Spring has something for everyone. The historic waterfront, equipped with a Victorian band shell and park benches, has unequaled views of the Hudson River; Main Street is packed with antiques shops, cafes, and restaurants; and the nearby mountains are perfect for surprisingly rigorous hikes. Cold Spring is within easy reach of lots of historic estates along the river, and the town's excellent handful of restaurants and inns could easily entice you to a much longer stay than you had planned. See chapter 7.

- **Aurora:** A tiny, picture-perfect village hugging the east shore of Cayuga Lake, Aurora, now in the throes of full-scale revitalization, could be a movie set. It pretty much consists of a main street, a village market, a pizza restaurant, an ice-cream parlor, a historic inn, a whimsical ceramics factory, and a women's college. The town owes its startling makeover to the efforts of the Aurora Foundation, set up by a single benefactor who made it big with American Girl dolls and set about overseeing the restoration of the village's historic buildings, including the beautiful 1833 Aurora Inn (like the town, on the National Register of Historic Places). Visiting the campus of ceramics maker MacKenzie-Childs is about as close to a Willy Wonka wonderland as you'll get. See chapter 11.

- **Cooperstown:** This chain-store-free town is best known for being home to the Baseball Hall of Fame. But sitting on the shores of Lake Otsego, it's also one of the state's cutest small towns. Tiny buildings and shops line the short Main Street, and you can walk its length in just a few minutes. You'll find cute inns, good restaurants, and plenty of baseball-card shops; then walk down to the water and have a picnic lunch overlooking the quiet, undeveloped lake. See chapter 10.

- **Skaneateles:** They don't come any cuter (or harder to pronounce) than this graceful town, which is more reminiscent of New England than upstate New York. The historic downtown, an attractive mix of 19th-century Greek Revival and Victorian homes and appetizing boutiques and antiques shops lining East Genesee Street, sits right on the north shore of Skaneateles Lake. The beautiful and crystal-clear lake is one of the prettiest and cleanest in the state, and charming inns and restaurants back right up to it. In summer, bands play on the lakefront at a picturesque gazebo, and in winter, costumed actors create a Dickensian holiday. See chapter 11.

- **Saranac Lake:** Less hectic than its neighbor, Lake Placid, this town boasts a charm all its own. With tiny clapboard shops mixed in with cute brick structures, the town has a couple of good restaurants, along with a pretty inn and clean streets. See chapter 12.

14 The Best Oddball Attractions

- **Big Duck, Long Island:** You knew Long Island was famous for its duck, but this statue on Route 24 at the Flanders/Hampton Bays border will likely surprise you—it's 20 feet tall. Even better, you can stop here and pick up tourist information. See p. 173.

- **Reviving the Borscht Belt:** The Catskill region has come a long way from the Borscht Belt vacationland where New York City families once retreated to day camps in the mountains. But there are still some of those old-school, all-in-one resorts, many of them ethnic enclaves of group entertainment and back-to-back activities like bowling, shuffleboard, and pale imitations of yesteryear game shows. They're nostalgic for some, high camp or cheese for others. Among the many resorts hanging onto old ways of summer fun in the mountains, one stands out: Scott's Oquaga Lake House, where generations of one family have been entertaining visitors, incredibly, since 1869. The resort is best known for the singing Scott family's nightly cabaret revues in which everyone from the costumed grandkids to the grandparents play a rousing part. See p. 248.

- **700 Mormons Interpreting the Bible in Full Technicolor:** The Mormon Church, also known as the Church of Jesus Christ of Latter-day Saints, got its miraculous start in the Finger Lakes region before heading west. Every year in July, hundreds of thousands of the faithful and curious make pilgrimages to witness the Hill Cumorah Pageant, a giant spectacle that constitutes the largest outdoor theatrical production in the U.S.: The show sports a costumed cast of 700, a nine-level stage, and music by the Mormon Tabernacle Choir. It has to be seen to be believed, but even nonbelievers enjoy the over-the-top show. See p. 335.

- **The Winery Impersonating Hooters:** Wine tasting is all about protocol and pompous, highbrow terms like bouquet, nose, and body, right? Not at Hazlitt 1852 Vineyards, in the Finger Lakes, where a visit to the vineyard is occasionally more akin to something you'd stumble upon at a college frat house. To start, the winery's bestseller is the mass-market "Red Cat," a low-rent party wine that has earned a reputation as an everyman's aphrodisiac. The winery revels in party atmosphere, rock-'n'-roll music, and irreverence toward traditional wine-tasting etiquette. Sometimes, wine tasting is accompanied by cheerful folks joining in chants laced with sexual innuendo; more than a few women have been known to doff their tops to demonstrate their preference for Hazlitt wines. See p. 316.

- **Kazoo Museum, Eden:** Who would go through the trouble of collecting wooden kazoos, gold kazoos, and liquor-bottle-shaped kazoos (celebrating the end of Prohibition)? People driven indoors by the brutal western New York winters. This museum has the oddest collection of this peculiar little instrument and until recently was making even more. See chapter 13.

- **Town of Mediums, Lily Dale:** This haven for those in touch with otherworldly spirits has been celebrating its odd collection of residents for nearly 130 years. You can stop by for a private reading any time of year, or come in the summer for daily events, along with meditation and healing services. See chapter 13.

2

Planning Your Trip to New York State

by Neil E. Schlecht

In the pages that follow, we've compiled everything you need to know to handle the practical details of planning your trip in advance—from tips on accommodations to finding great deals on the Internet, plus a calendar of events and more.

1 The Regions in Brief

NEW YORK CITY Residents in the surrounding areas of New York, New Jersey, and Connecticut refer to it simply as "the City," as if there were no other. The city comprises about 300 square miles divided into five boroughs—the Bronx, Brooklyn, Manhattan, Queens, and Staten Island. Best known for world-class museums, Broadway theater, Madison Avenue shopping, four-star cuisine, and glamorous nightlife, it's also a great place for more low-key adventures, like grabbing a hot dog at Yankee Stadium or spending a sunny afternoon in Central Park. For more about New York City, see chapter 5.

LONG ISLAND & THE HAMPTONS At 188 miles, "long" is an accurate description of the island situated to the east of Manhattan, dividing the waters of the Long Island Sound from the Atlantic Ocean. As you may have guessed, the sea is the dominant theme here—charming ports, sandy beaches, and fresh seafood abound. Surprisingly, it's also an agricultural area that supports numerous farms and vineyards. The north shore, or "Gold Coast," is strewn with mansions formerly belonging to Astors and Vanderbilts, now transformed into museums open to the public. See chapter 6.

THE HUDSON RIVER VALLEY The stunning landscape along the 100-mile stretch of the Hudson River from Albany to New York City has been immortalized on canvas by the painters of the Hudson River School and on paper in classics such as *The Legend of Sleepy Hollow* and *Rip Van Winkle*. The Appalachian Trail cuts through the valley, offering hikers an up-close view of the river and wilderness. Antiquing is a favorite pastime here, as is touring grand, historic estates built by America's great industrialists. See chapter 7.

THE CATSKILL MOUNTAIN REGION The Catskill Park and Forest Preserve lies in the heart of the Catskill Mountains, about 100 miles to the northwest of New York City. Nature lovers can explore 300 miles of trails up and down mountain peaks and amid unspoiled forests, lakes, and rivers. The Borscht Belt image of yesteryear is subsiding as more sophisticated travel and residents take root. See chapter 8.

THE CAPITAL REGION: SARATOGA SPRINGS & ALBANY Albany's impressive architecture reflects its status as the state's capital since 1797. Saratoga Springs, about 20 miles north of Albany, is named for the natural mineral waters that have drawn visitors to the town's spas and baths since the 1800s. It's also home to the Saratoga Race Course, the oldest thoroughbred racetrack in the U.S. See chapter 9.

CENTRAL NEW YORK Just west of the Finger Lakes, this largely rural area is legendary among sports fans for the National Baseball Hall of Fame and Museum in Cooperstown. See chapter 10.

THE FINGER LAKES REGION Bounded by Lake Ontario to the north and the Pennsylvania border to the south, the aptly named Finger Lakes region has 11 long, slender lakes plus rivers, streams, waterfalls, and smaller bodies of water. The lakes offer lots of water-related fun, from swimming to kayaking to fishing. Finger Lakes wine is another big attraction here; more than 70 wineries are located around Canandaigua, Keuka, Seneca, and Cayuga lakes. See chapter 11.

THE NORTH COUNTRY Massive Adirondack Park, full of lakes, hiking trails, and rustic "camps," accounts for the majority of land in New York State north of I-90. At 6.1 million acres, the park is almost the size of the neighboring state of Vermont. See chapter 12.

WESTERN NEW YORK On its journey from Lake Ontario to Lake Erie, the Niagara River pours between 50,000 and 100,000 cubic feet of water per second over spectacular Niagara Falls. Buffalo—the second-largest city in New York State and a good bet for restaurants and nightlife—is just a 30-minute drive from the falls. See chapter 13.

2 Visitor Information & Maps

Call or write the **New York State Division of Tourism,** P.O. Box 2603, Albany, NY 12220-0603 (© **800/CALL-NYS** or 518/474-4116; www.iloveny.com), for a stack of free brochures, including the informative *I Love New York Travel Guide,* the *Official NYC Guide,* and pamphlets about seasonal events. They even throw in a free state map that's just as useful as any for which you'd pay $5 at the gas station. While on the road, you can pick up brochures at one of the state's **information centers.** Call the toll-free number above or check the *I Love New York Travel Guide* for the locations along your route. For regional tourist offices and websites, see the listings in destination chapters later in this book.

If you're planning a tour of the great outdoors, contact the **New York State Office of Parks, Recreation and Historic Preservation,** Albany, NY 12238 (© **518/474-0456,** or 518/486-1899 for hearing- or speech-impaired callers; www. nysparks.state.ny.us), to request a free brochure, order admission passes, or find out about camping, hiking, and a host of other activities within the state's parks and historic sites. To reserve a campsite or other accommodations, book online or call © **800/456-2267.**

3 Entry Requirements

PASSPORTS

For information on how to get a passport, go to **"Passports"** in the **"Fast Facts"** section of this chapter—the websites listed provide downloadable passport applications as well as the current fees for processing passport applications. For an up-to-date, country-by-country listing of passport requirements around the world, go to the Web page of the U.S. State

U.S. Entry: Passport Required

New regulations issued by the Homeland Security Department now require virtually every air traveler entering the U.S. to show a passport—and future regulations will cover land and sea entry as well. As of January 23, 2007, all persons, including U.S. citizens, traveling by air between the United States and Canada, Mexico, Central and South America, the Caribbean, and Bermuda are required to present a valid passport. Similar regulations for those traveling by land or sea (including ferries) are expected as early as January 1, 2008.

Department at **http://travel.state.gov.** Click on "International Travel" and "Document Requirements," then "U.S. Citizens—Visas for Entry into Foreign Countries" and "Foreign Entry Requirements." International visitors can obtain a visa application at the same website. *Note:* Children are required to present a passport when entering the United States at airports. More information on obtaining a passport for a minor can be found at **http://travel.state.gov.**

VISAS

For specifics on how to get a Visa, go to **"Visas"** in the **"Fast Facts"** section of this chapter.

The U.S. State Department has a **Visa Waiver Program (VWP)** allowing citizens of the following countries (at press time) to enter the United States without a visa for stays of up to 90 days: Andorra, Australia, Austria, Belgium, Brunei, Denmark, Finland, France, Germany, Iceland, Ireland, Italy, Japan, Liechtenstein, Luxembourg, Monaco, the Netherlands, New Zealand, Norway, Portugal, San Marino, Singapore, Slovenia, Spain, Sweden, Switzerland, and the United Kingdom. Canadian citizens may enter the United States without visas; they will need to show passports and proof of residence, however. *Note:* Any passport issued on or after October 26, 2006, by a VWP country must be an **e-Passport** for VWP travelers to be eligible to enter the U.S. without a visa. Citizens of these nations also need to present a round-trip

air or cruise ticket upon arrival. E-Passports contain computer chips capable of storing biometric information, such as the required digital photograph of the holder. (You can identify an e-Passport by the symbol on the bottom center cover of your passport.) If your passport doesn't have this feature, you can still travel without a visa if it is a valid passport issued before October 26, 2005, and includes a machine-readable zone, or between October 26, 2005, and October 25, 2006, and includes a digital photograph. For more information, go to **www.travel.state.gov/ visa.**

Citizens of all other countries must have (1) a valid passport that expires at least 6 months later than the scheduled end of their visit to the United States, and (2) a tourist visa, which may be obtained without charge from any U.S. consulate.

As of January 2004, many international visitors traveling on visas to the United States will be photographed and fingerprinted on arrival at Customs in airports and on cruise ships in a program created by the Department of Homeland Security called **US-VISIT.** Exempt from the extra scrutiny are visitors entering by land or those (mostly in Europe; see p. 53) that don't require a visa for short-term visits. For more information, go to the Homeland Security website at **www. dhs.gov/dhspublic.**

MEDICAL REQUIREMENTS

Unless you're arriving from an area known to be suffering from an epidemic (particularly cholera or yellow fever), inoculations or vaccinations are not required for entry into the United States. If you have a medical condition that requires **syringe-administered medications,** carry a valid signed prescription from your physician; syringes in carry-on baggage will be inspected. Insulin in any form should have the proper pharmaceutical documentation. If you have a disease that requires treatment with **narcotics,** you should also carry documented proof with you—smuggling narcotics aboard a plane carries severe penalties in the U.S.

For **HIV-positive visitors,** requirements for entering the United States are somewhat vague and change frequently. For up-to-the-minute information, contact **AIDSinfo** (© **800/448-0440** or 301/519-6616 outside the U.S.; www.aidsinfo.nih. gov) or the **Gay Men's Health Crisis** (© **212/367-1000;** www.gmhc.org).

CUSTOMS

For information on what you can bring into and take out of New York State, see **"Customs"** in the **"Fast Facts"** section of this chapter.

4 When to Go

Since New York State is a four-season destination, the best time to visit depends on what you want to do.

Summer is peak season, accounting for about 40% of New York State tourism. From June to August, the weather is pleasant and mostly sunny, though it tends to be humid. Temperatures usually remain below 85°F (29°C), except in the vicinity of New York City and Long Island, which is about 10°F (6°C) warmer than the rest of the state year-round. Summer weather is ideal for travel; the problem is that everyone else thinks so, too. Parklands and campgrounds are filled with vacationers, especially on weekends. Cities throng with sightseers, making for long lines, sold-out events, and high prices.

Average Monthly Temperatures

Albany	Jan	Feb	Mar	Apr	May	June	July	Aug	Sept	Oct	Nov	Dec
°F	22	25	35	47	58	66	71	69	61	49	39	28
°C	–6	–4	2	8	14	19	22	21	16	9	4	–2

Buffalo	Jan	Feb	Mar	Apr	May	June	July	Aug	Sept	Oct	Nov	Dec
°F	25	26	34	45	57	66	71	69	62	51	40	30
°C	–4	–3	1	7	14	19	22	21	17	11	4	–1

New York City	Jan	Feb	Mar	Apr	May	June	July	Aug	Sept	Oct	Nov	Dec
°F	33	35	42	52	62	72	77	76	69	58	48	38
°C	1	2	6	11	17	22	25	24	21	14	9	3

Syracuse	Jan	Feb	Mar	Apr	May	June	July	Aug	Sept	Oct	Nov	Dec
°F	23	25	34	45	57	66	71	69	61	50	40	29
°C	–5	–4	1	7	14	19	22	21	16	10	4	–2

Fall, from September to November, is another extremely popular time to visit. Upstate, the air turns to crisp jacket weather in September, but farther south summertime lingers until early October.

New York's beautiful fall foliage is a huge draw, especially in mid-October—the best time to catch trees sporting brilliant reds and golds. Expect country inns, B&Bs, and state and national parks to be particularly busy over Columbus Day weekend.

Contrary to popular belief, winter temperatures aren't miserable—they normally range from about 15°F (–9°C) to as high as 40°F (4°C) in New York City. The snow, on the other hand, can be brutal. Infamous "lake-effect" snowstorms can dump several feet at once on Buffalo and surrounding towns, prompting Thruway and airport closings. Most of upstate New York is blanketed in snow from December to March. Although statistically winter is the slowest time for tourism in New York, it's high season for the state's ski destinations, and parks are still active with winter-sports lovers. New York City, which welcomes a steady flow of visitors all year long, is extra-jammed during the holidays thanks to Christmas festivities at Rockefeller Center, holiday shopping, and New Year's Eve in Times Square.

The spring thaw begins in March, but it's not unusual for snow to fall in April, or even May. There are spring showers, but the average amount of precipitation is no heavier than in summer or fall. Rainfall remains fairly constant from May to November at approximately 3 to 4 inches per month. If you enjoy the quietly melting snow and fresh spring breezes, this season may be your golden opportunity to indulge in outdoor activities before the summer rush.

NEW YORK STATE CALENDAR OF EVENTS

For an exhaustive list of events beyond those listed here, check http://events.frommers.com, where you'll find a searchable, up-to-the-minute roster of what's happening in cities all over the world.

January

World Cup Freestyle, Lake Placid. The world's best aerial skiers take off and fly, tucking and spinning their way to a championship. You'll see mogul action, too, as the athletes' skis zigzag among the mounds of snow. Call © 518/523-1655 or visit www.orda. org. Mid-January.

February

Chinese New Year, New York City. Every year, Chinatown rings in its own new year (based on a lunar calendar) with 2 weeks of celebrations, including parades with dragon and lion dancers, plus vivid costumes of all kinds. Call the New York City Visitor's hot line at © 212/484-1222 or the Asian American Business Development Center at © 212/966-0100. February 7 to 21, 2008.

Olmsted Winterfest, Buffalo. Delaware Park becomes a magnet for fun seekers, with sledding, skating, snowmobiling, softball, ice sculpting, a chili cook-off, and races taking place all over the park. There's a Friday Fish Fry, naturally, and fireworks. Call © 716/838-1249 or visit www.buffaloolmstedparks.org. Four days in mid-February.

Empire State Winter Games, Lake Placid. The games for New York State's premier amateur athletes. Call © 518/523-1655 or visit www.orda.org. Mid-February.

March

St. Patrick's Day Parade, New York City. More than 150,000 marchers join in the world's largest civilian parade, as Fifth Avenue from 44th to 86th streets rings with the sounds of bands and bagpipes. The parade usually starts at 11am, but go extra early if you want a good spot. Irish bars throughout the city throb with revelers. Call © 212/484-1222. March 17.

April

Easter Parade, New York City. No marching bands, no baton twirlers, no protesters. It's more about flamboyant exhibitionism, with hats and costumes that get more outrageous every year—and anybody can join right in for free.

It's along Fifth Avenue from 48th to 57th streets on Easter Sunday, from about 10am to 3 or 4pm. Call © 212/484-1222.

May

Lilac Festival, Rochester. More than 1,000 lilac trees in Highland Park, with dozens of varieties of fragrant lilacs in full bloom, are the excuse for a big civic party. There is music and food, but the highlight is easily the lilacs. Call © 585/256-4960 or visit www.lilacfestival.com. Mid-May.

Bike New York: The Great Five Borough Bike Tour, New York City. The largest mass-participation cycling event in the United States attracts about 30,000 cyclists from all over the world. Call © 212/932-BIKE (2453) or visit www.bikenewyork.org to register. First or second Sunday in May.

Tulip Festival, Albany. For more than 50 years, Albany has celebrated its Dutch heritage with this colorful festival, where, in addition to thousands of beautiful tulips in Washington Park, there is plenty of food, entertainment, and crafts—not to mention the annual crowning of the tulip queen! Call © 518/434-2032 or visit www.albany events.org/tulip_festival/index.cfm. First or second week of May.

Falls Fireworks & Concert Series, Niagara Falls, Ontario. Every Friday and Sunday, you can enjoy free concerts by the falls at 8pm, followed by a fireworks show at 10pm, which bathes the falls in color. Call © 877/642-7275 or visit www.niagaraparks.com. Mid-May through mid-September.

Fleet Week, New York City. About 10,000 U.S. Navy and Coast Guard personnel are "at liberty" in New York for the annual Fleet Week, an event immortalized on *Sex and the City.* Usually from 1 to 4pm daily, you can watch the ships and aircraft carriers as they dock at the piers on the west side of Manhattan, tour them with on-duty personnel, and watch some dramatic exhibitions by the U.S. Marines. Call © 212/245-0072, or visit www.fleet week.com. Late May.

June

Annual Hall of Fame Game, Cooperstown. The day begins with a lecture by Hall of Famers and moves into a game between pro teams. There's a home run contest, and, of course, lots of hot dog eating. Call © 888/HALL-OF-FAME or visit www.baseballhall offame.org. Early June.

Belmont Stakes, Elmont (Long Island). The third jewel in the Triple Crown is held at the Belmont Park Race Track. If a Triple Crown winner is to be named, it will happen here. For information, call © 516/488-6000. Early June.

Shakespeare in the Park, New York City. The Delacorte Theater in Central Park is the setting for first-rate free performances under the stars—including at least one Shakespeare production. Call © 212/539-8500 or point your browser to www.publictheater.org. Early June to early September.

Caramoor International Music Festival, Katonah (Hudson River Valley). This idiosyncratic house-museum and performing arts center hosts one of the state's best music festivals, with a full slate of summer outdoor chamber and symphonic music concerts. Call © 914/232-1252 or visit www.caramoor.com. June 21 through August 3, 2008.

Hudson Valley Shakespeare Festival, Garrison (Hudson River Valley). On the gorgeous grounds of Boscobel Restoration, one of the prettiest spots along the Hudson, the summer theater performance of Shakespeare seems suitably grand, and perfect for a summer's eve picnic. Call © 845/265-7858

(845/265-9575 for tickets) or visit www.hvshakespeare.org. Mid-June to early September.

Shakespeare in Delaware Park, Buffalo. Free Shakespeare under the stars has been a Buffalo tradition for almost 30 years. Call ✆ 716/856-4533 or visit www.shakespeareindelawarepark.org. Mid-June to mid-August.

Chautauqua season opens, Chautauqua Institution. This arts camp in western New York is one of the most prestigious in the nation. Its extensive grounds, right on the shores of Chautauqua Lake, play host to all manner of arts classes, lectures, and performances. Call ✆ 800/836-ARTS or go to www.chautauqua-inst.org. Mid-June to mid-August.

Museum Mile Festival, New York City. Fifth Avenue from 82nd to 104th streets is closed to cars from 6 to 9pm as 20,000-plus strollers enjoy live music, street entertainers, and free admission to nine Museum Mile institutions, including the Metropolitan Museum of Art and the Guggenheim. Call ✆ 212/606-2296 or visit www.museummile festival.org. Usually the second Tuesday in June.

Lesbian and Gay Pride Week and March, New York City. A week of cheerful happenings, from simple parties to major political fundraisers, precedes a zany parade commemorating the Stonewall Riot of June 27, 1969, which for many marks the beginning of the gay liberation movement. Call ✆ 212/807-7433 or check www.hopinc.org. Mid- to late June.

U.S. Open Golf Championship, Farmingdale. In 2009, this major tournament returns to New York, to the Black Course at Bethpage State Park. Come see if Tiger can put another major tournament under his belt. Call

the USGA at ✆ 908/234-2300 or visit www.usopen.com for more information. June 15–21, 2009.

Lake Placid Horse Show, Lake Placid. Watch horses take to the air in this prestigious horse show set against the gorgeous Adirondacks. Call ✆ 518/523-9625 or visit www.lakeplacidhorseshow.com. Late June to early July.

July

Glimmerglass Opera, Cooperstown. Central New York's famous opera gears up for another impressive season. Call ✆ 607/547-2255 or go to www.glimmerglass.org. Early July through end of August.

Hill Cumorah Pageant, Palmyra (Finger Lakes region). Near the site where the Mormon religion was founded, the Church of Jesus Christ of Latter-day Saints puts on an amazing theatrical spectacle, in the tradition of Middle Ages pageants, with 700 actors. Call ✆ 315/597-2757 or 315/597-5851. First 2 weeks of July.

Independence Day Harbor Festival and Fourth of July Fireworks Spectacular, New York City. Start the day amid the patriotic crowds at the Great July Fourth Festival in Lower Manhattan, and then catch Macy's great fireworks extravaganza (one of the country's most fantastic) over the East River (the best vantage point is from the FDR Drive, which closes to traffic several hours before sunset). Call ✆ 212/484-1222, or Macy's Visitor Center at 212/494-2922. July 4th.

Hurley Stone House Tour, Hurley (Catskill region). Unlike New Paltz, where the ancient stone structures are open in season to visitors, Hurley's collection of two dozen stone houses, most privately owned, open only once a year for visits. Call ✆ 845/331-4121. Mid-July.

Finger Lakes Wine Festival, Watkins Glen International Racetrack. The Finger Lakes is one of the country's great (but still up-and-coming) wine regions, and everybody gets together—locals, visitors, and some five dozen or so wineries—for tastings, crafts, food, and good spirits. It's anything but stuffy, though, as the annual toga party (or "Launch of the Lakes") attests. Call ☎ 866/461-7223 or visit www.fl winefest.com. Usually the third weekend in July.

Windham Chamber Music Festival, Windham (Catskill region). Opera stars from the Metropolitan in New York City descend upon the Catskill Mountains for some high culture at a higher altitude. Call ☎ 518/734-3868 or visit www.windhammusic.com. July through August.

Belleayre Music Festival, Highmount (Catskill region). The ski mountain of Belleayre races in summer with a wide-ranging mix of high-brow and popular music and entertainment, from classical and opera to folk and puppetry. Call ☎ 800/254-5600 or visit www.belleayremusic.org. July through August.

Annual Wine Country Classic Boat Show & Regatta, Hammondsport (Finger Lakes region). At the southern end of Keuka Lake, this antique- and classic-boat show features more than 100 boats, with judging, water parades, and demonstrations. On Sunday is the race regatta. Call ☎ 585/394-3044. Third weekend in July.

Saratoga Summer Culture, Saratoga Springs. In July, the New York City Ballet makes its off-season home at the National Museum of Dance & Hall of Fame, and during the month of August, the Philadelphia Orchestra is in residence at the Saratoga Performing Arts Center (SPAC). Who would think that high culture could compete stride-for-stride with the horses over at the track for the big event of the summer? Call ☎ 518/584-2225 or 518/584-9330, or visit www.saratoga.com. July and August.

Baseball Hall of Fame Induction Weekend, Cooperstown. Come see which legendary swingers will make it in this year. Call ☎ 888/HALL-OF-FAME or visit www.baseballhallof fame.org. Late July.

Thoroughbred Horse Racing, Saratoga Springs (Capital region). At the famed Race Course, the oldest in the country, the race season lasts 6 weeks and turns the town upside down. Call ☎ 518/584-6200 or visit www.nyra.com/index_saratoga.html End of July through early September.

Bounty of the Hudson, Hudson Valley. A 2-day food and wine festival showcasing the best of the Hudson Valley, including cooking workshops and live music held at one of the local wineries. Tickets and more information at www.shawangunkwinetrail.com. Last weekend in July.

August

Antique Boat Show & Auction, Clayton (Thousand Islands). It's the oldest continuous boat show in the world—you can even bid on a boat at the auction. Cruise the commercial marketplace and flea market, sit in on an educational forum, listen to music, and sample food. Lots of kids' programs, too. Call ☎ 315/686-4104. Early August.

Maverick Concert Series, Woodstock. America's oldest summer chamber music series, continuous since 1916, is this agreeable version of "Music in the Woods." Call ☎ 845/679-8217 or visit www.maverickconcerts.org. August through early September.

Harlem Week, New York City. The world's largest black and Hispanic cultural festival actually spans almost the whole month to include the Black Film Festival, the Harlem Jazz and Music Festival, and the Taste of Harlem Food Festival. Call ☎ **212/484-1222.** Throughout August.

NASCAR Winston Cup at the Glen, Watkins Glen. Among legions of race fans, this huge event is unparalleled in the Northeast, and it draws NASCAR fans from across the state and region, filling up just about every bed in the Finger Lakes. Call ☎ **607/535-2486** (for tickets, **866/461-RACE** [7223]) or visit www.theglen.com. Second week in August.

Toy Fest, East Aurora. The home of Fisher-Price toys (western New York) comes to life with a toy parade along Main Street, an antique toy show, rides, and other activities. Call ☎ **716/687-5151** or visit www.toytownusa.com. Late August.

National Buffalo Wing Festival, Buffalo. This festival features many restaurants and sauces from Buffalo and around the country. Best wing and sauce competitions, wing-eating contests, and more. Call ☎ **716/565-4141** or visit www.buffalowing.com. Late August.

New York State Fair, Syracuse (Finger Lakes region). New York State's massive 12-day agricultural and entertainment fair, with all kinds of big-name music acts and food you'll be glad only comes 'round once a year. Call ☎ **800/475-FAIR** or visit www.nysfair.org. Late August to early September.

U.S. Open Tennis Championships, New York City. The final Grand Slam event of the tennis season is held at the Arthur Ashe Stadium at the USTA National Tennis Center, the largest public tennis center in the world, at Flushing Meadows Park in Queens. Tickets go on sale in May or early June, and the event sells out immediately. Call ☎ **888/OPEN-TIX** or 718/760-6200 well in advance; visit www.usopen.org or www.usta.com for additional information. Two weeks around Labor Day.

September

Turn-of-the-Century Day, Roxbury (Catskill region). Reliving the glory days of baseball and hoop skirts, the town of Roxbury sheds about 100 years and celebrates with a vintage "base ball" game, horse-drawn wagon rides, and period foods and costumes on the former estate of Helen Gould Shepard in this Labor Day tradition. Call ☎ **607/326-3722.** Labor Day weekend.

West Indian–American Day Parade, New York City. This annual Brooklyn event is New York's largest and best street celebration. Come for the extravagant costumes, pulsating rhythms (soca, calypso, reggae), bright colors, folklore, food (jerk chicken, Caribbean soul food), and two million hip-shaking revelers. Call ☎ **212/484-1222** or 718/625-1515. Labor Day.

Adirondack Balloon Festival, Glens Falls, Queensbury, and Lake George. Watch a rainbow of colors soar into the sky as 60-plus hot-air balloons lift off. Tons of activities surround this annual event. Call ☎ **800/365-1050** or visit www.adirondackballoonfest.org. Mid-September.

Naples Grape Festival, Naples (Finger Lakes region). To celebrate the harvest of the grape in this grape-growing and wine-producing region, grape pie lives for a weekend in the tiny town of Naples. Connoisseurs rejoice, scarfing down as much pie as possible, and there's a "World's Greatest Grape Pie" contest and live entertainment. Call

© 585/374-2240 or visit www.naples valleyny.com/grapefestival.php. End of September.

October

Legend Weekend at Sleepy Hollow and Philipsburg Manor, Tarrytown (Hudson River Valley). At Washington Irving's Sunnyside home, as well as up the road at Philipsburg Manor, the specter of the Headless Horseman returns for one last ride. So as not to scare all concerned, there are also walks in the woods, storytelling, and puppet shows. Call © 914/631-8200 or visit www.hudsonvalley.org. Last week in October.

Halloween at Howe Caverns (near Utica). Come check out the underground scare-a-thon with pumpkin-decorating contests, scary stories, and a special kids' buffet. Call © 518/296-8900 or visit www.howecaverns.com. October 31.

Greenwich Village Halloween Parade, New York City. This is Halloween at its most outrageous. You may have heard Lou Reed singing about it on his classic album *New York*—he wasn't exaggerating. Drag queens and assorted other flamboyant types parade through the Village in wildly creative costumes. Call the *Village Voice* parade hot line at © 212/475-3333, ext. 4044, or go to www.halloween-nyc. com for the exact route so you can watch—or participate, if you have the threads and the imagination. October 31.

November

New York City Marathon, New York City. Some 30,000 hopefuls from around the world participate in the largest U.S. marathon, and more than a million fans cheer them on as they follow a route that touches on all five New York boroughs and finishes at Central Park. Call © 212/423-2249 or 212/860-4455, or visit www.nyrrc. org, where you can find applications to run. First Sunday in November.

Lights in the Park, Buffalo. Delaware Park is transformed into a colorful wonderland throughout the holidays, with animated lighting displays and a collection of holiday scenes. Call © 716/856-4533. Begins mid-November.

Winter Festival of Lights, Niagara Falls, Ontario. A visual lighting extravaganza featuring Disney's motion light displays in Queen Victoria Park. Call © 800/563-2557 or 905/374-1616 or visit www.wfol.com. November to early January.

Macy's Thanksgiving Day Parade, New York City. The procession of huge hot-air balloons from Central Park West and 77th Street and down Broadway to Herald Square at 34th Street continues to be a national tradition. The night before, you can usually see the big blowup on Central Park West at 79th Street; call in advance to see if it will be open to the public again this year. Call © 212/484-1222, or Macy's Visitor Center at 212/494-2922. Thanksgiving Day.

Christmas Traditions, New York City. Look for these holiday favorites: Radio City Music Hall's Christmas Spectacular (© 212/247-4777; www.radiocity. com); the New York City Ballet's staging of *The Nutcracker* (© 212/870-5570; www.nycballet.com); *A Christmas Carol* at The Theater at Madison Square Garden (© 212/465-6741; www.thegarden.com); and the National Chorale's singalong performances of Handel's *Messiah* at Avery Fisher Hall (© 212/875-5030; www.lincolncenter. org). Call for schedules. Late November through December.

Dickens Christmas, Skaneateles (Finger Lakes region). Sweet nostalgia takes over this quaint Finger Lakes town as costumed characters—Father Christmas, Mother Goose, and Scrooge—roam the streets. Locals go door-to-door caroling, and there are carriage rides and free roasted chestnuts. Call ℭ **315/685-0552** or visit www.skaneateles.com/dickens.shtml. Last weekend in November to just before Christmas.

December

Great Estates Candlelight Christmas Tours, Hudson River Valley. Some of the grandest mansions lining the Hudson River—Boscobel, Sunnyside, Van Cortlandt Manor, Lyndhurst, Olana, and others—get all decked out for the holidays, with special candlelight house tours, caroling, bonfires, and hot cider. It's one of the best times to experience the pageantry and customs of another era. Throughout December.

Holiday Trimmings, New York City. Stroll down festive Fifth Avenue and you'll see doormen dressed as wooden soldiers at FAO Schwarz, a 27-foot sparkling snowflake floating over the intersection outside Tiffany & Co., the Cartier building ribboned and bowed in red, wreaths warming the necks of the New York Public Library's lions, and fanciful figurines in the windows of Saks Fifth Avenue and Lord & Taylor. Madison Avenue between 55th and 60th streets is also a good bet; Sony Plaza usually displays something fabulous, as does Barneys New York. Throughout December.

New Year's Eve, New York City. The biggest party of them all happens in Times Square, where thousands of raucous revelers in unison count down the year's final seconds until the new lighted ball drops at midnight at 1 Times Square. Hate to be a party pooper, but this one, in the cold surrounded by thousands of very drunk revelers, is a masochist's delight. Call ℭ **212/768-1560** or 212/484-1222, or visit www.timessquarebid.org. December 31.

5 Getting There

BY PLANE

With flights from across the country and around the world converging in New York City, many visitors to New York State may find it convenient to arrive in New York City first and move on from there.

The Port Authority of New York and New Jersey operates three major airports in the New York City area: **John F. Kennedy International Airport (JFK), LaGuardia Airport (LGA),** and **Newark Liberty International Airport (EWR).** Together they're served by most major domestic airlines, including **AirTran Airways** (ℭ 800/247-8726; www.airtran.com), **American Airlines** (ℭ 800/433-7300; www.aa.com), **America West Airlines** (ℭ 800/327-7810; www.americawest.com), **ATA** (ℭ 800/435-9282; www.ata.com), **Continental** (ℭ 800/525-0280; www.continental.com), **Delta** (ℭ 800/221-1212; www.delta.com), **Jet-Blue Airways** (ℭ 800/538-2583; www.jetblue.com), **Midwest Airlines** (ℭ 800/452-2022; www.midwestairlines.com), **Northwest** (ℭ 800/225-2525; www.nwa.com), **Spirit Airlines** (ℭ 800/772-7117; www.spiritair.com), **United** (ℭ 800/864-8331; www.ual.com), and **US Airways** (ℭ 800/28-4322; www.usair.com).

However, arriving in New York City isn't the only option. For those traveling elsewhere in the state, several of the airlines listed above offer direct or connecting flights to Albany, Buffalo, Rochester, Syracuse, Ithaca, and 10 other cities. US Airways covers more New York destinations than any other carrier. AirTran Airways, American Airlines, Continental,

Delta, JetBlue Airways, Northwest, and United also offer service, as do **Air Canada** (© 888/247-2262; www.air canada.ca) and **Southwest** (© 800/435-9792; www.southwest.com). For more information about intrastate flights, see "Getting Around New York State," later in this chapter.

ARRIVING AT THE AIRPORT

IMMIGRATION & CUSTOMS CLEARANCE Foreign visitors arriving by air, no matter what the port of entry, should cultivate patience and resignation before setting foot on U.S. soil. U.S. airports have considerably beefed up security clearances in the years since the terrorist attacks of 9/11, and clearing Customs and Immigration can take as long as 2 hours.

People traveling by air from Canada, Bermuda, and certain Caribbean countries can sometimes clear Customs and Immigration at the point of departure, which is much faster.

BY CAR

Drivers approaching from the west or east can take **I-90,** a toll road that crosses the country from Seattle to Boston and runs straight through New York, connecting Buffalo, Rochester, Syracuse, Utica, Schenectady, and Albany. **Route 17 (I-86** in western New York) roughly follows the state's southern border through Jamestown, Olean, Corning, Elmira, and Binghamton, then heads southwest into the Catskills and Orange County.

I-95 connects major cities along the East Coast from Florida to Maine, including New York City. **I-87** runs north to south, from New York City to Newburgh, Kingston, Albany, Saratoga Springs, and Plattsburgh; it then crosses into Canada where the road extends to Montreal.

Travelers from the south can also use **I-81,** which enters the state near Binghamton and continues north to Cortland, Syracuse, and Watertown. **I-88** links Binghamton and Schenectady. **I-390** provides a route between I-90 and NY Route 17 in the Finger Lakes region.

There is a toll on the **New York State Thruway,** which is I-90 from western New York to Albany and I-87 from Albany to New York City. The New York State Thruway Authority hot line dispenses recorded updates on road conditions; dial © **800/THRUWAY,** or check the website for construction schedules at www.thruway.state.ny.us.

The **American Automobile Association** (© 800/836-2582; www.aaa.com) will help members find the best routes to their destinations and provide free customized maps. AAA also offers emergency roadside assistance; members can call © **800/AAA-HELP.**

Another great way to plan your route is on the Internet site **MapQuest** (www.mapquest.com). Simply type in your start and end points, and MapQuest will give full step-by-step directions to your destination. A free state map is also available from the **New York State Division of Tourism.** See "Visitor Information & Maps," earlier in this chapter.

All the major rental-car companies operate in New York State, including **Alamo** (© 800/462-5266; www.goalamo. com), **Avis** (© 800/230-4898; www.avis. com), **Budget** (© 800/527-0700; www. budget.com), **Dollar** (© 800/800-4000; www.dollar.com), **Enterprise** (© 800/ 736-8222; www.enterprise.com), **Hertz** (© 800/654-3131; www.hertz.com), **National** (© 800/227-7368; www. nationalcar.com), and **Thrifty** (© 800/ 847-4389; www.thrifty.com). It's worth noting that the only companies located at Kennedy, LaGuardia, and Newark airports are Avis, Budget, Dollar, Hertz, and National. Enterprise is also available at LaGuardia and Newark, but not at Kennedy.

When you're renting a car, there is always some kind of deal to be found—check company websites or ask reservations agents about specials before you rent. If you're a member of AAA, AARP, or another organization, find out if you qualify for a discount.

BY TRAIN

Rail travel can be less cramped than airline flights and affords some amazing views of the American landscape. **Amtrak** (© **800/USA-RAIL**; www.amtrak.com) connects New York with many American cities from coast to coast, and a handful of Canadian cities, too. However, a cross-country trip can last for days (Los Angeles to New York City is about 70 hr.) and requires one or more connections. Unfortunately, despite the extended travel time, there isn't much savings here; train reservations cost almost as much as air travel, and sometimes more.

Three main Amtrak routes cross New York State, connecting major metropolitan areas and the towns along the way. Several trains, including **Metroliner** shuttle service and high-speed **Acela Express** trains, travel the Northeast Corridor from Washington, D.C., to Philadelphia, New York City, and Boston. **Empire Service** runs north from New York City to Albany, then west to Syracuse, Rochester, Buffalo, and Niagara Falls; the **Maple Leaf** runs daily, extending the same route through Toronto, Canada. The **Adirondack** travels the Hudson River Valley north to Albany (making stops in Yonkers, Croton-on-Hudson, Poughkeepsie, Rhinecliff, and Hudson), then follows along Lake Champlain to Plattsburgh and finally Montreal, Canada.

Check the website for Internet-only deals or ask your phone representative about regional and seasonal promotions before you reserve tickets. Seniors automatically receive 15% off regular fares, and membership discount programs are available to veterans and students. Families should note that for each adult ticket purchased, two kids under 15 may ride for half-price, and one child under 2 comes along for free.

Amtrak Vacations (© **877/YES-RAIL**; www.amtrak.com) can put together a complete travel package including train, hotel, car rental, and sightseeing. Through a partnership with United Airlines, Amtrak has created the **Air Rail** program, which allows travelers to explore destinations at leisure by rail, then make a speedy return home by plane.

6 Money & Costs

It's always advisable to bring money in a variety of forms on a vacation: a mix of cash, credit cards, and traveler's checks. You should also exchange enough petty cash to cover airport incidentals, tipping, and transportation to your hotel before you leave home, or withdraw money upon arrival at an airport ATM.

New York City is consistently ranked among the top 15 most expensive cities in the world, and the most expensive in the U.S. Hotel costs in the city far outstrip those of pretty much anywhere else in the country. Thankfully, costs elsewhere in the state are closer to the national average, and even in New York City, there are deals to be found.

ATMs

Nationwide, the easiest and best way to get cash away from home is from an ATM (automated teller machine), sometimes referred to as a "cash machine," or "cashpoint." The **Cirrus** (© **800/424-7787**; www.mastercard.com) and **PLUS** (© **800/843-7587**; www.visa.com) networks span the country; you can find them even in remote regions. Go to your bank card's website to find ATM locations at your destination. Be sure you know your daily withdrawal limit before you depart.

Note: Many banks impose a fee every time you use a card at another bank's ATM, and that fee is often higher for international transactions (up to $5 or more) than for domestic ones (where they're rarely more than $2). In addition, the bank from which you withdraw cash may charge its own fee. To compare banks' ATM fees within the U.S., use **www.bankrate.com**. Visitors from outside the U.S. should also find out whether their bank assesses a 1% to 3% fee on charges incurred abroad.

The State of New York Banking Department has compiled a comparison of bank fees by region at **www.banking.state.ny. us/bf.htm**. You can also use this chart to see if your own bank operates in the area you plan to visit.

CREDIT CARDS & DEBIT CARDS

Credit cards are the most widely used form of payment in the United States: **Visa** (Barclaycard in Britain), **Master-Card** (EuroCard in Europe, Access in Britain, Chargex in Canada), **American Express, Diners Club,** and **Discover.** They also provide a convenient record of all your expenses, and offer relatively good exchange rates. You can withdraw cash advances from your credit cards at banks or ATMs, but high fees make credit-card cash advances a pricey way to get cash.

It's highly recommended that you travel with at least one major credit card. You must have a credit card to rent a car, and hotels and airlines usually require a credit card imprint as a deposit against expenses.

ATM cards with major credit card backing, known as **"debit cards,"** are now a commonly acceptable form of payment in most stores and restaurants. Debit cards draw money directly from your checking account. Some stores enable you to receive cash back on your debit-card purchases as well. The same is true at most U.S. post offices.

TRAVELER'S CHECKS

Though credit cards and debit cards are more often used throughout New York State, traveler's checks are still widely accepted. (However, where they are rarely seen, especially outside many larger cities, it may feel impractical to use them if it requires explaining to merchants how traveler's checks should be treated.) Foreign visitors should make sure that traveler's checks are denominated in U.S. dollars; foreign-currency checks are often difficult to exchange.

You can buy traveler's checks at most banks. Most are offered in denominations of $20, $50, $100, $500, and sometimes $1,000. Generally, you'll pay a service charge ranging from 1% to 4%.

The most popular traveler's checks are offered by **American Express** (✆ **800/807-6233;** 800/221-7282 for card holders—this number accepts collect calls, offers service in several foreign languages, and exempts Amex gold and platinum cardholders from the 1% fee); **Visa** (✆ **800/732-1322)**—AAA members can obtain Visa checks for a $9.95 fee (for checks up to $1,500) at most AAA offices or by calling ✆ **866/339-3378;** and **MasterCard** (✆ **800/223-9920)**.

Be sure to keep a copy of the traveler's checks' serial numbers separate from your checks in the event that they are stolen or lost. You'll get a refund faster if you know the numbers.

Another option is the new **prepaid traveler's check cards,** reloadable cards that work much like debit cards but aren't linked to your checking account. The **American Express Travelers Cheque Card,** for example, requires a minimum deposit ($300), sets a maximum balance ($2,750), and has a one-time issuance fee of $15. You can withdraw money from an

ATM ($2.50 per transaction, not including bank fees), and the funds can be purchased in dollars, euros, or pounds. If you lose the card, your available funds will be refunded within 24 hours.

7 Travel Insurance

The cost of travel insurance varies widely, depending on the cost and length of your trip, your age and health, and the type of trip you're taking, but expect to pay between 5% and 8% of the vacation itself. You can get estimates from various providers through **InsureMyTrip.com.** Enter your trip cost and dates, your age, and other information, for prices from more than a dozen companies.

For **U.K. citizens,** insurance is always advisable when traveling in the States. Travelers or families who make more than one trip abroad per year may find that an annual travel insurance policy works out cheaper. Check **www.moneysupermarket. com**, which compares prices across a wide range of providers for single- and multi-trip policies.

Most big travel agents offer their own insurance and will probably try to sell you their package when you book a holiday. Think before you sign. **Britain's Consumers' Association** recommends that you insist on seeing the policy and reading the fine print before buying travel insurance. **The Association of British Insurers** (✆ 020/7600-3333; www.abi. org.uk) gives advice by phone and publishes *Holiday Insurance,* a free guide to policy provisions and prices. You might also shop around for better deals: Try **Columbus Direct** (✆ 0870/033-9988; www.columbusdirect.net).

MEDICAL INSURANCE

Although it's not required of travelers, health insurance is highly recommended. Most health insurance policies cover you if you get sick away from home—but check your coverage before you leave.

International visitors should note that unlike many European countries, the United States does not usually offer free or low-cost medical care to its citizens or visitors. Doctors and hospitals are expensive, and in most cases will require advance payment or proof of coverage before they render their services. Good policies will cover the costs of an accident, repatriation, or death. Packages such as **Europ Assistance's "Worldwide Healthcare Plan"** are sold by European automobile clubs and travel agencies at attractive rates. **Worldwide Assistance Services, Inc.** (✆ 800/777-8710; www. worldwideassistance.com), is the agent for Europ Assistance in the United States.

Though lack of health insurance may prevent you from being admitted to a hospital in nonemergencies, don't worry about being left on a street corner to die: The American way is to fix you now and bill the living daylights out of you later.

If you're ever hospitalized more than 150 miles from home, **MedjetAssist** (✆ 800/527-7478; www.medjetassistance.com) will pick you up and fly you to the hospital of your choice in a medically equipped and staffed aircraft 24 hours a day, 7 days a week. Annual memberships are $225 individual, $350 family; you can also purchase short-term memberships.

Canadians should check with their provincial health-plan offices or call **Health Canada** (✆ 866/225-0709; www. hc-sc.gc.ca) to find out the extent of their coverage and what documentation and receipts they must take home in case they are treated in the United States.

8 Health

STAYING HEALTHY

For the latest information about health issues affecting travelers, visit the **Centers for Disease Control and Prevention**'s travel page at www.cdc.gov/travel or call the **Travelers' Health Hotline** at © 877/ FYI-TRIP. The **New York State Department of Health** website (www.health. state.ny.us) is geared toward residents rather than visitors but provides more specifics about issues concerning New York.

GENERAL AVAILABILITY OF HEALTHCARE

There's no shortage of doctors, hospitals, and pharmacies in New York. But it's true that cities have more facilities than rural areas. The New York State Department of Health provides a list of hospitals by county at www.health.state.ny.us/nysdoh/hospital/main.htm.

Pharmacy chains like **Rite Aid** (www.riteaid.com), **CVS** (www.cvs.com), and **Walgreens** (www.walgreens.com) are pretty easy to find should you need to fill or refill a prescription. Bring your doctor's telephone number with you so that the pharmacist can confirm the prescription with your doctor's office. It's also helpful to have the number of your home pharmacy on hand in case your doctor can't be reached.

Contact the **International Association for Medical Assistance to Travelers** (IAMAT) (© 716/754-4883 or, in Canada, 416/652-0137; **www.iamat.org**) for tips on travel and health concerns in the countries you're visiting, and for lists of local, English-speaking doctors. The United States **Centers for Disease Control and Prevention** (© 800/311-3435; www.cdc.gov) provides up-to-date information on health hazards by region or country and offers tips on food safety. The website **www.tripprep.com**, sponsored by

a consortium of travel medicine practitioners, **Travel Health Online,** may also offer helpful advice on traveling abroad. You can find listings of reliable clinics overseas at the **International Society of Travel Medicine** (www.istm.org).

COMMON AILMENTS

BUGS & BITES   Mosquitoes are a familiar annoyance, particularly in late summer and early fall when New York's mosquito population peaks. They were upgraded from pest to public health issue, however, when the first U.S. case of the mosquito-borne **West Nile virus** was reported in New York City back in 1999. The virus can lead to a flulike bout of West Nile fever, or more serious diseases such as West Nile encephalitis or meningitis. Even if you get a few bites, though, the risk of illness is low. Not all mosquitoes carry the virus, and most people who are infected never become sick, although people over 50 are more susceptible. Symptoms include fever, headache, stiff neck, body ache, muscle weakness or tremors, and disorientation. If you think you've been infected, see a doctor right away or go to the emergency room.

The best defense is an effective bug repellent worn whenever you're in a mosquito-friendly environment—this includes warm and wet urban areas as well as forests and fields. They can bite right through lightweight fabrics, so it's smart to give clothes a spritz, too. If possible, stay inside when mosquitoes are busiest: dawn, dusk, and early evening.

Ticks are common in the Northeast. They stay close to the ground and prefer damp, shady grass and stone walls. **Lyme disease** is carried by deer ticks, which are 2 millimeters or less in size (smaller than dog ticks or cattle ticks). If you've been bitten by a tick, there's no reason to assume you've contracted the disease. Not all ticks are carriers, and removing the offender within the first 36 hours usually prevents transmission of the harmful bacteria. Seek medical aid if symptoms develop, such as the trademark "bull's-eye" bruise or red rash that grows outward from the area of the bite, or other signs like joint pain, fever, fatigue, or facial paralysis. If left unchecked, Lyme disease can lead to serious complications affecting the heart or nervous system.

OTHER WILDLIFE CONCERNS
New York's national and state parks are great places to glimpse wild creatures. This can be exciting; but remember that wild animals are unpredictable, and it's wise not to get too close.

Raccoons, foxes, skunks, and bats are the most likely to spread **rabies.** The virus can be transmitted through the bite or scratch of an infected animal, or by contact with the animal's saliva or nervous tissue through an unhealed cut. This means it's unsafe to poke around dead carcasses as well. If contact occurs, wash the wound thoroughly with soap and water and report to a doctor or hospital for treatment. Let a park ranger or other official know so the animal can be captured and tested for the disease.

Black bears are indigenous to the Adirondack, Catskill, and Allegany mountains. Although they're naturally inclined to avoid humans, they'll often raid campsites in search of food. Tuck food away and clean up campsites after meals to keep them from sniffing around. And never approach a baby bear. The mother bear is usually not far away and may perceive you as a threat to the cub. A useful source for black-bear safety tips is the Citizens for Responsible Wildlife Management website at **www.responsiblewildlifemanagement. org/bear_safety.htm.**

Deer are frequently sighted in upstate New York—often crossing the road in front of your car. Hitting a deer can be an awful experience. Besides feeling as if you've just killed Bambi, you could also sustain major damage to your vehicle or yourself in the accident. Warning signs are posted at well-known deer crossings, but keep your eyes peeled in any wilderness area, especially during breeding season (Oct–Dec).

EXTREME WEATHER EXPOSURE
It's not typically cold enough in New York for **frostbite** to take hold during normal activities like sightseeing. But if you plan to spend all day on the slopes or take long winter hikes, dress appropriately and warm up indoors periodically. This is especially important for kids—they lose heat faster than adults and may not notice the cold if they're having fun. In summer, high temperatures and humidity combined with too much exercise can provoke **heat illness.** Stop and rest in the shade when you feel too hot, tired, or dehydrated, and always carry water with you.

STAYING SAFE
The crime rate in New York State has been steadily dropping for the past decade. New York City, once famous for muggings, is now considered one of the safest large cities in the country. That said, it's never a good idea to take your safety for granted.

First and foremost, know where you're going. If you look lost or distracted, you may seem like an easy mark. Ask for directions at the front desk before leaving your hotel, and try not to be obvious about checking maps on the street. Be wary of strangers who offer to act as guides. They may expect you to tip them, or they may try to lead you to a secluded place where they can rob you. Try not to use the subway to get around late at night; opt for the bus or a taxi instead.

Keep on the lookout for thieves and pickpockets. Common tactics include bumping into you, accompanying you through a revolving door, or spilling something on your clothes to distract you. When withdrawing money from an ATM at a bank after hours, note who enters the foyer with you or who is already inside. If it doesn't seem safe, find another ATM.

At the hotel, keep the door locked and use the bolt when you're inside the room. Before you answer the door, make sure you know who it is. If it's an unexpected visit from room service or maintenance, don't be embarrassed to call the front desk to make sure it's legitimate. Remember that the staff has passkeys, and your room is frequently opened when you're not there. Use the in-room safe for cash, traveler's checks, and valuables like your jewelry or your laptop. If there's no safe in your room, inquire about using the hotel safe.

Since the September 11, 2001, terrorist attacks, counteracting terrorism has become a major concern. The police urge everyone to report unattended bags or suspicious-looking packages through the **Statewide Public Security Tips Hotline** at © **866/SAFE-NYS,** or 888/NYC-SAFE in New York City.

10 Specialized Travel Resources

TRAVELERS WITH DISABILITIES

Most disabilities shouldn't stop anyone from traveling. There are more options and resources out there than ever before.

Several travel agencies offer services for travelers with disabilities who are eager to explore the natural and cultural wonders of New York State. **People and Places** (© **716/937-1813** or 716/496-8826; www.people-and-places.org) offers escorted tours for vacationers with developmental disabilities to the Adirondacks, Catskills, Thousand Islands, Finger Lakes, and other destinations in New York State. **Next Stop New York** (© **800/434-7554** or 718/264-2300; www.nextstopnewyork.com) designs theater, food-tasting, and sightseeing tours of Manhattan for groups or individuals. **Alternative Leisure Co. & Trips Unlimited** (© **781/275-0023;** www.alctrips.com) offers group excursions in New York and New England as well as a "Traveling Companion" program, which provides staff members to accompany individuals on customized trips.

The **America the Beautiful—National Park and Federal Recreational Lands Pass—Access Pass** (formerly the **Golden Access Passport**) gives travelers who are visually impaired or permanently disabled (regardless of age) free lifetime entrance to federal recreation sites administered by the National Park Service, including the Fish and Wildlife Service, the Forest Service, the Bureau of Land Management, and the Bureau of Reclamation. This may include national parks, monuments, historic sites, recreation areas, and national wildlife refuges.

The America the Beautiful Access Pass can be obtained only in person at any NPS facility that charges an entrance fee. You need to show proof of medically determined disability. Besides free entry, the pass also offers a 50% discount on some federal-use fees charged for such facilities as camping, swimming, parking, boat launching, and tours. For more information, go to www.nps.gov/fees_passes.htm or call © **888/467-2757.**

Organizations that offer a vast range of resources and assistance to travelers with disabilities include **MossRehab** (© **800/CALL-MOSS;** www.mossresourcenet.org); the **American Foundation for the Blind (AFB)** (© **800/232-5463;** www.afb.org); and **SATH (Society for Accessible Travel & Hospitality)** (© **212/447-7284;** www.sath.org). **AirAmbulanceCard.com** is now partnered with SATH and allows you to preselect top-notch hospitals in case of an emergency.

Access-Able Travel Source (© 303/232-2979; www.access-able.com) offers a comprehensive database on travel agents from around the world with experience in accessible travel; destination-specific access information; and links to such resources as service animals, equipment rentals, and access guides.

Many travel agencies offer customized tours and itineraries for travelers with disabilities. Among them are **Flying Wheels Travel** (© 507/451-5005; www.flyingwheelstravel.com) and **Accessible Journeys** (© 800/846-4537 or 610/521-0339; www.disabilitytravel.com).

Flying with Disability (www.flying-with-disability.org) is a comprehensive information source on airplane travel. **Avis Rent a Car** (© 888/879-4273) has an "Avis Access" program that offers services for customers with special travel needs. These include specially outfitted vehicles with swivel seats, spinner knobs, and hand controls; mobility scooter rentals; and accessible bus service. Be sure to reserve well in advance.

Also check out the quarterly magazine *Emerging Horizons* (www.emerginghorizons.com), available by subscription ($16.95 year U.S.; $21.95 outside U.S).

The "Accessible Travel" link at **MobilityAdvisor.com** (www.mobility-advisor.com) offers a variety of travel resources to persons with disabilities.

British travelers should contact **Holiday Care** (© 0845/124-9971 in UK only; www.holidaycare.org.uk) to access a wide range of travel information and resources for travelers with disabilities and seniors.

GAY & LESBIAN TRAVELERS

New York City is home to a gay, lesbian, bisexual, and transgender community of more than a million strong by some estimates. The highlight of the events calendar is the annual Pride Week (p. 29), but visitors year-round have plenty to explore in the many gay-owned restaurants, bars, boutiques, bookstores, and art galleries found largely in Manhattan's Greenwich Village and Chelsea neighborhoods. The central bulletin board for meetings, cultural events, and resources in New York City is **The Lesbian, Gay, Bisexual, and Transgender Community Center** (© 212/620-7310; www.gaycenter.org). Click on "NYC Resources" and "Accommodations" on its home page for a list of gay-friendly places to stay.

However, there's more to gay and lesbian life in the Empire State than cruising Chelsea and the Village. Travelers will find thriving networks in upstate, central, and western New York. **Outcome Buffalo** (www.outcomebuffalo.com), **Gay-Buffalo Online** (www.gaybuffalo.org/nfgc), **Gay Rochester Online** (www.gayrochester.com), and **Capital District Gay and Lesbian Community Council, Inc.** (© 518/462-6138; www.cdglcc.org), are great sources of information about nightlife, social groups, news, and links to other gay and lesbian organizations. **Sullivan County** in the Catskill Mountain region is proudly gay-friendly in tourist matters, and it operates a website with plenty of information for gay and lesbian travelers (www.outinthecatskills.com).

The **International Gay and Lesbian Travel Association (IGLTA)** (© 800/448-8550 or 954/776-2626; www.iglta.org) is the trade association for the gay and lesbian travel industry, and offers an online directory of gay- and lesbian-friendly travel businesses and tour operators.

SENIOR TRAVEL

Mention the fact that you're a senior when you make your travel reservations. Although all of the major U.S. airlines except America West have canceled their senior discount and coupon book programs, many hotels still offer discounts for seniors. In most cities, people over the age of 60 qualify for reduced admission to theaters, museums, and other attractions, as well as discounted fares on public transportation.

Members of **AARP**, 601 E St. NW, Washington, DC 20049 (© **888/687-2277**; www.aarp.org), get discounts on hotels, airfares, and car rentals. AARP offers members a wide range of benefits, including *AARP: The Magazine* and a monthly newsletter. Anyone over 50 can join.

The U.S. National Park Service offers an **America the Beautiful—National Park and Federal Recreational Lands Pass—Senior Pass** (formerly the **Golden Age Passport**), which gives seniors 62 years or older lifetime entrance to all properties administered by the National Park Service—national parks, monuments, historic sites, recreation areas, and national wildlife refuges—for a one-time processing fee of $10. The pass must be purchased in person at any NPS facility that charges an entrance fee. Besides free entry, the America the Beautiful Senior Pass also offers a 50% discount on some federal-use fees charged for such facilities as camping, swimming, parking, boat launching, and tours. For more information, go to www.nps.gov/fees_passes.htm or call © **888/467-2757.**

FAMILY TRAVEL

New York's varied cultural landscape offers plenty of opportunities for family fun. You can pack up the station wagon for a *Brady Bunch*–style camping trip through the wilderness, visit the National Baseball Hall of Fame and Museum in quaint Cooperstown, or take in a Broadway show amid the bright lights of Manhattan's now-family-friendly Times Square. To locate accommodations, restaurants, and attractions that are particularly kid-friendly, refer to the "Kids" icon throughout this guide.

A good source for family vacation suggestions is the **I Love NY** website (www.iloveny.com)—click on "Travel Ideas." New York City's official tourism website, **NYC & Company** (www.nycvisit.com), details restaurants, museums, and tours designed to fascinate kids, plus a list of activities and neighborhoods that even the most blasé teen might enjoy.

Familyhostel (© **800/733-9753**) takes the whole family, including kids ages 8 to 15, on moderately priced domestic and international learning vacations. Lectures, fields trips, and sightseeing are guided by a team of academics.

11 Sustainable Tourism/Ecotourism

Each time you take a flight or drive a car, carbon dioxide is released into the atmosphere. You can help neutralize this danger to our planet through "carbon offsetting"—paying someone to reduce your carbon dioxide emissions by the same amount you've added. Carbon offsets can be purchased in the U.S. from companies such as **Carbonfund.org** (www.carbonfund.org) and **TerraPass** (www.terrapass.org), and from **Climate Care** (www.climatecare.org) in the U.K.

Although one could argue that any vacation that includes an airplane flight can't be truly "green," you can go on holiday and still contribute positively to the environment. In addition to purchasing carbon offsets from the companies mentioned above, you can take other steps toward responsible travel. Choose forward-looking companies that embrace responsible development practices, helping preserve destinations for the future by working alongside local people. An increasing number of sustainable tourism initiatives can help you plan a family trip and leave as small a "footprint" as possible on the places you visit.

Responsible Travel (www.responsibletravel.com), run by a spokesperson for responsible tourism in the travel industry, contains a great source of sustainable travel ideas.

You can find eco-friendly travel tips, statistics, and touring companies and associations—listed by destination under "Travel Choice"—at The International Ecotourism Society (TIES) website, **www.ecotourism.org**. Also check out **Conservation International** (www.conservation.org)—which, with *National Geographic* *Traveler,* annually presents **World Legacy Awards** to those travel tour operators, businesses, organizations, and places that have made a significant contribution to sustainable tourism. **Ecotravel.com** is part online magazine and part ecodirectory that lets you search for touring companies in several categories (water-based, land-based, spiritually oriented, and so on).

12 Staying Connected

TELEPHONES

Generally, hotel surcharges on long-distance and local calls are astronomical, so you're better off using your **cellphone** or a **public pay telephone.** Many convenience stores, groceries, and packaging services sell **prepaid calling cards** in denominations up to $50; for international visitors these can be the least expensive way to call home. Many public pay phones at airports now accept American Express, MasterCard, and Visa credit cards. **Local calls** made from pay phones in most locales cost either 25¢ or 35¢ (no pennies, please).

Most long-distance and international calls can be dialed directly from any phone. **For calls within the United States and to Canada,** dial 1 followed by the area code and the seven-digit number. **For other international calls,** dial 011 followed by the country code, city code, and the number you are calling.

Calls to area codes **800, 888, 877,** and **866** are toll-free. However, calls to area codes **700** and **900** (chat lines, bulletin boards, "dating" services, and so on) can be very expensive—usually a charge of 95¢ to $3 or more per minute, and they sometimes have minimum charges that can run as high as $15 or more.

For **reversed-charge or collect calls,** and for person-to-person calls, dial the number 0, then the area code and number; an operator will come on the line, and you should specify whether you are calling collect, person-to-person, or both.

If your operator-assisted call is international, ask for the overseas operator.

For **local directory assistance** ("information"), dial 411; for long-distance information, dial 1, then the appropriate area code and 555-1212.

CELLPHONES

Just because your cellphone works at home doesn't mean it will work everywhere in the U.S. (thanks to our nation's fragmented cellphone system). It's a good bet that your phone will work in major cities, but take a look at your wireless company's coverage map on its website before heading out; T-Mobile, Sprint, and Nextel are particularly weak in rural areas. If you need to stay in touch at a destination where you know your phone won't work, **rent** a phone that does from **InTouch USA** (✆ **800/872-7626;** www.intouch global.com) or a rental-car location, but beware that you'll pay $1 a minute or more for airtime.

If you're not from the U.S., you'll be appalled at the poor reach of our **GSM (Global System for Mobile Communications) wireless network,** which is used by much of the rest of the world. Your phone will probably work in most major U.S. cities; it definitely won't work in many rural areas. To see where GSM phones work in the U.S., check out www.t-mobile.com/coverage/national_popup.asp. And you may or may not be able to send SMS (text messaging) home.

Online Traveler's Toolbox

Veteran travelers usually carry some essential items to make their trips easier. Following is a selection of handy online tools to bookmark and use.

- **Airplane Food** (www.airlinemeals.net)
- **Airplane Seating** (www.seatguru.com and www.airlinequality.com)
- **Foreign Languages for Travelers** (www.travlang.com)
- **Maps** (www.mapquest.com)
- **Subway Navigator** (www.subwaynavigator.com)
- **Time and Date** (www.timeanddate.com)
- **Travel Warnings** (http://travel.state.gov, www.fco.gov.uk/travel, www.voyage.gc.ca, and www.dfat.gov.au/consular/advice)
- **Universal Currency Converter** (www.xe.com/ucc)
- **Visa ATM Locator** (www.visa.com), **MasterCard ATM Locator** (www.mastercard.com)
- **Weather** (www.intellicast.com and www.weather.com)

In New York City, you can rent cell-phones at **Roberts Rent-a-Phone,** 226 E. 54th St., New York, NY 10022 (© **800/964-2468** or 212/832-7143; www.roberts-rent-a-phone.com) or **Cellhire USA,** 45 Broadway, 20th Floor, New York, NY 10006 (© **866/235-5447;** www.cellhire.com).

INTERNET/E-MAIL WITHOUT YOUR OWN COMPUTER

To find cybercafes in your destination check **www.cybercaptive.com** and **www.cybercafe.com**.

Most major airports have **Internet kiosks** that provide basic Web access for a per-minute fee that's usually higher than cybercafe prices. Check out copy shops like **Kinko's** (FedEx Kinkos), which offers computer stations with fully loaded software (as well as Wi-Fi).

WITH YOUR OWN COMPUTER

More and more hotels, resorts, airports, cafes, and retailers are going Wi-Fi (wireless fidelity), becoming "hot spots" that offer free high-speed Wi-Fi access or charge a small fee for usage. Wi-Fi is even found in campgrounds, RV parks, and even entire towns. Most laptops sold today have built-in wireless capability. To find public Wi-Fi hot spots at your destination, go to **www.jiwire.com**; its Hotspot Finder holds the world's largest directory of public wireless hot spots.

For dial-up access, most business-class hotels in the U.S. offer dataports for laptop modems, and a few thousand hotels in the U.S. and Europe now offer free high-speed Internet access.

Wherever you go, bring a **connection kit** of the right power and phone adapters, a spare phone cord, and a spare Ethernet network cable—or find out whether your hotel supplies them to guests.

For information on electrical currency conversions, see **"Electricity,"** in the **"Fast Facts"** section at the end of this chapter.

13 Packages for the Independent Traveler

Package tours are simply a way to buy the airfare, accommodations, and other elements of your trip (such as car rentals, airport transfers, and sometimes even activities) at the same time and often at discounted prices.

One good source of package deals is the airlines themselves. Most major airlines offer air/land packages, including **American Airlines Vacations** (℡ 800/321-2121; www.aavacations.com), **Delta Vacations** (℡ 800/654-6559; www.deltavacations. com), **Continental Airlines Vacations** (℡ 800/301-3800; www.covacations. com), and **United Vacations** (℡ 888/854-3899; www.unitedvacations.com). Several big **online travel agencies**—

Expedia, Travelocity, Orbitz, Site59, and Lastminute.com—also do a brisk business in packages.

Be sure to check out the deals and packages on **HotNewYorkDeals.com** (http://hotnewyorkdeals.com). **Gorp Travel** (www.gorptravel.com) lists outdoor-oriented trips to New York State, such as biking in the Finger Lakes wine country and along the Erie Canal.

Travel packages are also listed in the travel section of your local Sunday newspaper. Or check ads in the national travel magazines such as *Arthur Frommer's Budget Travel Magazine, Travel + Leisure, National Geographic Traveler,* and *Condé Nast Traveler.*

14 Escorted General-Interest Tours

Escorted tours are structured group tours, with a group leader. The price usually includes everything from airfare to hotels, meals, tours, admission costs, and local transportation.

Despite the fact that escorted tours require big deposits and predetermine hotels, restaurants, and itineraries, many people derive security and peace of mind from the structure they offer. Escorted tours—whether they're navigated by bus, motorcoach, train, or boat—let travelers sit back and enjoy the trip without having to drive or worry about details. They take

you to the maximum number of sights in the minimum amount of time with the least amount of hassle. They're particularly convenient for people with limited mobility and they can be a great way to make new friends.

On the downside, you'll have little opportunity for serendipitous interactions with locals. The tours can be jam-packed with activities, leaving little room for individual sightseeing, whim, or adventure—plus they often focus on the heavily touristed sites, so you miss out on many a lesser-known gem.

15 Getting Around New York State

New York State is considerably larger than many people realize; the drive from New York City to Niagara Falls can take 7 or 8 hours, while the nearest point in the Finger Lakes is 4 hours from the city. Before you commit to hours of drive time, you may want to weigh the alternatives.

BY CAR

Unless you plan to spend the bulk of your vacation in a city where walking is the

best way to get around (read: New York City), the most cost-effective way to travel is by car.

If you're visiting from abroad and plan to rent a car in the United States, keep in mind that foreign driver's licenses are usually recognized in the U.S., but you should get an international one if your home license is not in English.

Check out **Breezenet.com,** which offers domestic car-rental discounts with some of the most competitive rates around.

For an explanation of major New York State roadways and the cities they connect, see "Getting There," earlier in this chapter.

Gas prices in New York State tend to be about 10¢ higher than the national average. Of the major cities, Albany and Binghamton have the cheapest gas. Not surprisingly, New York City's is the most expensive (as much as 50¢ higher per gallon).

If you plan to travel between December and March, be advised that winter weather can present significant obstacles, such as wet or icy pavement, poor visibility, or routes that are just plain shut down. Make sure that your vehicle is adequately prepared with snow tires and working windshield wipers, battery, and defrosters. Most likely, though, you won't run into too many problems. Roads are well maintained in the winter, and even after a storm, side streets and highways alike are cleared fairly quickly.

Highway speed limits are 55 or 65 mph. The speed limit in New York City is 30 mph unless otherwise posted. "Right on red" (making a right turn at a red light after coming to a complete stop) is permitted, except in New York City. Motorcyclists must wear helmets, and goggles if helmets are not equipped with face shields. Everyone should buckle up, but at the minimum, state law requires drivers, front-seat passengers, and children under 10 to wear seat belts. Children under 4 must ride in safety seats. Fines can run up to $100. Talking on a hand-held cellphone while driving (without an earpiece) is punishable by a fine of up to $100 (exceptions are made for emergency situations, such as calls to the police). Drivers can be charged with driving while intoxicated (DWI) for having a blood alcohol content of .08% or higher and sentenced to a fine or jail time upon conviction.

BY TRAIN

The train won't get you where you're going any faster, but it will cut down on the amount of time you have to spend behind the wheel. Once you get where you're going, though, you'll probably need to rent a car anyway since public transportation is not very extensive beyond New York City.

Amtrak (© 800/USA-RAIL; www. amtrak.com) basically follows the same paths as the New York State Thruway and the Adirondack Northway (routes 90 and 87), leaving much of the state inaccessible by rail. For more information on cities served by Amtrak, see "Getting There," earlier in this chapter.

Visitors to Long Island can take the **Long Island Rail Road (LIRR; © 718/217-5477;** www.mta.nyc.ny.us/lirr). With service from New York City's Penn Station, the LIRR is the main mode of transportation for commuters as well as Manhattanites weekending in the Hamptons. Since seating is normally unreserved, trains are often standing-room-only during the summer vacation season. **Hamptons Reserve Service** (© 718/558-8070) guarantees passengers a seat on the Friday express train for an extra fee in addition to the regular fare.

Metro-North Railroad (© 800/METRO-INFO or 212/532-4900; www. mta.nyc.ny.us/mnr/index.html) makes the Hudson Valley region easily reachable from New York City's Grand Central Station with commuter lines extending as far north as Poughkeepsie and Wassaic, and west to Port Jervis.

International visitors can buy a **USA Rail Pass,** good for 5, 15, or 30 days of unlimited travel on **Amtrak** (© 800/USA-RAIL;** www.amtrak.com). The pass is available online or through many overseas travel agents. See Amtrak's website for the cost of travel within the western, eastern, or northwestern United States. Reservations are generally required and should be made as early as possible. Regional rail passes are also available.

BY PLANE

CommutAir (www.commutair.com), a partner of **Continental Airlines** (© 800/525-0280; www.continental.com), offers flights from its Albany hub to Buffalo, Rochester, Syracuse, Elmira, White Plains, Islip, Plattsburg, and Lake Placid. Reservations must be made through Continental.

JetBlue Airways (© 800/538-2583; www.jetblue.com) is hard to beat, with consistently low ticket prices and daily runs from New York City (JFK Airport) to Buffalo, Rochester, and Syracuse.

US Airways (© 800/428-4322; www.usairways.com) and its partner **Colgan Air** (www.colganair.com) provide direct flights from New York City to Albany, Buffalo, Ithaca, Rochester, and Syracuse, as well as service from Albany to Buffalo and Islip.

Northwest Airlines (© 800/225-2525; www.nwa.com) now flies to Ithaca.

Overseas visitors can take advantage of the APEX (Advance Purchase Excursion) reductions offered by all major U.S. and European carriers. In addition, some large airlines offer transatlantic or transpacific passengers special discount tickets under the name **Visit USA,** which allows mostly one-way travel from one U.S. destination to another at very low prices. Unavailable in the U.S., these tickets must be purchased abroad in conjunction with your international fare. This is the easiest, fastest, cheapest way to see the country.

16 Tips on Accommodations

New York offers a wide range of accommodations—from the superchic luxury hotels of Manhattan and the Victorian B&Bs of Saratoga Springs to the rustic mountain retreats of the Catskills and Adirondacks and the salty seaside motels of Long Island.

The **New York State Hospitality and Tourism Association** (© 518/465-2300; www.nyshta.org) covers the gamut of hotel and motel options and provides a free map listing the names and basic rates of its members statewide.

The perfect bed-and-breakfast can be hard to track down since few are well known outside their local areas. The **Empire State Bed & Breakfast Association** (© 800/841-2340; www.esbba.com) makes the task easier with its free, color guide to 150 inns and B&Bs across the state. Another good bet is **Bed & Breakfast Inns Online** (www.bbonline.com),

where you can view interior and exterior photos of almost every property profiled, including several listed on the National Register of Historic Places. The site offers last-minute, midweek, and seasonal specials besides a variety of other packages.

House swaps aren't for everyone—clean freaks and people with control issues may skip ahead to the next section. However, you may consider staying in a private home while the owners stay in yours to be a comfortable and cost-effective alternative to booking a hotel. **HomeLink International** (© 800/638-3841 or 813/975-9825; www.homelink.org) is an established house-swapping service. Apartment swaps in Manhattan, Brooklyn, and other New York City boroughs can be found through **Craigslist.org.** People over 50 may register their homes with **Seniors Home Exchange** (www.seniorshomeexchange.com).

FAST FACTS: New York State

American Express For the location of the nearest American Express Travel office, call ✆ **800/297-3429** or log on to www.americanexpress.com. If you have questions about traveler's checks, call ✆ **800/221-7282**. For help with your credit card account, call ✆ **800/528-4800**. See "Lost & Found," below, for what to do in the event of lost or stolen credit cards or traveler's checks.

Area Codes Several changes have been made to area-code dialing in New York over the past several years. New area codes have been added in western New York, Long Island, New York City, and the Hudson Valley/Catskill region, bringing the state total to 14. In addition, callers in New York City are now required to dial the area code for both local and long-distance calls (1 + the area code + the seven-digit local number) whether calling another borough or calling across the street. For a list of New York State area codes, consult the phone book or go to www.verizon.com.

Business Hours Business hours in New York State don't differ much from those of the rest of the country, and are generally 9am to 5pm, with one notable exception: It may be a tired cliché, but they don't call New York City "the city that never sleeps" for nothing. Although some stores close at 7pm, many are open until 9pm, and a few as late as 11pm. Most restaurants serve until 11pm, and later on weekends. Some diners serve breakfast all night to bar-crawlers and club kids, and 24-hour convenience stores on every other block sell an assortment of items you might need during the night, such as groceries, beer, ice cream, cigarettes, and cold remedies.

Currency The most common bills are the $1 (occasionally called a "buck"), $5, $10, and $20 denominations. There are also $2 bills (seldom encountered), $50 bills, and $100 bills (the last two are usually not welcome as payment for small purchases).

Coins come in seven denominations: 1¢ (1 cent, or a penny); 5¢ (5 cents, or a nickel); 10¢ (10 cents, or a dime); 25¢ (25 cents, or a quarter); 50¢ (50 cents, or a half dollar); the gold-colored Sacagawea coin, worth $1; and the rare silver dollar.

For additional information see "Money & Costs" on p. 35.

Customs **What You Can Bring into New York State:** Every visitor more than 21 years of age may bring in, free of duty, the following: (1) 1 liter of wine or hard liquor; (2) 200 cigarettes, 100 cigars (but not from Cuba), or 3 pounds of smoking tobacco; and (3) $100 worth of gifts. These exemptions are offered to travelers who spend at least 72 hours in the United States and who have not claimed them within the preceding 6 months. It is altogether forbidden to bring into the country foodstuffs (particularly fruit, cooked meats, and canned goods) and plants (vegetables, seeds, tropical plants, and the like). Foreign tourists may carry in or out up to $10,000 in U.S. or foreign currency with no formalities; larger sums must be declared to U.S. Customs on entering or leaving, which includes filing form CM 4790. For details regarding U.S. Customs and Border Protection, consult your nearest U.S. embassy or consulate, or **U.S. Customs** (✆ **202/927-1770**; www.customs.ustreas.gov).

What You Can Take Home from New York State:

Canadian Citizens: For a clear summary of Canadian rules, write for the booklet *I Declare,* issued by the **Canada Border Services Agency** (✆ **800/461-9999** in Canada, or 204/983-3500; **www.cbsa-asfc.gc.ca**).

U.K. Citizens: For information, contact **HM Customs & Excise** at ✆ **0845/010-9000** (from outside the U.K., 020/8929-0152), or consult their website at **www.hmce.gov.uk**.

Australian Citizens: A helpful brochure available from Australian consulates or Customs offices is *Know Before You Go.* For more information, call the **Australian Customs Service** at ✆ **1300/363-263,** or log on to **www.customs.gov.au**.

New Zealand Citizens: Most questions are answered in a free pamphlet available at New Zealand consulates and Customs offices: *New Zealand Customs Guide for Travellers, Notice no. 4.* For more information, contact **New Zealand Customs,** The Customhouse, 17–21 Whitmore St., Box 2218, Wellington (✆ **04/473-6099** or 0800/428-786; **www.customs.govt.nz**).

Drinking Laws The legal age for purchase and consumption of alcoholic beverages is 21; proof of age is required and often requested at bars, nightclubs, and restaurants, so it's always a good idea to bring ID when you go out.

In general, grocery and convenience stores sell beer and other products that are less than 6% alcohol by volume (like wine coolers). Many of these stores are open 24 hours, but state law forbids them to sell alcohol from 3am to noon on Sunday. Wine and spirits are sold at liquor stores, also called package stores. Hours vary, but by law they must remain closed from midnight to 8am Monday through Saturday. Some stores may be open from noon to 9pm on Sunday, but many are closed. All liquor stores are closed Christmas Day.

Restaurants and bars can't serve drinks before 8am Monday through Saturday, or before noon on Sunday. Closing time for bars, taverns, and nightclubs varies by county. Albany, Buffalo, and New York City bars close at 4am; in Rochester and Syracuse they close at 2am. In quieter areas, closing time comes as early as 1am. Do not carry open containers of alcohol in your car or any public area that isn't zoned for alcohol consumption. The police can fine you on the spot. And nothing will ruin your trip faster than getting a citation for DWI ("driving while intoxicated"), so don't even think about drinking and driving.

Driving Rules See "Getting Around New York State" on p. 45.

Electricity Like Canada, the United States uses 110 to 120 volts AC (60 cycles), compared to 220 to 240 volts AC (50 cycles) in most of Europe, Australia, and New Zealand. Downward converters that change 220–240 volts to 110–120 volts are difficult to find in the United States, so bring one with you.

Embassies & Consulates All embassies are located in the nation's capital, Washington, D.C. Some consulates are located in major U.S. cities, and most nations have a mission to the United Nations in New York City. If your country isn't listed below, call for directory information in Washington, D.C. (✆ **202/555-1212**), or log on to **www.embassy.org/embassies**.

The embassy of **Australia** is at 1601 Massachusetts Ave. NW, Washington, DC 20036 (✆ **202/797-3000;** www.austemb.org). There are consulates in New York City, Honolulu, Houston, Los Angeles, and San Francisco.

The embassy of **Canada** is at 501 Pennsylvania Ave. NW, Washington, DC 20001 (© **202/682-1740;** www.canadianembassy.org). Other Canadian consulates are in Buffalo (New York), Detroit, Los Angeles, New York City, and Seattle.

The embassy of **Ireland** is at 2234 Massachusetts Ave. NW, Washington, DC 20008 (© **202/462-3939;** www.irelandemb.org). Irish consulates are in Boston, Chicago, New York City, San Francisco, and other cities. See website for complete listing.

The embassy of **New Zealand** is at 37 Observatory Circle NW, Washington, DC 20008 (© **202/328-4800;** www.nzemb.org). New Zealand consulates are in Los Angeles, Salt Lake City, San Francisco, and Seattle.

The embassy of the **United Kingdom** is at 3100 Massachusetts Ave. NW, Washington, DC 20008 (© **202/588-7800;** www.britainusa.com). Other British consulates are in Atlanta, Boston, Chicago, Cleveland, Houston, Los Angeles, New York City, San Francisco, and Seattle.

Emergencies Call © **911** to report a fire, call the police, or get an ambulance anywhere in the United States. This is a toll-free call. (No coins are required at public telephones.)

Gasoline (Petrol) At press time, in the U.S., the cost of gasoline (also known as gas, but never petrol) is abnormally high. Gasoline in New York State is just above the national average, while filling the tank in New York City is about as expensive as you'll find in the country. Taxes are already included in the printed price. One U.S. gallon equals 3.8 liters or .85 imperial gallons. Fill-up locations are known as gas or service stations.

Holidays Banks, government offices, post offices, and many stores, restaurants, and museums are closed on the following legal national holidays: January 1 (New Year's Day), the third Monday in January (Martin Luther King, Jr., Day), the third Monday in February (Presidents' Day), the last Monday in May (Memorial Day), July 4 (Independence Day), the first Monday in September (Labor Day), the second Monday in October (Columbus Day), November 11 (Veterans' Day/Armistice Day), the fourth Thursday in November (Thanksgiving Day), and December 25 (Christmas). The Tuesday after the first Monday in November is Election Day, a federal government holiday in presidential-election years (held every 4 years, and next in 2008).

For more information on holidays, see "New York State Calendar of Events," earlier in this chapter.

Hotlines In New York City, the main hotline for all things metropolitan is © **311.** For tourism matters and questions across the state, call © **800-CALL NYS.** For issues of safety, call the **Statewide Public Security Tips Hotline** at © **866/SAFE-NYS,** or 888/NYC-SAFE in New York City.

Legal Aid If you find yourself in need of legal representation, contact the **New York State Bar Association's Lawyer Referral and Information Service** (© **800/342-3661** or 518/487-5709; www.nysba.org).

Lost & Found Be sure to tell all of your credit card companies the minute you discover that your wallet has been lost or stolen, and file a report at the nearest police precinct. Your credit card company or insurer may require a police report number or record of the loss. Most credit card companies have an emergency toll-free number to call if your card is lost or stolen; they may be able to wire you a cash advance immediately or deliver an emergency credit card in a day or two. Visa's U.S. emergency number is © 800/847-2911 or 410/581-9994. American Express clients should call © 800/221-7282 regarding traveler's checks and © 800/528-4800 regarding credit cards. MasterCard holders should call © 800/307-7309 or 636/722-7111. For other credit cards, call the toll-free number directory at © 800/555-1212.

If you need emergency cash over the weekend when all banks and American Express offices are closed, you can have money wired to you via **Western Union** (© 800/325-6000; www.westernunion.com).

Mail   At press time, domestic postage rates were 26¢ for a postcard and 41¢ for a letter. For international mail, a first-class letter of up to 1 ounce costs 90¢ (69¢ to Canada and Mexico); a first-class postcard costs the same as a letter. For more information, go to **www.usps.com** and click on "Calculate Postage."

If you aren't sure what your address will be in the United States, mail can be sent to you, in your name, c/o General Delivery at the main post office of the city or region where you expect to be. (Call © 800/275-8777 for information on the nearest post office.) The addressee must pick up mail in person and must produce proof of identity (driver's license, passport, and so on). Most post offices will hold your mail for up to 1 month, and are open Monday to Friday from 8am to 6pm, and Saturday from 9am to 3pm.

Always include zip codes when mailing items in the U.S. If you don't know your zip code, visit www.usps.com/zip4.

Maps   The **New York State Division of Tourism,** P.O. Box 2603, Albany, NY 12220-0603 (© 800/CALL-NYS or 518/474-4116; www.iloveny.com/main.asp), will mail you a free map, or you can download state and regional maps from its website. You can also find maps at state **information centers,** or ask for one at the **rental-car company** when you pick up your car. **MapQuest** (www.mapquest.com) can instantly plot your route online. Maps can also be purchased at most bookstores, gas stations, and rest stops.

Measurements   See the chart on the inside front cover of this book for details on converting metric measurements to U.S. equivalents.

Newspapers & Magazines   The *New York Times,* the *Wall Street Journal,* and *USA Today* are sold at newsstands everywhere in New York City and are generally available in hotels and corner newspaper boxes throughout the state. Major cities have their own daily papers. The largest of these are the *Buffalo News, Rochester Democrat and Chronicle, Syracuse Post-Standard,* and *Albany Times Union.* In Manhattan, magazine stores carrying all kinds of domestic and international publications are located in most neighborhoods. In other cities, bookstore chains such as Barnes & Noble carry a wide selection of magazines.

Passports   **For Residents of Australia:** You can pick up an application from your local post office or any branch of Passports Australia, but you must schedule an interview at the passport office to present your application materials. Call the **Australian Passport Information Service** at © 131-232, or visit the government website at www.passports.gov.au.

For Residents of Canada: Passport applications are available at travel agencies throughout Canada or from the central **Passport Office,** Department of Foreign Affairs and International Trade, Ottawa, ON K1A 0G3 (© **800/567-6868;** www.ppt.gc.ca). *Note:* Canadian children who travel must have their own passport. However, if you hold a valid Canadian passport issued before December 11, 2001, that bears the name of your child, the passport remains valid for you and your child until it expires.

For Residents of Ireland: You can apply for a 10-year passport at the **Passport Office,** Setanta Centre, Molesworth Street, Dublin 2 (© **01/671-1633;** www.irlgov.ie/iveagh). Those under age 18 and over 65 must apply for a 3-year passport. You can also apply at 1A South Mall, Cork (© **021/272-525**), or at most main post offices.

For Residents of New Zealand: You can pick up a passport application at any New Zealand Passports Office or download it from their website. Contact the **Passports Office** at © **0800/225-050** in New Zealand or 04/474-8100, or log on to www.passports.govt.nz.

For Residents of the United Kingdom: To pick up an application for a standard 10-year passport (5-yr. passport for children under 16), visit your nearest passport office, major post office, or travel agency, or contact the **United Kingdom Passport Service** at © **0870/521-0410** or search its website at www.ukpa.gov.uk.

Police In nonemergency situations, call the nearest police station. Local police precinct telephone numbers can be found in the blue "government" pages of the phone book. In an emergency, call © **911,** a toll-free call (no coins are required at public telephones).

Smoking The legal age to purchase cigarettes and other tobacco products in New York State is 18. But you won't find many places left to smoke them, aside from your hotel room. A state law passed in 2003 prohibits smoking in almost all public venues and in the workplace. This includes bars and restaurants, although smokers can still light up in cigar bars, designated outdoor areas of restaurants, and some private clubs. The law does not affect Native American–run casinos, and smoking is still permitted there.

Taxes Sales tax in New York State varies between 7.25% and 8.75% (the state tax is 4.25%, and counties generally tack on another 3% or 4%). On top of the sales tax, hotel occupancy taxes can add as much as 5% to hotel and motel bills; an additional 5% typically applies to car rentals as well.

Telegraph, Telex & Fax **Telegraph and telex services** are provided primarily by Western Union. You can telegraph money, or have it telegraphed to you, very quickly over the Western Union system, but this service can cost as much as 15% to 20% of the amount sent.

Most hotels have **fax machines** available for guest use (be sure to ask about the charge to use it). Many hotel rooms are even wired for guests' fax machines. A less expensive way to send and receive faxes may be at stores such as **The UPS Store** (formerly Mail Boxes Etc.).

Time The continental United States is divided into **four time zones:** Eastern Standard Time (EST), Central Standard Time (CST), Mountain Standard Time

(MST), and Pacific Standard Time (PST). Alaska and Hawaii have their own zones. New York State is located in Eastern Standard Time. So, for example, noon in New York City (EST) is 11am in Chicago (CST), 10am in Denver (MST), 9am in Los Angeles (PST), 8am in Anchorage (AST), 7am in Honolulu (HST), 5pm in London (GMT), and 2am the next day in Sydney. **Daylight saving time** is in effect from 1am on the second Sunday in March to 1am on the first Sunday in November, except in Arizona, Hawaii, the U.S. Virgin Islands, and Puerto Rico. Daylight saving time moves the clock 1 hour ahead of standard time.

Tipping Tips are a very important part of certain workers' income, and gratuities are the standard way of showing appreciation for services provided. (Tipping is certainly not compulsory if the service is poor!) In hotels, tip **bellhops** at least $1 per bag ($2–$3 if you have a lot of luggage) and tip the **chamber staff** $1 to $2 per day (more if you've left a disaster area for him or her to clean up). Tip the **doorman** or **concierge** only if he or she has provided you with some specific service (for example, calling a cab for you or obtaining difficult-to-get theater tickets). Tip the **valet-parking attendant** $1 every time you get your car.

In restaurants, bars, and nightclubs, tip **service staff** 15% to 20% of the check, tip **bartenders** 10% to 15%, tip **checkroom attendants** $1 per garment, and tip **valet-parking attendants** $1 per vehicle.

As for other service personnel, tip **cab drivers** 15% of the fare; tip **skycaps** at airports at least $1 per bag ($2–$3 if you have a lot of luggage); and tip **hairdressers** and **barbers** 15% to 20%.

Useful Phone Numbers U.S. Dept. of State Travel Advisory: ℂ **202/647-5225** (manned 24 hr.); U.S. Passport Agency: ℂ **202/647-0518;** U.S. Centers for Disease Control International Traveler's Hot Line: ℂ **404/332-4559.**

Visas For information about U.S. Visas go to **http://travel.state.gov** and click on "Visas." Or go to one of the following websites:

Australian citizens can obtain up-to-date visa information from the **U.S. Embassy Canberra,** Moonah Place, Yarralumla, ACT 2600 (ℂ **02/6214-5600**), or by checking the U.S. Diplomatic Mission's website at **http://usembassy-australia. state.gov/consular.**

British subjects can obtain up-to-date visa information by calling the **U.S. Embassy Visa Information Line** (ℂ **0891/200-290**) or by visiting the "Visas to the U.S." section of the American Embassy London's website at **www.usembassy. org.uk.**

Irish citizens can obtain up-to-date visa information through the **Embassy of the USA Dublin,** 42 Elgin Rd., Dublin 4, Ireland (ℂ **353/1-668-8777;** or by checking the "Consular Services" section of the website at **http://dublin.usembassy.gov.**

Citizens of **New Zealand** can obtain up-to-date visa information by contacting the **U.S. Embassy New Zealand,** 29 Fitzherbert Terrace, Thorndon, Wellington (ℂ **644/472-2068**), or get the information directly from the website at **http://wellington.usembassy.gov.**

3

Suggested New York State Itineraries

If you want to experience the best of a large and diverse state like New York in a relatively short amount of time, you need a workable and efficient travel schedule. That's the point of this chapter. Of course, these are merely suggestions, and infinite variations and combinations are possible. We suggest you concentrate on one region—the Adirondacks or the Finger Lakes, for example—rather than trying to cover too much ground in one trip. These itineraries are designed for travel in a car, and some of the highlights below are particular to summer (or to a lesser degree, spring or fall); winter in New York State may be ideal for skiers, but parts of the state virtually close up in the dead of winter.

1 The Best of New York City in 2 Days

Seeing the best of New York City in 2 days requires endurance, patience, perseverance, very good walking shoes, a $7 daily fun pass MetroCard (p. 82), and a good map of the city subway system. You'll also need to get an early start and have a plan of attack. If you've seen many or all of these sites before, try some of the other listings in chapter 5. Or pick a few neighborhoods you don't know as well, and explore. See *Time Out New York* and the *New York Times* for festivals and events. **Start:** *42nd Street at Twelfth Avenue.*

Day ❶: Major Buildings & Landmarks

On Day 1, take the **Circle Line Sightseeing Cruise** ✻✻ (p. 138) for an overview of Manhattan and a view of the Statue of Liberty. Then take the M42 42nd Street crosstown bus to Fifth Avenue and head to the **New York Public Library** ✻✻ (p. 132). Don't miss the incredible reading room. While you're here, take a look at the library's backyard, **Bryant Park.** (If tents are up, you're visiting during one of the two Fashion Weeks held yearly in the park.) Head east on 42nd Street to Lexington Avenue for a view of our favorite skyscraper, the **Chrysler Building** ✻✻ (p. 131). Take a stroll through **Grand Central Terminal** ✻✻ (p. 122), then walk down Fifth Avenue into the **Empire State Building** ✻✻✻ (p. 122), and head to the top for a pristine panoramic view. Take the B or D train uptown to Seventh Avenue, and walk east across 53rd Street to the completely renovated **Museum of Modern Art** ✻✻ (p. 124). Yes, the $20 suggested admission is outrageous, but this is New York and you are slowly getting used to outrageous. Then spend the rest of the afternoon strolling around **Rockefeller Center** ✻✻ (p. 124) and **Fifth Avenue** (p. 143). If your timing is right, you may be able to squeeze in the 70-minute **NBC Studio Tour** (p. 125).

Finally, cap off the evening with dinner, then a **Broadway show in Times Square** (p. 144 for ticket details) and see the area in all its noisy, illuminated glory.

Day ❷: Downtown & Major Museums

On your second day, head downtown in the morning and explore the city where it began. Take the no. 1 subway to South Ferry or no. 4 or 5 to Bowling Green, and check out **Wall Street** attractions (p. 128), including the impressive **U.S. Customs House,** which houses the **National Museum of the American Indian,** and the **New York Stock Exchange,** where, if you are someone significant, they might let you ring the opening day's bell, at 9:30am. Take the A or C train at Broadway/Nassau Street to High Street, the first stop in Brooklyn, and take a half-hour stroll back to Manhattan over the **Brooklyn Bridge** 𝕲𝕲 (p. 121), an absolute must,

with a spectacular view of the skyline. You'll exit the bridge near the no. 6 train at Brooklyn Bridge/City Hall, which you can take uptown to 77th Street and Lexington Avenue. There, you can explore a few Upper East Side attractions, like the exciting (and manageable in size) **Whitney Museum of American Art** 𝕲 (p. 129) and sprawling, spectacular **Metropolitan Museum of Art** 𝕲𝕲𝕲 (p. 123). Take an hour-long museum highlights tour, or stick with exploring a few rooms. The Met's backyard is **Central Park** 𝕲𝕲𝕲 (p. 133), which you enter at either 79th Street or 85th Street. If you have time, check out the fantastic **American Museum of Natural History** 𝕲𝕲𝕲 (p. 120) at the western side of the park. As with the Met, pick a few highlights. At night, check out a comedy club, or try a barhop and bond with the locals.

2 The Hudson Valley & Saratoga Springs in 3 Days

The Hudson River is more than 300 miles long and loaded with historical homes, museums, Victorian hamlets, and outdoor sporting opportunities, so you have a lot to choose from during a 3-day trip. If you live in or around New York City, you could easily make a day trip or a weekend in any of these spots. See chapter 7 for more ideas, and watch for wineries along your route. ***Start:*** *New York City.*

Day ❶: Lower Hudson Valley

Drive north from Manhattan up the east side of the Hudson River, quickly entering Westchester County (take either I-87 or the Sawmill Pkwy. to Rte. 9N) and traveling through Tarrytown. (If traveling with kids, you may want to squeeze in **Philipsburg Manor** 𝕲𝕲 [p. 186], a surprising living-history museum in Sleepy Hollow.) Perhaps the biggest attraction in the Lower Hudson Valley is **Kykuit** 𝕲𝕲𝕲 (p. 188), the famed Rockefeller estate, where you'll need at least 2 to 3 hours to enjoy one of the tours of the house, gardens, and modern artwork. For lunch, head upriver (25 miles, Rte. 9N) to the riverside town of **Cold Spring** 𝕲 (p. 190), which has several

nice restaurants on or near Main Street. After lunch, check out some of the antiques shops or stroll down to the river for a great view of the Hudson. In the afternoon, visit **Boscobel Restoration** 𝕲𝕲 (p. 188), a mansion not only handsomely restored, but picked up and moved to its spectacular current site, on the banks of the Hudson in nearby Garrison. Fans of contemporary art will prefer to head upriver to **Dia:Beacon** 𝕲𝕲𝕲 (p. 201), a huge repository of minimalist art housed in an old factory. For a special dinner outing, check out **The Valley Restaurant at The Garrison** 𝕲𝕲𝕲 (p. 198) or **The Bird & Bottle Inn** 𝕲𝕲 (p. 195). Spend the night at one of the inns in either Cold Spring or Garrison.

Day ❷: The Mid-Hudson Valley

Continue your Great Estates tour of the Hudson Valley in Hyde Park, home to the **FDR Presidential Library and Home (Springwood)** 🎯🎯🎯 (p. 202), as well as **Eleanor Roosevelt's Val-Kill Cottage** and FDR's private getaway **Top Cottage** 🎯 (p. 204). You'll need most of the morning to explore all three. Have lunch at one of the restaurants at the esteemed **Culinary Institute of America** 🎯🎯🎯 (p. 206). (Foodies should check the tour schedule in advance for a behind-the-scenes look at one of the foremost culinary-arts programs in the country.) After lunch head to the storied **Vanderbilt Mansion** 🎯🎯🎯 (p. 202), one of the finest estates of the Gilded Age. *Note:* Fans of modern art may wish to take a different tack for Day 2 and head west across the Hudson (take I-84W toward Newburgh and the bridge) for one of the most unique art museums in the country, **Storm King Art Center** 🎯🎯🎯 (p. 189), 500 acres of rolling hills and monumental

sculpture by the top names of 20th-century art. To get to Storm King, head south from Newburgh on Route 9W to Mountainville, near Cornwall.

Day ❸: Upper Hudson River

Head north on route 9W or 9G, up to **Hudson** 🎯🎯 (p. 216), and shop on Warren Street, the best spot in the state for antiquing. You can easily spend a morning and an afternoon here. Also check out the Persian castle architecture and panoramic landscapes of the **Olana State Historic Site** 🎯🎯🎯 (p. 216). If you have time, try the **Shaker Museum** 🎯 (p. 218). Then you can eat and sleep in either Tivoli or Hudson (and take the 2½-hr. trip back to New York City in the morning via the Taconic State Pkwy.). If you don't have another night to spend in the region, you could leave the Upper Hudson in late afternoon and make your way south along the west side of the river (along either I-87, the faster route, or 9W), perhaps stopping for dinner in the attractive town of **Nyack** 🎯 (p. 192) before making your way back to New York City.

3 The Adirondacks & the North Country in 1 Week

For outdoors lovers, the North Country is the heart of New York State. Blessed with deep pine forests, softly rounded mountain peaks, and isolated islands set on quiet lakes, the Adirondacks and the Thousand Islands region can make for endless days of adventure. If you're staying in hotels, settle in Old Forge before starting off, then switch lodgings throughout the tour as you see fit. For camping information, see listings in chapter 12. *Start: Old Forge.*

Days ❶ & ❷: Blue Mountain Lake & Raquette Lake Area

From Old Forge, drive east on Route 28 and go north on Route 30 to start off the week with a great overview of the park at the **Adirondack Museum** 🎯🎯 (p. 368). Along with the history, flora, and fauna you'd expect, you'll also find great interactive exhibits, making this museum perfect for kids as well as adults. It's easy to spend a full morning here. Be sure to pack a

picnic lunch and enjoy it out on the shores of gorgeous **Blue Mountain Lake.** Then strap on your hiking boots, make sure you have drinking water, and tackle **Bald Mountain,** just east of Old Forge— it's a short but steep climb, and the summit will reward you with a great view. With your remaining energy, drive back to Old Forge and wander the town, enjoying the kitschy rides and games.

On the second day, hit the water. This area is famous for its chain of lakes; the only way to really get a sense of them is to go out with a canoe or kayak. **Mountain-man Outdoor Supply Company** (p. 366) in both Old Forge and Inlet can set you up with the equipment; then spend the morning paddling as the mist rises from the lake. Drive over Route 28 to Raquette Lake and see how people with the name of Vanderbilt went "camping" (in 27 rooms, with a bowling alley!), at **Great Camp Sagamore** 𝒢𝒢 (p. 367). You can tour what was their retreat for more than 50 years, just south of Raquette Lake.

Day ❸: Lake George

Part of this park's appeal is that it makes for great driving. Take your time heading east on Route 28 over to the Lake George area. Then go out onto the lake with **Lake George Steamboat Company** (p. 365) on one of its narrated cruises aboard a steamship paddle-wheeler. Drive up to Bolton Landing and enjoy a drink or dinner at **The Sagamore** 𝒢𝒢𝒢 (p. 369), one of the few historic hotels left in the park.

Day ❹: Lake Placid

Meander up I-87, then cut over Route 73 and take Route 86 into the town of Lake Placid, which is famous for hosting both the 1932 and 1980 Winter Olympics and remains a center for Olympic training. Get a taste of history in the **Winter Olympic Museum** 𝒢 (p. 373) at the Olympic Center, and check out the rinks where Sonja Henie and Eric Heiden captured hearts and gold medals. Then get ready for some Olympic adventures yourself, out at the Verizon Sports Complex, 20 minutes west of town. You can jump in a bobsled (don't worry, professionals drive it), either on wheels or on ice. Grab a bite in town, then go off to **High Falls Gorge** (p. 375), 8 miles east of town, which allows for a great stroll along the **Ausable River.** The trail runs past 700 feet of waterfalls and across bridges as you admire the water spilling over ancient granite cliffs. Come back into town as the sun starts to set and casts its rosy glow over Mirror Lake. Enjoy dinner and stay overnight in Lake Placid.

Days ❺, ❻ & ❼: The Thousand Islands

Spend the morning saying goodbye to the Adirondacks aboard the **Adirondack Scenic Railroad** 𝒢 (p. 375) on a 1-hour journey through the forest between Lake Placid and Saranac Lake. Then say a longer goodbye as you drive west on Route 86, out of the park on Route 3 to Watertown, then on Route 12 up to the Thousand Islands region. Count on a few hours for the drive. You have a few options for the rest of Day 5: Either delay your departure from the 'dacks by stopping in a few towns like Childwold and Cranberry Lake; or test out the **St. Regis Canoe Wilderness Area** (p. 372); or just head straight to the Thousand Islands, to **Clayton,** the center of the area's activity, and explore the town. Dine and stay in Clayton.

On your second day here, check out some of the area castles, built by wealthy industrialists in the early 20th century. Pack a picnic lunch for your castle outing, then hop on the two-castle tour run by **Uncle Sam Boat Tours** 𝒢𝒢 (p. 385). You'll get a good overview (or rather, water view) of the many islands that lie in the middle of the **St. Lawrence River.** You'll stop off at Dark Island and take a guided tour of **Singer Castle** 𝒢𝒢 (p. 384), built by the director of the Singer Sewing Company and just opened to the public in 2003. Then it's over to **Boldt Castle** 𝒢 (p. 383), on Heart Island, built by Waldorf=Astoria owner George C. Boldt. Enjoy your picnic lunch on the 5 acres of grounds, then explore the turrets, admire the 365 windows, and wander among the formal gardens. You have an unlimited stop here, so whenever you're ready, just catch the shuttle back to the mainland. In the late afternoon, head over to the **1000**

Islands Skydeck ⊛ (p. 384), 400 feet off the ground and with a 25-mile view over the St. Lawrence River. It's over the Canadian border, so bring your passport.

Start off Day 3 with a fine tradition here—**fishing,** followed by a **shore dinner** ⊛⊛⊛ (p. 388). Many of the fishing charter companies run these trips and they've been happening up here since the early 1900s. You'll spend the morning fishing and then stop on a deserted island.

Your guide fries up the just-caught fish in grease rendered from pig fat, then serves it up with potatoes, corn, and dessert. Walk off your decadent lunch by heading over to the **Antique Boat Museum** ⊛⊛⊛ (p. 383), which boasts the largest collection of inland freshwater boats in the U.S. You'll see more than 200 boats, from a 19th-century dugout canoe to 1920s racing boats. The sunset is gorgeous, so grab a table on the water to enjoy it.

4 The Finger Lakes & Western New York in 1 Week

This itinerary covers a large swath of central and western New York. It begins with the natural beauty of the Finger Lakes, a series of deep, slender bodies of water formed by glaciers many thousands of years ago at the end of the ice age. The local wine industry, the state's biggest, is deservedly winning accolades for its cool-climate wines, and a tour of the wineries hugging the banks of the lakes is one of the most scenic (and delicious) trips in the state. You'll see more scenic beauty at the spectacular gorges of Watkins Glen and Letchworth, as well as the world-famous Niagara Falls. *Start: Ithaca (Cayuga Lake).*

Day ❶: Ithaca

Hugging the southern shore of Cayuga Lake, Ithaca is an attractive, relaxed college town with a superb setting, and it's a good place to start your tour of the region. In the morning, visit the campus of Ivy League **Cornell University** (p. 303), which sits on a hilltop above town. Its **Johnson Museum of Art** has a particularly strong collection of Asian art and spectacular fifth-floor views of Cayuga Lake. From the museum, you can take a short walk along a path leading to a suspension bridge over deep **Fall Creek Gorge** (p. 304). Also part of the university is **Cornell Plantations,** a wonderful spot for garden lovers. Head down the hill for lunch downtown at either a spot near Ithaca Commons, such as **Just a Taste Wine & Tapas Bar** (p. 311), or **Moosewood** (p. 313). After lunch, take a stroll around **The Commons,** the pedestrian zone of shops, galleries, and restaurants.

In the afternoon, families will enjoy a visit to **Sciencenter** (p. 306), a hands-on science museum with a walk-in camera, outdoor playground, and "piano stairs." The **Sagan Planet Walk** (p. 306) is an outdoor scale model of the sun and nine planets, built as a memorial to Cornell astronomer Carl Sagan. Have dinner in town at **Maxie's** (p. 311). Alternatively, if you want to see some of southern Cayuga Lake, take the 7-mile drive up Route 89 to **Taughannock Falls State Park** (p. 306), with an easy hike to a free-falling waterfall that outdoes even Niagara Falls. You could then head up to Sheldrake Point Winery, along Route 96, for dinner at **Simply Red Lakeside Bistro** (p. 311).

Day ❷: Wineries of Cayuga & Seneca Lakes

If you didn't visit **Taughannock Falls State Park** on Day 1 (see above), you can catch it on your way to exploring the wineries that dot Cayuga Lake.

Getting a taste of the Finger Lakes means exactly that: tasting some of the excellent wines that come from this respected viticultural region. Starting out on the west side of Cayuga Lake, you can visit a few of the wineries that belong to the **Cayuga Wine Trail** and several on the east side of Seneca Lake, part of the **Seneca Lake Wine Trail** (p. 316). Sheldrake Point, Hosmer, and Goose Watch, all about halfway up Route 89 on the west side of the lake, are some of our favorites on Cayuga. Head south along Route 414 past Lodi to visit some of the wineries belonging to the **Seneca Lake Wine Trail,** such as Lamoreaux Landing, Wagner, Standing Stone, and Red Newt. Depending on which wineries you visit and the hour, Sheldrake Point, Wagner, and Red Newt all have restaurants and are good spots for lunch. Spend the night at an inn near Watkins Glen, along either the east or west side of Seneca Lake.

Day ❸: Watkins Glen/Keuka Lake

Begin by trekking through **Watkins Glen State Park** (p. 315), a 776-acre park with a walking trail that wends through a spectacular gorge formed at the end of the last ice age. Then drive west toward **Keuka Lake** (p. 328). You can stop at more wineries along the way, or merely enjoy the drive around perhaps the prettiest of the Finger Lakes. Head north along Route 54, on the east side of the lake, toward Penn Yan. **Route 54A** (p. 329), which travels between the two prongs of the lake and south along the west side of the lake, is a gorgeous drive, one of the best in the region. Stop at Esperanza Mansion for lunch and magnificent lake views. After lunch, hit perhaps the most famed winery in the region, Dr. Frank's, and a couple of the other wineries of the **Keuka Lake Wine Trail** (p. 330), and then head down to the cute town of **Hammondsport** (p. 329) for shopping and dinner at the Village Tavern Restaurant. Spend the night here, either in one of the rooms owned by Village Tavern or at Black Sheep Inn. You could also base yourself just west, in another adorable

Finger Lakes town, **Naples** (along Route 53), where the place for dinner is Brown Hound Bistro.

Day ❹: Letchworth Park

Starting in Corning, drive on the New York State Thruway (I-90) west to Route 400 south and take the East Aurora exit. Turn left onto Route 20A east. Follow 20A to Warsaw. Make a right onto Route 19 south to Route 19A, to Denton Corners Road. Turn left on Denton Corners Road and into the park. **Letchworth State Park** 👍👍 (p. 407) is a gorgeous gash in the earth and has been formed over the millenniums by the Genesee River. You'll find 66 miles of trails here, but it's best to stick to the southern end, where cliffs climb as high as 600 feet. Pack a snack and hike on the **Gorge Trail,** a 7-mile one-way trek that's moderately difficult, so don't do the whole thing unless you're feeling adventuresome. Then reward yourself with a great all-American dinner at the **Glen Iris Inn** 👍👍 (p. 408) in Castile. You can even spend the night here.

Days ❺ & ❻: Buffalo

Head back to I-90 and drive west to **Buffalo.** This city may just surprise you with its collection of famous architecture. It's worth taking a walking tour of downtown to check out some of these buildings. Start at **Market Arcade** (p. 393) on Main Street and walk south—you'll see neoclassical, Beaux Arts, and Art Deco buildings galore. Stop off for lunch at the **Ellicott Square** (p. 394) building and try some "Beef on Weck" (p. 396) done right by Charlie the Butcher. Then head over to the **Darwin D. Martin House** 👍👍👍 (p. 396), where a painstaking restoration is beautifully showcasing the mastery of the home's architect, Frank Lloyd Wright. If your passion tends more toward painting and sculpture, visit the **Albright-Knox Art Gallery** 👍👍👍 (p. 396), a winner of a gallery that houses some 5,000 works. Finish up the daytime hours with a stroll through **Delaware Park,** designed by Frederick Law Olmsted,

Weekend Excursions from New York City

When New Yorkers tire of the big city, it only takes a couple of days in the "country," as they call it, to make them yearn to come back. Here are some popular getaways, also handy for travelers in the city on extended business.

Long Island Wine & History Tour   On Day 1, head out of New York onto the Long Island Expressway (LIE) to exit 41 north (NY 106 north). Take 106 north to Oyster Bay and follow signs to **Sagamore Hill** ✶✶✶ (p. 152), Theodore Roosevelt's 23-room Victorian estate—full of animal trophies and other things masculine—that he used as the summer White House from 1902 to 1908. It's an easy drive to **Planting Fields Arboretum/Coe Hall** ✶✶ (p. 152), a grand expanse of historic buildings and greenhouses. Have lunch in tiny **Locust Valley,** peruse its collection of antiques shops, and then head out to the **Vanderbilt Museum and Planetarium** ✶✶ (p. 153) in Centerport. Have dinner and overnight in the **Centerport** area. On Day 2, try hopping between some of the 50 wineries on the North Fork. Fortunately, lots of wineries are east on Route 25, which is a much nicer drive than the LIE. Out past Jamesport, you can stop at **Bedell Cellars** and sample its merlot; then it's just a half-mile to **The Lenz Winery.** See p. 160 for more listings. End up in the town of Greenport for dinner.

Beach Party in the Hamptons   Note that the quickest way to get here by train is the express off-peak train from Hunter's Point in Queens (near the 7 subway stop). If you're driving, take the LIE. Remember, it's best to choose your beach before you go. In Southampton, **Cooper's Beach** is the main public stretch of sand, beautiful but crowded and with pricey parking. **Old Town Beach** is less crowded but parking can be a problem. **Main Beach** in East Hampton is gorgeous and in view of some giant mansions. **Montauk** is away from the crowds, at the end of the island. Then dine among the celebrities in **East Hampton** and go clubbing in town. On Day 2, check out the **chic shops of East Hampton,** drive by the enormous estates in Southampton's **Gin Lane** and **Coopers Neck,** and then have a happy-hour home brew at the

creator of Central Park. Today it's a 350-acre gem. For dinner, drop by the home of the original chicken wing, **Anchor Bar** (p. 400). Honestly, the wings are nothing special, but when in Buffalo . . . .

Then, the area surrounding Buffalo has more than enough cool and quirky museums and sites to keep you occupied for another day. Start off at **Graycliff** ✶✶✶ (p. 402), a stunning Frank Lloyd Wright creation. Then drive over to the tiny, charming town of **East Aurora,** where

Elbert Hubbard started his furniture-building movement and founded the **Roycroft Arts and Crafts Community** (p. 404) more than 100 years ago. Browse some of the craft shops, then have lunch at the **Roycroft Inn** ✶✶ (p. 405). Make a stop at **Vidler's 5 & 10,** which has been selling candy and knickknacks since 1930. Then drive farther west on I-90 to Route 60 and over to America's largest community of mediums, the **Lily Dale Assembly** ✶✶ (p. 403). In summertime, there

Southampton Publick House ⟨⟨ (p. 178). Have dinner in Southampton, then check out some live music at the **Stephen Talkhouse** ⟨⟨⟨ (p. 179) in Amagansett. See coverage in chapter 6 for complete Hamptons details.

Catskill Mountain Region   **Ulster County,** just 90 minutes by car from New York City, is not the most pastoral part of the Catskills, but it offers the greatest diversity of attractions in a relatively compact area. Cross the George Washington Bridge, then take the Palisades Parkway to I-87 north about 80 miles to **New Paltz** (p. 227) and explore the town. After lunch, outdoors types can hike or bike in the **Mohonk Preserve** ⟨⟨ or **Minnewaska State Park Preserve** or even rock-climb the awesome **Shawangunk Mountains** ("the 'Gunks"). Or take a scenic drive from New Paltz to Gardiner and up **Route 44/55,** just beyond the Minnewaska Preserve. Watch for a handful of nearby wineries. Stay at the legendary **Mohonk Mountain House** ⟨⟨⟨ (p. 232), a Victorian fantasy on a cliff with activities galore, or return east toward High Falls or nearby Rosendale for dinner. Spend the night in Stone Ridge, Gardiner, along the Hudson in Milton, or even in Mount Tremper, about 35 to 40 miles northwest. On Day 2, head up I-87 to Route 28 west, toward Mount Tremper (or Rte. 213 to 28A, which is more scenic but longer). Off Route 28 is the beautiful **Ashokan Reservoir** (p. 230). Then, Mount Tremper's **Emerson Place** ⟨ or the town of **Phoenicia** ⟨ (a mile west) are perfect for shopping. After lunch, head east along Route 212 (just outside of Mt. Tremper) toward **Woodstock** ⟨ and check out the town, or explore the legendary **Byrdcliffe Arts Colony** ⟨ (p. 229). Then head east along the road (Rte. 212) to **Saugerties** ⟨, about 10 miles away, where you'll find a host of homegrown antiques stores. Or head across the river to **Hudson** ⟨⟨ (I-87N to Rte. 23E, about 20 miles), site of the best antiques shopping in upstate New York. Enjoy dinner, then head back to the city (the drive will take 2–2½ hr.).

are public readings, but you can come anytime for a private reading. Don't count on any chairs rattling, but some of these folks are frighteningly good at telling you about anyone who has "passed over." Have dinner and stay overnight back in Buffalo.

Day ❼: Niagara Falls
Get back on to I-90 and drive west to check out the beautiful gushing water of **Niagara Falls** ⟨⟨⟨ (p. 411). Some daredevils attempt the falls in a barrel, while others just come to admire the view. We recommend the latter. We also recommend bringing your passport, since you'll want to see the falls from both the American side and the Canadian side. Pick up the discount card Passport to the Falls at **Niagara Falls State Park** (p. 413), then walk out onto the newly renovated Observation Tower that stretches into the river. At the bottom of the tower is the famous *Maid of the Mist* boat ride ⟨⟨⟨ (p. 414), a very cool (but very wet) way to see the falls from

below. Then visit the **Cave of the Winds** ⋪ (p. 413) to walk around the base of the falls. Walk over the border (it's faster than driving, especially in summer), have lunch, and check out the stunning Niagara Falls view from the Canadian side. Then peruse the area of **Clifton Hill,** Niagara's answer to Disney. Head back to the American side to have dinner at one of the excellent new restaurants in the **Seneca Niagara Casino & Hotel** ⋪⋪⋪ (p. 417) and finish off the day by trying your luck on the casino floor.

4

The Active Vacation Planner

by Neil E. Schlecht

Perhaps because New York City is—despite the giant green oasis of Central Park—the ultimate in asphalt adventure, New York State doesn't quite get its due as an outdoors destination. But New York is much more rural, mountainous, and crisscrossed with water than many people realize, and it's a splendid, incredibly diverse state with terrain and opportunities to satisfy the most discriminating outdoors enthusiasts. New York is, after all, where the **American Conservation Movement** began, and the state has benefited from the active presence of committed environmentalists like native son Theodore Roosevelt, the 26th president of the U.S.

Niagara Falls State Park was designated the first state park in the U.S., and state parks and forest preserves in the **Adirondack and Catskill mountains** were declared "forever wild" by the New York State Constitution. Adirondack Park, totaling more than 6 million acres of public and private lands—roughly one-fifth of the state—ranks as the largest park in the country.

From Long Island and Great Lakes beaches to Adirondack lakes and Catskill rivers, there are myriad opportunities for water fun, including swimming, boating, fishing, canoeing, and kayaking. The Catskill region is famous among anglers as one of the fly-fishing capitals of the world.

The rugged mountains and dense forests that dominate upstate New York beckon avid hikers, mountain bikers, and winter-sports fans. In the Catskills, 35 peaks reach 3,500 feet, while in the Adirondacks, more than 40 mountains rise above 4,000 feet. Lake Placid has hosted the Winter Olympics, and ski mountains in the Catskills draw enthusiasts from across the Northeast, as do the hundreds of miles of terrain for cross-country skiing.

In warm months, New York State plays host to professional golf and tennis championships, including the U.S. Open, and an impressive roster of public and private courses make the state one of the nation's best for golf.

The website of the **I Love New York** Travel and Tourism board—www.iloveny.com/Outdoors/Default.aspx—contains exhaustive listings of parks, outfitters, facilities, and more for outdoors adventure.

1 Visiting New York's National Parks

New York State's 24 national parks include splendid natural spots like the Appalachian National Scenic Trail, the Upper Delaware Scenic and Recreational River, and Fire Island National Seashore, in addition to famous historic monuments. One is the **Upper Delaware Scenic and Recreational River,** part of the National Wild and Scenic Rivers System; it runs 73 miles along the New York–Pennsylvania border, making it the Northeast's longest free-flowing river. Perfect for boating and kayaking, the

Upper Delaware is known for its Class I and II rapids, public fishing, and wintering bald eagles. An interesting fact: Nearly all the land along the Upper Delaware River is privately owned; only 30 acres belong to the U.S. government. The **Erie Canalway National Heritage Corridor,** the newest national park in New York State, comprises four navigable waterways (Erie, Champlain, Oswego, and Cayuga-Seneca) and sections of the first Erie Canal, totaling more than 500 miles in upstate New York. More than 230 trail miles along the corridor have been equipped for biking and hiking. The **Fire Island National Seashore,** located in Patchogue (1 hr. east of New York City), is the site of beautiful ocean shores, an ancient maritime forest, and historic lighthouses and estates. Outdoor activities include backpacking and birding.

Crossing New York State are two of the nation's most important scenic trails. The famous **Appalachian National Scenic Trail (A.T.)** (www.appalachiantrail.org), which opened as a continuous trail in 1937 and was designated the first National Scenic Trail in 1968, is a 2,167-mile footpath that crosses the Appalachian Mountains from Maine to Georgia. The trail is very popular with day, weekend, and other short-term hikers, section hikers, and through-hikers (who hike the entire length of the trail in one season). The **North Country National Scenic Trail (NST)** (www.northcountrytrail.org) crosses seven northern states: New York, Pennsylvania, Ohio, Michigan, Wisconsin, Minnesota, and North Dakota.

Detailed national park information covering travel and transportation, facilities, fees and permits, hours, wildlife, and more is available through the National Park Service website at **www.nps.gov.**

NATIONAL & STATE PARK PASSES

The best way to visit national parks not just in New York State but across the country is with the **National Parks Interagency Annual Pass** ($80, valid for 1 year), which provides admission to any national park that charges an entrance fee. The pass covers the pass holder and three accompanying adults. It can be purchased at national park sites, online at http://store.usgs.gov/pass or http://www.recreation.gov, by calling ℂ **888-ASK-USGS**, ext. 1, or by sending a check or money order payable to the National Park Service for $80 (plus $3.95 for shipping and handling) to National Park Foundation, P.O. Box 34108, Washington, DC 20043-4108. The new Senior Pass ($10, for seniors only; lifetime membership) replaced the old Golden Age Passport in January 2007. Other old passes, including the National Parks Pass, Golden Eagle Hologram, and Golden Access and Golden Eagle Passports, will continue to be honored until they expire. For additional information, call ℂ **888-ASK-USGS.**

The **Empire Passport** provides unlimited day use and vehicle access to most New York State parks ($59, valid Apr 1–Mar 31 of the following year), and it is available at www.nysparks.com/passport.

2 Outdoor Activities from A to Z

BICYCLING

New York State has thousands of excellent roads and mountain trails for cycling. The **Hudson Valley** has moderate hills, Hudson River views, farm landscapes, and the allure of historic estates such as those in Hyde Park. Excellent off-trail riding is possible in the Catskill Mountain region in the **Mohonk Preserve** (ℂ **914/255-0919;** www.mohonkpreserve.org) and **Minnewaska State Park Preserve** (ℂ **845/256-0579;**

http://nysparks.state.ny.us/parks/info.asp?parkID=78). For mountain-biking trails, road-cycling routes, and trip reports in the **Shawangunk Mountains,** at the edge of the Catskills, see www.gunks.com; fat-tire fans should also contact GUMBA (Gunks Mountain Biking Association) (℡ **914/255-3572;** www.gumba.us). The **Finger Lakes** region is ideal for cyclists who want to circle the lakes, perhaps stopping off at wineries en route. Cyclists are very fond of scenic lake loops around several of the larger Finger Lakes, such as the 100-mile loop around **Cayuga Lake** and the 40-mile loop around **Skaneateles Lake.** In the Catskills, **Plattekill Mountain** is one of the top five mountain-biking destinations in North America, and other mountains, such as **Windham** and **Hunter,** also cater to mountain bikers in summer. There's easy cycling along the **Catskill Scenic Trail** (℡ **607/652-2821**), a 19-mile "Rails to Trails" pathway. Farther upstate, **The Seaway Trail,** a scenic road route, runs 450 miles from Massena to Niagara Falls and goes along the south shore of Lake Ontario and the St. Lawrence River. Near the shores of Lake Champlain, **Lake Champlain Bikeways** is a series of demarcated bicycling loops.

A terrific cycling option for cyclists of all abilities is along the historic **New York State Canal System,** comprising more than 230 miles of trails across upstate New York. Multiuse trails include the 25-mile **Hudson-Mohawk Bikeway** in the Capital-Saratoga region, the 36-mile **Old Erie Canal State Park** in central New York, the 90-mile **Erie Canal Heritage Trail** in the northern Finger Lakes region, and the 8-mile **Glens Falls Feeder Canal Trail** in the foothills of the Adirondacks near Lake Champlain. For additional information, contact the **New York State Canal Corporation,** 200 Southern Blvd., P.O. Box 189, Albany, NY 12201-0189 (℡ **800/4-CANAL-4;** www.canals.state.ny.us). For information on bike tours along the Erie Canal, call ℡ **518/434-1583**. New York City may not seem like a place to hop on a bike, but it is home to a great many dedicated cyclists. The 6.25-mile loop within **Central Park** is a classic urban cycling destination—but look out for in-line skaters, joggers, dogs, and even horses. The multiuse **Manhattan Waterfront Greenway** runs along the Hudson River, from Battery Park at Manhattan's southernmost tip, north to 181st Street, with a couple of still incomplete sections and a consequent street break from 125th Street to 145th Street. Eventually, the plan is to complete a greenway that encircles the entire island (currently about 20 of the targeted 32 miles are completed). Another favorite of locals is the ride from the city across the George Washington Bridge up to **Nyack** along the west side of the Hudson River, a perfect 50-mile round-trip. Each May some 25,000 intrepid cyclists take to the New York streets for the **Great Five Boro Bike Tour,** which covers 42 miles and touches all five of the city's boroughs; get more information at www.bikenewyork.org.

A great resource, with information on organizations, trails, and guided trips, is the website of **A1 Trails** (www.a1trails.com/biking/bike_ny.html). Most areas—especially the major leisure destinations, such as the Hamptons, Catskills, Adirondacks, and Finger Lakes—have bicycle shops that rent bikes. There are loads of guidebooks dealing specifically with biking in New York State. Following are some recommended titles: *25 Mountain Bike Tours in the Adirondacks* (Countryman Press); *30 Bicycle Tours in the Finger Lakes Region* (Countryman Press); *Bicycling the Canals of New York: 500 Miles of Bike Riding along the Erie, Champlain, Cayuga-Seneca & Oswego Canals* (Vitesse Press); *The Catskills: A Bicycling Guide* (Purple Mountain Press); *Cranks from Cooperstown: 50 Bike Rides in Upstate New York* (Tourmaster Publications); *Paths Along the*

Hudson: A Guide to Walking and Biking (Rutgers University Press); *Ride Guide: Hudson Valley, New Paltz to Staten Island* (Anacus Press).

BOATING

New York is blessed with thousands of miles of rivers and streams, as well as 500 miles of the New York State Canal System, hundreds of lakes, and the Long Island Sound. From Saratoga Lake to the Delaware River and the 11 scenic Finger Lakes, there are plenty of great opportunities for boating enthusiasts.

On the **New York State Canal System,** you can cruise the waterway's 57 locks. The canal system stretches more than 500 miles and is normally navigable from May through mid-November. There are four canals, all easily accessible by boat. From the south, the Hudson River opens onto the Erie Canal; farther north is the Champlain Canal. The Erie Canal travels east to west, with access to the Great Lakes from the Oswego Canal or the western end of the Erie Canal, with access to Lake Erie. The Cayuga-Seneca Canal connects with the Erie Canal in central New York, allowing access to the Finger Lakes region.

You can rent an authentic, old-fashioned canal boat for a few days or a week. For more information on tour boat and cruise operators, canal passes, boats for hire, and the many sites and attractions (including state parks, canal villages, museums, and urban cultural parks) along the canal system, contact the **New York State Canal Corporation,** 200 Southern Blvd., P.O. Box 189, Albany, NY 12201-0189 (© 800/4-CANAL-4; www.canals.state.ny.us). The organization puts out the *Cruising Guide to the New York State Canal System,* which you can purchase by calling © 800/422-1825. Individual counties also put out canal-specific tourism brochures. See chapters 11 and 13 for additional regional canal information.

Several cruises and riverboat tours are offered along the majestic **Hudson River,** passing some of the great estates, historic river towns, and even West Point Military Academy. Another option is to rent a houseboat in the Thousand Islands and sail the St. Lawrence River, which makes its way around an estimated 1,000 to 1,800 small islands. For more information, contact the **Thousand Islands International Council** (© 800/8-ISLAND).

Fans of regattas may want to check out the annual **New York YC Regatta,** which celebrated its 150th year in 2004. **Lake Champlain,** on the New York/Vermont border, plays host to a number of regattas throughout the season.

The free *New York State Boater's Guide* is available from **New York State Parks Marine and Recreational Vehicles,** Empire State Plaza, Albany, NY 12238 (© 518/474-04545). You may also want to visit www.nysparks.state.ny.us/boating/resource.asp, where you'll find a link to the **New York State Boater's Guide,** a reference guide detailing the rules and regulations for boating in New York State.

CAMPING

New York State has more than 500 public and privately owned campgrounds across the state. Above all, the wilderness, forests, lakes, and rivers of the Adirondack and Catskill mountains offer the best backwoods camping in the state. The Hudson Valley and Finger Lakes regions, while not as remote, also offer fine camping with easy access to towns and regional attractions. The **Adirondack Camping Association** (www.adirondackcampgrounds.com) is a good resource for campsite information in that region. **Ausable Point Campground** (© 518/561-7080) sits on a stunning patch of land overlooking Lake Champlain, with 123 sites. But to really get away from everyone, reserve a spot on one of the **Saranac Lake Islands,** Saranac Lake (© 518/ 891-3170), and prepare to canoe there. Detailed listings of campgrounds large and small are available at © **800/CALL-NYS** or www.iloveny.com/search/accommodations_ camp.asp, www.nysparks.com, and www.gocampingamerica.com/newyork.

The Department of Environmental Conservation (DEC) operates 52 campgrounds in the Adirondack and Catskill state parks and publishes the free booklet *Camping in New York State Forest Preserves.* For camping reservations and additional information, call © **518/457-2500,** and for reservations, contact **Reserve America** (© **800/456- CAMP;** www.reserveamerica.com). Guidebooks include what some consider to be the bible of New York camping, *The Campgrounds of New York: A Guide to the State Parks and Public Campgrounds* (North Country Books), and *Adventures in Camping: An Introduction to Adirondack Backpacking* (North Country Books).

CANOEING, KAYAKING & RAFTING

From the Hudson River to the Adirondacks and rivers in the Catskills, New York State has thousands of miles for canoeing, kayaking, and rafting. In the Adirondacks alone, there are 1,200 miles of rivers designated wild, scenic, and recreational rivers—little-changed since first used by Native Americans. One of the most popular routes is the **Adirondack Canoe Route,** which begins at Old Forge and flows 140 miles through the Fulton Chain of Lakes to Raquette Lake and north to the Saranac Lakes through Long Lake and then on to Tupper Lake, or east to Blue Mountain Lake. Nick's Lake is excellent for beginning paddlers, and the north branch of Moose River is more challenging. Another great spot for canoeing is the **St. Regis Canoe area** near Saranac Lake, with 57 interconnecting lakes and ponds. For information about canoeing in the Adirondacks, contact the **Department of Environmental Conservation, Preserve Protection and Management,** 50 Wolf Rd., Albany, NY 12233-4255 (© **518/457-7433**), or the **Adirondack Regional Tourism Council** (© **518/846-8016**). The **Delaware River** in the Catskills is one of the longest (73 miles) and cleanest free-flowing rivers in the Northeast, and it's excellent for tubing, rafting, kayaking, and canoeing. Also excellent for kayaking is the historic **Hudson River,** especially in the Mid-Hudson Valley around Cold Spring. For more information, including access points, contact the **Upper Delaware Scenic and Recreational River** (© 570/685-4871; www.nps.gov/upde), which maintains a 24-hour River Hotline recording from April to October: © **845/ 252-7100.**

Guided **white-water rafting trips** of varying difficulty, lasting a single day or even less, are available on several New York State rivers. White water is the most challenging in the springtime, although some companies offer rides throughout the summer and fall. In western New York, excellent rafting is done on Cattaraugus Creek through Zoar Valley or the Genesee River in Letchworth State Park. In the Adirondacks, the Black River near Watertown is best for advanced rafters, while Indian Lake is considered "the Whitewater Capital of New York State." Moose River is another favorite of experts, while the Sacandaga River is a long and serene trip through the Adirondacks with an exciting finish.

A detailed list of canoeing, kayaking, and rafting operators is available on www.ilove ny.com. You can also visit the DEC Bureau of Public Lands website at www.dec. state.ny.us, or call © **518/402-9428.**

FISHING

The trout streams and rivers of the **southwestern Catskills,** such as Beaver Kill and the Delaware River, are among the best in North America—or the world, for that matter—for fly-fishing. For additional information, contact the **Delaware County Chamber of Commerce** (✆ 800/642-4443; www.delawarecounty.org) or **Sullivan County Visitors Association** (✆ 800/882-CATS; www.scva.net).

The **Hudson River** is very good for striped bass and trout fishing from mid-March to the end of May. For more information, visit www.hudsonriver.com/stripers.htm.

At the eastern end of Long Island, **Montauk** is a sport-fishing capital known for its shark fishing (peaks in late June). Sport-fishing boat rentals and charters are available. For a list of fishing charters and outfitters, see www.montauk-ny.worldweb.com/tours activitiesadventures/fishingtrips/index.html. Charter fishing on **Lake Ontario,** a celebrated freshwater fishery, brings in large chinook and Atlantic salmon, as well as brown, rainbow, and lake trout; walleye; and smallmouth bass. Contact the **Lake Ontario Sportfishing Promotion Council** (✆ 800/338-7890).

The **Thousand Islands** isn't a world-class fishing area for nothing. Grab a charter in tiny Clayton—the river serves up walleye, pike, perch, muskellunge (get your muscles ready—these grow up to 35 lb.), and bass. In **Eastern Lake Ontario,** you'll hook onto salmon, lake trout, steelhead, and walleye. For information on fishing charters and guides, see www.visit1000islands.com.

State fishing licenses are required for anyone over the age of 16 for fishing in New York freshwater. Many tackle shops and fishing outfitters issue them, as do town clerk offices. Call ✆ **518/357-2049** or visit www.dec.ny.gov/outdoor/fishing.html for more information on fishing in New York State, and www.dec.ny.gov/outdoor/365.html for specific information on permits. Guidebooks on fishing in New York State include *Flyfisher's Guide to New York* (Wilderness Adventures Press); *Gone Fishin': The 100 Best Spots in New York* (Rutgers University Press); and *Good Fishing in the Catskills: A Complete Angler's Guide* (Countryman Press).

GOLF

New York State boasts a preponderance of courses routinely rated by golfing magazines and organizations to be among the country's best. There are more than 600 public and private golf courses, many in gorgeous natural settings. Some of the nation's most prestigious golf tournaments, including the U.S. Open and the PGA Championship, are routinely held in New York. Championship status has been awarded to James Baird and Rockland Lake North in the Hudson Valley; Saratoga Spa and Battle Island in Fulton; Chenango Valley in Binghamton; Green Lakes in Fayetteville; Beaver Island in Grand Island; and Montauk Downs and Bethpage on Long Island.

But throughout the state, in the Catskill region, Long Island, Finger Lakes, Hudson Valley, Adirondacks, western New York, and the area around Saratoga Springs,

---

Tips **When You Don't Go It Alone**

The New York State Outdoor Guides Association (NYSOGA) offers licensed guide services for guided wilderness trips—whether your interests are hunting, fishing, rock and ice climbing, or cross-country skiing and snowshoeing. Contact NYSOGA, 211 Saranac Ave., #150, Lake Placid, NY 12946 (✆ **866/4-NYSOGA**; www.nysoga.com).

there are dozens of superb courses for golfers of all abilities. Many of the large resort hotels in regions like the Catskills and Adirondacks have their own golf courses, many of them quite good.

For information about golfing in state parks, contact **New York State Parks** (© 518/474-0456; www.nysparks.state.ny.us/golf). For complete listings of courses across the state, visit www.iloveny.com/Outdoors/Golfing.aspx and www.golfguideweb.com/new york/newyork.html. Golf fans and those looking to play extensively on a trip to New York would do well to consult the **New York State Golf Association** (www.nysga.org), which maintains a ratings list of courses.

HIKING

Few places on the East Coast have the variety of mountains, forest preserves, and hiking trails of New York State, making it a superb destination for anyone from hard-core trail hounds to casual day hikers. The wild, remote **Adirondacks**—an area that covers nearly one-fifth of the state—are probably the state's top location for hiking, with a great hiking trail system to high peaks, waterfalls, and secluded lakes. Serious hikers will want to head to the High Peaks region. **Mount Marcy,** at 5,300 feet, is New York State's highest mountain, but with a heavy tree cover, there are peaks with better views to be found. One of them is **Bald Mountain,** east of Old Forge, a 2-mile (steep) climb with gorgeous vistas. The trail to **Avalanche Lake** is extraordinary, and **Phelps Mountain** is a moderate climb rewarded by 360-degree views of the high peaks. The DEC's Preserve Protection and Management (© 518/457-7433; www.dec.ny.gov/outdoor/7865.html) publishes free trail maps and literature. Information on the Adirondacks can also be obtained from the **Adirondack Mountain Club,** or ADK, in Lake George (© 518/668-4447; www.adk.org), New York's oldest hiking club.

The **Catskill Mountain region** abounds with fantastic hiking possibilities. Particularly good are trails in the Minnewaska Preserve and Mohonk Preserve. Hugely popular with climbers, the **Shawangunks** (commonly known as the 'Gunks), at the southeastern edge of the Catskills, also have great hiking trails. For trail information throughout the region, see www.catskillguide.com/hiking.htm. The **Hudson River Valley** is more hilly than mountainous, but there are great hikes in Bear Mountain, Hudson Highlands, and Fahnestock state parks.

The **Finger Lakes** are a real sleeper region as far as hiking goes. The numerous gorges and glens in and around the lakes are terrific for hiking. The 16,000-acre **Finger Lakes National Forest** (between Cayuga and Seneca lakes) contains nine trails of up to 12 miles in length. See www.fs.fed.us/r9/gmfl/fingerlakes for more information. In terms of sheer length, nothing (save the Appalachian Trail and North Country Trail, both of which cross through New York State) is on a par with the **Finger Lakes Trail** (© 716/288-7191; www.fingerlakestrail.org), a hard-core 559-mile system of wilderness foot trails across the state. It's part of the North Country National Scenic Trail, which upon completion will extend 4,200 miles from eastern New York State all the way to North Dakota. The main Finger Lakes Trail connects the Catskill Mountains with the Allegheny Mountains.

The **New York State Canalway System** comprises 230 miles of multiuse trails across upstate, including the 90-mile Erie Canal Heritage Trail; the 36-mile Old Erie Canal Park Trail in central New York; the 25-mile Mohawk Hudson Bikeway in eastern New York; and the 8-mile Glens Falls Feeder Canal Trail in the foothills of the Adirondacks (near Lake Champlain). For a free map of the **Canalway Trail System,** call © 800/4-CANAL-4.

A good website for information on hiking in **western New York,** from Letchworth State Park to Niagara Falls, is www.wnyhikes.com/hiking-trails.htm.

For trail information and maps, contact the conservation group (composed of hiking clubs, environmental organizations, and individuals) **New York–New Jersey Trail Conference,** 232 Madison Ave., #802, New York, NY 10016 (© **212/685-9699;** www.nynjtc.org). The **New York State Office of Parks, Recreation and Historic Preservation** publishes the comprehensive *Empire State Trails;* for a free copy, contact NYS Parks, Empire State Plaza, Agency Building 1, Albany, NY 12238 (© 518/474-0456). Trail information is also available online at http://nysparks.state.ny.us/news/public. **New York Parks and Conservation Association** (© 518/434-1583) has an online trail-finder maps feature, with details on more than 90 trails and over 850 miles of walking, biking, in-line skating, and cross-country skiing. Another excellent resource, with information on organizations, trails, and more, is the **A1 Trails** website, **www.a1trails.com,** which has a section specifically dealing with guided hikes and adventure: www.a1trails.com/guides/gdesny.html.

The **Adirondack Mountain Club (ADK),** based in Lake George but with chapters in all major regions in the state, has more than 20,000 members and publishes guidebooks and the *Adirondack* magazine. It also manages trail maintenance and operates two lodges in the Adirondacks. For more information on specific trails, call © **800/395-8080** or visit www.adk.org. **The New York Ramblers** in New York City offers hiking and snowshoeing trips. Visit www.nyramblers.org. The **Views from the Top** bulletin board has postings on the latest trail conditions across New York State; consult www.viewsfromthetop.com/trail/ny/index.html.

Following are just a few recommended guidebooks devoted to hiking in New York State; local bookstores will have more options: *50 Hikes in Central New York: Hikes & Backpacking Trips from the Western Adirondacks to the Finger Lakes* (W.W. Norton & Co.); *50 Hikes in the Adirondacks: Short Walks, Day Trips & Backpacks Throughout the Park* (Countryman Press); *50 Hikes in Western New York: Walks & Day Hikes from the Cattaraugus Hills to the Genesee Valley* (Countryman Press); *Hiking New York State* (Falcon Press); and *Paths Less Traveled: The Adirondack Experience for Walkers, Hikers & Climbers of All Ages* (Pinto Press).

HUNTING

Hunting, especially big-game hunting, is big with New Yorkers upstate and more than a few visitors. The New York State Department of Environmental Conservation estimates that 700,000 New Yorkers and more than 50,000 nonresidents hunt in the state for a large variety of wildlife, including big game, small game, game birds, and fur bearers. Small- and big-game licenses are required in New York State.

For information on hunting in the Adirondacks and Catskills, the two principal hunting destinations, check out the information on seasons, regulations, and more at © **518/402-8924** or www.dec.ny.gov/outdoor/hunting.html.

ROCK CLIMBING

The sheer white cliffs of the **Shawangunk Mountains,** colloquially called the 'Gunks, near Minnewaska Preserve in the Catskill/Hudson Valley region, allow for some of the best rock climbing on the East Coast—but this is probably not the place for beginners. Experienced rock climbers will delight in more than 1,000 technical climbing routes. For articles, route suggestions, and information on climbing, see www.gunks.com or www.mohonkpreserve.org. There is also good rock climbing in and around Lake

High-Flying Adventures

Elmira, in the southern Finger Lakes region, is where the first 13 national soaring contests in the U.S. were held, which is why the city is sometimes called "the Soaring Capital of America." You can hop aboard a glider or soaring plane at the **Harris Hill Soaring Center** (© 607/796-2988 or 607/734-0641; www.harrishill soaring.org), which offers soaring rides over the rolling countryside of Chemung County, and check out the **National Soaring Museum** (© 607/734-3128; www. soaringmuseum.org) in Elmira. If you're more interested in motorized flight, you can take to the air in a PT-17 warplane at the **National Warplane Museum** (© 607/739-8200; www.warplane.org), in Horseheads, near Elmira. For amazing balloon rides (Apr–Oct) over one of the state's most beautiful parks, contact **Balloons Over Letchworth** (© 585/493-3340; www.balloonsoverletchworth.com) for a trip high above Letchworth State Park.

Placid and Lake George in the **Adirondacks;** contact the **Adirondack Mountain Club** in Lake George (© 518/668-4447; www.adk.org) for locations and outfitters.

SKIING & WINTER SPORTS

Though New York may not be in the league of Vermont or New Hampshire for classic East Coast skiing, it has a considerable number of downhill skiing areas and quite respectable mountains appealing to expert skiers, novices, and families. You'll find the east's only Olympic mountain (and its greatest vertical drop) at **Whiteface Mountain,** Wilmington (© **518/946-2223;** www.whiteface.com), just outside of Lake Placid. The top downhill areas overall are in the Catskills region. **Hunter Mountain** in Hunter (© **888/HUNTER-MTN;** www.huntermtn.com) and **Windham Mountain** in Windham (© **518/734-4300;** www.skiwindham.com) have plenty of good trails for practiced skiers, but now also cater to beginners and families. **Belleayre Mountain** in Highmount (© **800/942-6904;** www.belleayre.com) has the highest skiable peak and longest trail in the Catskills, while **Plattekill Mountain** (© **800/NEED-2-SKI;** www.plattekill.com) is a small '50s-style resort. There are also good skiing mountains in the Adirondacks and near the Hudson Valley and Finger Lakes regions. Lift tickets are in line with those of most ski resorts in the Northeast (that is to say, not inexpensive), though many offer very good ski packages, especially for beginners.

Cross-country trails are scattered throughout the state, from the grounds of historic homesteads to state parks. Rural areas like the Adirondacks, Catskills, and Finger Lakes couldn't be better for Nordic skiing, but virtually anywhere you go in upstate New York, you'll find trails. Sections of the massive 559-mile **Finger Lakes Trail** (© **716/288-7191;** www.fingerlakestrail.org) are equipped for cross-country skiing.

5

New York City

by Brian Silverman

We New Yorkers have heard the proud refrain from local politicos many times: New York is better than ever. The FBI has rated New York as the safest big city in the United States. It's cleaner than it ever was. The number of hotels, restaurants, and clubs keeps growing and they get better every year. This rebirth helped bring in more than 44 million tourists in 2006, and even more are projected in the next few years. Everything seems rosy. Why, then, are some of us worried about our city? With this boom, those of us who have been here a long time and have seen the city evolve into what it is today fret that this renaissance is one without character. We worry that with a Starbucks on every corner and new glass-and-steel condos sprouting like mushrooms at the expense of an old favorite bookstore or our local Cuban/Chinese joint, we are slowly losing our identity. The fear is that we will become like everycity USA.

But change is inevitable and though we might mourn loss, we also anticipate and expect change—it's part of our way of life. We know that a restaurant, show, club, or store might be the hottest thing now, but in a couple of months, the next one will open or be discovered—and the former hot spot will quickly become passé.

But some icons and institutions are so entrenched in our daily lives that we could never accept their loss. What would we do without that reassuring sight of the Lady of the Harbor or the gleaming spire of the Empire State Building? Or the perfect pizza? Or a Sunday in Central Park? Or the rumbling of the trains beneath the street? Or the sounds of jazz from a Village club? So while New York is ever-changing, as long as its core remains the same, we might complain a bit but we aren't going anywhere.

1 Arriving

BY PLANE

Three major airports serve New York City: **John F. Kennedy International Airport** (© 718/244-4444) in Queens, about 15 miles (1 hr. driving time) from midtown Manhattan; **LaGuardia Airport** (© 718/533-3400), also in Queens, about 8 miles (30 min.) from Midtown; and **Newark International Airport** (© 973/961-6000) in nearby New Jersey, about 16 miles (40 min.) from Midtown. Information about all three airports is available online at **www.panynj.gov**; click on the "All Airports" tab on the left.

Even though LaGuardia is the closest airport to Manhattan, it has a hideous reputation for flight delays and terminal chaos, in both ticket-desk lines and baggage claim. Hopefully, airport officials will have rectified the problems by the time you fly, but you may want to use JFK or Newark instead. (JFK has the best reputation for timeliness among New York–area airports.)

Almost every major domestic carrier serves at least one of the New York–area airports; most serve two or all three. Among them are **American** (© 817/967-2000; www. aa.com), **America West** (© 800/327-7810; www.americawest.com), **Continental** (© 800/525-3273; www.continental.com), **Delta** (© 800/221-1212; www.delta.com), **Northwest** (© 800/225-2525; www.nwa.com), **United** (© 800/864-8331; www.united. com), and **US Airways** (© 800/428-4322; www.usairways.com).

In recent years, there has been rapid growth in the number of start-up, no-frills airlines serving New York. You can check out Atlanta-based **AirTran** (© 800/AIR-TRAN; www.airtran.com), Chicago-based **ATA** (© 800/225-2995; www.ata.com), Denver-based **Frontier** (© 800/432-1359; www.flyfrontier.com), Milwaukee- and Omaha-based **Midwest Airlines** (© 800/452-2022; www.midwestairlines.com), or Detroit-based **Spirit Airlines** (© 800/772-7117; www.spiritair.com). The JFK-based airline **JetBlue** ✈ (© 800/JETBLUE; www.jetblue.com) has taken New York by storm with its low fares and classy service to cities throughout the nation. The nation's leading discount airline, **Southwest** (© 800/435-9792; www.iflyswa.com), flies into MacArthur (Islip) Airport on Long Island, 50 miles east of Manhattan.

TRANSPORTATION TO & FROM THE NEW YORK–AREA AIRPORTS

For transportation information for all three airports (JFK, LaGuardia, and Newark), call **Air-Ride** (© **800/247-7433**), which provides 24-hour recorded details on bus and shuttle companies and car services registered with the New York and New Jersey Port Authority. Similar information is available at **www.panynj.gov/airports**; click on the airport at which you'll be arriving.

The Port Authority also runs staffed Ground Transportation Information counters on the baggage-claim level in each terminal at each airport, where you can get information and book all manner of transport once you land. Most transportation companies also have courtesy phones near the baggage-claim area.

Generally, travel time between the airports and midtown Manhattan by taxi or car is 45 to 60 minutes for JFK, 20 to 35 minutes for LaGuardia, and 35 to 50 minutes for Newark. Always allow extra time, though, especially during rush hour, in peak holiday travel times, and if you're taking a bus.

BY TRAIN

Amtrak (© **800/USA-RAIL;** www.amtrak.com) runs frequent service to New York City's **Penn Station,** on Seventh Avenue between 31st and 33rd streets, where you can easily pick up a taxi, subway, or bus to your hotel. To get the best rates, book early (as much as 6 months in advance) and travel on weekends.

BY BUS

Buses arrive at the **Port Authority Terminal,** on Eighth Avenue between 40th and 42nd streets, where you can easily transfer to your hotel by taxi, subway, or bus. Call **Greyhound Bus Lines** (© **800/229-9424;** www.greyhound.com).

BY CAR

From the **New Jersey Turnpike** (I-95) and points west, there are three Hudson River crossings into the city's west side: the **Holland Tunnel** (lower Manhattan), the **Lincoln Tunnel** (Midtown), and the **George Washington Bridge** (upper Manhattan).

From **upstate New York,** take the **New York State Thruway** (I-87), which crosses the Hudson on the Tappan Zee Bridge and becomes the **Major Deegan Expressway** (I-87) through the Bronx. For the east side, continue to the Triborough Bridge and then down the FDR Drive. For the west side, take the Cross Bronx Expressway (I-95) to the Henry Hudson Parkway, or the Taconic State Parkway to the Saw Mill River Parkway to the Henry Hudson Parkway south.

From **New England,** the **New England Thruway** (I-95) connects with the **Bruckner Expressway** (I-278), which leads to the Triborough Bridge and the FDR Drive on the east side. For the west side, take the Bruckner to the Cross Bronx Expressway (I-95) to the Henry Hudson Parkway south.

Note that you'll have to pay tolls along some of these roads and at most crossings.

Once you arrive in Manhattan, park your car in a garage (expect to pay at least $20–$55 per day) and leave it there. Don't use your car for traveling within the city. Public transportation, taxis, and walking will easily get you where you want to go without the headaches of parking, gridlock, and dodging crazy cabbies.

VISITOR INFORMATION
INFORMATION OFFICES

For information before you leave home, your best source (besides this book!) is **NYC & Company,** the organization that fronts the New York Convention & Visitors Bureau (NYCVB), 810 Seventh Ave., New York, NY 10019. You can call ℂ **800/NYC-VISIT** to order the **Official NYC Visitor Kit,** which contains the *Official NYC Guide* detailing hotels, restaurants, theaters, attractions, events, and more; a foldout map; a newsletter on the latest goings-on; and brochures on attractions and services. The guide is free and will arrive in 7 to 10 days. (*Note:* I've received complaints that the packets sometimes take longer to arrive.)

You can also find a wealth of free information on the bureau's website, **www.nyc visit.com**. To speak with a live person who can answer specific questions, call ℂ **212/ 484-1222,** staffed weekdays from 8:30am to 6pm EST, weekends from 9am to 5pm EST.

CITY LAYOUT

The city comprises five boroughs: **Manhattan,** where most of the visitor action is; the **Bronx,** the only borough connected to the mainland United States; **Queens,** where JFK and LaGuardia airports are located and which borders the Atlantic Ocean and occupies part of Long Island; **Brooklyn,** south of Queens, which is also on Long Island and is famed for its attitude, accent, and Atlantic-front Coney Island; and **Staten Island,** the least populous borough, bordering Upper New York Bay on one side and the Atlantic Ocean on the other.

When most visitors envision New York, they think of Manhattan, the long finger-shaped island pointing southwest off the mainland—surrounded by the Harlem River to the north, the Hudson River to the west, the East River (really an estuary) to the east, and the fabulous expanse of Upper New York Bay to the south. Despite the fact that it's the city's smallest borough (13½ miles long, 2¼ miles wide, 22 sq. miles), Manhattan contains the city's most famous attractions, buildings, and cultural institutions. For that reason, almost all of the accommodations and restaurants suggested in this chapter are in Manhattan.

In most of Manhattan, finding your way around is a snap because of the logical, well-executed grid system by which the streets are numbered. If you can discern uptown and downtown, and East Side and West Side, you can find your way around pretty easily. In real terms, **uptown** means north of where you happen to be and **downtown** means south.

Avenues run north–south (uptown and downtown). Most are numbered. **Fifth Avenue** divides the East Side from the West Side of town and serves as the eastern border of Central Park north of 59th Street. **First Avenue** is all the way east and **Twelfth Avenue** is all the way west. The three most important unnumbered avenues on the East Side are between Third and Fifth avenues: **Madison** (east of Fifth), **Park** (east of Madison), and **Lexington** (east of Park, just west of Third). Important unnumbered avenues on the West Side are **Avenue of the Americas,** which all New Yorkers call Sixth Avenue; **Central Park West,** which is what Eighth Avenue north of 59th Street is called since it borders Central Park on the west; **Columbus Avenue,** which is what Ninth Avenue is called north of 59th Street; and **Amsterdam Avenue,** which is what Tenth Avenue is called north of 59th.

Broadway is the exception to the rule—it's the only major avenue that doesn't run straight uptown–downtown. It cuts a diagonal path across the island, from the northwest tip down to the southeast corner. As it crosses most major avenues, it creates **squares** (Times Sq., Herald Sq., Madison Sq., and Union Sq., for example).

Streets run east–west (crosstown) and are numbered consecutively as they proceed uptown from Houston (pronounced *House*-ton) Street. So to go uptown, simply walk north of, or to a higher-numbered street than, where you are. Downtown is south of (or a lower-numbered street than) your current location.

As I've already mentioned, Fifth Avenue is the dividing line between the **East Side** and **West Side** of town (except below Washington Sq., where Broadway serves that function). On the East Side of Fifth Avenue, streets are numbered with the distinction "East"; on the West Side of that avenue, they are numbered "West." East 51st Street, for example, begins at Fifth Avenue and runs east to the East River, while West 51st Street begins at Fifth Avenue and runs west to the Hudson River.

Unfortunately, the rules don't apply to neighborhoods in Lower Manhattan, south of 14th Street—like Wall Street, Chinatown, SoHo, TriBeCa, the Village—since they sprang up before engineers devised this brilliant grid scheme. A good map is essential when exploring these areas.

MANHATTAN NEIGHBORHOODS IN BRIEF

Downtown

Lower Manhattan: South Street Seaport & the Financial District Lower Manhattan constitutes everything south of Chambers Street. **Battery Park,** the point of departure for the Statue of Liberty, Ellis Island, and Staten Island, is on the southern tip of the island. The **South Street Seaport,** now touristy, but still a reminder of times when shipping was the lifeblood of the city, lies a bit north on the east coast; it's just south of the Brooklyn Bridge, which stands proudly as the ultimate engineering achievement of New York's 19th-century Industrial Age.

The rest of the area is considered the **Financial District,** but may be more famous now as **Ground Zero.** Until September 11, 2001, the Financial District was anchored by the **World Trade Center,** with the World Financial Center complex and residential Battery Park City to the west, and **Wall Street** running crosstown a little south and to the east.

Just about all of the major subway lines congregate here before they either end up in or head to Brooklyn.

TriBeCa Bordered by the Hudson River to the west, the area north of Chambers Street, west of Broadway, and south of Canal Street is the *Tri*angle *Be*low *Ca*nal Street, or TriBeCa. Since the 1980s, as SoHo became saturated with chic, the spillover has been quietly transforming TriBeCa into one of the city's hippest residential neighborhoods, where celebrities and families quietly coexist in cast-iron warehouses converted into spacious, expensive loft apartments. Artists' lofts and galleries as well as hip antiques and design shops pepper the area, as do some of the city's best restaurants.

Chinatown New York City's most famous ethnic enclave is bursting past its traditional boundaries and has seriously encroached on Little Italy. The former marshlands northeast of City Hall and below Canal Street, from Broadway to the Bowery, are where Chinese immigrants arriving from San Francisco were forced to live in the 1870s. This booming neighborhood is now a conglomeration of Asian populations. It offers tasty cheap eats in cuisine ranging from Szechuan to Hunan to Cantonese to Vietnamese to Thai. Exotic shops sell strange foods, herbs, and souvenirs; bargains on clothing and leather are plentiful.

One of the Canal Street (J, M, N, Q, R, W, Z, 6) subway stations will get you to the heart of the action. The streets are crowded during the day and empty out after around 9pm; they remain quite safe, but the neighborhood is more enjoyable during the bustle.

Little Italy Little Italy, traditionally the area between Broadway and Bowery, south of Houston Street and north of Canal Street, is a shrinking community today, due to the encroachment of thriving Chinatown. It's now limited mainly to **Mulberry Street,** where you'll find most restaurants, and just a few offshoots. With rents going up in the increasingly trendy Lower East Side, a few chic spots are moving in, further intruding upon the old-world neighborhood. The best way to reach Little Italy is to walk east from the Spring Street station, on the no. 6 line, to Mulberry Street; turn south for Little Italy (you can't miss the year-round red, green, and white street decorations).

The Lower East Side The Lower East Side boasts the best of both old and new New York: Witness the stretch of Houston between Forsyth and Allen streets, where Yoneh Shimmel's Knish Shop sits shoulder-to-shoulder with the city's newest art-house cinema—and both are thriving.

The neighborhood makes a fascinating itinerary stop for both nostalgists and nightlife hounds. Still, the blocks well south of Houston can be grungy in spots, so walk them with confidence and care after dark.

There are some remnants of what was once the largest Jewish population in America along **Orchard Street,** where you'll find great bargain hunting in its many old-world fabric and clothing stores still thriving between the club-clothes boutiques and trendy lounges. Keep in mind that the old-world shops close early on Friday afternoon and all day on Saturday (the Jewish Sabbath).

Take the F or V trains to Second Avenue and walk east on Houston; when you see Katz's Deli, you'll know you've arrived. You can also reach the neighborhood from the Delancey Street station on the F line, and the Essex Street station on the J, M, and Z lines.

SoHo & Nolita No relation to the London neighborhood of the same name, **SoHo** got its moniker as an

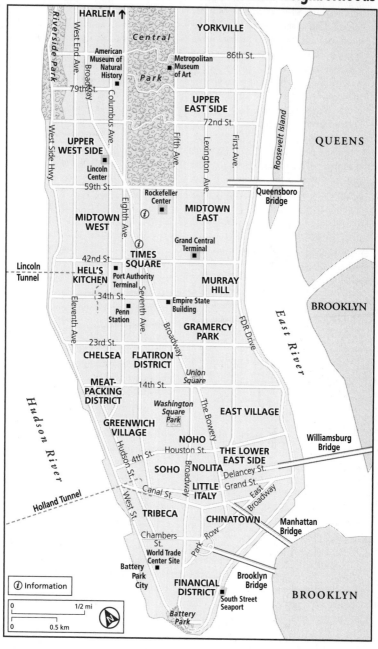

Manhattan Neighborhoods

HARLEM ↑

YORKVILLE

Central

Riverside Park

West End Ave.

86th St.

American
Museum of
Natural
History ■

Metropolitan
Museum
of Art ■

Park

79th St.

Broadway

Columbus Ave.

UPPER
EAST SIDE

72nd St.

West Side Hwy

Fifth Ave.

Lexington Ave.

First Ave.

Roosevelt Island

QUEENS

UPPER
WEST
SIDE ■

Lincoln
Center
59th St.

Rockefeller
Center
■ ①

MIDTOWN
EAST

Queensboro
Bridge

MIDTOWN
WEST

Eighth Ave.

Grand Central
Terminal ■

① TIMES
SQUARE

Lincoln
Tunnel

42nd St.

HELL'S
KITCHEN

Port Authority
Terminal ■

34th St.

MURRAY
HILL

Seventh Ave.

■ Empire State
Building

■ Penn
Station

Eleventh Ave.

BROOKLYN

East River

GRAMERCY
PARK

FDR Drive

23rd St.

Broadway

CHELSEA

FLATIRON
DISTRICT

*Union
Square*

MEAT-
PACKING
DISTRICT

14th St.

*Washington
Square
Park*

EAST VILLAGE

The Bowery

GREENWICH
VILLAGE

Williamsburg
Bridge

NOHO

Houston St.

Hudson River

Hudson St.

4th St.

SOHO

NOLITA

THE LOWER
EAST SIDE

Delancey St.

West St.

Canal St.

LITTLE
ITALY

Broadway

Grand St.

East Broadway

Holland Tunnel

TRIBECA

CHINATOWN

Manhattan
Bridge

Chambers
St.

Park Row

World Trade
Center Site ■

Battery
Park
City

Brooklyn
Bridge

① Information

FINANCIAL
DISTRICT ■

South Street
Seaport

BROOKLYN

0 ——— 1/2 mi

*Battery
Park*

0 ——— 0.5 km

abbreviation of "*So*uth of *Ho*uston Street." This superfashionable neighborhood extends down to Canal Street, between Sixth Avenue to the west and Lafayette Street (1 block east of Broadway) to the east. It's easily accessible by subway: Take the N, R, or W to the Prince Street station; the C, E, or 6 to Spring Street; or the B, D, F, or V trains to the Broadway–Lafayette Street stop.

An industrial zone during the 19th century, SoHo retains the impressive cast-iron architecture of the era. Once a haven for artists seeking cheap rents, SoHo is now a prime example of urban gentrification and is more a ritzy shopping district than an art center.

In recent years SoHo has been crawling its way east, taking over Mott and Mulberry streets—and white-hot Elizabeth Street in particular—north of Kenmare Street, an area now known as **Nolita** for its *No*rth of *Li*ttle I*tal*y location. Nolita is becoming increasingly well known for its hot shopping prospects, which include a number of pricey antiques and home-design stores. Taking the no. 6 to Spring Street will get you closest by subway, but it's just a short walk east from SoHo proper.

The East Village & NoHo The **East Village,** which extends between 14th Street and Houston Street, from Broadway east to First Avenue and beyond to Alphabet City—avenues A, B, C, and D—is where the city's real bohemia has gone. It's a fascinating mix of affordable ethnic and trendy restaurants, upstart clothing designers and kitschy boutiques, punk-rock clubs, and folk cafes. A half-dozen Off-Broadway theaters also call this place home. The gentrification that has swept the city has made a huge impact on the East Village, but there's still a seedy element that some of you won't find appealing—and some of you will.

The East Village isn't very accessible by subway; unless you're traveling along 14th Street (the L line will drop you off at Third and First aves.). Your best bet is to take the N, Q, R, W, 4, 5, or 6 to 14th Street/Union Square; the N, R, or W to 8th Street; or the 6 to Astor Place and walk east.

The southwestern section of the East Village, around Broadway and Lafayette between Bleecker and 4th streets, is called **NoHo** (for *No*rth of *Ho*uston), and has a completely different character. The area has developed much more like its neighbor to the south, SoHo. The Bleecker Street stop on the no. 6 line will land you in the heart of it, and the Broadway-Lafayette stop on the B, D, F, and V lines will drop you at its southern edge.

Greenwich Village Tree-lined streets crisscross and wind, following ancient streams and cow paths. Each block reveals yet another row of Greek Revival town houses, a well-preserved Federal-style house, or a peaceful courtyard or square. This is "the Village," from Broadway west to the Hudson River, bordered by Houston Street to the south and 14th Street to the north. It defies Manhattan's orderly grid system with streets that predate it—so be sure to take a map along as you explore.

The Seventh Avenue line (nos. 1, 2, and 3) is the area's main subway artery, while the West 4th Street stop (where the A, C, and E lines meet the B, D, F, and V lines) serves as its central hub.

The Village is probably the most chameleon-like of Manhattan's neighborhoods. Some of the highest-priced real estate in the city runs along lower Fifth Avenue, which dead-ends at **Washington Square Park.** Serpentine **Bleecker Street** stretches through most of the neighborhood and is emblematic of the area's historical bent. The tolerant anything-goes attitude in the Village has fostered a large gay community, which is still largely in evidence around **Christopher Street** and Sheridan Square. The streets west of Seventh Avenue, an area known as the **West Village,** boast a more relaxed vibe and some of the city's most charming and historic brownstones. Three colleges—New York University, Parsons School of Design, and the New School for Social Research—keep the area thinking young.

Streets are often crowded with weekend warriors and teenagers, especially on Bleecker, West 4th, 8th, and surrounding streets.

Midtown

Chelsea & the Meat-Packing District

Chelsea has come on strong in recent years as a hip address, especially for the gay community. A low-rise composite of town houses, tenements, lofts, and factories, the neighborhood comprises roughly the area west of Sixth Avenue from 14th to 30th streets. (Sixth Ave. itself below 23rd St. is actually considered part of the Flatiron District; see below.) Its main arteries are Seventh and Eighth avenues, and it's primarily served by the C or E and no. 1 subway lines.

New restaurants, cutting-edge shopping, and superhot nightspots pop up daily in the still-beefy **Meat-Packing District,** while the area from West 22nd to West 29th streets between Tenth and Eleventh avenues is home to the cutting edge of today's New York art scene. With galleries and bars tucked away in converted warehouses and former meat lockers, browsing can be frustrating. Your best bet is to have a specific destination (and an exact address) in mind, be it a restaurant, gallery, boutique, or nightclub, before you come.

The Flatiron District, Union Square & Gramercy Park

These adjoining and sometimes overlapping neighborhoods are some of the city's most appealing. Their streets have been rediscovered by New Yorkers and visitors alike, largely thanks to the boom-to-bust dot.com revolution of the late 1990s; the Flatiron District served as its geographical heart and earned the nickname "Silicon Alley" in the process. These neighborhoods boast great shopping and dining opportunities and a central-to-everything location that's hard to beat.

The **Flatiron District** lies south of 23rd Street to 14th Street, between Broadway and Sixth Avenue, and centers on the historic Flatiron Building on 23rd (so named for its triangular shape) and Park Avenue South, which has become a sophisticated new Restaurant Row. Below 23rd Street along Sixth Avenue (once known as the Ladies' Mile shopping district), mass-market discounters such as Filene's Basement, Bed Bath & Beyond, and others have moved in. The shopping gets classier on Fifth Avenue, where you'll find a mix of national names and hip boutiques.

Union Square is the hub of the entire area; the L, N, Q, R, W, 4, 5, and 6 trains stop here, making it easy to reach from most other city neighborhoods. Union Square is best known as the setting for New York's premier green market every Monday, Wednesday, Friday, and Saturday.

From about 16th to 23rd streets, east from Park Avenue South to about Second Avenue, is the leafy, largely residential district known as **Gramercy Park.**

Times Square & Midtown West

Midtown West, the vast area from 34th to 59th streets west of Fifth Avenue to the Hudson River, encompasses several famous names: Madison Square Garden, the Garment District, Rockefeller Center, the Theater District, and Times Square. This is New York's tourism central, where you'll find the bright lights and bustle that draw people from all over the world.

The nos. 1, 2, 3 subway line serves the massive neon station at the heart of Times Square, at 42nd Street between Broadway and Seventh Avenue, while the B, D, F, V line runs up Sixth Avenue to Rockefeller Center. The N, Q, R, W line cuts diagonally across the neighborhood, following the path of Broadway before heading up Seventh Avenue at 42nd Street. The A, C, E line serves the west side, running along Eighth Avenue.

Longtime New Yorkers like to kvetch about the glory days of the old peep-show-and-porn-shop **Times Square.** The area is now cleaned up and there really is not much here for the native New Yorker. The revival, however, has been nothing short of an outstanding success for tourism. Grand old theaters have come back to life as Broadway playhouses. Expect dense crowds, though; it's often tough just to make your way along the sidewalks.

To the west of the Theater District, in the 40s and 50s between Eighth and Tenth avenues, is **Hell's Kitchen,** an area that is much nicer than its ghoulish name and one of my favorites in the city. The neighborhood resisted gentrification until the mid-'90s, but has grown into a charming, less touristy adjunct to the neighboring Theater District. Ninth Avenue, in particular, has blossomed into one of the city's finest dining avenues; just stroll along and you'll have a world of great cuisine, ranging from American diner food to rustic Mediterranean to traditional Thai.

Unlike Times Square, gorgeous **Rockefeller Center** has needed no renovation. Situated between 46th and 50th streets from Sixth Avenue east to Fifth, this Art Deco complex contains some of the city's great architectural gems, which house hundreds of offices, and a number of NBC studios.

Between Seventh and Eighth avenues and 31st and 33rd streets, **Penn Station** sits beneath unsightly behemoth

Madison Square Garden, where the Liberty and the Knicks play. Taking up all of 34th Street between Sixth and Seventh avenues is **Macy's,** the world's largest department store; exit Macy's at the southeast corner and you'll find more famous-label shopping around **Herald Square.**

Midtown West is also home to some of the city's most revered museums and cultural institutions, including **Carnegie Hall,** the **Museum of Modern Art,** and **Radio City Music Hall,** to name just a few.

Midtown East & Murray Hill Midtown East, the area including Fifth Avenue and everything east from 34th to 59th streets, is the more upscale side of the Midtown map. This side of town is short of subway trains, served primarily by the Lexington Avenue no. 4, 5, 6 line.

Midtown East is where you'll find the city's finest collection of grand hotels. The stretch of **Fifth Avenue** from Saks at 49th Street extending to 59th Street is home to the city's most high-profile haute couture shopping.

Magnificent architectural highlights include the recently repolished **Chrysler Building,** with its stylized gargoyles glaring down on passersby; the Beaux Arts tour de force that is **Grand Central Terminal; St. Patrick's Cathedral;** and the glorious **Empire State Building.**

Farther east, swank Sutton and Beekman places are enclaves of beautiful town houses, luxury living, and tiny pocket parks that look out over the East River. Along this river is the **United Nations,** which isn't officially in New York City, or even the United States, but on a parcel of international land belonging to member nations.

Claiming the territory east from Madison Avenue, **Murray Hill** begins somewhere north of 23rd Street (the line between it and Gramercy Park is fuzzy), and is most clearly recognizable north of 30th Street to 42nd Street. This brownstone-lined quarter is largely a quiet residential neighborhood, most notable for its handful of good budget and midprice hotels.

Uptown

Upper West Side North of 59th Street and encompassing everything west of Central Park, the Upper West Side has **Lincoln Center,** arguably the world's premier performing arts venue, and the **Time Warner Center** with its upscale shops, such as **Hugo Boss, A/X Armani,** and **Sephora.** It's also the home for **Jazz at Lincoln Center.**

Unlike the more stratified Upper East Side, the Upper West Side is home to an egalitarian mix of middle-class yuppiedom, laid-back wealth (lots of celebs and moneyed media types call the grand apartments along Central Park West home), and ethnic families who were here before the gentrification.

Two major subway lines service the area: the no. 1, 2, 3 line runs up Broadway, while the B and C trains run up glamorous Central Park West, stopping right at the historic Dakota apartment building (where John Lennon was shot and Yoko Ono still lives) at 72nd Street, and at the Museum of Natural History at 81st Street.

Upper East Side North of 59th Street and east of Central Park is some of the city's most expensive residential real estate. This is New York at its most gentrified: Walk along Fifth and Park avenues, especially between 60th and 80th streets, and you're sure to encounter some of the wizened WASPs and Chanel-suited socialites that make up the most rarefied of the city's population. Madison Avenue from 60th Street well into the 80s is the main shopping strip—so bring your platinum card.

The main attraction of this neighborhood is **Museum Mile,** the stretch of Fifth Avenue fronting Central Park, which is home to no fewer than 10 terrific cultural institutions, including the mind-boggling **Metropolitan Museum of Art.**

The Upper East Side is served solely by the crowded Lexington Avenue line (4, 5, 6 trains), so wear your walking shoes (or bring taxi fare) if you're heading up here to explore.

Harlem Harlem has benefited from a dramatic image makeover in the past few years, and with new restaurants, clubs, and stores, it's slowly becoming a neighborhood in demand.

Harlem proper stretches from river to river, beginning at 125th Street on the West Side, 96th Street on the East Side, and 110th Street north of Central Park. This area is benefiting greatly from the revitalization that has swept so much of the city. The commercial area is served primarily by the A, B, C, D and nos. 2, 3, 4, and 5 lines.

Washington Heights & Inwood Located at the northern tip of Manhattan, Washington Heights (the area from 155th St. to Dyckman St., with adjacent Inwood running to the tip) is home to a large segment of Manhattan's Latino community, plus an increasing number of yuppies who don't mind trading a half-hour subway commute to Midtown for much lower rents. **Fort Tryon Park** and **the Cloisters** are the two big reasons for visitors to come up this way. The Cloisters houses the Metropolitan Museum of Art's stunning medieval collection, in a building perched atop a hill, with excellent views across the Hudson to the Palisades. Committed off-the-beaten-path sightseers might also want to visit the **Dyckman Farmhouse,** a historic jewel built in 1783 and the only remaining Dutch Colonial structure in Manhattan.

2 Getting Around

Frankly, Manhattan's transportation systems are a marvel. It's simply miraculous that so many people can gather on this little island and move around it. For the most part, you can get where you're going pretty quickly and easily using some combination of subways, buses, and cabs.

But during rush hours, you'll easily beat car traffic while on foot, as taxis and buses stop and groan at gridlocked corners (don't even *try* going crosstown in a cab or bus in Midtown at midday). You'll also see a whole lot more by walking than by riding beneath the street in the subway or flying by in a cab. So pack your most comfortable shoes and hit the pavement—it's the best, cheapest, and most appealing way to experience the city.

BY SUBWAY

Run by the **Metropolitan Transit Authority (MTA),** the much-maligned subway system is actually the fastest way to travel around New York, especially during rush hours. The subway runs 24 hours a day, 7 days a week.

PAYING YOUR WAY

The subway fare is $2 (half-price for seniors and those with disabilities), and children under 44 inches tall ride free (up to three kids per adult).

Tokens are no longer available. People pay fares with the **MetroCard,** a magnetically encoded card that debits the fare when swiped through the turnstile (or the fare box on a city bus). Once you're in the system, you can transfer to any subway line that you can reach without exiting your station. MetroCards also allow you **free transfers** between the bus and subway within a 2-hour period.

MetroCards can be purchased from staffed booths, where you can pay only with cash; at the ATM-style vending machines located in just about every subway station, which accept cash, credit cards, and debit cards; from a MetroCard merchant, such as most Rite Aid drugstores or Hudson News at Penn Station and Grand Central Terminal; or at the MTA information desk at the Times Square Information Center, 1560 Broadway, between 46th and 47th streets.

MetroCards come in a few different configurations:

Pay-Per-Ride MetroCards can be used for up to four people by swiping up to four times (bring the whole family). You can put any amount from $4 (two rides) to $80 on your card. Every time you put $10 or $20 on your Pay-Per-Ride MetroCard, it's automatically credited 20%—that's one free ride for every $10, or five trips. You can buy Pay-Per-Ride MetroCards at any subway station; an increasing number of stations now have automated MetroCard vending machines, which allow you to buy Metro-Cards using your major credit card or debit card. MetroCards are also available from shops and newsstands around town in $10 and $20 values. You can refill your card at any time until the expiration date on the card, usually about a year from the date of purchase, at any subway station.

Unlimited-Ride MetroCards, which can't be used for more than one person at a time or more frequently than 18-minute intervals, are available in four values: the **daily Fun Pass,** which allows you a day's worth of unlimited subway and bus rides for $7; the **7-Day MetroCard,** for $24; and the **30-Day MetroCard,** for $76. Seven- and 30-day Unlimited-Ride MetroCards can be purchased at any subway station or from a MetroCard merchant. Fun Passes, however, cannot be purchased at token booths—you can buy them only at a MetroCard vending machine; from a MetroCard merchant; or at the MTA information desk at the Times Square Information Center. Unlimited-Ride MetroCards go into effect not at the time you buy them, but the first time you use them—so if you buy a card on Monday and don't begin to use it until Wednesday, Wednesday is when the clock starts ticking on your MetroCard. A Fun Pass is good from the first time you use it until 3am the next day, while 7- and 30-day MetroCards run out at midnight on the last day. These MetroCards cannot be refilled; throw them out once they've been used up and buy a new one.

To locate the nearest MetroCard merchant, or for any other MetroCard questions, call © **800/METROCARD** or 212/METROCARD (212/638-7622) Monday through Friday between 7am and 11pm, Saturday and Sunday from 9am to 5pm. Or go online to **www.mta.nyc.ny.us/metrocard**, which can give you a full rundown of MetroCard merchants in the tri-state area.

USING THE SYSTEM

The subway system basically mimics the lay of the land aboveground, with most lines in Manhattan running north and south, like the avenues, and a few lines east and west, like the streets.

Lines have assigned colors on subway maps and trains—red for the no. 1, 2, 3, line; green for the 4, 5, and 6 trains; and so on—but nobody ever refers to them by color. Always refer to them by number or letter when asking questions. Within Manhattan, the distinction between different numbered trains that share the same line is usually that some are express and others are local. **Express trains** often skip about three stops for each one that they make; express stops are indicated on subway maps with a white (rather than solid) circle. Local stops are usually from 5 to 10 blocks apart.

Directions are almost always indicated using "Uptown" (northbound) and "Downtown" (southbound), so be sure to know in which direction you want to head. The outsides of some subway entrances are marked UPTOWN ONLY or DOWNTOWN ONLY; read carefully, as it's easy to head in the wrong direction. Once you're on the platform, check the signs overhead to make sure that the train you're waiting for will be traveling in the right direction. If you do make a mistake, it's a good idea to wait for an express station, like 14th Street or 42nd Street, so you can get off and change for the other direction without paying again.

SUBWAY SAFETY TIPS   In general, the subways are safe, especially in Manhattan. There are panhandlers and questionable characters like anywhere else in the city, but subway crime has gone down to 1960s levels. Still, stay alert and trust your instincts. Always keep a hand on your personal belongings.

When using the subway, **don't wait for trains near the edge of the platform** or on extreme ends of a station. During non–rush hours, wait for the train in view of the token-booth clerk or under the yellow DURING OFF HOURS TRAINS STOP HERE signs, and ride in the train operator's or conductor's car (usually in the center of the train; you'll see his or her head stick out of the window when the doors open). Choose crowded cars over empty ones—there's safety in numbers.

Avoid subways late at night, and splurge on a cab after about 10 or 11pm—it's money well spent to avoid a long wait on a deserted platform. Or take the bus.

BY BUS

Cheaper than taxis and more pleasant than subways (they provide a mobile sightseeing window on the city), MTA buses are a good transportation option. However, they can get stuck in traffic, sometimes making it quicker to walk. They stop every couple of blocks, rather than the 5 to 10 blocks that local subways traverse between stops. So for long distances, the subway is your best bet; but for short distances or traveling crosstown, try the bus. Bus stops are located every 2 or 3 blocks on the right-side corner of the street (facing the direction of traffic flow). Watch for the blue-and-white sign with the bus emblem.

PAYING YOUR WAY

Like the subway fare, **bus fare** is $2, half-price for seniors and riders with disabilities, free for children under 44 inches (up to three kids per adult). The fare is payable with a **MetroCard** or **exact change.** Bus drivers don't make change, and fare boxes don't accept dollar bills or pennies. You can't purchase MetroCards on the bus, so you'll have to have them before you board; for details on where to get them, see "Paying Your Way" under "By Subway," above.

If you pay with a MetroCard, you can transfer to another bus or to the subway for free within 2 hours. If you pay cash, you must request a **free transfer** slip that allows you to change to an intersecting bus route only (legal transfer points are listed on the transfer paper) within 1 hour of issue. Transfer slips cannot be used to enter the subway.

BY TAXI

If you don't want to deal with public transportation, find an address that might be a few blocks from the subway station, or share your ride with 3.5 million other people, then take a taxi. Cabs can be hailed on any street and will take you right to your destination.

Official New York City taxis, licensed by the Taxi and Limousine Commission (TLC), are yellow, with the rates printed on the door and a light with a medallion number on the roof. You can hail a taxi on any street. *Never* accept a ride from any other car except an official city yellow cab (private livery cars are not allowed to pick up fares on the street).

The base fare on entering the cab is $2.50. The cost is 40¢ for every ⅕ mile or 40¢ per 2 minutes in stopped or slow-moving traffic (or for waiting time). There's no extra charge for each passenger or for luggage. However, you must pay bridge or tunnel tolls (sometimes the driver will front the toll and add it to your bill at the end; most times, however, you pay the driver before the toll). You'll also pay a $1 surcharge between 4 and 8pm and a 50¢ surcharge after 8pm and before 6am. A 15% to 20% tip is customary. (At press time, the cab drivers were lobbying the city for a fare hike due to increased fuel costs.)

The TLC has posted a **Taxi Rider's Bill of Rights** sticker in every cab. Drivers are required by law to take you anywhere in the five boroughs, to Nassau or Westchester counties, or to Newark Airport. They are supposed to know how to get you to any address in Manhattan and all major points in the outer boroughs. They are also required to provide air-conditioning and turn off the radio on demand, and they cannot smoke while you're in the cab. They are required to be polite.

Tips Taxi-Hailing Tips

When you're waiting on the street for an available taxi, look at the **medallion light** on top of the oncoming cabs. If the light is out, the taxi is in use. When only the center part (the number) is lit, the taxi is available—this is when you raise your hand to flag the cab. If all the lights are on, the driver is off duty. A taxi can't take more than four people, so expect to split up if your group is larger.

FAST FACTS: New York City

American Express Travel-service offices are at many Manhattan locations, including 295 Park Avenue S. at 23rd Street (✆ **212/691-9797**); 1535 Broadway, in the eighth-floor lobby (✆ **212/575-6580**); on the mezzanine level at Macy's Herald Square, 34th Street and Broadway (✆ **212/695-8075**); and 374 Park Ave., at 53rd Street (✆ **212/421-8240**). Call ✆ **800/AXP-TRIP** or go online to **www.american express.com** for other city locations or general information.

Area Codes There are four area codes in the city: two in Manhattan, the original **212** and the new **646,** and two in the outer boroughs, the original **718** and the new **347.** Also common is the **917** area code, which is assigned to cellphones, pagers, and the like. All calls between these area codes are local calls, but you'll have to dial 1 + the area code + the 7 digits for all calls, even ones made within your area code.

Business Hours In general, **retail stores** are open Monday through Saturday from 10am to 6 or 7pm, Thursday from 10am to 8:30 or 9pm, and Sunday from noon to 5pm. **Banks** tend to be open Monday through Friday from 9am to 3pm and sometimes Saturday mornings.

Doctors For medical emergencies requiring immediate attention, head to the nearest emergency room (see "Hospitals," below). For less-urgent health problems, New York has several walk-in medical centers, such as **DOCS at New York Healthcare,** 55 E. 34th St., between Park and Madison avenues (✆ **212/252-6001**), for nonemergency illnesses. The clinic, affiliated with Beth Israel Medical Center, is open Monday through Thursday from 8am to 8pm, Friday from 8am to 7pm, Saturday from 9am to 3pm, and Sunday from 9am to 2pm. The **NYU Downtown Hospital** offers physician referrals at ✆ **212/312-5000.**

Embassies & Consulates See "Fast Facts" in chapter 2.

Emergencies Dial ✆ **911** for fire, police, and ambulance. The **Poison Control Center** can be reached at ✆ **800/222-1222** toll-free from any phone.

Hospitals The following hospitals have 24-hour emergency rooms. Don't forget your insurance card.

   Downtown: New York University Downtown Hospital, 170 William St., between Beekman and Spruce streets (✆ 212/312-5063 or 212/312-5000); **St. Vincent's Hospital and Medical Center,** 153 W. 11th St., at Seventh Avenue (✆ 212/604-7000); and **Beth Israel Medical Center,** First Avenue and 16th Street (✆ 212/420-2000).

   Midtown: Bellevue Hospital Center, 462 First Ave., at 27th Street (✆ 212/252-94571); **New York University Medical Center,** 550 First Ave., at 33rd Street (✆ 212/263-7300); and **St. Luke's/Roosevelt Hospital,** 425 W. 59th St., between Ninth and Tenth avenues (✆ 212/523-4000).

   Upper West Side: St. Luke's Hospital, 1111 Amsterdam Ave. at 114th Street (✆ 212/523-4000); and **Columbia Presbyterian Medical Center,** 622 W. 168th St., between Broadway and Fort Washington Avenue (✆ 212/305-2500).

   Upper East Side: New York Presbyterian Hospital, 525 E. 68th St., at York Avenue (✆ 212/472-5454); **Lenox Hill Hospital,** 100 E. 77th St., between Park and Lexington avenues (© 212/434-2000); and **Mount Sinai Medical Center,** Fifth Avenue at 100th Street (© 212/241-6500).

Hot Lines The 24-hour **Rape and Sexual Abuse Hot Line** is © 212/267-7273. The **Bias Crimes Hot Line** is © 212/662-2427. The **LIFENET Hot Line** for suicide prevention, substance abuse, and other mental health crises is © 800/543-3638. For **Mental Health and Alcoholism Services Crisis Intervention,** call © 212/219-5599. You can reach **Alcoholics Anonymous** at © 212/647-1680 (general office) or 212/ 647-1680 (intergroup, for alcoholics who need immediate counseling from a sober, recovering alcoholic). The **Domestic Violence Hot Line** is © 800/621-4673. Other useful numbers include the **Crisis Help Line,** © 212/532-2400, and the **Samaritans' Suicide Prevention Line,** © 212/673-3000. To locate local **police** precincts, call © 646/610-5000 or 718/610-5000. For the **Department of Consumer Affairs,** call © 212/487-4444, and for **taxi complaints,** call © 212/NYC-TAXI or 212/676-1000. If you suspect your car may have been towed, call the **Department of Transportation TOWAWAY Help Line** at © 212/869-2929.

Libraries The **New York Public Library** is on Fifth Avenue at 42nd Street (© **212/ 930-0830**). This Beaux Arts beauty houses more than 38 million volumes, and the beautiful reading rooms have been restored to their former glory. More efficient and modern, if less charming, is the mid-Manhattan branch at 455 Fifth Ave., at 40th Street, across the street from the main library (© **212/340-0833**). There are other branches in almost every neighborhood; you can find a list online at **www. nypl.org**.

Liquor Laws The minimum legal age to purchase and consume alcoholic beverages in New York is 21. Liquor and wine are sold only in licensed stores, which are open 6 days a week, with most choosing to close on Sunday. Liquor stores are closed on holidays and election days while the polls are open. Beer can be purchased in grocery stores and delis 24 hours a day, except Sunday before noon. Last call in bars is at 4am, although many close earlier.

Newspapers & Magazines There are three major daily newspapers: the *New York Times,* the *Daily News,* and the *New York Post.* For arts and entertainment listings, try *Time Out New York,* the *Village Voice,* and www.nytoday.com (see information listed under "New York City After Dark," later in this chapter).

If you want to find your hometown paper, visit **Universal News & Magazines,** at 234 W. 42nd St., between Seventh and Eighth avenues (© **212/221-1809**), and 977 Eighth Ave., between 57th and 58th streets (© **212/459-0932**); or **Hotalings News Agency,** 624 W. 52nd St., between Eleventh and Twelfth avenues (© **212/974-9419**). Other good bets include the **Hudson** newsdealers, located in Grand Central Terminal (42nd St. and Lexington Ave.) and Penn Station (34th St. and Seventh Ave.).

Pharmacies **Duane Reade** (www.duanereade.com) has 24-hour pharmacies in Midtown at 224 W. 57th St., at Broadway (© 212/541-9708); on the Upper West Side at 2465 Broadway, at 91st Street (© **212/663-1580**); and on the Upper East Side at 1279 Third Ave., at 74th Street (© **212/744-2668**).

Police Dial © **911** in an emergency; otherwise, call © **646/610-5000** or 718/ 610-5000 (NYPD headquarters) for the number of the nearest precinct.

Restrooms Public restrooms are available at the visitor centers in Midtown (1560 Broadway, between 46th and 47th sts.; and 810 Seventh Ave., between 52nd and 53rd sts.). Grand Central Terminal, at 42nd Street between Park and Lexington avenues, also has clean restrooms. Your best bet on the street is Starbucks or another city java chain—you can't walk more than a few blocks without seeing one. The big chain bookstores are good for this, too. You can also head to hotel lobbies (especially the big Midtown ones) and department stores like Macy's and Bloomingdale's. On the Lower East Side, stop into the Lower East Side BID Visitor Center, 261 Broome St., between Orchard and Allen streets (open Sun–Fri 10am–4pm, sometimes later).

Salon Services Need a haircut or a manicure while you're here in town? Bold, bustling **Warren-Tricomi**, 16 W. 57th St., just west of Fifth Avenue (© 212/ 262-8899; www.warrentricomi.com), can meet all of your salon needs. For a dash of downtown style (and slightly lower prices), make an appointment at **Arte**, 284 Lafayette St., SoHo (© 212/941-5932). If it's a good manicure or pedicure you need, visit **Pinky**, which has five locations on the Upper West Side, including 2050 Broadway, at 70th Street (© 212/362-9466); 312 Columbus Ave., at 74th Street (© 212/787-0390); and 2240 Broadway, at 80th Street (© 212/877-4992).

Smoking Smoking is prohibited on all public transportation; in the lobbies of hotels and office buildings; in taxis, bars, and restaurants; and in most shops.

Taxes **Sales tax** is 8.625% on meals, most goods, and some services, but is not charged on clothing and footwear under $110. **Hotel tax** is 13.25% plus $2 per room per night (including sales tax). **Parking-garage tax** is 18.25%.

Time For the correct local time, dial © 212/976-1616.

Transit Information For information on getting to and from the airport, see section 1, "Arriving," earlier in this chapter, or call **Air-Ride** at © 800/247-7433. For information on subways and buses, call the **MTA** at © 718/330-1234, or see "Getting Around," earlier in this chapter.

Traveler's Assistance **Travelers Aid** (www.travelersaid.org) helps distressed travelers with all kinds of problems, including accidents, sickness, and lost or stolen luggage. There is an office on the first floor of Terminal 6 (JetBlue terminal) at JFK Airport (© 718/656-4870), and one in Newark Airport's Terminal B (© 973/623-5052).

Weather For the current temperature and next day's forecast, look in the upper-right corner of the front page of the *New York Times* or call © 212/976-1212. If you want to know how to pack before you arrive, point your browser to **www.cnn.com/weather** or **www.weather.com**.

3 Where to Stay

New York City may be the most expensive place to live in the United States. It only follows that hotel rates here will also be more expensive than in almost any other city in the country. If you want to spend less than 100 bucks a night, you're probably going to have to put up with some inconveniences, such as sharing a hall bathroom with

Downtown Accommodations, Dining & Attractions

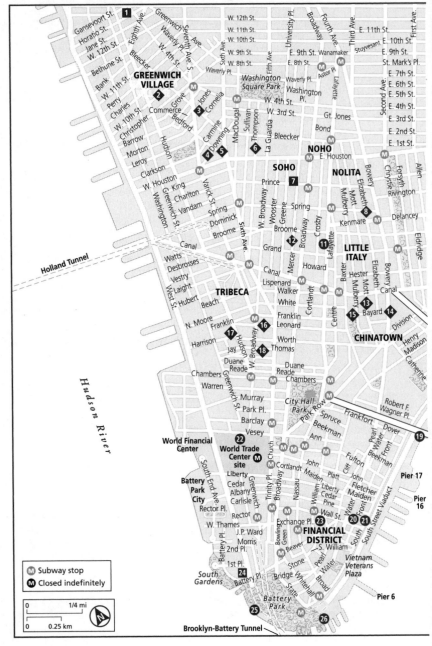

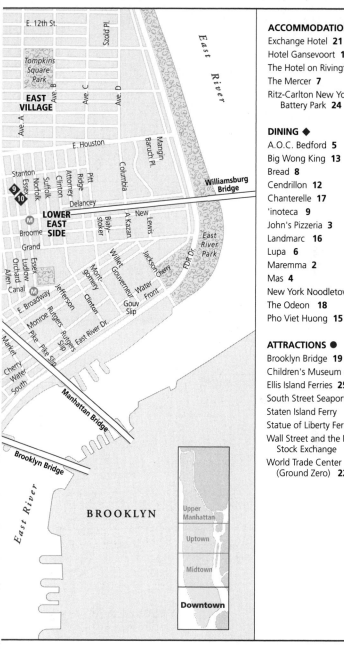

ACCOMMODATIONS ■
Exchange Hotel **21**
Hotel Gansevoort **1**
The Hotel on Rivington **10**
The Mercer **7**
Ritz-Carlton New York,
Battery Park **24**

DINING ◆
A.O.C. Bedford **5**
Big Wong King **13**
Bread **8**
Cendrillon **12**
Chanterelle **17**
'inoteca **9**
John's Pizzeria **3**
Landmarc **16**
Lupa **6**
Maremma **2**
Mas **4**
New York Noodletown **14**
The Odeon **18**
Pho Viet Huong **15**

ATTRACTIONS ●
Brooklyn Bridge **19**
Children's Museum of the Arts **11**
Ellis Island Ferries **25**
South Street Seaport & Museum **20**
Staten Island Ferry **26**
Statue of Liberty Ferry **25**
Wall Street and the New York
Stock Exchange **23**
World Trade Center Site
(Ground Zero) **22**

Midtown Accommodations, Dining & Attractions

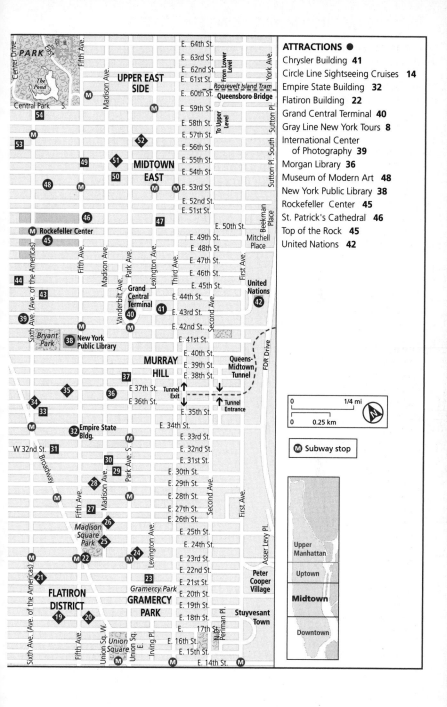

ATTRACTIONS ●

Chrysler Building **41**
Circle Line Sightseeing Cruises **14**
Empire State Building **32**
Flatiron Building **22**
Grand Central Terminal **40**
Gray Line New York Tours **8**
International Center
of Photography **39**
Morgan Library **36**
Museum of Modern Art **48**
New York Public Library **38**
Rockefeller Center **45**
St. Patrick's Cathedral **46**
Top of the Rock **45**
United Nations **42**

Ⓜ Subway stop

Uptown Accommodations, Dining & Attractions

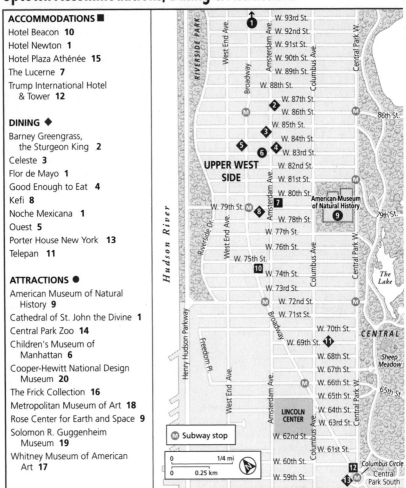

ACCOMMODATIONS ■

Hotel Beacon **10**
Hotel Newton **1**
Hotel Plaza Athénée **15**
The Lucerne **7**
Trump International Hotel
&Tower **12**

DINING ◆

Barney Greengrass,
the Sturgeon King **2**
Celeste **3**
Flor de Mayo **1**
Good Enough to Eat **4**
Kefi **8**
Noche Mexicana **1**
Ouest **5**
Porter House New York **13**
Telepan **11**

ATTRACTIONS ●

American Museum of Natural
History **9**
Cathedral of St. John the Divine **1**
Central Park Zoo **14**
Children's Museum of
Manhattan **6**
Cooper-Hewitt National Design
Museum **20**
The Frick Collection **16**
Metropolitan Museum of Art **18**
Rose Center for Earth and Space **9**
Solomon R. Guggenheim
Museum **19**
Whitney Museum of American
Art **17**

your fellow travelers. If you want a room with standard amenities, plan on spending at least $150 a night or so. If you do better than that, you've landed a deal.

THE FINANCIAL DISTRICT
VERY EXPENSIVE

Ritz-Carlton New York, Battery Park ✦✦✦   Perfect on almost every level, the only drawback to this Ritz-Carlton is its remote downtown location. But that location, on the extreme southern tip of Manhattan, is also one of its strengths. Where else can you get, in most rooms anyway, magnificent views of New York Harbor from your bedroom—complete with telescope for close-ups of Lady Liberty? Where else can you have a cocktail in your hotel bar and watch the sun set over the harbor? And where else can you go for a morning jog around the Manhattan waterfront? This modern, Art Deco–influenced high-rise differs from most Ritz-Carlton properties with an English

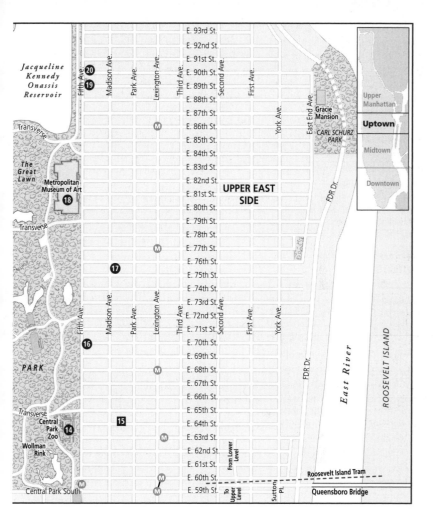

countryside look, including its sister hotel on Central Park (p. 96), but that's where the differences end. You'll find the full slate of comforts and services typical of Ritz-Carlton here, from Frette-dressed feather beds to the chain's signature Bath Butler, who will draw a scented bath for you in your own deep soaking tub. Standard rooms are all very large and have huge bathrooms, while suites are bigger than most New York apartments.

2 West St., New York, NY 10004. (C) **800/241-3333** or 212/344-0800. Fax 212/344-3801. www.ritzcarlton.com. 298 units. $350–$545 double; from $750 suite. Extra person 12 and over $30 (starting from $100 on club level). Check website for promotional weekend packages. AE, DC, DISC, MC, V. Valet parking $60. Subway: 4, 5 to Bowling Green. **Amenities:** Restaurant; lobby lounge (w/outdoor seating) for afternoon tea and cocktails; 14th-floor cocktail bar w/light dining and outdoor seating; state-of-the-art health club w/views; spa treatments; 24-hr. concierge; well-equipped business center w/24-hr. secretarial services; 24-hr. room service; laundry service; dry cleaning; Ritz-Carlton Club Level w/5 food presentations daily; technology butler and bath butler services. *In room:* A/C, TV w/pay movies and video games, dataport, minibar, fridge, hair dryer, safe, CD player, DVD w/surround sound in suites and Club rooms, Wi-Fi and high-speed Internet connectivity.

EXPENSIVE/MODERATE

Exchange Hotel ⭐ This cozy hotel is a solid, midpriced choice if you are looking for a downtown location. A short walk from Wall Street, the South Street Seaport, Brooklyn Bridge, and Chinatown, the Exchange Hotel features personalized service and a few perks like Wi-Fi and a complimentary continental breakfast. Recently renovated in a sleek, contemporary style, standard and deluxe guest rooms are on the small size, but outfitted nicely with plasma televisions, minirefrigerators, and microwaves. The suites are roomy with a separate living room, black leather furniture, and a full-sized kitchen. Bathrooms are tight in both the guest rooms and the suites and include those fashionable marble bowl sinks that look good but don't leave much space for any of your toiletries. That minor complaint aside, the Exchange is a welcome addition to an area quite lacking in lodging.

129 Front St. (between Wall and Pine sts.), New York, NY 10005. © 212/742-0003. Fax 212/742-0124. www.exchange hotel.com. 53 units. $299–$469. Rates include continental breakfast. AE, DC, MC, V. Parking $25. Subway: 2, 3 to Wall St. **Amenities:** Lounge; access to nearby fitness club; laundry/valet service. *In room:* A/C, TV, VCR, full-sized kitchens in suites, minifridge, microwave, iron/ironing board, safe, Wi-Fi.

LOWER EAST SIDE
EXPENSIVE

The Hotel on Rivington ⭐⭐ The contrast of a gleaming 21-story, glass-tower luxury hotel in the midst of 19th- and early-20th-century Lower East Side low-rise tenement buildings is striking, but an accurate representation of what that neighborhood has become. From the floor-to-ceiling windows of your room, surrounded by amenities such as flat-panel televisions, Japanese soaking tubs in the bathrooms, and Tempur-Pedic mattresses, not only do you have incredible and unobstructed city views, but you can look down and spot ancient Lower East Side landmarks such as the sign for the Schapiro Kosher wine factory, the Economy Candy store (est. 1937), or the shops of Orchard Street. You may not be close to the center of Manhattan at The Hotel on Rivington, but you will be in a dually historic and trendy location, where old-world customs and institutions coexist with the new and the supercool. The Hotel on Rivington is most definitely new and supercool, but the comforts the hotel offers are timeless. Along with the aforementioned views, three-quarters of the rooms have private terraces, the option of in-room spa services, and heated, tiled floors in the large bathrooms where you can enjoy your view of the city as you bathe—which means someone with binoculars might have a view of you as well.

107 Rivington St. (between Ludlow and Essex sts.), New York, NY 10002. © 212/475-2600. Fax 212/475-5959. www. hotelonrivington.com. 110 units. From $325 double. AE, DC, MC, V. Parking $50. Subway: F to Delancey St. **Amenities:** Restaurant; fitness center; in-room spa services available; concierge; 24-hr. room service; laundry service; dry cleaning. *In room:* A/C, TV, dataport, Wi-Fi, fridge, hair dryer, CD players and JBL On Stage iPod speaker system available.

SOHO
VERY EXPENSIVE

The Mercer ⭐⭐⭐ The best of the downtown, celebrity-crawling, hip, and trendy hotels, The Mercer is a place where even those who represent the antithesis of hip (and I'm speaking personally) can feel very much at home. Though SoHo can be a bit over the top with its high-end boutiques, cutting-edge restaurants, and a constant parade of too-serious fashionistas on the streets, it is still a very exciting place to be. And the corner of Mercer and Prince streets, the location of the hotel, is probably the epicenter of SoHo. Still, once inside the hotel, there is a pronounced calm—from the postmodern library lounge and the relaxed Mizrahi-clad staff to the huge soundproof loftlike guest rooms; the hotel is a perfect complement to the scene outside your big window. The tile-and-marble bathrooms have a steel cart for storage, and an oversize shower stall or oversize two-person tub (state your preference when booking). Just off the lobby is the Kitchen restaurant, one of Jean-Georges Vongerichten's earlier endeavors that is still going strong.

147 Mercer St. (at Prince St.), New York, NY 10012. ✆ **888/918-6060** or 212/966-6060. Fax 212/965-3838. www.mercerhotel.com. 75 units. $440–$480 double; $550–$680 studio; from $1,250 suite. AE, DC, DISC, MC, V. Parking $35 nearby. Subway: N, R to Prince St. **Amenities:** Restaurant; lounge; food and drink service in lobby; free access to nearby Crunch fitness center; 24-hr. concierge; secretarial services; 24-hr. room service; laundry service; dry cleaning; video, DVD, and CD libraries. *In room:* A/C, TV/DVD, dataport, Wi-Fi, minibar, safe, CD player, ceiling fan.

THE MEAT-PACKING DISTRICT

EXPENSIVE

Hotel Gansevoort ★★ Built from the ground up by hotelier Henry Kallan (of New York's Hotel Giraffe and The Library) and opened in 2004, the Gansevoort became the first major hotel in the white-hot Meat-Packing District. And now this sleek, 14-floor zinc-colored tower, with its open, sprawling clubby lobby, the very popular Japanese restaurant **Ono,** and the indoor/outdoor rooftop bar and pool (with music piped underwater), is the symbolic anchor of the district. Despite its potentially excessive trendiness, the Gansevoort offers excellent, personable service, as do all of Henry Kallan's hotels. Rooms are a good size with comfortable furnishings in soft tones and hi-tech amenities like plasma televisions and Wi-Fi. Suites have a living room and separate bedroom and some have small balconies and bay windows. Corner suites have adjoining guest rooms for families or larger parties. The generous-size bathrooms are done up in ceramic, stainless steel, and marble and are impeccably appointed. In all the guest rooms and throughout the hotel, original art by New York artists is on display.

18 Ninth Ave. (at 13th St.), New York, NY 10014. ✆ **877/426-7386** or 212/206-6700. Fax 212/255-5858. www.hotelgansevoort.com. 187 units. From $450 double; from $795 suite. AC, DC, DISC, MC, V. Parking $40. Subway: A, C, E to 14th St. Pet-friendly floors. **Amenities:** Restaurant; rooftop bar and lounge; indoor/outdoor pool; fitness center; spa; concierge; business center; 24-hr. room service; laundry service; dry cleaning; rooftop garden. *In room:* A/C, TV, dataport, Wi-Fi and high-speed Internet, minibar, hair dryer, iron, safe, dual-line telephones, voice mail.

CHELSEA

MODERATE

Inn on 23rd Street ★★★ *Finds* Behind an unassuming entrance in the middle of bustling 23rd Street is one of New York's true lodging treasures: a real urban bed-and-breakfast with as personal a touch as you'll find anywhere. All 14 guest rooms are spacious. Each has a king- or queen-size bed outfitted with a supremely comfy pillow-top mattress and top-quality linens, satellite TV, a large private bathroom with thick Turkish towels, and a roomy closet. Rooms have themes, like the Rosewood Room, with '60s built-ins; the elegantly Asian Bamboo Room; and Ken's Cabin, a large, lodgelike room with cushy, well-worn leather furnishings and wonderful Americana relics. The Inn has a lovely library where the complimentary breakfast is served, and it also has an honor bar where you can make yourself a drink for less money than you would pay in any other hotel in the city. Other perks include free high-speed Internet access in the rooms, Wi-Fi in the library, and wine and cheese served on Friday and Saturday. The only drawback: The Inn is so comfortable you might be tempted to lounge indoors and miss the city sights.

131 W. 23rd St. (between Sixth and Seventh aves.), New York, NY 10011. ✆ **877/387-2323** or 212/463-0330. Fax 212/463-0302. www.innon23rd.com. 14 units. $219–$259 double; $359 suite. Rates include continental breakfast. Extra

person $25. Children under 12 stay free in parent's room. AE, DC, DISC, MC, V. Parking $20 nearby. Subway: F, 1 to 23rd St. **Amenities:** Fax and copy service; cozy library w/stereo, VCR, and W-Fi. *In room:* A/C, TV, dataport, high-speed Internet access, hair dryer, iron.

UNION SQUARE, THE FLATIRON DISTRICT & GRAMERCY PARK
VERY EXPENSIVE

Gramercy Park Hotel 🕉🕉🕉   Shuttered for 2 years, this 1925-built legend borders charming Gramercy Park and has been stunningly redone by famed hotelier Ian Schrager. Start with the lobby, with its eclectic mix of art: Julian Schnabel–designed lamps (Schnabel was a main contributor to the design concept of the hotel and his pieces abound), two 10-foot Italian fireplaces, red velvet curtains, Moroccan tiles, bronze tables, and a magnificent Venetian glass chandelier. What once was a 500-plus-room hotel now has only 185 rooms, so where the former version had tiny rooms, now there is space. More than half of the rooms are suites, some with views overlooking Gramercy Park. All have mahogany English drinking cabinets where the minibar and DVD player are hidden, along with some variation of the overstuffed lounge chair and a portrait of Schnabel's friend, the late Andy Warhol. Beds are velvet upholstered, tables have leather tops, and photos by world-famous photojournalists adorn the walls. Bathrooms are large and feature wood-paneled walls. If you choose to leave your room, the hotel's magnificent **Rose Bar** is where you should venture first, but make sure you are on the "list."

2 Lexington Ave. (at 21st St.), New York, NY 10010. 📞 **212/920-3300.** Fax 212/673-5890. www.gramercyparkhotel.com. 185 units. From $525 double; from $675 suite. AE, DC, DISC, MC, V. Parking $55. Subway: 6 to 23rd St. **Amenities:** Restaurant; 2 bars; fitness center; spa; 24-hour concierge; 24-hour room service; laundry service; dry cleaning. *In room:* A/C, TV w/DVD/CD, dataport, Wi-Fi and high-speed Internet, minibar, hair dryer, safe, iPod and docking station.

INEXPENSIVE

Gershwin Hotel 🕉 *Kids*   Nestled between Le Trapeze, an S&M club, and the Museum of Sex, and with its own glowing protruding horns as your landmark, the close proximity to erotica is really just a coincidence. This creative-minded, Warhol-esque hotel caters to up-and-coming artistic types—and well-established names with an eye for good value—with its bold modern-art collection and wild style. The lobby was recently renovated, and along with a new bar called Gallery at the Gershwin, much of the original art remains. The standard rooms are clean and bright, with Picasso-style wall murals and Philippe Starck–ish takes on motel furnishings. Superior rooms are best, as they're newly renovated, and well worth the extra $10; all have either a queen bed, two twins, or two doubles, plus a new, private bathroom with cute, colorful tile. If you're bringing the brood, two-room suites or family rooms are a good option. The hotel is more service oriented than you usually see at this price level, and the staff is very professional.

7 E. 27th St. (between Fifth and Madison aves.), New York, NY 10016. 📞 **212/545-8000.** Fax 212/684-5546. www.gershwinhotel.com. 150 units. $109–$300 double; $230–$300 family room. Extra person $20. Check website for discounts or other value-added packages. For hostel rooms, use this website: www.gershwinhostel.com. AE, MC, V. Parking $25 3 blocks away. Subway: N, R, 6 to 28th St. **Amenities:** Bar; tour desk; babysitting; laundry service; dry cleaning; Internet access. *In room:* A/C, TV, dataport, Wi-Fi, hair dryer, iron.

TIMES SQUARE & MIDTOWN WEST
VERY EXPENSIVE

Ritz-Carlton New York, Central Park 🕉🕉🕉 *Kids*   This undoubtedly luxurious hotel manages to maintain a homey elegance and does not intimidate you with an overabundance of style. Rooms are spacious and decorated in traditional English countryside style. Suites are larger than most New York City apartments. Rooms facing Central Park come with telescopes, and all have flatscreen TVs with DVD; the hotel even has a library of Academy Award–winning films available. The marble bathrooms are also oversize and provide a choice of bathrobes, terry or linen, and extravagant Frederic Fekkai bath amenities. For families who can afford the very steep prices, the hotel is extremely kid-friendly. Suites have sofa beds, and cribs and rollaway beds can be brought in. Children are given in-room cookies and milk. You can even bring your dog (under 60 lb.); if it rains, the pooch gets to wear a Burberry trench coat. Now that's homey elegance. While the kids and dogs are entertained, the older folks can be pampered with facials or massages at Swiss-based La Prairie Spa.

50 Central Park S. (at Sixth Ave.), New York, NY 10019. ℂ 212/308-9100. Fax 212/207-8831. www.ritzcarlton.com. 260 units. $650–$1,295; from $995 suite. Package and weekend rates available. AE, DC, DISC, MC, V. Parking $50. Subway: N, R, W to Fifth Ave. and F to 57th St. Pets under 60 lb. accepted. **Amenities:** Restaurant; bar; lobby lounge for tea and cocktails; fitness center; La Prairie spa and facial center; concierge; complimentary Bentley limousine service; business center; 24-hr. room service; babysitting; overnight laundry; dry cleaning; technology butler and bath butler services. *In room:* A/C, TV/DVD, dataport, high-speed Internet access, minibar, hair dryer, iron, safe, telescopes in rooms w/park view.

EXPENSIVE

Doubletree Guest Suites-Times Square 👪 *Kids* For many, the location of this 43-story Doubletree, in the heart of darkness known as Times Square, might offer a more Vegas-like experience than a true New York one. Just outside the hotel's entrance, the streets are constantly gridlocked, the bright neon burns holes into your eye sockets, and the noise level is earsplitting—and lucky you, there's an Olive Garden across the street and a McDonald's next door. But at times we all must make sacrifices for our children, and this Doubletree, location and all, is perfect for the kids. From the fresh-baked chocolate-chip cookies given out upon arrival, the spacious and affordable suites big enough for two 5-year-olds to play hide-and-seek (as mine did), and the all-day children's room-service menu to the proximity of the gargantuan Toys "R" Us, the TKTS Booth, and other kid-friendly Times Square offerings, this Doubletree is hard to beat for families. Bathrooms have two entrances so the kids don't have to traipse through the parents' room; and every suite has two televisions with PlayStation, so while Nickelodeon is on one, CNN is on the other.

1568 Broadway (at 47th St. and Seventh Ave.), New York, NY 10036. ℂ 800/222-TREE or 212/719-1600. Fax 212/921-5212. www.doubletree.com. 460 units. From $349 suite. Extra person $20. Children under 18 stay free in parent's suite. Ask about senior, corporate, and AAA discounts and special promotions. AE, DC, DISC, MC, V. Parking $35. Subway: N, R to 49th St. **Amenities:** Restaurant; lounge; fitness center; concierge; limited room service; babysitting; laundry service; dry cleaning. *In room:* A/C, 2 TVs w/pay movies and video games, dataport, high-speed Internet access, minibar, fridge, microwave, wet bar w/coffeemaker, hair dryer, iron, safe.

Le Parker Meridien 👪👪 *Kids* Not many hotels in New York have attributes that rival those at this hotel. Its location on 57th Street, not too far from Times Square and a close walk to Central Park and the shopping of Fifth Avenue, is practically perfect. The 17,000-square-foot fitness center, called Gravity, features state-of-the-art equipment, a basketball court, a racquetball court, a spa, and a rooftop pool. It has three excellent restaurants, including **Norma's,** where breakfast is an art, and the aptly named **Burger Joint,** rated by many as serving the best hamburger in the city. The gorgeous, bustling lobby also serves as a public space. Elevators have televisions that continuously show *Tom and Jerry* and *Rocky and Bullwinkle* cartoons and Charlie Chaplin shorts that are a wonder for the kids. The spacious hotel rooms, though a bit on the IKEA side, have a fun feel to them, with hidden drawers and swirling television platforms, inventively exploiting an economical use of space. Rooms have wood platform beds with feather mattresses, built-ins that include large work desks, stylish Aeron chairs, free high-speed Internet, and 32-inch flatscreen televisions with VCR/DVD and CD players. The slate-and-limestone bathrooms are large, but unfortunately come only with a shower.

118 W. 57th St. (between Sixth and Seventh aves.), New York, NY 10019. ℂ 800/543-4300 or 212/245-5000. Fax 212/307-1776. www.parkermeridien.com. 731 units. $600–$800 double; from $780 suite. Extra person $30. Excellent packages and weekend rates often available (as low as $225 at press time). AE, DC, DISC, MC, V. Parking $45. Subway: F, N, Q, R to 57th St. Pets accepted. **Amenities:** 3 restaurants; rooftop pool; fantastic fitness center; spa; concierge (2 w/Clefs d'Or distinction); weekday morning courtesy car to Wall St.; full-service business center; 24-hr. room service; laundry service; dry cleaning. *In room:* A/C, 32-in. TV w/VCR/DVD, dataport, high-speed Internet access, minibar, hair dryer, iron, safe, CD player, nightly complimentary shoeshine.

Sofitel New York ✦✦✦ *(Finds)*   There are many fine hotels on 44th Street between Fifth and Sixth avenues, but the newest (built in 2000) and best, in this writer's estimation, is the soaring Sofitel. Upon entering the hotel and the warm, inviting lobby with check-in tucked off to the side, you wouldn't think you were entering a hotel that is this young—which is one of the reasons the hotel is so special. The designers have successfully melded modern, new-world amenities with European old-world elegance. The rooms are spacious and ultracomfortable, adorned with art from New York and Paris. The lighting is soft and romantic, the walls and windows soundproof. Suites are extraspecial, equipped with king-size beds, two televisions, and pocket doors separating the bedroom from a sitting room. Bathrooms in all rooms are magnificent, with separate showers and soaking tubs. Owned by the Accor Hotels & Resorts company of France, Sofitel reflects its heritage with a greeting of *"bonjour"* or *"bonsoir"* at reception; a unique gift shop with hard-to-find French products, including perfumes and cosmetics; and a stylish French restaurant called **Gaby** that bakes delicious croissants for breakfast.

45 W. 44th St. (between Fifth and Sixth aves.), New York, NY 10036. ℂ 212/354-8844. Fax 212/354-2480. www. sofitel.com. 398 units. $299–$599 double; from $439 suite. 1 child stays free in parent's room. AE, DC, MC, V. Parking $45. Subway: B, D, F, V to 42nd St. Pets accepted. **Amenities:** Restaurant; bar; exercise room; concierge; 24-hr. room service; laundry service; dry cleaning. *In room:* A/C, TV w/pay movies and Internet access, dataport, high-speed Internet access, minibar, hair dryer, iron, safe, CD player.

MODERATE

Casablanca Hotel ✦✦ *(Value)*   Try to picture the exotic, romantic setting of the movie *Casablanca*—ceiling fans, mosaic tiles, and North African–themed art—and then try to picture that setting in the heart of neon-blinding, cacophonous Times Square. The combination seems unlikely, but really, who wouldn't want a desert oasis in the middle of all that mayhem? And that's what the Casablanca Hotel really is: a calming refuge where you can escape from the noise and crowds. It's where, in **Rick's Café,** the Casablanca's homey guest lounge, you can sit by a fire, read a paper, check your e-mail, watch television on the gargantuan-size screen, or sip a cappuccino from the serve-yourself cappuccino/espresso machine. Or, if the days or nights are balmy, you can lounge on the rooftop deck or second-floor courtyard. Or you can just retreat to your room. The rooms here might not be the biggest around, but they are well outfitted with the aforementioned ceiling fans, bathrobes, free bottles of water, complimentary high-speed Internet access, and beautifully tiled bathrooms. Because of its location, moderate prices, and size (only 48 rooms), the Casablanca is in high demand, so book early.

147 W. 43rd St. (just east of Broadway), New York, NY 10036. ℂ **888/922-7225** or 212/869-1212. Fax 212/391-7585. www.casablancahotel.com. 48 units. $249–$299 double; from $399 suite. Rates include continental breakfast, all-day cappuccino, and weekday wine and cheese. Check website for Internet rates and other special deals. AE, DC, MC, V. Parking $25 next door. Subway: N, R, 1, 2, 3, 9 to 42nd St./Times Sq. **Amenities:** Cyber lounge; free access to New York Sports Club; concierge; business center; limited room service; laundry service; dry cleaning; video library. *In room:* A/C, TV/VCR, dataport, minibar, hair dryer, CD player, ceiling fan.

Hotel Metro 🐾🐾 *Kids*   The Metro is the choice in Midtown for those who don't want to sacrifice either style or comfort for affordability. This lovely Art Deco–style jewel has larger rooms than you'd expect for the price. They're outfitted with smart retro furnishings, playful fabrics, fluffy pillows, and small but beautifully appointed marble bathrooms, plus alarm clocks. Only about half the bathrooms have tubs, but the others have shower stalls big enough for two (junior suites have whirlpool tubs). The family room is an ingenious invention: a two-room suite that has a second bedroom in lieu of a sitting area; families on tighter budgets can opt for a roomy double/double. The neo-Deco design gives the whole place an air of New York glamour that I've not otherwise seen in this price range. A great collection of black-and-white photos, from Man Ray classics to Garbo and Dietrich portraits, adds to the vibe. The comfy, fire-lit library/lounge area off the lobby, where the complimentary buffet breakfast is laid out and the coffeepot is on all day, is a popular hangout. Service is attentive, and the well-furnished rooftop terrace boasts a breathtaking view of the Empire State Building and makes a great place to order up room service from the stylish—and very good—Metro Grill.

45 W. 35th St. (between Fifth and Sixth aves.), New York, NY 10001. ℂ **800/356-3870** or 212/947-2500. Fax 212/279-1310. www.hotelmetronyc.com. 179 units. $210–$365 double; $245–$420 triple or quad; $255–$425 family room; $275–$475 suite. Rates include buffet breakfast. Extra person $25. 1 child under 13 stays free in parent's room. Rates include continental breakfast. Check with airlines and other package operators for great-value package deals. AE, DC, MC, V. Parking $20 nearby. Subway: B, D, F, N, R, V to 34th St. **Amenities:** Restaurant; alfresco rooftop bar in summer; good fitness room; salon; limited room service; laundry service; dry cleaning. *In room:* A/C, TV, dataport, high-speed Internet access, fridge, hair dryer, iron.

Hotel QT 🐾🐾 *Value*   Owned by Andre Balazs, of The Mercer (p. 94), Hotel QT offers much of The Mercer's style without the hefty rates. From its Midtown location, to many extras such as a swimming pool in the lobby, steam room and sauna, free high-speed Internet, complimentary continental breakfast, and good-size rooms including a number with bunk beds, Hotel QT is now one of the best moderate options in the Times Square area. Upon entering, you check in at a kiosk/front desk where you pick up periodicals and essentials for stocking your minibar. Making your way to the elevators, you might see guests swimming in the lobby pool or having a drink at the swim-up bar, an unusual sight in the Big Apple. The rooms are sparse in tone, but the queen- and king-sized platform beds are plush and dressed with Egyptian-cotton sheets. The biggest drawback is the bathrooms: There are no doors on the bathrooms—sliding doors conceal the shower (none of the rooms has a tub) and the toilet. But for prices this low along with the extras, who are we to quibble?

125 W. 45th St. (between Sixth Ave. and Broadway), New York, NY 10036. ℂ **212/354-2323.** Fax 212/302-8585. www.hotelqt.com. 140 units. $199–$350 double. Rates include continental breakfast. AE, DC, MC, V. Parking nearby $25. Subway: B, D, F, V to 47th–50th St./Rockefeller Center. **Amenities:** Bar; swimming pool; gym; sauna; steam room. *In room:* A/C, TV, free high-speed Internet access, Wi-Fi, minifridge, hair dryer, iron/ironing board, safe, CD player, DVD player, free local calls, 2-line speakerphones.

INEXPENSIVE

Red Roof Inn 🏆🏆 *(Value)*   Manhattan's first, and only, Red Roof Inn offers relief from Midtown's high-priced hotel scene. The hotel occupies a former office building that was gutted and laid out fresh, allowing for more spacious rooms and bathrooms than you'll usually find in this price category. The lobby feels smart, and elevators are quiet and efficient. In-room amenities—including coffeemakers and TVs with on-screen Web access—are better than most competitors', and furnishings are new and comfortable. Wi-Fi is available throughout the property. The location—on a bustling block lined with nice hotels and affordable Korean restaurants, just a stone's throw from the Empire State Building and Herald Square—is excellent. Check both Apple Core Hotel's reservation line (the management company) and Red Roof's line; prices can vary wildly. Free continental breakfast adds to the good value.

6 W. 32nd St. (between Broadway and Fifth Ave.), New York, NY 10001. ℰ 800/567-7720, 800/RED-ROOF, or 212/643-7100. Fax 212/643-7101. www.applecorehotels.com or www.redroof.com. 171 units. $189–$329 double (usually less than $189). Rates include continental breakfast. Children under 13 stay free in parent's room. AE, DC, DISC, MC, V. Parking $26. Subway: B, D, F, N, R, V to 34th St. **Amenities:** Breakfast room; wine-and-beer lounge; exercise room; concierge; laundry service; dry cleaning. *In room:* A/C, TV w/pay movies and Internet access, dataport, Wi-Fi, fridge, coffeemaker, hair dryer, iron, video games.

Travel Inn *(Kids)*   Extras such as a huge outdoor pool and sun deck, a sunny and up-to-date fitness room, and absolutely free parking (with in-and-out privileges!) make the Travel Inn a terrific deal. It may not be loaded with personality, but it does offer the clean, bright regularity of a good chain hotel—an attractive trait in a city where "quirky" is the catchword at most affordable hotels. Rooms are oversize and comfortably furnished, with extrafirm beds and work desks; even the smallest double is sizable and has a roomy bathroom, and double/doubles make great affordable shares for families. A total renovation over the past couple of years has made everything feel like new, even the nicely tiled bathrooms. Though it's a bit off the track, Off-Broadway theaters and great affordable restaurants are at hand, and it's a 10-minute walk to the Theater District.

515 W. 42nd St. (just west of Tenth Ave.), New York, NY 10036. ℰ 888/HOTEL58, 800/869-4630, or 212/695-7171. Fax 212/268-3542. www.newyorkhotel.com. 160 units. $105–$250 double. Extra person $10. Children under 16 stay free in parent's room. AAA discounts available; check website for special Internet deals. AE, DC, DISC, MC, V. Free self-parking. Subway: A, C, E to 42nd St./Port Authority. **Amenities:** Coffee shop; terrific outdoor pool w/deck chairs and lifeguard in season; fitness center; Gray Line tour desk; 24-hr. room service. *In room:* A/C, TV, dataport, hair dryer, iron.

MIDTOWN EAST & MURRAY HILL
VERY EXPENSIVE

The Peninsula New York 🏆🏆🏆   The paparazzi was waiting outside as I lugged my overnight bag into the hotel lobby, and for a moment they contemplated an explosion of flashbulbs. It didn't take them long, however, to realize I was no celeb—just a fortunate soul spending a night at the marvelous Peninsula hotel. Housed in a beauty of a landmark Beaux Arts building, The Peninsula is the perfect combination of old-world charm and modern, state-of-the art technology. Rooms are huge with plenty of closet and storage space, but best of all is the bedside control panel that allows you to regulate lighting, television, stereo, and air-conditioning and to signal the DO NOT DISTURB sign on your door. Though you really don't have to leave the comfort of your bed, eventually you will need to go to the bathroom, and when you do, you won't be disappointed. The huge marble bathrooms all have spacious soaking tubs with yet another control panel at your fingertips, including the controls for, in most rooms, a television you can watch while taking your bubble bath (now that's happy excess). The

Peninsula also features one of the best and biggest New York hotel health clubs and spas, the rooftop Pen-Top Bar, and a faultless concierge desk.

700 Fifth Ave. (at 55th St.), New York, NY 10019. ℂ 800/262-9467 or 212/956-2888. Fax 212/903-3949. www. peninsula.com. 239 units. $650–$850 double; from $1,110 suite. Extra person $50. Children under 12 stay free in parent's room. Winter weekend package rates from $585 at press time. AE, DC, DISC, MC, V. Valet parking $55. Subway: E, V to Fifth Ave. Pets accepted. **Amenities:** Restaurant; rooftop bar; library-style lounge for afternoon tea and cocktails; heated pool; tri-level rooftop health club and spa w/treatment rooms; exercise classes; whirlpool; sauna; sun deck; 24-hr. concierge; business center; 24-hr. room service; in-room massage; babysitting; laundry service; dry cleaning. *In room:* A/C, TV w/pay movies, fax, T-1 Internet connectivity, Wi-Fi, minibar, hair dryer, laptop-size safe, complimentary "water bar" w/5 choices of bottled water.

St. Regis 🐦🐦🐦 When John Jacob Astor built the St. Regis in 1904, he set out to create a hotel that would reflect the elegance and luxury he was used to in hotels in Europe. Over a hundred years later, the St. Regis, now a New York landmark, still reflects that European splendor. Located on Fifth Avenue and close to Rockefeller Center, St. Patrick's Cathedral, and Saks, this Beaux Arts classic is a marvel. Antique furniture, crystal chandeliers, silk wall coverings, and marble floors adorn both the public spaces and the high-ceilinged, airy guest rooms. The suites are particularly ornate, some with French doors, four-poster beds, and decorative fireplaces. The marble bathrooms are spacious and feature separate showers and bathtubs. In a nod to the future, plasma televisions were recently added in all the rooms, along with LCD screens in the bathrooms. Service is efficiently white-gloved and every guest is assigned a personal, tuxedoed butler, on call 24 hours to answer any reasonable requests. The hotel has a large fitness center and a spa that is the first in New York to offer the skin-care line from the renowned Carita Spa of Paris.

2 E. 55th St. (at Fifth Ave.), New York, NY 10022. ℂ 212/753-4500. Fax 212/787-3447. www.stregis.com. 256 units. $695–$750 double; from $1,150 suite. Check Internet for specials as low as $400 at press time. AE, DC, DISC, MC, V. Parking $40. Subway: E, V to Fifth Ave. **Amenities:** Restaurant; historic bar; tea lounge; fitness center; spa; concierge; 24-hr. room service; babysitting; laundry; valet service; 24-hr. butler service. *In room:* A/C, TV, high-speed Internet access, minibar, hair dryer, safe, DVD/CD player.

EXPENSIVE

The Benjamin 🐦🐦🐦 From the retro sign and clock on Lexington Avenue to the high-ceilinged marble lobby, The Benjamin makes you feel as if you've suddenly stepped into the jazz era of New York of the 1920s. But once you get to your spacious room and notice the numerous hi-tech amenities, such as Bose Wave radios, Internet browsers and video games for the TVs, high-speed Internet access, fax machines, ergonomic chairs, and movable workstations, you'll know you're most definitely in the 21st century. Many of the amenities are geared toward business travelers, but why should they be the only ones to experience all this comfort and luxury? All rooms are airy, but the deluxe studios and one-bedroom suites are extra-large. And don't forget the pillow menu featuring 11 options, including buckwheat and Swedish Memory, in which foam designed by NASA reacts to your body temperature. If you are a light sleeper, however, book a room away from Lexington Avenue, which can get very busy most weekdays. Bathrooms feature Frette robes, TV speakers, and water pressure from the shower head strong enough to make you think you've just experienced a deep-tissue massage. The hotel also features a good fitness center and the Woodstock Spa and Wellness Center.

125 E. 50th St. (at Lexington Ave.), New York, NY 10022. ℂ 888/4-BENJAMIN, 212/320-8002, or 212/715-2500. Fax 212/715-2525. www.thebenjamin.com. 209 units. From $459 superior double; from $499 deluxe studio; from $559 suite. Call or check website for special weekend-stay offers. AE, DC, DISC, MC, V. Parking $45. Subway: 6 to 51st

St.; E, F to Lexington Ave. Pets accepted. **Amenities:** Restaurant; cocktail lounge; state-of-the-art exercise room; full-service spa; concierge; sleep concierge; business services; 24-hr. room service; dry cleaning; valet service. *In room:* A/C, TV w/pay movies/video games/Internet access, fax/copier/printer, high-speed Internet access, kitchenette, minibar, microwave, coffeemaker, laptop-size safe, china.

Hotel Elysée ✹✹ This little romantic gem of a hotel in the heart of Midtown might be easy to miss: It's dwarfed by modern glass towers on either side of it. But the fact that it's so inconspicuous is part of the Elysée's immense romantic appeal. Built in 1926, the hotel has a storied past as the preferred address for artists and writers including Tennessee Williams, Jimmy Breslin, Maria Callas, Vladimir Horowitz (who donated a Steinway, which still resides in the Piano Suite), John Barrymore, Marlon Brando, and Ava Gardner, who once had a tryst here with football legend Paul Hornung. The hotel still retains that sexy, discreet feel and now is run expertly by HK Hotels, which also oversees the Hotel Gansevoort (p. 95) and The Library. Rooms have been renovated and have many quirky features; some have fireplaces, others have kitchens or solariums, and all are decorated in country French furnishings. Good-size bathrooms are done up in Italian marble and are well outfitted. Off the gorgeous black-and-white marble-floored lobby is the legendary Monkey Bar.

60 E. 54th St. (between Park and Madison aves.), New York, NY 10022. © **800/535-9733** or 212/753-1066. Fax 212/980-9278. www.elyseehotel.com. 101 units. From $295 double; from $425 suite. Check the website for seasonal specials. Rates include continental breakfast and weekday evening wine and cheese. AE, DC, DISC, MC, V. Parking $30. Subway: E, V to Fifth Ave. **Amenities:** Restaurant; bar; free access to nearby gym; concierge; limited room service; laundry service; dry cleaning. *In room:* A/C, TV/VCR, dataport, Wi-Fi, minibar, hair dryer, iron, safe.

The Kitano New York ✹✹✹ *(Finds)* Owned by the Kitano Group of Japan, this elegant Murray Hill gem offers a unique mix of East and West sensibilities. The marble and mahogany lobby, with its Y-shaped staircase and Botero bronze *Dog,* is one of the most attractive in New York. The hotel was first opened in 1973; in the mid-1990s, along with an 1896 landmark town house acquired next door, The Kitano was fully renovated. If you're a very lucky (and wealthy) individual, you'll get the opportunity to stay in one of three one-bedroom town house suites, each with a sunken living room, bay windows, and original, eclectic art. Or, if your sensibilities are Eastern-oriented, the hotel offers a Tatami suite, with tatami mats, rice-paper screens, and a Japanese Tea Ceremony room. Most rooms are not quite that luxurious or unique, but all include tasteful mahogany furniture, soundproof windows, and, for a real taste of Japan, green tea upon arrival; marble bathrooms are large and have heated towel racks and removable shower heads. The sky-lit **Garden Café,** residing in the town house, serves contemporary American cuisine, while **Hakubai** serves traditional multicourse kaiseki cuisine. There's also an interesting gift shop in the lobby specializing in unique Japanese items. But best of all is the mezzanine-level bar that's home to the acclaimed **Jazz at the Kitano** Wednesday through Saturday evenings.

66 Park Ave. (at 38th St.), New York, NY 10016. © **212/885-7000.** Fax 212/885-7100. www.kitano.com. 149 units. $480–$605 double; from $715 suite. Check website for specials, as low as $239 at press time. AE, DC, DISC, MC, V. Parking $40. Subway: 4, 5, 6, 7, S to Grand Central. **Amenities:** 2 restaurants; bar w/live jazz; access to a nearby health club; concierge; complimentary limo service to Wall St. on weekdays; limited room service; laundry service; dry cleaning. *In room:* A/C, TV, fax, high-speed Internet access, hair dryer, iron, complimentary tea.

The Roger ✹✹ The hotel's namesake, Roger Williams, in time, abandoned his puritanical roots to become a secular leader. This Murray Hill hotel, formerly known as the Roger Williams, shed its traditional, slightly worn veneer and was reborn in 2005 with a glitzy, colorful new look and style—not to mention a hip name. This

Roger wears its new look well, starting with the welcoming lobby and its odd assortment of modern yet comfortable seating, where small jazz combos entertain 3 nights a week. With its many varieties of rooms—some small, some generous, some with huge landscaped terraces, others with views of the nearby Empire State Building, and all with impressive amenities such as colorful quilts, flat-panel televisions, free high-speed Internet, and good-size marble bathrooms—the Roger is now one of the top choices in a quiet yet convenient Midtown location. A floating granite staircase leads from the lobby to a mezzanine lounge, where you can have breakfast in the morning and drink cocktails by candlelight at night.

131 Madison Ave. (at E. 31st St.), New York, NY 10016. ℂ **888/448-7788** or 212/448-7000. Fax 212/448-7007. www.hotelrogerwilliams.com. 200 units. $250–$300 double. AE, DC, DISC, MC, V. Subway: 6 to 28th St./Lexington Ave. **Amenities:** Lounge; fitness center; concierge; laundry service; dry cleaning; Wi-Fi; conference suite. *In room:* A/C, flat-screen TV, high-speed Internet access, minibar, iron/ironing board, safe.

INEXPENSIVE

Thirty Thirty 🏨🏨 *Value*   This hotel is just right for bargain-hunting travelers looking for a splash of style with an affordable price tag. Rooms are mostly on the smallish side, but do the trick for those who intend to spend their days out on the town rather than holed up here. Configurations are split between twin/twins (great for friends), queens, and queen/queens (great for triples, budget-minded quads, or shares that want more spreading-out room). Nice features include cushioned headboards, firm mattresses, two-line phones, nice built-in wardrobes, and spacious, nicely tiled bathrooms. A few larger units have kitchenettes, great if you're in town for a while.

30 E. 30th St. (between Madison and Park aves.), New York, NY 10016. ℂ **800/497-6028** or 212/689-1900. Fax 212/689-0023. www.thirtythirty-nyc.com. 243 units. $169–$225 double; $189–$249 double with kitchenette; $245–$325 quad. Call for last-minute deals, or check website for special promotions (as low as $99 at press time). AE, DC, DISC, MC, V. Parking $30 1 block away. Subway: 6 to 28th St. Pets accepted with advance approval. **Amenities:** Restaurant; concierge; laundry service; dry cleaning. *In room:* A/C, TV, Internet access, hair dryer.

UPPER EAST SIDE

EXPENSIVE

Hotel Plaza Athénée 🏨🏨🏨   This hideaway in New York's most elegant neighborhood (the stretch of Madison Ave. in the 60s) is a mirror image of that elevated social strata; it's elegant, luxurious, and oozing with sophistication. With antique furniture, hand-painted murals, and the Italian-marble floor that adorns the lobby, the Plaza Athénée has a European feel. In that tradition, service here is as good as it gets, with personalized check-in and staff at every turn.

The rooms come in a variety of shapes and sizes, and are all high-ceilinged and spacious; entrance foyers give them a real residential feel. They are designed in rich fabrics and warm colors that help set a tone that makes you want to lounge in your room longer than you should. The suites have so much closet space that it made this New Yorker, used to minuscule apartment closets, very envious. Many of the suites have chaises, which you don't see too often in New York hotels, and a few have terraces large enough to dine out on. The Portuguese-marble bathrooms are outfitted with thick robes made exclusively for the hotel; put one on and you might never want to take it off. The lush, leather-floor lounge is appropriately called **Bar Seine** and is a welcome spot for a predinner cocktail.

37 E. 64th St. (between Madison and Park aves.), New York, NY 10021. ℂ **800/447-8800** or 212/734-9100. Fax 212/772-0958. www.plaza-athenee.com. 149 units. $555–$825 double; from $1,200 suite. Check for packages and seasonal specials (as low as $495 at press time). AE, DC, DISC, MC, V. Parking $53. Subway: F to Lexington Ave.

Amenities: Restaurant; bar; fitness center; Clefs d'Or concierge; business center; 24-hr. room service; laundry service; dry cleaning. *In room:* A/C, TV, fax, dataport, high-speed Internet access, minibar, hair dryer, safe.

UPPER WEST SIDE
VERY EXPENSIVE
Trump International Hotel & Tower 🏵🏵🏵   From the outside, it's the prototypical, not-very-attractive Trump creation—a tall, dark monolith, hovering over Columbus Circle and lower Central Park. But go inside and spend a night or two at the Trump International and experience services such as your own Trump Attaché, a personal concierge who will provide comprehensive services (your wish is his command). Take advantage of such first-class facilities as the 6,000-square-foot health club with a lap pool and a full-service spa. Order room service from the hotel's signature restaurant, the four-star Jean Georges. Not only will you immediately dispel any prejudices you might have toward The Donald, but you might even comprehend why someone would sell his or her soul to become the Master Builder's apprentice.

Guest rooms are surprisingly understated, with high ceilings and floor-to-ceiling windows, some with incredible views of Central Park and all with telescopes for taking in the view, and marble bathrooms with Jacuzzi tubs. But if that's not enough—it certainly was for me—you also get two complimentary bottles of Trump water, complete with a picture of The Donald on each one. For a hotel this well run, you can forgive the man for his excesses.

1 Central Park W. (at 60th St.), New York, NY 10023. 📞 212/299-1000. Fax 212/299-1150. www.trumpintl.com. 167 units. From $765 double; from $1,200 1- or 2-bedroom suite. Children stay free in parent's room. Check website for special rates and package deals; also try booking through www.travelweb.com for discounted rates. AE, DC, DISC, MC, V. Parking $48. Subway: A, B, C, D, 1 to 59th St./Columbus Circle. **Amenities:** Restaurant; spa and health club w/steam, sauna, and pool; Clefs d'Or concierge; staffed business center w/secretarial services; 24-hr. room service; in-room massage; babysitting; laundry service; dry cleaning; butler (personal attaché); CD library. *In room:* A/C, TV/VCR w/pay movies and video games, fax/copier/printer, dataport, high-speed Internet access, minibar, coffeemaker, hair dryer, iron, laptop-size safe, DVD/CD player.

MODERATE
Hotel Beacon 🏵🏵 *Kids* *Value*   Okay, so you're not in Times Square or in trendy SoHo, but when you're at the Hotel Beacon, you're on the Upper West Side, and for families, you won't find a better location—or value. Close to Central Park and Riverside Park, the Museum of Natural History and Lincoln Center, and major subway lines, it's not as if the Beacon were in a desolate spot. Rooms here are a generous size and feature kitchenettes, roomy closets, and new marble bathrooms. Virtually all standard rooms have two double beds, and they're plenty big enough to sleep a family on a budget. The large one- and two-bedroom suites are some of the best bargains in the city; each has two closets and a pullout sofa in the well-furnished living room. The two-bedroom suites have a second bathroom, making them well-outfitted enough to house a small army—including my own. The view from our room and many others in the hotel is a true New York vista: the magnificent, turn-of-the-20th-century Ansonia building; ballet dancers limbering up at a dance studio; and fresh fruit and vegetables constantly being replenished at Fairway market directly across the street. There's no room service, but a wealth of good budget dining options that deliver, along with excellent markets like the aforementioned Fairway, make the Beacon even more of a home away from home.

2130 Broadway (at 75th St.), New York, NY 10023. 📞 800/572-4969 or 212/787-1100. Fax 212/724-0839. www.beaconhotel.com. 236 units. $210–$225 single or double; from $270 1- or 2-bedroom suite. Extra person $15. Children under 17 stay free in parent's room. Check website for special deals (doubles from $145; 1-bedroom suites as low as $195 at press time). AE, DC, DISC, MC, V. Parking $41 1 block away. Subway: 1, 2, 3 to 72nd St. **Amenities:** Coffee shop adjacent; access to health club in the building; concierge; laundry service; dry cleaning; coin-op laundry; fax and copy service; Internet center. *In room:* A/C, TV w/pay movies, kitchenette, hair dryer, iron, laptop-size safe.

The Lucerne *Finds* This magnificent 1903 landmark building has had many incarnations over the years, including one as a dormitory for Columbia University students. But most recently it has been transformed into a luxury boutique hotel, and that transformation has been a triumph on many levels. As a longtime resident of the Upper West Side, I can easily say The Lucerne best captures the feel of that very special neighborhood. Service here is impeccable, especially for a moderately priced hotel; the attentive GM is on top of every detail and everything is fresh and immaculate. The rooms are all comfortable and big enough for kings, queens, or two doubles, with attractive bathrooms complete with travertine counters. Some of the rooms have views not only of the Hudson River, but also of one of my favorite pubs, the Dublin House. The suites are extraspecial here and each has a kitchenette, a stocked minifridge, a microwave, and a sitting room with a sofa and extra television. The highly rated **Nice Matin** offers room service or breakfast, lunch, and dinner. But if you don't want to dine there, you can sample the food at nearby Zabar's or H&H Bagels.

201 W. 79th St. (at Amsterdam Ave.), New York, NY 10024. ☎ **800/492-8122** or 212/875-1000. Fax 212/579-2408. www.thelucernehotel.com. 216 units. $310–$430 super queen or double room; $330–$450 super king; $390–$500 deluxe queen suite. Extra person $20. Children under 16 stay free in parent's room. AAA discounts offered; check website for special Internet deals. AE, DC, DISC, MC, V. Parking $29 nearby. Subway: 1 to 79th St. **Amenities:** Restaurant; fitness center; business center; limited room service; laundry service; dry cleaning. *In room:* A/C, TV w/Nintendo and Internet access, dataport, coffeemaker, hair dryer, iron.

INEXPENSIVE

Hotel Newton *Value* Located on the burgeoning northern extreme of the Upper West Side, the Newton, unlike many of its peers, doesn't scream "budget" at every turn. As you enter the pretty lobby, you're greeted by a uniformed staff that's attentive and professional. The rooms are generally large, with good, firm beds, work desks, and sizable new bathrooms, plus roomy closets in most (a few of the cheapest have wall racks only). Some are big enough to accommodate families, with two doubles or two queen-size beds. The suites feature two queen-size beds in the bedroom and a sofa in the sitting room, plus niceties such as a microwave, minifridge, and iron, making them well worth the few extra dollars. The bigger rooms and suites have been upgraded with cherrywood furnishings, but even the older laminated furniture is much nicer than I usually see in this price range. The AAA-approved hotel is impeccably kept. The 96th Street express subway stop is a block away, providing convenient access to the city, and the Key West Diner next door serves huge, cheap breakfasts.

2528 Broadway (between 94th and 95th sts.), New York, NY 10025. ☎ **888/HOTEL58** or 212/678-6500. Fax 212/678-6758. www.newyorkhotel.com. 110 units. $95–$175 double or junior suite. Extra person $25. Children under 15 stay free in parent's room. AAA, corporate, senior, and group rates available; check website for special Internet deals. AE, DC, DISC, MC, V. Parking $27 nearby. Subway: 1, 2, 3 to 96th St. **Amenities:** 24-hr. room service. *In room:* A/C, TV, Wi-Fi, hair dryer.

4 Where to Dine

Attention, foodies: Welcome to your mecca. No other culinary capital spans the globe as successfully as the Big Apple. *Tip:* Reservations are always a good idea in New York, and a virtual necessity if your party is bigger than two. For some popular spots, you'll need to call a month in advance—or take a chance with a late-night walk-in.

TRIBECA
VERY EXPENSIVE

Chanterelle 𝒢𝒢𝒢 CONTEMPORARY FRENCH   This is one of New York's best "special occasion" restaurants mainly because, well, they treat you so special here. The dining room is a charmer with daily floral displays and an interesting modern-art collection. Tables are far enough apart to give diners plenty of intimacy, something rare in many New York restaurants these days. Your server will work with you on your choices, pairing items that go best together. The French-themed menu is seasonal and changes every few weeks, but one signature dish appears on almost every menu: a marvelous grilled seafood sausage. Cheese lovers should opt for a cheese course—the presentation and selection can't be beat. The wine list is superlative but expensive. Still, you don't come to Chanterelle on the cheap—you come to celebrate.

2 Harrison St. (at Hudson St.). ⓒ 212/966-6960. www.chanterellenyc.com. Reservations recommended well in advance. Fixed-price lunch $42; a la carte lunch $22–$30; 3-course fixed-price dinner $95; tasting menu $125. AE, DISC, MC, V. Mon–Wed 5:30–10:30pm; Mon–Sat noon–2:30pm; Thurs–Sat 5:30–11pm; Sun 5–10pm. Subway: 1 to Franklin St.

EXPENSIVE

Landmarc 𝒢𝒢 *Finds* MEDITERRANEAN   This cozy, intimate TriBeCa restaurant is too good to just be considered a neighborhood joint. Chef/owner Marc Murphy has put his own distinctive spin on this Italian/French rendition of a bistro. Here you'll find excellent smoked mozzarella and ricotta fritters alongside escargots bordelaise. It will be up to you to decide whether you imagine yourself in a Tuscan trattoria or a Provençal bistro. Or you can mix and match cuisines. Try the pasta of the day accompanied by mussels with a choice of sauce—Provençal, dijonnaise, or the comforting blend of shallots, parsley, and white wine. Steaks and chops are cooked over an open fire and the steaks are also served with a variety of sauces; I had the hangar with a shallot bordelaise that complemented the meat perfectly. What keeps the neighbors pouring into Landmarc along with the excellent food are the remarkably affordable wines sold, not by the glass but by the bottle or half bottle. Desserts are simple and small, and none is more than $3. For a special treat or if you've brought the kids, ask for the cotton candy. Now you won't find that in a Tuscan trattoria.

179 W. Broadway (between Leonard and Worth sts.). ⓒ 212/343-3883. www.landmarc-restaurant.com. Reservations recommended. Main courses $15–$34. AE, DC, DISC, MC, V. Mon–Fri noon–2am; Sat–Sun 9am–2pm and 5:30pm–2am. Subway: 1 to Franklin St.

MODERATE

The Odeon 𝒢 AMERICAN BRASSERIE   For over 2 decades, The Odeon has been a symbol of the TriBeCa sensibility; in fact, the restaurant can claim credit for the neighborhood's cachet—it was the first to lure artists, actors, writers, and models to the area below Canal Street before it was given its moniker. Why did they come? They came to drink, to schmooze, and to enjoy the hearty no-frills brasserie grub like the still-splendid country frisee salad with bacon, Roquefort cheese, and pear vinaigrette; the truffled poached egg; the grilled skirt steak; *moules frites* (mussels with fries); and sautéed cod. Though the restaurant has not always been the celebrity magnet it was in its heyday of the 1980s, the food, drink, and that inviting, open, Deco-ish room have withstood the test of time, and the place has surpassed trendy to now claim well-deserved New York establishment status.

145 W. Broadway (at Thomas St.). ⓒ 212/233-0507. Reservations recommended. Main courses lunch $13–$35; main courses dinner $19–$35 (most less than $21); fixed-price lunch $27. AE, DC, DISC, MC, V. Mon–Fri noon–11pm; Sat 11:30am–midnight; Sun 11:30am–11pm. Subway: 1, 2, 3 to Chambers St.

CHINATOWN
INEXPENSIVE

Big Wong King ⊛ CANTONESE   Last year, Big Wong was called New Big Wong; this year, it wants to be called Big Wong King. No matter. It will always be Big Wong and that's a good thing. Why mess with success? For more than 30 years, Big Wong has been an institution for workers from the nearby courthouses and Chinese families who come to feast on *congee* (rice porridge) and fried crullers for breakfast. They come not only for the *congee,* but for the superb roasted meats, the pork and duck seen hanging in the window, the comforting noodle soups, and the terrific barbecued ribs. This is simple, down-home Cantonese food—lo mein, chow fun, bok choy in oyster sauce—cooked lovingly, and so very cheap. If you don't mind sharing a table, Big Wong is a must no matter what time of day.

67 Mott St. (between Canal and Bayard sts.). ⓒ 212/964-0540. Appetizers $1.50–$5; *congee* $1.50–$6; soups $3–$5; Cantonese noodles $5.25–$11. No credit cards. Daily 8:30am–9pm. Subway: N, Q, R, 6 to Canal St.

New York Noodletown ⊛⊛ CHINESE/SEAFOOD   So what if the restaurant has all the ambience of a school cafeteria? I'm wary of an overadorned dining room in Chinatown; the simpler the better, I say. And New York Noodletown is simple, but the food is the real thing. Seafood-based noodle soups are spectacular, as is the platter of chopped roast pork. Those two items alone would make me very happy. But I'm greedy and wouldn't leave the restaurant without one of its perfectly prepared shrimp dishes, especially the salt-baked shrimp. If you're lucky and your hotel has a good-size refrigerator, take the leftovers home—they'll make a great snack the next day. New York Noodletown keeps very long hours, which makes it one of the best late-night bets in the neighborhood, too.

28½ Bowery (at Bayard St.). ⓒ 212/349-0923. Reservations accepted. Main courses $4–$15. No credit cards. Daily 9am–3:30am. Subway: N, Q, R, 6 to Canal St.

Pho Viet Huong ⊛ (Value VIETNAMESE   Chinatown has its own enclave of Vietnamese restaurants, and the best is Pho Viet Huong. The menu is vast and needs intense perusing, but your waiter will help you pare it down. The Vietnamese know soup, and *pho,* a beef-based soup served with many ingredients, is the most famous, but the hot-and-sour *canh* soup, with either shrimp or fish, is the real deal. The small version is more than enough for two to share, while the large is more than enough for a family. The odd pairing of barbecued beef wrapped in grape leaves is another of the restaurant's specialties and should not be missed, while the *bun,* various meats and vegetables served over rice vermicelli, are simple, hearty, and inexpensive. You'll even find Vietnamese sandwiches here: French bread filled with ham, chicken, eggs, lamb, and even pâté. All of the above are best washed down with an icy cold Saigon beer.

73 Mulberry St. (between Bayard and Canal sts.). ⓒ 212/233-8988. Appetizers $3–$8.50; soups $6–$7; main courses $10–$25. AE, MC, V. Sun–Thurs 10am–10pm; Fri–Sat 10am–11pm. Subway: N, Q, R, 6 to Canal St.

SOHO & NOLITA
MODERATE

Cendrillon ⊛⊛ (Finds FILIPINO/ASIAN   Cendrillon serves authentic yet innovative Filipino food in a comfortable setting with exposed brick, a skylight in the main dining room, and cozy booths up front. How authentic? Try a shot of *lambagong,* also known as coconut grappa. It's a potent drink distilled from the coconut flower sap and blended with sugar-cane sap, and as far as I know, Cendrillon is the only restaurant in New York to serve this Filipino specialty. The drink will ignite your appetite for the flavors to follow, like the squash soup with crab dumplings or the fresh *lumpia* with tamarind and peanut sauce (Asian vegetables wrapped in a purple-yam-and-rice wrapper). Cendrillon's chicken *adobo* (chicken braised in a marinade of vinegar, soy, chiles, and garlic) renders the bird as tender and tasty as you could imagine, while Romy's (the chef/owner's) spareribs, marinated in rice wine and garlic, rubbed with spices, and cooked in a Chinese smokehouse, are as good as any ribs cooked in a Texas smokehouse. You'll be tempted by just about everything, but save room for the exotic desserts like the *Buko* pie, made with coconut and topped with vanilla-bean ice cream, or the *halo halo,* a parfait stuffed with ice creams and sorbets with flavors like avocado, jackfruit, and purple yam.

45 Mercer St. (between Broome and Grand sts.). © 212/343-9012. www.cendrillon.com. Main courses $15–$24. AE, DISC, MC, V. Sun 11am–10pm; Tues–Sat 11am–10:30pm. Subway: N, R to Prince St.; 6 to Spring St.; A, C, E, 1, 9 to Canal St.

Lupa *Value* ROMAN ITALIAN   Since it opened in late 1999, this Roman-style osteria has remained a hot ticket. For one, it's blessed with an impeccable pedigree: One of its owners is Mario Batali, the Food Network "Iron Chef" who has built a miniempire in the Manhattan restaurant world. Second, it offers high-quality food at good value—you can eat well here and not have to max out your credit card. And finally, the food is consistently tasty—but don't expect big portions. That's part of the secret to the good value, but don't worry—you won't starve. The menu is thoughtful and creative, focusing on lusty Roman fare like ricotta gnocchi with sausage and fennel, or pork saltimbocca. Wines, too, have been thoughtfully chosen, and you can order a bottle from the extensive list or sample one of several varieties that come in a carafe. Here, perhaps more than at any other Batali enterprise, the service hits the right notes: Servers are warm and supremely knowledgeable. Make a reservation, or go early to snag one of the tables set aside for walk-ins.

170 Thompson St. (between Houston and Bleecker sts.). © 212/982-5089. www.luparestaurant.com. Reservations recommended. *Primi* $9–$16; *secondi* $16–$20. AE, MC, V. Daily noon–midnight. Subway: A, B, C, D, E, F, Q to W. 4th St.

INEXPENSIVE

Also consider **Lombardi's Pizza,** 32 Spring St., between Mott and Mulberry streets.

Bread ITALIAN   Bread does bread like no other sandwich shop. The bread comes from Balthazar Bakery down the street, but it's what they do with it that makes this eatery so special. For example, they take a rustic ciabatta loaf; slather it with Sicilian sardines, Thai mayonnaise, tomato, and lettuce; and then turn it over to their panini press. The result is a gooey convergence of flavors that you will attempt to gobble down gracefully. It *will* fall apart, but that's okay; someone will be along very shortly with more napkins. Besides the spectacular sardine sandwich, the Italian tuna with mesclun greens and tomatoes in a lemon dressing and the fontina with grilled zucchini, eggplant, arugula, and tomato in a balsamic vinaigrette are also standouts. Really, there are no losers on the bread side of Bread's menu, which also includes salads, pastas, and "plates." The 32-seat restaurant is located in fashionably chic Nolita, and if you are lucky, you might even be treated by the sight of a breathtakingly thin model doing her best to keep the contents of one of Bread's sandwiches from staining her custom-made designer duds.

20 Spring St. (between Mott and Elizabeth sts.). © 212/334-1015. Reservations not accepted. Breads $7–$9.50; plates $6–$16. AE, DC, DISC, MC, V. Daily 10:30am–midnight. Subway: 6 to Spring St.

THE LOWER EAST SIDE, EAST VILLAGE & NOHO
MODERATE
'inoteca ⁄⁄ Finds ITALIAN SMALL PLATES   The Lower East Side was once the home to many Kosher wine factories, but you'll find only Italian wines at cozy 'inoteca. The list is more than 250 bottles long, but even better are the exquisitely prepared small plates that complement the wines. Though the Italian-language menu is a challenge, servers are helpful. The panini stand out in their freshness and delicacy, with the *coppa* (a spicy cured ham) with hot peppers and *rucola* (arugula) being the standout. The *tramezzini,* a crustless sandwich, is nothing like the crustless sandwiches served at high tea. Here, among other things, you can have yours stuffed with tuna and chickpeas or with *pollo alla diavola,* spicy shredded pieces of dark-meat chicken. The "Fritto" section includes a wonderful mozzarella *in corroza,* breaded mozzarella stuffed with a juicy anchovy sauce and lightly fried. Whatever you order, don't rush; 'inoteca is a place to go slow, to savor both wine and food.

98 Rivington St. (at Ludlow St.). ℂ 212/614-0473. www.inotecanyc.com. Reservations accepted for parties of 6 or more. Panini $8–$17; *piatti* (small plates) $8–$11. AE, MC, V. Daily noon–3am. Brunch Sat–Sun 10am–4pm. Subway: F, J, M, Z to Delancey St.

INEXPENSIVE
One of the most famous delis in the world is **Katz's Delicatessen** at 205 E. Houston St., at Ludlow Street (ℂ **212/254-2246**).

GREENWICH VILLAGE & THE MEAT-PACKING DISTRICT
EXPENSIVE
A.O.C. Bedford ⁄⁄ Finds MEDITERRANEAN   You'll find this brick-walled, cozy, romantic charmer tucked away on equally cozy and romantic Bedford Street in the West Village. Here the A.O.C. in the restaurant name stands for *appellation d'origine controlee*—the French designation for high-quality food products. But on the menu you'll find not only A.O.C. products from France, but D.O.C., the Italian designation, and D.O., the Spanish. You really won't need all those designations to know that what you are eating is of high quality—just a few bites will suffice. The paella marinara, a constant on the menu, is prepared for two, stuffed with jumbo shrimp (heads on for more flavor), squid, scallops, mussels, and clams and cooked in Spanish Calasparra rice. Another standout is the duck, a crispy breast prepared best medium rare, and served with a Bosc pear. Finish with a selection of cheeses, A.O.C.-, D.O.C.-, and D.O.-quality only, of course. The restaurant has an impressive wine list and bottles are, as they should be, decanted at your table.

14 Bedford St. (between Sixth Ave. and Downing St.). ℂ 212/414-4764. Reservations recommended. Main courses $21–$32. AE, DC, MC, V. Sun–Thurs 5:30–11pm; Fri–Sat 5:30–11:30pm. Subway: 1 to Houston St.

Mas ⁄⁄ Finds FRENCH   I've never had the pleasure of dining in a French country farmhouse, but if the experience at Mas is anything like it, I know now what I've been missing. This "farmhouse" is in the West Village, and though there are nods to the rustic in the decor with wood beams and a bar of sandstone with stools made from tree trunks, there is also an atmosphere of sophistication. A glass-enclosed wine cellar is visible from the small dining room, the restaurant stays open late, and you'll find hipsters in jeans and T-shirts as well as folks in power suits eating here. And it's that combination, along with the creative menu, that makes Mas so special. The dishes are innovative and the ingredients are fresh, many of them supplied by upstate New York farms. The tender, perfectly prepared braised pork belly, from Flying Pig Farm, is served with polenta and a stew of escargot and lima beans; and the duck breast, from Stone Church Farm, melds magically with apple purée and sautéed Brussels sprouts. Service is low-key but attentive, and the seating, though somewhat cramped, is not enough to dim the romantic aura.

39 Downing St. (between Bedford and Varick sts.). © 212/255-1790. Reservations recommended. 4-course tasting menu $68; 6-course $95; main courses $32–$36. AE, DC, DISC, MC, V. Mon–Sat 6pm–4am (small-plate tasting menu after 11:30pm). Subway: 1 to Houston St.

MODERATE

Maremma ★★ *Finds* ITALIAN/WESTERN   Named after the rocky, rough coastal region of Tuscany where cowboys roam the land, Maremma is New York's first and only spaghetti Western restaurant. Here you'll find small plates on the menu like Casella's spin on the traditional sloppy Joe he calls "sloppy Giuseppe," made with tender pieces of shredded beef over thick-crusted Tuscan bread, or the *bordatino di mare*, sticks of fried seafood with a crispy polenta crust served with spicy "Tuscan ketchup." The addition of chocolate to the wild-boar ragout that covers the fresh pappardelle is Casella's nod to the West, while a touch of bourbon westernizes the tomato-and-*grana-padano* sauce served over artisanal pasta. The Tuscan fries, traditional fries but with herbs and garlic sprinkled on them, are an addictive revelation. Not only is Maremma the only Italian/Western restaurant in New York, but it is also probably the only restaurant in New York that serves Rocky Mountain oysters (also known as bull's testicles). Are you cowboy enough to try them?

228 W. 10th St. (between Bleecker and Hudson sts.). © 212/645-0200. Reservations recommended. Small plates $9–$12; big plates $16–$28. AE, DC, DISC, MC, V. Mon–Wed 5:30–11pm; Thurs–Sat 5:30pm–midnight. Subway: 1 to Christopher St.

INEXPENSIVE

The original **John's Pizzeria** (there are now four of them) is at 278 Bleecker St., near Seventh Avenue (© **212/243-1680**); it's the most old-world romantic of the group and my favorite.

CHELSEA
EXPENSIVE

Buddakan ★ ASIAN   My expectations of Buddakan were of a loud dance-club scene in a 16,000-square-foot bi-level space where the food would be showy, but flavorless. I was right about the loud dance-club scene, but I was wrong about the flavorless food. The "Brasserie" is the main dining room on the lower level and the steps can seem steep after a few too many cocktails in the upstairs lounge, like the signature *Heat*, a combination of tequila, Cointreau, and chilled cucumbers. However, they were not steep enough to deter a man from being carried down in his wheelchair on the night I dined there. To fortify yourself after those cocktails, don't hesitate to order some of Buddakan's superb appetizers like the edamame dumplings, the crab and corn fritters, and, most notably, the crispy calamari salad. In fact, you can make your meal out of sharing appetizers—the extensive menu at Buddakan works best for large parties and has the now-obligatory "communal" table. But if you order one entree, make sure it's the sizzling short rib, tender and removed from the bone and sitting on top of a bed of mushroom chow fun.

75 Ninth Ave. (at 16th St.). © 212/989-6699. www.buddakannyc.com. Dim sum appetizers $9–$13; main courses $17–$35. AE, DC, MC, V. Sun–Wed 5:30pm–midnight; Thurs–Sat 5:30pm–1am. Subway: A, C, E to 14th St.

MODERATE

RUB 🦃🦃 BARBECUE   RUB is short for Righteous Urban Barbecue—a contradiction in terms if ever there was one. The New York arrival of RUB, co-owned by Kansas City pit master Paul Kirk, who has won seven World Barbecue Championships and is a member of the Barbecue Hall of Fame, was eagerly anticipated by those barbecue fanatics who are aware there is a Barbecue Hall of Fame. Could chef Kirk replicate his cuisine in New York, where pollutant-inducing smokers are illegal? The answer is no. You will never get that true smoked taste without creating some serious smoke, but that doesn't mean what you get at RUB is bad. On the contrary, the smoked turkey and barbecued chicken are the best I've had, moist inside with a distinctive smoked flavor, and the ribs, St. Louis style, were delicate and crispy, yet tender and meaty. The "burnt ends," the fatty part of the brisket, however, were a bit tough. The restaurant is cramped and loud and the prices are urban (meaning high); but the food at RUB will provide all the comfort you need.

208 W. 23rd St. (between Seventh and Eighth aves.). ℂ **212/524-4300**. www.rubbbq.net. Sandwiches $9–$12; platters $15–$23; Taste of the Baron $46. AE, MC, V. Tues–Thurs noon–11pm; Fri–Sat noon–midnight. Subway: 1 to 23rd St.

UNION SQUARE, THE FLATIRON DISTRICT & GRAMERCY PARK
EXPENSIVE

A Voce 🦃🦃 MODERN ITALIAN   The kind of food that is served at A Voce—rustic Italian, for the most part, with exceptional nods to innovation—seems somewhat out of place in the loud, postmodern dining room in a sleek high-rise just off Madison Park. You can start with something peasanty like Sardinian sheep's milk ricotta and slather it on thick, crusty grilled bread, or you can sample the hip, wild *branzini tartara* (Mediterranean sea bass)—something no peasant would ever dare eat. The same can be said for the "secondi." Chef Carmellini offers "My Grandmother's meat ravioli," and though my grandmother never made it, Carmellini's grandmother's meat ravioli is so good it certainly was *not* from a can. Continuing on that rustic theme, the "country-style Tuscan tripe," with barlotti beans, tomato, fried duck egg, and grilled ciabatta bread, would have made my normally dour Calabrese grandfather happy. A Voce offers daily specials called "del mercato," which usually feature the chef's unique creations like, on the day I visited, a "rabbit terrina" with salt-cured foie gras. You won't go wrong whether you try the rustic or the modern. The chef's palate-cleansing citrus tiramisu is the perfect conclusion.

41 Madison Ave. (at 26th St.). ℂ **212/545-8555**. www.avocerestaurant.com. Main courses $18–$39. AE, DC, MC, V. Mon–Fri 11:45am–2:30pm and 5:30–11pm; Sat–Sun 5:30–11pm. Subway: N, R, W to 23rd St.

Devi 🦃🦃 INDIAN   With the preponderance of Indian restaurants in New York City, you'd think another one would be welcomed with a big yawn. But few come along like Devi, which opened in late 2004. Devi offers $55 tasting menus (vegetarian and nonvegetarian) and that's really the way to go here. The menu features nine small courses that will let you sample much of what the restaurant serves. Some of the highlights include tender tandoori chicken stuffed with spicy herbs; halibut coated in a cilantro rub and accompanied by mint coconut chutney and lemon rice; *zimikand koftas,* delicate yam koftas in a creamy tomato-onion sauce; and the addictive, crispy okra, the Indian equivalent of french fries. With the tasting menus, you get a choice of desserts; of them, I strongly recommend the fabulous *falooda,* an Indian sundae that's a refreshing combination of noodles with honey-soaked basil seeds, mango, and strawberry sorbet in lemon-grass-infused coconut milk. Seating is comfortable and service is knowledgeable, though servers regrettably don bright orange uniforms that look a bit too much like prison garb.

8 E. 18th St. (between Fifth Ave. and Broadway). ℭ 212/691-1300. www.devinyc.com. Reservations recommended. Main courses $15–$31; tasting menus $60. AE, DISC, MC, V. Mon–Fri noon–2:30pm; Mon–Sat 5:30–11pm. Subway: N, Q, R, W, 4, 5, 6 to 14th St./Union Sq.

INEXPENSIVE

Also consider Danny Meyer's popular **Shake Shack,** in Madison Square Park (ℭ **212/ 889-6600**). For healthy burgers, try either outlet of the **New York Burger Co.,** 303 Park Ave. S., between 23rd and 24th streets (ℭ **212/254-2727**), and 678 Sixth Ave., between 21st and 22nd streets (ℭ **212/229-1404**). For a burger with boutique quality meat, try **Brgr,** 287 Seventh Ave., at 26th St. (ℭ **212/488-7500**).

City Bakery 𝄢 (Kids) ORGANIC AMERICAN　City Bakery offers comfort food that manages to be delicious, nutritious, *and* eco-friendly. Its salad bar is unlike any you'll find in the city, where the integrity of the ingredients is as important as the taste. This is health food, all right—roasted beets with walnuts, glistening sautéed greens, lavender eggplant tossed in miso—but with heart and soul, offering such classic favorites as French toast with artisanal bacon, deeply flavorful mac 'n cheese, fried chicken, tortilla pie, and even smoked salmon with all the trimmings on Sunday. The "bakery" in the name refers to the plethora of sinful desserts; kids love the spinning wheel of chocolate and the homemade marshmallows. *One caveat:* It's a bit pricey for a salad bar, but oh, what good eats.

3 W. 18th St. (between Fifth and Sixth aves.). ℭ 212/366-1414. Salad bar $12 per lb.; soups $4–$7; sandwiches $5–$10. AE, MC, V. Mon–Fri 7:30am–7pm; Sat 7:30am–6:30pm; Sun 9am–6pm. Subway: N, Q, R, 4, 5, 6 to Union Sq.

TIMES SQUARE & MIDTOWN WEST
EXPENSIVE

Frankie & Johnnie's 𝄢𝄢 STEAKHOUSE　When restaurants open other branches, red flags go up. Does that mean the restaurant has become a chain and thus quality has eroded to chain-food status? In the case of Frankie & Johnnie's, the legendary Theater District former-speakeasy-turned-steakhouse, which opened another outlet in 2005 in the two-story town house once owned by actor John Barrymore, those fears are quickly allayed after one bite of their signature sirloin. It also helps that the dining room on the second floor of the town house is gorgeous, especially the Barrymore room, the actor's former study with stained-glass ceiling panels, dark wood walls, and a working fireplace. Not only are Frankie & Johnnie's steaks underrated in the competitive world of New York steakhouses, but the other options are superb as well. The crab-cake appetizer had an overwhelmingly high crab-to-cake ratio—and that's a good thing in my book—while the side of hash browns was the best I've had. Service is steakhouse oldschool, and if you are staying in Midtown, the restaurant provides complimentary stretch-limo service to and from the restaurant.

32 W. 37th St. (between Fifth and Sixth aves.). ℭ 212/947-8940. www.frankieandjohnnies.com. Reservations recommended. Main courses $25–$36. AE, DC, DISC, MC, V. Mon–Fri noon–2:30pm; Mon–Thurs 4–10:30pm; Fri–Sat 4–11pm. Subway: B, C, D, N, Q, R, V, W to 34th St./Herald Sq. Also at 269 W. 45th St. (at Eighth Ave.). ℭ 212/997-9494. Subway: 1, 2, 3, 7, A, C, E, N, Q, R, S, W to 42nd St.

Keens Steakhouse 𝄢𝄢𝄢 STEAKHOUSE　Up until the latter part of the 20th century, Keens, which was established in the same location in 1885, referred to itself as a "chop house." It is now known as a steakhouse, but I wish they had remained true to their roots and hadn't submitted to modern-day marketing and made that change.

To its credit, it is a steakhouse in name only. It not only serves the basics of a steakhouse—the porterhouse for two, aged prime T-bone steak, and filet mignon with the requisite sides such as creamed spinach and hash browns—but also serves chops: lamb chops, prime rib, short ribs, and, most notably, mutton chops. It is the mutton chop that has made Keens the original that it is. The monstrous cut has two flaps of long, thick, rich, subtly gamy meat on either side of the bone, which looks kind of like mutton-chop sideburns. Keens is no gussied-up remake: It's the real thing, from the thousands of ceramic pipes on the ceiling (regular diners were given their own personal pipes, including celebrities like Babe Ruth, George M. Cohan, and Albert Einstein) to the series of rooms on two floors with wood paneling, leather banquettes, fireplaces (in some), a bar with a three-page menu of single malts, and even the framed playbill Lincoln was reading at the Ford Theater that infamous evening in 1865.

72 W. 36th St. (at Sixth Ave.). © **212/947-3636**. www.keens.com. Reservations recommended. Main courses $26–$45. AE, DC, DISC, MC, V. Mon–Fri 11:45am–10:30pm; Sat 5–10:30pm; Sun 5–9pm. Subway: B, D, F, N, Q, R, V, W to 34th St./Herald Sq.

Molyvos ✿✿ GREEK   When Molyvos opened in 1997 it was heralded as a trailblazer of upscale and innovative Greek cuisine. Now, more than 10 years later, upscale and innovative Greek is the current "in vogue" cuisine in Manhattan. Molyvos's long-term success is based on its ability to please those who want simple, unpretentious, traditional Greek food as well as exciting, original-Greek-accented creations. For those who like their Greek unadulterated, you won't go wrong with cold *mezedes* (appetizers), such as the spreads *tzatziki, melitzanosalata,* and *taramosalata,* and hot *mezedes* like spinach pie or grilled octopus. For Greek food with an edge, there is ouzo-cured salmon on a chickpea fritter or the terrific seafood Cretan bread salad. Just a sampling of the *mezedes* alone should be enough for anyone's hearty appetite, but with entrees as good as grilled *garides,* wild head-on prawns barbecued "souvlaki-style," and the *chios* pork and *gigante* bean stew, not ordering one would be a mistake. The knowledgeable sommelier will pair your choices with a comparable Greek wine, of which there are many. Or, skip the wine and sample one or two of the dozens of ouzos available, but don't skip the desserts. Sure you've had baklava before, but have you ever had chocolate baklava? Yes, it's as good as it sounds.

871 Seventh Ave. (between 55th and 56th sts.). © **212/582-7500**. www.molyvos.com. Reservations recommended. Main courses lunch $17–$29 (most less than $20); main courses dinner $20–$36 (most less than $25); fixed-price lunch $24; pre-theater 3-course dinner $36 (5:30–6:45pm). AE, DC, DISC, MC, V. Mon–Thurs noon–11:30pm; Fri–Sat noon–midnight; Sun noon–11pm. Subway: N, R to 57th St.; B, D, E to Seventh Ave.

MODERATE

Becco ✿ *Finds* ITALIAN   If you're a fan of *Lidia's Italian-American Kitchen* on PBS, you'll be happy to know you can sample Lidia Bastianich's simple, hearty Italian cooking here. Becco, on Restaurant Row, is designed to serve her meals "at a different price point" (read: cheaper) than at her East Side restaurant, Felidia. The prices are not rock-bottom, but in terms of service, portions, and quality, you get tremendous bang for your buck at Becco (which means to "peck, nibble, or savor something in a discriminating way"). The main courses can head north of the $20 mark, but take a look at the prix-fixe menu for $17 at lunch, $22 at dinner, which includes either a Caesar salad or antipasto plate, followed by a "Symphony of Pasta," unlimited servings of the three fresh-made daily pastas. There's also an excellent selection of Italian wines at $20 a bottle. If you can't make up your mind about dessert, have them all: A tasting plate includes gelato, cheesecake, and whatever else the dessert chef has whipped up that day. Lidia herself does turn up at Becco and Felidia regularly; you can even "Dine with Lidia" (see website for details).

355 W. 46th St. (between Eighth and Ninth aves.). © 212/397-7597. www.becconyc.com. Reservations recommended. Main courses lunch $13–$25; dinner $19–$35. AE, DC, DISC, MC, V. Mon noon–3pm and 5–10pm; Tues and Thurs–Fri noon–3pm and 5pm–midnight; Wed and Sat 11:30am–2:30pm and 4pm–midnight; Sun noon–10pm. Subway: C, E to 50th St.

Virgil's Real BBQ 𝒜𝒜 *Kids* BARBECUE/SOUTHERN   Located in the heart of the theme-restaurant wasteland known as Times Square is a theme restaurant that actually has good food. The "theme" is Southern barbecue and the restaurant, sprawling with dining on two levels, is made to look and feel like a Southern roadhouse with good-ol'-boy decorations on the walls and blues on the soundtrack. Virgil's does a very admirable job in re-creating that authentic flavor that's so hard to find north of the Mason-Dixon line. The spice-rubbed ribs are slow-cooked and meaty, but it's the Owensboro Lamb (smoked slices of lamb) and the Texas beef brisket that are the standouts. Both are melt-in-your-mouth tender; the lamb is sprinkled with a flavorful mustard sauce, while the brisket is perfect with a few dabs of Virgil's homemade spicy barbecue sauce. Desserts are what you would expect from a restaurant emulating a Southern theme: big and sweet. Try the homemade ice-cream sandwich made with the cookie of the day. Virgil's is a great place to bring the kids; they can make as much noise as they want and no one will notice.

152 W. 44th St. (between Sixth and Seventh aves.). © 212/921-9494. www.virgilsbbq.com. Reservations recommended. Sandwiches $10–$13; main courses and barbecue platters $15–$24 (most less than $19). AE, DC, DISC, MC, V. Sun–Mon 11:30am–11pm; Tues–Sat 11:30am–midnight. Subway: 1, 2, 3, 7, N, R to 42nd St./Times Sq.

INEXPENSIVE

If you're looking for the quintessential New York Jewish deli, you have a choice between the **Stage Deli,** 834 Seventh Ave., between 53rd and 54th streets (© 212/245-7850), known for its jaw-distending celebrity sandwiches; and the **Carnegie Deli,** 854 Seventh Ave., at 55th Street (© 800/334-5606), for the best pastrami, corned beef, and cheesecake in town.

There is a very nice outlet of **John's Pizzeria** in Times Square, 260 W. 44th St., between Seventh and Eighth avenues (© 212/391-7560).

Sapporo 𝒜 *Finds* JAPANESE NOODLES   Peruse the community bulletin board as you enter Sapporo and you might find a deal on an apartment—that is, if you can read Japanese characters. Thankfully, the menu is in English at this longtime Theater District noodle shop. If the mostly Japanese clientele doesn't convince you of Sapporo's authenticity, the constant din of satisfied diners slurping at huge bowls of steaming ramen (noodle soup with meat and vegetables) surely will. And though the ramen is Sapporo's well-deserved specialty, the *gyoza* (Japanese dumplings) and the *donburi* (pork or chicken over rice with soy-flavored sauce) are also terrific. Best of all, nothing on the menu is over $10 and that's not easy to accomplish in the oft-over-priced Theater District.

152 W. 49th St. (between Sixth and Seventh aves.). © 212/869-8972. Reservations not accepted. Main courses $6–$9. No credit cards. Mon–Sat 11am–11pm; Sun 11am–10pm. Subway: N, R, W to 49th St.

Wondee Siam 𝒜 *Finds* THAI   Hell's Kitchen offers countless ethnic culinary variations and one of the most prevalent is Thai—there are at least six in a 5-block radius.

My favorite among these is the tiny, zero-ambience Wondee Siam. I don't need color-ful decorations or a big fish tank to enjoy authentic, uncompromisingly spicy Thai food, and that's what I get at Wondee Siam. Here you don't have to worry that your waiter will assume you want a milder form of Thai. If there is a little red asterisk next to your item, you can be sure it is appropriately spicy. The soups are terrific, especially the sinus-clearing Tom Yum. In fact, there is a whole section of Yum (chiles) dishes on the menu, my favorite being the Larb Gai, minced ground chicken with ground toasted rice. The curries are also first-rate, as are the noodles, including the mild pad Thai. This is strictly BYOB and you'll want to do so to complement the spicy food. If you want a bit more comfort, try Wondee Siam II, 1 block up. But make sure you ask your waiter not to dumb down the spices, but serve up the food authentic Thai style.

792 Ninth Ave. (between 52nd and 53rd sts.). ⓒ 212/459-9057. Reservations not accepted. Main courses $8.50–$18 (most under $10). No credit cards. Daily 11am–11pm. Subway: C, E to 50th St. Also, Wondee Siam II, 813 Ninth Ave. (between 53rd and 54th sts.). ⓒ 917/286-1726. Same hours.

MIDTOWN EAST & MURRAY HILL
EXPENSIVE

Aquavit ⓐⓐⓐ SCANDINAVIAN I'll miss the waterfall and the intimate town house setting that Aquavit regrettably vacated in early 2005. Thankfully, however, the food and staff have had no trouble adjusting to the transition. Everything remains impeccably first-rate. The restaurant is now housed in the bottom of a glass tower on East 55th Street and designed in sleek Scandinavian style with modernist furniture. In the front of the restaurant is an informal and less expensive cafe, while past a long bar is the main dining room.

After the move, if anything, the food has improved. The smoked fish—really all the fish—is prepared perfectly. I often daydream about the herring plate: four types of herring accompanied by a tiny glass of Aquavit, distilled liquors not unlike vodka fla-vored with fruit and spices, and a frosty Carlsberg beer. The hot smoked Arctic char on the main a la carte menu, served with clams and bean purée in a mustard green broth, is also a winner. Most fixed-price menus offer a well-chosen beverage accompa-niment option.

65 E. 55th St. (between Park and Madison aves.). ⓒ 212/307-7311. www.aquavit.org. Reservations recommended. Cafe main courses $9–$32; 3-course fixed-price meal $24 at lunch, $35 at dinner. Main dining room fixed-price meal $39 at lunch, $82 at dinner ($39 for vegetarians). Main dining room 3-course pre-theater dinner (5:30–6:15pm) $55; tasting menus $58 at lunch, $115 at dinner ($90 for vegetarians); supplement for paired wines $30 at lunch, $80 at din-ner. AE, DC, MC, V. Mon–Fri noon–2:30pm; Sun–Thurs 5:30–10:30pm; Fri–Sat 5:15–10:30pm. Subway: E, F to Fifth Ave.

BLT Steak ⓐⓐⓐ STEAKHOUSE/BISTRO Steakhouses are often stereotyped as bastions of male bonding—testosterone-fueled with red meat and hearty drinks. But BLT (Bistro Laurent Tourendel) Steak breaks that mold in a big way; on the night I visited, I noticed fewer men than women—slinky and model-like—chomping on thick cuts of beef. That doesn't mean men can't also enjoy the beef here—served in cast-iron pots and finished in steak butter with a choice of sauces: béarnaise, red wine, horseradish, and blue cheese, to name a few. The signature is the porterhouse for two (a whopping $70), but I recommend the New York strip or the succulent short ribs braised in red wine. Both dishes can be shared, which may be a good idea, especially after you've devoured the airy complimentary popovers and sampled an appetizer like the incredible tuna tartare or a side of onion rings, potato gratin, or creamy spinach. Even after sharing one of the meats, you might not have room for the memorable chestnut-chocolate sundae or peanut butter chocolate mousse, and that would be a shame. This is not a restaurant for intimate conversation; even the music was muffled by the cacophonous din of the diners.

106 E. 57th St. (between Park and Lexington aves.). ✆ 212/752-7470. www.bltsteak.com. Reservations highly recommended. Main courses $24–$39. AE, DC, MC, V. Mon–Fri 11:45am–2:30pm; Mon–Thurs 5:30–11pm; Fri–Sat 5:30–11:30pm. Subway: 4, 5, 6, N, R, W to 59th St.

Country ✾✾ FRENCH/AMERICAN   Stunningly elegant and urbane, there is really nothing country about Country—and that's not a knock. Gorgeously designed by David Rockwell, the restaurant's centerpiece is the 200-square-foot Tiffany skylight dome that was hidden over the years by a dropped ceiling. The prix-fixe menu changes every 2 weeks and matches the decor's sophisticated style. When I visited in early spring, warm asparagus in a light lemon vinaigrette was an outstanding first-course option, while the lamb cannelloni (tender pieces of shredded lamb in a wonton-thin dumpling) made the perfect second-course accompaniment. Of the third-course options, the striped bass with crushed herbs, potatoes, and clams was the standout. A selection of cheeses is offered as a dessert option and it's hard to resist. Downstairs are the more countrified, darker, wood-paneled booths of Café at Country.

90 Madison Ave. (at 29th St.). ✆ 212/889-7100. Reservations required. Prix-fixe $105; 4-course tasting menu $105, 5-course $110, 6-course $135. AE, DC, DISC, MC, V. Sun–Thurs 5:30–10pm; Fri–Sat 5:30–11pm. Café at Country main courses $15–$27. Mon–Sat 11:30am–3pm and 5:30–11pm; Sun 10:30am–3pm. Subway: 6, N, R to 28th St.

UPPER WEST SIDE
VERY EXPENSIVE
Porter House New York ✾✾ STEAKHOUSE   The space, located in the Time Warner Center on Columbus Circle, is sleek with large leather banquettes for groups, along with smaller, white tableclothed tables by the floor-to-ceiling windows overlooking Central Park. But even if there were no view, this steakhouse would satisfy the essentials of the best red meat emporiums, with a few inventive twists. I gambled by ordering the chili-rubbed rib-eye—would chili obscure the natural flavor of the meat? My gamble paid off; the chili was subtle and actually brought out the cut's essence. If you want your steak straight ahead, the dry-aged prime strip steak, cooked to perfection and bursting with flavor, won't let you down. Sides are unconventional for a steakhouse, such as pieces of thick smoky bacon added to the creamed spinach, and porcini mushrooms on a bed of polenta offered as an alternative to mashed potatoes. But it's the meat—and eating it overlooking Central Park—that makes Porter House New York so special.

10 Columbus Circle (4th Floor) in the Time Warner Center (at 60th St.). ✆ 212/823-9500. www.porterhousenewyork. com. Main courses $24–$39. AE, DC, DISC, MC, V. Mon–Sat noon–4pm; Sun noon–3pm; Mon–Thurs 5–10:30pm; Fri–Sat 5–11pm. Subway: A, B, C, D, 1 to 59th St./Columbus Circle.

EXPENSIVE
Ouest ✾✾✾ CONTEMPORARY AMERICAN   With plush red banquettes and an intimate balcony area, Ouest is both cozy and clubby. Service is personable but also professional—so good you'll need to keep reminding yourself that you're on the Upper West Side. But what really draws the crowds is chef Tom Valenti's mastery in the kitchen, especially with meats such as his signature braised lamb shank or his melt-in-your-mouth braised beef short ribs. The sautéed skate is perfectly prepared with a simple sauce of parsley and olive oil, while the baby calamari in a spicy tomato sopressata sauce appetizer was so good, I actually smiled as I ate it.

2315 Broadway (at 84th St.). ✆ 212/580-8700. www.ouestny.com. Reservations required well in advance. Main courses $23–$36. AE, DC, DISC, MC, V. Mon–Thurs 5:30–11pm; Fri–Sat 5:30–11:30pm; Sun 11am–10pm. Subway: 1 to 86th St.

Telepan 🌟🌟 AMERICAN   The venue for Telepan is an Upper West Side town house with a dining room painted in soothing lime green. The cool design complements the menu, which changes seasonally, but always features farm-fresh products. I had the good fortune to dine in the spring and was greeted with fresh ramps, fiddleheads, and young peas in many of the dishes I sampled. There was no fresh produce, however, in the foie gras donuts listed as a "share." The "donuts" are dusted with cocoa and cinnamon and might work as well with a cup of java as with a cocktail. Of the appetizers, the standout was the wild green frittata that did indeed come with in-season ramps. Telepan offers Mid Courses, and of them, the pea pancakes with pea agnolotti looked and, more important, tasted greenmarket fresh. Save room for an entree, specifically the haddock with a sweet lobster sauce. Whatever you choose to eat, you'll have no problem finding a complimentary wine from the restaurant's long and impressive list. Telepan has become a pre–Lincoln Center favorite, so if you want to avoid the crush, make a reservation for after curtain.

72 W. 69th St. (at Columbus Ave.). ℂ 212/580-4300; www.telepan-ny.com. Reservations recommended. Main courses $29–$36; 4-course tasting menu $59; 5-course tasting menu $69. AE, DC, MC, V. Lunch Wed–Fri 11:30am–2:30pm; dinner Mon–Thurs 5–11pm, Fri–Sat 5–11:30pm, Sun 5–10:30pm; brunch Sat–Sun 11am–2:30pm. Subway: B, C to 72nd St.

MODERATE

Kefi 🌟🌟🌟 *Finds* GREEK   Chef/owner Michael Psilakis has transformed what was formerly the nouveau-Greek restaurant Onera back to something much closer to your Greek mother's (if you had a Greek mother) kitchen. In fact, the restaurant is inspired by Psilakis's mother and her traditional recipes. So gone is the Offal Tasting menu of Onera and back are Greek standards like moussaka, spinach pie, Greek salad, and grilled fish. But oh, what Psilakis does with the standards. The *mezes* (Greek appetizers) are good enough to make up a meal; it's hard to resist the selection of spreads accompanied by pita, the warm feta, tomatoes, capers and anchovies, and especially the sublime grilled octopus salad, as good as I've had anywhere. But something's got to go if you want to save room for entrees like the flat noodles with braised rabbit; the grilled whole branzino with potatoes, olives, tomatoes, and feta; or the slow-cooked, comforting lamb shank on a bed of orzo. If it is humanly possible after indulging in all of the above, don't miss out on the desserts, most notably the walnut cake with maple walnut ice cream. Service is casual and the space is a bit cramped, but not enough to deter you from the many pleasures of Kefi.

222 W. 79th St. (between Broadway and Amsterdam Ave.). ℂ 212/873-0200. Reservations not taken. Main courses $10–$20. No credit cards. Tues–Thurs 5–10:30pm; Fri–Sat 5–11pm; Sun 5–10pm. Subway: 1 to 79th St.

INEXPENSIVE

For breakfast or lunch, also consider **Barney Greengrass, the Sturgeon King,** 541 Amsterdam Ave., between 86th and 87th streets (ℂ **212/724-4707**), one of the best Jewish delis in town.

Celeste 🌟🌟 *Finds* ITALIAN   This is another very welcome addition to the Upper West Side dining scene. Tiny but charming Celeste features its own wood-burning pizza oven, which churns out thin-crusted, simple but delicious pizzas. But pizza is not the only attraction here; the "fritti" (fried) course is unique; the *fritto misto de pesce* (fried mixed seafood) is delectable, but the fried zucchini blossoms, usually available in the summer and fall, are amazing. The fresh pastas are better than the dried pasta; I never thought the fresh egg noodles with cabbage, shrimp, and sheep's cheese would work, but it was delicious. Not on the menu but usually available are plates of rare, artisanal Italian cheeses served with homemade jams. Though the main courses are

The Soul of Harlem

There is much soul to go around in Manhattan, but Harlem seems to possess the mother lode—at least when it comes to food. Here is one man's primer to Harlem's soul food:

Amy Ruth's, 112 W. 116th St., between Lenox and Seventh avenues (© **212/ 280-8779**). Claiming to be authentic soul, Amy Ruth's has become a mecca for Harlem celebs, with the kitschy gimmick of naming platters after some of them, such as the Rev. Al Sharpton (chicken and waffles) and the Rev. Calvin O. Butts III (chicken wings and waffles). You can't go wrong with anything here as long as waffles are included.

Charles' Southern Style Kitchen 🐦, 2841 Eighth Ave., between 151st and 152nd streets (© **877/813-2920** or 212/926-4313). Nothing fancy about this place, just a brightly lit, 25-seater on a not-very-attractive block in upper Harlem. But you don't come here for fancy, you come for soul food at its simplest and freshest. And you'd better come hungry. The $11 all-you-can-eat buffet features crunchy, incredibly moist, pan-fried chicken; ribs in a tangy sauce, with meat falling off the bone; macaroni and cheese; collard greens with bits of smoked turkey; black-eyed peas; and corn bread, warm and not overly sweet. Hours can be erratic, so call ahead before you make the trek.

Copeland's, 547 W. 145th St., between Broadway and Amsterdam Avenue (© **212/234-2357**). With food almost as good as Charles' but in a much more elegant setting (you'll find tables adorned with china and white tablecloths), Copeland's has been dishing out excellent soul food for 40 years. Fried chicken is its trademark, but I favor the braised short ribs. The jazz buffet on Tuesday, Wednesday, and Thursday nights is a double treat.

also good, stick with the pizzas, antipasto, frittis, and pastas. For dessert, try the gelato; the pistachio was the best I've ever had in New York. The restaurant has been "discovered," so go early, go late, or expect a wait.

502 Amsterdam Ave. (between 84th and 85th sts.). © **212/874-4559**. Reservations not accepted. Pizza $10–$12; antipasto $7–$10; pasta $10; main courses $14–$16. No credit cards. Mon–Sat 5–11pm; Sun noon–3pm. Subway: 1 to 86th St.

Flor de Mayo *Finds* CUBAN/CHINESE Cuban/Chinese cuisine is a New York phenomenon that started in the late 1950s when Cubans of Chinese heritage immigrated to New York after the revolution. Most of the immigrants took up residence on the Upper West Side, and Cuban/Chinese restaurants flourished. Many have disappeared, but the best one, Flor de Mayo, still remains and is so popular that a new branch opened farther south on Amsterdam Avenue. The kitchen excels at both sides of the massive menu, but the best dish is the *la brasa* half-chicken lunch special— beautifully spiced and slow-roasted until it's fork tender and falling off the bone, served with a pile of fried rice, bounteous with roast pork, shrimp, and veggies. Offered Monday through Saturday until 4:30pm, the whole meal is $6.95, and it's

I don't speak sign language.

A hotel can close for all kinds of reasons.
Our Guarantee ensures that if your hotel's undergoing construction, we'll
let you know in advance. In fact, we cover your entire travel experience.
See www.travelocity.com/guarantee for details.

travelocity
You'll never roam alone.

M&G Diner, 383 W. 125th St., at St. Nicholas Avenue (✆ 212/864-7325). All the soul food joints I've listed here serve top-notch fried chicken, but the best I've had is the perfectly pan-fried, supermoist bird at the M&G. This small, no-frills diner, open 24 hours, is a treat any time of day. Start your day here with a soul breakfast of eggs with salmon croquettes or eggs with grits, or finish it with the celebrated chicken, chitterlings, or meatloaf. All the sides are freshly made and the desserts, especially the sweet-potato pie, are phenomenal. There's also a great jukebox loaded with soul to complement the food.

Miss Mamie's Spoonbread Too, 366 W. 110th St., between Columbus and Manhattan avenues (✆ 212/865-6744). Entering this bright, strawberry-curtained charmer is like stepping straight into South Carolina. But you are in Harlem, or at least the southern fringe of Harlem, and you won't be paying South Carolina soul prices, or Harlem soul prices, either. Still, despite the somewhat inflated prices, Miss Mamie's is the real deal, especially the barbecued ribs, falling off the bone and smothered in a sweet peppery sauce, and the smothered chicken, fried and then covered with thick pan gravy.

Sylvia's, 328 Lenox Ave., between 126th and 127th streets (✆ 212/996-0660; www.sylviassoulfood.com). Sylvia is the self-proclaimed queen of not only Harlem soul food but all soul food. In reality, Sylvia is queen of self-promotion. Sylvia's now has become a franchise, with canned food products, beauty and hair products, and fragrances and colognes. With all that attention to merchandising, the food at her original Harlem restaurant has suffered and now has regressed into a tourist trap. If you plan to go, however, make it on Sunday for the gospel brunch, which is an absolute joy.

enough to fortify you for the day. Service and atmosphere are reminiscent of Chinatown: efficient and lightning-quick. My favorite combo: the noodles-, greens-, shrimp-, and pork-laden Chinese soup with yellow rice and black beans.

2651 Broadway (between 100th and 101st sts.). ✆ 212/663-5520 or 212/595-2525. Reservations not accepted. Main courses $4.50–$19 (most under $10); lunch specials $5–$7 (Mon–Sat to 4:30pm). AE, MC, V ($15 minimum). Daily noon–midnight. Subway: 1 to 103rd St. Also at 484 Amsterdam Ave. (between 83rd and 84th sts.). ✆ 212/787-3388. Subway: 1 to 86th St.

Good Enough to Eat ⚐ *(Kids* *(Finds* AMERICAN HOME COOKING   For 23 years, the crowds have been lining up on weekends outside Good Enough to Eat to experience chef/owner Carrie Levin's incredible breakfasts; as a result, lunch and dinner have been somewhat overlooked. Too bad, because these meals can be just as great as the breakfasts. The restaurant's cow motif and farmhouse knickknacks imply hearty, home-cooked food, and that's what's done best here. Stick with the classics: meatloaf with gravy and mashed potatoes; traditional turkey dinner with cranberry relish, gravy, and cornbread stuffing; macaroni and cheese; griddled corn bread; Vermont spinach salad; and the barbecue sandwich—roasted chicken with barbecue sauce and homemade potato chips. Save room for the homemade desserts; though the selection is often overwhelming, I can never resist the coconut cake. This is food you loved as a kid, one reason why the kids will love it as well.

There are only 20 tables here, so expect a wait on weekends during the day or for dinner after 6pm.

483 Amsterdam Ave. (between 83rd and 84th sts.). (*) 212/496-0163. www.goodenoughtoeat.com. Breakfast $5.25–$12; lunch $8.50–$15; dinner $8.50–$23 (most under $18). AE, MC, V. Breakfast Mon–Fri 8:30am–4pm, Sat–Sun 9am–4pm; lunch Mon noon–4pm, Tues–Fri 11:30am–4pm; dinner Mon–Thurs and Sun 5:30–10:30pm, Fri–Sat 5:30–11pm. Subway: 1 to 86th St.

Noche Mexicana *finds* MEXICAN   This tiny restaurant serves some of the best tamales in New York. Wrapped in cornhusks, as a good tamale should be, they come in two varieties: in a red mole sauce with shredded chicken or in a green tomatillo sauce with shredded pork. There are three tamales in each order, which costs only $5, making it a cheap and almost perfect lunch. The burritos are authentic and meals unto themselves. The *tinga* burrito, shredded chicken in a tomato-and-onion chipotle sauce, is my favorite. Each is stuffed with rice, beans, and guacamole. Don't get fancy here; stick with the tamales, burritos, and soft tacos, the best being the taco *al pastor*, a taco stuffed with pork marinated with pineapple and onions.

852 Amsterdam Ave. (between 101st and 102nd sts.). (*) 212/662-6900 or 212/662-7400. Burritos $6.50–$8.50; tacos $2; tamales $6; Mexican dishes $9.50–$11. AE, DISC, MC, V. Sun–Thurs 10am–11pm; Fri–Sat 10am–midnight. Subway: 1 to 103rd St.

HARLEM
INEXPENSIVE
Also consider **Patsy's Pizzeria,** 2287 First Ave. (between 117th and 118th sts.; (*) 212/ 534-9783), my favorite pizzeria (and the late Frank Sinatra's, too).

5 Exploring New York City

A word of advice for newcomers: Don't try to tame New York—you can't. Decide on a few must-see attractions, and then let the city take you on its own ride.

THE TOP ATTRACTIONS
American Museum of Natural History *find find find*   Founded in 1869, this 4-block museum houses the world's greatest natural science collection in a group of buildings made of towers and turrets, pink granite and red brick—a mishmash of architectural styles, but overflowing with neo-Gothic charm. The diversity of the holdings is astounding: some 36 million specimens ranging from microscopic organisms to the world's largest cut gem, the Brazilian Princess Topaz (21,005 carats). If you don't have a lot of time, you can see the best of the best on free **highlights tours** offered daily at 15 minutes after every hour from 10:15am to 3:15pm. **Audio Expeditions,** high-tech audio tours that allow you to access narration in the order you choose, are available to help you make sense of it all.

The museum excels at **special exhibitions,** so check to see what will be on while you're in town in case advance planning is required. The magical **Butterfly Conservatory** *find*, a walk-in enclosure housing nearly 500 free-flying tropical butterflies, has developed into a can't-miss fixture from October to May; check to see if it's open while you're in town.

The four-story-tall planetarium sphere in the **Rose Center for Earth and Space** *find* hosts the excellent "Cosmic Collisions," possibly the most technologically advanced show on the planet.

Value CityPass Combo Ticket Deal

CityPass may be New York's best sightseeing deal. Pay one price ($53, or $44 for kids 12–17) for admission to six major attractions: The American Museum of Natural History (admission only; does not include Space Show), the Guggenheim Museum, the Empire State Building, the Museum of Modern Art, and a 2-hour Circle Line harbor cruise. Individual tickets would cost more than twice as much.

More important, CityPass is not a coupon book. It contains actual tickets, so you can bypass lengthy lines. This can save you hours, since sights such as the Empire State Building often have ticket lines of an hour or more.

CityPass is good for 9 days from the first time you use it. It's sold at all participating attractions and online at **www.citypass.com**. To avoid online service and shipping fees, you may buy the pass at your first attraction (start at an attraction that's likely to have the shortest admission line, such as the Guggenheim, or arrive before opening to avoid a wait at such spots as the Empire State Building). However, if you begin your sightseeing on a weekend or during holidays, when lines are longest, online purchase may be worthwhile.

For more information, call CityPass at © **208/787-4300** (note, however, that CityPass is not sold over the phone).

Central Park West (between 77th and 81st sts.). © **212/769-5100** for information, or 212/769-5200 for tickets (tickets can also be ordered online). www.amnh.org. Suggested admission $14 adults, $11 seniors and students, $8 children 2–12; Space Show and museum admission $22 adults, $17 seniors and students, $13 children under 12. Additional charges for IMAX movies and some special exhibitions. Daily 10am–5:45pm; Rose Center 1st Fri of every month until 8:45pm. Subway: B, C to 81st St.; 1 to 79th St.

Brooklyn Bridge *Moments*   Its Gothic-inspired stone pylons and intricate steel-cable webs have moved poets like Walt Whitman and Hart Crane to sing the praises of this great span, the first to cross the East River and connect Manhattan to Brooklyn. Completed in 1883, the beautiful Brooklyn Bridge is now the city's best-known symbol of the age of growth that seized the city during the late 19th century.

Walking the Bridge: Walking the Brooklyn Bridge is one of my all-time favorite New York activities. A wide wood-plank pedestrian walkway is elevated above the traffic, making it a relatively peaceful, and popular, walk. It's a great vantage point from which to contemplate the New York skyline and the East River.

There's a sidewalk entrance on Park Row, just across from City Hall Park (take the 4, 5, or 6 train to Brooklyn Bridge/City Hall). But why take this walk *away* from Manhattan, toward the far less impressive Brooklyn skyline? Instead, for Manhattan skyline views, take an A or C train to High Street, one stop into Brooklyn. From there, you'll be on the bridge in no time: Come aboveground, then walk through the little park to Cadman Plaza East and head downslope (left) to the stairwell that will take you up to the footpath. (Following Prospect Place under the bridge, turning right onto Cadman Plaza E., will also take you directly to the stairwell.) It's a 20- to 40-minute stroll over the bridge to Manhattan, depending on your pace, the amount of foot traffic, and the number of stops you make to behold the spectacular views (there are benches along the way). The footpath will deposit you right at City Hall Park.

Subway: A, C to High St.; 4, 5, 6 to Brooklyn Bridge–City Hall.

Ellis Island 𝒦𝒦   One of New York's most moving sights, the restored Ellis Island opened in 1990, slightly north of Liberty Island. Roughly 40% of Americans (myself included) can trace their heritage back to an ancestor who came through here. For the 62 years when it was America's main entry point for immigrants (1892–1954), Ellis Island processed some 12 million people. The statistics can be overwhelming, but the **Immigration Museum** skillfully relates the story of Ellis Island and immigration in America by placing the emphasis on personal experience.

It's difficult to leave the museum unmoved. Today, you enter the Main Building's baggage room, just as the immigrants did, and then climb the stairs to the **Registry Room,** with its dramatic vaulted tiled ceiling, where millions waited anxiously for medical and legal processing. A step-by-step account of the immigrants' voyage is detailed in the exhibit, with haunting photos and touching oral histories. What might be the most poignant exhibit is **"Treasures from Home,"** 1,000 objects and photos donated by descendants of immigrants, including family heirlooms, religious articles, and rare clothing and jewelry. Outside, the **American Immigrant Wall of Honor** commemorates the names of more than 500,000 immigrants and their families, from Myles Standish and George Washington's great-grandfather to the forefathers of John F. Kennedy, Jay Leno, and Barbra Streisand. You can even research your own family's history at the interactive **American Family Immigration History Center.** *Touring tips:* Ferries run daily to Ellis Island and Liberty Island from Battery Park and Liberty State Park at frequent intervals; see the Statue of Liberty listing (p. 127) for details.

In New York Harbor. 🕐 **212/363-3200** (general info), or 212/269-5755 (ticket/ferry info). www.nps.gov/elis or www. ellisisland.org. Free admission (ferry ticket charge). Daily 9:30am–5:15pm (last ferry departs around 3:30pm). For subway and ferry details, see the Statue of Liberty listing on p. 127 (ferry trip includes stops at both sights).

Empire State Building 𝒦𝒦𝒦   It took 60,000 tons of steel, 10 million bricks, 2.5 million feet of electrical wire, 120 miles of pipe, and seven million man-hours to build. King Kong climbed it in 1933. A plane slammed into it in 1945. The World Trade Center superseded it in 1972 as the island's tallest building. On that horrific day of September 11, 2001, it once again regained its status as New York City's tallest building, after 29 years of taking second place. Through it all, the Empire State Building has remained one of the city's favorite landmarks, and its signature high-rise. Completed in 1931, the limestone-and-stainless-steel Streamline Deco dazzler climbs 102 stories (1,454 ft.) and now harbors the offices of fashion firms and, in its upper reaches, a jumble of high-tech broadcast equipment.

Always a conversation piece, the Empire State Building glows every night, bathed in colored floodlights to commemorate events of significance (you can find a complete lighting schedule online). The familiar silver spire can be seen from all over the city. But the views that keep nearly three million visitors coming every year are the ones from the 86th- and 102nd-floor **observatories.** The lower one is best—you can walk out on a windy deck and look through coin-operated viewers (bring quarters!) over what, on a clear day, can be as much as an 80-mile visible radius. The citywide panorama is magnificent. Starry nights are pure magic.

350 Fifth Ave. (at 34th St.). 🕐 **212/736-3100.** www.esbnyc.com. Observatory admission $18 adults, $16 seniors and children 12–17, $12 children 6–11, free for children under 6. Daily 8am–2am, last elevator at 1:15am. Subway: B, D, F, N, Q, R, V, W to 34th St.; 6 to 33rd St.

Grand Central Terminal 𝒦𝒦   Restored in 1998, Grand Central Terminal is one of the most magnificent public spaces in the country. Even if you're not catching one of the subway lines or Metro-North commuter trains that rumble through the bowels of this great place, come and visit. And even if you arrive and leave by subway, be sure to exit the station, walking a couple of blocks south, to about 40th Street, before you turn around to admire Jules-Alexis Coutan's neoclassical sculpture *Transportation* hovering over the south entrance, with a majestically buff Mercury, the Roman god of commerce and travel, as its central figure.

The greatest visual impact comes when you enter the vast **main concourse.** The high windows once again allow sunlight to penetrate the space, glinting off the ½-acre Tennessee marble floor. The brass clock over the central kiosk gleams, as do the gold- and nickel-plated chandeliers piercing the side archways. The masterful **sky ceiling,** again a brilliant greenish blue, depicts the constellations of the winter sky above New York. On the east end of the main concourse is a grand **marble staircase** where there had never been one before, though it had always been in the original plans.

This dramatic Beaux Arts splendor serves as a hub of social activity as well. Excellent-quality retail shops and restaurants have taken over the mezzanine and lower levels. The highlight of the west mezzanine is **Michael Jordan's–The Steak House,** a gorgeous Art Deco space that allows you to dine within view of the sky ceiling. Off the main concourse at street level, there's a nice mix of specialty shops and national retailers, as well as the truly grand **Grand Central Market** for gourmet foods.

42nd St. at Park Ave. ℂ 212/340-2210 (events hot line). www.grandcentralterminal.com. Subway: S, 4, 5, 6, 7 to 42nd St./Grand Central.

Metropolitan Museum of Art ✮✮✮ Home of blockbuster after blockbuster exhibition, the Metropolitan Museum of Art attracts some five million people a year, more than any other spot in New York City. And it's no wonder—this place is magnificent. At 1.6 million square feet, this is the largest museum in the Western Hemisphere. Nearly all the world's cultures are on display through the ages—from Egyptian mummies to ancient Greek statuary to Islamic carvings to Renaissance paintings to Native American masks to 20th-century decorative arts—and masterpieces are the rule. You could go once a week for a lifetime and still find something new on each visit.

So unless you plan on spending your entire vacation in the museum (some people do), you cannot see the entire collection. One good way to get an overview is to take advantage of the little-known **Museum Highlights Tour,** offered every day at various times throughout the day (usually 10:15am–3:15pm; tours also offered in Spanish, Italian, German, and Korean). Visit the museum's website for a schedule of this and subject-specific walking tours (Old Master Paintings, American Period Rooms, Arts of China, Islamic Art, and so on); you can also get a schedule of the day's tours at the Visitor Services desk when you arrive. A daily schedule of **Gallery Talks** is available as well.

Highlights include the American Wing's **Garden Court,** with its 19th-century sculpture; the terrific ground-level **Costume Hall;** and the **Frank Lloyd Wright room.** The beautifully renovated **Roman and Greek galleries** are overwhelming, but in a marvelous way, as are the collections of **Byzantine Art** and later **Chinese art.** The highlight of the astounding **Egyptian collection** is the **Temple of Dendur,** in a dramatic, purpose-built glass-walled gallery with Central Park views. The **Greek Galleries,** which at last fully realize McKim, Mead & White's grand neoclassical plans of 1917, and the **Ancient Near East Galleries** are particularly noteworthy.

The big news at the Met this season is that after 50 years of being used as a dining area, the **Greek and Roman galleries** reopened in the spring of 2007. It follows a $220-million renovation that includes the redesign and expansion of the galleries to

---

Tips **Free Art on Friday**

Many museums have free admission (or "pay what you wish") on Friday evenings. They include **The American Folk Art Museum,** 45 W. 53rd St. (*©* **212/265-1040**) from 6 to 8pm; the **Asia Society,** 725 Park Ave. (*©* **212/327-9276**), from 6 to 9pm; **MoMA** (see below), from 4:30 to 8pm; the **Guggenheim** (p. 125), from 6 to 8pm; the **Whitney** (p. 129), from 6 to 9pm; and the **International Center of Photography** (p. 129), 1133 Sixth Ave. (*©* **212/857-0000**), from 6:30 to 8pm. Most other museums have late hours on Friday and Saturday, so even if you don't get free admission, you'll likely beat the crowds, which tend to thin out at night.

57,000 square feet. The galleries now exhibit ancient artifacts that had been in storage, with 30,000 of the square footage devoted to Roman collections.

Fifth Ave. at 82nd St. *©* **212/535-7710.** www.metmuseum.org. Admission (includes same-day entrance to the Cloisters) $15 adults, $10 seniors and students, free for children under 12 when accompanied by an adult. Sun, holiday Mon (Memorial Day, Labor Day), and Tues–Thurs 9:30am–5:15pm; Fri–Sat 9:30am–8:45pm. Closed Monday. Strollers are permitted in most areas—inquire at Information Desks for gallery limitations. Oversized and jogging strollers are prohibited. Subway: 4, 5, 6 to 86th St.

Museum of Modern Art 𝘈𝘈   The newer, larger MoMA, after a 2-year renovation, is almost twice the space of the original. The renovation, designed by Yoshio Taniguchi, highlights space and light, with open rooms, high ceilings, and gardens— a beautiful work of architecture and a perfect complement to the art within. This is where you'll find Van Gogh's *Starry Night,* Cézanne's *Bather,* Picasso's *Les Demoiselles d'Avignon,* and the great sculpture by Rodin, *Monument to Balzac.* Whenever I visit, I like to browse the fun "Architecture and Design" department, with examples of design for appliances, furniture, and even sports cars. MoMA also features edgy new exhibits and a celebrated film series that attracts serious cinephiles. But the heart of the museum remains the **Abby Aldrich Rockefeller Sculpture Garden,** which has been enlarged; the museum's new design affords additional views of this lovely space from other parts of the museum. MoMA is one of the most expensive museums in New York, but it does have a "free" day: on Fridays from 4 to 8pm.

11 W. 53rd St. (between Fifth and Sixth aves.). *©* **212/708-9400.** www.moma.org. Admission $20 adults, $16 seniors, $12 students, free for children under 16 accompanied by an adult. Sat–Mon and Wed–Thurs 10:30am–5:30pm; Fri 10:30am–8pm. Subway: E, V to Fifth Ave.; B, D, E to Seventh Ave.

Rockefeller Center 𝘈𝘈 *Moments*   A Streamline Art Deco masterpiece, Rockefeller Center is one of New York's central gathering spots for visitors and New Yorkers alike. Designated a National Historic Landmark in 1988, it's now the world's largest privately owned business-and-entertainment center, with 18 buildings on 21 acres.

For a dramatic approach to the entire complex, start at Fifth Avenue between 49th and 50th streets. The builders purposely created the gentle slope of the Promenade, known here as the **Channel Gardens** because it's flanked to the south by La Maison Française and to the north by the British Building (the Channel, get it?). The Promenade leads to the **Lower Plaza,** home to the famous ice-skating rink in winter (see next paragraph) and alfresco dining in summer in the shadow of Paul Manship's freshly gilded bronze statue *Prometheus,* more notable for its setting than its magnificence as an artwork. All around, the flags of the United Nations' member countries flap in the breeze. In December and early January, just behind *Prometheus,* towers the city's official and majestic Christmas tree.

The **Rink at Rockefeller Center** ✸ (© 212/332-7654; www.rockefellercenter.com) is tiny but positively romantic, especially during December, when the giant Christmas tree's multicolored lights twinkle from above. The rink is open from mid-October to mid-March.

The focal point of this "city within a city" is the **GE Building** ✸, at 30 Rockefeller Plaza, a 70-story showpiece towering over the plaza. It's still one of the city's most impressive buildings; walk through for a look at the granite-and-marble lobby, lined with monumental sepia-toned murals by José Maria Sert.

NBC television maintains studios throughout the complex. *Saturday Night Live* and *Late Night with Conan O'Brien* originate in the GE Building. NBC's *Today* show is broadcast live on weekdays from 7 to 10am from the glass-enclosed studio on the southwest corner of 49th Street and Rockefeller Plaza; come early if you want a visible spot, and bring your HI MOM! sign.

The 70-minute **NBC Studio Tour** (© 212/664-3700) will take you behind the scenes at the Peacock network. The tour changes daily, but may include the *Today* show, *NBC Nightly News, Dateline NBC,* and/or *Saturday Night Live* sets. Tickets are $18 for adults, $15 for seniors and children 6 to 16. You can reserve your tickets for either tour in advance (reservations are recommended) or buy them right up to tour time at the **NBC Experience** store, on Rockefeller Plaza at 49th Street. They also offer a 75-minute **Rockefeller Center Tour,** hourly every day between 10am and 4pm, costing $10 for adults, $8 for seniors and children 6 to 16; two-tour combination packages are available for $21.

The newly restored **Radio City Music Hall** ✸, 1260 Sixth Ave., at 50th Street (© 212/247-4777; www.radiocity.com), is perhaps the most impressive architectural feat of the complex. Designed by Donald Deskey and opened in 1932, it's one of the largest indoor theaters, with 6,200 seats. But its true grandeur derives from its magnificent Art Deco appointments. The crowning touch is the stage's great proscenium arch that from distant seats evokes a faraway sun setting on the horizon of the sea. The theater hosts the annual **Christmas Spectacular,** starring the Rockettes. The illuminating 1-hour **Stage Door Tour** is offered Monday through Saturday from 10am to 5pm, Sunday from 11am to 5pm; tickets are $16 for adults, $10 for children under 12.

Between 48th and 50th sts., from Fifth to Sixth aves. © 212/332-6868. www.rockefellercenter.com. Subway: B, D, F, V to 47th–50th sts./Rockefeller Center.

Solomon R. Guggenheim Museum ✸

It's been called a bun, a snail, a concrete tornado, and even a giant wedding cake; bring your kids, and they'll probably see it as New York's coolest opportunity for skateboarding. Whatever description you choose to apply, Frank Lloyd Wright's only New York building, completed in 1959, is best summed up as a brilliant work of architecture—so consistently brilliant that it competes with the art for your attention. If you're looking for the city's best modern art, head to MoMA or the Whitney first; come to the Guggenheim to see the house.

It's easy to see the bulk of what's on display in 2 to 4 hours. Inside, a spiraling rotunda circles over a slowly inclined ramp that leads you past changing exhibits that, in the past, have ranged from "The Art of the Motorcycle" to "Norman Rockwell: Pictures for the American People," said to be the most comprehensive exhibit ever of the

Heading for the Top of the Rock

Giving the Empire State Building some friendly competition when it comes to spectacular views, the observation deck of 30 Rockefeller Plaza is known as the **Top of the Rock** 👓👓. The deck that comprises floors 67 to 70 had been closed since 1986, but reopened in late 2005. The stately deck was constructed in 1933 to resemble a luxury ocean liner in all its grandeur, and unlike the Empire State Building, the observation deck here is more spacious and the views, though not quite as high, are just as stunning. You'll have just as much fun getting up to the deck as you will on the deck itself; the sky-shuttle elevator with a glass ceiling projects images from the 1930s through the present day as it zooms its way up. Reserved-time tickets help minimize the lines and are available online at **www.topoftherocknyc.com**. The observation deck is open daily from 8:30am to midnight; admission rates are $18 for adults, $16 for seniors, $11 for ages 6 to 11, and free for children under 6. For more information, call ℂ **877/NYC-ROCK** (877/692-7625) or 212/698-2000 or visit www.topoftherocknyc.com.

beloved painter's works. Usually the progression is counterintuitive: from the first floor up, rather than from the sixth floor down. If you're not sure, ask a guard before you begin. Permanent exhibits of 19th- and 20th-century art, including strong holdings of Kandinsky, Klee, Picasso, and the French Impressionists, occupy a stark annex called the **Tower Galleries,** an addition accessible at every level, but which some critics claim make the original look like a toilet bowl backed by a water tank (judge for yourself— I think there may be something to that view).

1071 Fifth Ave. (at 89th St.). ℂ 212/423-3500. www.guggenheim.org. Admission $18 adults, $15 seniors and students, free for children under 12, pay what you wish Fri 6–8pm. Sat–Wed 10am–5:45pm; Fri 10am–7:45pm. Subway: 4, 5, 6 to 86th St.

Staten Island Ferry 👓 𝘝𝘢𝘭𝘶𝘦   Here's New York's best freebie—especially if you just want to glimpse the Statue of Liberty and not climb her steps. You get an enthralling hour-long excursion (round-trip) into the world's biggest harbor. This is not strictly a sightseeing ride, but commuter transportation to and from Staten Island. As a result, during business hours you'll share the boat with working stiffs reading papers and drinking coffee inside, blissfully unaware of the sights outside.

You, however, should go on deck and enjoy the busy harbor traffic. The old orange-and-green boats usually have open decks along the sides or at the bow and stern; try to catch one of these boats if you can, since the newer white boats don't have decks. Grab a seat on the right side of the boat for the best view. On the way out of Manhattan, you'll pass the Statue of Liberty (the boat comes closest to Lady Liberty on the way to Staten Island), Ellis Island, and, from the left side of the boat, Governor's Island; you'll see the Verrazano Narrows Bridge spanning the distance from Brooklyn to Staten Island in the distance.

There's usually another boat waiting to depart for Manhattan. The skyline views are simply awesome on the return trip. It's all well worth the time spent.

Departs from the Whitehall Ferry Terminal at the southern tip of Manhattan. © 718/815-BOAT. www.ci.nyc.
ny.us/html/dot. Free admission ($3 for car transport on select ferries). 24 hr.; every 20–30 min. weekdays, less fre-
quently on off-peak and weekend hours. Subway: N, R to Whitehall St.; 4, 5 to Bowling Green; 1 to South Ferry (ride
in one of the 1st 5 cars).

Statue of Liberty ★★★ *Kids*   For the millions who first came by ship to America
in the last century—either as privileged tourists or needy, hopeful immigrants—Lady
Liberty, standing in the Upper Bay, was their first glimpse of America. No monument
so embodies the nation's, and the world's, notion of political freedom and economic
potential. Even if you don't make it out to Liberty Island, you can get a spine-tingling
glimpse from Battery Park, from the New Jersey side of the bay, or during a free ride
on the Staten Island Ferry (see above). It's always reassuring to see her torch lighting
the way.

Proposed by French statesman Edouard de Laboulaye as a gift from France to the
United States, commemorating the two nations' friendship and joint notions of liberty, the statue was designed by sculptor Frédéric-Auguste Bartholdi with the engineering help of Alexandre-Gustave Eiffel (who was responsible for the famed Paris
tower) and unveiled on October 28, 1886. *Touring tips:* Ferries leave daily every half-
hour to 45 minutes from 9am to about 3:30pm, with more frequent ferries in the
morning and extended hours in summer. Try to go early on a weekday to avoid the
crowds that swarm in the afternoon, on weekends, and on holidays.

A stop at **Ellis Island** (p. 122) is included in the fare, but if you catch the last ferry,
you can visit only the statue or Ellis Island, not both.

Note that you can **buy ferry tickets in advance** via **www.statuereservations.com**,
which will allow you to board the boat without standing in the sometimes-long ticket
line; however, there is an additional service charge attached. Even if you've already
purchased tickets, arrive as much as 30 minutes before your desired ferry time to allow
for increased security procedures prior to boarding the ferry. The ferry ride takes about
20 minutes.

Once on Liberty Island, you'll start to get an idea of the statue's immensity: It
weighs 225 tons and measures 152 feet from foot to flame. Its nose alone is 4½ feet
long, and the index finger is 8 feet long.

On Liberty Island in New York Harbor. © 212/363-3200 (general info), or 212/269-5755 (ticket/ferry info). www.
nps.gov/stli or www.circlelinedowntown.com. Free admission; ferry ticket to Statue of Liberty and Ellis Island $12
adults, $9.50 seniors, $4.50 children 3–17. Daily 9am–3:30pm (last ferry departs around 3:30pm); extended hours in
summer. Subway: 4, 5 to Bowling Green; 1 to South Ferry. Walk south through Battery Park to Castle Clinton, the fort
housing the ferry ticket booth.

Times Square *Overrated*   There's no doubting that Times Square has evolved into
something much different than it was over a decade ago when it had a deservedly
sleazy reputation. Yet there is much debate among New Yorkers about which incarnation was better. Times Square is a place New Yorkers go out of their way to avoid. The
crowds, even by New York standards, are stifling; the restaurants, mostly national
chains, aren't very good; the shopping, also mostly national chains, is unimaginative;
and the attractions, like **Madame Tussaud's New York** wax museum, are kitschy. I
suppose it's a little too Vegas for us. Still, you've come all this way—you've got to at
least take a peek, if only for the amazing neon spectacle of it all.

Most of the Broadway shows are centered on Times Square, so plan your visit
around your show tickets. For your predinner meal, walk 2 blocks west to Ninth

Avenue where you'll find a number of relatively inexpensive, good restaurants. If you are with the kids, the Ferris wheel in the **Toys "R" Us** store makes a visit to Times Square worthwhile.

Subway: A, C, E, N, Q, R, S, W, 1, 2, 3, 7 to 42nd St./Times Sq.

Wall Street & the New York Stock Exchange   Wall Street—it's an iconic name, and the world's prime hub for bulls and bears everywhere. This narrow 18th-century lane (you'll be surprised at how little it is) is appropriately monumental, lined with neoclassical towers that reach as far skyward as the dreams and greed of investors who built it into the world's most famous financial market.

At the heart of the action is the **New York Stock Exchange (NYSE),** the world's largest securities trader, where you can watch the billions change hands and get a fleeting idea of how the money merchants work. NYSE came into being in 1792, when merchants met daily under a nearby buttonwood tree to try to pass off to each other the U.S. bonds that had been sold to fund the Revolutionary War. By 1903 they were trading stocks of publicly held companies in this Corinthian-columned Beaux Arts "temple" designed by George Post. About 3,000 companies are now listed on the exchange, trading nearly 314 billion shares valued at about $16 trillion.

World Trade Center Site (Ground Zero)

Do you call a place where more than 3,000 people lost their lives an "attraction"? Or do you now call it a shrine? This is the quandary of the World Trade Center site. What had been a big hole for 5 years is a little more than that; construction began in early 2006 on the proposed "Freedom Tower" to be built at the site. But even though work is ongoing, there is still political bickering on what will rise from that hole. The new design retains essential elements of the original—soaring 1,776 feet into the sky, its illuminated mast evoking the Statue of Liberty's torch. From the square base, the Tower will taper into eight tall isosceles triangles, forming an octagon at its center. An observation deck will be located 1,362 feet aboveground. Of course, all this could change by the time this book comes out.

For now, you can see the site through a viewing wall on the Church Street side of the site; on that "Wall of Heroes" are the names of those who lost their lives that day along with the history of the site, including photos of the construction of the World Trade Center in the late 1960s and how, after it opened in 1972, it changed the New York skyline and downtown. A walk along the Wall of Heroes remains a painfully moving experience.

The site is bordered by Church, Barclay, Liberty, and West streets. Call ℂ 212/484-1222 or go to www.nycvisit.com or www.southstseaport.org for viewing information; go to www.downtownny.com for lower-Manhattan area information and rebuilding updates. The Tribute Center gives guided tours of the site. Call ℂ 212/422-3520 or visit www.tributewtc.org for more information. Tours are given Monday through Friday at 11am, 1pm, and 3pm; Saturday and Sunday at noon, 1pm, 2pm, and 3pm. The fee is $10 for adults; under 12 free.

20 Broad St. (between Wall St. and Exchange Place). (C) 212/656-3000. www.nyse.com. Subway: J, M, Z to Broad St.; 2, 3, 4, 5 to Wall St.

Whitney Museum of American Art ⭐

What is arguably the finest collection of 20th-century American art in the world is an imposing presence on Madison Avenue—an inverted three-tiered pyramid of concrete and gray granite with seven seemingly random windows designed by Marcel Breuer, a leader of the Bauhaus movement. The rotating permanent collection consists of an intelligent selection of major works by Edward Hopper, Georgia O'Keeffe, Roy Lichtenstein, Jasper Johns, and other significant artists. A pleasing second-floor exhibit space is devoted exclusively to works from its permanent collection from 1900 to 1950, while the rest of the space is dedicated to rotating exhibits.

The springtime **Whitney Biennial** (2004, 2006, and so on) is a major event on the national museum calendar. It serves as the premier launching pad for new American artists working on the vanguard in every media. Free **gallery tours** are offered daily, and music, screenings, and lectures fill the calendar.

945 Madison Ave. (at 75th St.). (C) 877/WHITNEY or 212/570-3676. www.whitney.org. Admission $15 adults, $10 seniors and students, free for children under 12, pay what you wish Fri 6–9pm. Wed–Thurs and Sat–Sun 11am–6pm; Fri 1–9pm. Subway: 6 to 77th St.

MORE MANHATTAN MUSEUMS

Cooper-Hewitt National Design Museum ⭐

Part of the Smithsonian Institution, the Cooper-Hewitt is housed in the Carnegie Mansion, built by steel magnate Andrew Carnegie in 1901 and renovated in 1996. Some 11,000 square feet of gallery space is devoted to changing exhibits that are invariably well conceived, engaging, and educational. Shows are both historic and contemporary in nature, and topics range from Charles and Ray Eames to Russell Wright to Disney theme parks. Many installations are drawn from the museum's own vast collection of industrial design, drawings, textiles, books, and prints.

2 E. 91st St. (at Fifth Ave.). (C) 212/849-8400. www.cooperhewitt.org. Admission $12 adults, $9 seniors and students, free for children under 12, free to all Fri 5–9pm. Mon–Thurs 10am–5pm; Fri 10am–9pm; Sat 10am–6pm; Sun noon–6pm. Subway: 4, 5, 6 to 86th St.

The Frick Collection ⭐⭐

One of the most beautiful mansions remaining on Fifth Avenue is a living testament to New York's vanished Gilded Age, graced with beautiful paintings rather than being a museum. Come here to see the classics by some of the world's most famous painters: Titian, Bellini, Rembrandt, Turner, Vermeer, El Greco, and Goya, to name only a few. A highlight of the collection is the **Fragonard Room,** with the sensual rococo series *The Progress of Love.* The portrait of Montesquieu by Whistler is also stunning. Sculpture, furniture, Chinese vases, and French enamels complement the paintings and round out the collection. Included in the price of admission, the AcousticGuide audio tour is particularly useful because it allows you to follow your own path rather than a prescribed route. In addition to the permanent collection, The Frick regularly mounts small, well-focused temporary exhibitions.

1 E. 70th St. (at Fifth Ave.). (C) 212/288-0700. www.frick.org. Admission $15 adults, $10 seniors, $5 students. Children under 10 not admitted; children under 16 must be accompanied by an adult. Tues–Sat 10am–6pm; Sun 11am–5pm. Closed all major holidays. Subway: 6 to 68th St./Hunter College.

International Center of Photography ⭐ *Finds*

The ICP is one of the world's premier educators, collectors, and exhibitors of photographic art. The state-of-the-art gallery space is ideal for viewing rotating exhibitions of the museum's 50,000-plus

> **Tips** *Intrepid* **in Dry Dock**
>
> The much-loved USS *Intrepid* battleship/museum is sitting in dry dock in Bay-onne, New Jersey, at the moment, and you won't be able to see it this time out. After getting stuck in the Hudson, the *Intrepid* was towed away from its home on the West Side piers for a much-needed refurbishment. It is scheduled to return to the pier at W. 46th St. sometime in 2008. For information and updates, call ℂ 212/245-0072 or visit www.intrepidmuseum.org.

prints as well as visiting shows. The emphasis is on contemporary photographic works, but historically important photographers aren't ignored. This place is a must on any photography buff's list.

1133 Sixth Ave. (at 43rd St.). ℂ 212/857-0000. www.icp.org. Admission $12 adults, $8 seniors and students, free for children under 12. Tues–Thurs and Sat–Sun 10am–6pm; Fri 10am–8pm. Subway: B, D, F, V to 42nd St.

Morgan Library ★★ *Finds*   This New York treasure, boasting one of the world's most important collections of original manuscripts, rare books and bindings, master drawings, and personal writings, has reopened after 2 years of extensive renovations. Those renovations include a welcoming entrance on Madison Avenue; new and reno-vated galleries, so that more of the library's holdings can be exhibited; a modern audi-torium; and a new Reading Room with greater capacity and electronic resources and expanded space for collections storage. Some of the Library's recent exhibitions include one on the life of **Bob Dylan** through music, letters, and memorabilia and an exhibit on illustrator **Saul Steinberg.** You can lunch in the intimate **Morgan Dining Room** as if you were dining in JP's own quarters.

225 Madison Ave. (between 36th and 37th sts). ℂ 212/590-0300. www.themorgan.org. Tues–Thurs 10:30am–5pm; Fri 10:30am–9pm; Sat 10am–6pm; Sun 11am–6pm. $12 adults, $8 seniors and students, free for children under 12. Subway: 4, 5, 6 to 33rd St.

South Street Seaport & Museum *Kids*   This landmark historic district on the East River encompasses 11 square blocks of historic buildings, a maritime museum, several piers, shops, and restaurants. The 18th- and 19th-century buildings lining the cobbled streets and alleyways are impeccably restored but nevertheless have a theme-park air about them, no doubt due to the mall-familiar shops housed within. The Sea-port's biggest tourist attraction is Pier 17, a historic barge converted into a mall, complete with food court and cheap jewelry kiosks.

Despite its rampant commercialism, the Seaport is well worth a look. There's a good amount of history to be discovered here, most of it around the **South Street Sea-port Museum,** a fitting tribute to the sea commerce that once thrived here.

In addition to the galleries—which house paintings and prints, ship models, scrimshaw, and nautical designs, as well as frequently changing exhibitions—there are a number of historic ships berthed at the pier to explore, including the 1911 four-masted *Peking* and the 1893 Gloucester fishing schooner *Lettie G. Howard.* A few of the boats are living museums and restoration works in progress; the 1885 cargo schooner ***Pioneer*** (ℂ 212/748-8786) offers 2-hour public sails daily from early May to September.

Even **Pier 17** has its merits. Head up to the third-level deck overlooking the East River, where the long wooden chairs will have you thinking about what it was like to cross the Atlantic on the *Normandie*. From this level you can see south to the Statue of Liberty, north to the Gothic majesty of the Brooklyn Bridge, and Brooklyn Heights on the opposite shore.

At the gateway to the Seaport, at Fulton and Water streets, is the **Titanic Memorial Lighthouse,** a monument to those who lost their lives when the ocean liner sank on April 15, 1912. It was erected overlooking the East River in 1913 and moved to this spot in 1968, just after the historic district was so designated.

At Water and South sts.; museum visitor center is at 12 Fulton St. © **212/748-8600** or 212/SEA-PORT. www.southst seaport.org. Museum admission $8 adults, $6 students and seniors, $4 children 5–12, free for children under 5. Museum Apr–Oct Tues–Sun 10am–6pm, Thurs 10am–8pm; Nov–Mar Fri–Mon 10am–5pm. Subway: 2, 3, 4, 5 to Fulton St. (walk east, or downslope, on Fulton St. to Water St.).

SKYSCRAPERS & OTHER ARCHITECTURAL HIGHLIGHTS

Cathedral of St. John the Divine ⟨⟩   The world's largest Gothic cathedral, St. John the Divine has been a work in progress since 1892. Its sheer size is amazing enough—a nave stretching the length of two football fields and with a seating capacity of 5,000—but keep in mind that there is no steel structural support. The church is being built using traditional Gothic engineering; blocks of granite and limestone are carved out by master masons and their apprentices—which may explain why construction is still ongoing, more than 110 years after it began, with no end in sight.

You can explore the cathedral on your own, or on the **Public Tour,** offered 6 days a week; also inquire about periodic (usually twice-monthly) **Vertical Tours,** which take you on a hike up the 11-flight circular staircase to the top for spectacular views. To hear the incredible pipe organ in action, attend the weekly **Choral Evensong and Organ Meditation** service, which highlights one of the nation's most treasured pipe organs, Sunday at 6pm.

1047 Amsterdam Ave. (at 112th St.). © **212/316-7490,** 212/932-7347 for tour information and reservations, 212/662-2133 for event information and tickets. www.stjohndivine.org. Suggested admission $2; tour $5. Mon–Sat 7am–6pm; Sun 7am–7pm. Tours offered Tues–Sat 11am; Sun 1pm. Worship services Mon–Sat 8 and 8:30am (morning prayer and holy Eucharist), 12:15pm, and 5:30pm (1st Thurs service 7:15am); Sun 8, 9, and 11am and 6pm; AIDS memorial service 4th Sat of the month at 12:15pm. Subway: B, C, 1 to Cathedral Pkwy.

Chrysler Building ⟨⟩⟨⟩   Built as Chrysler Corporation headquarters in 1930 (they moved out decades ago), this is perhaps the 20th century's most romantic architectural achievement, especially at night, when the lights in its triangular openings play off its steely crown. As you admire its facade, be sure to note the gargoyles reaching out from the upper floors. The observation deck closed long ago, but you can visit its lavish ground-floor interior, which is Art Deco to the max. The ceiling mural depicting airplanes and other early marvels of the first decades of the 20th century evince the bright promise of technology. The elevators are works of art, masterfully covered in exotic woods (especially note the lotus-shaped marquetry on the doors).

405 Lexington Ave. (at 42nd St.). Subway: S, 4, 5, 6, 7 to 42nd St./Grand Central.

Flatiron Building   This triangular masterpiece, so called for its resemblance to the laundry appliance, was one of the first U.S. skyscrapers. Its knife-blade wedge shape was the only building design possible for the triangular property created by the intersection of Fifth Avenue and Broadway, and that happy coincidence created one of the city's most distinctive landmarks. Built in 1902 and fronted with limestone and terra cotta (not iron), the Flatiron measures only 6 feet across at its narrow end. There's no observation deck, and the building mainly houses publishing offices; but there are a few shops on the ground floor. The building's existence has served to name the neighborhood around it: the Flatiron District, home to a bevy of smart restaurants and shops.

175 Fifth Ave. (at 23rd St.). Subway: R to 23rd St.

New York Public Library ⟨R⟩⟨R⟩   The New York Public Library, designed by Carrère & Hastings (1911), is one of the country's finest examples of Beaux Arts architecture, a majestic structure of white Vermont marble with Corinthian columns and allegorical statues. Before climbing the broad flight of steps to the Fifth Avenue entrance, take note of the famous lion sculptures—*Fortitude* on the right and *Patience* on the left—so dubbed by whip-smart former mayor Fiorello LaGuardia. At Christmastime, they don natty wreaths to keep warm.

This library is actually the **Humanities and Social Sciences Library,** only one of the research libraries in the New York Public Library system. The interior is one of the finest in the city and features **Astor Hall,** with high arched marble ceilings and grand staircases. The stupendous **Main Reading Rooms** have now reopened after a massive restoration and modernization that returned them to their stately glory and moved them into the computer age. Even if you don't stop in to peruse the periodicals, you may want to check out one of the excellent rotating **exhibitions.** Call or check the site for show schedules.

Fifth Ave. at 42nd St. ⟨C⟩ 212/930-0830 (exhibits and events) or 212/661-7220 (library hours). www.nypl.org. Free admission to all exhibitions. Thurs–Sat 10am–6pm; Tues–Wed 11am–7:30pm; Sun 1–5pm. Subway: B, D, F, V to 42nd St.; S, 4, 5, 6, 7 to Grand Central/42nd St.

St. Patrick's Cathedral   This incredible Gothic white-marble-and-stone structure is the largest Roman Catholic cathedral in the United States, as well as the seat of the Archdiocese of New York. Designed by James Renwick, begun in 1859, and consecrated in 1879, St. Patrick's wasn't completed until 1906. Strangely, Irish Catholics picked one of the city's WASPiest neighborhoods for St. Patrick's. After the death of the beloved John Cardinal O'Connor in 2000, Pope John Paul II installed Bishop Edward Egan, whom he elevated to cardinal in 2001. The vast cathedral seats a congregation of 2,200; if you don't want to come for Mass, you can pop in between services to get a look at the impressive interior.

Fifth Ave. (between 50th and 51st sts.). ⟨C⟩ 212/753-2261. Free admission. Sun–Fri 7am–8:30pm; Sat 8am–8:30pm. Mass Mon–Fri 7, 7:30, 8, and 8:30am, noon, and 12:30, 1, and 5:30pm; Sat 8 and 8:30am, noon, and 12:30 and 5:30pm; Sun 7, 8, 9, and 10:15am (Cardinal's mass), noon, and 1, 4, and 5:30pm; holy days 7, 7:30, 8, 8:30, 9, 11, and 11:30am, noon, and 12:30, 1, 5:30, and 6:30pm. Subway: B, D, F, V to 47th–50th sts./Rockefeller Center.

United Nations   In the midst of New York City is this working monument to world peace. The U.N. headquarters occupies 18 acres of international territory—neither the city nor the United States has jurisdiction here—along the East River from 42nd to 48th streets. Designed by an international team of architects (led by American Wallace K. Harrison and including Le Corbusier) and finished in 1952, the complex along the East River weds the 39-story glass slab Secretariat with the free-form General Assembly on beautifully landscaped grounds donated by John D. Rockefeller, Jr. A total of 180 nations use the facilities to arbitrate worldwide disputes.

Guided tours leave every half-hour or so and last 45 minutes to an hour.

At First Ave. and 46th St. ⟨C⟩ 212/963-8687. www.un.org/tours. Guided tours $12 adults, $9 seniors, $8.50 high-school and college students, $6.50 children 5–14. Children under 5 not permitted. Tours every half-hour Mon–Fri 9:30am–4:45pm and Sat–Sun 10am–4:30pm; closed weekends Jan–Feb; limited schedule may be in effect during the general debate (late Sept to mid-Oct). Subway: S, 4, 5, 6, 7 to 42nd St./Grand Central.

CENTRAL PARK

Without the miracle of civic planning that is **Central Park** ✸✸✸, Manhattan would be a virtual unbroken block of buildings. Instead, smack in the middle of Gotham, an 843-acre natural retreat provides a daily escape valve and tranquilizer for millions of New Yorkers.

On just about any day, Central Park is crowded with New Yorkers and visitors alike. On nice days, especially weekend days, it's the city's party central. The crowds are part of the appeal—folks come here to peel off their urban armor and relax, and the common goal puts a general feeling of camaraderie in the air. On these days, people-watching is more compelling here than anywhere else in the city. But even on the most crowded days, there's always somewhere to get away from it all, if you just want a little peace and quiet and a moment to commune with nature.

ORIENTATION & GETTING THERE   Look at your map—that great green swath in the center of Manhattan is Central Park. It runs from 59th Street (also known as Central Park S.) at the south end to 110th Street at the north end, and from Fifth Avenue on the east side to Central Park West (the equivalent of Eighth Ave.) on the west side. A 6-mile rolling road, **Central Park Drive,** circles the park, and has a lane set aside for bikers, joggers, and in-line skaters.

A number of subway stops and lines serve the park, and which one you take depends on where you want to go. To reach the southernmost entrance on the west side, take an A, B, C, D, or 1 train to 59th Street/Columbus Circle. To reach the southeast corner entrance, take the N or R to Fifth Avenue; from this stop, it's an easy walk into the park to the Information Center in the **Dairy** (✆ 212/794-6564; open daily 11am–5pm, to 4pm in winter), midpark at about 65th Street. Here you can ask questions, pick up park information, and purchase a good park map.

If your time for exploring is limited, I suggest entering the park at 72nd or 79th streets for maximum exposure (subway: B or C to 72nd St. or 81st St./Museum of Natural History). From here, you can pick up park information at the visitor center at **Belvedere Castle** (✆ 212/772-0210; open Tues–Sun 10am–5pm, to 4pm in winter), midpark at 79th Street. There's also a third visitor center at the **Charles A. Dana Discovery Center** (✆ 212/860-1370; open daily 11am–5pm, to 4pm in winter), at the northeast corner of the park at Harlem Meer, at 110th Street between Fifth and Lenox avenues (subway: 2 or 3 to Central Park N./110th St.). The Dana Center is also an environmental education center hosting workshops, exhibits, music programs, and park tours, and lends fishing poles for fishing in Harlem Meer (park policy is catch-and-release).

Food carts and vendors are set up at all of the park's main gathering points, selling hot dogs, pretzels, and ice cream, so finding a bite to eat is never a problem. You'll also find a fixed food counter at the **Conservatory,** on the east side of the park north of the 72nd Street entrance, and both casual snacks and more sophisticated New American dining at **The Boat House,** on the lake near 72nd Street and Park Drive North (✆ 212/517-2233).

SAFETY   Even though the park has the lowest crime rate of any of the city's precincts, keep your wits about you, especially in the more remote northern end. It's a good idea to avoid the park entirely after dark, unless you're heading to one of the restaurants for dinner or to **Shakespeare in the Park.**

VISITOR INFORMATION   Call ✆ 212/360-3444 for recorded information, or 212/310-6600 or 212/628-1036 to speak with a live person. Call ✆ **888/NY-PARKS**

for special-events information. The park also has two comprehensive websites that are worth checking out before you go: The city parks department's site at **www.central park.org** and the Central Park Conservancy's site at **www.centralparknyc.org**, both of which feature excellent maps and a far more complete rundown of park attractions and activities than there is room to include here. If you have an **emergency** in the park, dial ℂ **800/201-PARK,** which will link you directly to the park rangers.

EXPLORING THE PARK

The best way to see Central Park is to wander along the park's 58 miles of winding pedestrian paths, keeping in mind the following highlights.

The southern part of Central Park is more formally designed and heavily visited than the relatively rugged and remote northern end. Not far from the Dairy is the **Carousel** with 58 hand-carved horses (ℂ **212/879-0244;** open daily Apr–Nov 10am–6pm, to 4:30pm in winter; rides are $1); the zoo (see below); and the Wollman Rink for roller- or ice-skating.

The **Mall,** a long a formal walkway lined with elms shading benches and sculptures of sometimes forgotten writers, leads to the focal point of Central Park, **Bethesda Fountain** ⓡ (along the 72nd St. transverse road). **Bethesda Terrace** and its grandly sculpted entryway border a large **lake** where dogs fetch sticks, rowboaters glide by, and dedicated early-morning anglers try their luck at catching carp, perch, catfish, and bass. You can rent a rowboat at or take a gondola ride from **Loeb Boathouse,** on the eastern end of the lake. Boats of another kind are at **Conservatory Water** (on the east side at 73rd St.), a stone-walled pond flanked by statues of both **Hans Christian Andersen** and **Alice in Wonderland.** On Saturday at 10am, die-hard yachtsmen race remote-controlled sailboats in fierce competitions that follow Olympic regulations.

If the action there is too intense, **Sheep Meadow** on the southwestern side of the park is a designated quiet zone, where Frisbee throwing and kite flying are as energetic as things get. Another respite is **Strawberry Fields** ⓡ, at 72nd Street on the West Side. This memorial to John Lennon, who was murdered across the street at the Dakota apartment building (72nd St. and Central Park W., northwest corner), is a gorgeous garden area centered around an Italian mosaic bearing the title of the lead Beatle's most famous solo song and his lifelong message: IMAGINE. In keeping with its goal of promoting world peace, the garden has 161 varieties of plants, donated by each of the 161 nations in existence when it was designed in 1985. This is a wonderful place for peaceful contemplation.

Bow Bridge, a graceful lacework of cast iron, designed by Calvert Vaux, crosses over the lake and leads to the most bucolic area of Central Park, the **Ramble.** This dense 38-acre woodland with spiraling paths, rocky outcroppings, and a stream is the best spot for bird-watching and feeling as if you've discovered an unimaginably leafy forest right in the middle of the city.

North of the Ramble, **Belvedere Castle** is home to the **Henry Luce Nature Observatory** (ℂ **212/772-0210**), worth a visit if you're with children. From the castle, set on Vista Rock (the park's highest point at 135 ft.), you can look down on the **Great Lawn,** where softball players and sun worshippers compete for coveted greenery, and the **Delacorte Theater,** home to Shakespeare in the Park. The small **Shakespeare Garden** south of the theater is scruffy, but it does have plants, herbs, trees, and other bits of greenery mentioned by the playwright. Behind the Belvedere Castle is the **Swedish Cottage Marionette Theatre** ⓡ (ℂ **212/988-9093**), hosting various marionette plays for children throughout the year; call to see what's on.

Central Park

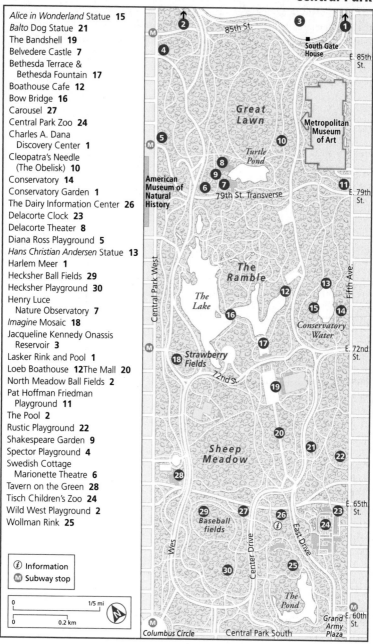

(i) Information
Ⓜ Subway stop

0   1/5 mi
0   0.2 km

Continue north along the east side of the Great Lawn, parallel to East Drive. Near the glass-enclosed back of the **Metropolitan Museum of Art** (p. 123) is **Cleopatra's Needle,** a 69-foot obelisk originally erected in Heliopolis around 1475 B.C. It was given to the city as a gift from the khedive of Egypt in 1880. (The khedive bestowed a similar obelisk to the city of London, which now sits on the Embankment of the Thames.)

North of the 86th Street Transverse Road is the **Jacqueline Kennedy Onassis Reservoir,** so named after the death of the beloved First Lady, who lived nearby and often enjoyed a run along the 1.5-mile jogging track that circles the reservoir.

North of the reservoir is my favorite part of the park. It's much less traversed and, in some areas, absolutely tranquil. The **North Meadow** (at 96th St.) features 12 baseball and softball fields.

North of the North Meadow, at the northeast end of the park, is the **Conservatory Garden** ✿ (at 105th St. and Fifth Ave.), Central Park's only formal garden, with a magnificent display of flowers and trees reflected in calm pools of water. **The Lasker Rink and Pool** (☎ 212/534-7639) is the only swimming pool in Central Park, and in the winter it's converted to a skating rink that offers a less hectic alternative to Wollman Rink. **Harlem Meer** and its boathouse have been renovated and look beautiful. The boathouse now berths the **Charles A. Dana Discovery Center,** near 110th Street between Fifth and Lenox avenues (☎ 212/860-1370), where children learn about the environment and borrow fishing poles for catch-and-release at no charge. **The Pool** (at W. 100th St.), possibly the most idyllic spot in all of Central Park, has been renovated and features willows, grassy banks, and a small pond populated by some very well-fed ducks. You might even spot an egret and a hawk or two lurking around here.

Central Park Zoo/Tisch Children's Zoo ✿ Kids

It has been over a decade since the zoo in Central Park was renovated, making it both more human and more humane. Lithe sea lions frolic in the central pool area with beguiling style. The gigantic but graceful polar bears (one of whom, by the way, made himself a true New Yorker when he began regular visits with a shrink) glide back and forth across a watery pool that has glass walls through which you can observe very large paws doing very smooth strokes. The monkeys seem to regard those on the other side of the fence with knowing disdain. In the hot and humid Tropic Zone, large, colorful birds swoop around in freedom, sometimes landing next to nonplused visitors.

Because of its small size, the zoo is at its best with the displays of smaller animals. The indoor multilevel Tropic Zone is a real highlight, its steamy rainforest home to everything from black-and-white colobus monkeys to Emerald tree boa constrictors to a leaf-cutter-ant farm; look for the new dart-poison-frog exhibit, which is very cool. So is the large penguin enclosure in the Polar Circle, which is better than the one at San Diego's Sea World. In the Temperate Territory, look for the Asian red pandas (cousins to the big black-and-white ones), which look like the world's most beautiful raccoons.

The entire zoo is good for short attention spans; you can cover the whole thing in 1½ to 3 hours, depending on the size of the crowds and how long you like to linger. It's also very kid-friendly, with lots of well-written and -illustrated placards that older kids can understand. For the littlest ones, there's the **Tisch Children's Zoo.** With pigs, llamas, potbellied pigs, and more, this petting zoo and playground are a real blast for the 5-and-under set. On the main path leading north from the Tisch Children's Zoo—at East Drive and 67th Street—is one of the most admired statues in the park: the bronze statue of the famous sled dog Balto, which stands on a rock outcropping and is a favorite with kids.

830 Fifth Ave. (at 64th St., just inside Central Park). © 212/439-6500. www.wcs.org/zoos. Admission $8 adults, $4 seniors, $3 children 3–12, free for children under 3. Summer hours (Apr–Oct) weekdays 10am–5pm, weekends 10am–5:30pm; winter hours (Nov–Mar) daily 10am–4:30pm. Last entrance 30 min. before closing. Subway: N, R to Fifth Ave.

ACTIVITIES IN THE PARK

The 6-mile rolling road circling the park, **Central Park Drive,** has a lane set aside for bikers, joggers, and in-line skaters. The best time to use it is when the park is closed to traffic: Monday to Friday 10am to 3pm (except Thanksgiving to New Year's) and 7 to 10pm. It's also closed from 7pm Friday to 6am Monday, but when the weather is nice, the crowds can be hellish.

BIKING   Off-road mountain biking isn't permitted; stay on Central Park Drive or your bike may be confiscated by park police.

You can rent 3- and 10-speed bikes as well as tandems in Central Park at the **Loeb Boathouse,** midpark near 74th Street and Park Drive North, just in from Fifth Avenue (© **212/517-2233** or 212/517-3623), for $9 to $15 an hour, with a complete selection of kids' bikes, cruisers, tandems, and the like ($200 deposit required); and at **Metro Bicycles,** 1311 Lexington Ave., at 88th Street (© **212/427-4450**). No matter where you rent, be prepared to leave a credit card deposit.

BOATING   From March to November, gondola rides and rowboat rentals are available at the **Loeb Boathouse,** midpark near 74th Street and Park Drive North, just in from Fifth Avenue (© **212/517-2233** or 212/517-3623). Rowboats are $10 for the first hour, $2.50 every 15 minutes thereafter, and a $20 deposit is required; reservations are accepted. (Note that rates were not set for the summer season at press time, so these may change.)

HORSE-DRAWN CARRIAGE RIDES   Horses belong on city streets as much as chamber pots belong in our homes. You won't need me to tell you how forlorn most of these horses look; if you insist, rides start at the entrance to the park at 59th Street and Central Park South, and cost about $50 for two for a half-hour, but I suggest skipping it.

ICE-SKATING   Central Park's **Wollman Rink** ⊛, on the east side of the park between 62nd and 63rd streets (© **212/439-6900;** www.wollmanskatingrink.com), is the city's best outdoor skating spot, more spacious than the tiny rink at Rockefeller Center. It's open for skating generally from mid-October to mid-April, depending on the weather. Rates are $8.50 for adults, $4.50 for seniors and kids under 12, and skate rental is $4.75; lockers are available (locks are $6.75). **Lasker Rink** (© **212/534-7639**), on the east side around 106th Street, is a less expensive alternative to the much more crowded Wollman Rink. Open November through March. Rates are $4.50 for adults, $2.25 for kids under 12, and skate rental is $4.75.

IN-LINE SKATING   Central Park is the city's most popular place for blading. See the beginning of this section for details on Central Park Drive, the main drag for skaters. On weekends, head to West Drive at 67th Street, behind Tavern on the Green, where you'll find trick skaters weaving through an NYRSA slalom course at full speed, or the Mall in front of the band shell (above Bethesda Fountain) for twirling to tunes. In summer, **Wollman Rink** converts to a hotshot roller rink, with half-pipes and lessons available (see "Ice-Skating," above).

You can rent skates for $20 a day from **Blades Board and Skate,** 120 W. 72nd St., between Broadway and Columbus Avenue (© 212/787-3911; www.blades.com). Wollman Rink (above) also rents in-line skates for park use at similar rates.

PLAYGROUNDS   Nineteen Adventure Playgrounds are scattered throughout the park, perfect for jumping, sliding, tottering, swinging, and digging. At Central Park West and 81st Street is the **Diana Ross Playground** 👧, voted the city's best by *New York* magazine. Also on the west side is the **Spector Playground,** at 85th Street and Central Park West, and, a little farther north, the **Wild West Playground** at 93rd Street. On the east side is the **Rustic Playground,** at 67th Street and Fifth Avenue, a delightfully landscaped space rife with islands, bridges, and big slides; and the **Pat Hoffman Friedman Playground,** right behind the Metropolitan Museum of Art at East 79th Street, is geared toward older toddlers.

RUNNING   Marathoners and wannabes regularly run in Central Park along the 6-mile **Central Park Drive,** which circles the park (please run toward traffic to avoid being mowed down by wayward cyclists and in-line skaters). The **New York Road Runners** (© 212/860-4455; www.nyrrc.org), organizers of the New York City Marathon, schedule group runs 7 days a week at 6am and 6pm, leaving from the park entrance at 90th Street and Fifth Avenue.

ORGANIZED SIGHTSEEING TOURS

Gray Line New York Tours   Gray Line offers just about every sightseeing tour option and combination you could want. There are bus tours by day and by night that run uptown, downtown, and all around the town, as well as bus combos with Circle Line cruises, helicopter flights, museum admittance, and guided visits of sights. There's no real point to purchasing some combination tours—you don't need a guide to take you to the Statue of Liberty, and you don't save any money on admission by buying the combo ticket.

777 Eighth Ave. (between 47th and 48th sts.). Tours depart from additional Manhattan locations. © 800/669-0051 or 212/445-0848. www.graylinenewyork.com. Hop-on, hop-off bus tours from $49 adults, $39 children 5–11.

Circle Line Sightseeing Cruises 👧👧   Circle Line is the only tour company that circumnavigates the entire 35 miles around Manhattan, and I love this ride. The **Full Island** cruise takes 3 hours and passes by the Statue of Liberty, Ellis Island, the Brooklyn Bridge, the United Nations, Yankee Stadium, the George Washington Bridge, and more, including Manhattan's wild northern tip. The panorama is riveting, and the commentary isn't bad. The big boats are basic but fine, with lots of deck room for everybody to enjoy the view. Snacks, soft drinks, coffee, and beer are available onboard for purchase.

If 3 hours is more than you or the kids can handle, go for either the **Semi-Circle** or **Sunset/Harbor Lights** cruises, both of which show you the highlights of the skyline in 1½ hours.

Departing from Pier 83, at W. 42nd St. and Twelfth Ave. Also departing from Pier 16 at South St. Seaport, 207 Front St. © 212/563-3200. www.circleline42.com and www.seaportmusiccruises.com. Sightseeing cruises $21–$30.50 adults, $17–$26 seniors, $13–$18 children under 13. Subway to Pier 83: A, C, E to 42nd St. Subway to Pier 16: J, M, Z, 2, 3, 4, 5 to Fulton St.

ESPECIALLY FOR KIDS

Some of New York's sights and attractions are designed specifically with kids in mind, and I've listed those below. But many of those I've discussed in the rest of this chapter are terrific for kids as well as adults; look for the kids icon next to the attraction.

MUSEUMS

In addition to the museums discussed below, which are designed specifically for kids, also consider the following, discussed elsewhere in this chapter: the **American Museum of Natural History** (p. 120), whose dinosaur displays are guaranteed to wow both you and the kids, and the **South Street Seaport & Museum** (p. 130), which little ones will love for its theme park–like atmosphere and old boats bobbing in the harbor.

Children's Museum of the Arts *Kids*   Interactive workshop programs for children ages 1 to 12 and their families are the attraction here. Kids dabble in puppet making and computer drawing or join in singalongs and live performances. Also look for rotating exhibitions of the museum's permanent collection featuring WPA work. Call or check the website for the current exhibition and activities schedule.

182 Lafayette St. (between Broome and Grand sts.). *C* **212/941-9198** or 212/274-0986. www.cmany.org. Admission $8 for everyone under 66, pay-what-you-wish Thurs 4–6pm. Wed–Sun noon–5pm (Thurs to 6pm). Subway: 6 to Spring St.

Children's Museum of Manhattan *Kids*   Here's a great place to take the kids when they're tired of being told not to touch. Designed for ages 2 to 12, this museum is strictly hands-on. Interactive exhibits and activity centers encourage self-discovery—and a recent expansion means that there's now even more to keep the kids busy and learning. The Time Warner Media Center takes children through the world of animation and helps them produce their own videos. The Body Odyssey is a zany, scientific journey through the human body. This isn't just a museum for the 5-and-up set—there are exhibits especially designed for babies and toddlers, too. The busy schedule also includes daily art classes and storytellers, and a full slate of entertainment on weekends.

212 W. 83rd St. (between Broadway and Amsterdam Ave.). *C* **212/721-1234.** www.cmom.org. Admission $9 children and adults, $6 seniors. School season Wed–Sun and school holidays 10am–5pm; summer Tues–Sun 10am–5pm. Subway: 1 to 86th St.

New York Hall of Science *Kids*   Children of all ages will love this huge hands-on museum, which bills itself as "New York's Only Science Playground." Exhibits allow visitors to be engulfed by a giant soap bubble, float on air in an antigravity mirror, and compose music by dancing in front of light beams. There's a Preschool Discovery Place for the really little ones. But probably best of all is the summertime Outdoor Science Playground for kids 6 and older—ostensibly lessons in physics, but really just a great excuse to laugh, jump, and play on jungle gyms, slides, seesaws, spinners, and more. The museum is located in **Flushing Meadows–Corona Park,** where kids can have even more fun beyond the Hall of Science. Not only are there more than 1,200 acres of park and playgrounds, but there are also a zoo, a carousel, an indoor ice-skating rink, an outdoor pool, and bike and boat rentals. Kids and grown-ups alike will love getting an up-close look at the Unisphere steel globe, which was not really destroyed in *Men in Black.* The park is also home to the Queens Museum of Art as well as Shea Stadium and the U.S. Open Tennis Center.

47–01 111th St., in Flushing Meadows–Corona Park, Queens. *C* **718/699-0005.** www.nyscience.org. Admission $11 adults, $8 seniors and children 2–17, free on Fri 2–5pm Sept–June 30. Additional $3 for Science Playground. Mon–Thurs 9:30am–2pm; Fri 9:30am–5pm; Sat–Sun 10am–6pm (Mon–Fri 9:30am–5pm July–Aug). Subway: 7 to 111th St.

SPECTATOR SPORTS

BASEBALL   With two baseball teams in town, you can catch a game almost any day from opening day in April to the beginning of the playoffs in October. (Don't bother trying to get subway series tix, though—they're the hottest seats in town. Ditto for opening day or any playoff game.)

Both teams have new stadiums in the works scheduled to open in 2009. For now, however, the Amazin' **Mets** play at **Shea Stadium** in Queens (subway: 7 to Willets Point/Shea Stadium). For tickets and information, call the **Mets Ticket Office** at © **718/507-TIXX,** or visit www.mets.com.

The **Yankees** play at the House That Ruth Built, otherwise known as **Yankee Stadium** (subway: C, D, or 4 to 161st St./Yankee Stadium; call **Ticketmaster** (© **212/307-1212** or 212/307-7171; www.ticketmaster.com) or Yankee Stadium (© **718/293-6000;** www.yankees.com). Serious baseball fans might check the schedule well in advance and try to catch **Old Timers' Day,** usually held in July, when pinstriped stars of years past return to the stadium to take a bow.

MINOR-LEAGUE BASEBALL 🎯   Boasting their very own waterfront stadium, the **Brooklyn Cyclones,** a Mets farm team, have been a major factor in the revitalization of Coney Island; spanking-new Keyspan Park sits right off the legendary boardwalk (subway: F, N, Q, or W to Stillwell Ave./Coney Island). The **SI Yanks** also have their own shiny new playing field, the Richmond County Bank Ballpark, just a 5-minute walk from the Staten Island Ferry terminal (subway: N or R to Whitehall St.; 4 or 5 to Bowling Green; 1 to South Ferry). What's more, with bargain-basement ticket prices at around $10, this is a great way to experience baseball in the city for a fraction of the major-league hassle and cost. Both teams have already developed a rabidly loyal fan base, so it's a good idea to buy your tickets for the summer season—which runs June through September—in advance. For the Cyclones, call © **718/449-8497** or visit www.brooklyncyclones.com; to reach the SI Yanks, call © **718/720-9200** or go online to www.siyanks.com.

BASKETBALL   For two pro teams, home court is **Madison Square Garden,** Seventh Avenue between 31st and 33rd streets (© **212/465-6741** or www.thegarden.com; 212/307-7171 or www.ticketmaster.com for tickets; subway: A, C, E, 1, 2, or 3 to 34th St.): the **New York Knicks** (© **877/NYK-DUNK** or 212/465-JUMP; www.nyknicks.com) and the **New York Liberty** (© **212/465-6080;** www.wnba.com/liberty). Knicks tickets are hard to come by, so plan ahead if you want a front-row seat near first fan Spike Lee.

ICE HOCKEY   The **New York Rangers** play at Madison Square Garden, Seventh Avenue between 31st and 33rd streets (© **212/465-6741;** www.newyorkrangers.com or www.thegarden.com; subway: A, C, E, 1, 2, or 3 to 34th St.). The Rangers have been going through tough times, but tickets are hard to get nevertheless; so plan well ahead. Call © **212/307-7171,** or visit www.ticketmaster.com for online orders.

6 Shopping Highlights

For a terrific Big Apple shopping guide that's loaded with store listings, I recommend *Suzy Gershman's Born to Shop New York* (Wiley Publishing, Inc.).

CHINATOWN

Don't expect to find the purchase of a lifetime on Chinatown's streets, but enjoy the quality browsing. The fish and herbal markets along Canal, Mott, Mulberry, and Elizabeth streets are fun for their bustle and exotica. Dispersed among them (especially along **Canal St.**), you'll find a mind-boggling collection of knockoff sunglasses and watches, cheap backpacks, discount leather goods, and exotic souvenirs. It's a fun day-time browse, but don't expect quality—and be sure to bargain before you buy. (Also, skip the bootleg CDs, video, and software—these are stolen goods, and you *will* be disappointed with the product.) **Mott Street,** between Pell Street and Chatham Square, boasts the most interesting of Chinatown's off-Canal shopping, with an antiques shop or two dispersed among the tiny storefronts selling blue-and-white Chinese dinnerware. Just around the corner, peek into **Ting's Gift Shop** (18 Doyer St.; ✆ 212/962-1081), one of the oldest operating businesses in Chinatown. Under a vintage pressed-tin ceiling, it sells good-quality Chinese toys, kits, and lanterns.

THE LOWER EAST SIDE

The bargains aren't quite what they used to be in the **Historic Orchard Street Shopping District**—which basically runs from Houston to Canal along Allen, Orchard, and Ludlow streets, spreading outward along both sides of Delancey Street—but prices on leather bags, shoes, luggage, and fabrics on the bolt are still quite good. Be aware, though, that the hard sell on Orchard Street can be pretty hard to take. Still, the district is a nice place to discover a part of New York that's disappearing. Come during the week, since most stores are Jewish-owned and, therefore, close Friday afternoon and all day Saturday. Sunday tends to be a madhouse.

The artists and other trendsetters who have been turning this neighborhood into a bastion of hip have also added a cutting edge to its shopping scene in recent years. You'll find a growing—and increasingly upscale—crop of alternative shops south of Houston and north of Grand Street, between Allen and Clinton streets. Before you browse, stop into the **Lower East Side Visitor Center,** 261 Broome St., between Orchard and Allen streets (✆ 866/224-0206 or 212/226-9010; **www.lowereastsideny.com**; subway: F to Delancey St.).

SOHO

People love to complain about superfashionable SoHo—it's become too trendy, too tony, too Mall of America. True, **J. Crew** is only one of many big names that have supplanted the artists and galleries that inhabited its historic cast-iron buildings. But SoHo is still one of the best shopping 'hoods in the city—and few are more fun to browse. It's the epicenter of cutting-edge fashion and still boasts plenty of unique boutiques. The streets are chock-full of tempting stores, so just come and browse.

SoHo's shopping grid runs from Broadway west to Sixth Avenue, and Houston Street south to Canal Street. **Broadway** is the most commercial strip, with such recognizable names as **Pottery Barn, Banana Republic, Sephora,** and **A/X Armani Exchange. H&M,** the popular Swedish department store with cutting-edge fashions sold at unbelievably low prices, has two stores that face one another on Broadway. **Bloomingdale's** has opened up a downtown branch in the old Canal Jean space. **Prada**'s flagship store, also on Broadway, is worth visiting for its spacious, almost soothing design alone (by Dutch architect Rem Koolhaus). A definite highlight is the two-story **Pearl River** Chinese emporium, which offers everything from silk *cheongsam* (traditional Chinese high-necked dresses) to teaware.

The big names in avant-garde fashion have landed in SoHo, but you'll also find one-of-a-kind boutiques, such as the **Hat Shop,** 120 Thompson St., between Prince and Spring streets (✆ 212/219-1445), a full-service milliner for women that also sells plenty of off-the-rack toppers, plus shoe stores galore and high-end home design and housewares boutiques.

THE EAST VILLAGE

The East Village personifies bohemian hip. The easiest subway access is the no. 6 train to Astor Place, and from there, it's just a couple of blocks east.

East 9th Street between Second Avenue and Avenue A is lined with an increasingly smart collection of boutiques, proof that the East Village isn't just for kids anymore. Designers, including **Jill Anderson** (331 E. 9th St.; ℂ **212/253-1747**) and **Huminska** (315 E. 9th St.; ℂ **212/677-3458**) sell excellent-quality and original fashions for women along here.

If it's strange, illegal, or funky, it's probably available on **St. Marks Place,** which takes over for 8th Street, running east from Third Avenue to Avenue A. This skanky strip is a permanent street market, with countless T-shirt and cheap-jewelry stands. The height of the action is between Second and Third avenues, which is prime hunting grounds for used-record collectors.

GREENWICH VILLAGE

The West Village is great for browsing and gift shopping. Specialty book- and record stores, antiques and craft shops, and gourmet food markets dominate. The Village isn't much of a destination for fashion hunters, with the exception of NYU territory: 8th Street between Broadway and Sixth Avenue for trendy footwear and affordable fashions, and Broadway from 8th Street south to Houston, anchored by **Urban Outfitters** at 628 Broadway, between Bleecker and Houston streets (ℂ **212/475-0009;** www.urbanoutfitters.com), and dotted with skate and sneaker shops. Clothes hounds looking for volume shopping are better off elsewhere.

But the biggest shopping boom of late has happened on **Bleecker Street** west of Sixth Avenue. Between Carmine Street and Seventh Avenue, foodies will delight in the strip of boutique food shops, including **Amy's Bread, Wild Edibles,** and **Murray's Cheese** (in a large new space). In between are record stores, guitar shops, and a sprinkling of artsy boutiques. On **Christopher Street,** the center of Village gay life, you'll find wonders like **Aedes De Venutas,** a gorgeous boutique selling fabulous perfumes and scented candles that are difficult to find in the States, and **The Porcelain Room,** 13 Christopher St. (ℂ **212/367-8206**), which is located below street level and offers amazing antique and contemporary porcelains that have to be seen to be believed. **The Oscar Wilde Bookshop,** the world's first gay bookstore, has been situated on the sleepy eastern end of Christopher Street since 1967. Follow Christopher Street westward where Bleecker becomes boutique alley and one jewel box of a shop follows another, among them **Intermix, Olive & Bette, Ralph Lauren, Lulu Guinness,** and **Marc Jacobs.**

Those who really love to browse should also wander **west of Seventh Avenue** and along **Hudson Street,** where charming shops like **House of Cards and Curiosities,** 23 Eighth Ave., between Jane and 12th streets (ℂ **212/675-6178**), the Village's own funky take on an old-fashioned nickel-and-dime store, are tucked among the brownstones.

THE FLATIRON DISTRICT & UNION SQUARE

When 23rd Street was the epitome of New York uptown fashion more than 100 years ago, the major department stores stretched along **Sixth Avenue** for about a mile from 14th Street up. These elegant stores stood in huge cast-iron buildings that were long ago abandoned and left to rust. In the past several years, however, the area has grown into the city's discount shopping center, with superstores and off-pricers filling up the renovated spaces: **Filene's Basement, T.J. Maxx,** and **Bed Bath & Beyond** are all at 620 Sixth Ave., near 18th Street, while **Old Navy** is next door, and **Barnes & Noble** is just a couple of blocks away at Sixth Avenue near 22nd Street.

On Broadway, just a few blocks north of Union Square, is **ABC Carpet & Home** (881 and 888 Broadway, at 19th St.; ℭ **212/473-3000;** www.abccarpet.com), a magnet for aspiring Martha Stewarts, if any of those are still out there. If it's actually a rug you're looking for, a whole slew of imported carpet dealers line Broadway from ABC north to about 25th Street.

Upscale retailers who have rediscovered the architectural majesty of **lower Fifth Avenue** include **Banana Republic, Victoria's Secret,** and **Kenneth Cole.** You won't find much that's new along here, but it's a pleasing stretch nonetheless.

HERALD SQUARE & THE GARMENT DISTRICT

Herald Square—where 34th Street, Sixth Avenue, and Broadway converge—is dominated by **Macy's** (W. 34th St. and Broadway; ℭ **212/695-4400;** www.macys.com), the self-proclaimed world's biggest department store. And a few blocks north of Macy's is that dowager of department stores, **Lord & Taylor** (424 Fifth Ave.; ℭ **212/391-3344;** www.lordandtaylor.com).

TIMES SQUARE & THE THEATER DISTRICT

This neighborhood has become increasingly family oriented, hence: Richard Branson's rollicking **Virgin Megastore;** the fabulous **Toys "R" Us** flagship on Broadway and 44th Street, which even has its own full-scale Ferris wheel; and the mammoth **E-Walk** retail and entertainment complex on 42nd Street between Seventh and Eighth avenues, overflowing with mall-familiar shops like the **Museum Company.**

West 47th Street between Fifth and Sixth avenues is the city's famous **Diamond District.** The street is lined shoulder-to-shoulder with showrooms, and you'll be wheeling and dealing with the mostly Hasidic dealers, who are quite a juxtaposition to the crowds. You'll also notice a wealth of **electronics stores** throughout the neighborhood, many suspiciously trumpeting GOING OUT OF BUSINESS sales. These guys have been going out of business since the Stone Age. That's the bait-and-switch: Pretty soon you've spent too much money for not enough stereo. If you want to check out what they have to offer, find out beforehand the going price on that PDA or digital camera you're interested in. You can make a good deal if you know exactly what the market is, but these guys will be happy to suck you dry given half a chance.

FIFTH AVENUE & 57TH STREET

The heart of Manhattan retail is the corner of Fifth Avenue and 57th Street. There was a time when only the very rich could shop these sacred crossroads. Such is not the case anymore, now that **Tiffany & Co.** (727 Fifth Ave.; ℭ **212/755-8000;** www.tiffany.com), which has long reigned supreme here, sits a stone's throw from **Niketown** (6 E. 57th St.; ℭ **212/891-6453;** http://niketown.nike.com) and the **NBA Store** (666 Fifth Ave.; ℭ **212/515-NBA1;** www.nbastore.com). In addition, a good number of mainstream retailers, like **Banana Republic,** have flagships along Fifth, further democratizing the avenue. Still, you will find a number of big-name, big-ticket designers and jewelers radiating from the crossroads, as well as chichi department stores like **Bergdorf Goodman** (754 Fifth Ave.; ℭ **212/753-7300**), **Henri Bendel** (712 Fifth Ave.; ℭ **212/247-1100**), and **Saks Fifth Avenue** (611 Fifth Ave.; ℭ **212/753-4000;** www.saksfifthavenue.com), all of which help the avenue maintain its classy cachet.

A few blocks east on Lexington is the world's flagship **Bloomingdale's,** 1000 Third Ave. (Lexington Ave. at 59th St.; *©* **212/705-2000;** www.bloomingdales.com), a great place to shop.

MADISON AVENUE

Madison Avenue from 57th to 79th streets boasts the most expensive retail real estate in the world. Bring lots of plastic. This ultradeluxe strip—particularly in the high 60s—is home to *the* most luxurious designer boutiques, with **Barneys New York** as the anchor. Don't be intimidated by the glamour or any of the celebrities you're likely to bump into. There are affordable treasures to be had, such as the Ginger Flower room spray at **Shanghai Tang** (714 Madison Ave.; *©* **212/888-0111**) or a pair of crystal cuff links at the **Lalique** boutique next door at 712 Madison Ave. (*©* **212/355-6550**).

UPPER WEST SIDE

The Upper West Side's best shopping street is **Columbus Avenue.** Small shops catering to the neighborhood's white-collar mix of young hipsters and families line both sides of the pleasant avenue from 66th Street (where you'll find an excellent branch of **Barnes & Noble**) to about 86th Street. Highlights include **Maxilla & Mandible** for museum-quality natural-science–based gifts, and **Harry's Shoes,** but you won't lack for good browsing along here. **The Shops at Columbus Circle,** in the new Time Warner Center, also has a world of upscale choices for shopping.

7 New York City After Dark

For the latest nightlife listings, check out *Time Out New York* (www.timeoutny.com), a comprehensive weekly magazine of events; the free *Village Voice* (www.villagevoice.com), the city's legendary alternative paper; and the *New York Times* website of events, **www.ny today.com.**

GETTING TICKETS   Buying tickets can be simple if the show you want to see isn't sold out. You need only call such general numbers as **TeleCharge** (*©* **212/239-6200;** www.telecharge.com), which handles most Broadway and Off-Broadway shows and some concerts; or **Ticketmaster** (*©* **212/307-4100;** www.ticketmaster.com), which also handles Broadway and Off-Broadway shows and most concerts.

DISCOUNT TICKETS   The best deal in town on same-day tickets for both Broadway and Off-Broadway shows is at the **Times Square Theatre Centre,** better known as the **TKTS** booth run by the nonprofit Theatre Development Fund in the heart of the Theater District. At press time, its long-time home at Duffy Square, 47th Street and Broadway, was undergoing renovation, and it was temporarily housed across the street outside the New York Marriott Marquis between Broadway and Eighth avenues. The new booth is set to open by the end of 2007. The booth is open 3 to 8pm for evening performances, 10am to 2pm for Wednesday and Saturday matinees, and from 11am to 8pm on Sunday for all performances. Tickets for that day's performances are usually offered at half-price, with a few reduced only 25%, plus a $2.50 per ticket service charge. Boards outside the ticket windows list available shows; you're unlikely to find certain perennial or outsize smashes, but most other shows turn up. Only cash and traveler's checks are accepted (no credit cards). There's often a huge line, so show up early for the best availability and be prepared to wait—but, frankly, the crowd is all part of the fun. If you don't care much what you see and you'd just like to go to a show, you can walk right up to the window later in the day and something will always be available.

Visit **www.tdf.org** or call **NYC/Onstage** at © **212/768-1818** and press "8" for the latest TKTS information.

THE PERFORMING ARTS

Brooklyn Academy of Music *(finds* BAM is the city's most renowned contemporary arts institution, presenting cutting-edge theater, opera, dance, and music. Offerings have included historically informed presentations of baroque opera by William Christie and Les Arts Florissants; pop opera from Lou Reed; Marianne Faithfull singing the music of Kurt Weill; dance by Mark Morris and Mikhail Baryshnikov; the Philip Glass ensemble accompanying screenings of *Koyannisqatsi* and Lugosi's original *Dracula;* the Royal Dramatic Theater of Sweden directed by Ingmar Bergman; and many more experimental works by both renowned and lesser-known international artists as well as visiting companies from all over the world. 30 Lafayette Ave. (off Flatbush Ave.), Brooklyn. © **718/636-4100.** www.bam.org. Subway: 2, 3, 4, 5, M, N, Q, R, W to Pacific St./Atlantic Ave.

Carnegie Hall *(finds(finds* Perhaps the world's most famous performance space, Carnegie Hall offers everything from grand classics to the music of Ravi Shankar. The **Isaac Stern Auditorium,** the 2,804-seat main hall, welcomes visiting orchestras from across the country and the world. Many of the world's premier soloists and ensembles give recitals. The legendary hall is both visually and acoustically brilliant; don't miss an opportunity to experience it if there's something on that interests you.

There's also the intimate 268-seat **Weill Recital Hall,** usually used to showcase chamber music and vocal and instrumental recitals. Carnegie Hall has also, after being occupied by a movie theater for 38 years, reclaimed the ornate underground 650-seat **Zankel Concert Hall.** 881 Seventh Ave. (at 57th St.). © **212/247-7800.** www.carnegiehall.org. Subway: N, Q, R, W to 57th St.

City Center Modern dance usually takes center stage in this Moorish dome-topped performing arts palace. The companies of Merce Cunningham, Martha Graham, Paul Taylor, Alvin Ailey, Twyla Tharp, the Dance Theatre of Harlem, and the American Ballet Theatre are often on the calendar. Don't expect cutting edge—but do expect excellence. Sightlines are terrific from all corners, and a new acoustical shell means the sound is pitch-perfect. 131 W. 55th St. (between Sixth and Seventh aves.). © **877/247-0430** or 212/581-1212. www.citycenter.org. Subway: F, N, Q, R, or W to 57th St.; B, D, or E to Seventh Ave.

Lincoln Center for the Performing Arts New York is the world's premier performing arts city, and Lincoln Center is its premier institution. Lincoln Center's many buildings serve as permanent homes to their own companies as well as major stops for world-class performance troupes from around the globe.

Resident companies include the **Metropolitan Opera** (© **212/362-6000;** www.metopera.org), which ranks first in the world. The opera house also hosts the **American Ballet Theatre** (www.abt.org) each spring, as well as visiting companies such as the Kirov, Royal, and Paris Opera ballets. The **New York State Theater** (© **212/870-5570**) is the home of the **New York City Ballet** (www.nycballet.com), with performances in winter and spring, and the New York City Opera (www.nycopera.com), a superb company with lower prices than the Met.

Symphony-wise, you'd be hard-pressed to do better than the phenomenal **New York Philharmonic** *(finds* (© **212/875-5656;** www.newyorkphilharmonic.org), which performs at Avery Fisher Hall.

Additional resident companies include the **Chamber Music Society of Lincoln Center** (© **212/875-5788;** www.chambermusicsociety.org), which performs at Alice

Tully Hall or the Daniel and Joanna S. Rose Rehearsal Studio. The **Film Society of Lincoln Center** (✆ **212/875-5600;** www.filmlinc.com) screens a daily schedule of movies at the Walter Reade Theater, and it hosts a number of important annual film and video festivals, as well as the Reel to Real program for kids, pairing silent-screen classics with live performances. **Lincoln Center Theater** (✆ **212/362-7600;** www.lct. org) consists of the Vivian Beaumont Theater, a modern and comfortable venue with great sightlines that has been home to much good Broadway drama, and the Mitzi E. Newhouse Theater, a well-respected Off-Broadway house that has also boasted numerous theatrical triumphs.

Check Lincoln Center's website to see what special events will be on while you're in town. **Tickets** for all performances at Avery Fisher and Alice Tully halls can be purchased through **CenterCharge** (✆ **212/721-6500**) or online at www.lincolncenter.org. Tickets for all Lincoln Center Theater performances can be purchased thorough **TeleCharge** (✆ **212/239-6200;** www.telecharge.com). Tickets for New York State Theater productions (New York City Opera and Ballet companies) are available through **Ticketmaster** (✆ **212/307-4100;** www.ticketmaster.com), while tickets for films showing at the Walter Reade Theater can be bought up to 7 days in advance by calling ✆ **212/496-3809.**

Offered daily, 1-hour **guided tours** of Lincoln Center tell the story of the great performing arts complex, and even offer glimpses of rehearsals; call ✆ **212/875-5350.** 70 Lincoln Center Plaza (at Broadway and 64th St.). ✆ **212/546-2656** or 212/875-5456. www.lincoln center.org. Subway: 1 to 66th St.

LIVE ROCK, JAZZ, BLUES & MORE

In addition to the listings below, you'll find a slew of music clubs on and around Bleecker Street in Greenwich Village, between 6th Avenue and Broadway.

Dizzy's Club Coca-Cola ✪   This beautiful, cozy new jazz club is part of the Jazz at Lincoln Center complex in the Time Warner Center on Columbus Circle. Acoustics and sightlines are excellent, and, though not nearly as dramatic as the window in the complex's Allen Room, there is a window behind the stage with views of Central Park and the city. The club attracts an interesting mix of both up-and-coming and established bands. Every Monday, the club features the Upstarts, a student showcase from local schools including Juilliard and the Manhattan School of Music. My only complaint is the high $30 cover every day of the week—even for the Upstarts. Time Warner Center, 60th St. and Broadway. ✆ **212/258-9598.** www.jalc.org. Subway: A, B, C, D, 1 to Columbus Circle.

The Knitting Factory   New York's premier avant-garde music venue has four separate spaces, each showcasing performances ranging from experimental jazz and acoustic folk to spoken-word and poetry readings to out-there multimedia works. Regulars who use the Knitting Factory as their lab of choice include former Lounge Lizard John Lurie; around-the-bend experimentalist John Zorn; guitar gods Vernon Reid and David Torn; and television's Richard Lloyd. (If these names mean nothing to you, chances are good that the Knitting Factory is not for you.) There are often two showtimes a night in the remarkably pleasing main performance space. 74 Leonard St. (between Broadway and Church St.). ✆ **212/219-3006.** www.knittingfactory.com. Subway: 1 to Franklin St.

Smoke ✪✪ (Value)   A superstar in the New York jazz scene and the best place to hear it on the Upper West Side, Smoke is a welcome throwback to the informal, intimate clubs of the past—the kind of place where on most nights you can just walk in and experience solid jazz. Though it seats only 65, for no more than a $30 cover, Smoke still manages to attract big names like the Steve Turre Quartet, Ron Carter, Eddie Henderson, and John Hicks. Sunday through Thursday, there is no cover. On Sundays, the club features Latin jazz; every Tuesday, I groove to my favorite Hammond organ riffs played by Mike LeDonne. There are three sets nightly and a very popular happy hour. 2751 Broadway (between 105th and 106th sts.). (℗ 212/864-6662. www.smokejazz.com. Subway: 1 to 103rd St.

S.O.B.'s If you like your music hot, hot, hot, visit S.O.B.'s, the city's top world-music venue, specializing in Brazilian, Caribbean, and Latin sounds. The packed house dances and sings along nightly to calypso, samba, mambo, African drums, reggae, or other global grooves, united in the high-energy, feel-good vibe. Bookings include top-flight performers from around the globe; Astrud Gilberto, Mighty Sparrow, King Sunny Ade, Eddie Palmieri, Buckwheat Zydeco, Beausoleil, and Baaba Maal are only a few of the names of those who have graced this lively stage. The room's Tropicana Club style has island pizazz that carries through to the Caribbean-influenced cooking and extensive tropical-drinks menu. This place is so popular that it's an excellent idea to book in advance, especially if you'd like table seating. Monday is dedicated to Latin sounds, Tuesday to reggae, Friday features a late-night French Caribbean dance party, while Saturday is reserved for samba. 204 Varick St. (at Houston St.). (℗ 212/243-4940. www.sobs.com. Subway: 1 to Houston St.

The Village Vanguard What CBGB was to rock, The Village Vanguard is to jazz. One look at the photos on the walls will show you who's been through since 1935, from Coltrane, Miles, and Monk to Wynton Marsalis and Chuchu Valdes. Expect a mix of established names and high-quality local talent, including the Vanguard's own jazz orchestra on Monday nights. The sound is great, but sightlines aren't; so come early for a front table. 178 Seventh Ave. S. (just below 11th St.). (℗ 212/255-4037. www.villagevanguard.net. Subway: 1, 2, 3 to 14th St.

6

Long Island & the Hamptons

by Rich Beattie

You've likely heard some joke about Long Island: its malls, its residents' distinctive accent, the ungodly traffic on the Long Island Expressway (LIE). Here's the truth about the largest island adjoining the continental U.S: Yes, there are malls; yes, some people have an accent; and absolutely, the traffic on the LIE can be nightmarish. Part of it is, after all, a gigantic suburb of New York City.

But look beyond that and you'll find an island ringed by some of the nation's—some would say the world's—best beaches, a thin stretch of land dotted with award-winning wineries, and an area that reflects America's earliest history.

The key to visiting is to stay close to the shoreline, where you'll enjoy beach-based recreation, along with great views of the Atlantic Ocean and the Long Island Sound. Long Island also has the most interesting remnants of its history, from the early seaside whaling villages to the homes of wealthy industrialists who co-opted the water views for themselves. Drive east along the north shore, through the towns of Sandy Point and Oyster Bay,

and you'll see where those barons built their palatial mansions.

Continue out to the North Fork and you'll find a laid-back world that in many ways has yet to catch up with the modern era: farmstands, vineyards, antiques shops, and little towns that still bear the marks of their 17th-century whaling past. But not everything is rooted in the past: You'll find a cutting-edge culinary scene here as well.

Along the southern shore, Jones Beach and Long Beach make great day trips from New York City, while Fire Island is a magical, car-free beach community and a world unto itself. Go out to the Hamptons, the beach playground for New York City–based celebs, and you may just catch an impromptu Billy Joel concert or dine with Martha Stewart. Just 100 miles from the New York City border to the island's easternmost tip at Montauk, the Hamptons have an entirely different culture, where playing hard is a way of life. And tucked in between the North and South forks is tiny Shelter Island, another piece of pristine earth that completes the Long Island playground.

1 The North Shore ★

From Great Neck to Wading River

Drive slowly along the quiet back roads of Long Island's north shore and you just might hear it: the faint murmur of a rollicking party, with ghostly musicians stirring up hot jazz as bootleg liquor flows as freely as the wealth. The towns that line the coast have been inhabited by some of America's richest citizens for decades, and that still holds true. Towns like Great Neck and Sea Cliff have cute village centers, while just outside their borders lie homes of mammoth proportions. Drive along Route 25A into

Suffolk County and the towns become even cuter: Northport, Stony Brook, and Port Jefferson give new meaning to the word *quaint.*

The **Gold Coast,** as it came to be known in the Roaring Twenties, was the domain of F. Scott Fitzgerald's *The Great Gatsby.* The area was famous for its glorious excess in everything from mansions to parties. It is where America's most powerful tycoons—bearing names like Astor and Vanderbilt—bought up to 1,000 acres of land and built 100-room mansions based on English manor houses and French châteaux. While fox hunts are a thing of the past, and the Long Island Expressway now cuts through many of those former estates, some of these homes still remain and can be glimpsed on a drive, along with great views of Long Island Sound. Start in the exclusive community of Great Neck and drive along the main road, Route 25A; its two lanes are responsible for moving tons of traffic. Continue east and the cars start to dissipate. You'll come to Sagamore Hill, Theodore Roosevelt's summer home. Pass through sleepy Centerport and eventually the terrain becomes even more rural, with farms cropping up as you approach the North Fork.

A word of advice for beach lovers: Stick with the south shore. The few beaches that do exist on the north shore tend to be on the rocky side.

ESSENTIALS
GETTING THERE
BY CAR   The **Long Island Expressway** (I-495) is your quickest way through here, when it's not packed with traffic. Avoid rush hour at all costs!

BY TRAIN   More than 80 million people ride the **Long Island Rail Road (LIRR).** For schedule and fare information, call ℂ **516/822-LIRR** or 631/231-LIRR or visit www.mta.info/lirr. The LIRR services 124 Long Island stations and makes more than 20 stops along the north shore, including Great Neck, Manhasset, Port Washington, Oyster Bay, Locust Valley, Glen Cove, Sea Cliff, Roslyn, Westbury, Hicksville, Syosset, Cold Spring Harbor, Huntington, Northport, St. James, Stony Brook, and Port Jefferson. Cab service is available at all stations; you can just show up and get a cab or check the LIRR website for phone numbers.

BY PLANE   LaGuardia and John F. Kennedy airports lie just over the Long Island Border in New York City (p. 72). **Long Island MacArthur Airport,** situated mid-island in Islip (ℂ **631/467-3210;** www.macarthurairport.com), is the closest airport and is served by **Southwest** (ℂ **800/435-9792;** www.southwest.com), **U.S. Airways** (ℂ **800/428-4322;** www.usairways.com), **Continental Express** (ℂ **800/523-3273;** www.continental.com), **Delta Express** (ℂ **800/325-5205;** www.delta.com), and **ATA** (ℂ **800/I-FLY-ATA;** www.ata.com).

BY FERRY   The **Bridgeport & Port Jefferson Ferry Company,** 102 W. Broadway, Port Jefferson (ℂ **631/473-0286;** www.bpjferry.com), makes the 1¼-hour trip between Port Jefferson and Bridgeport, Connecticut, every 90 minutes from 6am to 9pm on weekdays and 16 times from Friday to Sunday. Car and driver cost is $45; foot passengers pay $15.

VISITOR INFORMATION   The **Long Island Convention and Visitors Bureau** (ℂ **877/FUN-ON-LI** or 631/951-3440; www.licvb.com) has an office at 330 Motor Pkwy., Suite 203, Hauppauge. It's open Monday to Friday from 9am to 5pm; call or visit for all the info you can handle.

Long Island

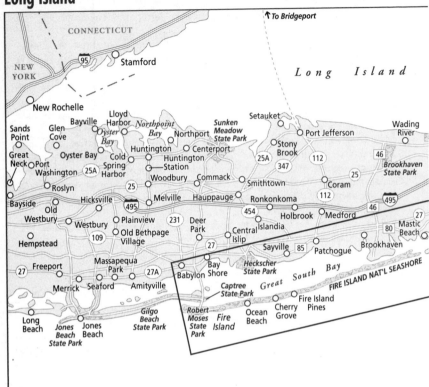

GETTING AROUND A car is essential on Long Island. **Avis** (© 800/331-1212; www.avis.com) has offices in Islip, Massapequa, Huntington Station, Smithtown, Stonybrook, Lynbrook, Roslyn, Melville, Port Jefferson, and Port Washington; **Budget** (© 800/527-0700; www.budget.com) has offices in Farmingdale, Garden City, Hicksville, and Huntington Station; **Dollar** (© 800/800-3665; www.dollar.com) has offices in Islip and Roslyn; and **Hertz** (© 800/654-3131; www.hertz.com) has offices in Islip, Great Neck, Huntington, West Hempstead, Middle Island, Lynbrook, Centereach, East Northport, Farmingdale, and Hicksville.

SPORTS & OUTDOOR PURSUITS

GOLF The Red Course at **Eisenhower Park**, East Meadow (© 516/572-0327), was home to the 1926 PGA Championship and was a stop for the PGA Seniors Tour in 2003. But it's a public course—so you can go make your own history. Or bring your clubs to **Bethpage State Park**, 99 Quaker Meeting House Rd., Farmingdale (© 516/249-0700), home to the 2002 U.S. Open and the host of the same event in 2009.

HITTING THE BEACH Though the north shore shouldn't be your first choice for beaches—they tend to be rocky and often quite small—there are a couple of nice ones that allow for swimming in the calm waters of Long Island Sound or for lounging on the sand. The beach in **Governor Alfred E. Smith/Sunken Meadow State Park**,

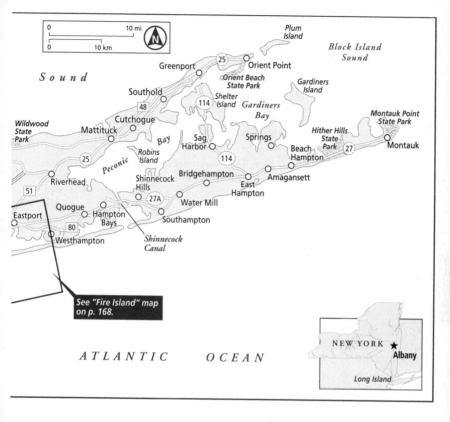

Kings Park (© **631/269-4333**), is 3 miles of sand with tall, glacier-formed bluffs at its western end. Farther east, **Wildwood State Park,** in Wading River (© **631/929-4314**), has 2 miles of beach.

SPECTATOR SPORTS   Long Island's only pro sports team is the NHL's **New York Islanders,** who play 40 of their 80 games from October to April at the Nassau Coliseum in Uniondale (© **800/882-ISLE;** www.newyorkislanders.com).

SHOPPING

ANTIQUES   Route 25A is dotted with lots of little antiques stores, and you'll find a town full of them when you reach Port Jefferson. Along the way, there are a couple of standout villages.

   Cold Spring Harbor is a quiet little town with a couple of nice places to shop. Of special note is the **Huntington Antiques Center,** 129 Main St. (© **631/549-0105**), where you'll find collections from about 20 dealers. There are lots of 18th- and early-19th-century items from England, France, and America, as well as an excellent collection of antique Oriental rugs.

   Tiny Locust Valley, rarely even plotted on Long Island maps, is a favorite of Long Island antiques hunters in the know. **Oster-Jensen,** 86 Birch Hill Rd. (© **516/676-5454**), carries everything from American country–style antiques to furniture in Federal,

> ## *Value* Getaway Trains
>
> From June to October, the LIRR offers 1-day getaways from New York City, which include train fare, connecting bus or ferry fees (if necessary), and entrance fees to museums. Some are specialty tours of Long Island Wine Country, for example, or the Montauk Lighthouse. Others are beach getaways to places like Fire Island. For trips that aren't guided tours, be sure to return on the same day or you'll end up paying twice for the return ride. Visit **www.mta.info/lirr/getaways** for details.

English Georgian, and Regency styles. There's a host of smaller items as well. **Locust Valley Antiques,** 94 Forest Ave. (© **516/676-5000**), boasts two large showrooms of European and Continental artwork and furniture. For a pleasant lunch break, grab one of the best burgers on Long Island at Buckram Stables Café, 31 Forest Ave. (© **516/671-3080**).

RETAIL   One of the most renowned shopping strips on the East Coast is the so-called "Miracle Mile." The real name is the **Americana Manhasset,** 2060 Northern Blvd., Manhasset (© **800/818-6767** or 516/627-2277), where you'll find such high-end retailers as Brooks Brothers, Tiffany, Talbots, Louis Vuitton, Burberry, Prada, and the ubiquitous Banana Republic and the Gap. Take a break for a fine lunch (salads, paninis, and more) at Cipollini (© **516/627-7172**).

GOLD COAST MANSIONS

Old Westbury Gardens 🎭🎭   Worshipers of formal gardens will be in heaven, and even casual nature lovers will adore the 160 landscaped and blooming acres of the former Phipps estate. Stroll among the wildflower-filled nooks, lilac-laden walkways, wide-open lawns, formal rose gardens, and meticulously maintained ponds—all in a constantly changing display of seasonal colors. Step inside the property's gorgeous, Charles II–style three-story mansion furnished with fine English antiques and decorative arts; it's virtually unchanged from when the Phipps family lived here in the early 20th century.

71 Old Westbury Rd., Old Westbury. © 516/333-0048. www.oldwestburygardens.org. Admission $10 adults, $8 seniors 62 and over, $5 children 7–12, free for children under 7. Mid-Apr to late Oct Wed–Mon 10am–5pm; last vehicle allowed on property at 4pm. Take LIE exit 39 (Glen Cove Rd.). Follow the service road east for 1 mile, turn right onto Old Westbury Rd., and continue ⅗ mile. The gate is on the left. LIRR to Westbury; it's just a 2½-mile taxi ride from there.

Planting Fields Arboretum/Coe Hall 🎭🎭   This grand expanse of historic buildings and greenhouses, the former estate of Standard Oil heiress Mai Rogers Coe and insurance king William Robertson Coe, is one of the few remaining Gold Coast properties to remain intact. As in its heyday of the 1920s, the 409 acres boast formal gardens, hiking trails, and two greenhouses with unique displays. The main building, Coe Hall, is a showy, 65-room Tudor Revival mansion that has many original pieces and furnishings, along with wood and stone carvings, stained-glass windows, and murals.

Planting Fields Rd., Oyster Bay. © 516/922-8600. www.plantingfields.com. Grounds daily 9am–5pm; $6 parking fee daily May–Oct, other times weekends only. Coe Hall admission $6.50 adults, $5 seniors and students, $2 children 7–12, free for children under 7. Coe Hall tours daily Apr–Sept noon–3:30pm. LIE to exit 41N. Take Rte. 106 north into Oyster Bay. Left on Lexington Ave., left on Mill River Rd., and follow the signs. LIRR to Oyster Bay; it's a 1½-mile taxi ride.

Sagamore Hill 🎭🎭🎭   Theodore Roosevelt's testosterone-laden tribute to hunting, oak, and all things manly still stands on 100 gorgeous acres overlooking Long Island

Sound. His 23-room Victorian estate, the so-called summer White House from 1902 to 1908, has been preserved just the way he liked it—full of animal heads, skins, and exotic treasures—and visiting is a fun experience that also gives you some good historical insight. The home reflects his travels as a Rough Rider in Cuba, big-game hunter in East Africa, and fearless explorer in the Brazilian Amazon. You must take a guided tour, which leaves on the hour and lasts about an hour. On summer weekends, arrive early—tour tickets tend to sell out by early afternoon.

Cove Neck Rd., Oyster Bay. © 516/922-4788. www.nps.gov/sahi. Admission $5 adults, free for children under 16. Daily tours of the house on the hour 10am–4pm. Grounds dawn–dusk. Labor Day to Memorial Day Wed–Sun only. LIE to exit 41 north (NY 106 north). Take 106 north to Oyster Bay and follow signs. LIRR to Oyster Bay or Syosset; it's a 3-mile taxi ride from Oyster Bay and 6 miles from Syosset, but it's easier to find cabs at the Syosset station.

Sands Point Preserve ✦   You'll think you've died and gone to medieval Europe at this place. The castles on these grounds are a stunning display of the extravagance and wealth from a different era. Created by Howard Gould, son of railroad tycoon Jay Gould, the 100,000-square-foot 1904 castle (Castlegould) and 1912 Tudor-style manor, Hempstead House (residence of second owner, Daniel Guggenheim), sit on gorgeous property. Unfortunately, due to renovations and recent administrative changes, those buildings may not be open. But also on the grounds is the beautiful Falaise, a Normandy-style manor house decked out in period furnishings, which was built by Harry F. Guggenheim in 1923.

   Bonus: The grounds have extensive nature trails. Pick up a picnic lunch (you can't miss with a sandwich from Best Bagels, 40 Middle Neck Rd., Great Neck; © **516/482-9860**) and make a day of it.

127 Middleneck Rd., Sands Point (Port Washington). © 516/571-7900. www.sandspointpreserve.org. It's $2 to visit the preserve on weekends Memorial Day to Labor Day (rest of the year it's free); weekdays are always free. 10am–5pm. Falaise: May–Oct Thurs–Sun noon–3pm. Admission $6 adults, $5 seniors. LIE to exit 36N, go straight 6 miles via Searingtown Rd., Port Washington Blvd., and Middleneck Rd. to entrance.

Vanderbilt Museum and Planetarium ✦✦ *Kids*   The word *planetarium* may conjure up memories of horrid grade-school road trips. But before you dismiss this domed building, know that the planetarium was opened by the county merely to help sustain the amazing mansion and museum adjoining it in back. The real reason to come to William K. Vanderbilt II's 43-acre estate is to see the overly extravagant, 24-room Spanish Revival mansion, built in three stages from 1910 to 1936. Rooms exemplify his eclectic taste and amazing worldwide collection from the fields of art and science. Don't miss the Hall of Fish, a collection of fish species unknown in this part of the world during Vanderbilt's lifetime. Don't completely dismiss the planetarium either—the shows are great for kids.

180 Little Neck Rd., Centerport. © 631/854-5555. www.vanderbiltmuseum.org. $10 adults, $9 seniors and students, $6 children under 12 for general admission and choice of guided mansion tour, daytime planetarium show, or daytime laser show; $3 for each additional. General admission only, $7 adults, $6 seniors and students, $3 children under 12. Late June to early Sept Tues–Sat 10am–5pm, Sun noon–5pm; early Sept to Oct Tues–Sun noon–5pm; Nov–Apr Tues–Fri noon–4pm, Sat–Sun noon–5pm; May to late June Tues–Sun noon–5pm. LIE to exit 51, go north on Deer Park Ave., bear left at the fork onto Park Ave. At 3rd light, turn right onto Broadway, continue for 5 miles to Rte. 25A. Cross 25A (to left of Shell gas station), and you're on Little Neck Rd.

MORE MUSEUMS & ATTRACTIONS

Heckscher Museum of Art ✦   It would be great if we all could afford a huge collection of eclectic artwork and build a small Beaux Arts museum to house it. But we all can't be like industrialist August Heckscher, who did just that in 1920. Today, this impressive and wide-ranging collection has more than 1,800 paintings, sculptures, and other works ranging from Egyptian artifacts to Renaissance art to the noted collection from the Hudson River and Long Island landscape schools.

2 Prime Ave., Huntington. © 631/351-3250. www.heckscher.org. Suggested $5 admission adults, $3 seniors and students, $1 children 5–12, free for children under 5. Tues–Fri 10am–5pm; Sat–Sun 1–5pm; 1st Fri of month until 8:30pm. LIE to exit 49N, take Rte. 110N into Huntington, turn right on 25A, make a left at the 1st light. LIRR to Huntington; it's a 3-mile taxi ride.

John P. Humes Japanese Stroll Garden 🦋🦋 Walking meditation is the goal at this extremely serene Japanese garden, set amid 4 acres of deep woodland. Step through the gate and you'll be awash in *yamazato,* or the transcendent feeling of a remote mountain hideout. Follow the trail, a symbolic path to enlightenment that takes you past a lake garden, as well as the shrubs and rocks that are essential to imperial garden design. The garden is the dream child of Ambassador Humes, who was inspired by a 1960 visit to Kyoto, Japan. Today, it's a refuge from the world. For a special treat, come to a tea ceremony held just a couple of days per month (no reservations required, but call for schedule).

Oyster Bay Rd. and Dogwood Lane, Mill Neck. © 516/676-4486. Admission $7 adults, free for children under 12; $12 for tour with tea ceremony. Mid-Apr to mid-Oct Sat–Sun 11:30am–4:30pm. LIE to exit 39N to Northern Blvd., turn right and go 3 miles to Wolver Hollow Rd., turn left to end, turn right on Chicken Valley Rd.; go 1¾ miles to Dogwood Lane, turn right.

Nassau County Museum of Art 🦋🦋 One of the finest suburban art museums in the nation, this surprisingly notable collection sits on 145 acres in a home once owned by steel baron Henry Clay Frick. Today, there's a wide variety of artwork to peruse. The permanent collection has more than 600 works of 19th- and 20th-century European and American artists like Edouard Vuillard, Roy Lichtenstein, and Robert Rauschenberg. You'll also find changing exhibits, along with formal gardens and an outdoor sculpture area that are glorious to walk through on a nice day. For an even bigger experience, the Tee Ridder Miniature Museum is also on the grounds.

1 Museum Dr., Roslyn Harbor. © 516/484-9338. www.nassaumuseum.com. Admission $10 adults, $8 seniors, $4 children and students, free for children under 5. Tues–Sun 11am–4:45pm. LIE to exit 39, go north 2 miles to Northern Blvd. (Rte. 25A) and turn left. At the 2nd light turn right. LIRR to Roslyn; it's a 2-mile taxi ride.

Walt Whitman Birthplace You don't have to be a *Leaves of Grass* fan to enjoy this famous poet's birthplace, a tiny historic home that looks oddly out of place in the heart of strip-mall country. Though Whitman left here at an early age, Long Island was always home for him. An interpretation center has a good collection of his manuscripts and photographs, and a chronology of his career as journalist, editor, and Civil War correspondent, along with recordings of Whitman reading his own work. The home is an interesting step back in time, since it looks much as it did when Whitman was born in 1819, though it has been outfitted with replacement furniture.

246 Old Walt Whitman Rd., West Hills. © 631/427-5240. Admission $4 adults, $3 seniors, free for children under 18. Mid-June to Labor Day Mon–Fri 11am–4pm, Sat–Sun noon–5pm; Labor Day to mid-June Wed–Fri 1–4pm, Sat–Sun 11am–4pm. LIE to exit 49N, north 1¾ miles, turn left on Old Walt Whitman Rd.

WHERE TO STAY

Many chain hotels put the Gold Coast within easy reach: **Holiday Inn Express,** 3131 Nesconset Hwy., Centereach (© 631/471-8000); **Hampton Inn,** 680 Commack Rd., Commack (© 631/462-5700); and the **Hilton,** 598 Broad Hollow Rd., Melville (© 631/845-1000).

Sunday Driving

While some north shore towns can't claim huge Vanderbilt mansions or sprawling gardens, they still are great places to take a drive. **Sea Cliff** began as a Methodist summer campground in 1871 and now boasts some two dozen homes on the National Register of Historic Places (as well as 900 structures built before World War II). Come to walk the steep streets and admire the Victorian homes with their gingerbread porches and Gothic gables. Then stop off at Memorial Park for spectacular sunsets over the water. You won't even find **Locust Valley** on many maps—this very cute small town (just 1 sq. mile) is full of great antiques shops and boutiques and is one of the island's biggest secrets. **Cold Spring Harbor** 🏕 is another antiques-filled haven right on the water; Route 25A takes you through town and offers some gorgeous water views. Stop in at the **Whaling Museum** 🏕, Main Street (🕾 631/367-3418), then walk the length of Main Street (it's only ¼ mile) and admire some of the structures dating back to the days when whaling was the backbone of industry here. Named after the third U.S. president, **Port Jefferson** is a bustling town on the water, full of restaurants, antiques shops, marinas, and cute storefronts. It's also a docking point for one of the Connecticut ferries, so it's constantly in motion, especially in the summer.

EXPENSIVE

Danford's on the Sound 🏕🏕🏕   A sprawling resort right on Long Island Sound, Danford's is its own Colonial New England–style village imbued with a nautical theme. The spacious quarters are decorated in navy blue, red, and gold with furniture that's comfortable, but perhaps a bit too formal for this laid-back seafaring town. Get a room with a view of the Port Jefferson harbor and it will be filled with light; balcony rooms let you take in the sea air.

25 E. Broadway, Port Jefferson, NY 11777. 🕾 **800/332-6367** or 631/928-5200. Fax 631/928-9082. www.danfords.com. 86 units. Apr–Oct $149–$229 double, $259–$409 suite; Nov–Mar $129–$169 double, $209–$409 suite. Weekend packages available. AE, DC, DISC, MC, V. **Amenities:** Restaurant; lounge; exercise room; spa; salon; limited room service; in-room massage; babysitting; laundry service; same-day dry cleaning. *In room:* A/C, TV w/pay movies, dataport, kitchenette (in some rooms), coffeemaker, hair dryer, iron.

The Three Village Inn 🏕🏕   You may have to duck to get through some of the doorways in this charming 1750s country inn, set on the harbor. That, of course, is just the point. With the exposed beams, narrow hallways, and antiques, you'll feel like you're padding around in your grandmother's attic. The all-nonsmoking rooms aren't huge, but they're comfy and decked out in pastels, with frilly drapes. Cottages give you a bit more space and some have extras you won't find in the inn, such as stone fireplaces and water views.

150 Main St., Stony Brook, NY 11790. 🕾 **631/751-0555.** Fax 631/751-0593. www.threevillageinn.com. 26 units. $139–$179 double Sun–Thurs, $179–$225 double Fri–Sat. Rates include breakfast. AE, DISC, MC, V. LIE to exit 62; north 10 miles to Rte. 25A; left 1½ miles at HISTORIC STONY BROOK sign to Main St.; right ½ mile to the inn. **Amenities:** Restaurant; lounge; small business center. *In room:* A/C, TV, dataport, hair dryer, iron.

MODERATE

Swan View Manor   A converted motel right on the main road and across the street from Cold Spring Harbor, this inn's main house is a beautiful historic home. But most of the nonsmoking rooms are in the single-story motel section that is oddly furnished with quasi-antiques. Though the floral and lace designs and friendly staff make it a welcoming place to stay, the traffic rolling by right outside your door means you shouldn't come searching for a quiet getaway.

45 Harbor Rd., Cold Spring Harbor, NY 11724. ✆ 631/367-2070. www.swanview.com. 19 units. May–Oct weekdays $145–$205 double, weekends $165–$225 double; rest of year weekdays $132–$192 double, weekends $147–$207 double. Rates include continental breakfast. AE, DC, DISC, MC, V. *In room:* A/C, TV.

INEXPENSIVE

Heritage Inn *Value*   The heritage of this inn is more value-driven than historical, but it's still a quality place to stay in Port Jefferson. Rooms are very sparsely furnished, and don't count on big bathrooms.

201 W. Broadway, Port Jefferson, NY 11777. ✆ 631/928-2400. Fax 631/474-0627. www.portjeffheritageinn.com. 30 units. Jan–Mar $79–$89 double; May–Aug weekdays $99–$119 double, weekends $129–$139 double. Spring and fall rates in between high and low season are priced according to demand. AE, DC, DISC, MC, V. **Amenities:** Nearby golf course; nearby outdoor tennis courts. *In room:* A/C, TV, dataport, kitchenette (in some rooms), coffeemaker, hair dryer, iron.

WHERE TO DINE
EXPENSIVE

La Plage ✮✮ NEW AMERICAN   With the salty air blowing in straight from the ocean across the street, this tiny bistro has washed tones, a rustic wooden floor, and some tables with great views. Sit out on the patio to make the most of them. The food is decidedly New American, weaving together flavors that work magic into hearty dishes, like the crispy duck confit with fresh chive risotto and exotic mushrooms.

131 Creek Rd., Wading River. ✆ 631/744-9200. Reservations requested. Main courses dinner $24–$36, lunch $13–$18. AE, MC, V. Memorial Day to Sept Mon–Sat noon–3pm, Mon–Thurs 4–9pm, Fri–Sat 4–10pm, Sun 2–9pm. Sept–May closed Mon–Tues. LIE to exit 68, go north to Rte. 25A, go east ¾ mile, turn left on Randalls Rd., turn right on North Country Rd., at stop sign turn left on Sound Rd., then left onto Creek Rd.

Peter Luger ✮✮✮ STEAKHOUSE   "Wow" is the only word that comes to mind when you bite into Luger's porterhouse. This famous steakhouse deserves its reputation as one of America's best—they take meat seriously and they do it right. The porterhouse is what you want—dry aged, brushed with a delicious glaze, and served up straightforward, just the way you want it cooked. They take no credit cards, so bring lots of cash.

255 Northern Blvd., Great Neck. ✆ 516/487-8800. Reservations recommended. Steak for 2 $81; other entrees $15–$37. No credit cards. Mon–Thurs 11:45am–9:45pm; Fri–Sat 11:45am–10:45pm; Sun 1–10pm. LIE to exit 33, Lakeville Rd., then left onto Northern Blvd.

MODERATE

Elk Street Grill ✮✮ CONTINENTAL   This friendly oasis in Port Jefferson is a neighborhood favorite. Skip the appetizers since you'll get a salad with great home-made dressings (try the sesame); entree winners are the pan-seared tuna with a tangy ginger sauce and a sesame-crusted rare ahi tuna with a honey-soy reduction, but meats score well, too.

201 Main St., Port Jefferson. ✆ 631/331-0960. Main courses $19–$32. AE, DC, DISC, MC, V. Tues–Thurs 4–9:30pm, Fri–Sat 4–11pm, Sun noon–3pm and 4–9pm. LIE to exit 64 (Rte. 112), head north for 15 min., pass over railroad tracks, go down steep hill, turn right at the Starbucks.

Tupelo Honey ✴✴✴ *Finds* AMERICAN   With mosaics forming ocean-life scenes, an open kitchen shaped like a mythic castle, and chandeliers shaped like wings, this north shore gem is fanciful, but not in a Disney way: It's actually tasteful and romantic. The food matches the unique decor, with flavor combinations that bring a Spanish influence to an otherwise American menu. Even old favorites are served with a twist. A changing menu may include grilled swordfish, for example, with whipped purple Peruvian potatoes, kiwi-melon salsa, and blood-orange coulis.

39 Roslyn Ave., Sea Cliff. ✆ 516/671-8300. Reservations strongly suggested. Main courses $19–$35. AE, DC, MC, V. Mon–Thurs 5–10pm; Fri–Sat 5–11pm; Sun 4–9pm. Take Rte. 25 to Glen Cove Rd., go north for 3 miles to the sign that says CEDAR SWAMP RD. to Sea Cliff, veer right to the 1st light, turn left onto Sea Cliff Ave., go 1 mile to Roslyn Ave.

INEXPENSIVE

Best Bagels ✴ BAGEL SHOP   If you're going to claim to be the best, your product had better live up to the boast. These bagels are not too dense, not too puffy, cooked on the outside, and not too mushy inside—done just right. Endless toppings and sandwich combos are available.

40 Middle Neck Rd., Great Neck. ✆ 516/482-9860. Bagel sandwiches $4–$9. AE, DC, DISC, MC, V. Mon–Fri 6:30am–5pm; Sat 6:30am–4pm; Sun 6:30am–3pm.

Renaissance Gourmet Shop ✴ *Finds* CAFE   It's hard to imagine a more delightful environment to grab a morning coffee or a lunchtime sandwich. The Garden Room is bursting with color and Italianate windows painted on the walls. Breakfast options include homemade muffins; for lunch you'll find delicious sandwiches, burgers, salads, and pizzas.

35A Gerard St., Huntington Village. ✆ 631/549-2727. Sandwiches $6–$7. AE, MC, V. Mon–Thurs 7am–9pm; Fri–Sat 7am–10pm; Sun 7am–8pm (closes 1 hr. earlier in winter).

THE NORTH SHORE AFTER DARK

There are a couple of outstanding places for music and other live events. The **Tilles Center,** 720 Northern Blvd., Brookville (✆ **516/299-3100**), part of the C. W. Post Campus of Long Island University, boasts a 2,242-seat hall and more than 70 events each season (Sept–June) in music, dance, and theater. Everyone from the Big Apple Circus to Wynton Marsalis has performed there. The **North Fork Theatre,** 960 Brush Hollow Rd., Westbury (✆ **516/334-0800**), tends to host performers of somewhat recent memory, like Tom Jones and Ringo Starr. The **Nassau Veterans Memorial Coliseum,** 1255 Hempstead Tpk., Uniondale (✆ **516/794-9303**), not only is home to professional hockey's New York Islanders, but also hosts big-name concerts (such as Justin Timberlake) and family shows like *Sesame Street Live.* Huntington's smaller but wonderful not-for-profit **Inter-Media Art Center (IMAC),** 370 New York Ave. (✆ **631/549-9666;** www.imactheater.org), presents an eclectic concert mix. One bar worth noting: **Chesterfields,** 330 New York Ave., Huntington (✆ **631/425-1457**), which serves up live music.

2 The North Fork ✴✴

Golden beaches and the sweet nectar of fermented grapes are the sirens that lure most travelers to this slender strip of Long Island. Though close to the Hamptons, the attitude is completely un-Hamptons; South Forkers refer to this area as "upstate."

Thank goodness. Right now it's a laid-back playground that's quaint, beautiful, and completely unpretentious. Wineries just took root out here less than 30 years ago, and

Long Island wines are growing in recognition—and numbers. There are now 23 places to sample them (see tour, p. 160). But this tiny tract of flat, beachy turf is also a great place to just relax. With a couple of bold new restaurants, the culinary scene on the North Fork is definitely picking up, though this area still can't compare to the South Fork in its range of dining (and lodging) options.

Just two roads slice through the North Fork: Route 25 and Route 25A. Take either of them past Riverhead and you'll trade malls for farmstands, wineries, and tiny towns brimming with antiques shops and small-town flair. The two roads come together in Greenport, where most of the area's action (such as it is) can be found. Take that road out to the tip at Orient Point for gorgeous views. You won't be alone: On summer weekends you can expect to find huge traffic jams. Yes, the roads are narrow, but more and more people are discovering the treasures of the North Fork—all while staying in hotels right on the beach, and spending their days shopping and tasting great wines.

ESSENTIALS

GETTING THERE   The **Long Island Expressway** runs to Riverhead; from there, take Route 25 East. The **Long Island Rail Road** (© 516/822-LIRR) stops in Mattituck, Southold, and Greenport. The **Hampton Jitney** (© 631/283-4600) provides bus service from New York City to Riverhead, Aquebogue, Jamesport, Laurel, Mattituck, Cutchogue, Peconic, Southold, Greenport, East Marion, Orient Village, and Orient Point for $18 one-way. **Long Island MacArthur Airport** (© 631/467-3210), situated mid–Long Island, is the closest airport and is served by several airlines mentioned in "Getting There," earlier in this chapter. From Connecticut, take the **Cross Sound Ferry** (© 631/323-2525; www.longislandferry.com), which sails from New London, Connecticut, to Orient Point, New York. Schedules change daily, leaving 8 to 12 times a day. Cars and passenger trucks are allowed.

VISITOR INFORMATION   Tourist information booths are located on Main Road in the towns of Laurel (© 631/298-5757) and Greenport (© 631/477-1383), but are open daily only during July and August (scattered hours at other times). You can also contact the **Long Island Convention and Visitors Bureau** (© 877/FUN-ON-LI or 631/951-3440).

GETTING AROUND   Cars may offer flexibility for visiting wineries, but for people who don't want to brave the summer traffic, the train is the best way to go.

BEACHES & OUTDOOR PURSUITS

BEACHES   There are lots of beaches out here, but check for signs—some are permit-only. For public beaches, your best bet is more than 8 miles of sand in **Orient Beach State Park,** Orient Point (© 631/323-2440), where you'll also find plenty of breathing room and a maritime forest of red cedar and prickly-pear cactus. Two permit-only beaches worth checking out are **Norman Klipp Marine Park** in Greenport and **Town Beach** in Southold, which is a popular family beach. Pick up your permit from the attendant at either beach (after 9:30am): It's $10 for a daily nonresident pass.

BOATING   One of the most unique ways to check out Greenport is aboard the electric *Glory,* a 30-foot fantail launch with varnished hardwood and brass. It sails all afternoon in the summer; $15 for adults, $5 for kids. Go to Preston's Dock at the foot of Main Street in Greenport, or call © 631/477-2515 for details. Or go boating yourself: Canoeing or kayaking on the inlets, creeks, and marshes is a great way to see herons, osprey, hawks, fish, and turtles. Rent from **Eagle's Neck Paddling Company,** 49295 Main Rd., Southold (© 631/765-3502). Rentals start at $30 for 2 hours.

FARMSTANDS   Once you pass Riverhead, Long Island becomes a collection of farms, not malls. Definitely plan to stop at one of them. From tomatoes and sweet corn in the summer to pumpkins and apples in the fall, get your produce at **Wickham's Fruit Farm,** Route 25, Cutchogue ((C) **631/734-6441**); **Harbes Family Farmstand,** Sound Avenue, Route 48, Mattituck ((C) **631/298-0800**); and **Punkinville USA,** Route 48, Peconic ((C) **631/734-5530**). **Briermere Farms,** 4414 Sound Ave., Riverhead ((C) **631/722-3931**), is famous for its divine selection of fruit-filled pies, from raspberry cherry to blueberry cream.

FISHING   The tradition of fishing lives on out here, with many boats made for the novice caster. In the summer, you may be after shark, tuna, or fluke. Other prime catches are sea bass and flounder. Fishing season generally runs from April or May to October, and local captains will set you up with all the gear you need. Go with **Captain Bob**'s fleet in Mattituck ((C) **631/298-5522**), or the *Peconic Star II* with **Capt. Dave Brennan** in Greenport ((C) **631/289-6899**), and expect to pay around $65 for a full day. If you want to go it alone, contact the **Southold Town Clerk's** office ((C) **631/765-1800**), **Warren's Bait & Tackle** in Aquebogue ((C) **631/722-4898**), or **Jamesport Bait & Tackle** in Mattituck ((C) **631/298-5450**) for beach-fishing permits.

GOLF   Your choices are limited. Try **Cherry Creek Golf Links,** 900 Reeves Ave., Riverhead ((C) **631/369-6500**), which has 18 holes and a driving range. To work on those chipping and putting skills, head to **Cedars Golf Club,** Cases Lane, Cutchogue ((C) **631/734-6363**).

WINERIES   Long Island's East End wine industry is relatively young; it turns out that with its well-drained, sandy soil, the North Fork is ideal for grapes, so the industry has taken off. See sidebar below.

SHOPPING

ANTIQUES   The North Fork is an old seafaring world, full of antiques shops and galleries. Step into some of these musty old shops and start digging. Most towns have one or two stores, but Greenport and Southold (and to a lesser extent, Jamesport) have some of the best selections on the North Fork. You'll find a wealth of stained-glass lamps and handmade furnishings at **Lydia's Antiques and Stained Glass,** 215 Main St., Greenport ((C) **631/477-1414**). **Jan Davis Antiques,** 45395 Main Rd., Southold ((C) **631/765-2379**), set in a country store that dates to the 1850s, sells antiques and collectible dolls. **Three Sisters Antiques,** 1550 Main Rd., Jamesport ((C) **631/722-5980**), specializes in linens, postcards, and paper, but you'll also find glass, china, kitchenware, books, and artwork. **Kapell's Antiques,** 400 Front St., Greenport ((C) **631/477-0100**), is the place for early whaling and marine items. And **Pastimes Antiques,** 56025 Main Rd., Southold ((C) **631/765-1221**), has five rooms of porcelain, cut glass, and sterling silver.

RETAIL   The last mall you'll see before you hit the fork is the **Tanger Outlet Center I & II,** 1770 W. Main St., Riverhead ((C) **631/369-2732**), with upscale shops like Kenneth Cole and Barneys New York, along with Nike, Old Navy, and Bose.

MUSEUMS

Horton Point Lighthouse (★)   It's a lighthouse. It's a museum. It's also a great place to bring a picnic lunch, since this 8-acre park has great views of the Long Island Sound, along with picnic tables. The lighthouse dates from 1857, and inside, the small museum has a collection of lighthouse and other early marine artifacts.

Along the Long Island Wine Trail

Long Island sustains some 50 vineyards, ranging in size from 2 to 600 acres, with 30 wineries producing a half-million cases annually. In just 30 years, wine production has transformed a sleepy farming community into a vibrant wine district, producing wines that appear on world-renowned wine lists. Here's why: Ever looked at the "hardiness zone" map in garden books? Eastern Long Island lies in a zone quite different from the rest of the state; a Zone 7, it shares company with Virginia, Kentucky, and northwestern Texas. Long Island's climate is often compared to that of Bordeaux, France.

Merlot, the most widely planted variety on the North Fork, ripens here beautifully and reliably. Chardonnay is second. Many North Fork wineries offer two styles: one that is fruity and crisp, fermented in steel tanks, and another that's more buttery, and rich, with vanilla flavors imparted from its fermentation in oak barrels. Some wineries even produce a third style somewhere in the middle.

The North Fork is becoming a destination in itself for gastronomes. Top contenders include the **Frisky Oyster** in Greenport (✆ 631/477-4265; p. 163), **The Seafood Barge** in Southold (✆ 631/765-3010), the **Red Door** in Mattituck (✆ 631/298-4800), and the **Jamesport Country Kitchen** in Jamesport (✆ 631/722-3537).

But you'll want to do some tasting yourself. If you plan to make several stops, make sure your encounters are of the swirl-sniff-sip-spit variety, designate a driver, or schedule one of the services that you can hire for the day to take you wine tasting. **Vintage Tours** (✆ 631/765-4689; www.northfork.com/tours) offers wine tours that include lunch ($55 per person weekends, $48 on weekdays). Or tour the vineyards on a trolley with the **North Fork Trolley Company** (✆ 631/369-3031; www.northforktrolley.com); a three-vineyard tour is $49, and you can add lunch for $10 per person more. The height of the season is in the autumn, during pumpkin-picking season.

Start your tour at Route 25 (Main Rd.) in Paumanok. Wineries are marked with a green and white **wine trail** sign. Here are some highlights:

Paumanok Vineyards   This is the only winery in the region to produce chenin blanc and a late-harvest sauvignon blanc. Paumanok (the original Indian name for Long Island) also offers two merlots, cabernet franc, and three chardonnays. Established in 1981, Paumanok is known to craft two, sometimes three, styles of cabernet sauvignon (and with certain vintages, a bordeaux blend they named "Assemblage"). Located at 1074 Main Rd., Aquebogue (✆ 631/722-8800; www.paumanok.com), it's open from 11am to 5pm daily. *Continue east on Route 25, just ⅓ mile, to Jamesport Vineyards, on your left.*

Jamesport Vineyards   This father-and-son collaboration also began in 1981, providing some of the North Fork's oldest vines. This "estate winery," using its 60 acres planted in vines as the sole source of fruit for the winery, specializes in sauvignon blanc and merlot, but also produces chardonnay, merlot, cabernet franc, and Riesling. A charmingly rustic, 150-year-old barn houses both the tasting room and the winery. Located at 1216 Main Rd., Jamesport (✆ 631/722-5256; www.jamesport-vineyards.com); open 11am to 6pm daily. *Continue east on Main Road (Rte. 25) for 9 miles to Bedell Cellars, on your left.*

Bedell Cellars   The Bedell Cellars group, owned by Michael Lynne, includes three vineyards (Bedell Cellars, Corey Creek Vineyards, and Wells Road Vineyards), two tasting rooms, and a winery. Known for its merlot, Bedell also produces chardonnay, cabernet sauvignon, viognier, and a late-harvest Riesling. The winery is at 36225 Main Rd., Cutchogue (✆ 631/734-7537; www.bedellcellars.com), and is open in summer Monday to Thursday 11am to 5pm and Friday to Sunday 11am to 6pm; off season daily 11am to 5pm. *Continue east on Route 25 another 1/2 mile to Lenz on your left.*

The Lenz Winery   Founded in 1979, Lenz is one of the oldest wineries on the East End, yielding three chardonnays, three merlots, Gewürztraminer, and cabernet sauvignon, plus a sparkling wine from pinot noir that spends 7 years *sur lie* (French for "on the lees" [or settled yeast cells]), a key element in quality in a traditional method sparkling wine, adding complexity. "Old Vines" merlot is produced here, from some of the oldest merlot vineyards found in North America. Visit them at Main Road, Peconic (✆ 631/734-6010; www.lenzwine.com), from 10am to 5pm daily. *Continue east on Route 25 another 4 miles to The Old Field on your right.*

The Old Field   First growing fruit for sale, The Old Field, established in 1974, began making wines with its first pinot noir released in 1997, and then moved on to merlot, cabernet franc, chardonnay, pinot noir blush, and, in the wings, a sparkling wine. Their address is 59600 Main Rd., Southold (✆ 631/765-2465; www.theoldfield.com); open Saturday and Sunday from 11am to 5pm. *Leaving Old Field, turn left on Route 25, driving west again 3 miles to Peconic Lane. Turn right (north) on Peconic Lane and proceed past the railroad tracks to The Tasting Room on your left.*

The Tasting Room   In May 2003, four small North Fork vineyards opened a tasting room with a nice old-world oak bar for sampling and sales: **Sherwood House** offers a chardonnay and merlot; **Schneider Vineyards** has cabernet franc and chardonnay; **Broadfields Wine Cellars** has merlot and cabernet franc; and **Le Clos Thérèse** offers merlots under the label Comtesse Thérèse. The location is 2885 Peconic Lane, in Peconic (✆ 631/765-6404). Summer hours are Monday to Friday 11am to 5pm, 11am to 6pm weekends; winter, Wednesday to Sunday 11am to 5pm, sometimes weekends only. Closed major holidays. *Continue north on Peconic Lane to the divided highway (Rte. 48/Sound Ave.). Turn left, heading west for 3 miles for Castello di Borghese on your left.*

Castello di Borghese Vineyard & Winery   The "founding" vineyard of the Long Island estate wine industry, Castello di Borghese (formerly Hargrave Vineyards, est. 1973) produces three chardonnays, pinot blanc, two sauvignon blancs, cabernet franc, two merlots, pinot noir, and Riesling. Don't miss the wonderful gift shop. Located on Route 48, Alvah's Lane, Cutchogue (✆ 631/734-5111; www.castellodiborghese.com), it's open April through December Monday to Friday 11am to 5pm, Saturday and Sunday 11am to 6pm; January through March Thursday to Sunday 11am to 5pm.

—Mary Foster Morgan

Lighthouse Rd., Southold. © **631/765-5500.** Suggested donation $2. Grounds open daily. Museum: Memorial Day to Columbus Day Sat–Sun 11:30am–4pm. From Rte. 48, make a left onto Young Ave., a right onto Old North Rd., then a left onto Lighthouse Rd.

Indian Museum 🔗 It's easy to overlook Long Island's Native American history. It's worth an hour to let this museum fill you in on the history of the area through interesting exhibits of old pots, arrowheads, pipes, wampums, toys, and fishing tools that have been dug up out here.

1080 Main Bayview Rd., Southold. © **631/765-5577.** $2 adults, 50¢ for kids. Sept–June Sun 1:30–4:30pm; July–Aug Sat–Sun 1:30–4:30pm.

WHERE TO STAY

Accommodations here are a mix of motels and B&Bs. Don't expect to see many chains. Some motels sit on waterfront property, but they date from the 1950s and many haven't changed much since then; increased tourism, however, is pushing some owners to renovate. In the meantime, however, you can enjoy cheap rooms, even if they aren't the height of luxury.

VERY EXPENSIVE

Jedediah Hawkins Inn 🔗🔗🔗 This new inn has raised the bar on North Fork luxury, yet it almost never came about. A Victorian mansion dating to the 1860s, it had fallen into such disrepair that it was slated for demolition in 2004. An amazing renovation has restored its elegance and makes for a romantic stay. Modern, comfortable, and filled with light, the rooms here come with flat-screen TVs and gas fireplaces, and each has its own personality. My favorite is the Cider Room, a bright mix of modern and antique, with touches like old mailboxes and contemporary sculptures. The most dramatic room is the Cocoa Room, with its chocolate-colored, textured walls and black-and-white photos. The bi-level suite built into the attic, with exposed brick and an upstairs sitting area, is nothing short of stunning. The terrific restaurant, Jedediah's, is reviewed below.

400 S. Jamesport Ave., Jamesport, NY 11947. © **631/722-2900.** Fax 631/722-2901. www.jedediahhawkinsinn.com. 6 units. May–Oct $325–$350 double, $500–$595 suite; Nov–Apr $290–$315 double, $465–$550 suite. Rates Include continental breakfast. 2-night minimum on weekends, 3-night minimum on holidays. AE, MC, V. **Amenities:** Restaurant, small fitness center, massage (can do in-room). *In room:* A/C, TV, hair dryer, iron, safe.

EXPENSIVE

Arbor View B&B 🔗🔗 Instead of going with the regular antique look, the affable innkeepers went with a muted decor that leans more toward the elegant than the rustic. All rooms are named for grapes, with shades of colors reflecting the names (Champagne, Rose, Merlot). Since the inn sits on the main drag, you'll likely hear some traffic, but not enough to be a deal breaker. The nicest room, the Zinfandel, boasts a gorgeous four-poster bed, but is downstairs right next to the entrance.

8900 Main Rd., East Marion, NY 11939. © **800/963-8777** or 631/477-8440. Call for fax. www.arborviewhouse.com. 4 units. Apr–Nov Mon–Thurs $255–$275 double, Fri–Sun $275–$295 double; Dec–Mar $185–$225 double midweek, $225–$255 double weekend. Rates include an excellent full breakfast. 2-night minimum May–Nov. AE, MC, V. Inn located about 2 miles east of Greenport. **Amenities:** Nearby golf courses; massages. *In room:* A/C, TV/DVD, fax, Wi-Fi, high-speed Internet access, hair dryer, CD player, no phone.

Bayview Inn 🔗 "Bayview" is a bit of a misnomer, since you have to squint past trees for a view of the bay. Still, the rooms in the main house are cozy and plainly furnished, but with smallish bathrooms. Snag room no. 8, which is a bit bigger than the others. The cottage is actually a separate house next door with two units; they're nice and modern, but sparsely furnished and quite sterile. All rooms are nonsmoking.

10 Front St., South Jamesport, NY 11970. ✆ 631/722-2659. www.northforkmotels.com. 9 units. Memorial Day to Labor Day $165–$185 double inn rooms, $200–$250 double cottage rooms; early Sept to late May $130–$150 double inn rooms, $150–$200 double cottages. 2-night minimum for inn rooms on summer weekends, 3-night minimum for cottage rooms. AE, DISC, MC, V. From Rte. 25, turn south on S. Jamesport Ave. to Front St. **Amenities:** Restaurant; lounge. *In room:* A/C, TV/VCR, full kitchens (cottage rooms), no phone.

MODERATE

The Inn at the Blue 🦞🦞 Renamed from its previous incarnation, the Blue Dolphin, "The Blue" is still as party-friendly as ever—the pool and bar areas are crowded all summer long. But even with its 1950s-era motel facade, this isn't a bad place to shack up, either: while standard rooms aren't large or luxe, they are comfortable and have the added benefit of kitchenettes. Quite nice, though, are the suites, which are done up with wood furniture, good lighting, and subdued colors.

7850 Main Rd., East Marion, NY 11939. ✆ 631/477-0907. www.stayattheblue.com. 31 units. Late May to late Sept $169–$199 double, $219–$299 suite; early May–Oct $129–$179 double, $189–$249 suite; Nov–Apr $99–$119 double, $139–$199 suite. AE, MC, V. **Amenities:** Restaurant; lounge; outdoor pool; spa; game room; courtesy stretch limo; coin-op washers and dryers. *In room:* A/C, TV, kitchenette, fridge, coffeemaker, no phone.

Silver Sands 🦞 Set back from the road, this motel sits on 36 acres with a quarter-mile of private beach—*the* reason to stay here. Rooms are far from glamorous: They're clean, but maintain their dated furniture, linoleum floors, and small bathrooms. Still, the owners are friendly, and if you stay in room no. 1 or 22, you'll get that wonderful view of the sound. Cabins are similarly furnished with two bedrooms, but not a lot of extra space. A huge wildlife preserve is also on the grounds, and a cool webcam lets you keep a close watch on a nearby osprey's nest.

Silvermere Rd., Greenport, NY 11944. ✆ 631/477-0011. www.silversands-motel.com. 40 units. Mid-June to Labor Day motel rooms $150–$200 double, cottages only by the week, double $1,500–$2,500; early Sept to mid-June motel rooms $100–$150 double, cottages $150 double. Motel rates include breakfast. AE, DC, DISC, MC, V. Head east on Rte. 25 out of Southold and at the 1st right after passing the Lutheran church, you'll see the sign for the motel on the right. **Amenities:** Outdoor heated pool; game room; laundry service; same-day dry cleaning. *In room:* A/C, TV, kitchenette or microwave and fridge (motel rooms), kitchens (cottages only), coffeemaker, iron.

WHERE TO DINE

Restaurants on the North Fork operate according to their own timetables: They close when people stop coming in, their "in season" starts up whenever the traffic warrants, and they may shut down at a moment's notice for a month's vacation. Especially in the winter months, it's best to call first.

EXPENSIVE

Frisky Oyster 🦞🦞🦞 ECLECTIC   This modern restaurant with a Manhattan ambience sits in an unassuming storefront in bustling Greenport. Step inside and you'll find a candle-lit space, house music, walls lined with colorful banquettes, and even more colorful wall coverings. You may not actually find oysters on the menu (it changes often), but you will discover an inventive cuisine that's often tweaked with Asian, French, or Mexican touches. The menu is split between meat and fish, and the restaurant serves both with a modern flourish and taste. Start with one of the excellent soups or salads, and continue on to entrees like the steak frites, a juicy strip steak with thin, crispy fries. Or try the pan-seared scallops with fresh corn salad and a coriander-and-carrot broth. And be sure to finish off with "The Best Key Lime Pie," which has sufficient cause to boast.

27 Front St., Greenport. ✆ **631/477-4265**. Reservations recommended. Main courses $18–$32. AE, DC, DISC, MC, V. Memorial Day to Labor Day Sun–Thurs 5–10pm, Fri–Sat 5–11pm; early Sept to late May closed Mon–Tues.

Jedediah's ★★★ CONTINENTAL   Helping to raise the North Fork's culinary ante is this new restaurant, part of the luxurious Jedediah Hawkins Inn. The two rooms that make up the dining area may be a bit too formal for the laid-back North Fork, with flowery drapes and classical music. But modern art and down-to-earth service keep it from crossing over into stuffiness. Besides, you'll likely be distracted by the symphony happening on your plate. Dig into diver scallops with saffron shellfish risotto in a bouillabaisse broth, or the roasted loin of venison with mulled cider sauce and a butternut squash flan.

400 S. Jamesport Ave., Jamesport (in the Jedediah Hawkins Inn). ✆ **631/722-2900**. Reservations recommended. Main courses $26–$35. AE, MC, V. May–Oct daily 5–10pm; Nov–Apr Sun–Thurs 5–9pm, Fri–Sat 5–10pm.

North Fork Table and Inn ★★★ CONTINENTAL   This newcomer opened in 2006 in the spot where Coeur des Vignes used to be, and it's been a significant addition to the area's dining scene. The new owners have given the first-floor restaurant a fresh look, and now the bright space is reminiscent of a country inn, with wood floors and ceiling beams. Frette tablecloths, muted tones, and cozy alcoves add a dash of romance to the atmosphere as well. Excellent food—from a kitchen led by Gerard Hayden, formerly of Aureole in New York City—makes the experience complete. Using very fresh local, seasonal ingredients, dishes are given a simple presentation with a perfect melding of flavors. An organic chicken, for example, comes with an organic sweet-pea risotto; my favorite, a delicious pork tenderloin and crisp confit belly, is served with a lemon-thyme apricot purée.

57225 Main Rd. (Rte. 25), Southold. ✆ **631/765-0177**. Reservations recommended. Main courses dinner $28–$39, lunch $16–$36. AE, DISC, MC, V. Wed–Mon 5–10pm, Sat–Sun noon–2:30pm.

MODERATE

Legends ★ AMERICAN   When you're steps from the water, you'd better serve fresh fish, and this casual restaurant doesn't disappoint. The bar area is rowdy, with 22 TVs and a stone fireplace, and serving some 200 beers to complement dishes that span from burgers to pad Thai. The dining room is quieter and classier. On the dining-room menu, you'll find a mix of starters like wild mushroom, filet and Gorgonzola tart, followed by entrees like pecan-crusted chicken with coconut-rum sauce and a delicious seafood potpie with several different kinds of fish.

835 First St., New Suffolk. ✆ **631/734-5123**. Reservations accepted in the dining room. Main courses $21–$33; pub $9–$16. AE, DC, DISC, MC, V. Sun–Thurs noon–9pm; Fri–Sat noon–10pm. From Cutchogue, turn left at the light (New Suffolk), go 1½ miles to the blinking lights, turn left onto New Suffolk Ave., then left onto First St.

Modern Snack Bar AMERICAN   When this North Fork eatery opens for the season in early April, people flock here for the home cooking. A dinerlike restaurant, it has grown from an actual snack bar in 1950 to a place serving all kinds of dishes today. The standard burgers and salads are complemented by mom-knows-best dishes like meatloaf and fried chicken.

628 Main Rd., Aquebogue. ✆ **631/722-3655**. Reservations not accepted. Main courses $10–$21. AE, DISC, MC, V. Early Apr to mid-Dec Tues–Thurs 11am–9pm; Fri–Sat 11am–10pm; Sun noon–9pm.

INEXPENSIVE

Bruce's Cheese Emporium and Café 𝒢𝒢 CAFE   Step into this Greenport market and you're immediately hit with the aromas of coffee and cheese mingled together. Tables are set in the middle of the market and surrounded by old-time photos and antiques. It's a great place to come for a morning omelet or a lunchtime sandwich, or just to buy bread and cheese to take to the waterfront.

208 Main St., Greenport. ℭ **631/477-0023.** Omelets and sandwiches $7–$9. AE, MC, V. July–Aug daily 8am–6pm; Sept–Dec and Apr–Jun Thurs–Mon 9am–5pm; Jan–Mar Fri–Sun 9am–5pm.

Harbourfront Deli DELI   This wide-open, light-flooded restaurant is a great place to start your morning or grab an afternoon sandwich. It's right on the main drag in charming Greenport and serves up several different kinds of burgers, grilled-chicken sandwiches, and homemade salads.

48 Front St., Greenport. ℭ **631/477-1878.** Sandwiches $6–$8. No credit cards. Daily 6am–7pm; summer until 9pm.

THE NORTH FORK AFTER DARK

While the North Fork nightlife scene is nothing like the Hamptons, summer weekend nights can get a bit crazy. If you want to stand elbow to elbow with tons of revelers on an outdoor wharf with the music blasting till all hours, check out **Claudio's Clam Bar,** 111 Main St., Greenport (ℭ **631/477-1889**), open May to October. Some people head out to drink at the **Inn at the Blue,** 7850 Main Rd., East Marion (ℭ **631/477-0907**), while others prefer to stay in town and party at its sister, the **Blue Harbor Café,** 110 Front St., Greenport (ℭ **631/477-1566**). And **Bay & Main,** 300 Main St. (ℭ **631/477-1442**), also comes alive after dark, right in the heart of Greenport.

3 South Shore Beaches 𝒢𝒢: Long Beach, Jones Beach & Robert Moses State Park

Standing in the heart of Manhattan, it's hard to believe that golden beaches are only an hour away. While Jones Beach, Long Beach, and Robert Moses State Park are the biggest stretches of sand, there are some smaller (and sometimes less crowded) beaches you may want to check out as well. Just watch out—they're also surfer havens. **Tobay Beach** is a half-mile of sand just east of Jones Beach, and **Gilgo Beach** is another gorgeous stretch 6 miles west of Robert Moses.

JONES BEACH

Jones Beach has a dual function, as both beach and concert venue. For more than 80 years, it's been swimming heaven; with more than 6 miles of ocean beach and a half-mile of bay beach, it can get crowded, but the water is surprisingly clean and nice. There are also swimming pools and locker rooms available. With a summertime stadium, the area sees some of music's biggest names. The beach and stadium are set out over a causeway and are not accessible by train. In fact, when Jones Beach opened in the 1920s, it was socially exclusionary; buses couldn't negotiate the low underpasses, and less wealthy people didn't own cars. Today, beach- and concertgoers travel the causeway by car and bus to walk the Jones Beach boardwalk.

   Tip: To escape the crushing crowds, head to the beach's west end—there you'll find the park's most undeveloped areas that are home to a variety of migratory birds and native plants. For even fewer crowds, head to Tobay or Gilgo beaches or Robert Moses State Park.

ESSENTIALS

GETTING THERE   From New York City, the **Long Island Rail Road** (© 516/822-LIRR) offers a Jones Beach Package in summer, which includes round-trip rail fare to Freeport plus round-trip Long Island Bus connections to the beach. By car, take the Long Island Expressway east or Grand Central Parkway east to Northern State Parkway east, to Wantagh Parkway south, to Jones Beach State Park or Belt/Southern State Parkway east, to Wantagh Parkway south, to the state park. It's $8 to park in summer.

VISITOR INFORMATION   The main number for **Jones Beach State Park** is © 516/785-1600.

ACTIVITIES & ATTRACTIONS

CONCERTS   From June to August, the Jones Beach Amphitheater (© 888/706-7600 or 516/221-1000) hosts the hottest outdoor music events around. Gwen Stefani, the Goo Goo Dolls, Def Leppard, the Allman Brothers, Taylor Hicks, and Aerosmith all played in 2007, for example.

GOLF   A fun way to pass some time with a great view of the ocean is at the **Pitch & Putt** (© 516/785-1600; Apr–Nov), a par-3 course that's right next to the boardwalk and the Atlantic Ocean. Park in field 4 or 5. Cost is $7 per 18 holes; club rental is $2.

NATURE   The **Theodore Roosevelt Nature Center,** at the west end of Jones Beach Park (© 516/679-7254), houses educational exhibits, interactive activities, environmental displays, and video programs. Children can dig in a mystery bone discovery area, explore a section of a shipwreck, and see a butterfly garden, along with exhibits on the dunes and endangered species. Open weekends year-round and Wednesday to Sunday 10am to 4pm from Memorial Day to Labor Day.

ROBERT MOSES STATE PARK

Technically part of Fire Island since it sits at the island's western end, this gorgeous stretch of beach is in a different world because you can actually drive here. Motor over to the eastern end of the park and you'll see the barriers that prevent access to the car-free area of Fire Island. So park and take a stroll on the 5 sandy miles, or take in a game of pitch-and-putt.

ESSENTIALS

GETTING THERE   Take the Southern State Parkway to Robert Moses Causeway (exit 40) and go south to the western end of Fire Island. Parking fee is $8 in summer.

VISITOR INFORMATION   The main number for **Robert Moses State Park** is © 631/669-0470.

LONG BEACH

Long Beach is also best experienced as a day trip from the city, since it's not set up for overnighters: All the beachfront property is occupied by apartments and retirement homes, and hotels (and boardwalk restaurants) are virtually nonexistent. People come for the beaches and to walk the lengthy boardwalk. With miles of surprisingly clean beach and water, sunbathers and surfers congregate here in mass quantities. Make no mistake: The beaches get supercrowded on summer weekends, and the skies are even more crowded, with planes on their way into and out of New York.

To actually get onto the beach, you have to purchase a beach pass ($10) on the weekends from late May to late June and then daily until early September. You can buy them from the cabanas on the boardwalk or with your train ticket from New York City. When you tire of the beach, the boardwalk makes for a great bike ride, with the sea breezes in your nose and the center lane reserved for bikes. For rentals, try **Buddy's,** 907 W. Beech St. (© **516/431-0804**); they'll set you up with a 3-hour rental for $15.

ESSENTIALS
GETTING THERE   The **Long Island Rail Road** (© **516/822-LIRR**) goes straight to Long Beach in about 50 minutes from Penn Station. Driving? Take Route 27 to Route 878. If street parking proves difficult—and it probably will—your best bet is the train station lot, which is just a couple of blocks from the ocean.

VISITOR INFORMATION   Contact the **Long Beach Chamber of Commerce,** 350 National Blvd. (© **516/432-6000**), or the **Long Island Convention and Visitors Bureau** (© **877/FUN-ON-LI** or 631/951-3440).

WHERE TO DINE
There are a few worthwhile restaurants, congregated on Park Avenue just west of the train station or on Beech Avenue, west of where the beach ends. **Billy's Beach Cafe,** 222 Park Ave. (© **516/889-2233**), sits a few blocks from the beach, but has good burgers and other casual fare. **John Henry's,** 150 E. Park Ave. (© **516/897-9551**), is a good old-fashioned pub with traditional pub fare along with tasty dishes like Yankee pot roast. Both the cuisine and the decor at **Duke Falcon's,** 36 W. Park Ave. (© **516/897-7000**), span the globe, and it takes a while to sift through the zillions of entrees that include everything from Italian and Japanese dishes to a delicious Chilean sea bass. Don't skip the creamy gelato for dessert.

4 Fire Island ★★★

A half-mile wide, 32 miles long, and car- and attitude-free, Fire Island is about as emotionally far from New York City as you can get within a couple of hours. A patchwork of national seashore and private property, the island has few formal addresses; folks ride beat-up bicycles barefoot and know places only by name. Regulars talk of "the mainland" as if it were a distant continent rather than right across the bay. And the word "ostentatious" hasn't even been coined yet—informality rules the day. With punishing winters, Fire Island is strictly a summertime getaway. When Memorial Day hits, the small hamlets fill with warm-weather revelers, while other parts of the island see only congregations of deer. And after September's over, almost everything shuts down.

Since cars are off-limits and the water taxi is expensive, it's best to decide what kind of experience you're after before you arrive here. Ocean Beach is the hub of island activity, where you'll find most of the island's hotels and restaurants, along with most of the party-hearty weekend visitors. The small hamlets of **Kismet** and **Ocean Bay Park** are mostly residential and great for crowd escape, but have few hotels or restaurants. **Cherry Grove** and **Fire Island Pines** are popular gay communities. And to get away from everyone, head to **Watch Hill** and points east—the area boasts a fantastic wildlife preserve, but no facilities other than camping. Walk the beach at night and it'll be just you, the surf, and the moonlight. Out here (and on the western end), beaches are clothing-optional, though going topless is tolerated everywhere.

Fire Island

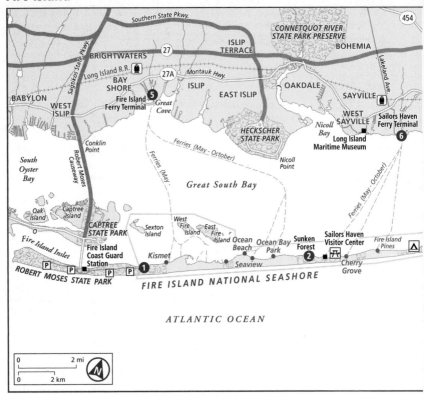

ESSENTIALS

GETTING THERE   Robert Moses wanted to build a superhighway through the island, but fervent residents put up a fight; and we thank them for it. Now, ironically, you can drive to the eastern end of Robert Moses State Park and walk over. But unless you're a world-class swimmer, the ferry is your only other option for getting out here. Though some boats operate year-round, they mostly run from May to October a few times daily, with very frequent service in July and August. Take the **Long Island Rail Road** (℃ 516/822-LIRR) to one of three stops: Bay Shore, Sayville, or Patchogue. Van taxis will be waiting to whisk you to a ferry for $5 per person. If you're planning on spending only a day, purchase one of the LIRR's packages and you'll save some money. **Fire Island Ferries** (℃ 631/665-3600; www.fireislandferries.com) gets you from Bay Shore to Ocean Beach, Kismet, Ocean Bay Park, and a few other communities from the Fire Island Ferry Terminal; **Sayville Ferry** (℃ 631/589-0810; www.sayvilleferry.com) takes you from Sayville to Cherry Grove, The Pines, and Sunken Forest from the Sailors Haven Ferry Terminal; and **Davis Park Ferry** (℃ 631/475-1665; www.pagelinx.com/dpferry/index.shtml) gets you from Patchogue to Watch Hill from the Watch Hill Ferry Terminal. Most ferries are $7 to $10 for the 20- to 30-minute jaunt across the bay.

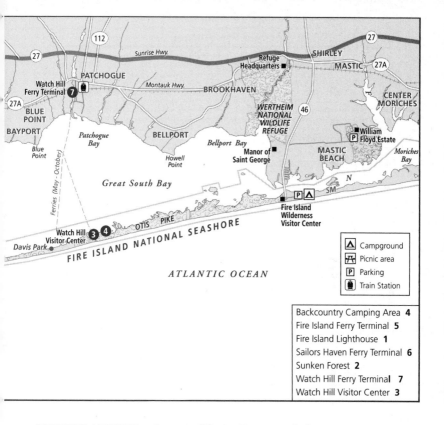

△	Campground
🛆	Picnic area
P	Parking
🚂	Train Station

Backcountry Camping Area **4**
Fire Island Ferry Terminal **5**
Fire Island Lighthouse **1**
Sailors Haven Ferry Terminal **6**
Sunken Forest **2**
Watch Hill Ferry Terminal **7**
Watch Hill Visitor Center **3**

GETTING AROUND   Cars are off-limits. You can walk from town to town, but distances are deceptively long, so consider calling **Fire Island Water Taxi** (② 631/665-8885) and they'll come and collect you from any pier.

Besides expensive water taxis and hoofing it, **bikes** are the only way to get around. Rent them from **Ocean Beach Hardware,** 482 Bayberry Walk, Ocean Beach (② 631/583-5826), for $15 per day.

VISITOR INFORMATION   There's no tourist office here, but the **Long Island Convention & Visitors Bureau** (② 877/386-6654) may provide some info.

SHOPPING

While tacky T-shirt shops and home-decor stores dominate the streets of Ocean Beach, you can find real art at the **Kenny Goodman Gallery,** 325 Denhoff Walk, Ocean Beach (② 631/583-8207), open weekends-only in May, June, September, and October, daily in July and August. Since 1968, Kenny has made beautiful wooden walking sticks and eerily disturbing wooden heads, along with gorgeous silver jewelry.

EXPLORING FIRE ISLAND

For a little history with a killer 360-degree view of island, bay, and ocean—you can even see Manhattan on a superclear day—climb the 182 steps to the top of the **Fire Island Lighthouse** (② 631/661-4876), near Kismet at the island's western end. The

Out & About: The Pines & Cherry Grove

While all of Fire Island has a reputation as a hangout for gays and lesbians, the action is mostly in The Pines (for men) and Cherry Grove (for women and men). Both are small communities: Cherry Grove, especially, gets the party going . . . and keeps it going every summer night, while The Pines tends to be quieter. The beaches are gorgeous; in fine weather don't be surprised to find people walking around in their birthday suits. The biggest day of the year out here is the Invasion of The Pines on July 4th, when boatloads of drag queens from Cherry Grove come and "terrorize" the posh Pines. You'll find a few places to stay. In The Pines, the most popular is **Hotel Ciel** (© 631/597-6500, ext. 26). Or look for a place to rent with **Pines Harbor Realty** (© 631/597-7575; www.pinesharborrealty.com), though be aware that real estate here is some of the most expensive on Fire Island. Over in Cherry Grove, shack up at the **Grove Hotel** (© 631/597-6600), or check into the **Belvedere Guest House** (© 631/597-6448). Nightclubs hop in these two towns until all hours of the night and morning. In The Pines, kick the party off with colorful concoctions during Low Tea (otherwise known as the "Tea Dance") from 5 to 8pm at the **Blue Whale** (© 631/597-6500, ext. 22). Then move on to High Tea from 8 to 10pm at the balcony above **The Pavilion** (© 631/597-6500, ext. 28), where you get the added benefit of checking out anyone coming off the ferries. Just stay at The Pavilion to get your dance-on.

In Cherry Grove the **Grove Hotel** (© 631/597-6600) is the hottest spot, with drag shows, live bands, and theme parties throughout the summer. For the best people-watching, snag a table overlooking the main walk. Another popular gathering place is **Cherry's Pit** (© 631/597-6820); you can catch a great view of the sunset over on the bayside deck. They also serve food. Eat with a view of the ocean at **Rachel's** (© 631/597-4174). Or go grab a great pie at **Cherry Grove Pizza** (© 631/597-6766).

Note that you may see some interesting scenes as you pass through the woods between Cherry Grove and The Pines, affectionately known as the "Meat Rack."

Look online for more gay listings and news for the area. The most comprehensive site is **www.fireislandqnews.com**, which also has a calendar of area events. Also try **www.asthegroveturns.net** and **www.fipines.com**.

---

light has been guiding ships since 1825. It's open 9:30am to 4pm daily from April to mid-December (and until 5pm during summer); January to March it's open weekdays 9:30am to 4pm and weekends noon to 4pm, but in winter call ahead to confirm. Admission is $6. Farther east, the **Sunken Forest** (© 631/597-6183) is a gorgeous nature preserve and a great walkabout that's free and always open. Set behind the dunes, this 250-year-old forest is a crowded collection of American holly and sassafras that twists and tangles to create a shady canopy. The dense growth has withstood the punishment of constant salt spray better than most of the homes. The marked boardwalk trail will help you sort out what's what.

WHERE TO STAY

With demand for accommodations far outweighing supply, it's decidedly a seller's market. Even tiny, moldy rooms with bathrooms down the hall still get away with charging more than $100 a night. Buyer beware!

Clegg's Hotel ⊛   The owners of this hotel, family-run since the 1940s, actually care about cleanliness. Plus, Clegg's occupies a prime position in the middle of the Ocean Beach action. Standard rooms are closet-size and sparsely furnished with either a full bed or two twins. You'll have to share a bathroom with several other rooms. A better choice? One of the studio apartments with a bay view: You'll also get a small private bathroom and a kitchenette.

478 Bayberry Walk, Ocean Beach, Fire Island, NY 11770. ℂ 631/583-5399. www.cleggshotel.com. 20 units. May–Oct Sun–Thurs $110 double, $210 suite; Fri–Sat $320 double, $420 suite. Off-season rates available upon request. Includes continental breakfast. 2-night minimum on weekends. AE, MC, V. *In room:* A/C, kitchenette in suites, no phone.

CAMPGROUNDS

Unless you know someone, camping at **Watch Hill** is the only way to sleep for free out here, and while it's far removed from any facilities or action, it's superquiet and in the island's most beautiful area. The official campground, which is not free, has 26 tent sites and one group site. It also books up a year in advance (get the rules and tips at www.nps.gov/fiis/planyourvisit/camping.htm). Last-minute campers, however, can get a free backcountry pass from the **Watch Hill Visitor Center** (ℂ 631/597-6455) and walk ¼ mile east on the beach into the Otis Pike Wilderness Area. Pop your tent anywhere behind the dunes.

RENTALS

Most people rent a home for their Fire Island vacations. For a place in Ocean Beach, Sea View, Robins Rest, or other points on the island's western end, call **Red Wagon Realty,** 431 Denhoff, Ocean Beach (ℂ 631/583-8158). For The Pines, call **Pines Harbor Realty** (ℂ 631/597-7575). In Cherry Grove, call **A Summer Place** (ℂ 631/597-6140).

WHERE TO DINE

Two words: Bring money. Restaurateurs have only a couple of months to make money, so it's not cheap to eat out here.

Matthew's Seafood House ⊛⊛ SEAFOOD   Get past the hokey fishnet decor and you'll find Fire Island's best seafood. As you sit on a wooden patio overlooking the bay, the cornbread comes warm and portions are supersized, making the high prices more tolerable. Stick with the fish: Shrimp and scallops are excellent, and tuna or swordfish steaks are prepared many ways. Come on Sunday (3–6pm) for the weekly party that includes deals on drinks, as well as clams, wings, and other bar food.

935 Bay Walk, Ocean Beach. ℂ 631/583-8016. Reservations recommended. Main courses $16–$33. AE, DISC, MC, V. Mother's Day to mid-June weekends only Fri–Sat noon–11pm; mid-June to mid-Sept Sun–Thurs noon–10pm, Fri–Sat noon–11pm.

Rachel's ⊛ *Value* DINER   This centrally located diner has been dishing up breakfast, lunch, and dinner for more than 30 years, and the fan-cooled, skylight-filled building is the town's closest thing to a reasonably priced diner. Breakfast is served from 7am to 4pm, and the blueberry pancakes are a great way to start the morning or afternoon. Dinners are fair, but your best bet is to have breakfast or lunch here. Want something to go? Hit the bakery next door.

325 Bay Walk, Ocean Beach. ℂ 631/583-5953. Breakfasts and burgers $5–$11; dinner entrees $12–$17. AE, MC, V. Mid-Apr to mid-Oct daily 7am–2pm, until 11pm July–Aug.

FIRE ISLAND AFTER DARK

Drinkers love the down-at-the-heels feel of **Housers,** Bayview Walk in Ocean Beach (ℂ **631/583-8900**); it's one of the biggest indoor scenes in town. To party on the water, head to **Casino Bar and Café,** on the ocean in Davis Park (ℂ **631/597-9414**), with its huge deck where DJs spin on the weekends.

5 The South Fork: The Hamptons ⟨★⟨★⟨★

Generally referred to as simply "the Hamptons," the South Fork actually consists of a group of towns, not all of which actually end in "Hampton" and each with its own flavor. Regardless of name, though, this is where the rich and famous spend their summers, and with good reason: Some of the most gorgeous land in New York State—and some of the best beaches in the world—is here. Ever since the railroad was built out to Southampton in 1870, people have been hooked on the South Fork.

While winters are relatively quiet, the summer season brings crushing crowds and a flashy nightclub scene. A drive along Route 27 requires immense patience, so it's worthwhile figuring out what kind of experience you seek so that there's not a lot of backtracking. **Eastport** is a tiny hamlet filled with antiques shops; **Westhampton** has tree-lined streets and Victorian mansions; **Southampton** boasts old money, huge estates, and chic stores; **East Hampton** is the trendy, new-money capital of Long Island (Jerry Seinfeld, Billy Joel, and Martha Stewart have homes here); **Sag Harbor** is a gorgeous town on the water where even the dry cleaner has antique irons in the window; **Amagansett** and **Bridgehampton** are cute little towns; and laid-back **Montauk** relishes its position at the island's tip—set apart from the more exclusive villages, it's also a big draw for fishermen and surfers.

To locate the towns in this section, please see the map on the inside back cover.

ESSENTIALS

GETTING THERE   The **Long Island Rail Road** (ℂ **516/822-LIRR**) makes stops in Westhampton, Hampton Bays, Southampton, Bridgehampton, East Hampton, Amagansett, and Montauk. By car, take the **Long Island Expressway** to Riverhead (where it ends) and head south to Route 27, which takes you all the way out to Montauk. The **Hampton Jitney** (ℂ **800/936-0440** or 631/283-4600) buses run daily. Pickup locations include Manhattan, LaGuardia, JFK, and Islip airports and several stops in the Hamptons. The complete route takes around 3½ hours, but allow for traffic delays at peak travel times. Count on around $25 each way. The buses run by **Hampton Luxury Liner** (ℂ **631/537-5800**) have more room than other bus lines, with just 33 reclining leather captain's seats for $28 each way. But if money is no object, grab an airplane and skip the traffic: **MacArthur Airport** (ℂ **631/467-3210**), situated mid–Long Island, is the closest airport (see section 1 of this chapter). **Viking Ferry** (West Lake Dr., Montauk; ℂ **631/668-5700**) runs a passengers-only service between Montauk and Block Island, as well as New London, Connecticut, and Martha's Vineyard, Massachusetts.

(Fun Fact   **Just Ducky**

Long Island is famous for its duck, but you won't likely see any duck farms out here—in fact, the only duck you may see is the landmark 20-foot-tall Big Duck statue (on Rte. 24 at the Flanders/Hampton Bays border). So what gives? Well, there used to be many farms, but the smell drove residents to get them closed. Now there are just a couple of farms, providing ducks to only a few select restaurants. Anyone else who calls it Long Island duck is just a quack.

VISITOR INFORMATION   The **Southampton Chamber of Commerce** is at 76 Main St., Southampton (© **631/283-0402**), or contact **the Long Island Convention and Visitors Bureau** (© **877/FUN-ON-LI** or 631/951-3440).

GETTING AROUND   Cars are your best option out here. Rent from **Hertz** (© **800/ 654-3131**) in Riverhead or **Avis** (© **800/331-1212**), which has an office in Southampton. For a taxi in Southampton, call **McRides Taxi** (© **631/283-1900**). In Montauk, call **Montauk Taxi** (© **631/668-2468**).

BEACHES & ACTIVE PURSUITS

BEACHES   Hamptons beaches are world-class for a reason: Not only are the grains of gold perfectly maintained, but they stretch on forever. Unlike some beaches that are interrupted by cliffs or rocks, these sandy stretches allow you to walk for hours, just getting lost in the grandness of the ocean—and if you look to the other side, the grandness of the homes. There's just one problem when it comes to enjoying these beaches: parking. Walk, ride a bike, take a taxi—do anything but drive to the beach. Nonresident parking permit fees run up to $275 and daily parking fees can be $25— if a spot's even available.

Your best option? Stay at a hotel that has beach rights. Hotels like Gurney's Inn are right on the water, so you'll have no problems. Some off-beach places like the Southampton Inn will shuttle you to the water for free.

So where do you go? In Southampton, **Cooper's Beach** is the main public beach; it's beautifully maintained and you'll find a concession stand; but it can get crowded, and parking costs as much as $35. **Old Town Beach** is much less crowded and there's no parking permit required; but it has only 30 spaces, so get there early. **Main Beach** in East Hampton is gorgeous and in view of some giant mansions. A weekday parking pass is $20, and there are no nonresident parking permits on weekends. **Westhampton Beach Village** has some of the best beaches on Long Island, but forget about parking. Even walking onto the beach requires a permit (call © **631/288-1654**).

If you want to tote your lunch along, pick up sandwiches to go at **Hampton Bagels;** there are outlets in East Hampton, 74 N. Main (© **631/324-5411**), and Hampton Bays, 252 W. Montauk Hwy. (© **631/728-7893**). For something fancier, check out the gourmet cheeses and huge salad bar at **Schmidt's Market,** 120 N. Sea Rd., Southampton (© **631/283-5777**).

BOATING   Go exploring on the water by kayak. **Mill Creek Kayaks,** 3253 Noyac Rd., Sag Harbor (© **631/725-4712**), will take you out for lessons ($30 per hour) or rent you a kayak ($16–$20 per hour). It also offers a wetlands wildlife tour and a children's tour ($45). Open May to October.

DRIVING   Wheel around Southampton and check out some of the amazing estates along Gin Lane and Coopers Neck; unfortunately, many are blocked by sky-high hedges.

FISHING   Montauk is renowned as one of the nation's best places for surf-casting. Start getting your muscles ready now: 40- and 50-pound bass migrate through these waters in the fall, and gigantic bass and stripers can be caught in the summer as well. Climb aboard with **Sea Otter Fishing Fleet** (© **631/668-2669**), where a half-day is $35 to $40. Or go with the larger **Viking Lines,** Montauk Harbor (© **631/668-5700**); a half-day's fishing is $36.

GOLF   **Montauk Downs,** on Fairview Avenue east of **Montauk** (© **631/668-5000**), has a beautiful course. For New York State residents, it's $36 to $41 for 18 holes. A great value course is the 9-hole **Sag Harbor State Golf Course,** off Route 114 between East Hampton and Sag Harbor (© **631/725-2503**). It's just $14 on weekdays, $21 on weekends. The famed **Shinnecock Hills,** 200 Tuckahoe Rd., Southampton, was home to the U.S. Open in 2004; but it's a private course, so you'll have to make friends with a member.

SURFING   Just below the Montauk Point Lighthouse, you'll find some of the biggest waves on Long Island—along with boarders who come out for some impromptu wave catching. The currents are very tricky where the ocean meets the sound, but experienced riders will have a blast. Pick up your supplies at **Plaza Surf & Sports,** 716 Main St., Montauk (© **631/668-9300**).

U-PICK FARMS   Have fun picking your own fruit. **Hank Kraszewski Farms** has a couple of outlets: For strawberries, head out Route 39, Southampton Bypass, Southampton (© **631/726-4667**), and for pumpkins, take Route 27, Water Mill (same number).

WINERIES   While you won't find a winery every mile like on the North Fork, the South Fork does boast three fine wineries: **Wölffer Estate,** 139 Sagg Rd., Sagaponack (© **631/537-5106**); **Duck Walk Vineyards,** 231 Montauk Hwy., Water Mill (© **631/726-7555**); and **Channing Daughters,** 1927 Scuttlehole Rd., Bridgehampton (© **631/537-7224**).

SHOPPING

For chic shopping, walk along Main Street in Southampton, where you'll find the country homes of upscale Manhattan shops like **Saks Fifth Avenue,** 50 Main St. (© **631/283-3500**), and the clothing and furnishings at **Edward Archer,** 85 Main St. (© **631/283-2668**). Gallery-wise, don't miss the collection of artists at the **Chrysalis Gallery,** 2 Main St. (© **631/287-1883**).

East Hampton also boasts loads of upscale shops like the **Coach Factory Stores,** 69 Main St. (© **631/329-1777**), and the **Polo Country Store Ralph Lauren,** 31–33 Main St. (© **631/324-1222**), plus many art galleries showing the work of highly regarded artists, including the **Arlene Bujese Gallery,** 66 Newtown Lane (© **631/324-2823**).

For antiques, two villages stand out: Eastport and Bridgehampton. In Eastport, drop by the **Eastport Antique Center,** 500 Montauk Hwy. (© **631/325-0388**), and **Ragamuffins,** 486 Montauk Hwy. (© **631/325-1280**). In Bridgehampton, it seems every other store sells antiques: Try **Hampton Briggs Antiques,** 2462 Main St. (© **631/537-6286**), for Asian pieces and the **Shinnecock Trading Post,** Montauk Highway, Southampton (© **631/287-2460**), for Native American arts and crafts.

MUSEUMS & ATTRACTIONS

Montauk Point Lighthouse Museum ⋆⋆   Up on a hill, overlooking the rocky coastline of Long Island's easternmost point, this museum boasts a bevy of artifacts and a great view. Commissioned by Congress under George Washington in 1792 and completed in 1796, the first lighthouse in New York State has old exhibits of historical documents and the lonely life of a lighthouse keeper. There's also a 110-foot tower that you can climb for a stunning view of the ocean, the coastline, and the dense scrub lining the road from the town of Montauk.

Located at the very end of Rte. 27. © 888/MTK-POIN or 631/668-2544. Admission $7 adults, $6 seniors, $3 children. Mid-May to mid-Oct daily, usually 10:30am–4:30 or 5:30pm; scattered hours in the off season, mostly weekends only.

Whaling Museum ⋆   Housed in a gorgeous 1845 Greek Revival mansion built by whaling-ship magnate Benjamin Huntting, the home is as cool as the collection inside, devoted to the industry that put this part of the world on the map. Highlights include 100-year-old genuine whale jawbones, a reconstructed 18th-century kitchen, tools and weapons of whalers, and samples of whale oil.

200 Main St. (at Garden St.), Sag Harbor. © 631/725-0770. Admission $5 adults, $3 seniors and students, free for children under 13. Mid-May to Sept Mon–Sat 10am–5pm, Sun 1–5pm.

WHERE TO STAY

Accommodations range from small motels to extravagant resorts to tiny historical inns, but they all have one thing in common: In summer, they require 2- and 3-night minimum stays.

EXPENSIVE

Gurney's Inn Resort & Spa ⋆⋆⋆   Set on a bluff over a gorgeous stretch of private ocean beach, Gurney's sprawls across several buildings and has a great European-style spa. Only some of the buildings are right on the ocean, and the range of rates reflects your view. Rooms are spacious and very modern, which translates to a bit sterile. The marble-and-glass interiors may not be overly charming, but a beige-and-green color scheme gives them some warmth, and they are comfortable and generally get plenty of light. Head to the full-service spa if you have a vision of getting a massage on the beach, for this is the place to make it a reality.

290 Old Montauk Hwy., Montauk, NY 11954. © 631/668-2345. Fax 631/668-3576. www.gurneys-inn.com. 109 units. Late May to Labor Day midweek $387–$479 double, weekend $407–$495 double, $711 and way up suite and cottages; Labor Day to mid-Oct and mid-Apr to late May midweek $294–$371 double, weekend $340–$402 double, $495 and way up suite and cottages; mid-Oct to mid-Apr midweek $255–$315 double, weekend $325–$385 double, $390 and way up suite and cottage. Rates include $26 dinner credit and $15 breakfast credit per person. Packages available. 2-night minimum in June, 3-night minimum July–Aug, 2-night weekend minimum off season. AE, DC, DISC, MC, V. Free valet parking. **Amenities:** 3 restaurants; lounge; heated indoor seawater pool; big exercise room overlooking ocean; spa; children's programs in summer; game room; concierge; courtesy bus; salon; limited room service; massage (in-room available); laundry service; same-day dry cleaning. *In room:* A/C, TV w/pay movies, dataport, kitchenette in cottages, fridge, coffeemaker, hair dryer, iron, safe.

Seatuck Cove House ⋆⋆⋆   If you've ever dreamed of staying in one of the enormous Victorian waterfront homes that dot the shoreline, then this inn is for you. Its country-furnished look gives it a laid-back feel, and you're just a stone's throw from the inn's small private beach. The rooms are painted white and, with one exception, they're spacious and bright, with separate sitting areas. The Dune Road room is amazing—huge with great water views, a temperature-controlled whirlpool tub, flatscreen digital TV with DVD player, stone fireplace, and high ceilings.

61 S. Bay Ave., Eastport, NY 11941. ℂ 631/325-3300. Fax 631/325-8443. www.seatuckcovehouse.com. 5 units. May–Oct weekdays $150–$400 double, weekends $175–$475 double, 2-night minimum on weekends; Nov–Apr weekdays $125–$225 double, weekends $150–$300 double. Rates include full breakfast. AE, DISC, MC, V. Go east through village of Eastport, turn right onto S. Bay Ave., travel to end of road. **Amenities:** Heated outdoor pool. *In room:* A/C, 4 units w/TV, hair dryer.

1708 House 🌟🌟🌟 This cozy Colonial actually does date from 1708 and you can stay in the original 18th-century rooms. The inn has just four rooms (nos. 1–4) in this style: They're not the world's largest, but they have original wood floors and exposed-beam ceilings, along with beautiful four-poster beds and claw-foot tubs. The other rooms were added in 1996 and are also decked out in gorgeous furniture and wood floors, but they're more modern. The cottages are beachy and contemporary.

126 Main St., Southampton, NY 11968. ℂ 631/287-1708. Fax 631/287-3593. www.1708house.com. 15 units. May–Oct weekdays $195–$495 double, weekends $275–$625 double; Nov–Apr weekdays $140–$250 double, weekends $150–$295 double. Rates include continental breakfast. 2-night weekend minimums apply May–June and Sept–Oct; 3-night minimum weekends apply July–Aug; holidays are 4-night minimum. AE, MC, V. **Amenities:** Lounge. *In room:* A/C, TV (some w/DVD), kitchens in 2 of the cottages, hair dryer, iron.

MODERATE
Inn at Quogue 🌟🌟 *(Finds)* A combination of quaint country inn and pool-centered resort, this 67-unit inn stretches across several different buildings off the beaten path of the eponymous town. It offers cheap, small, poolside rooms as well as the more formal, but much nicer inn rooms. These were designed by Ralph Lauren's people and outfitted with his stuff. They're tiny but bright and gorgeously decorated. If you can, grab room no. 1 in the main house, a bright, big split-level room with original floors from 1785.

47–52 Quogue St., Quogue, NY 11959. ℂ 631/653-6560. Fax 631/653-8026. www.innatquogue.com. 67 units. Mid-June to mid-Sept $175–$395 double, $450 and up cottages, Mon–Wed half-price in July and Aug; mid-Mar to mid-June $135–$275 double, $300 and up cottages; mid-Sept to mid-Mar $95–$115 double, $225 and up cottages. AE, DISC, MC, V. **Amenities:** Restaurant; lounge; outdoor pool; bike rental. *In room:* A/C, TV, kitchenette and hair dryer in some rooms.

Southampton Inn 🌟🌟 *(Kids)* Set on extensive grounds with a conference center, pool, tennis court, and kids' programs, this inn is more of a resort destination, but it's just around the corner from the town's chic shops and restaurants. And with the inn's free shuttle to the beach in summer, the nightmare of parking near Southampton sand vanishes. It's the kind of place that caters to everyone—families, groups, couples, even pet lovers—and does a good job making everyone happy. Standard rooms are nothing extravagant, but they are very comfortable and spacious and come loaded with amenities, making for a good value, even in the heart of summer.

91 Hill St., Southampton, NY 11968. ℂ 800/832-6500 or 631/283-6500. Fax 631/283-6559. www.southamptoninn. com. 90 units. Nov–Apr $129–$199 double, $319 and way up suite; May–Oct $149–$489 double, $399 and way, way up suite. Packages available. 2-night minimum on weekends May–Sept; 3-night minimum summer holiday weekends. AE, DC, DISC, MC, V. Pets allowed with $39 fee. **Amenities:** Outdoor heated pool; outdoor tennis court; exercise room; children's programs; game room; complimentary beach shuttle; babysitting; laundry service; same-day dry cleaning. *In room:* A/C, TV w/pay movies, dataport, fridge, hair dryer.

INEXPENSIVE
Harborside Resort Motel A solid, affordable option that's just 3 blocks from the sound and one of its beaches, this small L-shaped motel provides decent rooms in a

quiet locale. Rooms are nothing extravagant and some are a tight fit; some are a little heavy on the wood paneling, while others are painted white. Still, when you need to get out, there's a pool and tennis court on the premises—and, of course, the beach nearby.

371 W. Lake Dr., Montauk, NY 11954. © 631/668-2511. www.montaukharborside.com. 28 units. Early June to early Sept midweek $105–$180 double, weekend $135-$198 double, $260 and up apt.; early Sept to late Nov and Apr to early June midweek $75-$118 double, weekend $95-$135 double, $170 and up apt.; late Nov to end of Mar midweek $56-$78 double, weekend $68-$88 double, $78 and up apt. 3 night weekend minimum in summer; 2-night weekend minimum in spring and fall. AE, DC, DISC, MC, V. 1 mile east of Montauk, turn left onto W. Lake Dr. (County Rd. 77). **Amenities:** Outdoor pool; tennis court. *In room:* A/C, TV, kitchenettes (in some apts. only), fridge.

CAMPGROUNDS

Hither Hills State Park, Montauk (© **631/688-2554**), is a gem of a beach park without the pretension of the Hamptons. It also has a rarity: camping just steps from the 2-mile-long white-sand beach. A campground in chic East Hampton seems like an anomaly (and it is), but **Cedar Point County Park** (© **631/852-7620**) is set in a densely wooded area of East Hampton overlooking the Long Island Sound. The 190 campsites, which are a few minutes' walk from the water, can be used for tents and campers, though none have electric hookups.

WHERE TO DINE

While you'll always find the well dressed (and well heeled) in Hamptons restaurants, you won't feel out of place in casual attire unless you're dining at a very formal place like East Hampton's The Palm (an outpost of the New York City steakhouse). Even servers at celebrity hangout Almond are clad in blue jeans. Of course, under intense pressure to be the next big thing, restaurants can come and go pretty quickly. Keep up-to-date with the comings and goings by picking up the ubiquitous *Dan's Papers.*

EXPENSIVE

Almond 𝒜𝒜𝒜 FRENCH BISTRO   This newcomer has quickly caught fire as the Hamptons' hottest bistro, attracting celebs—Billy Joel and Joy Behar were there the night I was—and making reservations sometimes hard to come by. If you can, get a table in the back for a more relaxed atmosphere. The menu offers traditional bistro fare that is as simple as the decor, with only a few selections each night. Steak frites is a delicious (and excellent) choice, and salmon and flounder come tender and flavorful; many dishes are helped along with subtle doses of saffron.

1970 Montauk Hwy., Bridgehampton. © 631/537-8885. Reservations recommended. Main courses $19–$29. AE, DC, DISC, MC, V. Memorial Day to Labor Day Mon–Thurs 6–11pm, Fri–Sat 6pm–midnight, Sun 6–10pm; early Sept to late May Mon–Tues and Thurs 6–10pm, Fri–Sat 6–11pm, Sun 6–9pm.

Tierra Mar 𝒜𝒜 SEAFOOD   You can get an amazing ocean view with your dinner if you don't mind eating before the sun goes down. The dining room itself is spectacular, with chandeliers and a formal yet beachy feel. Appetizers fall short, so head straight for the entrees, paired with a wine from the extensive list. Hanger steak comes with a green peppercorn cream, and the Maine salmon is served with a lemon-caper vinaigrette. And if you like bouillabaisse, try this one: Atlantic fish and shellfish stew in a light garlic saffron broth and served with toasted Tuscan bread.

At the Bath & Tennis Hotel, 231 Dune Rd., Westhampton Beach. © 631/288-2700. Reservations recommended. Main courses $24–$45. AE, DC, MC, V. Memorial Day to Labor Day Mon–Thurs 9:30am–9pm; Fri–Sun until 10pm. Off-season days and hours vary; call first.

MODERATE

Rowdy Hall ✹ AMERICAN   The acclaimed burger at this English-pub-style restaurant is well worth the hype. Stacked high with all the fixin's, it's also well worth the $13. Even if you're not a burger fan, this place, tucked back among the shops of tony East Hampton, serves a good selection of upscale pub food and beers, which makes it perfect for lunch or dinner.

10 Main St., East Hampton. ✆ **631/324-8555**. Reservations not accepted. Main courses $13–$36. AE, MC, V. Daily noon–10pm, until 11pm July–Aug.

Southampton Publick House ✹✹ *Finds* PUB   This bustling pub is the only microbrewery out here, so come to it for a meal or just for the party that rages continuously. You'll find summer wheat beers and winter stouts on their inventive beer menu—formulas that have won them all kinds of awards. The menu covers the basics, but they're done well—from ale-battered fish and chips to great baby back ribs and lemon-pepper chicken with mango chutney. And if you come on Tuesdays, you can get a bonus: two-for-one entrees.

40 Bowden Sq., Southampton. ✆ **631/283-2800**. AE, DC, DISC, MC, V. Main courses $13–$25. Mon–Thurs 11:30am–10pm; Fri–Sat 11:30am–11pm; Sun noon–9pm.

INEXPENSIVE

Golden Pear COFFEE SHOP   With great coffee, fresh-baked muffins, and fluffy omelets, the three small Golden Pears are consistently good and quaint. They're the perfect place to grab a Sunday morning coffee with your *New York Times*. Or come by later in the day for lunch, when you'll find soups and salads.

Locations: 99 Main St., Southampton; ✆ **631/283-8900**. 34 Newtown Lane, East Hampton; ✆ **631/329-1600**. 2426 Montauk Hwy., Bridgehampton; ✆ **631/537-1100**. Sandwiches $7–$9. AE, MC, V. 7am–5:30pm daily.

Provisions ✹ WHOLE FOODS   This natural-foods market and cafe is a great quiet place to relax and bite into a breakfast nosh like a scrambled tofu wrap or a tempeh reuben with melted soy cheese and organic sauerkraut. And don't miss the smoothies and organic juices.

Corner of Bay and Division St., Sag Harbor. ✆ **631/725-3636**. Sandwiches $6.95–$11. AE, MC, V. Daily 8:30am–4pm.

Sip 'n Soda ✹✹ *Kids* *Value* DINER   This old-fashioned soda fountain dates from 1958 and is a fun place for kids and adults alike. It also boasts prices that haven't hit the new millennium yet, making for some of the cheapest eats in Southampton.

40 Hampton St., Southampton. ✆ **631/283-9752**. Entrees from $4, burgers from $3.35. No credit cards. July–Aug Fri–Mon and Wed 7:30am–10pm, Tues and Thurs until 8pm; rest of year Mon–Sat 7:30am–5pm, Sun until 4pm.

THE HAMPTONS AFTER DARK

As you might imagine, Hamptons nightlife can be quite the scene. Bars can fill up quickly and some even roll out the velvet rope to restrict their clientele to models and people with movie deals. And while the über-chichi (and now infamous) Conscience Point Inn in Southampton closed its doors, you'll never be lacking for nightlife; just wander around Southampton or East Hampton and you may well mistake it for ancient Rome right before its decline. Grab a copy of *Dan's Papers* or pick up the *East Hampton Star* or the *Southampton Press* for listings.

NIGHTCLUBS & LIVE MUSIC

Le Flirt ✹✹   Formerly the Resort Lounge, this East Hampton hot spot reopened in 2007 as more of a restaurant, albeit one with a chic cabaret nightclub. The dramatically designed main dining area is used for live cabaret performances and dancing with a DJ. Expect longtime regulars like Betsey Johnson, Russell Simmons, P. Diddy, Carson Daly, and Star Jones to be returning to check out the new scene. Open Thursday to Saturday 10pm to 4am. 44 Three Mile Harbor Rd., East Hampton. ✆ 631/329-6000. Admission free except when there's a band or live cabaret. AE, MC, V.

Stephen Talkhouse ✶✶✶ Year-round live music draws folks in droves to this small Amagansett club for events that are often standing-room-only. Covers range from $5 to $100 depending on the act, which could be local blues acts or bigger names like Suzanne Vega or Todd Rundgren. The space gets a bit cramped, but the music is almost always great. And folks like Billy Joel, Paul Simon, and Paul McCartney have been known to show up unannounced and party with the band. Open nightly 7pm to 4am. 161 Main St., Amagansett. ✆ 631/267-3117. Admission $10–$20. AE, MC, V.

6 Shelter Island

Tiny and secluded, nestled between Long Island's two forks, Shelter Island has for centuries been a sheltered getaway spot. Relaxed and barely developed, it has some nice beaches, secluded coves great for boating and swimming, and an atmosphere unlike anything on the North or South forks. More than one-third of Shelter Island is owned by the Nature Conservancy and maintained as a nature preserve. There's lots of lush greenery and dense woods all across the island; the only "townlike" area is around Shelter Island Heights on the island's northwest corner. One hotel, a couple of antiques shops, a coffee shop, and a couple of restaurants are really all that's here.

ESSENTIALS
GETTING THERE   Shelter Island is accessible only by boat, but it's just about a 10-minute ferry trip from the mainland. If you're driving, the **LIE** runs out to Riverhead; then head north to Greenport or south to Sag Harbor. From Greenport on the North Fork, the **North Ferry Co.** (✆ 631/749-0139) runs every 15 to 30 minutes from 6am to midnight. The price is $9 for car and driver one-way, $2 per extra person or for walk-ons. From Sag Harbor, the **South Ferry** (✆ 631/749-1200) runs every 10 to 12 minutes from 5:40am to 11:45pm year-round, with extended hours in the summer and extended weekend hours the rest of the year. The price is $10 per car one-way, $1 per person for walk-ons. Since Shelter Island is so small, it doesn't matter which ferry you take, but if you don't want to bother with a car, you can take the **Long Island Rail Road** (✆ 516/822-LIRR) to Greenport; the ferry is right next to the train station.

VISITOR INFORMATION   Contact the **Long Island Convention and Visitors Bureau** at ✆ 877/FUN-ON-LI or 631/951-3440.

GETTING AROUND   If you just want to relax at your hotel, someone will pick you up from the ferry. But if you want to venture out, you'll need a car. Check out the South Fork section of this chapter for information on car rentals. On the island, you can get a taxi by calling **Shelter Island Go-fors** (✆ 631/749-4252).

BEACHES & OUTDOOR PURSUITS
BEACHES   Beaches here tend to be narrow strips of sand, but the protected waters are perfect for swimming. Head to **Crescent Beach** and **Silver Beach,** both along the southwestern area of the island.

FISHING   Take off among the rich waters around the island in search of striped bass and bluefish (May–July), then catch stripers, blues, and false albacore on a half- or full-day charter with **Light Tackle Challenge,** 91 W. Neck Rd. (© **631/749-1906**).

HIKING   The **Mashomack Preserve,** Route 114 (near the South Ferry office; © **631/749-1001**), encompasses more than 2,000 acres in southeastern Shelter Island, more than a third of the island. Ex–hunting club territory, the Nature Conservancy purchased it in 1980 and has protected its oak woodlands, marshes, freshwater ponds, and tidal creeks ever since. Car-free, it's a great place to go for easy hikes and look for osprey, ibis, hummingbirds, muskrats, foxes, harbor seals, and terrapins. It's open daily July to August from 9am to 5pm; September to June 9am to 4pm, closed Tuesdays. Park just inside the preserve entrance and pick up a trail map and hike the four well-marked trails of varying lengths and difficulty (up to 11 miles).

KAYAKING   The protected waters of Shelter Island's bays make for a scenic place to slice through on a kayak. You'll likely see the island's deer, osprey, and other wildlife. Go with **Shelter Island Kayak Tours,** Route 114 and Duvall Road (© **631/749-1990**). Rent a kayak ($30 per hour, 2-hr. minimum) or take a 2-hour tour ($60). The **Nature Conservancy** (© **631/749-1001**) also runs a few kayaking trips around Mashomack Preserve in the summer.

WHERE TO STAY
With a couple of exceptions, don't count on rooms with tons of space.

EXPENSIVE
Sunset Beach 🌟🌟🌟   Designed by Andre Balazs of L.A.'s Chateau Marmont fame, this hotel drips all the hipness you'd expect. The minimalist rooms are done all in white, with contemporary aluminum lamps and splashes of color (like bold orange sinks). But the prize in these rooms is outside: enormous balconies on all of them, looking out onto the water, which more than makes up for the teeny bathrooms and small kitchenettes.

35 Shore Rd., Shelter Island, NY 11965. © **631/749-2001.** Fax 631/749-1843. www.sunsetbeachli.com. 20 units. July–Aug weekday $305–$330 double, weekend $450–$480 double; mid-May to June and Sept weekday $215–$245 double, weekend $370–$400 double. 2-night weekend minimum. AE, DC, DISC, MC, V. Closed Oct to mid-May. From the North Ferry, take Rte. 114 south to W. Neck Rd., which becomes Shore Rd. Pets allowed with $100 fee. **Amenities:** Restaurant; free use of mountain bikes; limited room service; laundry service. *In room:* A/C, TV/VCR, kitchenettes (some units), minibar, hair dryer, iron.

MODERATE
The Pridwin 🌟 *Kids*   Sitting on the same stretch of beach as the Sunset Beach hotel (see above), this larger inn is decidedly less hip but offers good value. With one big inn and several small cottages, the grounds are fairly extensive and many rooms have good water views. The smallish hotel rooms have a retro look; get one with a water view, which is spectacular. Cottages have the same '70s feel and small bathrooms, but with big decks and kitchenettes.

P.O. Box 2009, Crescent Beach, Shelter Island, NY 11964. © **800/273-2497** or 631/749-0476. Fax 631/749-2071. www.pridwin.com. 49 units. Open early May to Oct. July to early Sept Sun–Thurs $187–$277 double, $257 and up cottages; Fri–Sat $237–$337 double, $317 and up cottages; rates include full breakfast; for dinner plan, add $50 for 2 people. June and Sept Sun–Thurs $159 and up double, cottages $179 and up; Fri–Sat $199 and up double, $229 and up cottages. Rates are lower in May and Oct. Outside of high season rates include continental breakfast on weekends only. 2-night weekend minimum June–Sept. AE, MC, V. From the North Ferry, take 114 south to West Neck Rd.; it becomes Shore Rd. and hotel is on the left. **Amenities:** Restaurant; lounge; outdoor saltwater pool; 3 tennis courts; extensive watersports rentals; bike rentals; game room; coin-op laundry. *In room:* A/C, TV, kitchenette (in cottages).

Ram's Head Inn 𝘍𝘍   Set on a small, private beach with extensive grounds, this inn is one of the island's most luxurious. Rooms have comfortable wicker furniture, lacy table coverings, and nice touches like pedestal sinks (though some have a shared bathroom). Rooms and bathrooms are small, but the grounds are gorgeous, with Adirondack chairs, hammocks, a small beach, and free use of the hotel's boats.

108 Rams Island Dr., Shelter Island, NY 11965. ℂ 631/749-0811. Fax 631/749-0059. www.shelterislandinns.com. 17 units, 5 with private bathroom. May–Oct $75–$150 double with shared bathroom; $165–$350 suite with semi-private bathroom; $135–$325 double with private bathroom. Special discount midweek rates available. Closed Nov-Apr. AE, MC, V. From North Ferry take 114 north, bear right onto Cartwright Rd., turn right at stop sign to Ram Island Rd., turn right onto Ram Island Dr. **Amenities:** Restaurant; lounge; tennis court; tiny fitness room; sauna; complimentary watersports; limited room service. *In room:* A/C.

WHERE TO DINE
EXPENSIVE

Ram's Head 𝘍𝘍𝘍 AMERICAN   Shelter Island's best restaurant is in the flowery, formal, and intimate dining room of the Ram's Head Inn. Both meat and seafood are done equally well. Dig into the jumbo lump crab and lobster risotto with chanterelles and wild asparagus, the American red snapper with wilted spinach, morels, and lemongrass butter, or the Opal Valley Australian rack of lamb with garlic *pommes anna* and rosemary jus. The service and wine list are also very good.

108 Rams Island Dr. ℂ 631/749-0811. Reservations recommended. Main courses $22–$35. AE, MC, V. May–Oct Wed–Mon 6–10pm, Sat–Sun 11:30am–2pm. From North Ferry take 114 north, bear right onto Cartwright Rd., turn right at stop sign to Ram Island Rd., turn right onto Ram Island Dr.

Vine Street Café 𝘍𝘍𝘍 *Finds* AMERICAN   This brand-new member of the Shelter Island scene is bound to cause a stir. The cafe's interior couldn't be more basic: wood floors, simple wooden tables and chairs, white walls, exposed beams. But the brief menu—relying on local, organic ingredients—presents intensively complex flavors, such as the miso-glazed salmon with bok choy, mushrooms, and jasmine rice. The seafood options only get better, with options like ceviches and a seasonal raw bar.

41 South Ferry Rd. ℂ 631/749-3210. Reservations preferred. Main courses $18–$32. AE, DISC, MC, V. Memorial Day to mid-Sept Sun–Thurs 5:30–11:30pm, Fri–Sat 5:30–midnight, Sat–Sun noon–3pm; mid-Sept to Memorial Day Thurs and Mon 5:30–10pm, Fri–Sat 5:30pm–midnight.

MODERATE

Sweet Tomato's 𝘍𝘍 AMERICAN   This eatery in the tiny town of Shelter Island Heights is quickly catching on as a good dinner stop after antiquing. The menu doesn't present any surprises, but in the bright, cheery restaurant with classic hardwood floors, the classics are served up nicely. Try the chicken Antonio: chicken breast chunks with sautéed onions and peas in a pink, cognac cream sauce with rigatoni.

15 Grand Ave. ℂ 631/749-4114. Main courses $12–$29. AE, DC, DISC, MC, V. July to Labor Day daily 5–10pm; rest of the year Tues–Sun 5–10pm.

INEXPENSIVE

Pat & Steve's Family Restaurant 𝘍 *Kids* DINER   This is a family favorite that fills with patrons for breakfast, lunch, and dinner. Bite into pancakes for just a couple of bucks, or snag perhaps the only $4 burger in town.

63 North Ferry Rd. ℂ 631/749-1998. Sandwiches $4–$8. No credit cards. Mon–Tues 6am–3pm; Thurs–Sat 6am–8pm, Sun 6am–3pm. Closed Wed.

7

The Hudson River Valley

by Neil E. Schlecht

The Mississippi is the longest and most famous river in the United States, but no river commands a larger place in American history than the Hudson. America's first great waterway flows from the Adirondacks down to New York City and the open sea. The rise of the United States from renegade colony to great nation is intrinsically linked at every stage to the mighty Hudson River. First sailed by Henry Hudson in 1609, it became the principal avenue of transportation for the emergent colonies in the 17th and 18th centuries and strategic territory during the war for American independence. As the young nation evolved, the Hudson became the axis along which some of America's most legendary families—among them, the Livingstons, Vanderbilts, Roosevelts, and Rockefellers—shaped the face of American industry and politics, leaving legacies of grand country estates and the towns that grew up around them.

Just over 300 miles long, the river is less mighty in size than stature. The Hudson River Valley spans eight counties along the east and west banks of the river, extending from Albany down to Yonkers. Divided into manageable thirds, the

Lower, Middle, and Upper Hudson together compose a National Heritage Area and one of the most beautiful regions in the eastern United States. The river valley's extraordinary landscapes gave birth to America's first art school, the Hudson River School of Painters, and writers like Edith Wharton and Washington Irving set their stories and novels along the banks of the Hudson. Though a place of immense historical importance and beauty, the river valley also has an impressive roster of sights and activities. The Hudson is lined with stunning country manor houses open to the public, unique museums, splendid historic sites, and easygoing Victorian hamlets. You can hike, golf, fish, boat, kayak, and even ski within easy reach of any of the towns along the Hudson. The valley—flush with organic farms and orchards, artisanal cheese makers, farmers' markets, and a growing number of wineries and small restaurants with Culinary Institute chefs at the helm—is fast becoming a real destination for gastronomes. For lovers of culture, history, the arts, the outdoors, and good food, the Hudson River Valley has few rivals anywhere in the country.

1 Orientation

ARRIVING

BY PLANE   Most visitors traveling by air will probably fly into one of three major airports in the New York City area. For information on those, see chapter 5. Other possibilities include **Albany International Airport,** 737 Albany-Shaker Rd. (© **518/242-2222;** flight information © **518/242-2359;** www.albanyairport.com), at the north end of the Upper Hudson Valley, and **Stewart International Airport,** Route

207, New Windsor (© **845/564-2100;** www.stewartintlairport.com), near New-burgh, which handles daily flights from major U.S. cities such as Atlanta, Chicago, Philadelphia, Raleigh/Durham, and Washington, D.C.

BY CAR   Most visitors embark on tours of the Hudson Valley by private automo-bile. Major car-rental companies, including Avis, Budget, Enterprise, Hertz, National, and Thrifty, have representatives at all the major airports. The Lower Hudson Valley begins just north of New York City, on either side of the river; take either I-87 (New York State Thruway) north or the Taconic State Parkway. From Albany south, take I-87 south to 9W or I-90 south to Route 9. Heading either east or west, the most direct route is along I-84.

BY TRAIN   **Amtrak** (© **800/USA-RAIL;** www.amtrak.com) has service to the Hudson Valley from New York City, Syracuse, Buffalo, Montreal, and Boston, with stops in Albany, Rensselaer, Poughkeepsie, Rhinecliff, New Rochelle, Yonkers, Croton Harmon, and Hudson.

The **Metro-North Railroad** (© **800/638-7646;** www.mta.nyc.ny.us/mnr) travels up and down the Hudson. The trip along the river on the east side is one of the most scenic train trips in the U.S. The commuter line runs from Grand Central Station in New York City and services Westchester, Orange, Rockland, Putnam, and Dutchess counties (with stops in Beacon, Chappaqua, Cold Spring, Garrison, Katonah, Pough-keepsie, Tarrytown, and Yonkers, among others). Some packages include round-trip train travel and admission to sights, such as the 1-day getaways to Dia:Beacon and the Rockefeller estate, Kykuit.

BY BUS   Bus service throughout the Hudson Valley is available on **Adirondack/ Pine Hills Trailways** (© **800/858-8555;** www.trailwaysny.com), with service to New York City, New Paltz, Kingston, and Albany; **Greyhound Bus Lines** (© **800/231-2222;** www.greyhound.com); and **Shortline Coach USA** (© **800/631-8405;** www.shortlinebus.com), with local service from New York City and throughout Orange, Rockland, and Dutchess counties.

VISITOR INFORMATION

General tourist information is available by calling **Hudson Valley Tourism, Inc.** (© **800/232-4782**) or by visiting the organization's website, www.travelhudsonvalley.org, for links to the very informative sites maintained by each of the eight counties that touch upon the Hudson River Valley. Tourist information offices or kiosks (and even cabooses) are found in a number of towns and at many historic sites, often oper-ated in season only. Offices that provide information and other resources for travelers include **Orange County Chamber of Commerce,** 11 Racquet Rd., Newburgh (© 845/567-6229; Mon–Fri 8:30am–5pm); **Greater Cornwall Chamber of Commerce,** 238 Main St., Cornwall (© 845/534-7826; Mon–Fri 9am–4:30pm); **Westchester County Office of Tourism,** 222 Mamaroneck Ave., Suite 100, White Plains (© 800/833-9282); **Putnam Visitors Bureau,** 110 Old Rte. 6, Building 3, Carmel (© 800/470-4854); **Dutchess County Tourism Promotion Agency,** 3 Neptune Rd., Suite M-17, Poughkeepsie (© 914/463-4000); **Rhinebeck Chamber of Commerce,** Route 9, Rhinebeck (© 914/876-4778); **Hudson Office of Tourism,** 401 State St., Hud-son (© 800/727-1846; Mon–Fri 8:30am–4pm); and the **County Office Building,** 10 Westbrook Lane, Kingston (© 845/340-3566; Mon–Fri 9am–5pm).

Many good free publications are widely available at hotels, restaurants, and other sites; look for *Hudson Valley Guide, Hooked on the Hudson River Valley, About Town,*

The Valley Table, and *Chronogram.* These all contain information on arts, entertainment, and dining.

AREA LAYOUT

The Hudson Valley extends from the banks of the river to the foothills of the Catskill Mountains in the west and approaches the Connecticut border in the east (and the Massachusetts border in the Upper Hudson Valley). This chapter is in an order contrary to the current of the Hudson River: from Lower to Upper. For the purposes of this chapter, the Lower Hudson includes the area from Yonkers and Nyack to Newburgh and Beacon (comprising Rockland, Orange, Westchester, and Putnam counties); the Mid-Hudson, from Newburgh to Rhinebeck (Ulster and Dutchess counties); and the Upper Hudson, west of the river and north to Chatham (Columbia County). These dividing lines are somewhat arbitrary, with occasional county overlap; if you're intending to explore only a single section of the Hudson Valley, be aware that attractions and lodgings in one part of the valley may be only minutes by car from those categorized in another. Towns that could certainly be considered part of the Hudson Valley, such as Saugerties and Catskill, are discussed instead in chapter 8, "The Catskill Mountain Region."

The Hudson River Valley is packed with sights from one end to the other, but the area is pretty manageable in size and easy to get around, especially if you have your own transportation. From the town of Hudson in the north to Yonkers, just outside New York City, is a distance of under 120 miles and just 2 hours by car. You could spend a couple of days or a couple of weeks making your way up the river. For this reason, note that in the sections that follow, attractions are grouped geographically, rather than alphabetically.

GETTING AROUND

BY CAR By far the easiest way to get around the Hudson Valley is by car. Public transportation, especially where it concerns county bus systems, is unduly complicated. Your best bet if not traveling by private automobile is one of the major bus carriers (see above), the train, or a tour operator. The main roads traversing the length of the Hudson Valley are I-87 and Route 9W on the west side of the river and Route 9 and the Taconic Parkway on the east.

The major car-rental agencies, which have outlets at airports and at several addresses throughout the region, include **Alamo** (© 800/327-9633), **Avis** (© 800/331-1212), **Budget** (© 800/527-0700), **Dollar** (© 800/800-4000), **Enterprise** (© 800/RENT-A-CAR), **Hertz** (© 800/654-3131), **National** (© 800/227-7368), and **Thrifty** (© 800/367-2277).

BY BUS OR TRAIN See "Arriving," above.

BY TAXI Local taxis are available at all the major train and bus stations, and in larger towns. Among taxi services throughout the Hudson Valley are **Rocket Cab** in Hyde Park (© 914/456-5783); **Yellow Cab Company** in Poughkeepsie (© 845/471-1100); **Rhinebeck Taxi** (© 845/876-5466); and **Howard's Taxi** in Hudson (© 518/828-7673).

BY ORGANIZED TOUR **Shortline Coach USA** (© 800/631-8405; www.shortline bus.com) offers Hudson Valley day trips and overnight packages and tours. **River Valley Tours** (© 800/836-2128; www.rivervalleytours.com) organizes weeklong, inn-to-inn, and boat and bus trips along the Hudson. They're not offered often and are a little

---

Tips **When to Go**

Many of the great Hudson River estates and other attractions in the region are closed during the long winter months. In **spring and summer,** a number of the estates have extensive formal gardens and are absolutely glorious in May and June, and many have special events like concerts. In **autumn,** the leaves are ablaze with color and gorgeously set off against the backdrop of the river.

---

pricey (at just under $2,000 per person), but they allow visitors to really experience the grandeur and history of the Hudson River. **New York Waterway** (© **800/53-FERRY**; www.nywaterway.com) offers tours by boat (including Sleepy Hollow, Autumn on the Hudson, and Kykuit cruises) from Pier 78 in Manhattan (weekends and Mon holidays May–Oct). **Metro-North Railroad** (© **800/METRO-INFO**; www.mta.nyc.ny.us/mnr/html/outbound.htm) has a series of "One-Day Getaways" to such places as Cold Spring, Dia:Beacon, Kykuit, and Woodbury Common, as well as organized 1-day hiking and biking tours.

2 The Lower Hudson Valley

The Lower Hudson Valley, just north of New York City, claims some of the region's most popular sights, including the literary legends and grand estates of Sleepy Hollow, West Point Military Academy, and important Revolutionary War sites. Two of the valley's most picturesque and enjoyable villages, Cold Spring and Nyack, cling to either side of the river, and the scenery, with the rocky Palisades framing the wide expanses of the river, is stunning.

EXPLORING THE LOWER HUDSON VALLEY
EAST SIDE OF THE HUDSON

Washington Irving's Sunnyside ⍟   Washington Irving—man of letters, diplomat, architectural historian, gentleman farmer, and first true international celebrity—designed an eclectic cottage in the country in 1835. Before he wrote *The Legend of Sleepy Hollow* and introduced the world to the Headless Horseman and Rip Van Winkle, Irving lived in England and was minister to Spain, where he rediscovered the Alhambra palace and reawakened its mystical architecture and magic aura with his *Tales of the Alhambra.* Sunnyside, with its mélange of historic and architectural styles, including a Dutch stepped-gable roofline, a Spanish tower, and master bedroom modeled after a Paris apartment, was Irving's very personal romantic retreat, a place to write and retire. Today the charming pastoral villa, swathed in vines and wisteria and nestled into the grounds along the Hudson, remains as he left it, with his books and writing papers in the study. The train rumbles by the riverfront property, as it did toward the end of Irving's life (he died here in 1859 at the age of 76). During the holidays, Sunnyside is festooned with Victorian Christmas decorations, and there are singalongs and storytelling—perfectly appropriate for a storybook house. The 45-minute tours are led by guides in 19th-century costume.

W. Sunnyside Lane, off Rte. 9, Tarrytown. © **914/591-8763.** www.hudsonvalley.org/sunnyside/index.htm. Admission $12 adults, $10 seniors, $6 students ages 5–17, free for children under 5. Grounds-only admission $5 adults and seniors, $3 students ages 5–17, free for children under 5. Apr–Oct Wed–Mon 10am–5pm (last tour at 4pm); Nov–Dec Wed–Mon 10am–4pm (last tour at 3pm); Mar weekends only 10am–4pm (last tour at 3pm). Closed Jan–Feb. Metro-North to Tarrytown.

Tips **Sleepy Hollow Cemetery**

Near Philipsburg Manor, in a gorgeous natural setting, is **Sleepy Hollow Cemetery,** 85 peaceful acres where several famous former residents of the Lower Hudson River Valley, including Andrew Carnegie, William Rockefeller, and Washington Irving, are buried. (Alas, you won't find either the Headless Horseman or Ichabod Crane, both fictional characters, entombed here.) The cemetery, on the east side of Route 9 just north of Tarrytown and the town of Sleepy Hollow, is open to the public; call *C* **914/631-0081** or visit www.sleepyhollow cemetery.org for more information. It's open Monday through Friday from 8am to 4:30pm and weekends from 8:30am to 4:30pm.

Lyndhurst *Kids*   One of the most impressive estates along the Lower Hudson, this handsomely restored Gothic Revival mansion, the finest of its style in the U.S., was designed by A. J. Davis in 1838 for a former New York City mayor. Later purchased by the railroad magnate and financier Jay Gould, the villa features an asymmetrical structure and grand Gothic interiors (including lots of faux stone and marble and stained-glass windows). The 67-acre estate, an excellent example of 19th-century landscape design, features a massive glass and steel-framed conservatory (the largest of its day), rose garden, and arboretum. Today the mansion, a National Trust Historic Site, is decorated with many original furnishings and decorative objects culled from the three families that inhabited the estate over 123 years. A number of lectures and other activities, including vintage "base ball" games staged on the front lawn and candlelight Christmas evenings, are held at Lyndhurst. The self-guided audio tour, included in the price of admission, is extremely well done, with an extended version that covers the entire property and Hudson Valley history and a children's version with entertaining features that will tune in the kids to history and architecture. Plan on at least an hour or two here, several if you wish to explore the grounds.

635 S. Broadway, Tarrytown. *C* **914/631-4481.** www.lyndhurst.org. Admission $10 adults, $9 seniors, $4 students ages 12–17, free for children under 12; grounds-only pass $4. Mid-Apr to Oct Tues–Sun and holiday Mon 10am–5pm; Nov to mid-Apr weekends and holiday Mon 10am–4pm. Guided tours at 10:30am, 11:45am, 2:15pm, 3:30pm, and 4:15pm Tues–Fri, more frequently on weekends. Metro-North to Tarrytown.

Philipsburg Manor *Kids*   Just a half-hour upriver from the 21st-century pace of New York City, this eye-opening and serenely beautiful agricultural estate is a jarring retreat to the late 17th and early 18th centuries. The bridge across the millpond of this Colonial farm and water-powered gristmill transports visitors to a complicated time in history, when this estate functioned as one of the largest slave plantations in the North—a shock to those who associate slavery only with the South. Organizers use that history to educate and place the estate, the entire Hudson Valley, and the influence of African culture in a historical context. Live demonstrations and scripted vignettes by interpreters in period dress bring to life the Colonial agricultural and merchant activities that took place here, re-creating the lives of the single caretaker and 23 skilled slaves who lived and worked at this provision plantation. Frederick Philipse made his fortune in shipping and export to the West Indies, commerce that included the human slave trade. The large original manor house dates from 1685; Philipse's landholdings in the area totaled more than 50,000 acres. When he died a bachelor, he left a 50-page inventory of his belongings, including the names of all his slaves, testimony to his extraordinary wealth. The site

Lower Hudson Valley

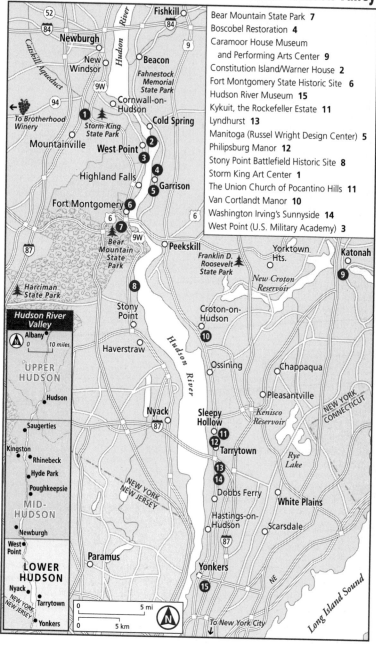

Bear Mountain State Park **7**
Boscobel Restoration **4**
Caramoor House Museum
  and Performing Arts Center **9**
Constitution Island/Warner House **2**
Fort Montgomery State Historic Site **6**
Hudson River Museum **15**
Kykuit, the Rockefeller Estate **11**
Lyndhurst **13**
Manitoga (Russel Wright Design Center) **5**
Philipsburg Manor **12**
Stony Point Battlefield Historic Site **8**
Storm King Art Center **1**
The Union Church of Pocantino Hills **11**
Van Cortlandt Manor **10**
Washington Irving's Sunnyside **14**
West Point (U.S. Military Academy) **3**

still functions as a working farm, with horses and sheep, wool spinning, milling of flour, and harvesting of rye in June and July. A great, educational outing for families (children will especially enjoy the special "Hands on the House" tours, featuring interactive "touch rooms," held on weekends at 11:30am, 2:30pm, and 4pm); allow a couple of hours.

Rte. 9, Sleepy Hollow. (✆ 914/631-3992. www.hudsonvalley.org/philipsburg/index.htm. Admission $12 adults, $10 seniors, $6 students ages 5–17, free for children under 5. Apr–Oct Wed–Mon 10am–5pm (last tour 4pm); Nov–Dec Wed–Mon 10am–4pm (last tour 3pm); Mar weekends only 10am–4pm (last tour 3pm). Closed Jan–Feb. Metro-North to Tarrytown.

Kykuit, the Rockefeller Estate ✫✫✫
The Hudson River is lined from one end to the other with grand manor houses, but none compares to Kykuit (pronounced "*Kye*-cut"). It's not the oldest or even the largest of the estates, but many people find it the most spectacular. When John D. Rockefeller, founder of Standard Oil, built Kykuit in its present classical Greek-Roman style in 1913, he was the richest man in the world. The estate, which became home to four generations of one of America's most famous business and philanthropic families, is architecturally grand and spectacularly sited and landscaped, with lovely stone terraces, fountains, and extensive Italianate formal gardens. Kykuit also houses Governor (and later Vice President) Nelson Rockefeller's incredible collection of 20th-century modern art, which graces the gardens and fills the entire lower level of the house. The sculpture collection includes important works by Alexander Calder, Henry Moore, Constantin Brancusi, and David Smith among its 70 works, all placed with great care to take maximum advantage of the gardens and their sweeping views of the Hudson (both of which are perhaps unequaled by any of the great river estates). Outstanding among the pieces in the very Sixties art gallery in the house is a unique series of giant and shockingly vibrant tapestries commissioned from Pablo Picasso.

Visits to Kykuit begin at Philipsburg Manor (see above); coaches shuttle visitors to Kykuit. Tours of Kykuit last between 2 and 3 hours. Choose from among seven different tours depending on your interest: House and Inner Garden Tour; Gardens and Sculpture Tour; in-depth Grand Tour; Modern Art Tour; Family Tour; Selected Highlights Tour; and Time Saver Tour. In high season, tours often sell out by midday; advance reservations for individuals are suggested for the Grand Tour and Modern Art Tour.

Pocantino Hills, Sleepy Hollow (Rte. 9, 2 miles north of the Tappan Zee Bridge). (✆ 914/631-9491. www.hudsonvalley. org/kykuit/index.htm. Admission, House and Inner Garden, Gardens and Sculpture, or Selected Highlights Tour $23 adults, $21 seniors and children; Grand Tour $38; Time Saver Tour $20; Modern Art Tour $30; Family Tour $15; indoor tours not recommended for children under 10. Late Apr to early Nov Wed–Mon House and Inner Garden Tour 10am–3pm (until 4pm on weekends and during daylight saving time); Gardens and Sculpture Tour 11am weekends; Grand Tour Wed–Mon 9:45am and 1:45pm, also 3:15pm weekends; Family Tour (1 hr.) 10:50am weekends; Selected Highlights Tour 11am and 1:15pm weekdays and 1:15pm weekends; Time Saver Tour 12:50 and 3:35pm weekdays and 3:35pm weekends; Modern Art Tour 12:50pm weekends. Closed Tues. Visitor center at Philipsburg Manor opens at 9am to sell Kykuit tickets for that day only; tickets also available online. Metro-North to Tarrytown.

Boscobel Restoration ✫✫
Two things about this magnificent mansion on the Hudson stand out: its splendid setting, among the finest in the entire Hudson Valley, and its incredible history. The house, an early-19th-century neoclassical Georgian mansion, was rescued from government destruction (it was sold at auction for $35 in the 1950s), moved piece by piece to its current location, and meticulously restored thanks to the generosity of the co-founder of *Reader's Digest*. The decorative arts of the Federal period that fill the house are indeed impressive, but they have a difficult time competing with the extraordinary river and gorge views afforded from the lawns, gardens, and orchards. No estate site along the river is more dramatic. Many activities are

held here and should not be missed, including the Hudson Valley Shakespeare Festival (advance reservations required; www.hvshakespeare.org) in the summer, dancing to big-band music in the fall, and pre-Victorian Christmas Candlelight tours.

1601 Rte. 9D, Garrison. ✆ 845/265-3638. www.boscobel.org. Admission $12 adults, $10 seniors, $7 students ages 6–14, free for children under 6; grounds only, $7 adults, $5 seniors, free for children under 15. Apr–Oct Wed–Mon 9:30am–5pm (last tour at 4:15pm); Nov–Dec Wed–Mon 9:30am–4pm (last tour at 3:15pm). Closed Jan–Mar and May 20. Metro-North to Tarrytown.

WEST SIDE OF THE HUDSON

West Point (U.S. Military Academy) ☆

West Point, the nation's oldest and foremost military college—which celebrated its 200th anniversary in 2002 and is the oldest continually used military post in the U.S.—has produced some of the greatest generals and leaders this country has known, including Robert E. Lee, Ulysses S. Grant, Douglas MacArthur, George Patton, and Dwight D. Eisenhower. (Edgar Allan Poe, however, dropped out!) West Point is one of the nation's most esteemed and rigorous science and engineering colleges. The most popular attraction in the entire Hudson Valley, West Point is no longer as visitor-friendly as it once was, however, due to heightened security concerns. In fact, whereas visitors once were free to roam the campus among the orderly cadets in their dress blues, for the foreseeable future the only way to visit is by organized 1- or 2-hour (June–Oct only) tours on a bus. It makes stops at the famous Cadet Chapel, which possesses stained-glass windows that were gifts of graduating classes and the largest church organ in the world, with more than 21,000 pipes; the Cadet Cemetery; and Trophy Point, where cannons captured from five wars are gathered in remembrance. The massive campus (home to just 4,000 student soldiers), with its Gothic Revival buildings perched on the west side above the Hudson River, is undeniably handsome, especially in fall. Tickets for all tours must be purchased at the visitor center. It's advisable to call ahead to confirm the tour schedule. Behind the visitor center, the West Point Museum is the oldest and largest collection of war memorabilia and war trophies in the U.S. See an atomic bomb, the cannon that fired the first American shot in World War I, Hitler's Lilliputian presentation pistol, and uniforms and artifacts that trace the history of warfare. For war and history buffs, it will be fascinating; for others, considerably less so. Allow 2 to 3 hours for the entire visit.

Rte. 218, Highland Falls. ✆ 845/446-4724. www.usma.edu or www.westpointtours.com. West Point 2-hr tours admission $12 adults, $10 children under 12; museum free; 1-hr. tours admission $10 adults, $7 children under 12. 1-hr tours Apr–Oct Mon–Sat 9:45am–3:30pm, Sun 11am–3:30pm; Nov Mon–Fri 10am–2:30pm, Sat 10am–3:30pm; Sun 11am–3:30pm; Dec–Mar daily 11:15am and 1:15pm. 2-hr. tours June–Oct daily 11:15am and 1:45pm; Nov 1:45pm only. No tours on Sat of home football games or during graduation 3rd week in May. Museum daily 10:30am–4:15pm.

Storm King Art Center ☆☆☆ (Kids)

A most unusual museum, this fabulous collection of modern, monumental sculpture benefits from one of the most stunning outdoor settings modern art has ever seen: 500 acres of rolling hills, meadows, and woodlands that, especially in autumn, are capable of converting contemporary-art doubters into passionate enthusiasts. Storm King's interplay between nature and human creativity is extraordinary. On view are nearly 100 large-scale works by some of the greatest American and European sculptors of the postwar 20th century, including Mark di Suvero, Henry Moore, Magdalena Abakanowicz, Isamu Noguchi, Alexander Calder, Richard Serra, Andy Goldsworthy, and, forming the nucleus of the collection, 13 works by David Smith (with the outdoor placement echoing Smith's

Finds Constitution Island/Warner House

From the end of June to the beginning of October, visitors to West Point can take a ferry out to **Constitution Island,** nearly forgotten in the middle of the Hudson River, 900 feet east of the military academy. The tiny island (287 acres) is home to the 1836 Warner mansion, the fully furnished Victorian home of the writers Susan and Anna Warner (Susan was the author of the million-selling *Wide, Wide World*), and Revolutionary War ruins of Fort Constitution (chains were floated across the Hudson here to delay advancing British troops). The sisters, who never married, lived on the island until their deaths (they are buried at West Point Cemetery). Costumed docents lead visitors on a most unexpected view of American history from the middle of one of its most historic rivers, and kids love it. Reservations are essential, as tours are limited to 40 people; ferries leave from the South Dock at West Point. Tours are given Wednesday and Thursday from the last week in June to mid-October at 1 and 2pm; www.constitutionisland.org. Admission is $10 adults, $9 seniors and children ages 6 to 16, $3 children 5 and under. Tours last 2 hours, 15 minutes. For reservations and information, call (C) **845/446-8676.**

studio in the Adirondacks). The most recent acquisition is di Suvero's *Joie de Vivre.* Every year Storm King presents a temporary exhibition of a couple of dozen works by a major sculptor (in the past it has focused on Smith and Calder). Though a warm, sunny day may be nicest to enjoy Storm King, the sculptures look and feel different under different conditions and in different seasons, so there is really no bad time to visit. Storm King is a great place to spend an entire day, and perfect for introducing children to art; bring a picnic lunch, as you are encouraged to do (no food concessions are on the grounds). You'll need several hours to see Storm King and could easily spend an entire day here.

Old Pleasant Hill Rd., Mountainville. (C) 845/534-3115. www.stormking.org. Admission $10 adults, $9 seniors and college students, $7 children K–12, free for children under 5; Acoustiguide audio tours $5. Apr to mid-Nov Wed–Sun 11am–5:30pm (on Sat late May to late Aug, grounds remain open until 8pm and trams until 7pm). Closed mid-Nov to Apr. Free docent-guided "Highlights of the Collection" tours at 2pm daily; free self-guided trams (hop on and off) run daily noon–4:30pm.

MORE TO SEE & DO
EAST SIDE OF THE HUDSON

In addition to the listings below, don't miss **Cold Spring,** one of the Hudson's most adorable waterfront towns located in Putnam County about an hour north of New York City. You'll find inviting views of the river, and a main street chockablock with antiques dealers, inns, cafes, and restaurants in Victorian cottages. Head 9 miles north on Route 9D, after the Bear Mountain Bridge.

Hudson River Museum *(Kids) (Value)* This large cultural complex in Yonkers, just north of New York City, covers several bases, including fine art, science, and history. It features six modern-art galleries (showing the works of George Segal and Andy Warhol, among others) and a high-tech planetarium. Also on the premises is a handsome restored 19th-century Victorian mansion overlooking the Hudson River and

Palisades. The museum hosts a variety of interesting temporary exhibits as well as concerts. *Bargain alert:* The planetarium is free for the 7pm show on Friday.

511 Warburton Ave., Yonkers. ⓒ 914/963-4550. www.hrm.org. Admission $5 adults, $3 seniors and children. Wed–Sun noon–5pm; Fri noon–8pm.

The Union Church of Pocantino Hills ★★ *Finds*

A short jaunt from the Rockefellers' Kykuit estate is this tiny country chapel, remarkable not for its architecture per se but for its unique collection of stained-glass windows by Marc Chagall and Henri Matisse, two masters of modern art better known for their works on canvas. The collection, commissioned by the Rockefeller family, features a large rose window by Matisse—the final work of his life—and a series of nine side windows by Chagall—his only cycle of church windows in the U.S.—that illustrate biblical passages. One, at the back right-hand corner, is a memorial to the son of Nelson Rockefeller, who died on an expedition to New Guinea in the early 1960s. Matisse's rose window is very soothing, while Chagall's painterly images swirl with brilliant color; try to visit the church on a sunny day, when it is ablaze with dramatic light and color.

Rte. 448 (Bedford Rd.), Sleepy Hollow. ⓒ 914/631-2069. www.hudsonvalley.org/unionchurch/index.htm. Admission $5. Apr–Dec Mon and Wed–Fri 11am–5pm; Sat 10am–5pm; Sun 2–5pm. Closed Jan–Mar.

Van Cortlandt Manor

Although superficially the least spectacular of the seven Historic Hudson Valley properties, this working estate and Revolutionary War–era country manor house is a living-history museum that reveals much about the life and activities of the 18th century. Guides don Federal period dress, and the massive open-hearth kitchen and grounds play host to cooking, blacksmithing, weaving, and brick-making demonstrations. The tavern on the premises served customers of a ferry business that carried people back and forth across the Croton River.

S. Riverside Ave. (off Rte. 9; Croton Point Ave. exit), Croton-on-Hudson. ⓒ 914/232-5035. www.hudsonvalley.org/vancortlandt/index.htm. Guided tours admission $12 adults, $10 seniors, $6 children 5–17, free for children under 5; grounds-only pass $5 adults, $3 children 5–17. Apr–Oct Wed–Mon 10am–5pm (last tour 4pm); Nov–Dec weekends only, 10am–4pm (last tour 3pm). Closed Jan–Mar.

Caramoor House Museum and Performing Arts Center *Finds*

Just east of the Hudson, a little off the beaten track for most Hudson Valley visitors, is this surprising mansion and performing arts center, well worth a visit for a summer concert or a view of the unusual Mediterranean villa constructed by a wealthy New York couple, Walter and Lucie Rosen. The Rosens purchased entire rooms from European palaces, churches, and country homes, then brought them to the U.S. Those rooms were reconstructed and incorporated into their sprawling mansion, built around a Spanish courtyard, designed with those exact rooms and furnishings in mind. It's hard to believe that the mansion and its bewildering array of Eastern, medieval, and Renaissance art and antiques were assembled on-site in the late 1930s. The collection contains treasures and furnishings of great value and others of highly personal taste. Caramoor is best known as a center of music and arts, and in particular for its summer outdoor Music Festival, which grew out of the Rosens' love for hosting concerts for their large circle of friends. The heart of the house is the extraordinary Music Room, a small palace unto itself, where chamber concerts are held throughout the year. Afternoon tea is served on the family's original china in the Summer Dining Room, Thursday and Friday afternoons at 3pm. Tours of the house last about an hour.

149 Girdle Ridge Rd. (off Rte. 22), Katonah. ⓒ 914/232-5035. www.caramoor.org. Admission (house museum) adults $10, free for children under 17. May–Dec guided tours Wed–Sun 1–4pm (last tour 3pm). Metro-North to Katonah.

Manitoga (Russel Wright Design Center) *Finds* Russel Wright, a preeminent midcentury American designer, tucked a unique country home into the woods and blurred the lines between interior and exterior, combining natural materials with industrial design. The only 20th-century modern home open to the public in New York, the 1962 house is very Zen-like, with abundant vegetation nearly camouflaging its simple lines. The house is sliced into a cliff above a dramatic waterfall and pond carved out of an abandoned quarry. Wright named the site Manitoga, which means "place of the great spirit," but he called the house "Dragon Rock," after his daughter's description of the massive rock that dips into the pond. In addition to the house, open for guided 90-minute tours, there are more than 4 miles of hiking trails on the property.

Rte. 9D, Garrison. ② 845/424-3812. www.russelwrightcenter.org. House tour admission $15 adults, $13 seniors, $5 children under 13; hiking trails $5 adults, $3 seniors and children under 12. Apr to late Oct guided tours Mon–Fri 11am, weekends 11am and 1:30pm; woodland garden paths open weekdays year-round 9am–4pm, weekends Apr–Oct 10am–6pm; reservations recommended.

WEST SIDE OF THE HUDSON

Nyack *Finds* One of the more charmingly "lived-in" river villages along the Lower Hudson, Nyack is a bedroom community of New York with a laid-back life all its own. The town has a smattering of antiques shops, cafes, booksellers, and restaurants. The American realist painter Edward Hopper was born and went to high school in Nyack, and his mid-19th-century Queen Anne childhood home, today the **Hopper House Art Center** (82 N. Broadway; ② **845/358-0774;** Thurs–Sun 1–5pm), is preserved as a small museum of the artist's life and career and gallery space for temporary exhibitions. The **Runcible Spoon** (37-9 N. Broadway; ② **845/358-9398**) is a great little bakery and favorite rest stop for cyclists who make the 50-mile round-trip from New York City.

Stony Point Battlefield Historic Site This site commemorates the historic 1779 Battle of Stony Point, during which American forces led by Brigadier General Anthony Wayne stormed a British stronghold at midnight and caught the enemy by surprise. The victory was the last major battle in the North and is credited with boosting American morale. Visitors can walk the battlefield and see an audiovisual presentation at the on-site museum. Stony Point Lighthouse, built on the site in 1826, is the oldest on the Hudson; lantern walks are offered several times a year.

Battlefield Rd. (off Rte. 9W), Stony Point. ② 845/786-2521. http://nysparks.state.ny.us/sites/info.asp?siteID=29. Free admission to grounds (but $5 parking fee); museum $2 adults, $1 seniors and children 5–12; audio tours $4 adults, $3 children under 13. Grounds Mon–Sat 10am–4:30pm; Sun noon–5pm. Museum closes 30 min. earlier.

Fort Montgomery State Historic Site Fort Montgomery was the site of a brave 1777 Revolutionary War battle to control the Hudson River. Patriot troops effectively stalled the British march to aid Burgoyne's army at Saratoga—which may have made the difference in the war. Visitors can view ruins of the fortifications and listen to an audio tour that explains the battle and importance of the Hudson to the Patriot and British war plans. A visitor center and trails are now open.

Rte. 9G, 1¼ miles north of Bear Mountain State Park, Bear Mountain. ② 845/786-2701. http://nysparks.state.ny.us/sites/info.asp?siteID=36. Free admission; audio tours $4 adults, $3 children under 13. Daily dawn–dusk; staffed mid-Apr to Oct Wed–Sun 10am–4:30pm.

ESPECIALLY FOR KIDS

The Lower Hudson Valley has a number of great activities for families and kids. Tops is **Bear Mountain State Park:** Besides its zoo, swimming lake and pool, ice-skating rink, and hiking trails, it has added an incredible $3-million carousel; the carved animals aren't just horses, but bobcats, rabbits, and bears—animals found in the park. The **Hudson River Museum** in Yonkers is a favorite of kids for its state-of-the-art planetarium. Although contemporary sculpture might not sound like most kids' idea of fun, the **Storm King Art Center,** with 100 monumental pieces spread over 500 beautiful acres, is a blast for children, who may have a more intuitive understanding of the works than their parents! Several of the historic houses and estates along the river are entertaining for children. Interpreters in period dress at **Sunnyside, Van Cortland Manor,** and **Philipsburg Manor** are entertaining and educational; the latter, a working farm that aims to present history lessons through actors and demonstrations, is particularly eye-opening. Occasional activities at **Lyndhurst,** such as vintage "base ball" games, should also delight kids.

SPORTS & OUTDOOR PURSUITS

The Lower Hudson Valley abounds in outdoor sports, from hiking and biking to cross-country skiing to kayaking and sailing.

BOATING & SAILING   **Hudson Maritime Services** of Cold Spring (© 845/265-7621; www.hudsonriver.cjb.net) offers sailing on Newburgh Bay and scenic cruises along the river. **Hudson Highlands Cruises** (© 845/534-7245; www.commander boat.com) embarks on 3-hour narrated cruises through the Hudson Highlands ($15 adults, $13 seniors and children under 12). **Hudson Valley Riverboat Tours** (© 845/788-4000) offers midweek cruises on *The River Queen,* a historic paddle-wheeler, in July and August.

CYCLING & MOUNTAIN BIKING   Bike rentals are available from **Bikeway,** 692 Rte. 6, in Mahopac (© 845/621-2800).

FISHING   The Hudson, which flows from the Adirondacks to the open sea, is excellent for striped bass from mid-March to the end of May. There is also good trout fishing. For more information, visit **www.hudsonriver.com/stripers.htm**.

GOLF   **Garrison Golf Club,** 2015 Rte. 9, Garrison (© 845/42436040; www.the garrison.com), is a stunning course in the Hudson Highlands overlooking the river; it's so pretty you may not care how you hit 'em. Rates are $40 to $85. There are more than 150 other golf courses in the Hudson River Valley; for specific information and course previews, see **www.hudsonrivergolf.com** and **www.golfhudsonvalley.com**.

HIKING   There are too many great hiking spots in state parks in the Lower Hudson Valley to mention. Near Cold Spring, **Hudson Highlands State Park** has a number of great day trails. Recommended hikes in the vicinity of Cold Spring include Breakneck Ridge and Bull Hill; in the southern highlands south of Garrison, popular trails include those to Anthony's Nose and White Rock. Pick up a map at **Hudson Valley Outfitters,** 63 Main St., Cold Spring (© 845/265-0221; www.hudsonvalley outfitters.com), which also offers guided hikes in the area, or contact the New York–New Jersey Trail Conference (p. 70). **Bear Mountain and Harriman state parks** make up the majority of the Palisades Interstate Park and afford dozens of splendid hiking opportunities, including a section of the Appalachian Trail. For trail maps and more information, visit the Palisades Interstate Park Commission at Bear Mountain (© 845/786-2701). See "Hiking" in the Mid-Hudson Valley section (p. 209) as well.

KAYAKING & RAFTING   **Hudson Valley Outfitters** (see "Hiking," above) is tops in the region for kayak rentals and guided tours. Its major competitor is **Pack & Paddle**

Adventures, 45 Beekman St., Beacon (© **845/831-1300;** www.hvpackandpaddle.com), which also handles kayak and canoe rentals and instruction.

SWIMMING **Bear Mountain State Park** allows for swimming in both Hessian Lake and the Bear Mountain pool, open in summer. There is also a public pool at Tallman State Park (Palisades Interstate Park Commission; © **845/359-0544**), just south of Nyack on Route 9W.

WINTER SPORTS For snowshoe and cross-country ski packages, contact Cold Spring's **Hudson Valley Outfitters** (see "Hiking," above). **Bear Mountain State Park** has cross-country ski trails, ski jumps, and an outdoor skating rink open late October through mid-March. **Croton Point Park**, Route 9 in Croton-on-Hudson, is also popular with Nordic skiers.

SHOPPING

The biggest draw by far among shopaholics is **Woodbury Common,** said to be the world's largest discount complex, about an hour north of New York City. It's in Central Valley, just south of Newburgh (498 Red Apple Court; © **845/928-4000;** Mon–Sat 10am–9pm, Sun 10am–8pm). There are more than 220 purveyors of clothing, home furnishings, jewelry, luggage, leather, and gift items, including Barneys New York, Burberry, Calvin Klein, Chanel, Coach, Dolce & Gabbana, Donna Karan, Giorgio Armani, Gucci, Max Mara, Neiman Marcus Last Call, Gap Outlet, Nike Factory Store, Saks Fifth Avenue, Polo Ralph Lauren Factory Store, Versace, and Williams-Sonoma. By car, take exit 16 off the New York State Thruway, or I-87. You can also hop a Gray Line bus from the Port Authority Bus Terminal at 42nd Street and Eighth Avenue in New York City. The bus leaves daily beginning at 8:30am and the last departs at 2:45pm ($37 adults, $19 children 5–11 round-trip). **Cold Spring** is the best antiques center in the Lower Hudson Valley. Main Street is lined with more than a dozen small antiques dealers and cute home-furnishings shops. **Taca-Tiques Antiques,** 109 Main St. (© **845/265-2655**), specializes in Victorian and estate sterling silver and beveled mirrors. **Nyack** is another town with a number of antiquing possibilities. Elsewhere, **Boscobel Restoration** in Garrison has one of the best gift shops attached to a historic site.

Though it's a bit removed from the Hudson Valley per se, lots of folks make the trip west to the **Sugar Loaf Art & Craft Village,** a hamlet in Orange County (north of Warwick, off Rte. 17) that features more than 50 shops and galleries dealing in jewelry, stained glass, and metalsmithing, among others. Sugar Loaf is open Tuesday to Sunday from 11am to 5pm; call © **914/469-9181** for events and more information.

WHERE TO STAY

The Lower Hudson Valley's proximity to New York City makes it popular as a day trip, but there is so much to see and do that it fortunately has the widest and most plentiful array of accommodations in the valley. There's a good mix of historic inns, modern hotels, and small B&Bs, as well as motel and hotel chains that are hard to come by farther up the Hudson.

VERY EXPENSIVE

Castle on the Hudson ⭐⭐⭐ This small, exclusive hotel (formerly The Castle at Tarrytown), in a grand 45-room castle built in 1910 on a bluff overlooking the river, offers some of the most extravagant accommodations in the Hudson Valley—at least since the Vanderbilts and company opened their estate to the public. If you're willing and able to live like a prince, this is the place. Reminiscent of castles in Scotland and Wales, it comes equipped with the requisite stone walls, turrets, and heavy medieval touches, though the property has been endowed with every possible luxury for guests. Rooms are elegant and extremely plush, but not over the top, with fine carpets, flowing drapes, and stylish linens on four-poster and canopied beds. The handsomely landscaped grounds don't skimp on fantastic views of the Hudson River. The Castle's fancy Equus restaurant is one of the most highly touted in the Lower Hudson Valley; even if you're not staying here, it's well worth it for a special seasonal four-course prix-fixe meal or one of the periodic wine-tasting dinners.

400 Benedict Ave., Tarrytown, NY 10591. © 800/616-4487 or 914/631-1980. Fax 914/631-4612. www.castleonthe hudson.com. 31 units. Weekdays $340 double, $385–$635 suite; weekends $360 double, $445–$810 suite. AE, DC, DISC, MC, V. Free parking. **Amenities:** Restaurant; bar; large outdoor pool; fitness center; tennis court; concierge; limited room service; massage; laundry service; same-day dry cleaning. *In room:* A/C, TV/VCR, minibar, hair dryer.

EXPENSIVE

The Bird & Bottle Inn ★★   Make a detour right into the Revolutionary War era at this charming inn, one of the oldest in New York State. Reopened in 2005 after a lengthy renovation by new owners, The Bird & Bottle began its business life on the Old Albany Post Road in 1761 as Warren's Tavern, and the wide floorboards, dark beams, and rustic flavor of the place bow very little to modernity. For anyone looking for a dose of history, this is it. Rooms are not fussy, as indeed they shouldn't be, but are very comfortable and inviting, with luxurious four-poster and canopied beds and working fireplaces stocked with wood. The restaurant, long one of the Hudson Valley's most sumptuous and formal, has been given a slight makeover, but it still reeks with Early American flavor and serves a very good prix-fixe dinner. The cozy first-floor bar, affectionately known as the Drinking Room, is a great place for exactly that.

1123 Old Albany Post Rd. (off Rte. 9D), Garrison, NY 10524. © 845/424-2333. Fax 845/424-2358. www.thebirdand bottleinn.com. 3 units. $180–$220 double. Rates include breakfast. Weekend 2-night minimum. AE, MC, V. Free parking. **Amenities:** Restaurant; tavern. *In room:* A/C, hair dryer, no phone.

Caldwell House ★★ (Finds)   A classic, New England–style B&B in a historic Colonial home, built in the early 19th century, this friendly and intimate inn is a perfect base for exploring the west side of the lower Hudson. The four rooms are lovingly decorated with period furnishings. The spacious Catherine Caldwell room is the choice for honeymooners, with its step-up Jacuzzi tub, antique sink, and gorgeous four-poster bed. The three-course breakfasts dreamed up by Carmela—who has published her own cookbook—are something to write home about: crème brûlée French toast, ginger scones, and pumpkin pancakes. Carmela even sells her hand-knitted items in the gift shop. Clearly, this is the kind of place for people who genuinely enjoy staying at B&Bs.

25 Orrs Mills Rd., Salisbury Mills, NY 12577. © 800/210-5565. Fax 845/496-5924. www.caldwellhouse.com. 4 units. Mon–Thurs $160–$195 double; Fri–Sat $185–$235. Rates include full gourmet breakfast. AE, MC, V. Free parking. *In room:* A/C, TV/VCR, Wi-Fi.

Cromwell Manor ★★   This sophisticated inn, in an imposing, historic house with white pillars, which was once owned by a descendant of Oliver Cromwell, sits on 7 acres next to a farm and is just minutes from Storm King Art Center and 5 miles from West Point. Well managed and largely successfully decorated in period style (rooms are elegant, but a few touches and bathrooms may strike some as a little modern and functional), it is one of the best B&Bs in the Hudson Valley. It faces a 4,000-acre

nature preserve that is spectacular in autumn. The 1820 manor house has nine rooms, six of which have wood-burning fireplaces. The Cromwell Suite has a private entrance and a bathroom so large that the owners have stuck a StairMaster in it (kid you not!). The separate Chimneys Cottage, the oldest part of the house (1764), is the most charming; it has four guest rooms, one of which has an enormous sitting room. Rooms are all quite different, so visit the website or call for additional details. The hands-on owners host a number of special events, such as weekend chef dinners and cooking classes, so check for scheduling as well as golf and spa packages and special offers.

174 Angola Rd., Cornwall, NY 12518. ℂ 845/534-7136. Fax 845/534-0354. www.cromwellmanor.com. 13 units. $165–$370 double. Rates include full gourmet breakfast. AE, MC, V. Free parking. **Amenities:** In-room massage; Wi-Fi. *In room:* A/C, hair dryer, robes.

Tarrytown House Estate & Conference Center *★★* *(Kids)* A sprawling hotel complex and conference estate, with one 1840s mansion and six or seven outpost buildings on the property, is tucked serenely behind gates just up the road from Washington Irving's Sunnyside home on the river. Loaded with amenities and sports facilities, but surprisingly easygoing and intimate, this is a perfect place for both business and leisure travelers, including families. Rooms are quite large and very comfortable; they were recently renovated in attractive contemporary style (brightly colored and flowered, but unfussy, bedcovers). The best rooms by far, though $100 more than others, are the 10 in the Georgian-style King House mansion. They have antiques, fireplaces, and large and nicely appointed bathrooms. Some even have terrific wraparound terraces with excellent views. Ask about the Passport to Sleepy Hollow Country package, which includes 2 nights' accommodations, breakfast, and admission to three nearby historic sights (Kykuit, Lyndhurst, and so on).

E. Sunnyside Lane, Tarrytown, NY 10591. ℂ 800/553-8118 or 914/591-8200. Fax 914/591-0059. www.tarrytownhouse estate.com. 212 units. Weekday $159–$309 double; weekend $119–$309 double. AE, DC, DISC, MC, V. Free parking. **Amenities:** Restaurant; bar; large indoor and outdoor pools; 3 tennis courts; basketball court; racquetball; fitness center with sauna; concierge; business center; executive business services; limited room service; massage; laundry service; same-day dry cleaning. *In room:* A/C, TV/VCR, Wi-Fi, minibar, hair dryer.

MODERATE

Hotel Thayer Ensconced within the grounds of the West Point campus, this landmark hotel is the best bet for anyone who always wanted to attend the military academy. A fine, large old hotel (constructed in 1926), built in a similar style to the Gothic campus and named for General Thayer, the "father of the academy," it has decent-size rooms with large, firm beds. Although one side looks over the beautiful campus and the other over the Hudson River, light sleepers should know that the train rumbles by right below on the river side, both late at night and early in the morning. You'll miss the river views, but the campus side is much quieter. The medieval-style restaurant in the basement is easily the best restaurant in the immediate area; Sunday brunch is especially popular. Don't even bother trying to get a room during West Point graduation week: The hotel is booked 4 years in advance.

674 Thayer Rd., West Point, NY 10996. ℂ 800/247-5047 or 845/446-4731. Fax 845/446-0338. www.thethayerhotel. com. 127 units. $155–$219 double. AE, DC, DISC, MC, V. Free parking. **Amenities:** Restaurant; fitness center; concierge; salon; limited room service; laundry service, dry cleaning. *In room:* A/C, TV w/pay movies, dataport, minibar, coffeemaker, hair dryer.

Hudson House River Inn *★★* *(Finds)* Facing a wide expanse of the Hudson River in one of the cutest towns in the valley, Cold Spring, this small but adorable inn (just 12 rooms) was built in 1832 and has operated as a hotel ever since, making it the second-longest continually operating inn in New York State. The historic building retains many period features but has been nicely updated. Rooms are sweetly decorated in a country style, with comfortable bedding. Room nos. 1 and 2 are equipped with river-front balconies; the views are enviable. The attractive restaurant, which has both a river room and a cozy old tavern with a fireplace, is one of the better places to stop for a meal in Cold Spring.

2 Main St., Cold Spring, NY 10516. © **845/265-9355.** Fax 845/265-4532. www.hudsonhouseinn.com. 13 units. Mon–Thurs $155–$185 double, Fri–Sun $165–$195 double; $225–$250 suite. Rates include continental breakfast on weekdays, full breakfast on weekends. See website for special packages. AE, DC, DISC, MC, V. Free parking. **Amenities:** Restaurant; laundry service. *In room:* A/C, TV w/pay movies, hair dryer.

Pig Hill Inn *Finds* Right on Cold Spring's Main Street, which is packed with antiques shops, this friendly and rustic little B&B is tucked behind a little antiques-and-gift shop of its own. In the cozy public rooms are plenty of decorative pigs on display, of course, while guest rooms are attractively done with Chippendale pieces, chinoiserie, and other antiques. Rooms have four-poster beds and comfortable quilts; many are equipped with fireplaces. Some rooms are very light and airy, while others are considerably darker and more masculine. A gourmet breakfast is served in the Victorian conservatory, out back in the cute terraced garden area, or in the main dining area.

73 Main St., Cold Spring, NY 10516. © **845/265-9247.** Fax 845/265-4614. www.pighillinn.com. 9 units, 5 with private bathroom. Mon–Thurs $150 double with shared bathroom, $170–$230 double with private bathroom; Fri–Sun $170 double with shared bathroom, $190–$250 double with private bathroom. Rates include full breakfast. Weekend and holiday 2-night minimum in high season. AE, DC, DISC, MC, V. Free parking. **Amenities:** Gift shop for tea and antiques. *In room:* A/C.

Storm King Lodge *Finds* Just down the road from the splendid Storm King Art Center, this charming, family-run, year-round B&B is a relaxing place to stay, ideal for art lovers and outdoorsy sorts (innkeeper Gay is a kayaker and can help organize outings on the Hudson). The home, once a carriage house on a 19th-century farm (converted into a guesthouse in the 1920s), is quiet and comfortable, with a high-ceilinged and cozy, wood-paneled great room and a serene, covered back deck, with stunning views past Storm King (including views of Andrew Goldsworthy's *The Wall That Went for a Walk*) to the Hudson Hills. The latter is a favorite gathering place of guests. The four guest rooms, three of which are upstairs off the great room, are very clean and spacious, with nice private bathrooms; two rooms (Pine and Lavender) have working fireplaces.

100 Pleasant Hill Rd., Mountainville, NY 10953. © **845/534-9421.** Fax 845/534-9416. www.stormkinglodge.com. 4 units. $150–$175 weeknights, $165–$190 weekends double. Rates include buffet breakfast. MC, V. Free parking. **Amenities:** Outdoor pool; massage. *In room:* A/C.

INEXPENSIVE

Bear Mountain Inn *Value Kids* *Main inn closed for renovations until 2008.* This sturdy wood-and-stone lodge hotel, opened in 1915 within the Bear Mountain State Park, is undergoing an ongoing $10-million renovation. This landmark of park architecture is being brought back to its rustic glory and Adirondack charm. The interior of the main lodge features original chestnut log posts and beams, massive stone fireplaces, timber framing, birch and iron light fixtures, and plenty of animal trophies. Accommodations—for now only the Overlook and Stone lodges a mile from the main inn across Hessian Lake are open—are simple. Those in the main inn have been undergoing renovation for the past 3 years and eventually will be transformed into suites. Still, about $100 for a double in such splendid surroundings constitutes a bargain. The inn's cozy Lobby Lounge, with its vaulted ceilings and handsome fireplace, is a great spot to relax after a day on the hiking trails. Kids will love all the activities just outside the door, including visiting the Trailside Museum and Wildlife Center, swimming in the lake, and hopping on the fantastic new Bear Mountain Merry-Go-Round. For weekend stays, it's advisable to make reservations at least a month in advance.

Bear Mountain State Park, Bear Mountain. © 845/786-2731. Fax 845/786-2543. www.bearmountaininn.com. 60 units. $99–$110 double. AE, DC, DISC, MC, V. Free parking. **Amenities:** Restaurant; bar; outdoor pool; skating rink. *In room:* A/C, TV.

CAMPGROUNDS
There are many campgrounds around the Hudson Valley. Among them are **Croton Point,** Route 9, Croton (© **914/271-3293;** open year-round; 180 sites, 48 with electricity); **Mills-Norrie State Park,** Old Post Road, Staatsburg (© **800/456-CAMP;** mid-May to late Oct; 55 sites); **Harriman State Park: Beaver Pond,** Route 106, Bear Mountain (© **800/456-CAMP;** mid-Apr to early Oct; 200 sites); and **Fahnestock State Park,** Route 301, Carmel (© **80/456-CAMP;** Memorial Day to Labor Day weekend; 86 sites).

WHERE TO DINE
Whether it's pizza for kids tired of touring grand estates or a romantic dinner in a historic inn or a casual meal in a riverfront restaurant, there is a good mix of dining options in the Lower Hudson Valley.

EAST SIDE OF THE HUDSON
Expensive
The Bird & Bottle Inn ★★ AMERICAN/CONTINENTAL   A tavern and inn since Colonial times, when travelers stopped along the Old Post Road to Albany for fortification, this inn, recently renovated and reopened with a new owner and chef, remains one of the most atmospheric places to dine in the Hudson Valley. The three separate dining rooms with fireplaces are models of rustic elegance. Dinner may be a la carte or a four-course prix-fixe or six-course tasting menu. Your appetizer might be grilled tiger shrimp over sautéed spinach and mango, followed by a nice salad and an entree of trout almondine or pan-seared sliced veal with wild mushroom risotto. The wine list has a number of surprisingly affordable choices. Jackets are requested for gentlemen at dinner. The Sunday four-course champagne brunch is also quite an affair, though more casual.

1123 Old Albany Post Rd. (off Rte. 9D), Garrison. © 845/424-2333. Reservations recommended weekends and holidays. Main courses $28–$38; dinner prix-fixe $54–$75; brunch $30. AE, MC, V. Thurs–Sat 6–10pm; Sun 4–8pm; Sat–Sun brunch 11:30am–3pm.

The Valley Restaurant at The Garrison ★★★ *Finds* CREATIVE AMERICAN
One of the finest new restaurants in the Hudson Valley—and very likely New York State—this serene and sophisticated spot, specializing in seasonal American cuisine, is unexpectedly tucked in among the perfect green lawns of The Garrison, a golf club, and a spa. High on the eastern bank of the Hudson is this smallish restaurant, a handsome contemporary dining room with rustic touches, pale woods, and a striking glass wine wall. The chef, Jeff Raider, makes excellent use of fresh ingredients and organic meats and poultry from nearby Hudson Valley farms. I recently had as fine a meal here as anywhere in New York outside of Manhattan: a deliciously Mediterranean appetizer

of baked artichoke-and-tomato casserole, accented with tasty olives and garlic (a sig-nature dish); and a beautifully presented and festive-looking Basque-like black sea bass, swimming in a puddle of bright green foam and topped by a tight rack of clams and piquillo peppers. In warm weather, the outdoor deck is a coveted spot, though I'm still partial to the elegantly understated dining room. For more casual dining, includ-ing lunch, check out the bar menu next door at World's End Bar.

2015 Rte. 9, Garrison. © **845/424-2339.** Reservations recommended. Main courses $21–$32. AE, DC, MC, V. Thurs–Sat 5:30–10pm; Sat–Sun 11:30am–3pm.

Moderate

Brasserie Le Bouchon ★★ *Value* FRENCH BISTRO   This new French restaurant

makes quite a statement in laid-back, antiques-mad Cold Spring: It's sexy and chic, with deep bordello red walls and ceilings, red banquettes, glittering mirrors, and bistro lighting. For the most part, it emphasizes classic, rich, home-cooked French fare like mussels, slow-braised pork tenderloin, and steak frites, steak tartare, and steak au poivre. Appetizers include duck and pork pâté. Desserts, such as Grand Marnier dou-ble-dark chocolate mousse, are similarly sinful. It's not the kind of place to worry about your waistline. The restaurant is very late-night cool, and it has a little bar at the back, a good spot to have a drink. If it's nice outside, you can dine on the patio, though it pales in comparison with the interior.

76 Main St., Cold Spring. © **845/265-7676.** Reservations recommended weekends and holidays. Main courses $13–$27. AE, MC, V. Sun–Mon and Wed–Thurs noon–9:30pm; Fri–Sat noon–10pm.

Cold Spring Depot AMERICAN/PUB FARE   In the old train station, built in

1893 by Cornelius Vanderbilt (the train still rumbles by at all hours), this easygoing restaurant is a favorite of both locals and weekend visitors on antiquing treks. It mainly serves comfort food, in either the popular tavern or the warmly decorated main dining room. Try the Guinness potpie, Ma Ralston's meatloaf, homemade chili, or fish and chips. Sophisticates who find those too pedestrian can opt for the filet mignon or seafood paella. There's a nice garden terrace for dining in warm months, and occasional live jazz on Saturday nights, and in summer an ice-cream parlor oper-ates next door. After you've had a couple of drinks, have a seat on the bench outside at 10:13pm and ask locals about "the ghost of the depot"—a woman murdered by her husband as she tried to escape on the train to Poughkeepsie in 1898.

1 Depot Sq., Cold Spring. © **845/353-8361.** Reservations recommended weekends and holidays. Main courses $13–$27. AE, MC, V. Mon–Thurs 11:30am–9pm; Fri–Sat 11:30am–11pm; Sun 11am–9pm. Sun brunch 11am–3:30pm.

Lanterna Tuscan Bistro ★★ TUSCAN   Nyack is a charming town, and in Lanterna

it gets what it deserves, a charming restaurant with flair but few pretensions. A small and mostly minimalist space with wood tables, white tablecloths, white walls, and slow-moving ceiling fans, it has one long corridor and two small sitting areas—one up front and the other back by the kitchen. The young chef, Rossano Gianni, turns out authentic Tuscan dishes and also gives cooking classes, demonstrations, and wine tast-ings. Lunch might be a simple affair of homemade pasta and soup or salad, while the dinner menu features risotto, fresh fish (monkfish sautéed with white wine and herbs is a good one), and hearty meat dishes such as filet mignon topped with Gorgonzola and a Barolo reduction. As you would hope, the wine list has some good Italian selec-tions, while the $29 pre-theater, prix-fixe dinner is an excellent deal. On a nice day, a few tables are set up on the sidewalk for alfresco dining.

3 S. Broadway, Nyack. © **845/353-8361.** Reservations recommended weekends and holidays. Main courses $14–$30. AE, MC, V. Mon–Sat 11:30am–3:30pm; Sun brunch 11am–3:30pm; Sun–Thurs 4:30–9:30pm; Fri–Sat 4:30–10:30pm.

Sushi Mike's ★★ *Finds* SUSHI   Locals claim the sushi here is every bit as good as what you'll find in New York City, and it's hard to disagree. My wife is a sushi snob, and she loves to detour off the Saw Mill River Parkway on the way out of the city to dip into Sushi Mike's, a friendly and fun little spot with excellent and creative rolls, sushi, and sashimi, as well as daily seafood specials. The owner, Mike, is a gregarious sort who greets regulars and newcomers at the door and comes around to the tables to make sure his diners are happy. There is sometimes live jazz on weekend and Monday nights, when a vocalist and keyboard player are crammed in next to the sushi bar; if you're not interested in being serenaded, sit in the lower dining room, or in warm weather, at one of the handful of tables on the street corner.

146 Main St., Dobbs Ferry, NY. © **914/591-0054.** Reservations recommended. Main courses $17–$24. AE, DC, MC, V. Mon–Fri 11:30am–3pm; Mon–Thurs 4:30–10pm; Fri 4:30–11pm; Sat noon–11pm; Sun 3–10pm.

WEST SIDE OF THE HUDSON
Moderate

Hotel Thayer ★★ *Value* AMERICAN   Eat where the parents of West Point cadets do, in this 1920s hotel on the campus of the famous military academy. Easily the best restaurant in the immediate area, the Hotel Thayer's elegant restaurant, with its dark wood, chandeliers, and exposed stone walls, keeps pace with the dramatic architecture of the West Point campus. It has a vaguely medieval feel, like dining in the workers' mess hall in a Gothic castle. Even if you're not staying here, it's worth passing through two or three security checkpoints for a meal. Entrees included pan-seared red snapper, baked stuffed shrimp with crabmeat, and rack of lamb with mint demi-glace. The restaurant is fairly priced and has attentive service and a good wine list. Sunday's champagne brunch is very popular, as are special events like comedy and dinner and dancing on Friday and Saturday evenings.

674 Thayer Rd., West Point. © **845/446-4731.** Reservations recommended. Main courses $12–$26; Sun brunch $26. AE, DC, DISC, MC, V. Daily 7–10:30am and 5:30–9pm; Mon–Sat 11am–2pm; Sun brunch 10am–2pm.

Prima Pizza ★★ *Kids* PIZZA/ITALIAN   An adorable family-owned and old-fashioned New York pizza joint, Prima has been in the same family since 1954. It's friendly and cozy, with bar stools at the counter and about 10 tables under hanging plants. The fresh dough is made daily, and sauces and meatballs are made on the premises. Besides some very creative pizzas, including lemon chicken and health-conscious no-fat and low-fat, it serves a mean hot meatball sub and more substantial dishes like lasagna and eggplant parmigiana. Cornwall, by the way, is a small town a stone's throw from West Point and Storm King Art Center in Mountainville—good to know if you're lugging kids around on art and history tours. If you find yourself back home with a hankering for Prima Pizza, you can even order it online at www.pizzaofnewyork.com and have it shipped overnight to your house.

252 Main St., Cornwall. © **845/534-7003.** Reservations not accepted. Main courses $13–$19. AE, DISC, MC, V. Tues–Thurs 10am–9pm; Fri 10am–10pm; Sat 11am–10pm; Sun noon–9pm.

THE LOWER HUDSON VALLEY AFTER DARK

The small towns along the Hudson River Valley provide just a few alternatives for evening entertainment; the biggest offering is of summertime concerts. In Katonah,

Caramoor Performing Arts Center, 149 Girdle Ridge Rd. (off Rte. 22; © 914/232-5035; www.caramoor.org), features the popular Summer Music Festival, with outdoor classical music concerts, as well as indoor chamber and cabaret performances in the spring and fall. **Boscobel Restoration** in Garrison, 1601 Rte. 9D (© 845/265-3638; www.boscobel.org), is home to the Hudson Valley Shakespeare Festival (www.hv shakespeare.org) on the lawn in the summer and dancing to big-band music in the fall. In Tarrytown, **The Music Hall Theatre,** 13 Main St. (© 914/631-1000; www.tarrytownmusichall.org), a terrific 1885 theater and National Historic Landmark that was saved from destruction, is a great place to see a theater production or music performance. Events range from *Sleeping Beauty*, the ballet, to Eddy Palmieri, the Latin jazz giant.

3 The Mid-Hudson Valley

The Mid-Hudson Valley is the Great Estates region, a stretch of river valley where families like the Vanderbilts and the Mills built truly spectacular spreads that epitomized the fantastic wealth and lofty aspirations of the Gilded Age. The region was also home to Franklin and Eleanor Roosevelt, pivotal 20th-century American figures who remained vitally connected to their roots here. Parts of the Mid-Hudson are undergoing greatly needed revitalization, especially on the west side of the river, with towns like Kingston and Newburgh taking advantage of their waterfront locations for development, spawning lively bar and restaurant scenes, and Beacon catapulting to life with the arrival of a stunning new contemporary-art museum. Though within easy reach of many towns on both sides of the Hudson, several places that lie at the edge of the Catskill Mountains, including New Paltz, High Falls, and the Minnewaska Preserve (and the Mohonk Mountain House), are covered in chapter 8.

EXPLORING THE MID-HUDSON VALLEY
EAST SIDE OF THE HUDSON
Dia:Beacon ✦✦✦   In a 1929 Nabisco box-printing factory on the banks of the Hudson, the Dia Art Foundation, begun by Heiner Friedrich and Philippa de Menil in the 1970s, has created the world's largest contemporary-art museum, an institution that adheres to the foundation's single-minded purpose. The new museum houses Dia's rarely seen permanent collection of pivotal conceptual, minimalist, and Earth artists, mostly men who came of age in the 1960s and 1970s. Nearly 250,000 square feet of gallery space—illuminated almost entirely by natural light that streams in through the factory's original skylights—were designed to exhibit the works of single artists. The museum's opening in 2003 represented the biggest development in the art world since the Guggenheim in Bilbao, Spain, and the new Modern in Fort Worth. As great as the space is, Dia is more about art than architecture. The museum exhibits 24 artists, including the sculptor Richard Serra (whose long gallery, the former train shed, is devoted to three of his massive *Torqued Ellipse* pieces), the fluorescent-light sculptures of Dan Flavin, Andy Warhol's work *Shadows* (a series of 102 brilliantly colored, silk-screen canvases), and mixed-media installations by Joseph Beuys. Other noted artists include Gerhardt Richter, Louise Bourgeois, Sol LeWitt, Walter De Maria, and Bruce Nauman (whose creepy installation documenting the nocturnal comings and goings of rats in his studio is perfectly suited to the basement). These are ambitious and challenging artists across the board, and their adventurously minimalist works will surely strike some viewers as head-scratchers; but even visitors who aren't

Take the Trolley

After your visit to Dia:Beacon, hop aboard Beacon's Main Street Trolley (Fri–Sun) for a spin through town and check out the city's self-described "Renaissance on the Hudson." The trolley makes several stops along Main Street (hop on and off all afternoon for $2), but be sure to check out the charming East End antiques district and the contemporary galleries that dot Main Street. Highlights include **Collaborative Concepts** (348 Main), **Concentric Gallery** (174 Main), and the brand-new **Hudson Beach Glass,** housed in a restored firehouse at 162 Main St. *Note:* If the trolley isn't running during your visit, it's just a 1-mile drive to downtown.

great fans of contemporary art are likely to find the museum space and the site on the river, with a landscape design by Robert Irwin, quite extraordinary.

Note: Metro-North Railroad offers a "1-day getaway fare" that includes round-trip train fare from New York City and admission to Dia:Beacon. See www.mta.info/mnr/html/getaways/outbound_diabeacon.htm for prices and additional information.

3 Beekman St., Beacon. (✆ 845/440-0100. www.diabeacon.org. Admission $10 adults, $7 seniors and students, free for children under 12. Mid-Apr to mid-Oct Thurs–Mon 11am–6pm; mid-Oct to mid-Apr Fri–Mon 11am–4pm. Metro-North to Beacon.

Vanderbilt Mansion National Historic Site 𝄇𝄇𝄇   One of the finest and most intact of the lavish estates built by wealthy 19th-century industrialists along the Hudson, Frederick William Vanderbilt's 54-room country palace in Hyde Park, built in 1898, is a no-holds-barred gem. One of the first steel-framed houses in the U.S., at 55,000 square feet (on 670 acres), it was the smallest and least expensive of the famed Vanderbilt mansions (others were in Newport, Bar Harbor, and Asheville), but it still epitomized the Gilded Age's nouveau riche. French in every respect, from Louise's Versailles-like bedroom to the grand dining room and Frederick's glittering master bedroom, it was decorated in impressively grand style. Yet the house, where the Vanderbilts spent only a few weeks each year in the spring and fall, functioned as a kind of spa retreat. Guests were encouraged to enjoy the outdoors: the majestic views of the Hudson and Catskills in the distance and the wonderful gardens and woodlands surrounding the house.

Rte. 9, Hyde Park. (✆ 845/229-9115. www.nps.gov/vama. Admission (guided 45-min. tour) $8 adults, free for children under 16. Daily 9am–5pm (by guided tour, the last at 4pm). Closed Thanksgiving, Christmas, and New Year's Day. Grounds daily year-round 7am–sunset (free admission). Metro-North and Amtrak to Poughkeepsie.

Franklin Delano Roosevelt Presidential Library and Museum/FDR Home (Springwood) 𝄇𝄇𝄇   Franklin Delano Roosevelt, the four-term president of the United States who was faced with not only the Great Depression and World War II, but living with polio, loved the Hudson River Valley. FDR designed his own presidential library, the nation's first, while still in his second term and built it next to his lifelong home in Hyde Park. He actually used the study while president and often would be in residence while the library was open to the public; it is the only presidential library to have been used by a sitting president. See his cluttered White House desk (left as it was the last day of his presidency), exhibits on the FDR presidency and times, and FDR's beloved 1936 Ford Phaeton, with the original hand controls that allowed him to travel all over the estate. Two wings added in memory of his wife,

Mid-Hudson Valley

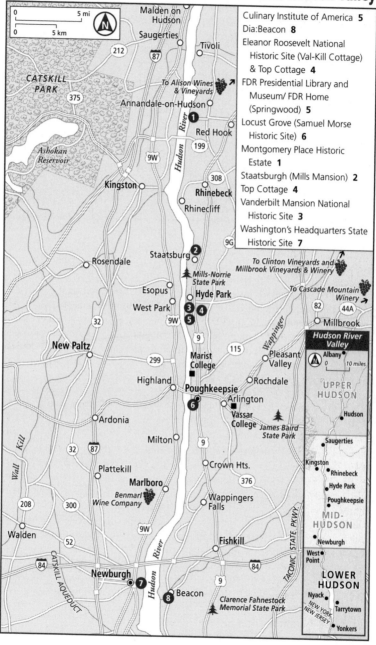

Culinary Institute of America **5**

Dia:Beacon **8**

Eleanor Roosevelt National Historic Site (Val-Kill Cottage) & Top Cottage **4**

FDR Presidential Library and Museum/ FDR Home (Springwood) **5**

Locust Grove (Samuel Morse Historic Site) **6**

Montgomery Place Historic Estate **1**

Staatsburgh (Mills Mansion) **2**

Top Cottage **4**

Vanderbilt Mansion National Historic Site **3**

Washington's Headquarters State Historic Site **7**

Value Hyde Park Discounts & National Parks Passes

With the purchase of admission to both the Vanderbilt estate and Roosevelt home, library, and museum, a third visit, to either of the Roosevelt retreats, Val-Kill or Top Cottage, is free.

These historic sites in Hyde Park belong to the extensive network of national parks. Several new discount passes are available to visitors, including the National Parks and Federal Recreation Lands Annual Pass, $80 (individuals; good for 1 year), and Interagency Senior Pass, $10 (for seniors only; lifetime membership). Older passes, including National Parks Passes, Golden Eagle, Golden Eagle Hologram, Golden Access, and Golden Age Passports, will continue to be honored according to the provisions of the pass. All park passes, good for free entry to any Vanderbilt-Roosevelt historic site tour, can be purchased at the national park sites in Hyde Park. For more information, see www.nps.gov or http://store.usgs.gov/pass.

Eleanor Roosevelt, make this the only presidential library to have a section devoted to a first lady. Springwood, the house next door, was built by FDR's father; FDR expanded the modest farmhouse in an eclectic Dutch Colonial style. The home isn't grand by the standard of the great river estates, but FDR entertained Churchill, the king and queen of England, and other dignitaries here. FDR and Eleanor are buried in the rose garden on the grounds. The Wallace Center, an impressive new visitor center at the entrance to the library (where tickets for all FDR sites are purchased), presents a short film on FDR and Eleanor. Advance reservations during the popular fall foliage season are a good idea (© **800/967-2283;** http://reservations.nps.gov), and reservations are accepted up to 5 months in advance.

4079 Albany Post Rd. (off Rte. 9), Hyde Park. © **800/FDR-VISIT** or 845/229-8114. www.nps.gov/hofr or www.fdr library.marist.edu. Admission (museum and guided tour of the Springwood home, good for 2 days) $14 adults, free for children under 16. Buildings daily 9am–5pm (last tour 4pm); grounds daily 7am–sunset. Metro-North and Amtrak to Poughkeepsie.

Eleanor Roosevelt National Historic Site (Val-Kill Cottage) & Top Cottage ✯

Both Eleanor Roosevelt—who like her husband grew up in the Hudson River Valley—and FDR maintained serene and simple private country retreats away from Springwood. When FDR was away, and after his death, Eleanor—one of the most admired and influential women in American history—lived and worked out of Val-Kill Cottage, the only home she ever owned. A simple, rustic, cabinlike home, Val-Kill is where Eleanor received world leaders and made her mark on civil rights legislation and international humanitarian issues (as a U.N. delegate, she chaired the committee that drafted the U.N. Human Rights Universal Declaration). The grounds were also the headquarters of Val-Kill Industries, which Eleanor and several other women established to teach trades to rural workers and produce Colonial Revival furniture and crafts.

FDR's retreat on a hilltop, which he christened Top Cottage, was more rustic still. He built it on Dutchess Hill in the 1930s as an informal place to get away from it all and think about issues confronting his presidency. FDR was at his most relaxed here, even allowing himself to be photographed in his wheelchair. Restored but unfurnished, Top Cottage has recently been opened to visitors who come to see FDR's cherished views of the Catskill and Shawangunk mountains from the famous porch, where he entertained guests such as Winston Churchill and King George VI and Queen Elizabeth of England (guests at his "scandalous" 1939 hot-dog dinner). A wooded trail leads from Springwood to Val-Kill and Top Cottage. Visits to both cottages are by guided tour only (tickets are available at the visitor center at the FDR Presidential Library and Museum).

Rte. 9G, Hyde Park. ℂ 845/229-9115. www.nps.gov/elro. Admission (45-min. guided tour) to either, $8 adults, free for children under 16. May–Oct daily 9am–5pm; Nov–Apr Thurs–Mon 9am–5pm (last tour at 4pm); grounds year-round daily sunrise–sunset. Metro-North and Amtrak to Poughkeepsie.

Staatsburgh (Mills Mansion) ⍟

One of the most opulent and elegant of the Hudson River estates, Staatsburgh, an 1896, 65-room Beaux Arts mansion on 1,600 acres (now the Mills-Norrie State Park), was the country home of Ogden and Ruth Livingston Mills. Mrs. Mills, a member of the prominent Livingston clan, inherited the simpler original home—one of five Mills family mansions—in 1890. She and her husband renovated it in grand European style, combining her aristocratic lineage with the big new money of the era, and the result is pure Gilded Age: 18-foot ceilings, a massive Louis XIV–style dining room with green Italian marble on the walls, sumptuous library, dramatic central staircase crowned by a ceiling mural, and 14 bathrooms. The house, the first in the area to have electricity, is outfitted with all original furnishings. Staatsburgh is thought to have been the model for the Bellomont estate in Edith Wharton's *The House of Mirth*. A number of special events (with special admission prices) are held here, including summer concerts, "Celtic Day in the Park" (Sept), "Scarborough Fair" (June), "Gilded Age Christmas," and an antique-car show in October. Note that the mansion continues to undergo extensive exterior and interior restoration (expected to last several years). Visits are by guided tour only.

Old Post Rd. (off Rte. 9), Staatsburgh. ℂ 845/889-8851. www.hvnet.com/houses/mills. Admission $5 adults, $4 seniors and students, $1 children 5–12, free for children under 5. Apr to Labor Day Wed–Sat 10am–5pm, Sun noon–5pm (last tour 4:30pm); Labor Day to last Sun in Oct Wed–Sun noon–5pm; Dec special extended hours for holiday program; Jan–Mar Sun 11am–4pm. Closed Nov. Metro-North and Amtrak to Poughkeepsie.

Montgomery Place Historic Estate ⍟

Main house currently closed for restoration but expected to reopen in 2008 (weekend-only, self-guided audio tours of the grounds only). Montgomery Place is one of the most lovingly sited and best preserved estates along the Hudson. This 434-acre, early-19th-century country Federal-style home enjoys splendid lawns and gardens and outstanding views overlooking the Hudson River and the distant Catskill Mountains. The most prominent designers of the day, the architect A. J. Davis and landscape designer Andrew Jackson Downing, built the home in fieldstone and stucco for Janet Livingston Montgomery, the widow of Revolutionary War hero General Richard Montgomery. Inside are family possessions from the late 1700s all the way to the second half of the 20th century. The house exhibits a very strong French influence, with hand-painted wallpaper and a formal parlor fashioned after Dolly Madison's White House parlor, though the massive kitchen in the basement and its original hearth are very Dutch in style. Many of the gardens were created in the 1930s, and they are some of the most beautiful of any estate along the Hudson. Montgomery Place is a great place to bring a picnic lunch and walk among the orchards, gardens, and woodland trails that lead to Sawkill falls.

Annandale Rd. (River Rd., off Rte. 9G), Annandale-on-Hudson. ℂ 914/758-5461. www.hudsonvalley.org/montgomery place. Admission (while restoration is underway): grounds-only pass $5 adults, $3 children under 18. May–Oct Sat–Sun only 10am–5pm. Metro-North and Amtrak to Rhinecliff.

WEST SIDE OF THE HUDSON

Washington's Headquarters State Historic Site ⚐   General George Washington established his military headquarters on the banks of the Hudson in Newburgh in 1782 and 1783, during the final years of the Revolutionary War. He, his wife, Martha, and his principal aides and their servants occupied a 1750 farmhouse donated to the army by a prosperous family, the Hasbroucks. Washington stayed here 16 months (and Martha 12 months), longer than at any other headquarters during the war. In 1850 the property was declared the nation's first public historic site. The farmhouse displays Washington's office (where he wrote the famous "circular letter" and Newburgh addresses) and the original tables and chairs of the general's aides de camp. A museum, opened in 1910, across the lawn displays memorabilia such as medals of honor (including a 1783 original badge of military merit), locks of Washington's hair, and Martha's pocket watch from her first marriage. Revolutionary War buffs may also wish to visit the **New Windsor Cantonment** (✆ **845/561-1765**), a few miles away on Route 300. The staff at Washington's Headquarters can give directions to reach this site where Washington's 7,500 troops and their families camped during the winter of 1782 and 1783. There are living-history presentations and military demonstrations in season.

84 Liberty St., Newburgh. ✆ **914/562-1195**. www.nysparks.com/sites/info.asp?siteID=32. Admission $4 adults, $3 seniors and students, $1 children 5–12, free for children under 5. Mid-Apr to Oct Wed–Sat 10am–5pm, Sun 1–5pm; July 1–Sept 6 also Mon 10am–5pm; also open Memorial Day, Independence Day, Labor Day, and Columbus Day.

OTHER ATTRACTIONS

EAST SIDE OF THE HUDSON

Culinary Institute of America   The nation's oldest culinary arts school and only residential college in the world dedicated to culinary training, the CIA (chefs, not spies) and its lovely 150-acre riverside campus (a former Jesuit seminary) are open for tours (not to mention culinary "boot camps" for serious nonprofessionals). The institute has trained thousands of chefs and food-service-industry professionals, including some of the most prominent chefs in the country, since its founding in 1946, and you'll see students on campus in their chef whites, a parallel to the West Point cadets across the river in their dress blues. You'll also smell what's cooking in the 41 kitchens and bake shops. If you're a foodie, a tour of this culinary temple is a must; others, with perhaps less interest in the behind-the-scenes of cooking school, may just want to have lunch or dinner at one of the excellent restaurants. CIA operates four restaurants and a bakery cafe, all staffed by students, open to the public (see "Where to Dine," later in this chapter) and a culinary bookstore and gift shop.

1946 Campus Dr., Hyde Park. ✆ **845/285-4627**. www.ciachef.edu. Admission $5. Tours Mon 10am and 4pm; Wed–Thurs 4pm. Closed July. Reservations required.

Rhinebeck ⚐   A historic, gracious small town marked by the oldest inn in America, the Beekman Arms, Rhinebeck is one of the most visitor-friendly spots along the Hudson. It has an expanding number of inns, sophisticated restaurants (including a tavern where George Washington dined), diverse furnishings and antiques shops, and even an art house movie theater. It's a perfect town to walk around and enjoy at a leisurely pace. Chief among its attractions are the **Old Rhinebeck Aerodome,** a museum of antique airplanes with 30 annual air shows, and **Wilderstein,** an elegant 19th-century Queen Anne mansion once occupied by Daisy Suckley, FDR's distant cousin and close confidant. The house, which features a five-story tower, massive veranda, and reams of family documents and belongings, has ongoing renovation, but is fascinating for the contrast it provides to the grander and somewhat more buttoned-up estates up and down the Hudson; the Suckleys' economic fortunes significantly declined during the Great Depression, and the house reflects that past. Lots of special programs, like formal teas and art exhibits, are scheduled.

RHINEBECK ATTRACTIONS   Old Rhinebeck Aerodome: Stone Church Rd. and Norton Rd., Rhinebeck. ℂ 845/752-3200. www.oldrhinebeck.org. Admission Mon–Fri (museum) $10 adults, $8 seniors, $3 children 6–10; Sat–Sun (museum and air show) $20 adults, $15 seniors, $5 children 6–10. Mid-May to Oct daily 10am–5pm; air shows every Sat–Sun mid-June to mid-Oct 2pm. Wilderstein: 330 Morton Rd., Rhinebeck. ℂ 845/876-4818. www.wilderstein. org. Admission is group tours only; call ahead for possibility of joining one. May–Oct Thurs–Sun noon–4pm.

Locust Grove (Samuel Morse Historic Site)

Locust Grove, a 150-acre estate and Tuscan-style villa, was purchased by Samuel Morse, painter-turned-inventor. The 19th-century artist invented the electric telegraph and Morse code and made a fortune that his paintings—though respected—never brought him. Morse purchased the 1830 Georgian estate from the Young family (today the art, furnishings, and decorative arts primarily recall their stay here) and brought in the noted architect A. J. Davis (designer of Lyndhurst and Montgomery Place) to expand and remodel it. The property has a man-made lake, waterfall, and lovely gardens. A recent addition to the estate is a small but well-done museum dedicated to the life, art, and inventions of Morse, and an excellent visitor center that shows a film on the estate and Morse's life.

2683 South Rd. (Rte. 9), Poughkeepsie. ℂ 845/454-4500. www.morsehistoricsite.org. Admission $9 adults, $5 students ages 6–18, free for children under 6. May–Nov daily 10am–3pm; call for special Dec hours. Grounds year-round daily 8am–dusk (free admission).

WEST SIDE OF THE HUDSON

Kingston ⚲   New York State's first capital, the old Dutch town of Kingston, on the west bank of the Hudson, has two distinct historic areas of great interest to visitors. In uptown Kingston is the historic **Stockade District,** a pleasant commercial area marked by the presence of 21 pre-Revolutionary, Dutch-style stone houses (all four corners at the intersection of John and Cross streets are occupied by 18th-century stone houses, unique in the U.S.). Chief among the historic landmarks is the **Senate House,** which housed the first New York State Senate in 1777 after the adoption of the first constitution, until British troops burned Kingston later that same year. The Senate House Museum contains Colonial artifacts and the paintings of John Vanderlyn. Along North Front and Wall streets is a pretty 2-block area of buildings with turn-of-the-20th-century-style canopied sidewalks, called the Pike Plan, home to a number of shops, galleries, restaurants, and cafes. The Old Town Stockade Farmers' Market is held Saturday, June through September. Opposite the Old Dutch Church is the **Fred J. Johnston Museum,** an 1812 Federal-style house with an excellent collection of American decorative arts. At the other end of town, Kingston's historic waterfront area, the **Rondout,** reached its pinnacle in the days of the D&H Canal in the early 19th century, but declined with the advent of the railroad. Today, it's a nicely revitalized commercial area with a burgeoning number of restaurants and bars. It is also home to the **Hudson River Maritime Museum and Lighthouse** (an old boat shop with exhibits on the history of boating and ships), weekend vintage trolley rides out to the Hudson (which begin in front of the Maritime Museum), Sampson opera house, and a handsome new visitor center. Boats leave from the Maritime Museum to go out along Rondout Creek to the 1913 Rondout Lighthouse (call ℂ **845/336-8145**

for information). The Rondout is also the spot to catch the larger **Hudson River Cruises** on the *Rip Van Winkle* ship (for more information, see p. 209).

KINGSTON ATTRACTIONS Senate House: 296 Fair St., Kingston. © 914/338-2786. Admission $3 adults, $2 seniors, $1 children 5–12. Apr 15–Oct Wed–Sat 10am–5pm; Sun 1–5pm. Fred J. Johnston Museum: 63 Main St., Kingston. © 845/339-0720. Admission $3. May–Oct Sat–Sun 1–4pm. Hudson River Maritime Museum: 1 Rondout Landing, Kingston. © 845/338-0071. www.hrmm.org. Admission museum only, $5 adults, $4 seniors and children; boat to lighthouse $15 adults, $12 seniors and children ($3 discount with admission to museum). May–Oct museum Fri–Mon noon–6pm; boat rides May–Oct weekends and holiday Mon noon–3pm.

ESPECIALLY FOR KIDS

Kids will love the **Rhinebeck Aerodome,** with its vintage airplanes and cool air shows. In Kingston, families can take a **Hudson River cruise** out to the lighthouse or hop aboard a vintage trolley car. Some of the great estates have extraordinary grounds and gardens with trails through the property; check out the **Vanderbilt Mansion, Staatsburgh,** and **Montgomery Place.** And finally, as an educational supplement to history classes, take the kids to **Washington's Headquarters** in Newburgh and the **FDR Presidential Library and Museum** in Hyde Park.

SHOPPING

In the Mid-Hudson Valley, **Beacon, Red Hook,** and **Rhinebeck** are the best towns for antiquing. Each has a couple of streets lined with good and interesting shops. In Beacon, now home to an exploding roster of antiques shops, gift stores, and galleries, **Relic,** 484 Main St. (© 845/440-0248), is the place for vintage housewares. **Beacon Hill Antiques** (474 Main St.; © 845/831-4577) peddles fine antiques while **Past Tense Antiques,** across the street at 457 Main (© 845/838-4255), offers well-priced antique and vintage pieces. **Hoffman's Barn Sale** in Red Hook, 19 Old Farm Rd. (© 845/758-5668), is an old barn with thousands of old, used, and antique items of varying quality. A particularly fine store in Rhinebeck is **Asher House Antiques,** 6380 Mill St. (© 845/876-1796), which deals in both elegant and country-rustic English and French pieces. Behind the Beekman Arms Hotel on Mill Street is the **Beekman Arms Antique Market,** with several dealers in an old barn (© 845/876-3477). **Gold Goat,** 6119 Rte. 9 (© 845/876-1582), is a small gallery with some cool pieces of American folk art. Rhinebeck hosts the **Rhinebeck Antiques Fair,** with three big shows annually featuring more than 200 dealers at the Dutchess County Fairgrounds, Route 9 (© 845/876-1989; www.rhinebeckantiquesfair.com). In Hyde Park the **Hyde Park Antiques Center,** 4192 Albany Post Rd. (© 845/229-8200), has 45 dealers and is open daily.

Those with a specific interest in arts and crafts should pick up the free *Explore Dutchess County Crafts and Arts Trail* brochure (available at many hotels, shops, and tourist information offices), which details more than two dozen craft shops and galleries on the east side of the Hudson, as well as craft shows.

A surprisingly good wine shop—in a strip mall without much going on—is **Liquorama Wine Cellars,** Hyde Park Mall, Route 9 (© 845/229-8177), with a number of coveted international wines and older vintages in stock.

SPORTS & OUTDOOR PURSUITS

The Mid-Hudson Valley is rich in outdoor activities, including river cruises, hiking and biking, and cross-country skiing. Besides more traditional outdoor sports, thrill seekers may want to check out barnstorming flights on biplanes over the Hudson Valley at the

Old Rhinebeck Aerodome (p. 206). Flights take off before and after air shows (15 min.; $40 per person).

BOATING & SAILING **Hudson River Cruises,** Rondout Landing at the end of Broadway, in Kingston (© **800/340-4700;** www.hudsonrivercruises.com), sets sail aboard the *Rip Van Winkle,* a modern 300-passenger vessel. The standard 2-hour cruises ($17 adults, $16 seniors, $10 children 4–11) visit the Mid-Hudson Valley in spring, summer, and fall; there are also specialty cruises, some with live music, and a 90-minute Sunset Sail ($11) on Wednesday. In Newburgh, **Hudson River Adventures** (Newburgh Landing; © **845/220-2120;** www.prideofthehudson.com) operates 2-hour sightseeing cruises ($17 adults, $16 seniors and children 4–11) from May to October on the *Pride of the Hudson,* a 130-passenger boat. **Scenic Hudson Sails** (© **845/546-1184;** norriepointsail@aol.com) offers weekend and sunset cruises and private charters aboard *Doxie,* a 31-foot sloop and traditional-style yacht.

The *Sloop Clearwater,* part of an environmental project to clean up the Hudson River, is a 75-foot, single-masted replica of a 19th-century ship, which embarks on 3-, 6-, and occasional 8-hour cruises along the Hudson from April to mid-November. It sets sail from Saugerties, Kingston, and New York City's 79th Street Boat Basin, among other ports of call along the river. Sail prices range from $25 to $80 for adults, with discounts available for children, students, and seniors. For schedules and more information, call © **800/67-SLOOP** (ext. 107) or visit www.clearwater.org/sail.html.

GOLF There are more than 150 golf courses in the Hudson River Valley. **Dinsmore Golf Course,** Old Post Road (Rte. 9), Staatsburgh (© **845/889-4071;** greens fees $18–$22), the second-oldest golf course in the United States, is part of the 1,000-acre Mills-Norrie State Park, which includes the Mills Mansion State Historic Site. With panoramic views of the Hudson River and majestic Catskill Mountains, it was named "Best Public Golf Course in the Hudson Valley" by *Hudson Valley Magazine.* Putnam County's **Centennial Golf Club,** Simpson Road, Carmel (© **845/225-5700;** www.centennialgolf.com; greens fees $55–$125), a hilly 1999 design by Larry Nelson, is one of the most picturesque in the Hudson Valley. **The Garrison,** 2015 Rte. 9, Garrison (© **845/424-3604;** www.garrisongolfclub.com; greens fees $35–$85), is a classic old 18-hole course with spectacular views high above the Hudson across from West Point. It has a yoga and spa center and distinguished restaurant on the premises.

For additional course information and course previews, see **www.hudsonrivergolf. com** and **www.golfhudsonvalley.com.**

HIKING Four miles north of Cold Spring on Route 9D, an excellent trail leads to **South Beacon Mountain,** the highest point in the East Hudson Highlands (a 6-mile round-trip). The 5-mile **Breakneck Ridge Trail,** also in Beacon, with views of the Hudson and Shawangunk and Catskill mountains, was voted the top hiking trail in New York State on www.trails.com. **Clarence Fahnestock Memorial State Park,** a 7,000-acre park southwest of Beacon (Rte. 301, Carmel; © **914/225-7207**), is also a terrific place for hiking, with a number of trails and loops (suggested hikes include Three Lakes Trail and East Mountain–Round Hill). Less strenuous trails can also be found in **Mills-Norrie State Park** (© **914/889-4100**), the site of the Staatsburgh Mills Mansion. On the other side of the Hudson, **Bear Mountain Loop** near Newburgh is a popular trail.

SWIMMING Canopus Lake in **Clarence Fahnestock Memorial State Park,** southwest of Beacon (Rte. 301, Carmel; © **914/225-7207**), has an attractive beach and swimming area open to the public.

WINTER SPORTS   Fahnestock Winter Park (Rte. 301, Carmel), part of Clarence Fahnestock Memorial State Park between Cold Spring and Beacon, is one of the best spots for Nordic skiing, snowshoeing, and sledding. Besides tons of trails, it also offers equipment rentals and lessons. For information and condition reports, call © **845/ 225-3998.**

WHERE TO STAY

The Mid-Hudson isn't loaded with accommodations options—there is little in the way of national chain hotels and motels—but the few it does have are quite special. Note that a good-value option is above the Raccoon Saloon in Marlboro (see "Where to Dine," below).

EXPENSIVE

Belvedere Mansion 🌟🌟   For unrestrained luxury in a country inn, none comes close to the Belvedere. The 1900 neoclassical mansion, with its pillared facade perched above the Hudson just south of Rhinebeck, features a carriage house, pond, and lodge on the property, and a bewildering choice of accommodations. The elegant interiors aim to re-create the grandeur of the Gilded Age estates along the Hudson, and indeed the 18th-century antiques, silk fabrics, rich colors, luxurious linens, and marble bathrooms are fit for a prince. The seven main-house rooms are the biggest and most expensive; several have fantastic river views and details like claw-foot tubs and canopied beds. The Henry Hudson Suite, in what was previously the servants' quarters, is a cool trio of rooms on the top floor, all sharing a bathroom—perfect for a genteel family or group of friends. The carriage-house rooms are smaller but also very nicely decorated; a nice bargain are the four small rooms called "cozies," which adequately describes their charm. Four additional luxury rooms with fireplaces occupy the Hunt Lodge.

Rte. 9, Staatsburgh, NY 12561. © 845/889-8000. www.belvederemansion.com. 22 units. "Cozies" $105–$125 double; Zen Lodge $125–$175; Carriage House $150–$195 double; Mansion Rooms $225–$275; Hunt Lodge $250–$450 suite. All rates include gourmet breakfast. 2-night minimum stay weekends; 3-night minimum some holidays. AE, DC, DISC, MC, V. Free parking. **Amenities:** Restaurant; tavern; laundry service. *In room:* A/C, hair dryer.

Buttermilk Falls Inn & Spa 🌟🌟🌟 *(Finds)*   Nestled in among 70 acres of wooded, river-hugging land fronting the Hudson, this spectacular inn is a real find in the Mid-Hudson Valley. Though small and friendly, with the feel of a hideaway, it provides the amenities of a much larger hotel. The main house, which holds 10 accommodations, is a 1764 Colonial that has been masterfully renovated and modernized; the bones of the historic home smartly have been respected and highlighted. Guest rooms are elegantly designed, with antique touches and period furnishings; they range from the intimate Lotus Room to the dramatic Grand Laurel, large enough to get lost in. For those interested in a bit of privacy, the nearby cottage-house rooms, newly constructed, are equally tasteful, though a touch more modern; one is a very comfortable, two-bedroom apartment with a full kitchen. Whirlpool tubs and plush linens are found in all. The Foxglove Room on the first floor of the main house is equipped for visitors with disabilities—a rarity in such an old house. Meander among the stunning grounds and you'll discover wooded trails, an art gallery housed in a barn, waterfalls and ponds, flowering and organic gardens, a bird house full of chickens and peacocks, and a riverfront esplanade (where music and events are staged). The expertly staffed spa has expanded into a larger facility with several treatment rooms, an indoor-outdoor saltwater pool, and a Jacuzzi.

220 North Rd., Milton-on-Hudson, NY 12547. ℂ 877/746-6772 or 845/795-1310. www.buttermilkfallsinn.com. 13 units. $225–$325 double; $425–$450 suite. All rates include gourmet breakfast. Special promotions available online. AE, DC, DISC, MC, V. Free parking. **Amenities:** Restaurant; day spa; laundry service; free high-speed Internet access; 1 room for those w/limited mobility. In room: A/C, TV, hair dryer, electric fireplaces, robes, whirlpool tubs.

MODERATE

Beekman Arms/Delamater House ⭐   The Beekman Arms has the distinction of being America's oldest continually operating inn; it's been around since 1761, and very much looks the part. How's this for pedigree? George Washington, Benedict Arnold, and Alexander Hamilton all drank, ate, and slept here. And the Colonial Tap Room (tavern) and lobby look like they could still welcome them, with their wide-plank floors, stone hearth, and hand-hewn beams. Rooms in the main inn are upstairs; updated in the mid-'90s, they are nicely decorated and perfectly comfortable, if not quite as special as the public rooms might lead you to expect. The Delamater House, just up the street on Mill Street/Route 9, is the new kid on the block; the noted architect A. J. Davis built the main American Gothic house in 1844. The main house has gorgeous verandas, while the property has seven separate buildings, both old and new, with 44 guest rooms total (more than half have working fireplaces). The oldest rooms are in the main house, carriage house, and gables; Courtyard and Townsend House rooms are the newest and blandest rooms, but they have working fireplaces and four have kitchenettes. Some rooms are a little frilly; the Carriage House rooms are the most interesting of the lot. A new addition is the one-bedroom suite in the 19th-century Stone House.

6387 Mill St./Montgomery St. (Rte. 9), Rhinebeck, NY 12572. ℂ 845/876-7077 or 845/876-7080. www.beekman delamaterinn.com. 63 units. Beekman Arms $140–$300 double; motel rooms $100–$130 double; Delamater Inn $100–$250 double; Carriage House $140–$170. Rates include breakfast. 2-night minimum stay on weekends May–Oct and all holiday weekends. AE, DC, DISC, MC, V. Free parking. **Amenities:** Restaurant; tavern; laundry service. In room: A/C, dataport, hair dryer, many have working fireplaces, several Delamater courtyard rooms have small kitchenettes with microwave and coffeemaker.

Journey Inn ⭐⭐ (Finds   A contemporary inn run by two sisters who've named rooms after favorite sojourns and stocked them with souvenirs, this exceedingly friendly and very comfortable B&B has one exclusive advantage going for it: It is literally right across the street from the gate of the Vanderbilt mansion and just minutes from all the FDR attractions in Hyde Park (as well as the Culinary Institute of America). While the inn isn't old and decorated with period furniture, for many travelers that will be a blessing: Instead, it has new, excellent bathrooms, great big comfortable beds, central air-conditioning, and no creaky floors. The sisters, Diane and Michele, wow visitors with their gourmet breakfast creations in the breakfast wing (one is the baker, the other the cook).

1 Sherwood Place, Hyde Park, NY 12538. ℂ 845/229-8972. www.journeyinn.com. 6 units. $130–$150 double; $170–$190 suite. Rates include full breakfast. Weekend 2-night minimum. No credit cards. Free parking. **Amenities:** Dial-up Internet access. In room: A/C, hair dryer.

WHERE TO DINE

With the Culinary Institute of America on the east bank of the Hudson, it's not surprising that there's some great eating in this section of the valley. Chief among the options are the student-staffed restaurants on the campus of the CIA, which are professionally run in every respect and require some foresight to nab reservations.

EAST SIDE OF THE HUDSON
Expensive

Culinary Institute of America (CIA) ✦✦✦ AMERICAN/FRENCH/ITALIAN/ BAKED GOODS   The nation's foremost culinary arts college has four on-campus restaurants and a bakery cafe, which are open to the public. They're staffed by students of CIA, but they hardly seem like training grounds. All are extremely professional, which is why it can be so hard to get a reservation (reservations are accepted 3 months in advance, and for weekends in season, you may need that much of a cushion). The three main restaurants are the elegant Escoffier Restaurant, serving classic French fare with a lighter touch; Ristorante Caterina de Medici, a handsome villa with a regionally varied Italian menu; and American Bounty Restaurant, which focuses on regional American specialties and ingredients from the Hudson River Valley. St. Andrew's Café is contemporary and casual, offering wood-fired pizzas, vegetarian dishes, and natural ingredients, while the newest addition to the roster is the Apple Pie Bakery Café, an informal place for baked goods and a nice lunch or early dinner. You'll know the nation's food-service industry is in good hands after a meal at one of the restaurants and a walk around CIA. The three main restaurants request business or "country club casual" (collared shirt and slacks or khakis) attire and no jeans, sneakers, or sandals. Reservations accepted online (often the best way to get in) at www.ciachef.edu; note that dining hours are limited. The restaurants are open only when CIA is in session.

1946 Campus Dr. (off Rte. 9), Hyde Park. ✆ 845/471-6608. www.ciachef.edu. Reservations essential (may be made online). Main courses $14–$32. AE, DC, DISC, MC, V. American Bounty Tues–Sat 11:30am–1pm and 6:30–8:30pm; Apple Pie Bakery Café Mon–Fri 8am–6:30pm; Escoffier Tues–Sat 11:30am–1pm and 6:30–8:30pm; Ristorante Caterina de Medici Mon–Fri 11:30am–1pm and 6:30–8:30pm (selected menu items available in Al Forno Room Mon–Fri 1–6pm); St. Andrew's Café Mon–Fri 11:30am–1pm and 6:30–8:30pm.

Terrapin Restaurant ✦✦✦ AMERICAN/INTERNATIONAL   Housed in an 1825 church, with soaring ceilings, this fine-dining restaurant and next-door bistro aims high. If you're in the mood for a sandwich or funky quesadilla, try the bistro. Otherwise, check out the elegant main dining room, where chef/owner Josh Kroner cooks up imaginative takes on American cuisine—adding Mexican and Asian twists— with the freshest of local ingredients. Start out with a selection of tapas, such as grilled lamb chop with chimichurri sauce, and proceed to an appetizer like potato gnocchi with sautéed duck livers, shiitake mushrooms, and leeks. Tempting main courses include Hudson Valley duck and horseradish-crusted, sushi-grade ahi tuna. Terrapin's extensive and well-priced wine list has received the *Wine Spectator* award of excellence and is one of the Valley's best.

⟮Tips⟯ The Other, Less-Secretive CIA

Throughout the Hudson Valley, inns and restaurants large and small count chefs and other personnel trained at the prestigious **Culinary Institute of America,** also known by its unfortunate acronym CIA, among their staffs. A diploma from the food-industry CIA is a real badge of distinction, and it is a terrific boon to the region to have so many culinary pros in the kitchens. If a local tells you about a new restaurant opened by a chef, in the local parlance, "from the Culinary," check it out; chances are you'll find a winner.

6426 Montgomery St., Rhinebeck. © **845/876-3330**. Reservations recommended on weekends. Main courses $18–$27. AE, DC, DISC, MC, V. Bistro Sun–Thurs noon–11pm, Fri–Sat noon–1am; dining room Sun–Thurs 5–9pm, Fri–Sat 5–10pm.

Moderate

The Piggy Bank ★★ *Value* *Kids* SOUTHERN BARBECUE   Beacon is definitely on the upturn, with the arrival of the Dia:Beacon Art Center, but the formerly sleepy river town isn't yet in a position to deal with too many Manhattanite hipsters. The Piggy Bank, though, has its own sense of cool. Serving authentic Southern barbecue out of a former 1880 bank (complete with a Remington & Sherman bank-vault-turned-wine-cellar), the restaurant is great looking, with scuffed wood tables, funky lighting fixtures, and a tin ceiling. The pit barbecue cranks out chili, hickory-smoked ribs, burgers, pulled-pork barbecue sandwiches, and grilled chicken breast with corn-bread and fantastic sweet-potato fries. On "Rack Attack Tuesdays," you can don a napkin and settle in for an all-you-can-eat rib dinner for $18. Live bands play on Friday nights and on Beacon's "Second Saturday" of each month (when shops and galleries stay open and a trolley service runs until 9pm), and during warm months, the outdoor patio is open.

448 Main St., Beacon. © **845/838-0028**. Reservations recommended on weekends. Main courses $7.75–$21. AE, DC, DISC, MC, V. Tues–Thurs 11am–9pm; Fri 11am–10pm; Sat noon–10pm; Sun noon–8:30pm.

Traphagen Restaurant & Colonial Tap Room (Beekman Arms) ★★ AMERICAN/CONTINENTAL   The official names of the restaurant and tavern of America's oldest continually operating inn are a bit unwieldy. But a stop here is almost obligatory. The tavern especially exudes Revolutionary War–era flavor, with its wide-plank floorboards and wood posts, paneling, and beams. It's a great place for a mug of ale and hearty soup—probably just what George Washington and his fellow war planners did when they dined here in the 1780s. I always eat in the Tap Room, just for the ambience, but the connected restaurant serves the same high-quality menu. Main courses include appropriately hearty items like *tournedos* of veal, aged Black Angus sirloin, Dutch-style turkey potpie, and slow-roasted duck. Slightly less macho dishes, such as baked crabmeat-stuffed brook trout with goat-cheese polenta, also make appearances.

6387 Mill St. (Rte. 9), Rhinebeck. © **845/876-1766**. Reservations recommended on weekends. Main courses $13–$29. AE, DC, DISC, MC, V. Mon–Sat 11:30am–3pm; Mon–Thurs 5:30–9pm; Fri–Sat 5:30–10pm; Sun 4–9pm; Sun brunch 10:30am–2pm.

Inexpensive

Eveready Diner *Kids* *Value* AMERICAN DINER   If you're not up for haute student cooking across the street at the Culinary Institute, or you've got the kids in tow, you can't beat this new, but obviously nostalgic, American diner. It's got the Deco styling down pat, and the menu has something for just about everyone, from soda fountain favorites to panini, New York deli sandwiches, pastas, and fajitas—even upscale dinners like filet mignon and stuffed shrimp, and stuffed sole Avalon. Desserts aren't just malts and cones; all the baked goods, including scrumptious fruit pies, are made on the premises. And for those with unscheduled cravings, Ed's famous breakfasts are served all day and include buttermilk pancakes and malted waffles.

Rte. 9 N., Hyde Park. © **845/229-8100**. Reservations not accepted. Main courses $4–$22. AE, DC, DISC, MC, V. Sun–Thurs 5am–1am; Fri–Sat 24 hr.

Foster's Coach House *(Kids)* *(Value)* PUB FARE A homey, historic restaurant where prices are about as cheap as you're going to find in this part of the country, Foster's has been in operation since just after World War I. An old tavern was converted into a full-scale restaurant, with horse stalls as dining booths. It is dark and cool but incredibly relaxed. The bar is a favorite watering hole for locals when there's a game on. On the menu nothing exceeds $14, and desserts like cheesecake and pecan pie are two measly bucks. Foster's is a perfect place to drop in for lunch or an informal dinner. Basics are best: chopped sirloin with onions and mushroom gravy, turkey with stuffing and gravy, shrimp scampi, and sandwiches and burgers for lunch. Beer is cheap, and so is wine by the glass.

22 Montgomery St., Rhinebeck. ⓒ 845/876-8052. Main courses $4–$17. AE, DC, DISC, MC, V. Tues–Sat 11am–11pm; Sun noon–11pm.

WEST SIDE OF THE HUDSON
Expensive
Raccoon Saloon *(★★)* *(Finds)* CREATIVE AMERICAN In a classic pre-Revolutionary saloon, this unassuming, family-owned and -operated restaurant and bar is hands-down one of the most charming spots along the Hudson. This longtime family-run place finally changed hands, but it remains a terrific find on the west side of the Hudson: a relaxed but great-looking bar with a couple of separate, vintage dining rooms and a small terrace with tables and stunning views high above a rushing waterfall and the mighty Hudson River. The Raccoon is the annual winner of a poll naming the Hudson Valley's best burgers (and they are truly fantastic, large and juicy, served with homemade ketchup and extras like guacamole, mushrooms, and bacon), and you might think it's just a bar if you peek in; but the menu offers many other, more sophisticated delights. Try the black truffle chicken-liver pâté, seared filet of salmon with mandarin orange sauce, or rib-eye steak au poivre with cracked peppercorn and cognac. Desserts are all homemade, and ice creams are imaginative and delicious: Flavors include basil, lavender, and honey. The homemade ginger ale is out of this world.

Rte. 9W, Marlboro-on-Hudson. ⓒ 845/236-7872. Reservations recommended weekends. Main courses $14–$26. AE, DISC, MC, V. Mon–Thurs 11am–9:30pm; Fri–Sat 11am–10pm; Sun noon–9:30pm.

Ship to Shore *(★★)* AMERICAN/STEAKHOUSE This cool, jazzy spot, one of the new arrivals in the revitalized Kingston waterfront district known as the Rondout, is a hip take on the classic New York steakhouse. The chef, a graduate of the Culinary Institute of America (always a good thing in these parts), prepares an extensive menu of steaks and chops as well as seafood and pastas, always augmented by a long list of fresh daily specials. Meat eaters can dive into broiled rib-eye with portobello-mushroom sauce or double-cut boneless pork loin, while seafood lovers can try dishes like semolina-crusted red snapper with linguine or seared ahi tuna with sticky rice and seaweed salad. For lunch, there are some great, creative sandwiches and an array of salads. Back past the bar are a couple of more intimate dining areas if the front gets too loud. There's live jazz on Friday and Saturday nights, and Wednesday is half-price wine night. For lunch, check out the bargain $11 three-course menu.

15 W. Strand (Rondout District), Kingston. ⓒ 845/334-8887. Reservations recommended on weekends. Main courses $14–$34. AE, DISC, MC, V. Daily 11am–11pm; brunch Sat–Sun 9am–3pm.

THE MID-HUDSON VALLEY AFTER DARK
The spectacular **Richard B. Fisher Center for the Performing Arts** *(★★★)*, on the campus of Bard College in Annandale-on-Hudson (ⓒ 845/758-7900; www.bard.edu/fisher center), is the work of the innovative architect Frank Gehry (designer of the Guggenheim

Bilbao and Disney auditorium in L.A.). This distinctive and intimate theater, which opened in 2003 and seats just 900 in the main hall, has featured performances by Elvis Costello, Merce Cunningham, the American Symphony Orchestra, and Ballet Hispánico, but it remains primarily a teaching space. If any public performances are scheduled, it's very much worth the trek. Poughkeepsie's legendary **Bardavon Opera House,** 35 Market St. (© **845/473-2072;** www.bardavon.org), which has hosted a variety of classical music, opera, and other musical and theatrical performances since 1869, is one of the top spots in the valley. Programs include music, dance, film, and theater; the schedule ranges from the Hudson Valley Philharmonic and Itzhak Perlman to Lily Tomlin and screenings of *King Kong.*

Beacon, basking in the attention of the Dia:Beacon Art Center, has initiated a program called **"Second Saturdays";** trolleys pick up passengers at the train station and ferry them down Main Street, where art galleries and shops stay open until 9pm on the second Saturday of every month and a number of bars and restaurants feature live music. For more information on scheduling, call © **845/838-4243.** Newburgh and Kingston's **revitalized waterfronts** are loaded with bars and restaurants. Both have become real scenes in the past couple of years. A Newburgh-Beacon commuter ferry is in the works, which will make it very easy to cross the Hudson and check out the restaurants and bars of either side. Rhinebeck has a number of congenial local bars, but its cool local art-house theater, **Upstate Films,** 6415 Montgomery St. (© **845/ 876-2515;** www.upstatefilms.org), is unique in these parts. One of the last of its kind, the 1950s-era **Hyde Park Drive-In Movie Theater,** Route 9 (across from the FDR presidential library and Springwood; © 845/229-4738), schedules first-run movies in summer ($7 adults, $4 children ages 4–11; Tuesday is $5 night).

4 The Upper Hudson Valley

The great estates also exist in the Upper Hudson Valley, one of the most pastoral segments of the region. The simple beauty of the landscape was a perfect complement to the Shakers, who established one of their largest communities in the area east of the Hudson, near Chatham; today, there's an excellent museum and library dedicated to the Shaker legacy in this part of the valley. Revitalization of this once-grand and then rundown region has been a struggle, but has now taken root in several towns along the Upper Hudson. Perhaps best known is the town of Hudson, which has exploded as an art and antiques destination, but unassuming Tivoli, tucked into the east bank of the river, has developed its own lively restaurant scene. The west side of the Upper Hudson, including the attractive town of Saugerties, is covered in chapter 8, as populations west of the Hudson tend to identify even more with the nearby Catskill Mountains than the river.

EXPLORING THE UPPER HUDSON VALLEY

Though the predominantly rural Upper Hudson Valley isn't as loaded with the must-see attractions that are in the Mid- and Lower Hudson Valley, it does have two splendid estates and the town of Hudson, the area's best antiquing center, as well as the fascinating traditions of the Shaker community. Just to the south are the charming historic villages of Tivoli and Red Hook, which though still small are teeming with shops, art galleries, and, especially, restaurants.

EAST SIDE OF THE HUDSON

Clermont State Historic Site 🔒 The oldest of the great estates on the Hudson, this 1750 Georgian manor house was home to seven successive generations of one of New York State's most prominent families, the Livingstons. Philip Livingston was one of the signatories of the Declaration of Independence, and Robert Livingston possessed one of the largest private libraries in the U.S., a large portion of which survives at Clermont. The family's important role in Revolutionary activities led the British to burn Clermont in 1777. The nearly 500-acre estate, on a 45-foot-high bluff with great views of the river below and the Catskill Mountains in the distance, has excellent woodland hiking trails out past the formal gardens, bar, and gardener's cottages. The house today for the most part evokes the 1920s, when the house was remodeled as a Colonial Revival, though it contains furnishings and belongings from more than 200 years of Livingstons at Clermont. The visitor center plays a short film that interviews the last resident of the house, Alice Livingston.

1 Clermont Ave. (off Rte. 9G), Germantown. ℂ 518/537-4240. www.friendsofclermont.org. Admission $5 adults, $4 seniors and students, $1 children 5–12, free for children under 5 ($5 vehicle fee on weekends and holidays Apr–Oct). Apr–Oct Tues–Sun and Mon holidays 11am–5pm; Nov to mid-Dec Sat–Sun 11am–4pm (last tour 30 min. before closing). Grounds year-round daily 8:30am–sunset.

Olana State Historic Site 🔒🔒 Olana, though not as massively grand as some of the homes built by the 19th-century industrialists, is surely the most unique of all the great Hudson Valley estates. A Persian fantasy perched on a hill high above the river, with stunning panoramic views, it was the home of the accomplished Hudson River School painter Frederick Church (1826–1900). Well traveled in the Middle East, Europe, and South America, Church made his home perhaps his most important work of art, an indoor and outdoor museum incorporating artifacts, design elements, and furnishings of his favorite places. He was particularly taken with Moorish-style architecture and design, which is reflected in the mansion's windows, courtyards, thick carpets, and decorative tile motifs; sumptuous parlors look like opium dens. The dark and heavy dining room, however, was meant to evoke a medieval castle. The landscaping on the 336-acre estate grew out of Church's romantic, painterly affection for the Hudson Valley. Inside is Church's collection of exotic treasures from around the world and a few of his most important paintings, such as his landscape of Petra in Jordan, as well as other works by Hudson River School painters like Thomas Cole. Guided tours last 45 minutes; in high season, tours (maximum 12 people) often sell out early in the day, and reservations are suggested on weekends.

Rte. 9G, Hudson. ℂ 518/828-0135. www.olana.org. Admission $7 adults, $5 seniors and students, $2 children 5–12, free for children under 5; grounds $5 vehicle fee on weekends and holidays. Apr–Nov Tues–Sun 10am–5pm; Dec weekends and holidays 10am–4pm; Jan–Mar Tues–Sun 10am–4pm. Last tour 1 hr. before closing.

Hudson 🔒🔒 Only a decade or so ago, Hudson was just a small upstate town with very little going for it save a setting near the river, some beautiful countryside, and run-down architecture. However, an influx of antiques dealers and part-time residents from the city has given it a remarkable makeover, resulting in a premier upstate shopping destination. Today it is *the* antiquing destination of the Hudson Valley and full of enjoyable shops and cafes. Most of its development and refurbishing is restricted to a single street, the long and charming **Warren Street,** which is packed end-to-end with antiques shops, several catering to those with an interest in contemporary and midcentury modern aesthetics. Also worth checking out in Hudson is the surprisingly

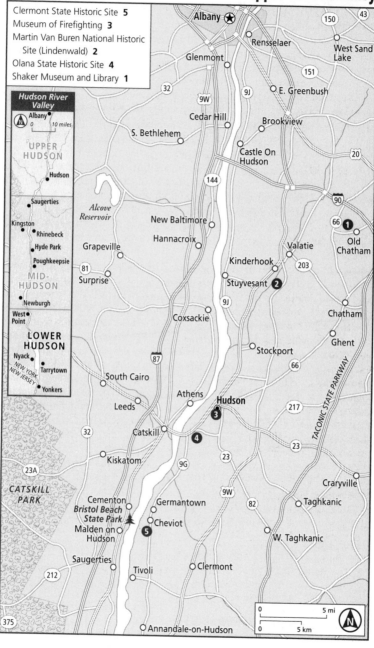

Upper Hudson Valley

Clermont State Historic Site **5**
Museum of Firefighting **3**
Martin Van Buren National Historic
  Site (Lindenwald) **2**
Olana State Historic Site **4**
Shaker Museum and Library **1**

Hudson River Valley

0   10 miles

UPPER HUDSON

Albany
Hudson
Saugerties
Kingston
Rhinebeck
Hyde Park
Poughkeepsie

MID-HUDSON

81
Surprise
Newburgh
West Point

LOWER HUDSON

Nyack
NEW YORK
NEW JERSEY
Tarrytown
Yonkers

Albany
Rensselaer
Glenmont
West Sand Lake
150
43
151
32
9W
9J
E. Greenbush
Cedar Hill
Brookview
S. Bethlehem
Castle On Hudson
20
144
Alcove Reservoir
New Baltimore
Hannacroix
Grapeville
Valatie
66
Old Chatham
1
Kinderhook
203
81
Surprise
Stuyvesant
2
9J
Coxsackie
Chatham
Ghent
Stockport
66
South Cairo
87
TACONIC STATE PARKWAY
Athens
Hudson
3
217
Leeds
Catskill
4
23
32
Kiskatom
9G
Craryville
23A
9W
CATSKILL PARK
Cementon
Bristol Beach State Park
Malden on Hudson
Germantown
Cheviot
82
Taghkanic
5
W. Taghkanic
Saugerties
212
Tivoli
Clermont
375
Annandale-on-Hudson

0   5 mi
0   5 km

N

engaging **FASNY Museum of Firefighting** (117 Harry Howard Ave. © **518/828-7695.** Donation suggested. Daily 9am–4:30pm). Hudson, home to the oldest volunteer fire department in the U.S., is also the site of this large and very well-organized museum, which has been around since 1925. It contains more than 80 fire apparatus, ranging from a 1725 Newsham wooden cart, the first fire "engine" in New York City, to wonderfully ornate, mid-19th-century carriages. A small 9/11 exhibit in the front reminds visitors of the importance and bravery of firefighters. For current information on gallery exhibits and other Hudson happenings, visit **www.warrenstreet.com**.

Martin Van Buren National Historic Site (Lindenwald)   The eighth president of the U.S.—admittedly, not one of the best-remembered presidents in American history—Martin Van Buren (1782–1862) grew up in the Upper Hudson Valley in the town of Kinderhook (it's said that "okay" comes from his references to Old Kinderhook by its initials). Van Buren bought the estate in 1839 during his presidency as a place to retire. He named the 226-acre farm Lindenwald and built a Georgian-style mansion here, where he lived out the final 21 years of his life.

Old Post Rd. (Rte. 9H), Kinderhook. © **518/758-9689.** www.nps.gov/mava. Admission $5 adults, $12 families (up to 4 adults and accompanying children). May–Oct 31 daily 9am–4:30pm; Nov 1–Dec 7 Sat–Sun only, 9am–4:30pm (tours hourly).

Shaker Museum and Library ✦✦ *(Finds)*   The Shakers, the Early American religious group known for not only their religious devotion and sexual abstinence, but also their exquisite craftsmanship and ingenious architectural simplicity that influenced legions of designers, established communities in upstate New York and New England at the end of the 18th century. The Shakers believed that every living act was an act of devotion, and they pursued their work like prayer. This rustic museum of nearly 20,000 objects and repository of books, journals, photographs, and papers—established in 1950 as the first public museum concerning the life, work, art, and religion of the United Society of Believers in Christ's Second Appearing, commonly known as the Shakers—contains one of the largest collections of the community's heavenly round baskets, furniture, textiles, kitchen implements, spinning wheels, farm tools, and machinery. The museum and library will eventually relocate to a state-of-the-art facility in the Shakers' Great Stone Barn (a stunning building and the largest stone barn in America) in nearby New Lebanon, New York, very close to the historic Mount Lebanon Shaker Village, from which more than three-quarters of the collection comes. When that happens, the Shaker site will become one of the top attractions in the Upper Hudson Valley.

88 Shaker Museum Rd., Old Chatham. © **518/794-9100.** www.shakermuseumandlibrary.org. Admission $8 adults, $4 children 8–17, free for children under 8. Late May to late Oct Wed–Mon 10am–5pm.

ESPECIALLY FOR KIDS

The **Museum of Firefighting** in Hudson is sure to delight kids—especially little boys—with its fantastic collection of vintage fire trucks. The grounds at the **Clermont** and **Olana** estates are great for exploring, with plenty of beautiful trails, and having a picnic.

SPORTS & OUTDOOR PURSUITS

HIKING   Nice and easy hiking trails can be found at the state historic sites **Clermont** (Clermont; © **518/537-4240**), **Olana** (Greenport; © **518/828-0135**), and **Martin Van Buren Park** (Kinderhook; © **800/724-1846**).

WINTER SPORTS   For downhill skiing, try **Catamount,** Route 23, Hillsdale (✆ **800/342-1840;** www.catamountski.com), on the Massachusetts border in the southern Berkshires. There are good cross-country ski trails at the state historic sites **Clermont** (Clermont; ✆ **518/537-4240**), **Olana** (Greenport; ✆ **518/828-0135**), and **Martin Van Buren Park** (Kinderhook; ✆ **800/724-1846**).

SHOPPING

Antiquing is a huge business and pastime in the Upper Hudson Valley. In the past decade, **Hudson** 🌟🌟 has been transformed from a sleepy and fairly run-down upstate town into one of the premier antiques destinations in New York State, with 65 shops and galleries spread out along 5 blocks of Warren Street and a few streets that fan out from there. It has many slick, high-end shops (though most shoppers find the prices a bit more accessible than in New York City) and a few stores for the rest of us. Pieces range from Egyptian to fine French and midcentury modern. There are far too many to mention, but among the nicest shops are **Eustace & Zamus,** 513 Warren St. (✆ **518/822-9200**); **Skalar Antiques,** 438½ Warrant St. (✆ 518/828-1170); **Neven and Neven Moderne,** 618 Warren St. (✆ 518-828-4214); **Vince Mulford,** 419 Warren St. (✆ **518/828-5489**); **Historical Materialism,** 601 Warren St. (✆ **518/671-6151**); and **Gottlieb Gallery,** 524 Warren St. (✆ **518/822-1761**). If those are too pricey, check out **Fern,** 554 Warren St. (✆ **518/828-2886**); **Cottage & Camp,** 521 Warren St. (✆ **518/822-9175**); and, above all, **The Armory Art & Antique Gallery,** State Street at North 5th (✆ **518/822-1477**), an eclectic and lower-priced assembly of some 60 dealers. Other non-antiques shops of interest, selling mostly housewares and gift items, include **Shop Naked,** 608 Warren St. (✆ **518/671-6336**); **Pieces,** 609 Warren St. (✆ **518/822-8131**); **Rural Residence,** 316 Warren St. (✆ **518/822-1061**); and the unique jewelry store **Ornamentum,** 506½ Warren St. (✆ **518/671-6770**). For a full list of stores and galleries, visit www.hudsonantiques.net.

The Shaker Museum & Library, in Old Chatham (88 Shaker Museum Rd.; ✆ **518/794-9100**), has a gift shop with an excellent selection of high-quality crafts based on Shaker traditions (such as oval boxes, furniture, and baskets), as well as books about the Shakers and other gift items.

WHERE TO STAY

Options in the Upper Hudson Valley are largely limited to small but charming and intimate bed-and-breakfasts. The area is close enough to other sections of the valley that you might also consider basing yourself farther downriver.

EXPENSIVE

Madalin Hotel 🌟🌟   A beautiful old hotel, originally built in 1909 and painstakingly restored in 2006, this inn and restaurant have quickly become the anchor of a lively scene in tiny Tivoli. The 11 rooms in the three-story building are spacious and understated, tastefully outfitted with Eastlake period pieces. Downstairs, the gorgeously carved 19-foot bar in the tavern is the centerpiece of the restaurant, Madalin's Table (see review below), which features a wraparound porch, a popular spot to be on warm evenings.

53 Broadway, Tivoli, NY 12583. ✆ 845/757-2100. www.madalinhotel.com. 11 units. $199–$299 double. AE, DC, MC, V. Free parking on street. **Amenities:** Restaurant, bar. *In room:* A/C, flat-screen TV, Wi-Fi.

Wine Trails & Farmers' Markets

The Hudson Valley, the nation's oldest winemaking region, is today home to about three dozen wineries. Though few of the area's wineries yet attained national followings, a number of them offer tours and tastings, and several are blessed with outstandingly scenic locations. If you'd like to visit a winery or two during your stay, all you have to do is follow the trail—either the **Dutchess Wine Trail** (© 845/266-5372; www.dutchesswinetrail.com), on the east side of the Hudson, or the **Shawangunk Wine Trail** (© 845/255-2494; www.shawangunkwinetrail.com), on the west side of the river. More than a dozen are open to regular visits. The following is merely a selection of my favorites: The Dutchess (Country) Trail consists of **Cascade Mountain Winery,** 835 Cascade Mountain Rd., Amenia (© 845/373-9021), which has a lovely setting and a very nice little restaurant with outdoor seating; **Clinton Vineyards,** Schultzville Road, Clinton Corners (© 845/266-5372), makers of a pretty nice white, a Seyval blanc; **Alison Wines & Vineyards,** 231 Pitcher Lane, Red Hook (© 845/758-6335), the newest of the bunch, with a garden shop, baked goods, and cut-your-own Christmas trees on the premises; and **Millbrook Vineyards & Winery** ★★, 26 Wing Rd., Millbrook (© 800/662-WINE), the largest and certainly one of the best of the lot. Millbrook makes an excellent pinot noir reserve, offers a full tour, features art exhibits and live music on Saturday nights in summer, and is worth the visit for the views over the rolling hillsides and horse farms alone.

Several of the nine family-owned wineries of the Shawangunk Trail, all sandwiched between the Shawangunk Mountains and the Hudson River in Ulster County, are easily visited on a Hudson Valley trip. Among them are **Brotherhood Winery,** 35 North St., Washingtonville (© 845/496-9101), the

MODERATE

The Country Squire B&B ★★   This stylish B&B, in the heart of Hudson and 2 blocks from the burgeoning expanse of shops and restaurants along Warren Street, is the perfect place to stay if you're an art and antiques hound. A well-designed and clutter-free but very comfortable Queen Anne Victorian, the sensitively restored home, built in 1900, features a wealth of interesting architectural details, such as parquet floors, leaded and stained-glass windows, pocket doors, and five fireplaces. The inn has five guest rooms, ranging from twin to king, that are sedately and elegantly decorated with a nice mix of handsome antique pieces and a few cool modern furnishings and accents. The most contemporary of the rooms has a private deck. The spacious private bathrooms, with wainscoting and claw-foot tubs, are particularly inviting, and bedding and linens are first-rate.

251 Allen St., Hudson, NY 12534. © 518/822-9229. www.countrysquireny.com. 5 units. May–Oct $155–$190 double; Nov 1–Dec 31 $115–$150 double; Jan–Apr $110–$130double. Rates include breakfast. AE, MC, V. Free parking on street. **Amenities:** Internet access. *In room:* Seasonal A/C, TV, Wi-Fi, and fax (in 1 room).

The Inn at Green River ★★   A luxurious B&B set in a serene residential area of Hillsdale, as accessible to the Hudson River Valley as it is to the Berkshires, this inn is oldest winery in the United States, in operation since 1839. Though the winery doesn't grow its own grapes (instead importing them from Long Island, the Finger Lakes, and California), its grounds constitute a well-stocked campus, with vast underground vaulted cellars and a whole host of shops and activities on-site. Claiming to be the oldest continuously operating vineyard in the U.S. is **Benmarl Wine Company,** 156 Highland Ave., Marlboro-on-Hudson (© **845/236-4265;** www.benmarl.com), a small, family-owned independent with awe-inspiring views from a hilltop location on the west side of the Hudson (between Newburgh and New Paltz). It also offers a small gallery of the owner's illustrations and artwork; Mark Miller was one of the best-known magazine illustrators in the world in the 1940s and 1950s. Other Shawangunk Trail wineries are covered in the Catskills region chapter (see chapter 8). Schedules for winery tours and tastings vary, though most are open to visitors throughout the Memorial Day–to–Labor Day season; for current hours and events, check the trail websites or pick up a brochure at any tourism information outlet.

Farmers' markets and **pick-your-own farm stands** are everywhere in this beautiful, bucolic region. There are dozens and dozens, so here are just a few: **Mead Orchards and Farm Stand,** 25 Scism Rd., Tivoli (9 miles north of Rhinebeck; © **914/756-5641**), with pick-your-own apples and pumpkins; **Greig Farm,** Pitcher Lane, Red Hook (© **914/758-1234**), which has pick-your-own fruits and vegetables and a farm market; **Millbrook Farmers' Market,** Franklin Avenue at Front Street, Millbrook village, every Saturday from 9am to 1pm; and **Tarrytown Farmers' Market,** Patriot's Park, Route 9, Tarrytown (© **914/923-4837**). Ask around and locals will come up with many more.

steeped in romance and relaxation. Rooms in the 1830s Federal-style farmhouse are exquisitely decorated with local antiques and art; most have fireplaces and soaking or Jacuzzi tubs. The property is surrounded by lovingly tended gardens overlooking a creek that flows into Green River. The proprietor Deborah Bowen is known for her sumptuous breakfasts, served in the candlelit dining room and featuring such delectables as lemon-ricotta hot cakes and fresh-baked scones. Deborah recently added a beautiful enclosed porch and deck.

9 Nobletown Rd., Hillsdale, NY 12529. © 518/325-7248. www.innatgreenriver.com. 7 units. $110–$255 double. Rates include breakfast. AE, DC, MC, V. Free parking on street. *In room:* A/C.

The Inn at Hudson ★★ *Value*   Just a few blocks from Hudson's main drag, teeming with antiques shops, is this elegant 1906 brick Dutch and Jacobean mansion, the Morgan Jones House. All rooms are named for their dominant decorative colors; three are especially spacious and handsomely decorated with antiques from local dealers. As impressive as they are, the carved woodwork of the dining room, library, and foyer is even more so. It will surely surprise some guests, especially those with a soft spot for '80s New Wave pop music, that the proprietors were once members of the flamboyant band Human Sexual Response (which had a hit with "I Want to Be Jackie Onassis"—a fact that makes the Jackie O memorabilia in the media room a bit more comprehensible). If you're planning to stay several days in the area, the inn rate policies make it a very good deal.

317 Allen St., Hudson, NY 12534. ☏ 518/822-9322. www.theinnathudson.com. 5 units. Large rooms $200 double 1st night, $100 double additional nights; smaller rooms $100 1st night, $75 additional nights. Rates include breakfast. AE, DISC, MC, V. Free parking. *In room:* A/C, cable TV, Wi-Fi.

Inn at Silver Maple Farm ★★ *(Finds)* A large converted barn complex on the outskirts of Chatham, not far from the Shaker Museum and Library and on the New York side of the Berkshire foothills, this picturesque 10-acre estate nestled into a hillside is a relaxing retreat. Rooms are varied, with a number of different views and designs. In all, you'll find comfortable beds, handsome linens, and down comforters, with other touches like antique trunks and hand-painted murals. The Pines suite has a downstairs living room, fireplace, and upstairs loft with a cathedral ceiling. The Lodge rooms are rustic and sedately decorated, without the frills of a few others. Breakfast is generous and includes items like French toast, apple-pie pancakes, and fresh-baked muffins.

Rte. 295, Canaan, NY 12029. ☏ 518/781-3600. Fax 518/781-3883. www.silvermaplefarm.com. 11 units. $100–$210 double; $235–$295 suite. Rates include full breakfast. AE, DISC, MC, V. Free parking. *In room:* A/C, TV.

WHERE TO DINE

You may have to search out a restaurant more in the northern section of the valley, since its best dining is quite spread out, but the restaurants below are every bit as good as those in the Mid- and Lower Hudson Valley.

MODERATE

Madalin's Table ★★ AMERICAN Part of the renovated Madalin Hotel (see above), this new restaurant is a welcome addition to the burgeoning scene on Broadway in out-of-the-way, but hip, Tivoli. The chef, Brian Kaywork, is a CIA grad, and he works with fresh local ingredients to prepare a seasonal menu that may not be particularly inventive, yet is certainly rewarding. Sample the straightforward tavern fare, such as a yummy burger, Baja fish tacos, or excellently prepared fresh seafood, pastas, and local meats, including molasses-brined pork tenderloin. The wine list isn't massive, but wines are very well chosen, with a few unexpected choices. The main dining room is an elegant turn-of-the-20th-century space tucked behind the foyer and outfitted with crisp white tablecloths. But on warm summer nights, it seems that everyone clamors for a table on the sweeping wraparound veranda, from which one can survey the local scene, made up of professors and students from nearby Bard College, weekenders, and a handful of celebrities who hide out in these parts.

53 Broadway, Tivoli, NY 12583. ☏ 845/757-2100. www.madalinhotel.com. Reservations recommended weekends. Main courses $12–$32; sushi $3.50–$10. AE, MC, V. Wed–Sun 5–9:30pm; Sun brunch 10am–2:30pm.

Osaka ★★ *(Finds)* SUSHI/JAPANESE In these parts, along the upper stretches of the Hudson, good sushi is probably less common than in your hometown. But this small and friendly little place, in a cute little slate-colored house on the adorable main street of Tivoli, is a most welcome find. People come from neighboring towns for the sushi, tempura, and teriyaki dishes. The interior is simple and contemporary, done up in pale woods; the sushi bar, though, is the place to be. The lunch specials, served Monday through Saturday from 11:30am to 2:30pm, are an excellent deal, though those with a big appetite might find themselves still hungry. Another branch of the restaurant can be found at 22 Garden St. in nearby Rhinebeck.

74 Broadway, Tivoli. ⓒ 845/757-5055. Reservations recommended weekends. Main courses $11–$23; sushi $3.50–$10. AE, MC, V. Mon and Wed–Thurs 11:30am–2:30pm and 4:30–9:30pm; Fri–Sat 11:30am–2:30pm and 4:30–10:30pm; Sun 3–9:30pm.

Swoon Kitchenbar ✹✹ *Value* CREATIVE BISTRO   The new place everybody seems to be falling for in Hudson, the ever-growing antiques destination of the Upper Valley, is Swoon. I have to admit it's become a favorite for me, too. The creative menu is impeccably prepared and prices are a bargain given the quality of ingredients and care that go into dishes. The long rectangular dining room is accented with an abundance of green plants and flowers—as if to communicate that you're about to have one very fresh meal—and a wonderful pressed-tin ceiling, marble tables, and an antique tile floor. The inventive menu includes a homemade charcuterie plate, with meats that come from local farms; the platter had my Argentine meat-loving friends licking their fingers. One of my favorite main courses is the iron-pot lamb shank, which is braised in red wine and, true to its name, comes in a small iron pot. Swoon's surprisingly long wine list has several excellent and accessibly priced choices, and the homemade pastries and desserts—one of the owners is the pastry chef—are most memorable. This is one restaurant that earns its boastful name.

340 Warren St., Hudson. ⓒ 518/822-8938. Reservations recommended weekends. Main courses $16–$21. AE, MC, V. Fri–Sat 11:30am–11pm; Thurs and Sun–Mon 5-10pm.

INEXPENSIVE
Red Dot ✹✹ *Value* CREATIVE BISTRO   As much bar as bistro, this groovy, dark two-room space is a popular watering hole for locals and visitors to Hudson, and though it's a great spot for an early or late-night drink, it's also a very good spot for dinner or brunch. Check out the generous salads, mussels marinière, braised short ribs, and specials like a salmon BLT. In summer, a seat on the lovely outdoor patio out back, swathed in ivy and featuring a stone waterfall, is particularly coveted. When I'm in Hudson hitting the antiques shops, I rarely fail to duck in for an Old Speckled Hen—a rarity, on tap—and some frites with Belgian mayonnaise.

321 Warren St., Hudson. ⓒ 518/828-3657. Reservations recommended weekends. Main courses $8–$19. MC, V. Wed–Sat 5–10pm; Sat–Sun 11am–3pm; Sun 5–9pm.

THE UPPER HUDSON VALLEY AFTER DARK
The nightlife is pretty quiet in the largely rural Upper Hudson Valley. When you tire from all the antiques shops and galleries in Hudson, pay a visit to the **Hudson Opera House,** housed in the Old City Hall, 327 Warren St. (ⓒ **518/822-1438;** www.hudson operahouse.org). It hosts a variety of events, including concerts, theater productions, workshops, lectures, and poetry readings. Check out theater productions, including children's theater, at **StageWorks/Hudson,** 41 Cross St., Hudson (ⓒ **518/822-9667**). Productions have included Tony Kushner's *The Illusion.* Tickets are $22 to $27 for adults, $20 to $25 for seniors, and $11 to $13 for students. Hudson is also home to a number of cafes and lively bar/restaurants. My favorite bar scene on Warren Street is **Red Dot,** 321 Warren St. (ⓒ **518/828-3657;** see restaurant review above).

8

The Catskill Mountain Region

by Neil E. Schlecht

The groundbreaking American conservation movement originated in the Catskill Mountains, 6,000 square miles of mountains, rivers, forests, and parkland considered **America's First Wilderness.** Though just 100 miles north of New York City, the region's natural state has been remarkably preserved, thanks to the state constitution that designated a quarter of a million acres of "forever wild" forest and the region's importance as the watershed for New York City and almost half the state. Yet natural beauty is not what many people have traditionally known the region for: Mention "The Catskills" and most Americans of a certain age still conjure either nostalgic or dreaded notions of resort vacations from another era.

Famous (or infamous) to many Americans through Hollywood movies like *Dirty Dancing* and *A Walk on the Moon,* the Catskill region is an area in transition. For most of a century, it was *the* summer vacation area for New Yorkers, beginning in the late 19th century, when steam trains deposited elegantly dressed vacationers at stations for their horse-drawn carriage rides to massive mountain lodges and boarding houses. That trend continued through the 1960s, when it became popular for the kind of resorts—many of them ethnic enclaves where family men from the city joined their wives, kids, and neighbors on weekends in the mountains and engaged in 9-to-5 schedules of planned activities—that earned it a perhaps unwelcome sobriquet, the "Borscht Belt."

Today, that type of vacationing has fallen wholly out of favor. The Catskill region, still boldly beautiful if less remote, is being transformed into a different kind of Catskills, open to new types of visitors and new forms of leisure activities. The new Catskill Mountain region not only has conspicuously renamed itself, but has set about recapturing its essence, the Great Outdoors, while holding onto an easygoing, rural lifestyle.

And so it should. The spiritual and natural heart of the region remains the 700,000-acre Catskill Park and Forest Preserve, a dense area with 35 peaks soaring to elevations of 3,500 feet. This scenic area overflows with lush hills and valleys, forests, farmland, waterfalls, trout streams, reservoirs, and six major river systems. It is regarded as one of the world's greatest fly-fishing areas, and anglers make pilgrimages from across the globe to wade in its trout streams. The Catskill Mountains practically beg for outdoors enthusiasts to sample the incredible variety of hiking and biking trails, sheer cliffs for rock climbing, and peaks for skiing. But you don't have to be a fleece-clad extreme-sports fan to enjoy the region, which is also home to a great number of historic homesteads, out-of-the-way antiques shops, pick-your-own co-ops and dairy farms, and nostalgic attractions like old trains and vintage "base ball" (yes, it was two words originally) teams.

The Catskill Mountain Region

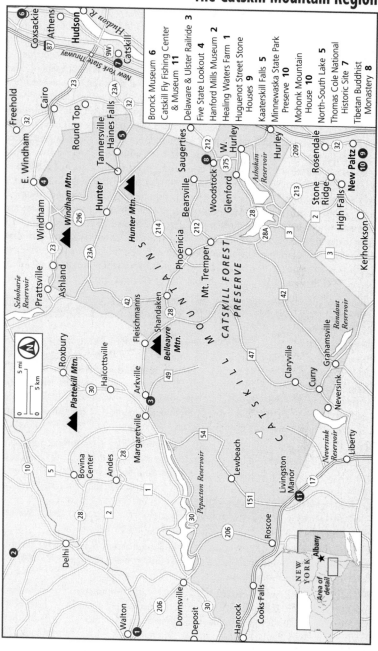

Bronck Museum **6**
Catskill Fly Fishing Center & Museum **11**
Delaware & Ulster Railride **3**
Five State Lookout **4**
Hanford Mills Museum **2**
Healing Waters Farm **1**
Huguenot Street Stone Houses **9**
Kaaterskill Falls **5**
Minnewaska State Park Preserve **10**
Mohonk Mountain House **10**
North-South Lake **5**
Thomas Cole National Historic Site **7**
Tibetan Buddhist Monastery **8**

Locals are anxious for visitors to know that this is no longer your granddad's Catskills. Today, mountain bikers plunge down Plattekill Mountain caked in mud, and luxury inns and spas have sprouted, offering individualized rather than mass service. City refugees are being reawakened to the natural beauty, small towns, and tranquil pleasures of the Catskill region. Young couples are moving in and starting up small businesses and inns, while chefs trained at the Hudson Valley's Culinary Institute of America have taken to the region's towns and proximity to local farms to gain a foothold for their restaurants and bars. And though prices have been steadily skyrocketing, weekenders weary of overdone destinations are finding what amount to second-home bargains in the area. Most of the region

has a revitalized feel that is far removed from the old Catskills; indeed, many new arrivals have little interest in, or perhaps even knowledge of, its less cool past.

Amazingly, a few old-school resorts hang on, in what can only be described as a nostalgic time warp, charmingly resistant to change. If you want a trip down a musty memory lane, you can still find a megaresort where you play shuffleboard at 11:30am, attend pool games at 1pm, and get your hair set before a bland buffet dinner and the night's entertainment of Rocco singing Italian love songs. But happening upon a yesteryear place today is more of a surprise than an expectation in the new Catskill region—one that is proudly returning to its progressive, outdoors roots while looking forward to a more dynamic future.

1 Orientation

ARRIVING

By Plane   Most visitors traveling by air will probably fly into one of the three major airports in the New York City area. For information on those, see chapter 5. Other visitors traveling by air will arrive via **Albany International Airport,** 737 Albany-Shaker Rd. (© **518/242-2299;** www.albanyairport.com), or **Stewart International Airport,** Route 207, New Windsor (© **845/564-2100;** www.stewartintlairport.com), near Newburgh, which handles 50 daily flights from major U.S. cities such as Atlanta, Chicago, Philadelphia, Raleigh/Durham, and Washington, D.C.

BY CAR   Most visitors tour the Catskill Mountain region by private automobile. The region begins about 90 miles, or about 2 hours, north of New York City; there is easy access via exits 16 through 21B of the New York State Thruway (I-87). From the south, Route I-81 and Route 17 (future I-86) also provide direct access. From New England, I-84 and I-90 connect with I-88, I-87, and Route 17 (future I-86).

Major car-rental companies, including Avis, Budget, Enterprise, Hertz, National, and Thrifty, have representatives at all the major airports.

BY TRAIN   **Amtrak** will get you as close as Poughkeepsie, Schenectady, Albany, or Syracuse. For more information and reservations, contact Amtrak at © **800/USA-RAIL** or visit www.amtrak.com.

BY BUS   **Greyhound** (© **800/231-2222;** www.greyhound.com) travels to Andes, Arkville, Bearsville, Catskill, Fleischmanns, Hensonville, Kerhonkson, Liberty, Livingston Manor, Monticello, Mountainville, New Paltz, Phoenicia, Rock Hill, Roscoe, Tannersville, Windham, and Woodstock, among other towns. **Adirondack, New York & Pine Hill Trailways** (© **800/776-7548;** www.trailwaysny.com) serves most of the Catskill region, including New Paltz, Woodstock, Phoenicia, Margaretville, Andes, Windham, Hunter, Cairo, Saugerties, Catskill, and more. **Shortline Coach**

USA (© **800/631-8405;** www.coachusa.com/shortline) covers the western section, from New York City to Ellenville, Hancock, Livingston Manor, Monticello, and Roscoe.

VISITOR INFORMATION

Get additional information before you go from the **Catskill Association for Tourism Services** in Catskill (© **800/NYS-CATS;** www.catskillregiontoday.com) or one of the four counties that make up the Catskill Mountain region: **Ulster County Tourism Office,** 10 Westbrook Lane, Kingston (© **800/342-5826;** www.ulstertourism.info); **Green County Promotion Department,** P.O. Box 527, Catskill (© **800/355-CATS** or 518/943-3223; www.greenetourism.com); **Delaware County Chamber of Commerce,** 114 Main St., Delhi (© **800/746-2281;** www.delawarecounty.org); and **Sullivan County Visitors Association,** 100 North St., Monticello (© **800/882-CATS** or 845/794-3000; www.scva.net).

2 Southeastern Catskill Region (Ulster County)

The southeastern section of the Catskill Mountains, centered in Ulster County and the closest to New York City (many parts are 2 hr. or less by car), is one of the most historic, sophisticated, and beautiful parts of the Catskill region. It's an area of bucolic farmlands and original settlers' stone houses belonging to French, Dutch, and English immigrants. The area straddles the easily blurred divide between the Catskill Mountains and the Mid-Hudson Valley and is thus easy to combine with tours of the west bank of the river valley. Some of the most legendary names are contained in this section that skirts the southern edge of the Catskill Forest Preserve: Mohonk Mountain House, Woodstock, and New Paltz, as well as up-and-comers like small but increasingly happening towns like Saugerties and Phoenicia.

ESSENTIALS

GETTING THERE From north and south, direct access by car is via exits 18 to 20 of the New York State Thruway (I-87).

VISITOR INFORMATION Contact the **Ulster County Tourism Office,** 10 Westbrook Lane, Kingston (© **800/342-5826;** www.ulstertourism.info). The **Woodstock Chamber of Commerce** operates an information kiosk, 10 Rock City Rd., Woodstock (© **845/679-6234;** Thurs–Sun 11am–6pm), which dispenses town and area maps.

NEW PALTZ & ENVIRONS ✿✿

The largest historical attraction in the southeastern Catskills is in New Paltz, a likable college town founded in 1678. The **Huguenot Street Stone Houses** ✿✿, 18 Broadhead Ave. (© **845/255-1660;** www.hhs-newpaltz.org; deluxe [90-min.] tour $10 adults, $9 seniors, $5 students ages 6–17, $24 families; standard [50-min.] tour $7 adults, $6 seniors, $3 students 6–17, free for children under 6; tours May 1–Oct 31 Tues–Fri hourly 10am–4pm, Sat–Sun every half-hour 10am–4pm), represent some of the oldest remaining architecture in the region. This collection of a half-dozen Colonial-era stone houses was built by a small group of French religious refugees, the Protestant Huguenots. A National Historic Landmark, the Huguenot district once occupied 40,000 acres at the edge of the Wallkill River. The original stone houses, the earliest built in 1692, have been restored with period furnishings and heirlooms and operate as house museums. Also on the site are the bright-yellow **1705 DuBois Fort**

Fun Fact **Historical Revisionism**

The esoteric science of dendrochronology, or dendrodating—by which wood samples are taken and rings counted and analyzed to determine age—has recently revealed that several houses along Huguenot Street, such as the Jean Hasbrouck House, are not quite as old as originally believed. Because the dates were off by a decade or so, it likely means that the house was built not by the paterfamilias but his sons.

(now a visitor center and museum shop, where tours begin) and the **French Church,** a reconstruction of the 1717 original. Visits are by guided tour only: The deluxe tour visits three of the houses and the church; the standard tour goes to one Colonial period house and the church. If visiting out of season, you can still stroll along the street and view the exterior of the houses (and maybe peek in a window or two).

In the tiny, charming village of **High Falls,** which backs up to the waters that flowed through what was once the Delaware and Hudson Canal, the **D&H Canal Museum,** in an 1885 church on Mohonk Road (© **845/687-9311;** www.canal museum.org; $4 adults, $2 children; May to Labor Day Thurs–Sat and Mon 11am–5pm; Sun 1–5pm; weekends only May and Sept–Oct), displays original locks and vignettes relating life along the 19th-century canal. A great spot for easy hikes is the **D&H Canal Heritage Corridor** (Rosendale; © **845/331-2100**), which runs 35 miles along the D&H towpaths and the Ontario & Western Railway from Ellenville to Kingston. The newly renovated **Five Locks Walk,** an enjoyable, easy half-hour hike in the woods, covers the ground between locks 16 and 20 alongside the canal. Another nearby village worth a look in the area is **Rosendale,** which is really on the upswing, with a cinema in the old town theater and lively new bars and restaurants that belie the village's small size.

The **Mohonk Preserve** ★★ is more than 6,000 acres of fabulously wild forests, fields, ponds, and streams, all part of the northern Shawangunk Mountains, with more than 60 miles of fantastic trails through dense woodlands and up bleached-white mountain crags. It is the largest privately held preserve (it's owned by a nonprofit environmental organization) in New York State. Not to be missed are the unmatched, breathtaking views from the climb to the tower at **Skytop**—at this spot, 1,500 feet above sea level, you can see into six states on a clear day. Day passes and more information are available at the Mohonk Preserve Visitor Center, Route 44/55 (© **845/255-0919;** www.mohonkpreserve.org). The legendary **Mohonk Mountain House** ★★★, a fantasy-like Victorian castle perched on a ridge within the preserve, is worth a visit even if you're not staying there—and it really has to be seen to be believed (see "Where to Stay," below). Day guests can hike the trails ($13), eat at the imposing lodge restaurant, and ice-skate at the beautiful outdoor pavilion.

Minnewaska State Park Preserve, Route 44/55 in Gardiner, is 12,000 acres ripe for hiking, biking, cross-country skiing, and lake swimming. There are 30 miles of footpaths and carriageways, as well as two lakes, waterfalls, and great mountain viewpoints. The panoramic views of the **Roundout Valley** from an overlook off Route 44/55, just beyond the Minnewaska Preserve, are breathtaking. A park preserve information office (© **845/255-0752**), which issues climbing permits, can be found along Route 44/55 as you climb on the road above Gardiner. The incredibly sheer white cliffs of the **Shawangunk Mountains** allow for some of the best rock climbing on the East Coast. The Eastern Mountain Sports shop next door to the Minnewaska Lodge provides guides and equipment. The **Wallkill Valley Rail Trail** (www.gorailtrail.org), which extends from New Paltz to Gardiner, is 12 miles of linear park, perfect for low-impact cycling, hiking, and skiing.

An excellent boutique winery, with gorgeous views of the Shawangunk cliffs, is **Whitecliff Vineyard and Winery,** a member of the Shawangunk Wine Trail (www. shawangunkwinetrail.com). Run by a husband-and-wife team, Whitecliff, 331 McKinstry Rd., Gardiner (© 845/255-4613; May–Oct Thurs–Fri and Sun noon–5pm, Sat 11am–6pm), produces nice European-style reds and whites. Other area wineries open for visits are **Adair Vineyards,** 52 Allhusen Rd., New Paltz (© 845/255-1377), set in a 200-year-old dairy barn, and **Rivendell Winery,** 714 Albany Post Rd., New Paltz (© 845/255-2494), which, despite a rather less-than-welcoming exterior, contains a vintage New York store that is one-stop shopping for Hudson Valley, Finger Lakes, and Long Island wines.

Though perhaps not as pristine as historic Huguenot Street in New Paltz, the two dozen stone houses that populate the downtown area of **Hurley,** off Route 209, are among the oldest and largest grouping of lived-in stone houses in the country. Main Street is lined with them, dating from the first half of the 18th century. Your only real opportunity to peek inside some of them is on Hurley Stone House Day, held the second Saturday in July, when guided tours are held. For more information, call © **845/ 331-4121.**

WOODSTOCK 🎯🎯 & SAUGERTIES 🎯

Woodstock has a name recognition any tourist town would die for. However, the watershed 1969 rock concert that defined a generation didn't actually take place here, but in an open field some 60 miles southwest of here, in Bethel. Woodstock, a long-time artists' community (beginning with the Byrdcliffe Arts Colony in 1902) with a vibe and creativity that fueled the '60s counterculture, has in recent years become a village with high-end boutiques as well as hippie shops. That said, it's still a pretty and enjoyable place, perfect for strolling, and *the* shopping destination in this part of the Catskill Mountains (hands-down, *the* place to satisfy your inner hippie with tie-dye tees and peace-sign art). The long main street, stuffed with shops and galleries, is Mill Hill Road, which becomes Tinker Street. **Byrdcliffe Arts Colony** 🎯, 34 Tinker St. (© 845/679-2079; www.woodstockguild.org), offers self-guided walking tours of the legendary Arts and Crafts colony (the largest surviving colony of its kind), as well as artists-in-residence programs. The **Woodstock Artists Association and Museum,** 28 Tinker St. (© 845/679-2940), is a long-standing cooperative with a large gallery space exhibiting work of local and nonlocal artists. The **Center for Photography at Woodstock,** 59 Tinker St. (© 845/679-6337), has excellent photography exhibits by well-known artists, along with workshops. Other galleries worth a look include the **Fletcher Gallery,** 40 Mill Hill Rd. (© 845/679-4411); **Art Forms,** 32 Mill Hill Rd. (© 845/679-1100); **Fleur de Lis Gallery,** 34 Tinker St. (© 845/679-2688); and **Clouds Gallery,** 1 Mill Hill Rd. (© 845/679-8155). Cool quilting classes are available at **Woodstock Quilt Supply,** 79 Tinker St. (© 845/679-0733; www.quilt stock.com).

Woodstock may not have been the site of the big concert, but it has plenty of year-round live-music concerts, poetry readings, and theater performances. The **Maverick concert series,** founded in 1916, is the oldest summer chamber music series in the

U.S. Check the events schedule at **www.maverickconcerts.org** and get information and tickets by calling $\textcircled{c}$ **845/679-8217. The Woodstock Playhouse** has performances of theater, music, and dance in the summer season ($\textcircled{c}$ **845/679-4101;** www. woodstockplayhouse.org). With a main stage, bar, and lounge, the **Bearsville Theater,** Rt. 212, Bearsville ($\textcircled{c}$ **845/679-4406;** www.bearsvilletheater.com) hosts diverse music groups, dancing, and arts performances year-round.

A worthwhile detour is to the **Tibetan Buddhist Monastery,** Meads Mountain Road (which begins as Rock City Rd.; $\textcircled{c}$ **845/679-5906**), high above Woodstock, a must not just for Buddhists, but for anyone with an interest in eclectic architecture. Tours are held for individuals on weekends.

Saugerties has been officially discovered. A cute little town upriver from Kingston and just 10 miles northeast of Woodstock, it has a sweet main drag called Partition Street, lined with good restaurants and suddenly teeming with art galleries, antiques dealers, and shops; it appears to be busy transforming itself into a mini-Hudson, the antiquing destination of the Upper Hudson River Valley. Still a peaceful and charming place, if a bit rough around the edges, it makes quite a good base for exploring both the Catskills and the Upper and Mid-Hudson Valley. Not to be missed is the enjoyable mile-long woodland walking trail out to the river and **Saugerties Lighthouse** (off Rte. 9W), built in 1838 (here's the kicker: you can actually sleep here; see "Where to Stay," below). In summer the formerly blue-collar town gives itself over to a very elite influx of equestrian fans with their fancy horses and trailers. The **HITS-on-the-Hudson National Show Jumping Championships,** 319 Main St. ($\textcircled{c}$ **845/ 246-8833;** www.hitsshows.com), are held in Saugerties from late May to mid-September. Admission is free weekdays and $5 on weekends.

MOUNT TREMPER & PHOENICIA ⋩

The busy main road to Mount Tremper, Route 28, skirts the northern shore of **Ashokan Reservoir,** a beautiful 12-square-mile lake. Follow Route 28A around the 40 miles of shoreline for spectacular views of mountains rising in all directions; it's especially scenic in the fall. A little farther on, **Emerson Place** (formerly Catskill Corners) ⋩, Route 28 in Mount Tremper, is a surprising empire of refined goods and services at the southern edge of the Catskill Forest Preserve purposely built as a tourist destination. **The Emporium,** inhabiting a mid-19th-century dairy barn, is a surprising array of upscale shops; see "Shopping," below. But the major attraction in these parts is the **Kaleidoscope at Emerson Place** ($\textcircled{c}$ **877/688-2828**). Like a planetarium, only trippier, the 60-foot kaleidoscope inside the old barn silo—according to the *Guinness Book of World Records* the world's largest—gives visitors an opportunity to climb inside the tube of a superhuman kaleidoscope. The psychedelic shows ($8, free for children under 12) are a blast, with different programs seasonally.

Tiny **Phoenicia** is perhaps the epitome of the new Catskills. Only a few years ago, this was just another forgotten little town with gorgeous mountain views. At the end of the 1990s, a small handful of restaurateurs and young people moved in and revamped the place; today it's a symbol, like Rosendale (see above), of the revitalization going on in the region. Its perfectly unassuming Main Street now has a handful of creative, stylish shops and an excellent restaurant, all of which cohabit nicely with the longtime local bars. The town is surrounded in all directions by the big peaks of the Catskill Forest Preserve. **The Town Tinker,** Bridge Street ($\textcircled{c}$ **845/688-5553;** www.towntinker.com), in a barn at the edge of town, rents inner tubes for floating down a 5-mile stretch of the Esopus River, something no kid could refuse. There are two river courses, one for novices and the other, which covers rapids and flumes, for expert floaters. Tubes are $10 to $12 per day, and the Tinker even provides tube taxi transportation ($5).

The **Catskill Mountain Railroad,** Route 28, Mount Pleasant (✆ **845/688-7400;** www.catskillmtrailroad.com), operates a Scenic Train ($14 adults, $8 children 4–11, free for children under 4), a 12-mile round-trip between Phoenicia and Boiceville; after departing the Mount Pleasant depot, the train travels along the Esopus Creek. An added bonus on the shuttle is that you can tube down the river from Phoenicia to Mount Pleasant and then take the train back. If you're lucky enough to be in the area in autumn, check out the Leaf Peeper Special.

SPORTS & OUTDOOR ACTIVITIES

BIKING & HIKING   For the best hiking (certainly some of the finest in the state), see the text on the Mohonk and Minnewaska preserves (near New Paltz), above. The widely available free brochure *Hiking Ulster County* has details of plenty more trails in the Catskill Forest Preserve and Overlook Mountain Wild Forest, near Woodstock; see also www.co.ulster.ny.us. Bike rentals are available from **Table Rock Tours and Bicycle Shop,** 386 Main St., Rosendale (next to the Red Brick Tavern; ✆ **845/658-7832**); **Cycle Path,** 138 Main St., New Paltz (✆ **914/255-8723**); and **Overlook Mountain Bikes,** 93 Tinker St., Woodstock (✆ **845/679-2122**).

KAYAKING   **Atlantic Kayak Tours,** 320 W. Saugerties Rd., Saugerties (✆ **845/ 246-2187;** www.atlantickayaktours.com), guides experts and novices on 40 different tours along the Hudson.

ROCK CLIMBING   **EMS,** 3124 Rte. 44/55, Gardiner (✆ **800/310-4504**), has equipment and climbing lessons.

SKIING   Northwest of Phoenicia, **Belleayre Mountain,** Route 28, Highmount (✆ **800/942-6904;** www.belleayre.com), has the highest skiable peak and longest trail in the Catskills, with 36 other trails and eight lifts, but also a lower mountain that's perfect for beginners and intermediates.

SHOPPING

Woodstock 𝄢𝄢 is the pinnacle among shoppers' destinations in the Catskill Mountains. It has everything from antiques and modern clothing to Tibetan crafts and tribal rugs. A neat little antiques shop is **Treasure Chest Antiques,** a tiny cottage down Waterfall Way (off Tinker St.). **The Golden Notebook,** 25–29 Tinker St. (✆ **845/ 679-8000**), is a great little bookshop, a real readers' hangout.

Saugerties is on the upswing, and its main drag, Partition Street, is a smaller cousin of Hudson's Warren Street across the river. Worth a look are **Saugerties Antiques Gallery,** 104 Partition St. (✆ **845/246-2323**); **Partition Street Antiques,** 114 Partition St. (✆ **845/247-0932**), full of antique wicker and Stickley and Arts and Crafts furniture; **Central Hotel Antiques,** 83 Partition St., Saugerties (✆ **845/246-6874**); and **Dust and Rust Antiques,** Route 32, Saugerties (✆ **845/246-7728**). **Arcadia,** 78 Partition St. (✆ **845/246-7321**), is a cute housewares shop with nice ceramic pieces.

New Paltz is, apart from Woodstock, the next best shopping town. It has a preponderance of Woodstock-like stores overflowing with tie-dye and incense, but it also has a couple of good antiques shops. One is **Medusa,** 2 Church St. (✆ **845/255-6000**). Also take a look at **Water Street Market,** 10 Main St. (www.waterstreetmarket.com), which contains several specialty craft shops, art galleries, restaurants, an excellent cheese shop, the Catskills photography of G. Steve Jordan, and The Antique Barn.

Don't miss the bevy of polished, upscale specialty shops at **The Emporium at Emerson Place** ✦, 5340 Rte. 28, Mount Tremper (✆ **845/688-5800**). From fine women's apparel, a bath-and-spa emporium, and Simon Pearce glassware to country furnishings and gardening shops and the amazing Kaleidostore, specializing in hundreds of fine-art kaleidoscopes, this is one shopping experience that will entertain you before making off with your wallet. Tiny **Phoenicia,** just down the road, has a handful of interesting home-furnishings and gift shops, including **The Tender Land,** 45 Main St. (✆ **845/688-2001); The Nest Egg,** 84 Main St. (✆ **845/688-5851**); and **Tender Land Home,** 64 Main St. (✆ **845/688-7213**).

WHERE TO STAY
VERY EXPENSIVE

Emerson Resort & Spa ✦✦   After a devastating fire in 2005, this chic inn and spa hotel reopened in the spring of 2007 in a new, but similarly elegant, form. The owners rebuilt across the road, next to the Lodge at Emerson Place (see below). While no longer inhabiting a historic house, the suites now all have gas fireplaces and decks overlooking the river. The inn caters to sybarites with a desire for big-city pampering in the country. Quality and service of this level don't come cheap, though. Although the rooms are still luxurious, they are more contemporary and less exotic than before the fire. The Asian-inspired spa is sophisticated and romantic, while the restaurant tempts epicures with exquisite menus of food and wine (and has a streamside deck for alfresco dining). The inn and resort are adults-only—the best kind of retreat for many weary parents.

5340 Rte. 28, Mt. Tremper, NY 12457. ✆ 877/688-2828. www.emersonresort.com. 25 units. $425–$595 double. AE, DC, DISC, MC, V. Free parking. **Amenities:** Restaurant; spa and fitness center; concierge; business center; laundry service. *In room:* A/C, flat-screen TV/DVD, Wi-Fi, hair dryer, fireplace, stocked 18-bottle wine cooler.

Mohonk Mountain House ✦✦✦ (Kids)   This National Historic Landmark, a mammoth mountaintop Victorian castle, is one of the country's great old hotel resorts. Like a mountain lodge in the great West, it commands huge views of the serene Shawangunk Mountains. The resort was built in 1869 by two brothers on a 2,200-acre rocky ridge overlooking a large glacial lake, pristine gardens, and the 6,400-acre Mohonk Forest Preserve, and its setting is incomparable. Still owned by the Smiley family, the fanciful, seven-story lodge is loaded with turrets, towers, porches, and parlors, as well as cozy sitting rooms with fireplaces. Rooms vary considerably as to size and views, which may be of the gardens, mountains, or lake, but all are warmly decorated with period Edwardian, Victorian, and Arts and Crafts furnishings. Many have fireplaces and balconies. Activities abound: ice-skating in the beautiful new open-air pavilion, snowshoeing, and cross-country skiing in winter; hiking, boating, tennis, and golf in warm-weather seasons; and plenty of children's programs and entertainment, including theme weeks and weekends. It's a hiker's paradise, with more than 85 miles of woodland trails. However, Mohonk is also a fabulous place to relax with a book in a rocker on the veranda, taking in the views, or at the luxury full-service spa with a massive, indoor heated pool, installed with some fanfare in the summer of 2005. In high season, though, it's packed with everyone from young families to groups of seniors.

1000 Mountain Rest Rd., Lake Mohonk, New Paltz, NY 12561. ✆ 800/772-6646 or 845/255-1000. Fax 845/256-2100. www.mohonk.com. 251 units. $445–$700 double; $730–$840 suite. $146 children over age 12; $82 children

4–12; free for children under 4. Rates include 3 meals plus afternoon tea and many complimentary activities and entertainment. Jackets are required for men at dinner. 2-night minimum stay most weekends. AE, DC, DISC, MC, V. Free valet parking. **Amenities:** Restaurant; swimming and boating lake; 9-hole golf course; 6 clay and Har-Tru tennis courts; fitness center; concierge; business center; massage and spa services; laundry service; ice-cream parlor/soda fountain; ice-skating pavilion; library. *In room:* A/C, hair dryer.

EXPENSIVE

Kate's Lazy Meadow Motel *★★* *(Finds)*   If someone told you a member of the New Wave band The B-52s bought and renovated a 1950s motel in the Catskills, it would look . . . exactly like this. Kate is Kate Pierson of that famously buoyant band from Athens, Georgia, and she and a team of hip designers from New York City have created a retro-kitsch retreat, a Love Shack in the mountains, for those cool enough to appreciate it. The funky motel rooms—which will soon be complemented by five Airstream trailers and, believe it or not, five heated and equipped tepees in the meadow by the river—are all with bright colors, paneled walls, and hip, Jetsons-esque midcentury furnishings. Several rooms have kitchenettes, and there are both two-bedroom and two-story loft cabins. One unit is pet-friendly (as long as your mutt doesn't weigh more than 25 lb.). Kate's Lazy Meadow certainly achieves what it sets out to do, even if you do get the feeling you're paying for the name recognition and novelty.

5191 Rte. 28, Mt. Tremper, NY 12457. *(C)* **845/688-7200.** www.lazymeadow.com. 8 units. $150–$175 double; $225–$275 suite. 2-night minimum on weekends. MC, V. Free parking. **Amenities:** Outdoor Jacuzzi. *In room:* A/C, TV, high-speed Internet access, DVD/CD players.

The Lodge at Emerson Place *★★* *(Kids)*   This casually upscale, contemporary Western-style lodge plays up the rustic side of the Catskills—in contrast to its sister property, the Emerson Resort & Spa. It features log-cabin beams and plaid woolen blankets, and many rooms have fireplaces and private decks overlooking the Esopus trout stream; you can almost fish off your balcony. Rooms are large and handsome, perfect for families and people who just want to kick back in jeans and Tevas. For families, the lodge is very convenient; it's next door to a complex of shops and a massive, kid-friendly kaleidoscope and within minutes of biking, hiking, skiing, and plenty more outdoor activities. Check the website for special package deals.

5368 Rte. 28, Mt. Tremper, NY 12457. *(C)* **877/688-2828** or 845/688-2828. Fax 845/688-5191. www.emersonresort. com. 27 units. $190–$220 double; $275–$400 suite. Rates include continental breakfast. Minimum 2-night stay most weekends. AE, DC, DISC, MC, V. Free parking. Pets allowed ($25). **Amenities:** Concierge. *In room:* A/C, TV, Wi-Fi, hair dryer.

MODERATE

The Inn at Canal House/Locktender Cottage *★★* *(Finds)*   Along the banks of the old Delaware & Hudson Canal, hovering between the Hudson Valley and the Catskill Mountains, is this surprising retreat attached to one of the finest restaurants in the region. A cute and cozy Victorian cottage that backs right up to the canal houses two charming, if not overly large, rooms. You'll also find a larger "Chef's Quarters" upstairs, with a low-peaked ceiling, kitchenette, and Jacuzzi, but without some of the flavor of the other two rooms. Across the street, near the famed and atmospheric Depuy Canal House restaurant, two more rooms have been created; they are larger suites and one has an outdoor garden patio and screened sitting area, but I prefer the rooms in the original cottage. For both dining and outdoors enthusiasts, and those on the lookout for the unique, this is a small slice of heaven: There are great trails for hiking, and the Mohonk Nature Preserve, with 90 miles of trails, is nearby. But it's a little idiosyncratic and won't suit everyone.

Rte. 213, High Falls, NY 12440. © 845/687-7700. Fax 845/687-7073. www.depuycanalhouse.net. 5 units. $99–$215 double. Rates include full breakfast. 2-night minimum on holiday and Oct weekends. AE, DC, DISC, MC, V. Free parking. **Amenities:** 2 restaurants. *In room:* A/C, suites have TV, 2 suites have kitchenettes and dinettes.

Minnewaska Lodge ⋆ Outdoors enthusiasts especially will appreciate this 3-year-old small lodge built at the base of the 1,200-foot Shawangunk cliffs on 17 acres. The area, adjacent to the Mohonk Preserve and a short distance from Minnewaska State Park (and just 6 miles from New Paltz), is a favorite of hikers and rock climbers. The lodge is woodsy and rustic, like a comfortable mountain inn, with high ceilings and lots of windows in common rooms. The terrific outdoor deck looks out onto the 'Gunks (cliffs), and some rooms have private decks (the suite has a private patio). Rooms on the second floor are handsomely decorated in a contemporary style and have cathedral ceilings and either cliff or forest views.

3116 Rte. 44/55, Gardiner (outside New Paltz), NY 12525. © 845/255-1110. Fax 845/255-5069. 26 units. www. minnewaskalodge.com. May–Oct $155–$229 double, $305–$329 suite; Nov–Apr $135–$175 double, $245–$255 suite. Rates include continental breakfast. 2-night minimum stay on weekends, 3-night minimum stay on holiday weekends. AE, DC, DISC, MC, V. Free parking. **Amenities:** Restaurant; fitness center; gift shop. *In room:* A/C, TV, dataport.

Sparrow Hawk B&B ⋆⋆ *Value* This handsome 1770 brick Colonial, originally a farmhouse, is a very professionally run inn that's both elegant and relaxed. It has a nice library, sitting room, fireplaces, and pretty grounds. The rooms are very large and nicely appointed with modern wicker furniture, plush bedding, towels, and robes. The high-ceilinged Grand Room features a 100-year-old Bechstein grand piano. Owner and chef Howard's excellent gourmet breakfasts are something to look forward to. The only drawback is that it's an old house on a main road, so there's some early-morning traffic noise; if that will spoil your stay, you should ask for one of the rooms facing the back of the property.

4496 Rte. 209, Stone Ridge, NY 12484. © 845/687-4492. www.sparrowhawkbandb.com. 5 units. $145–$220 double. Rates include full breakfast. AE, DISC, MC, V. Free parking. **Amenities:** Library, TV lounge. *In room:* A/C.

The Villa at Saugerties ⋆⋆ *Finds* A uniquely stylish and chic take on a country inn—modern boutique hotel rather than same-old Victorian B&B—this cutting-edge place, opened by a couple of young Manhattan refugees in 2002, is one of the coolest and least expected spots in the region. A 1929 Mediterranean villa on 4 acres of woodland bordering on two brooks, it turns the notion of country rustic on its head, substituting a hip midcentury modern aesthetic that appeals to hipsters from the city (if you're not one, you may feel out of place). Rooms are enlivened with original art, yet they don't sacrifice comfort for style. Each room is uniquely decorated and inviting; beds and linens are top-of-the-line. Two rooms have private entrances. Gourmet breakfasts are served on the outdoor patio in season, and a 40-foot outdoor pool beckons. Saugerties is on the upswing, with new hip restaurants and a wealth of antiques shops and art galleries, and Woodstock and the Catskills (including Hunter Mountain) are only minutes away.

159 Fawn Rd., Saugerties, NY 12477. © 845/246-0682. www.thevillaatsaugerties.com. 5 units. Nov–May $135–$165 double, $195 suite; June–Oct $145–$185 double, $235 suite. All rates include full breakfast. MC, V. Free parking. **Amenities:** Outdoor swimming pool. *In room:* A/C, TV.

INEXPENSIVE

Twin Gables *Value* A former boardinghouse for artists, this charming and easygoing old guesthouse on Woodstock's main drag has the perfect feel of the town. Rooms are colorful, clean, and very sweetly decorated; most feature pretty quilts and hooked rugs. Quite a variety of accommodations are available. Some have shared bathrooms,

Finds Unique Lodging in Saugerties

Saugerties, fast becoming one of the hippest little spots between the Upper Hudson Valley and the Catskill Mountains, is still being discovered. Two "inns" offer unique and "in the know" small-scale accommodations. **The Inn at Café Tamayo,** 89 Partition St., Saugerties, NY 12477 (© **845/246-9371;** www.cafetamayo.com; four units; $110 double, $160 suite; rates include full breakfast), a great value and one of the best restaurants in the region, is housed in an 1864 building on the main drag; upstairs are two simple but very affordable rooms and one suite with queen-size brass beds, comfortable reading chairs, and TVs. One of the regular rooms has a claw-foot tub, while the suite has two separate bedrooms and a sitting room. What could be better than having a terrific dinner and then stumbling upstairs to bed? Another restaurant with rooms to rent in Saugerties is **Miss Lucy's Kitchen,** 90 Partition St., Saugerties, NY 12477 (© **845/246-9240**; www.misslucyskitchen. com/guesthouse.html), which has attractive and nicely equipped one- and two-bedroom apartments available ($150–$175 double); pets are welcome.

Even more unexpected is **Saugerties Lighthouse** ⊛, off 9W and Mynderse Street, Saugerties, NY 12477 (© **845/247-0656**; www.saugertieslighthouse. com; two units; $160–$175 double; rates include breakfast). Not just a poetic name for an inn, it's an actual B&B within an 1869 lighthouse at water's edge. It may not be the most conveniently located B&B you'll ever stay at—access is by a mile-long trail through wood- and wetlands—but it surely will be one of the most interesting: How often do you get to sleep in the upstairs of a historic lighthouse overlooking the Hudson River? Inside the lighthouse are a small museum, keeper's quarters, two bedrooms, a kitchen, and a living room. Rooms are nicely furnished. The smaller one has windows facing both south down the Hudson and west up the Esopus Creek toward town, while the larger room has two windows looking out on the river. Linens, towels, and soap are provided, but it's suggested that you take only a few belongings in a backpack. A single downstairs bathroom, with a sink, shower with hot water, and composting toilet, is shared by everyone staying in the lighthouse. Area restaurants will deliver to the lighthouse; guests can also make use of the kitchen, refrigerator, and gas grill. Pets are allowed if guests rent both rooms.

others large private ones. A couple have twin beds, and there's even a single, which is becoming harder and harder to find. My favorite would have to be room no. 11, which is lavender with a large private bathroom. The young couple that owns and operates Twin Gables has ensured that it maintains a very high quality-to-price ratio. 73 Tinker St., Woodstock, NY 12498. © **845/679-9479.** Fax 845/679-5638. www.twingableswoodstockny.com. 9 units. $99–$129 double. Rates include continental breakfast. DISC, MC, V. Free parking. *In room:* A/C.

CAMPGROUNDS

Blue Mountain Campground, 3783 Rte. 32, Saugerties (© **845/246-7564**), has 50 sites with electricity.

WHERE TO DINE

In addition to the restaurants described below, an excellent place for breakfast or lunch is the superb bakery **Bread Alone,** which has branches in Boiceville (Rte. 28; © **914/657-3328**), just east of Mount Tremper, and in Woodstock, 22 Mill Hill Rd. (© **845/679-2108**). It features splendid artisanal breads, creative panini and other sandwiches, and homemade soups and salads.

Bear Café ☆☆ *(Finds* CREATIVE AMERICAN   In a theater complex that was the original playground of the founder of Bearsville Records (and manager of Dylan, Joplin, and The Band), this excellent restaurant with a rock-'n'-roll pedigree is a sophisticated but refreshingly casual eatery a couple of miles from Woodstock. The decor is charmingly rustic and warm, with peaked old-wood ceilings overlooking a flowing brook. Although you could opt for something simple like a half-pound burger, this is a place to indulge; meat eaters should try the signature dish, filet mignon with port garlic sauce and Stilton blue cheese, a French classic of sweet and sharp tastes. There is a long list of specials daily, and an extensive regular menu. At the front there's a nice and lively bar with a good mix of locals, weekenders, and visitors. Service is excellent, as are the delectable homemade desserts. The wine list is outstanding, with several interesting and hard-to-find choices, like the Priorats from Spain and several interesting kinds of Shiraz from Australia. Big spenders will enjoy the fantastic collection of rare bordeaux vintages, the "Off List," from which the restaurant donates 10% to the Windows of Hope Foundation, which benefits the families of restaurant workers lost in the 9/11 attacks.

Rte. 212 (The Bearsville Theatre Complex), Bearsville. © **845/679-5555.** Reservations recommended. Main courses $18–$36. AE, MC, V. Sun–Mon and Wed–Thurs 5–10pm; Fri–Sat 5–10:30pm.

Bywater Bistro ☆ *(Finds* CREATIVE AMERICAN BISTRO   This new restaurant has taken the reins from the Rosendale Cement Co., the former restaurant in a house that was once a bordello in the 1860s. The restaurant, popular with locals, remains stylishly relaxed and warmly contemporary, although with some new Southwestern accents. Chef Sam Ullman's menu uses the best of local ingredients, but looks to Asia, France, and the Americas for inspiration. Among the entrees are slow-roasted pork in pineapple barbecue sauce, served with chipotle creamed corn; teriyaki grilled sea scallops; and ale-braised short ribs. All bistro dinners are available in either half or full plates, a nice option for those with smaller appetites or kids in tow, and the wine list includes more wines by the glass than are available in bottles, a rarity. Out back is a seductive terrace for dining. The bistro takes full advantage of its location across the street from Rosendale's movie theater, offering a special "dinner and a movie" option: $20 gets you a two-course dinner plus a movie ticket—a budget-conscious guy's dream date.

419 Main St., Rosendale. © **845/658-3210.** Reservations recommended on weekends. Main courses $10–$25. MC, V. Mon, Thurs, and Sun 5–9:30pm; Fri–Sat 5–10pm; Sun 11am–2pm.

Café Tamayo ☆☆ CREATIVE AMERICAN   A saloonlike, romantic, and even modestly sexy spot in an original 1864 tavern with several spectacular features—including a gorgeous old carved mahogany bar with antique mirrors and slow-moving ceiling fans powered by a cool original pulley system—this is one of the most attractive restaurants in the region. Run by a husband-and-wife team, the restaurant focuses on local produce and organic meats and poultry, and the chef, a Culinary Institute of America (CIA) grad, puts a creative twist on American fare. There are good daily specials and dishes such as braised beef brisket and shell steak au poivre with Madeira sauce, but very little to tempt a committed vegetarian. The wine list is remarkably affordable and includes a large number of New York State wines. The owners have opened a new casual spot, Mediterranean Kitchen, next door (at 91 Partition St.; open daily for lunch and dinner), serving vegetarian dishes, seafood, and grilled pizzas.

89 Partition St., Saugerties. ⓒ 845/246-9371. Reservations recommended weekends. Main courses $16–$32. MC, V. Wed–Sun 5–10pm; Sun 11:30am–3pm.

Depuy Canal House ⭐⭐⭐ NOUVELLE AMERICAN/CONTINENTAL   An evocative 200-year-old stone tavern is home to one of the most creative and pleasurable restaurants in the entire Hudson Valley. Perched on the edge of the Catskills, the restaurant is the work of executive chef John Novi, who for more than 30 years has used fresh local products to fire his imagination. The restaurant couldn't be better looking; it rambles throughout a series of intimate and sumptuous dining rooms with roaring fires and elegant place settings. The menu, which changes daily, is either a la carte or by three- (not available on Sat), five- or seven-course prix fixe; entrees are on the order of sea bass filet with roasted-red-pepper cellophane noodles, or goat meat barbecued with black-bean Polish prosciutto strudel. For an incredible experience, reserve a table on the balcony and watch the kitchen from above. Downstairs in the atmospheric wine cellar is a more informal, but also excellent, bistro and bakery, called Chefs on Fire (it features a large wood-fired brick oven). It's open for lunch and dinner Wednesday and Thursday and breakfast, lunch, and dinner Friday through Sunday. If you want to stick around for another meal, ask about the charming cottage rooms across the street and next door.

Rte. 213, High Falls. ⓒ 845/687-7700. Reservations essential. Main courses $25–$44; prix-fixe menus $35–$75. AE, DISC, MC, V. Depuy Canal House dinner Thurs–Sun 5:30–9pm; Sun 11:30am–2pm. Chefs on Fire Wed–Thurs 11am–9pm; Fri–Sun 8am–10pm.

Oriole 9 (Value) MEDITERRANEAN   This popular new restaurant—inhabiting the space of the erstwhile cafe Heaven—is cool and casual, using only all-natural and organic products. The owners are a chef trained in Holland and a woman whose parents once ran Café Espresso in Woodstock in the '60s (where Dylan and Joan Baez hung out). Lunch is informal, with great salads and sandwiches; breakfast is yummy, with great omelets; and dinner includes local meats, fish, and vegetarian entrees.

17 Tinker St., Woodstock. ⓒ 845/679-5763. Reservations not accepted. Main courses $9–$24. MC, V. Daily 8:30am–4:30pm; Wed–Sun 5–10pm.

Sweet Sue's ⭐⭐ (Finds) BISTRO/BREAKFAST CAFE   Plenty of locals will tell you that Sue's, which has been around for 2 decades but suffered a devastating fire in 2003, is the stuff of legend. That's big praise for an informal breakfast-and-lunch place, but Sue's, now restored and reopened (and for my tastes, a tad too antiseptic), is still the real deal, a terrific neighborhood cafe. Breakfast is extraordinary, with pecan-crusted French toast, 25 kinds of pancakes (including pumpkin), and amazing home fries. The lunch menu changes weekly but always makes use of the finest handpicked produce and locals meats, with vegetarian specials. You'll surely have to wait for a table, but you will be happy you did.

Main St., Phoenicia. ⓒ 845/688-7852. Reservations recommended. Main courses $7–$12. MC, V. Thurs–Mon 7am–3pm.

3 Northeastern Catskill Region (Greene County)

The upper reaches of Ulster County extend along the Upper Hudson Valley, where, in the glory days of train travel from New York City in the late 19th century, steam trains brought thousands of people seeking country refuge at grand hotels like the Catskill Mountain House and Mohonk Mountain House to the station at Catskill. There they were met by horse-drawn carriages for their long rides up into the mountains. But most of the northeastern section of the Catskills is rural Greene County, the biggest ski destination in the Catskill Mountains. Though for years, much of the region lived off of ski tourism and little else, today a number of the sleepy little towns in Greene County are receiving new injections of life in the form of inns, restaurants, and cultural organizations.

ESSENTIALS

GETTING THERE   By car, there is easy access via exits 21 through 21B of the New York State Thruway (I-87).

VISITOR INFORMATION   The **Greene County Promotion Department,** P.O. Box 527, Catskill (© **800/355-CATS** or 518/943-3223; www.greenetourism.com), operates a visitor center at exit 21 of the New York State Thruway (I-87) on the right after the tollbooth.

EXPLORING THE NORTHEASTERN CATSKILL REGION

Catskill, a historic town across the river from Hudson, frankly has seen better days, though it is pinning its hopes on a rebound. Its riverfront zone and marina are slowly being developed, and in addition to a restaurant and public boat dock, there's a small museum and interpretation center of the area's history in the old freight master's building on **The Point** overlooking Catskill Creek and the Hudson River. A Saturday farmers' market and concerts are held here in summer, including the Catskill Jazz Festival the first week of August. The most important historic sight in Catskill is the **Thomas Cole National Historic Site (Cedar Grove),** 218 Spring St. (© **518/943-7465;** www.thomascole.org; admission $7 adults, $5 students and seniors; May–Oct Fri–Sun 10am–4pm; Memorial Day, Labor Day, Columbus Day, and Independence Day 1–4pm; other visits by appointment only). A large yellow 1815 Federal-style home, it once sat on 88 prime acres with unimpeded Catskills views and was the home of Thomas Cole, founder of the Hudson River School of Painting. A painter, poet, musician, and architect, Cole lived in the house for 12 years after his marriage and died here in 1848; it was in this house that he tutored Frederick Church. Until the 1970s, Cole's descendants lived in the house. Cedar Grove was recently restored with surprising alacrity; it has some of Cole's personal effects and original family items, but the period furnishings aren't original to the house. The house is worth a visit mostly for fans of Cole's romantic American landscape painting. Worth a brief peek in downtown Catskill is the **Greene County Council on the Arts,** 398 Main St., with two floors of exhibit area for local artists.

   Farther north along Route 9W in Coxsackie, the **Bronck Museum** ⭐⭐, 90 County Rte. 42 (© **518/731-6490;** www.gchistory.org; guided tours $5 adults, $3 students ages 12–15, $2 children 5–11, free for children under 5; Memorial Day to mid-Oct Wed–Fri noon–4pm, Sat 10am–4pm, Sun and holidays 1–4pm), is distinguished by a real rarity, the oldest surviving home in upstate New York. This beautifully solid stone Dutch medieval house was built in 1663 by the cousin of the man who would settle the Bronx. How old is that? Enough to predate the Constitution by 113 years. The museum is actually an entire complex of architecturally significant buildings. The homestead was a working farm and home to eight generations of Broncks, original Dutch settlers, until 1939. The original house has massive beams, wide floorboards, a cellar hatchway, and an early Dutch door; rooms feature Federal, Empire, and Victorian furniture. Also on the premises are a 1785 Federal brick house and three barns (including the unique 1835 "13-Sided Barn," the oldest multisided barn in New York). Coxsackie is a small but attractive town, a good place to grab a bite (see "Where to Dine," below).

If your surname begins with O' and you want to get your Irish up, you might pop in to see a couple of sights in East Durham. The **Our Lady of Knock Shrine,** Route 145, features stained-glass and mahogany carvings from County Mayo, Ireland. The **Irish American Heritage Museum,** 2267 Rte. 145 (© **518/634-7497;** www.irish americanheritagemuseum.org), has exhibits and educational programs about the Irish experience in America. On the agenda in East Durham is a future Irish Village. More interesting for most is the **Five State Lookout,** a spectacular overlook with distant views of—but of course—five states, on Route 23 (The Mohican Trail) in East Windham. The village of **Freehold** is yet another small town emblematic of the revitalization going on in the Catskill Mountain region; this unassuming place has a couple of very nice restaurants, a country store, and a pub, a local hangout. On Route 23A in Jewett is another ethnic contribution to the area, one of interest to architects. **St. John the Baptist Ukrainian Catholic Church and Grazhda** (© **518/734-5330;** www. brama.com/stjohn) is a small, wonderfully crafted, rustic wooden basilica, built without nails or cement. You may have to get the non-English-speaking priest to open it up so you can see the wooden chandelier, but it's worth a look.

Several of the small towns in this region get their biggest jolt from winter downhill skiing and snowboarding at **Windham and Hunter mountains** (see "Sports & Outdoor Activities," below), though the areas, with their golf courses and summer music and arts festivals, are also good year-round destinations. The village of **Hunter** has a newly thriving arts scene due to the efforts of the **Catskill Mountain Foundation,** Route 23A (© **518/263-4908**), which operates an arts center, a farm market, an excellent bookstore, and a cool movie theater. The town hosts an impressive roster of music festivals and summer concerts; see p. 243. In Tannersville, next door to Hunter, is a sight for naturalists: the **Mountain Top Arboretum,** Route 23C (© **518/589-3903;** www.mtarbor.org), a pretty 10-acre spot surrounded by mountains and containing nice woodland walking trails and flowering trees, evergreens, wildflowers, and shrubs; it's especially beautiful in summer.

Tip: The **Kaaterskill Trolley** (© **518/589-6150;** $1, free for children under 5) runs from the village of Hunter to Tannersville and South and North Lake beaches, between noon and 9:30pm; the weekend schedule begins Friday at 5:30pm.

The natural highlight of the area, though, is **Kaaterskill Falls** 👁👁, Route 23A, Haines Falls (© **518/589-5058**), the highest waterfall in New York State (higher even than Niagara). There's a beautiful and easy half-mile hike along a path from the bottom that wends along the creek, though you have to park in a small lot on Route 23A, cross the road, and walk along it to the beginning of the path. You can also see the falls from the top by taking Route 23A to North Lake Road and turning right on Laurel House Lane. A short path there takes you right to the edge of the precipitous drop; some folks are brave enough to sit on the flat rocks dangling their feet over the edge of the falls. Nearby is **North-South Lake,** the former site of the famed Catskill Mountain House, the first great mountain resort in the U.S. If you have time, I suggest you take both paths to see the falls from both ends.

SHOPPING

Ann Stewart, 384 Main St., Catskill (© 518/943-0975; www.kiltshop.com), is a maker of authentic Scottish kilts, one of only a handful in the U.S. Her shop could easily be called "All Things Scottish." The **Bookstore,** run by the Catskill Mountain Foundation, Main Street, Hunter (© 518/263-5157), is the only—yes, only—new-edition bookstore in Greene County. **The Barn,** Route 23 West at Jewett Road, Windham (© 888/883-0444), is a restored barn full of antique furnishings, clothing, toys, and other collectibles. **Ulla Darni at the Blue Pearl,** 7751 Rte. 23, East Windham (© 518/734-6525), features the fanciful lamps, sconces, and chandeliers of renowned lighting artist Ulla Darni. Her colorful, handcrafted lamps fetch huge prices. A nice traditional gallery is **Windham Fine Arts,** in a 19th-century house at 5380 Main St., Windham (© 518/734-6850; www.windhamfinearts.com); it focuses mostly on regional painters and sculptors. The **Windham Mini Mall,** 5359 Main St., Windham (© 518/734-5050), is a general store with gourmet foods, a tempting candy display, books, jewelry, and camping and fishing supplies. **Village Candle, Pottery & Gifts,** Main Street, Tannersville (© 518/589-6002), has an outstanding collection of scented candles and outdoors goods. **The Snowy Owl,** Main Street, Tannersville (© 518/589-9939), is a cool home-furnishings and gift store with a decidedly mountain look.

SPORTS & OUTDOOR ACTIVITIES

GOLF There are nearly a dozen golf courses in the northeastern Catskills. Call © 866/840-GOLF or check out the website www.greenecountygolf.com for additional information. The finest is **Windham Country Club,** South Street, Windham (© 518/734-9910; www.windhamcountryclub.com), a championship course highly rated by *Golf Digest.*

WINTER SPORTS Skiing is the big draw in these parts. **Hunter Mountain,** Route 23A West, Hunter (© 888/HUNTER-MTN; www.huntermtn.com), is a skier's (and boarder's) mountain—the closest "big mountain" to New York City, its management likes to say—that's long been popular with hard-core, rowdy singles who party it up afterward at the bars in Tannersville. A couple of years ago, the mountain added The Learning Center, a huge and superb beginner's ski facility that's doing much to attract families. It features excellent learners' packages. The resort itself has some great black-diamond runs and a nostalgic clubhouse where the drinking cranks up. In off season, there is a host of festivals, such as Oktoberfest and Celtic, German Alps, and Micro-brew festivals. **Mountain Trails Cross-Country Ski Center,** Route 23A, Tannersville (© 518/589-5361), has 20 miles of groomed trails, along with instruction, rentals, and a warming hut. Bike rentals are available at **Twilight Mountain Sports,** North Lake Road and Route 23A, Haines Falls (© 518/589-6480).

  Windham Mountain, C.D. Lane Road, Windham (© 518/734-4300; www.skiwindham.com), has a nice variety of trails and facilities. If you're not into the singles scene and, perhaps, less of a hard-core skier, Windham is an excellent choice. Both Windham and Hunter mountains feature mountain biking on trails in the off season and chairlifts up for the views (a great idea in fall foliage season). Check out **Windham**

Mountain Outfitters, Route 296 and South Street, Windham (© **518/734-4700**), for ski and snowboard rentals and other equipment, including bicycle and kayak rentals.

WHERE TO STAY

The northeastern section of the Catskill Mountains is home to a number of the classic old resorts and attractions that have been here for years. The area around Cairo and Round Top, tucked in the fold of the Catskill Forest Preserve, has a number of small, family-run resorts.

Albergo Allegria ★★ *Value*   This stellar family-owned and -operated midsize inn is top-of-the-line all the way, and it couldn't be any friendlier. It strikes a great balance of comfort, cleanliness, and character. The building has 19th-century heritage, though it's been nicely updated. Rooms in the main house are all uniquely decorated and different in size, offering something for just about everybody and every budget; many have excellent mountain views. Even the cheapest, called the "cozy rooms," are pretty spacious. The large "requested rooms," named for months of the year, are probably the best value. Carriage House Suites are new construction within the old carriage house; they have cathedral ceilings and separate entrances, perfect for skiers and anyone wanting a bit of privacy. For a splurge, but at prices that are still somewhat reasonable, indulge in the Master or Millennium suites, both of which are humongous and very well appointed. The inn, an AAA Four-Diamond property, is immaculate and provides lots of luxury details for the price, like free beverages in the kitchen 24 hours a day, luxurious linens and towels, and excellent, comfortable beds. Check online for Internet specials and other packages. Families should inquire about sister properties: the Farmhouse and the Mountain Streams Cottage.

Rte. 296, Windham, NY 12442. © **518/734-5560.** Fax 518/734-5570. www.albergousa.com. 21 units. $83–$189 double; $169–$299 suite. Rates include full breakfast. AE, DC, DISC, MC, V. Free parking. *In room:* A/C, TV, dataport, hair dryer.

Stewart House ★★ *Finds* *Value*   This funky old place, formerly the late-Victorian 1883 Athens Hotel, is a slightly bohemian inn and restaurant on the west bank of the Hudson. It's got lots of artsy character, though rooms are welcoming and nicely appointed for the price (though some may find the decor a bit spare). One room, called the Meryl Streep Room, is where the death scene with the Oscar winner was filmed in the movie version of William Kennedy's Pulitzer Prize–winning book *Ironweed*. Actors in town for the summer Shakespeare on the Hudson Festival (run by the inn's owners) often stay on the top floor. On the river are a nice gazebo and a bar at the boat dock. The stylish bistro restaurant, with a CIA-trained chef at the helm, serves northern Italian fare and has all the makings of a hipster hangout, even if it's a little tough to imagine in this out-of-the-way spot.

2 N. Water St., Athens, NY 12015. © **518/945-1357.** www.stewarthouse.com. 9 units. $118–$145 double. Rates include continental breakfast. MC, V. Free parking. **Amenities:** Restaurant; bar. *In room:* A/C.

Washington Irving Lodge ★★ *Value*   A charming Victorian ambience pervades this lovely 1890 house, outfitted with nice antiques, modern bathrooms, a fantastic reading room and parlor, fully equipped cocktail lounge, and large dining room. Some rooms on the third floor are very large, while those in the original tower (my favorite) are very cozy and rustic, with paneled walls and tower windows. All are very warmly decorated and have a 19th-century feel. The house sits on 8 acres and has an outdoor pool and a tennis court, rarities for an inn of this size. The friendly owner, Stephanie, is sometimes helped out by her equally gregarious son Nick, whom you may find tending bar. Midweek ski packages are available.

Rte. 23A, Hunter, NY 12442. ℂ 518/589-5560. Fax 518/589-5775. www.washingtonirving.com. 15 units. $130–$160 double. Rates include full breakfast. 2-night minimum stay on weekends in season. AE, DC, DISC, MC, V. Free parking. **Amenities:** Bar; outdoor pool; tennis court. *In room:* A/C, TV, dataport, hair dryer.

WHERE TO DINE

In addition to the restaurants below, if you're up near Athens, check out the cool restaurant at the **Stewart House** (see above).

The Catskill Mountain Country Store and Restaurant ★★ *Finds* *Kids* BREAK-FAST/CAFE   This cute and casual gourmet country store hides one of the best places for breakfast in the Catskills. The morning menu is as impressively creative as it is long, and portions are gigantic. The eight kinds of signature pancakes are outstanding, as are items like banana pecan French toast and the slightly spicy Italian wrap. Breakfast is served all day. The lunch menu features mostly healthy and organic-based items, using the store's own farm-fresh produce, such as spicy arugula salad, homemade soups, great wraps, chili, and burgers, with a few Tex-Mex offerings as well. Children will love the minizoo and gardens out back, where they'll find the pigs Priscilla and Daisy, as well as chickens, roosters, and more.

5510 Rte. 23, Windham. ℂ 518/734-3387. Reservations not accepted. Main courses $6–$9. DISC, MC, V. Mon–Fri 9am–3pm; Sat 8am–4pm; Sun 8am–3pm.

Last Chance Cheese & Antiques AMERICAN   The name doesn't lie: This casual spot, with a country-store ambience, is part restaurant, part antiques, gifts, and gourmet-foods shop. It's decorated with hanging musical instruments and antiques, and it has a deli with a few tables and an enclosed patio dining area. The menu is surprisingly diverse. Start with a homemade soup, or perhaps cheese fondue or a nice, large salad, followed by specialty sandwiches, or light fare like quiches, or go whole-hog with substantial entrees, such as St. Louis ribs, meatloaf, or stuffed filet of sole. An even bigger surprise is that this little place has a phenomenal beer list to go with 100 imported cheeses: Choose from among 300 imported beers, including several very select Belgian ales.

Main St., Tannersville. ℂ 518/589-5424. Reservations not accepted. Main courses $8–$23. AE, MC, V. Daily 11am–7pm.

Maggie's Krooked Café & Juice Bar ★★ *Finds* BREAKFAST/CAFE   Named for the crooked floor, if not the exuberant personality of the eponymous chef and owner, this friendly and cool little two-room bohemian cafe is done up in funky colors. Maggie's does an amazing breakfast (which she serves all day), with a long list of egg dishes and omelets and great buckwheat and potato pancakes. Lunch—the cafe menu—is mainly burgers and simple items like veggie melts, salads, and grilled-chicken sandwiches. I recently had a delicious veggie melt at Maggie's. The home-baked muffins and cakes are incredible; get 'em to go.

Main St., Tannersville. ℂ 518/589-6101. Reservations not accepted. Main courses $7–$14. AE, MC, V. Daily 7am–4pm.

Ruby's Hotel & Restaurant ★★ *Finds* ECLECTIC   A converted 19th-century hotel in the village of Freehold, a town on the upswing, Ruby's is a funky venture by a dynamic New York City chef, Ana Sporer, who has inhabited the cool space with a light hand but tons of vigor. Unassuming from the street, the restaurant features an amazing Deco bar, a classic 1938 soda fountain, hand-blocked Victorian wallpaper, and the original tables and chairs found in the place. Fortunately, the menu and execution are anything but afterthoughts. Though the menu changes frequently according to the whims of the chef and seasonal ingredients, standards are coq au vin, braised lamb shank with saffron Israeli couscous, and homey favorites like turkey chili, chicken pot-pie, and a Cuban sandwich. At press time, a few rooms upstairs were in the process of being renovated for overnight stays.

3689 Rte. 67, Freehold. (C) 518/634-7790. Reservations recommended. Main courses $9–$24. AE, MC, V. Winter Fri–Sat 5–10pm; summer (June–Aug) Thurs–Sat 5–10pm.

Vesuvio 🌟🌟 *(Kids* NORTHERN ITALIAN   This romantic and surprisingly formal, family-owned restaurant—with the same chef, Joseph Baglio, for more than 25 years—has two large dining rooms and an outdoor space. Pastas, such as fettuccine matriciana (with prosciutto, pancetta, and more), are excellent, as are traditional items like veal chops, rack of lamb, and filet mignon. The children's menu (cheese ravioli or penne with meatballs, followed by ice cream) should keep the kids happy. Vesuvio features a nice wine list and superb service.

Goshen Rd., Hensonville. (C) 518/734-3663. Reservations recommended. Main courses $16–$26. AE, DC, DISC, MC, V. Mon–Thurs 4–10pm; Fri–Sat 4–11pm; Sun 3–10pm.

SPECIAL EVENTS & HUNTER/WINDHAM AFTER DARK

The summertime **Shakespeare on the Hudson Festival** ((C) 877/2-MCDUFF; www.shakespeareonthehudson.com), with actors from New York City and elsewhere, is held at a great space along the river in Athens, 1 mile north of the Rip Van Winkle Bridge on Route 385. The **Windham Chamber Music Festival,** 740 Rte. 32C, Windham ((C) 518/738-3852; www.windhammusic.com), features a sophisticated lineup of chamber-music concerts from January to Labor Day at the Historic Windham Civic Center on Main Street. The renovated **Catskill Mountain Foundation Movie Theater,** Main Street, Hunter ((C) 518/263-4702), features first-run Hollywood and foreign and independent films in two great theaters. A wide array of classical music, theater, dance, and popular music performances are held across the street at the foundation's red-barn **Performing Arts Center and Gallery,** Main Street, Hunter ((C) 518/263-4908; www.catskillmtn.org). Nostalgia buffs may want to catch a flick at the **Drive-In Movie Theater** ((C) 877/742-7675) on Route 296 between Hunter and Jewett; it's open seasonally, from May to September. A handful of bars and clubs on Main Street in Tannersville (just east of Hunter) cater to après-ski buffs in search of singles and dance action, though they've been a little more sophisticated and less rowdy in recent years.

4 Northwestern Catskill Region (Delaware County)

The intensely rural Catskill region gets even more rural and remote in Delaware County, home to just 25,000 New Yorkers—but to 700 miles of fishing streams and 11,000 acres of reservoirs and other waterways. This is a land of long uninterrupted vistas, deep green valleys, rivers, streams, and isolated dairy farms, with a handful of covered bridges and historic towns tossed in. Though just over 3 hours from New York City, it's one of the best places in the state to get away from it all and get outdoors to hike, mountain-bike, kayak, or ski. How rural is it? Well, you can pick up a brochure from the **Catskill Center for Conservation and Development** in Arkville ((C) 845/586-2611; www.catskillcenter.org) and spend several days doing a self-guided tour of the *Barns of Delaware County.* Hmm. Sounds like a movie.

ESSENTIALS

GETTING THERE   Route 28 is a 110-mile corridor running west from Kingston to Cooperstown, bisecting Delaware County and providing easy access to the entire county.

VISITOR INFORMATION   **Delaware County Chamber of Commerce,** 114 Main St., Delhi (© **800/746-2281** or 607/746-2281; www.delawarecounty.org).

EXPLORING THE NORTHWESTERN CATSKILL REGION

Roxbury today is a graceful and fairly somnolent burg, but it wasn't always that way. Its Main Street is lined with impressive Tudor and Victorian homes and maple shade trees. Helen Gould Shepard, daughter of the famous financier and railroad magnate—and Roxbury native—Jay Gould, was the town benefactor in the late 1800s. She was responsible for the **Gould Memorial Church** ⚔ (Main St./Rte. 30), built in 1894 by the same architect who designed the state capitol and the famous Dakota apartment building in New York City. Inside are four Tiffany stained-glass windows and a monumental pipe organ. Behind the church is pretty **Kirkside Park,** formerly Helen Gould's estate. The site has been cleaned up and restored in recent years, with rustic bridges built over the stream and trails and walkways added. A **vintage "base ball"** team, the Roxbury Nine, plays its games (according to strict 1864 rules and uniforms) here May through August (admission is free). On Labor Day, the town celebrates "Turn of the Century Day": Locals dress in period costume, and the opposing team is brought in by vintage train. (Look for additional costumed circa-1898 "railrides into yesteryear" in May and July; check the schedule at www.roxburyny.com.) The **John Burroughs Homestead and Woodchuck Lodge,** John Burroughs Memorial Road (© **607/326-372;** www.roxburyny.com; open occasionally in summer), was the rustic summer retreat of the renowned naturalist and essayist. The 1860s farmhouse, a National Historic Landmark, remains as it was when Burroughs lived and wrote here. To get to it, turn west off of Route 30 heading north to Grand Gorge from Roxbury; the house is several miles up on the right.

The **Hanford Mills Museum,** routes 10 and 12, East Meredith (© **800/295-4992;** www.hanfordmills.org; May–Oct Tues–Sun 10am–5pm; admission $7 adults, $5 seniors, $3.50 children, free for children under 6; last tour at 4pm), is a restored farmstead with 16 historic buildings, including a working, water-powered sawmill, an antique boxcar, a woodworking shop, and special events like an Old-Fashioned 4th of July, Quilt Show, and Lumberjack Festival. One of the most enjoyable attractions in this section of the Catskill region is **Healing Waters Farm** ⚔, Route 206, Walton (© **888/HWFarms** or **607/865-4420;** www.healingwatersfarms.com; Apr–Dec Thurs–Fri 11am–5pm, Sat 10am–4pm, Sun 11am–4pm; admission $5 adults, $4 children), a splendid all-in-one agrotourism attraction for families. Kids will be delighted by Little Boy Blue Animal Land, the petting zoo with an amazingly friendly (and rotating) roster of exotic and barnyard animals like a camel, llamas, emus, and baby goats, and hayrides across the rolling acres of farmland. Also on-site, in a 19th-century dairy barn, are the Walton Carriage Museum (a collection of antique horse-drawn carriages), a country antique shop, and a cool Western clothing and gift shop. The two dynamo guys behind this ever-expanding project plan all sorts of special events and seasonal programs.

The Penn Central Railroad arrived in these parts in 1872. The **Delaware & Ulster Railride** ⚔, 43510 Rte. 28, in Arkville (© **800/225-4132;** www.durr.org), south of

Take Me Out to Last Century

Vintage "base ball"—America's pastime as it was played pre-Ruth, when it was spelled "base ball"—has taken off as the ultimate in retro sporting style. Players wear thick period woolen uniforms and for the most part use no gloves; balls and bats are constructed strictly according to regulations of the day. There are about 100 teams in the U.S., and quite a number in New York State and the Northeast. Roxbury's opponents are the New York Gothams, Brooklyn Atlantics, Providence Grays, and Hartford Senators, among others. What no one seems able to agree on is which era should be faithfully reproduced. Some teams play by 1860 rules, while others adopt 1864 rules, and still others prefer to live in 1872, 1887, or 1898. The Roxbury Nine—which counts Mrs. Gould Shepard's grandson on its roster—is one of the most active in the Northeast, playing 16 to 20 games every summer and drawing as many as 3,000 people in attendance. Turn-of-the-Century Days are celebrated on Labor Day weekend. For more information on vintage "base ball," visit www.roxburyny.com and www.vbba.org.

Roxbury, is a tourist excursion train that takes visitors through the Catskill Mountains in a historic train or open-air flat car, departing from the old depot, a must for train fans. The Ulster & Delaware Railroad was one of the most scenic of the day, traversing dramatic mountain scenery from the Hudson to Oneonta. Special events include train runs with staging of a "Great Train Robbery" and "Twilight on the Rails," a slow-moving party excursion with live music and food onboard. From the end of May to the end of October, trains depart for the trip to Roxbury's 1872 depot at 11am and 2pm on weekends and in July and August at 11am and 2pm Thursdays and Fridays; admission is $12 adults, $9 seniors, and $7 children 3 to 12. A new service, the Rip Van Winkle Flyer Dinner Train, runs on selected dates ($45 adults, including dinner and train fare). Check the website or call for current schedules and special-event trains.

Margaretville is the most commercially developed of the small rural towns in Delaware County, with a cute Main Street (where the indie flick *You Can Count On Me,* with Laura Linney and Matthew Broderick, was filmed) lined with several antiques shops, a village pub, and a couple of restaurants. **Andes** (www.andesny.org) is a similar historic village with an interesting past and hopes for a bright future, one of those Catskills towns undergoing a style makeover, with new shops and galleries going in on Main Street. During the Anti-Rent War of the 1840s in New York, the local sheriff and his deputies arrived at the Moses Earle farm to collect overdue rents. Locals disguised themselves as Indians, killing the sheriff and resulting in the arrest of 100 men and two death sentences. Today, though, it's much more peaceful and definitely on the upswing, with the arrival of several new restaurants, shops, and, likely, accommodations. The **Hunting Tavern Museum,** Main Street (© **845/676-3775;** Memorial Day to Columbus Day Sat 10am–3pm), is housed in one of the oldest buildings in Andes and tells the story of village life in the 19th century.

SHOPPING

As rural as Delaware County is, it's not exactly a shopper's mecca. However, a number of tourist-oriented shops are in old barns, which makes it fun. Besides the shops of Healing Waters Farm in Walton, described above, **Pakatakan Farmer's Market** is held Saturday from May to October in a fantastic 1899 Round Barn, one of the oldest such structures, on Route 30 in Halcottsville. In season you'll see dozens of farms selling produce across the region.

If you must shop for man-made things, Margaretville is your place. The **Margaretville Antique Center,** Main Street (© 845/586-2424), has several dealers under one room, while **The Commons in Margaretville,** Main Street, has antiques, clothing, kitchenware, flowers, and Internet hookups. Walton's **Country Emporium,** 134 Delaware St. (© 607/865-8440; www.countryemporiumltd.com), is a marketplace in a historic building with lots of gourmet foods, antiques, and crafts. A funky flea market is held Saturday and Sunday in summer, along Route 28 in Arkville. Andes has an impressive new contemporary art gallery (which also features jewelry designs) called **Blink,** 454 Lower Main St. (© 845/676-3900), and a couple of interesting antiques shops on Main Street. In Fleischmanns, **Robert's Auction House,** Main Street, holds court every Saturday night from 7:30pm to midnight, providing entertainment and shopping excuses to locals and visitors to the area. It's low-rent but a lot of fun, like a yard sale, except with an auctioneer at the helm. The folding chairs have locals' names on them.

SPORTS & OUTDOOR ACTIVITIES

CANOEING & KAYAKING   With all the water around, **canoeing** and **kayaking** are big, especially along the east and west branches of the Delaware River. Rentals, and in some cases canoe and kayak tours, are available from **Al's Sport Store,** routes 30 and 206 in Downsville (© 607/363-7740; www.alssportstore.com); **Catskill Outfitters,** Delaware and North Street, Walton (© 800/631-0105; www.catskilloutfitters. com); and **Susan's Pleasant Pheasant Farm,** 1 Bragg Hollow Rd., Halcottsville (© 607/326-4266; www.pleasantpheasantfarm.com).

FISHING   The western Catskills are one of North America's top fishing destinations. You'll find great tailwater, still-water, and freestone fishing. Fly-fishing is huge in the east and west branches of the Delaware River, Beaverkill River, and Willowemoc. The junction pool at Hancock, where the east and west branches join to form the main stem of the Delaware River, is legendary for large brown and rainbow trout. **Pepacton Reservoir** is a great open-water brown-trout fishery. **Al's Sport Store,** routes 30 and 206 in Downsville (© 607/363-7740; www.alssportstore.com), is the best resource in the area for equipment and knowledge. Al knows everything about fishing the Catskills. For more information on fishing in the northern Catskills, request a **Delaware County Chamber Fishing Guide** (© 800/642-4443; www. delawarecounty.org) or an **I Love NY Fishing Map** (© 607/652-7366). The **West Branch Angler & Sportsman's Resort** in Deposit is a terrific upscale cabin resort targeting anglers (see "Where to Stay," below).

Remember, state licenses are required for fishing (p. 68).

GOLF   For golf, check out the sweet and hilly **Shepard Hills Golf & Tennis Club,** Golf Course Road (1 mile off Rte. 30), Roxbury (© 607/326-7121; www.shepard hills.com). The 9-hole course dates from 1916.

HIKING & BIKING   The **Catskill Scenic Trail** (© 607/652-2821) is 19 gentle miles of Rails-to-Trails (hard-packed rail paths) that run from Grand Gorge to Bloomville; it's terrific for hiking, biking, and cross-country skiing (in winter, watch out for snowmobiles roaring by). The best spot to pick up the trail is Railroad Avenue in Stamford. Within 15 miles of Margaretville, there are 12 peaks above 3,000 feet; **Balsam Lake Mountain** has nice marked trails. **Dry Brook Trail** begins at a trail head in Margaretville and passes Pakatakan Mountain, Dry Brook Ridge, and Balsam Lake Mountain. In **Andes** a nice hike is around the Pepacton Reservoir to Big Pond and Little Pond; from the trail heads, you can hike to the summits of **Cabot or Touchmenot mountains.** The **Catskill Center for Conservation and Development,** Route 28, Arkville (© 845/586-2611; www.catskillcenter.org), offers guided hikes, snowshoe excursions, and bird walks. Birders and naturalists may be interested in "Talons: A Birds of Prey Experience" (Andes; © 845/676-4885; www.talonsbirdsof prey.com), guided hawk walks with a licensed falconer.

Mountain bikers have lots to choose from, but **Plattekill Mountain** (© 800/ GOTTA BIKE; www.plattekill.com) is one of the top-five mountain-biking destinations in North America; it's very popular with extreme downhill crazies in head-to-toe gear and caked in mud, but there are also trails for novices and intermediates.

WINTER SPORTS   Skiers and boarders have two good options: **Belleayre Mountain** (p. 231) and **Plattekill Mountain** (© 800/NEED-2-SKI; www.plattekill.com), a small, laid-back 1950s-era resort that's good for families and novice-to-intermediate skiers.

SPECIAL EVENTS

One of the big annual events in the area is the **Great County Fair** (© 607/865-4763; www.delawarecountyfair.org), held in mid-August in Walton (closing in on 120 years of tradition). You'll find live music, tractor pulls, midway rides, goat shows, livestock auctions, and more. The **Belleayre Music Festival** (© 800/942-6904; www.belleayre music.org) in July and August brings big-name musicians, such as Wynton Marsalis and the Neville Brothers, to the mountain in Highmount. See also the information above about vintage "base ball" and Turn-of-the-Century Day in Roxbury.

WHERE TO STAY

In addition to the hotels and inns listed below, **The Andes Hotel** in Andes, despite its name, is primarily known for its restaurant and tavern, but it also has inexpensive, simple motel rooms ($85 double; see p. 249).

Margaretville Mountain Inn *(Value*   An 1866 Queen Anne, slate-roofed Victorian, up a long road from downtown Margaretville, this comfortable, informal inn has stupendous mountain views on its side. The panoramic view from the porch, overlooking Catskill Mountain State Park, is worth the price of a night's stay. Rooms have some period antiques and modern bathrooms; the Emerald Room inhabits the turret, but I prefer the cozy Birch Room. The owners also have a property in the village of Margaretville, with two two-bedroom suites with full kitchens, fireplaces, and a private yard (each sleeps as many as six—a real bargain for close-knit families).

Margaretville Mountain Rd., Margaretville, NY 12455. © 845/586-3933. Fax 845/586-1699. www.margaretville inn.com. 4 units. $85–$115 double; $120–$140 suite; $125–$150 2-bedroom village suite. AE, DISC, MC, V. Free parking. *In room:* A/C, TV, VCR (in village suites), Wi-Fi, kitchen (in village suites).

The Roxbury ✦✦✦ *(Value)*   This hugely appealing lodging is all about fun, contemporary design, as unexpected as it is welcome in these rural parts. Just 1 block back from Main Street, it's a large Colonial home with an attached wing, a 1960s motor lodge, updated with colorful, hipster styling (the bright-green doors are a hint of what lies behind them). There are motel units, boundary-pushing and whimsically named studio theme rooms, and swanky suites, including a full two-bedroom suite, a bit more restrained and elegant, and ideal for families, occupying the upstairs of the main house. Most accommodations feature full kitchenettes. Rooms are sleek and modern, with Day-Glo colors, chrome accents, and tastefully modern furnishings. From the widow's watch or the screened-in porch out back are great views of the verdant Catskills and nearby creek. A terrific new wrinkle is the small Shimmer Spa, with a hot tub, sauna, fireplace, and shower made of river rock.

2258 County Hwy. 41, Roxbury, NY 12474. © 607/326-7200. www.theroxburymotel.com. 18 units. $90–$155 studio room; $115–$145 kitchenette room; $160–$290 suite. Rates include breakfast. AE, DC, DISC, MC, V. Free parking. **Amenities:** Cocktail lounge; spa; Wi-Fi; DVD library. *In room:* A/C, TV, hair dryer, DVD player.

Scott's Oquaga Lake House *(Kids) (Finds)*   This family-owned resort has, incredibly, been in the same family since 1869 and continues with oddball stubbornness. But that's not even the most notable fact about it: What's really unique is that several generations of the "singing Scott family" continue to perform in nightly cabaret revues for their guests all summer. The shows have to be seen to be believed. For some guests, it will be like time travel to another, gentler planet: planet 1940s Americana. Their literature says it best: "the excitement of a cruise; the friendliness of a bed & breakfast." Actually, the marketing tag line I like better is "Be our guest, be our guest, put our service to the test." The resort's accommodations are pretty modest, but the place is ensconced on 1,100 lakefront acres, and spring-fed Oquaga Lake is stunning. All recreational activities, meals, and, best of all, cabaret shows are included in the price, and the family is strict about enforcing a "no tipping" policy. You can take free ballroom- or square-dancing lessons, water-ski, or play tennis, golf, or volleyball; the possibilities for fun are endless. The Scott house is popular with families, who, like the migratory Scotts (who flee to Florida in winter), return year after year.

Oquaga Lake Rd., Deposit, NY 13754. © 607/467-3094. www.scottsfamilyresort.com. 135 units. $234–$296 double; $338–$454 2-bedroom suite. Rates include 3 meals daily and all activities and entertainment. Weekly rates available. AE, MC, V. Free parking. **Amenities:** Restaurant; bar; 9-hole golf course; 3 outdoor and 1 indoor tennis courts; sail- and rowboats; cabaret shows. *In room:* A/C, TV.

West Branch Angler & Sportsman's Resort ✦✦ *(Kids)*   Though this great setup of very well outfitted cabins on the banks of the west branch of the Delaware River— one of the world's most famous tailwater trout fisheries—is all about fly-fishing, you don't have to come with your waders and rods to enjoy the place. Far from it. If you want something out of the ordinary, with good amenities and services but lots of contact with nature, this is the place. It sits on 300 acres of mountain forests, with lots of hiking and biking trails, and has a very nice restaurant and bar, swings, and a playground overlooking the river, as well as miniature golf and a large outdoor pool. The one- and two-bedroom cabins are upscale rustic, with porches facing the river, picnic areas, and nice kitchens; some have fireplaces. If fishing is what your stay in the Catskills is all about, this is really your kind of place. There's a full-service fly shop, expert instruction, and guides. New for 2007 are 12 riverview one-bedroom cabins that can accommodate up to four people, but are more economical than the executive cabins. As expected from such an outdoorsy place, the hotel is dog-friendly.

Tips Gone Fishin'

Anglers who really just want to concentrate on the fish and don't want any-thing fancy or expensive should check out the **Downsville Motel,** routes 30 and 206, Downsville (**( ) 607/363-7575**; $60 double). The eight rooms are standard motel rooms, but they have private balconies overlooking the east branch of the Delaware River, and they're just paces from Al's Sports Store, which dis-penses just about anything a fisherman could need.

Faulkner Rd., Deposit, NY 13754. **( ) 800/201-2557.** Fax 607/467-2215. www.westbranchangler.com. 36 units. $180–$232 1-bedroom cabin; $242–$266 2-bedroom executive cabin (double occupancy). Rates include breakfast. 2-night minimum stay on weekends in season. AE, DC, DISC, MC, V. Free parking. Dogs welcome. **Amenities:** Restau-rant; bar; swimming pool; exercise room; miniature golf. *In room:* A/C, TV, hair dryer.

WHERE TO DINE

The Andes Hotel *(Value* CREATIVE AMERICAN   Sally and Ed O'Neill bought and restored this classic 1850 inn, with a massive front porch, in the center of Andes. Ed is a Culinary Institute grad, and the restaurant strikes a nice balance between creative impulses and down-to-earth good food and good value. The decor is simple, with reddish brown paneling and simple white tablecloths and drop ceilings. Appetizers include an excellent warm wild-mushroom salad. A nightly special (on Mon it's baby back ribs) complements the unpretentious but consistently well-pre-pared menu, which features items like a double-cut pork chop, roasted brook trout, and bacon-wrapped sea scallops. Lunch menu items are simpler, such as pulled-pork barbecue, and a good value. The gregarious tavern next door, where there's live music on Saturday nights, serves bar comfort foods, like popcorn chicken and buffalo wings, so that folks of all stripes and means feel comfortable. The owners are still hoping to spruce up the hotel's 10 accommodations, which at this point are still pretty basic but not bad and not expensive ($85 double).

110 Main St., Andes. **( ) 845/676-3980.** Reservations recommended. Main courses $13–$18. AE, MC, V. Daily noon–3pm and 5–10pm.

The Old Schoolhouse Inn & Restaurant *(Finds* AMERICAN   A hunter's paradise, this restaurant, although in a 1903 schoolhouse, looks more like a hunting lodge. It is crammed to the rafters with taxidermy and hunting trophies of all shapes, sizes, and species. The Sunday brunch is a big local affair, with a huge spread under the watch-ful eyes of moose and elk in the front room and a shrimp-and-salad bar. Entrees are upscale and sophisticated, with a large array of fresh trout preparations, steaks, and pastas. The Saturday Special is roast prime rib au jus. Vegetarians and animals-rights activists beware: This may not be your kind of place!

Main St., Downsville. **( ) 607/363-7814.** Reservations recommended on weekends. Main courses $12–$29. AE, MC, V. Wed–Sun noon–3pm and 5–10pm; Sun brunch 10am–2pm.

River Run Restaurant & Trout Skeller Bar *(/* AMERICAN/GRILL   Tucked into the riverfront acreage of the West Branch Angler & Sportsman's Resort, this nice restaurant is a perfect place to unwind (and, if you're staying in one of the cabins, easy to get to) after a long day of—what else?—fishing. It's got the requisite, masculine lodge feel; and the tavern downstairs has a fancy, huge plasma TV behind the bar, so you can kick back with a beer and watch big-screen sports. The restaurant is the spot for fine dining. It features a number of nice pastas, including spinach ravioli, and shrimp and scallop carbonara, and entrees are pretty evenly divided between meat and fish, with a grilled burgundy filet, veal tenderloin, and grilled scarlet-red snapper among the well-prepared options. The tavern menu includes items like club sandwiches and big, juicy burgers.

At the West Branch Angler & Sportsman's Resort, 150 Faulkner Rd., Hancock. (C) **607/467-5533**.. Reservations recommended. Main courses $8.95–$23. AE, MC, V. Daily 5–10pm; Sun brunch 10am–3pm; bar menu only in Trout Skeller lounge daily 5–10pm. Closed Oct–Apr.

5 Southwestern Catskill Region (Sullivan County)

Rivers are, even more so than mountains, the defining characteristic of Sullivan County, in the southwestern quadrant of the Catskills. The Upper Delaware River paints the southwestern border of Sullivan County, separating New York State from Pennsylvania and running about 75 miles, all the way from Hancock to Sparrowbush. In addition to the Delaware, considered one of the top-10 fishing rivers in the world, the county boasts Beaverkill and Willowemoc creeks, making it one of the most important destinations in North America for trout fly-fishing. River sports like canoeing and kayaking are also huge. Beyond the area's natural bounty, Sullivan County is a picturesque region of covered bridges, scattered historic sights, and a sprinkling of towns undergoing revitalization and positioned to take advantage of growing outdoors and cultural tourism, like Narrowsburg, Livingston Manor, and Roscoe.

ESSENTIALS

GETTING THERE   Route 17 (future I-86 "Quickway") cuts northwest across Sullivan County, running from the New York State Thruway (I-87) and passing through Rock Hill on the way west to Deposit.

VISITOR INFORMATION   Contact **Sullivan County Visitors Association,** 100 North St., Monticello ((C) **800/882-CATS** or 845/794-3000; www.scva.net), or the **National Park Service Upper Delaware Scenic and Recreational River** information center, Narrowsburg ((C) **570/685-4871;** www.nps.gov/upde), for more information.

EXPLORING THE SOUTHWESTERN CATSKILL REGION

Roscoe *(R)*, which bills itself as "Trout Town USA," is a pleasant, laid-back town with an attractive downtown that's lined with shops set up to capitalize on the tourist trade, which consists almost wholly of outdoors enthusiasts and fishermen. Roscoe is one of the primary base camps in the Catskill region for anglers; it's perched at the edge of one of the most famous fishing spots in the country, **Junction Pool** *(R)*—the confluence of the renowned trout-fishing streams, Beaverkill and Willowemoc creeks. The kickoff of fly-fishing season is celebrated here every April 1. Legend holds that the fish are detained long enough at this crossroads, unsure of which direction to swim, that they grow exponentially in size and then offer themselves up as catch-and-release trophies. The **Roscoe O&W Railway Museum,** Railroad Avenue ((C) **607/498-5500;** Memorial Day to Columbus Day Sat–Sun 11am–3pm; free admission), across from the red NY O&W car, is a minor museum that contains artifacts and memorabilia from the old O&W railway line, a scale-model railroad, and exhibits on the area's major attractions and industry.

Anglers have their own cultural institution to celebrate: the **Catskill Fly Fishing Center & Museum** *(R)(R)*, 1031 Old Rte. 17 (between exits 94 and 96 off Rte. 17), Livingston Manor ((C) **845/439-4810;** www.cffcm.net; Apr–Oct daily 10am–4pm;

Nov–Mar Tues–Fri 10am–1pm, Sat 10am–4pm; $3 adults and students, $1 children under 12), is a handsomely built and displayed exhibit touting the achievements, art, science, and folklore of fly-fishing. Especially interesting are the numerous displays of wet, dry, nymph, and streamer flies and the actual tying tables of several of the most renowned tiers in the business. A stuffed doll of a 6-pound fish gives kids an idea of what it would be like to catch a big one. Expert fly-fishers conduct demonstrations on Saturday from April to October.

Fans of **historic covered bridges** have a number to choose from in Sullivan County, including ones in **Willowemoc** (built in 1860, 2 miles west of town); **Beaverkill** (1865, in Beaverkill State Campground); and **Livingston Manor** (1860, just north of town). All are signed. A different type of bridge, but well worth seeking out, is the centerpiece of the **Stone Arch Bridge Historical Park,** Route 52 near Kenoza Lake. The three-arched stone bridge was built in 1880 by Swiss-German immigrants.

Down Route 17 from Livingston Manor, the town of **Liberty** is distinguished by an attractive historic district with classic Gothic Revival, Romanesque, and Greek Revival buildings. Revitalization efforts got an unlikely boost from the recent arrival of the historic (1948) **Munson Diner**—featured on *Seinfeld* and *Law & Order,* and once frequented by Andy Warhol—which was uprooted from Hell's Kitchen in Manhattan and relocated to Liberty, purchased by a local group of investors. Nostalgic pilgrims have already made the trip to Liberty to relive memories of the diner, which should be up and running, again a 24-hour diner, by the time you read this. The **Apple Pond Farming Center** (✆ 845/482-4674; www.applepondfarm.com; Tues–Sun 10am–5pm), Hahn Road, in Callicoon Center, is a traditional horse-powered organic farm that offers demonstrations of milking, work and sport horses, and border collies, as well as goat-cheese-making classes and horse-drawn wagon rides. It's a great spot for families. **Bethel,** on Route 178 west of Route 17, is the site of the 1969 Woodstock Festival, the famous rock-'n'-roll party where Jimi Hendrix, Janis Joplin, and others jammed for a seriously mind-altered audience. The **Bethel Woods Center for the Arts,** 200 Hurd Rd., Bethel (✆ 866/781-2922; www.bethelwoodslive.org), now occupies the hallowed grounds with a beautiful pavilion that seats 4,800 for pop, jazz, rock, and classical concerts. In 2008, the center expects to open the **Museum at Bethel Woods,** containing exhibits on the 1960s political and social transformation and the legendary Woodstock concert.

Farther south, the surprising village of **Narrowsburg** ✿, perched on the Upper Delaware River and nestled between the Catskills and Pennsylvania's Poconos, is on the upswing, with a number of galleries and restaurants now populating its main street and a rich cultural life for such a small town, with an opera company in summer residence at the Tusten Theater, a film series, and chamber music concerts. Its biggest attraction, aside from its picturesque location at the edge of Big Eddy, is the **Fort Delaware Museum of Colonial History** ✿, 6615 Rte. 97 (✆ 845/252-6660; www. co.sullivan.ny.us; Memorial Day to Labor Day Sat–Mon 10am–5pm; admission $4.50 adults, $3.50 seniors, $2.50 children 6–16, $13 families), a fascinating living-history museum. Originally established as a museum in 1959, Fort Delaware was a stockaded settlement of the Connecticut Yankees in the Delaware Valley in the mid–18th century. Interpreters in 18th-century period dress reenact the work habits and traditions of the day, including candle making, spinning and weaving, woodworking, blacksmithing, and cooking over open fire pits. Interactive exhibits and children's workshops are intelligently designed and really involve kids in history; children can

---

Tips Gay-Friendly Sullivan County

Sullivan County is one of the few predominantly rural counties around that openly court gay visitors and promote gay-friendly establishments. Look for the "Out in the Catskills" rack card that highlights certain gay-friendly businesses and other informational brochures with a gay and lesbian rainbow symbol on them.

---

even be a part of daylong apprentice programs, craft days, and 3-day camps in which they learn an 18th-century skill. The **Delaware Arts Center,** 37 Main St. (© 845/ 252-7576), is an active cultural center with art exhibits and concerts held in the historic Arlington Hotel.

Minisink Battleground Park (© 845/794-3000; www.co.sullivan.ny.us; daily 8am–dusk; free admission), County Road 168 near Route 97 in Minisink Ford, is a 57-acre park on the site of a 1779 Revolutionary War battle, the only one that took place along the Upper Delaware. A tiny Colonial militia took on Tories and Native Americans who were aligned with the British. On-site are self-guided trails and an interpretive history center.

SHOPPING

There are a number of good antiques stores in Sullivan County; pick up a copy of the "Antiques Trail Map," available at many hotels and restaurants, as well as antiques shops. Among the best are **Ferndale Marketplace Antiques & Gardens,** 52 Ferndale Rd., Ferndale (© 845/292-8701), a very large, 120-year-old country general store with seven dealers; **Antiques of Callicoon,** 26 Upper Main St., Callicoon (© 845/ 887-5918), in a 19th-century building across from the train station; **Artisans Gallery,** 110 Mill St., Liberty (© 845/295-9278); **Memories,** Route 17 Quickway, Parksville (© 845/292-4270), a massive gallery between Livingston Manor and Liberty; **Town & Country Antiques,** 1 N. Main St., Liberty (© 845/292-1363), distinguished by its fabulous storefront; and **Hamilton's Antique Shoppe,** Route 55/Main Street, Neversink (© 845/985-2671). Roscoe has a number of cute shops (in addition to all the fishing gear and tackle stores), including **Annie's Place,** Stewart Avenue, Roscoe (© 607/498-4139), with contemporary country gifts; and the perfectly named **The Fisherman's Wife,** Stewart Avenue, Roscoe (© 607/498-6055), a purveyor of antiques and collectibles.

Narrowsburg has a nice art gallery, **River Gallery,** Main Street (© 845/252-3230), showing contemporary artists and photographers, while its **Delaware Arts Alliance,** 37 Main St. (© 845/252-7576), shows local artists.

SPORTS & OUTDOOR ACTIVITIES

FISHING   Anglers will be in heaven in this part of the Catskill Mountains. Sullivan County possesses several of the best trout streams in North America; the Delaware River and Beaverkill and Willowemoc creeks are among the most storied trout-fishing rivers in the world, and the famed fly fisher Lee Wulff established a fly-fishing school here. The fishing season, which attracts anglers from across the globe, begins in April. Pick up a copy of the *Sullivan County Visitors Guide* for a full listing of lakes, streams, and fishing preserves in the county. The **Catskill Fish Hatchery,** 402 Mongaup Rd., Livingston Manor (© 845/439-4328), open year-round, is the site of more than one million brown trout raised annually. For instruction and guided incursions into the world of fly-fishing, try **Catskill Flies & Fishing Adventures,** Roscoe (© 607/498-6146); **Baxter House River Outfitters & Guide Services,** Old Route 17, Roscoe (© 800/905-5095 or 607/498-5811); or **Tite-Line Fly Fishing School,** 563 Gulf Rd., Roscoe (© 607/498-5866). **Gone Fishing Guide Service,** 20 Lake St., Narrowsburg (© 845/252-3657), also offers half- and full-day float fishing trips. Among the many providers of equipment and tackle are **Beaverkill Angler,** Stewart Avenue, Roscoe (© 607/498-5194), and **The Little Store,** 26 Broad St., Roscoe (© 607/498-5553).

GOLF Golf fans can tee it up at some fine courses in scenic locales. Try the championship courses at **Grossinger Country Club,** 26 Rte. 52 E., Liberty (© 914/292-9000; www.grossingergolf.net; greens fees $45–$95), whose "Big G," which features an island green on hole 13, is considered one of the most beautiful and difficult in the Northeast; **Concord Resort & Golf Club,** Route 17/Concord Road, Kiamesha Lake (© 888/448-9686 or 845/794-4000; www.concordresort.com; greens fees $35–$95), which has two championship courses, one called "the Monster," a *Golf Digest* top-100 course for more than 25 years; and **Villa Roma Country Club,** 356 Villa Roma Rd., Callicoon (© 800/727-8455 or 845/887-5080; www.villaroma.com; greens fees $30–$65; open Apr–Nov).

HIKING In Sullivan County, there's very good hiking along the **Tusten Mountain Trail,** a moderately difficult but immensely scenic 3-mile round-trip trail maintained by the National Park Service. The trail head is near the Ten Mile River access site off Route 97 between Barryville and Narrowsburg, and the trail climbs to an elevation of more than 1,100 feet. For more information, call © 570/685-4871 or visit www.nps. gov/upde. A nice easy trail with great distant views is **Walnut Mountain Park** (© 845/292-7690), in Liberty, open May through September.

RAFTING & KAYAKING The rivers of Sullivan County, lacing the foothills of the Catskills and Pocono Mountains, are ideal for rafting, canoeing, tubing, and kayaking. The most experienced operator for boat rentals of all sorts is **Lander's River Trips** in Narrowsburg (© 800/252-3925 or 845/557-8783; www.landersrivertrips.com; rates $37–$42 per day). The company also operates campgrounds along the Delaware River and rents mountain bikes (and offers combined canoeing or rafting plus camping trips).

WILDLIFE Sullivan County plays host to more **bald eagles** than any other spot on the East Coast, and the state set aside more than 1,200 acres specifically for the protection of the migrant eagle population of about 100 that return every winter. **The Eagle Institute,** Barryville (© 845/557-6162; www.eagleinstitute.org; weekends Dec–Mar), offers interpretive programs and guided eagle watches on weekends during the winter migrating season. Along Route 55A is a bald-eagle observation site on the **Neversink Reservoir,** just outside the village of Neversink. Guided bald-eagle habitat trails are found in **Pond Eddy,** with the Upper Delaware Scenic and Recreational River National Park Services; the best times to see bald eagles are December and early March (call © 570/729-8251 for additional information).

WHERE TO STAY

A legendary old hotel in Roscoe, the 1890 **Antrim Lodge** (Highland Ave. at Union St.), was scheduled to open in the spring of 2007 after a full-scale restoration. Alas, the property has had a streak of awful luck: after extensive flooding in the region in June 2006, the hotel suffered a devastating fire on the top floors. Too bad, because it definitely stood to be one of the most attractive places to stay in the region. The owners still hope to rebuild, but don't plan on it being functional before spring 2009. For updates, see www.antrimlodge.com.

EXPENSIVE

The Inn at Lake Joseph ★★★ Although pricey, this professionally run luxury country inn, secluded on a 20-acre estate and surrounded by forest and down a wooded path from beautiful Lake Joseph, may be just the place for a very relaxing and pampering getaway. Formerly a summer residence and then a retreat for two Catholic cardinals, the 135-year-old Victorian estate exudes elegance and tranquillity. Rooms are divided among the main house, the carriage house, and the mountain lodge–like cottage; rooms in the outbuildings are nicely secluded, and though they're more modern and rustic than the manor house, I think they're even more special. Several of those rooms are plain gigantic, with cathedral ceilings; many have private sun decks and a couple have full kitchens. All but one room has a gas fireplace, and a guest kitchen is open around the clock. Pets are welcome in the outbuildings and on the grounds. Bargain hunters or solo travelers should check out the solitary, no-frills "spare room" in the cottage house, which goes for just $82 double ($52 single). The inn overflows with relaxing spots, from the lovely pool to hammocks strewn in the woods.

400 Saint Joseph Rd., Forestburgh, NY 12777. ☎ 845/791-9506. Fax 845/794-1948. www.lakejoseph.com. 15 units. $170–$310 double; $310–$385 suite. Rates include full breakfast. AE, DC, DISC, MC, V. Free parking. **Amenities:** Outdoor swimming pool; tennis court; bicycles; boating facilities. *In room:* A/C, TV/VCR, fridge (in some rooms), microwave, coffeemaker, hair dryer, Jacuzzi.

New Age Health Spa ★★ *Finds* A country-style, intimate destination spa tucked away in the hills at the edge of the Catskills State Forest Preserve, this is the perfect place for a relaxing retreat without the factory feel of some larger, more institutional spas. All kinds of treatments and classes, including tai chi, aqua aerobics, yoga, and meditation, are available; classes are included in the price. Guest rooms are located in five lodges and are very comfortable but not overly fancy; healthful spa-cuisine meals are served in the rustic dining room, which has a nice deck area for eating outdoors. Beautiful hiking trails wind through the 280-acre property (guided hikes are scheduled), and horses roam down by the stable. Lots of outdoor activities are programmed, as are frequent mind-and-body lectures. Guests are not allowed nicotine, caffeine, or alcohol, and guests caught smoking or drinking will be asked to leave. Check the website for specials.

658 Rte. 55, Neversink, NY 12765. ☎ 800/682-4348 or 845/985-7600. Fax 845/985-2467. www.newagehealthspa. com. 37 units. $408–$798 double. Rates include 3 meals daily, classes, and activities (spa treatments extra). 2-night minimum required. AE, DC, DISC, MC, V. Free parking. **Amenities:** Restaurant; 2 outdoor tennis courts; full spa facilities; TV and computer lounge with Internet access. *In room:* A/C.

MODERATE

Carrier House Bed & Breakfast ★★ *Finds* In a quiet residential neighborhood, on a gentle hill above downtown Liberty, sits this wholly unique retreat masquerading as a B&B. It is that, of course, but it has so much personality that it seems unfair to lump it in with more generic places that merely give you a place to sleep and something to eat in the morning. Occupying a detached guesthouse—behind a pale yellow 1906 main house with a massive wraparound porch—are two cozy and private apartments, decorated in a charming, winking 1950s style, with vintage furnishings. Downstairs is the cabin, a huge room done up in Adirondack style, with a kitchenette, sofa, stove-chimney-equipped living room, writing desk, and reading chair. Upstairs is the loft, a

> ## ⟨*Tips* A Fine Catch
>
> Folks with fishing on their minds, but who prefer stocked ponds to world-class trout streams, might check out **Eldred Preserve**, Route 55, Eldred, NY 12732 (ⓒ **800/557-FISH**; $75–$95 double). The motel complex—rooms are simple but large—is built around a fishing preserve and ponds stocked with trout and catfish for either catch-and-release or catch-and-keep. An outdoor pool and a restaurant are on the premises.

two-story space with a full galley kitchen and an upstairs writing desk with a perfectly framed view of the distant mountains. It's a warm and inviting place, contributed to, in no small part, by the proprietor Allan, a writer/historian and committed community activist (who was instrumental in bringing New York City's historic Munson Diner to Liberty). Breakfast is brought to your door in a picnic basket—just one of the many details that make staying here such a relaxed pleasure. The inn also functions as a writer's retreat; as inspired and thoughtful as its execution is, I wouldn't be surprised to hear someday that Carrier House played a part in a breakthrough novel.

64 Carrier St., Liberty, NY 12754. ⓒ 845/292-9742. Fax 845/796-3130. www.carrierhouseny.com. 2 units. $135–$150 cabin suite (double); $150–$165 loft suite (double). Rates include continental breakfast. MC, V. Free parking. *In room:* A/C, TV/VCR, coffeemaker, hair dryer, CD player.

The Lodge at Rock Hill ⭐   This surprising hotel, on 65 acres facing a major road, was an old Howard Johnson, but you'd never know it once inside. It was completely and handsomely redone in 2001 with sedate colors, warm tones, and excellent furnishings. Rooms are very large and impeccably clean. Out back, there are hiking trails through the entire property. Take my word for it: Behind a boring facade, which reveals its HoJo origins, is an excellent and very good-value hotel. The indoor pool with a deck and a nice big Jacuzzi is a huge bonus, as is the fact that the hotel is pet-friendly.

283 Rock Hill Dr., Rock Hill, NY 12775. ⓒ 866/RH-LODGE or 845/796-3100. Fax 845/796-3130. www.lodgeatrockhill.com. 73 units. $139–$189 double; $159–$239 suite. Rates include continental breakfast. AE, DC, DISC, MC, V. Free parking. Pets accepted. **Amenities:** Indoor swimming pool; Jacuzzi; video-game room; business center. *In room:* A/C, TV, dataport, coffeemaker, hair dryer.

INEXPENSIVE

The Reynolds House Inn and Motel ⟨*Finds*⟩ ⟨*Value*⟩   The oldest operational B&B in the county, this welcoming inn was built in 1902 as a "tourist home," or boardinghouse. John D. Rockefeller, a fishing fanatic, used to stay here, and "his" room, the largest and with a claw-foot tub, retains his name. The rooms are cozy and very attractively decorated, though bathrooms are on the small side. Today a charming Irishman and his wife run the inn, which also has inexpensive motel rooms and a cottage out back—perfect for long-term fishermen.

1934 Old Rte. 17 S., Roscoe, NY 12776. ⓒ 607/498-4422. Fax 607/498-5808. www.reynoldshouseinn.com. 7 units (in main house); 8 motel rooms. Main house $85–$110 double; motel rooms $65–$75 double. Rates include full breakfast. 2-night minimum on weekends May–Oct. AE, DC, DISC, MC, V. Free parking. *In room:* A/C, TV.

WHERE TO DINE
EXPENSIVE
Manny's Steakhouse & Seafood ⭐⭐ ⟨*Finds*⟩ STEAKHOUSE   Hiding behind an undistinguished exterior that would seem appropriate for a strip-mall chain restaurant,

Manny's surprises with a spacious and nice, even elegant, interior of warm tones and lots of wood. For lunch, there are good wraps (like the filet mignon) and sandwiches, while the classic steakhouse dinner menu emphasizes steaks and seafood (the name pretty much tells it like it is). Meat eaters can't go wrong with the prime porterhouse, prime rib, and baby back ribs; among fish and seafood, try the king crab legs or broiled flounder. There is also a number of good pastas, as well as a pretty decent and affordable wine list.

79 Sullivan Ave., Liberty. © 845/295-3170. Reservations recommended. Main courses $12–$29. AE, MC, V. Daily 11:30am–10pm.

The 1906 Restaurant 🦀🦀 AMERICAN ECLECTIC/GRILL   This 15-year-old upscale restaurant, a favorite of visitors and second-home owners in the area, has one of the best reputations in Sullivan County. The interior is almost homey, with tin ceilings and lots of pine paneling, exposed brick, and ceiling fans, as well as an odd overdose of pink tablecloths. The menu is also a bit of a surprise, featuring anything but comfort food; it includes several exotic meats, such as ostrich and buffalo. Other signature dishes include steak au poivre, baby rack of lamb, and the 1906 burger, prepared with sautéed onions and mushrooms, Swiss cheese, and bourbon or chili corn sauce (it tries hard to prove its worth at $14). Specials exhibit some flair: They include Cajun shrimp over fettuccine with jalapeño sauce, and veal rollatini with mushrooms and Marsala sauce. The wine list, with more than 175 selections, is one of the most extensive in the Catskills, and it's been continually recognized by *Wine Spectator.*

41 Lower Main St., Callicoon. © 845/887-1906. Reservations not accepted. Main courses $15–$30. AE, MC, V. Daily 5–10pm.

MODERATE

Cobblers 🦀 AMERICAN   This casual, genial spot is exactly the kind of neighborhood restaurant you'd expect to find in a transitional but historic town like Liberty. It has a *Cheers*-like bar of regulars and a simple attached dining room, with black leather-backed booths, and it's known for its home-cooked dishes that are a cut above the norm. Known far and wide (or at least throughout Liberty) for its mandarin-orange salad with sliced almonds and scallions (they even sell the vinaigrette by the bottle), it also serves a nice variety of soups, pastas, and hearty meat dishes.

77 N. Main St., Liberty. © 845/292-2970. Reservations recommended on weekends. Main courses $11–$19. MC, V. Daily 11:30am–10pm.

AFTER DARK

The Bethel Woods Center for the Arts 🦀, 100 Hurd Rd., Bethel (© 866/781-2922; www.bethelwoodslive.org), on the grounds of the 1969 Woodstock concert, plays host to a wide range of mainstream rock, pop, jazz, and classical concerts, including Bob Dylan and Crosby, Stills, Nash & Young (the 21st-century version), the Boston Pops, Lynyrd Skynyrd, and Earth, Wind & Fire. The pavilion seats 4,800, with room for another 12,000 on the lawn. **Callicoon Theater,** 30 Olympia St., Callicoon (© 845/887-4460), is a cool single-screen 1948 "post-Deco" theater still in use, showing first-run and art and independent films. **Tusten Theater,** 210 Bridge St., Narrowsburg (© 845/252-7576), is a fantastic, nicely renovated Deco-style theater that seats 160 for live music, including blues, jazz, chamber, and theater performances; the Delaware Valley Opera is in residence at the theater during the summer. The annual summer **Jazzfest** at the theater produces a great lineup of bands in May and June; call © 845/252-7576 for schedules.

The Capital Region:
Saratoga Springs & Albany

by Neil E. Schlecht

Sandwiched between the gentility of the Upper Hudson River Valley and the wilds of the Adirondack Mountains are two upstate towns at polar opposites. The oft-maligned capital city of the Empire State, Albany is an everyman's working city, home to state legislators, lobbyists, and banking and insurance industry workers. Just a half-hour away, charming Saratoga Springs is all about leisure: Its relaxed pace and cultural refinement override such prosaic matters as work.

Virtually equidistant from New York City, Boston, and Montreal, Albany is ideally placed for a state capital. On the banks of the Upper Hudson, Albany, now 350 years old, lays claim to being the oldest chartered city in the United States. The original Dutch settlement Beverwyck is today a city dominated by government business, one much more accustomed to lobbyists than tourists, but

it can claim a surprisingly full slate of cultural and architectural offerings sufficient to entertain anyone visiting without an official government or business agenda.

Saratoga Springs, a graceful and historic resort town, lies just north of the state capital. The site of the tide-turning 1777 Battle of Saratoga, the town later transformed itself into one of the country's most popular vacation destinations, renowned for its therapeutic mineral springs, expansive urban parks, and beautiful downtown dominated by Victorian architecture. By the mid–19th century, Saratoga had earned the moniker "Queen of the Spas." Saratoga Springs especially thrives in warm months, when its elegant Race Course hosts one of the nation's most prestigious thoroughbred-racing seasons and the city simmers with a rich platter of cultural events, including prestigious ballet and music companies in residence.

1 Orientation

ARRIVING

BY PLANE   Most visitors traveling by air will arrive via **Albany International Airport,** 737 Albany-Shaker Rd. (© **518/242-2222,** or 518/242-2359 for flight information; www.albanyairport.com), located about 10 minutes from downtown Albany and about a half-hour from Saratoga Springs. The airport is served by most major domestic and several international airlines. The information desk can provide details on getting to either Albany or Saratoga Springs, as well as basic lodging and tourist information.

Ground transportation to Albany or Saratoga Springs is by bus, airport shuttle, private car, charter limo, courtesy car, or taxi. To Albany, the Capital District Transit

Authority (CDTA) operates **ShuttleFly** buses that depart the airport Monday through Friday several times each hour between 6am and 11pm (on weekends, service begins about a half-hour earlier). For additional information, call CDTA at (C) **518/482-8822.** Taxis are also on hand at airport arrival gates. You can make airport transportation reservations by calling **Albany Yellow Taxi** ((C) **518/869-2258**), **Saratoga Taxi** ((C) **518/584-2700**), or **Saratoga Capitaland Taxi** ((C) **518/583-3131**) among taxis, and **Premiere Limo** ((C) **800/515-6123** or 518/459-6123) or **A Destiny Limousine of Saratoga** ((C) **518/587-5221**) among limousine services. From the airport, taxi fares to Albany and Saratoga Springs are about $15 and $40, respectively; a limo should cost about $50 to Albany and $90 to Saratoga.

Driving from Albany International Airport To downtown Albany, you can either take Albany-Shaker Road south, which will put you close to the visitor center and Broadway, or take I-87 south to I-90 west. The highways that ring Albany are notoriously confusing, though, and if you go the wrong way, you may end up circling around for a seemingly interminable length of time.

The fastest way to reach Saratoga Springs is to take I-87 north to exit 13N. Follow Route 9 north about 5 miles to downtown Saratoga Springs.

BY CAR Most major car-rental companies, including **Avis** ((C) 800/331-1212), **Budget** ((C) 800/527-0700), **Enterprise** ((C) 800/Rent-A-Car), **Hertz** ((C) 800/654-3131), **National** ((C) 800/227-7368), and **Thrifty** ((C) 800/THRIFTY), have representatives at Albany International Airport.

To get to Albany from points north, take the Adirondack Northway (I-87) south to I-90 east to I-787 south. From points south, take the New York State Thruway (I-87) to exit 23 to I-787 north. From the western part of the state, take the New York State Thruway (I-87) to exit 24 and follow I-90 to I-787 south.

To Saratoga Springs from points south, take I-87 to exit 13 south and Route 9 right into town; from the north, take I-87 south to exit 15 and Route 50 south. Saratoga Springs is about 3 hours by car from New York City. From Albany, the drive to Saratoga Springs is about a half-hour.

BY TRAIN The new **Albany-Rensselaer Rail Station,** 525 East St., Rensselaer ((C) **518/462-5763**), receives Amtrak trains from western New York (Empire Service), the Midwestern U.S. and Massachusetts (Lake Shore Limited), Canada (Maple Leaf), and points north and south of the capital (Adirondack and Ethan Allen Express Lines). Taxis are available for travel to downtown Albany.

To Saratoga Springs, there is daily service on Amtrak's Adirondack (originating in New York City and Montreal) and Ethan Allen Express (traveling from New York City to Vermont) lines. The Saratoga station is located at West Avenue and Station Lane; there are taxis as well as Enterprise and Thrifty car-rental agencies at the station. For more information and reservations, contact Amtrak at (C) **800/USA-RAIL** or visit www.amtrak.com.

BY BUS Greyhound ((C) **518/434-8095** or 845/339-4230; www.greyhound.com) and **Adirondack Trailways** ((C) **800/776-7548;** www.trailways.com) travel to both Albany and Saratoga Springs. The **Upstate Transit Albany-Saratoga Bus Service** ((C) **518/584-5252**) travels between Albany and Saratoga.

2 Saratoga Springs ✶✶✶

35 miles N of Albany; 190 miles N of New York City; 290 miles E of Buffalo; 200 miles NW of Boston

Saratoga residents proudly call their town a city in the country, one that offers the sophistication and culture of a major metropolis, but the greenery and unhurried pace of a rural area. A historic and stately town that saw its fortunes rise with the explosion of casino and thoroughbred-racing tourism in the late 19th century, Saratoga has confidently bounced back from its postwar, 20th-century malaise (when corruption and scandals led to a gambling prohibition, the closing of the race course, and widespread urban decline). Today, Saratoga is again proudly strutting its stuff as a resort hot spot in upstate New York. In warm months, Saratoga hits high stride with the advent of 6 weeks of horse racing at one of the world's prettiest tracks, public parks in full bloom, and an enviable offering of culture, with both the New York City Ballet and Philadelphia Orchestra in summer residence. Horse-mad, cigar-smoking track bettors mingle with urban sophisticates in designer outfits at outdoor cocktail parties, while families hit the trails in Saratoga State Spa Park and soak up classical music concerts and outdoor picnics.

Saratoga today is indistinguishable from horse racing and its attendant galas, but its historic importance is well established. Nearby is the site of the most famous battle of the Revolutionary War, the 1777 Battle of Saratoga, which marked the turning point in favor of General Washington's American forces. At the end of the 1800s, Saratoga was touted for the healing properties of its naturally carbonated mineral springs; at its apex, the small town counted two of the largest hotels in the world, each with more than 1,000 rooms. Saratoga lost many of its famous hotels to postwar razing, but this graceful small town retains an outstanding collection of predominantly Victorian architecture. Saratoga Springs remained very popular with the horse set and culture vultures, but over the past decade or so has welcomed droves of new visitors who discover that this delightful town's elegant, time-honored traditions live on.

VISITOR INFORMATION

Saratoga has one of New York's best-organized tourism information offices. The **Urban Heritage Area Visitors Center,** 297 Broadway (② 518/587-3241), has a wealth of helpful information, on not only Saratoga Springs but much of upstate New York. It also has regional displays, videos, and memorabilia, and offers walking tours in season. From April to November, it's open daily from 9am to 4pm; from December to March, it's open Monday through Saturday from 9am to 4pm. The Saratoga County Chamber of Commerce also operates an **Information Booth** (② 518/584-3255), Broadway at Congress Park, open July and August from 9am to 5pm daily. You can also visit the chamber's website at **www.saratoga.org**. Free area maps are available at both the visitor center and the information booth.

CITY LAYOUT

Saratoga Springs is relatively small and very easy to navigate. Everything revolves around the main axis, Broadway, which is the name for Route 9 once you come into town. Most restaurants and shops are located on the small streets off Broadway (though there are plenty on Broadway, too), such as Phila, Caroline, and Spring streets. Saratoga Spa State Park is just a mile southwest of downtown on Broadway, while Union Avenue, site of grand Victorian homes and the Saratoga Race Course, is a couple of blocks due west of Broadway. Skidmore College is a couple of miles straight up North Broadway.

Moments **Rewards for Early Risers**

Early morning before races is a great time to come out to the track; expert commentary accompanies the thoroughbreds as they go through their morning workouts, and a buffet breakfast is served each racing day on the Clubhouse Porch from 7 to 9:30am.

GETTING AROUND

BY PUBLIC TRANSPORTATION   Most of Saratoga is easily walked, but in summer (late June to Labor Day) a **Saratoga Springs Visitor Trolley** (© 518/584-3255) operates a Broadway loop ($1 round-trip).

BY CAR   Car-rental agencies in and around Saratoga Springs include **Enterprise Rent-A-Car,** 180 S. Broadway (© 518/587-0687); **New Country Saratoga Auto Park,** Route 50 (© 518/584-7272); and **Saratoga Car Rental, Inc.,** 360 Maple Ave. (© 518/583-4448).

BY TAXI   Taxi services include **Saratoga Taxi,** 15 W. Harrison St. (© 518/584-2700); **A Destiny Limousine,** 80 Church Ave., Ballston Spa (© 518/587-5221); and **Saratoga Capitaland Taxi,** 285 Broadway (© 518/583-3131).

EXPLORING SARATOGA SPRINGS

Saratoga is a delight to explore on foot, whether through its plentiful parks and gardens or its historic streets that are graced with fine examples of late-19th and early-20th-century architecture. But exploring Saratoga also means doing what visitors have come to this resort town to do for many decades: see a horse race at the internationally renowned Saratoga Race Course; walk or ski in Saratoga Spa State Park; and take advantage of some of the best summer cultural life any city has to offer. Saratoga Springs may be at its most enjoyable in summer, but the other seasons reveal a pleasant, slower pace.

THE "MANE" ATTRACTIONS 🐎🐎🐎

Saratogians like to say that their town isn't just about horses, but during the race season, everything else definitely takes a back seat to the track. Saratoga's race season lasts 6 weeks, from late July to Labor Day. The Saratoga Race Course, built in 1864, is the oldest thoroughbred track in the nation, acclaimed as perhaps the most beautiful in the country; its fans are legion. If you're in Saratoga during the meet, it's an obligatory visit to join the socialites and the hard-core race fans and bettors. Races are held Wednesday through Monday, with the first race post time at 1pm. **The Saratoga Race Course** (© 518/584-6200), a 350-acre, 1⅛-mile track, is located at 267 Union Ave. General admission is $3 and Clubhouse admission is $5. Reserved seats in the Clubhouse are $8, grandstand $5. For advanced ticket purchase, contact the **New York Racing Association** at © 718/641-4700, or during race season, © 518/584-6200, ext. 360. You can also visit their website, **www.nyra.com/index_saratoga.html,** or call © 800/814-7846 for tickets, schedules, and additional information.

Race fans may also enjoy a bit of harness racing, which you can witness year-round at the **Saratoga Equine Sports Center,** Nelson Avenue (© 518/584-2110). Races generally start at 7:40pm, but see **www.saratogaraceway.com** for the exact schedule. Polo, anyone? From June to September, **Saratoga Polo** organizes matches played at

Downtown Saratoga Springs

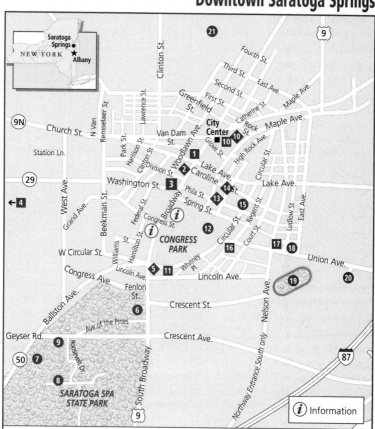

ACCOMMODATIONS ■
Adelphi Hotel **3**
Batcheller Mansion Inn **11**
Circular Manor B&B **16**
The Mansion Inn of Saratoga **4**
Saratoga Arms **1**
The Saratoga Hotel
and Conference Center **10**
Union Gables B&B **17**

DINING ◆
Beverly's **13**
Chez Sophie **10**
Chianti Il Ristorante **5**
Sperry's Restaurant **14**
The Wine Bar **2**

ATTRACTIONS ●
The Children's Museum
at Saratoga **15**
The Gardens at Yaddo **20**
National Museum of Dance
& Hall of Fame **6**
National Museum of Racing
and Hall of Fame **18**
Roosevelt Baths and Spa **8**
Saratoga Automobile Museum **9**
Saratoga Performing Arts Center **7**
Saratoga Race Course **19**
Saratoga Spa State Park **7**
Saratoga Springs History Museum **12**
The Tang Teaching
Museum and Art Gallery **21**

Lodge Field (corner of Crescent and Nelson aves.) and Whitney Field (corner of Bloomfield and Denton roads), usually 4 nights a week at 5:30pm. For more information, call ✆ **518/584-8108.**

MORE TO SEE & DO

The Children's Museum at Saratoga (Kids)
Less a museum than a terrific playground, the space includes adorable areas meant to create a little person's Main Street around 1920: There are a bank, a general store, a diner, a schoolhouse, and a fire station (complete with a sliding pole). Kids will be entertained for at least an hour or two.

69 Caroline St. ✆ 518/584-5540. www.childrensmuseumatsaratoga.org. Admission $5, free for children under 1. July to Labor Day Mon–Sat 9:30am–4:30pm; early Sept to June Tues–Sat 9:30am–4:30pm, Sun noon–4:30pm.

National Museum of Dance & Hall of Fame 🏆 (Kids)
Housed in the old Washington Bath House, a handsome European-style mineral spa built in 1918, this is the only museum in the country dedicated to American professional dance. Its archives, photographs, and exhibits of sets and costumes chronicle a century of dance. The museum is also a place that makes new contributions to the field; on-site are three full-size dance studios modeled after those of the New York City Ballet, which not coincidentally takes up residence in Saratoga Springs every July. Visitors have the opportunity to view rehearsals as well as participate in workshops, classes, and lectures. For children or adults interested in dance, the museum's programs are excellent learning tools. Plan on about a half-hour, unless there are rehearsals or workshops.

99 S. Broadway (Rte. 9). ✆ 518/584-2225. www.dancemuseum.org. Admission $6.50 adults, $5 seniors and students, $3 children under 12. Apr–Oct Tues–Sun 10am–5pm; Nov–Mar Sat–Sun 10am–5pm.

National Museum of Racing and Hall of Fame (Kids)
Across the road from the famous Saratoga Race Course, this midsize museum pays tribute to 3 centuries of thoroughbred racing in the U.S. Trophies, memorabilia, artwork, and film tell the story of the sport that grips the attention of so many in Saratoga during summer race season. The Hall of Fame celebrates the greatest names, both jockeys and horses, in the sport's history. Uniforms and artifacts are on display, and interactive screens allow visitors to relive great moments in racing. The museum is mostly for true fans, though even those without much interest in horse racing can pick up some interesting tidbits (including facts that kids are likely to enjoy and ponder). For example, did you know that the average racehorse weighs 1,000 pounds? And whereas a Ferrari can go from zero to 60 mph in 5.5 seconds, a racehorse can accelerate to 42 mph in just 2.5 seconds. The museum is unlikely to detain you for more than 45 minutes.

191 Union Ave. ✆ 800/562-5394 or 518/584-0400. www.racingmuseum.org. Admission $7 adults, $5 seniors and students, free for children under 5. Mon–Sat 10am–4pm; Sun noon–4pm (during the Saratoga racing meet, the museum is open daily 9am–5pm).

Saratoga Automobile Museum 🏆 (Kids)
Housed in an old bottling plant in the middle of Saratoga Spa State Park, this surprising museum will delight car lovers. On view are some interesting classic automobiles representing the once-vital New York State auto industry, such as Charles A. Lindbergh's 1928 Franklin, made in Syracuse, and an extraordinary 1931 Pierce Arrow, manufactured in Buffalo. The top floor is devoted to race cars, and there are curiosities like the 1957 BMW Isetta 300, called the "Rolling Egg." Kids into cars will love the tables set up with pads of paper and crayons and an invitation to draw and display their "dream car." A spin through the museum should take about 45 minutes.

110 Ave. of the Pines (Saratoga Spa State Park). ℂ **518/587-1935**. www.saratogaautomuseum.org. Admission $8 adults, $5 seniors, $3.50 children 6–16, free for children 5 and under. May–Oct daily 10am–5pm; Nov–Apr Tues–Sun 10am–5pm.

Saratoga National Historical Park ★

Saratoga was no less than the turning point in the American Revolution. In 1777 American troops defeated the British army—considered to be one of the most significant military victories in history—and forced its surrender on October 17, prompting France to recognize American independence and sign on as its ally. Today, this historical area is a national park, which comprises the 4-square-mile battlefield in Stillwater, the General Philip Schuyler House, and the Saratoga Monument in the nearby village of Victory. A 9½-mile battlefield tour road traces American defensive positions, battle sites, and British defensive positions, with a series of 10 interpretive stops along the way. Also on the grounds is the 4-mile Wilkinson Trail for hiking and cross-country skiing. Living-history demonstrations are presented in summer months.

The Schuyler House, located 8 miles north in Schuylerville, was the residence of General Philip Schuyler. Burned by the British, the present reconstruction was built after the American victory. The Saratoga Monument is a 155-foot memorial that marks Burgoyne's surrender. Plan on several hours if you go to all the sites.

648 Rte. 32 (at Rte. 4), Stillwater (15 miles southeast of Saratoga Springs). ℂ **518/664-9821**. www.nps.gov/sara. Admission $5 private vehicle, $3 individual (on foot, bike, or horse) or by National Parks Pass or Golden Pass (see p. 64 and p. 42 for details). Visitor center year-round daily 9am–5pm; Tour Road Apr 1 to mid-Nov daily 9am–7pm; The Schuyler House, Memorial Day to Labor Day, guided tours Wed–Sun 9:30am–4:30pm.

Saratoga Spa State Park ★ Kids

Saratoga Springs rose to prominence in the mid–19th century as a spa town, on the strengths of mineral springs and baths that drew wealthy patrons to exercise and "take the waters." Now a National Historic Landmark—and certainly one of the prettiest urban parks in the country—Saratoga Spa State Park is still a relaxing place to escape from daily pressures. The 2,200-acre park is a pine forest with natural geysers; it's home to a swimming pool complex, two golf courses, endless trails for walking and cross-country skiing in winter, picnic pavilions, a skating rink, tennis courts, and two restored bathhouses, designed in the classical European spa tradition. Also tucked into the park are a large historic hotel, three restaurants, the renowned Saratoga Performing Arts Center, and two small museums. You could easily spend all day in the park, depending on the diversions you choose. Special events, great for families, include the wildflower walk spring tour and trail races.

19 Roosevelt Dr. ℂ **518/584-2535**. www.saratogaspastatepark.org. Admission charged for some activities. Year-round dawn–dusk.

Saratoga Springs History Museum

In its heyday in the late 19th century, Saratoga was the elegant refuge of high-society high rollers. The Canfield Casino, built in 1870 in Congress Park, is a stately red-brick Victorian that today is home only to the ghosts of gamblers past and a museum and historical collection that chronicles Saratoga Springs' era as a resort known the world over. The original casino was built by John Morrissey, a heavyweight champion boxer turned entrepreneur, and later made over in haute style by a wealthy gambler, Richard Canfield, at the turn of the 20th century. Canfield's lavish decor included marble tables, massive mirrors, grand chandeliers, and the world's largest seamless rug. In the casino's parlors, Amelia Earhart was feted and grand balls and teas attracted the Gilded Age's fabulous wealthy.

Finds Hyde Collection Art Museum

Saratoga Springs' charms can make the resort town difficult to leave, but art fans may be pried loose by the presence of a splendid collection of old and modern masters just 20 minutes north of town in Glens Falls. The **Hyde Collection Art Museum** *Finds*, housed in a gorgeous renovated mansion, is reminiscent of New York City's Frick Collection in its breadth and beautiful setting. Among the treasures assembled in the 1912, neo-Renaissance Florentine-style villa are works by Raphael, Da Vinci, Van Dyck, Tiepolo, El Greco, Rubens, Tintoretto, Homer, Whistler, Turner, Degas, Seurat, Renoir, Picasso, and Van Gogh. The most remarkable works are Rembrandt's unusual *Portrait of Christ* (1655–57), purchased from the Russian government in 1934, and Botticelli's small *Annunciation* (1492), the first piece collected by the Hydes. Louis and Charlotte Hyde were a wealthy industrialist couple who began collecting European art in the 1920s; their mansion is furnished as they maintained it, with French and Italian 17th- and 18th-century pieces and massive tropical plants in the sky-lit central courtyard. A new wing hosts temporary exhibits and a gift shop. You'll need at least an hour here. The museum is located about 8 miles north of Saratoga Springs at 16 Warren St. in Glens Falls (© **518/792-1761**; www.hydeartmuseum.org). Admission is free, but donations are accepted. It's open Tuesday through Saturday from 10am to 5pm; and Sunday from noon to 5pm. Docent-led tours daily from 1 to 4pm.

The Historical Society's exhibitions of photography depict Saratoga Springs in all its splendor, and on the second floor is a re-creation of the high-stakes room and parlors with an original collection of handcrafted John Henry Belter furnishings. On the top floor, eight rooms re-create Pine Grove, the prominent Walworth family's Victorian home that was demolished in the 1950s. Allow about an hour to tour the museum.

Congress Park (off Broadway). © **518/584-6920**. www.saratogasprings-historymuseum.org. Admission $5 adults, $4 seniors, $3 children 12–17, free for children under 12. Memorial Day to Labor Day daily 10am–4pm; winter Wed–Sat 10am–4pm, Sun 1–4pm. Free guided casino tours, summer Tues 1pm and Wed–Thurs 11am.

The Tang Teaching Museum and Art Gallery *Finds*   The first art museum in Saratoga Springs, on the campus of Skidmore College, The Tang is most notable for its striking modern architecture. A visit here is a must for any fan of modern architecture. The stunning building in stone, concrete, and stainless steel by Antoine Predock slopes gently out of the ground and is surrounded by white pines, tucked neatly into the landscape; two large exterior staircases ascend and effectively create a short cut across campus that goes over the top of the building. The irregularly shaped galleries inside the 39,000-foot museum host often challenging contemporary art and cross-disciplinary exhibits focusing on fields like music and physics (highlighting its role as a teaching institution). Allow about an hour to explore.

815 N. Broadway. © **518/580-8080**. http://tang.skidmore.edu. Free admission (suggested donation). Tues–Wed and Fri 10am–5pm; Thurs 10am–9pm; Sat–Sun noon–5pm.

ESPECIALLY FOR KIDS

Saratoga Springs is a nice and relaxed place for families, with plenty of parks and sights that should entertain children of all ages. Most kids would love to attend a thorough-bred horse race at the **Saratoga Race Course,** one of the most famous and beautiful tracks in the world (p. 260). There are great features for kids at the track, including free walking tours of the stable area, a tram ride, and a starting gate demonstration. An interactive exhibit, the Discovery Paddock, teaches children how horses and jock-eys prepare for races, and kids can even ride the "Equipony" and dress up like a jockey, "weigh in" on a scale, and hammer a shoe on a mock-horse hoof. Open every racing day from 8am to 9am in season.

The **Saratoga Children's Museum,** with its cute play areas, is a no-brainer for tots, and the **Saratoga Automobile Museum** (p. 262) is also a fun outing. Older children, especially those budding ballerinas, will enjoy the **National Museum of Dance & Hall of Fame. Saratoga Spa State Park** is a delightful urban park with miles of hik-ing trails, two swimming pools, and a skating rink, fun in any season. The Urban Her-itage Area Visitors Center publishes a brochure called *Things to Do with Kids!*

ORGANIZED TOURS

Saratoga Race Course, Union Avenue (© **518/584-6200;** www.nyra.com), offers free walking tours of the stable area and a tram ride and starting gate demonstration daily from 8am to 9am in season. The **Upper Hudson River Railroad,** 3 Railroad Place, North Creek (© **518/251-5334**), is a scenic passenger-train ride that departs

Saratoga's Spas & Springs

Native Americans believed the waters of Saratoga Springs had natural thera-peutic properties, and so did early Americans such as George Washington and Alexander Hamilton. Saratoga Springs became a famous spa town in the 19th century, and was known as "Queen of the Spas," with hotels host-ing visitors seeking the local mineral waters for drinking and mineral baths. A geological fault line runs through Saratoga Springs and a solid layer of shale produces naturally carbonated waters from deep limestone beds. Saratoga Springs' heritage as a mineral spa resort town lives on, if on a smaller scale. **Roosevelt Baths and Spa,** 39 Roosevelt Dr., in Saratoga Spa State Park (© **518/226-4790;** www.gideonputnam.com), makes the most of the town's heritage with a full-service spa in one of the old classic spa build-ings, built in 1935. Charmingly low-tech and reminiscent of old-world Euro-pean spas, it even retains old steam cubicles and instruments. Services include mineral baths, massages, reflexology, body wraps, and hot stone therapy. More modern is **The Crystal Spa,** 120 S. Broadway (© **518/584-2556;** www.thecrystalspa.com), also offering clay and mud wraps, facials, and "pamper packages." Credit cards are not accepted.

You can also take a **self-guided tour** of Saratoga's mineral springs. There are 16 spots in and around the city, in Congress Park, Saratoga Spa State Park, and High Rock Park. Pick up the tour brochure *Tasting Tour of Saratoga's Springs* at the Saratoga Springs Visitor Center.

Architectural Tours

Saratoga Springs is awash in splendid examples of Victorian and other diverse styles of architecture, from Queen Anne and Colonial Revival to early Federal, Greek Revival, and English Gothic. To get a feel for the array of styles, simply stroll down Union Avenue, Circular Street, and others in the historic district, or take a more systematic approach by following the self-guided walking tours laid out in brochures of Saratoga's Historic West and East Sides, available at the visitor center. Each highlights about two dozen buildings in a manageable walking area.

The small town **Ballston Spa**, about 5 miles south of Saratoga Springs off Church Avenue (Rte. 50), is a Victorian village with about 20 or so notable houses and churches. Pamphlets for self-guided tours of Ballston Spa are also available at the visitor center.

from the North Creek depot and runs along the Hudson into the Adirondacks (May–Oct; $14 adults, $13 seniors, $9 children 3–11). For guided hiking, cycling, rock climbing, and snowshoeing adventures, as well as equipment rentals, contact **All Outdoors,** 35 Van Dam St. (© **518/587-0455**).

OUTDOOR PURSUITS

For additional information on outdoor activities in Saratoga Springs, consult the website **www.saratoga.org** and click on "Things to Do."

BIKING, IN-LINE SKATING & JOGGING   The 2,200-acre Saratoga Spa State Park is by far the best place in town, with tons of trails in a gorgeous park just minutes from downtown—in fact, within walking or jogging distance.

BOATING & FISHING   Saratoga Lake, on the outskirts of town, is the place for boating and fishing enthusiasts. **Lake Lonely Boat Livery,** 378 Crescent Ave., Saratoga Springs (© **518/587-1721**), has a tackle shop and rowboat and canoe rentals; there are largemouth bass, northern pike, and panfish in the lake. **Point Breeze Marina,** 1459 Rte. 9P, Saratoga Lake (© **518/587-3397**), is the largest marina in town and rents boats, canoes, and pontoons. **Saratoga Boatworks,** 549 Union Ave., Route 9P, Saratoga Lake (© **518/584-2628**), rents ski boats, pontoons, and fishing boats. **Saratoga Rowing Center,** 251 County Rte. 67, Saratoga Springs (© **518/584-7844**), is a sports shop dedicated solely to rowing, with rentals and instruction.

GARDENS   Garden and horticultural enthusiasts should visit **The Gardens at Yaddo,** handsome turn-of-the-20th-century gardens and a working artists' community created by a philanthropist couple. A Rose Garden with a fountain, terraces, and a pergola was inspired by Italian Renaissance gardens, while the Rock Garden features ponds and fountains. The Yaddo Gardens, on Union Avenue (near exit 14 of I-87), are open to the public free of charge, with guided tours on weekends at 11am, from mid-June to Labor Day and also Tuesday during racing season. **Congress Park,** off Broadway, was developed beginning in 1826; it has nature walks and ponds, and a wealth of tree species; the visitor center even publishes a free guide for easy identification. **Saratoga**

Spa State Park comprises 2,200 acres of woodlands and trails featuring naturally carbonated mineral springs.

GOLF   Saratoga Lake Golf Club, 35 Grace Moore Rd. (off Lake Rd.), Saratoga Springs (© **518/581-6616;** www.saratogalakegolf.com), is a public 18-hole course, opened in 2001 on 200 acres near the lake. Greens fees are $18 to $32. **Saratoga Spa Championship & Executive Golf,** 60 Roosevelt Dr. (© **518/584-2006;** www.saratogaspagolf.com), is an 18-hole course in the pine forests of Saratoga Spa State Park. Greens fees are $17 to $29. **Saratoga National Golf Club** ⟨★★, 458 Union Ave., Saratoga Springs (© **518/583-4653;** www.golfsaratoga.com), sits on 400 acres of rolling hills in wetlands within pitching range of the Race Course and gets all kinds of accolades. It was named Golf Course of the Year (2005) by the National Golf Course Owners Association, named the no. 2 ranked Best Public Access Course in New York by *Golfweek,* and ranked no. 5 among "Best New Upscale Public Courses in the U.S." in 2001 by *Golf Digest.* You'll pay for the privilege of playing at a noteworthy course, of course: Greens fees are $85 to $175.

HORSE RACING   see "The 'Mane' Attractions," earlier in this chapter.

TENNIS   Use of the eight hard-court and clay tennis courts in Saratoga Spa State Park is free to park visitors.

WINTER SPORTS   Saratoga Spa State Park (© **518/584-2535;** www.saratogaspastatepark.org) is the place for ice-skating, snowshoeing, and cross-country skiing, with several miles of groomed and ungroomed trails for the latter two sports. Winter-use trail maps are available at the Park Office.

SHOPPING

Until recently, Saratoga Springs had no national chain stores in its historic downtown. Today, inevitably, local independent shops mingle with a small number of chains, such as the Gap, Eddie Bauer, and Banana Republic. In the heart of downtown, there are also about a half-dozen antiques dealers, mostly on Broadway and Regent Street, including **Forty Caroline Antiques,** 454 Broadway, in the Downstreet Marketplace (© **518/424-4201**), and **Regent Street Antique Center,** 153 Regent St. (© **518/584-0107**), with 30 dealers under its historic roof. A good antiquarian bookseller is **Lyrical Ballad Bookstore,** 7–9 Phila St. (© **518/584-8779**), and a popular antiques shop is **Saratoga Collectible Closet,** 474 Maple Ave. (5 min. north of Saratoga on Route 9; © **518/682-2002**). Jewelry, clothing, home furnishings and accessories, and gift shops line Broadway and dot other streets in historic downtown Saratoga Springs. A particularly interesting shop, specializing in contemporary American glass, is **Symmetry Gallery,** 348 Broadway (© **518/584-5090**). Check out **deJonghe Original Jewelry,** 470 Broadway (© **518/587-6422**), for, well, it's all in the name.

SARATOGA'S FARMS

The Saratoga area is blessed with a surfeit of farms, including dairy and horse farms, orchards, and farm stands. **Saratoga Farmers' Market,** 110 Spring St. (© **518/638-8530**), is located in High Rock Park and open May to October, Wednesday 3 to 6pm and Saturday 9am to 1pm. **Saratoga Apple,** 1174 Rte. 29, Schuylerville (© **518/695-3131**), is a year-round farmers' market and pick-your-own apple orchard with wagon rides in autumn. **Weber's Farm,** 115 King Rd., Saratoga Springs, has a pick-your-own vegetable operation from May to December. **Hanehan's Pumpkins,** 223 County Rte. 67, Saratoga Springs, is a farmstand that sells pumpkins, squash, and corn in season.

Clark Dahlia Garden & Greenhouses, 139 Hop City Rd., Ballston Spa (© 518/ 885-7356), has homemade jams, seasonal produce, and fruit and flowers. **Bliss Glad Farm,** 129 Hop City Rd., Ballston Spa (© 518/885-9314), specializes in gladiolus bulbs and has cut flowers and perennials. There are many others in easy reach of Saratoga Springs; pick up a brochure of Saratoga farms at the visitor center.

WHERE TO STAY

Many of the city's most charming Victorian homes have been converted into welcoming bed-and-breakfast inns, making Saratoga a great place for those who prefer staying in a character-filled old house rather than a generic hotel. Hotel rates rise meteorically (doubling or even tripling) when most in demand during racing season. But they also climb considerably during Skidmore College's graduation in May, the Jazz Festival in late June, and other special events, when many hotels and inns require at least 2-night stays. In general, weekend rates are higher than midweek rates; be sure to confirm rates when booking. In addition, not all hotels and inns are open year-round. For race season, depending on the type of accommodations you want, I'd recommend booking 6 months to 1 year in advance. The Saratoga Chamber of Commerce and the visitor center (see "Visitor Information," earlier in this chapter) can help with reservations in high season; their website, **www.saratoga.org**, may be useful for finding additional hotels. Also, see "More Places to Stay," below.

EXPENSIVE

Batcheller Mansion Inn   This fanciful, fairy tale Victorian castle, built in 1873, is extraordinary from the outside. A riot of turrets and minarets, it looks like something hatched from the fertile imagination of Walt Disney or Antoni Gaudí. Inside, the grand home—the first to be patented in the U.S.—is quirky and rambling, with loads of interesting parlors and Victorian furnishings. That said, some of the accommodations are a bit disappointing, with heavy executive-style desks and older-style furnishings that aren't quite period or as nice as the common rooms. The raspberry-colored Trask Room, though, has its own grand balcony, and the Brady Room, for those of you looking for something out of the ordinary, has a regulation-size pool table within the room, as well as a massive Jacuzzi tub.

20 Circular St. (at Whitney), Saratoga Springs, NY 12866. © 800/616-7012 or 518/584-7012. Fax 518/581-7746. www.batchellermansioninn.com. 9 units. Nov to Mar Sun–Thurs $120–$200, Fri–Sat $150–$235 double; Apr–Oct Sun–Thurs $135–$230, Fri–Sat $180–$295 double; racing season $285–$410 double. Rates include breakfast. 2-night minimum stay on weekends. AE, MC, V. Free parking. *In room:* A/C.

Saratoga Arms 🏵🏵   Perfectly situated on the main drag in the heart of the historic district, this family-owned small hotel is like a grown-up B&B, elegant but very relaxed. A one-time boardinghouse converted to a luxury inn in 1999, it's in a beautiful 1870 "Second Empire" red-brick building with a terrific wraparound porch; from its antique wicker chairs, you can watch the world go by. Rooms are a good size and nicely appointed, with period antiques, handsome ornamental molding, and nice details like luxury robes and towels. Several rooms have electric fireplaces, and a number have claw-foot bathtubs. Prices vary according to season, as well as bed and room types; the highest prices are for rooms with king beds, fireplaces, and whirlpool tubs.

495–497 Broadway, Saratoga Springs, NY 12866. © 518/587-1775. Fax 518/581-4064. www.saratogaarms.com. 31 units. $175–$475 double; suite $325–$595. Rates include breakfast. AE, DC, DISC, MC, V. Free parking. *In room:* A/C, TV, dataport, minibar, hair dryer, CD player.

The Saratoga Hotel & Conference Center ★★ A massive lodging right on Broadway downtown, this revamped and remodeled business hotel presents something no others do in Saratoga: chic, modern, and luxurious rooms with all the big-city amenities. Anyone living in fear of Saratoga's perhaps overused Victorian decor should make a beeline here. Rooms are spacious and uncluttered, decorated with warm, soothing colors. An added bonus is that Saratoga's finest restaurant, Sophie's Bistro, moved to new digs here in 2006. Check online for specials, packages, and getaway deals, as low as $99 per night (and a racing-season package beginning at $230 a night).

354 Broadway, Saratoga Springs, NY 12866. ⓒ 866/937-7746 or 518/584-4000. Fax 518/584-7430. www.thesaratoga hotel.com. 240 units. $199–$329 double, $239–$529 suite; race season $429 double, $529 suite. AE, DC, DISC, MC, V. **Amenities:** Restaurant; indoor swimming pool; fitness center; concierge. *In room:* A/C, TV, Wi-Fi.

MODERATE

Adelphi Hotel ★★★ In a world of increasingly homogenized hotels, it's a treat to discover the Adelphi, an eclectic and eccentric midsize hotel that wears its exuberant personality on its sleeve. Behind a brown-and-yellow 1877 brick facade is one of the funkier places you're likely to stay, with just the right touch of high Victorian decadence. The Adelphi survived the demolitions of most of Saratoga Springs' great old hotels from the town's tourism heyday, and this classic hotel has undergone a recent renovation to again take its place as one of the coolest spots in town (though the lobby, with no air-conditioning, can get pretty hot in the summer). Its atmosphere is born of interesting old-world touches and Victorian clutter. Period antiques, old engravings and photographs, lacy curtains, and charming print wallpaper adorn rooms, which are all uniquely decorated; styles range from English country house, French provincial, and high Victorian to Adirondack, Arts and Crafts, and folk art. Yet it all works (visit the website for a smorgasbord of Quick-Time tours of the varied room styles). The second-floor piazza is ideal for people-watching, outfitted with antique wicker and Adirondack furniture, and there's a charming pool with leafy landscaping and a lovely pergola out back. Closed in winter.

365 Broadway, Saratoga Springs, NY 12866. ⓒ 518/587-4688. Fax 518/587-0851. www.adelphihotel.com. 39 units. May–July and Sept–Oct weekdays $125–$165 double, $200–$220 suite; May–June and Sept–Oct weekends $150–$190 double, $220–$250 suite; July weekends, Jazz Fest, and Skidmore week $180–$220 double, $275–$295 suite; race meet weekdays $235–$310 double, $375–$400 suite; race meet weekends $270–$390, $475–$510 suite. Rates include continental breakfast. Some weekends 2-night minimum stay; during race weekends 3-night minimum stay. AE, DC, DISC, MC, V. Free parking. **Amenities:** 2 cafes; outdoor swimming pool. *In room:* A/C, TV.

Circular Manor B&B ★★ *Finds* A warm and stately 1903 Colonial Revival, on a quiet street in the historic district within walking distance of both downtown and the Race Course, this small B&B owned by Dieter and Michele Funicello is gracious and friendly. The large and marvelously restored home has Victorian flourishes, including a welcoming Queen Anne circular porch and quartersawn oak staircase banisters, floors, and pocket doors. All the rooms are handsomely decorated; most bathrooms have marble floors and antique fixtures, including claw-foot tubs and Deco sinks. The sun-filled Hydrangea Suite, with a sitting room and French doors, is one of the better rooms you'll find at a B&B. Breakfast is a gourmet repast. Open mid-May to mid-October only.

120 Circular St., Saratoga Springs, NY 12866. ⓒ 518/585-6593. www.circularmanor.com. 5 units. $160–$240 double; racing season $260–$340 double. Rates include full breakfast. MC, V. Free parking on street. *In room:* A/C.

The Mansion Inn of Saratoga ★★★ *Value* Seven miles west of downtown Saratoga Springs is one of the finest places to stay in the area, a magnificently restored 1866 Victorian on 4 acres. The period details in the house—impressively carved wood

More Places to Stay

Reflecting its past as a prime resort town, Saratoga Springs has a surfeit of hotels, motels, and, especially, inns for a small town (many more are located within 10 miles). In prime horse-racing and culture season, July and August, even though prices rise (nearly doubling at some spots), places can really fill up. Try one of the following hotels and inns, or contact the **Saratoga Chamber of Commerce** (28 Clinton St.; © **518/584-3255**; www.saratoga.org) for a list of available accommodations.

Brunswick B&B (143 Union Ave.; © **800/585-6751** or 518/584-6741; www.brunswickbb.com; 12 units; $109–$169 double, higher during racing season), an attractive and comfortable 1886 Victorian Gothic home.

Hilton Garden Inn (125 S. Broadway; © **800/445-8667** or 518/587-1500; www.saratogasprings.gardeninn.com; 112 units; $119–$329 double), a well-placed standard hotel with high-speed Internet access.

Holiday Inn (232 Broadway; © **800/465-4329** or 518/584-4550; www.spa-hi.com; 168 units; $149–$195 double, racing season $279–$319 double), very large but conveniently located and with new indoor and outdoor pools; pet-friendly.

The Inn at Saratoga (231 Broadway; © **800/274-3573** or 518/583-1890; www.theinnatsaratoga.com; 42 units; $119–$193 double, $294–$349 double during racing season), the oldest operating hotel in Saratoga, today a modern hotel with frilly rooms, housed in an 1880 Victorian right on the main drag (Broadway).

Lewis House B&B (38 E. High St., in Ballston Spa, 5 miles south of Saratoga Springs; © **518/884-9857**; www.lewishouse.com; 6 units; $95–$125 double, racing season $150–$250 double), an Italianate Victorian dating from 1865.

Longfellows Inn & Restaurant (500 Union Ave., Rte. 9P S.; © **518/587-0108**; www.longfellows.com; 50 units; $135–$495 double), a large, modern place a few miles east of downtown that occupies a converted 1915 dairy barn.

Six Sisters B&B (149 Union Ave.; © **518/583-1173**; www.sixsistersbandb.com; 8 units; $80–$175 double, $285–$400 during racing season), an 1880 Victorian across from the Race Course. Its handsome porch sits under a striped awning, and some rooms have private balconies.

and marble mantelpieces, a Tiffany chandelier, etched-glass doors, and a gracious parlor with a grand piano—make this a very romantic and sophisticated place for a luxury getaway. Each unique room is sumptuously decorated with bold colors and inviting large beds dressed with top-of-the-line linens. The gourmet breakfast is taken in the handsome dining room in front of a massive fireplace. In the early evening, wine and cocktails are served in the parlor. The owners have done a remarkable job of renovating the inn in a very short time, and they have big plans for the place, including the addition of a terrace off the porch for sipping cocktails and a renovation of the barn for cabaret performances or other functions. Given the level of luxury in the rooms and general pampering, room rates are very reasonable. Open year-round.

801 Rte. 29, Rock City Falls, NY 12863. ℂ 888/996-9977 or 518/885-1607. www.themansionsaratoga.com. 10 units. May–Oct (excluding racing season) $135–$160 double, $200–$225 suite; racing season $240–$285 double, $300–$325 suite; Nov–Apr $125–$150 double, $160–$180 suite. Rates include breakfast. See website for special packages. AE, DISC, MC, V. Free parking. *In room:* A/C, TV.

Union Gables B&B ⊛ *Value*   A spectacularly rambling, 1901 Queen Anne Victorian—marked by distinctive turrets and gables—this pet-friendly B&B is lived in and not too perfect or fussy. For the most part, rooms are quite large, and they're named for the siblings of two families. The rooms facing Union Avenue are the best; "Linda" is full of pastel pinks and light green, while "Annie" is huge and very light, decorated in lilac and purple. "Bruce," a more masculine room, has a peaked attic ceiling. The handsome common areas include a massive wraparound porch and large living room. Unusual for a B&B, there are plenty of body-conscious amenities, including a tennis court, exercise room, and outdoor hot tub.

55 Union Ave., Saratoga Springs, NY 12866. ℂ 800/398-1558 or 518/584-1558. Fax 518/583-0649. www.uniongables. com. 10 units. Nov–Apr $140–$210 double; May–Oct $160–$235 double; racing season $360–$410 double. Rates include breakfast. AE, MC, V. Free parking. **Amenities:** Tennis court; exercise room; outdoor hot tub. *In room:* A/C, TV.

CAMPGROUNDS

Whispering Pines Campsites & RV Park, 560 Sand Hill Rd., Greenfield Center (ℂ 518/893-0416; www.saratogacamping.com), is 8 miles northwest of Saratoga Springs and set on 75 acres of pines with a new outdoor pool and restroom facility.

WHERE TO DINE

Saratoga Springs has a very nice little roster of fine dining and laid-back eateries, with something to appeal to picky gourmands and fussy families. Like the majority of inns, almost all are independently and locally owned, and most are within easy walking distance of the main drag downtown.

EXPENSIVE

Chez Sophie ⊛⊛⊛ *Value* FRENCH BISTRO   Now in a new location downtown, within the stylish Saratoga Hotel (the restaurant used to be out of town, in a 1950s stainless-steel diner), this insiders' favorite continues to serve simple but sophisticated French bistro fare. The young chef is the son of Sophie, who began her eponymous restaurant up this way in 1969; now Paul and his wife, Cheryl, continue the tradition but have added some new wrinkles—not the least of which is the chic modern ambience of the new location. The menu is creative without being fussy, focusing on fresh ingredients and the best organic produce, meats, and fish from local suppliers. The menu changes frequently, but mains have included a yummy roast pork loin with honeybell gastrique and black currant, and veal scaloppine with cream and lemon (a Sophie's specialty since 1969). There's a superb, expertly chosen and almost entirely French wine list, with several moderately priced bottles and a surprisingly well-chosen beer list (featuring 40 Belgian beers). In "honor of the restaurant's diner heritage," it offers a terrific midweek (Mon–Thurs) bargain, the Pink Plate Special, a prix-fixe, three-course meal for $30. Breakfast is now served daily, and brunch is served on Sundays, accompanied by a jazz pianist.

534 Broadway. ℂ 518/583-3538. Reservations recommended. Main courses $28–$38. Pink Plate Special prix-fixe (Mon–Thurs) $30. AE, DC, MC, V. Daily 7–10am and 5–10pm; Mon–Fri 11:30am–2pm. Sun brunch 7am–2pm.

MODERATE

Chianti Il Ristorante ⊛⊛⊛ *Value* NORTHERN ITALIAN   Ask Saratogians for their favorite restaurant in town and they're almost sure to tell you Chianti. Charmingly

Mediterranean, with deep-red curtains, flickering candlelight, an open kitchen, a main dining room lined with racks of wine bottles, and a warm and inviting Italian host (the owner, who greets you at the door), the restaurant sets the stage for a delightful meal. And the kitchen doesn't disappoint, with items such as porcini risotto in a light cream sauce, *filetto al Gorgonzola* (beef filet prepared with Gorgonzola cheese), dry-aged filet mignon, and grilled homemade sausage. There are also many good-value pastas such as *costa ligure* (linguine with scampi, olives, and capers in a spicy tomato sauce), and the salads are huge and excellently prepared (the *misticanza toscano* is a winner, with mixed greens, Tuscan white beans, Gorgonzola, walnuts, and roasted tomatoes). The extensive and impressive wine list includes many well-chosen Brunellos and Super Tuscans, but not too many at the lower end. You'd never know it, but Chianti is in a former Long John Silver's fast-food restaurant; talk about a transformation!

208 S. Broadway. © 518/580-0025. Reservations recommended. Main courses $14–$29. AE, MC, V. Daily 5:30–11pm.

Sperry's Restaurant (Value) AMERICAN BISTRO   Sperry's, known for its grilled seafood and crab cakes, is a dependable local favorite that's been around since the '30s, and it rarely disappoints. It's an attractive bistro with black-and-white tile floors, a few high-backed booths, and a welcoming bar on one of Saratoga Springs' cutest streets. The restaurant has a long list of daily specials, with entrees such as chicken Dijon, 14-ounce steak au poivre, and Maryland crab cakes; lunch specialties include jambalaya and a Cuban sandwich. There's outdoor seating on the back patio.

30½ Caroline St. © 518/584-9618. Reservations recommended on weekends for dinner. Main courses $13–$25. AE, MC, V. Mon–Sat 11:30am–3pm; daily 5:30–10pm.

The Wine Bar ✪ CREATIVE AMERICAN   With more than 50 wines by the glass and a ventilated smoking lounge where cigars are welcomed, this is the joint for would-be high rollers to celebrate their winnings at the track (or drown their sorrows in a good glass of wine and a nice meal). Trendy but moderately priced, with an upstairs bar and attractively modern and clean decor, it features a menu that will appeal to both wine-and-cigar guys and fashionable sorts. Dishes are available in both small-plate (tapas) and entree portions, and they change seasonally; among recent offerings were lobster poached in truffle butter with roasted beet and citrus salad; rare ahi crusted with Asian spices and served with a calamari stir-fry; and a beef filet with braised vegetables, forest mushrooms, and a foie gras demisauce. For dessert, the best idea is a good dessert wine and one of the many cheese plates. The select wine list changes on a weekly basis. On Friday and Saturday nights, there's live piano music.

417 Broadway. © 518/584-8777. Reservations recommended. Main courses $17–$23. AE, MC, V. Sept–June Tues–Sat 4–10pm; July–Aug Tues–Sun 4–10pm.

INEXPENSIVE

Beverly's ✪ (Value) BREAKFAST/CREATIVE AMERICAN   This small, slender cafe should be your first stop in the morning if your hotel doesn't include breakfast. The morning menu is extraordinary, with both creative dishes and traditional fresh-baked comfort foods and great coffee. The standard menu includes baguette French toast, eggs Benedict, and pancakes with a touch of wheat germ. Daily breakfast specials include whimsical dishes like poached eggs on roasted eggplant with dill hollandaise, or banana-and-walnut pancakes. Beverly's is also open for lunch, which might be a chicken teriyaki salad, grilled chicken breast with roasted peppers and pesto, or the quiche of the day.

47 Phila St. © 518/583-2755. Reservations not accepted. Main courses $3.75–$9.95. AE, MC, V. Daily 7am–3pm.

SARATOGA SPRINGS AFTER DARK

The **Saratoga Performing Arts Center** ✿✿✿, or SPAC, is in a class by itself. From June to September, this is *the* place to be in Saratoga Springs (after you've already been to the Race Course, of course) to see the amazing roster of high-culture talent that takes up summer residence, including the New York City Ballet and the Philadelphia Orchestra. SPAC is also the host of the Saratoga Chamber Music Festival, Freihofer's Jazz Festival in late June (with top-flight jazz talent, 26 years and counting), the Lake George Opera, and the 3-day Saratoga Wine & Food Festival. Set within the Saratoga Spa State Park grounds, perfect for walks and picnics, the center has a sheltered amphitheater and an intimate Spa Little Theatre. The box office opens May 11, but preseason discounts are available (up to 50% off ticket prices). Other discounts are SPACWIRE Internet specials and season lawn passes. Call ✆ **518/587-3330** or check the website, **www.spac.org**, for schedules and tickets.

Lake George Opera is celebrating a decade of performances, including "The Barber of Seville" and "La Bohème" in the Spa Little Theatre in the Saratoga Performing Arts Complex, 480 Broadway, Suite 336. For current schedule information, visit their website at www.lakegeorgeopera.org or call ✆ **518/584-6018** for tickets.

Caffé Lena, 47 Phila St. (✆ **518/583-0022**), is a legendary upstairs folk-music coffeehouse that's a little tattered but still reeks of all the folkies that have played here since 1960. There's mostly live acoustic music (and some blues, jazz, and poetry) Thursday to Sunday nights, and some relatively big names, like Tish Hinojosa, still drop by. Reservations are recommended; covers are generally $10 to $15. **9 Maple Avenue,** named for its address (✆ 518/583-CLUB), features live jazz on Friday and Saturday nights, as well as a huge selection of single-malt scotches and a martini menu. The **Tin & Lint,** 2 Caroline St. (✆ **518/587-5897**), is a pub popular with Skidmore students; it's where Don McLean, a former waiter, wrote the '70s pop anthem "American Pie" on a cocktail napkin. **Luna Lounge,** 17 Maple Ave. (✆ **518/583-6955**), is a flashy late-night lounge and dance club with an industrial look of brushed-steel and copper walls, owned by the proprietor of the more sedate Chianti Il Ristorante. It's open 10pm to 4am on Friday and Saturday nights. **The Wine Bar** ✿, 417 Broadway (✆ **518/584-8777**), has a cigar lounge, an upstairs bar, loads of wine by the glass, and live piano music on weekends. (See review above.) The local movie theater, **Saratoga Film Forum,** 320 Broadway (✆ **518/584-FILM**), shows first-run films. For a romantic end to the evening (or a nice afternoon activity), **Saratoga Horse & Carriage Company** (✆ **518/584-8820**) provides horse-drawn carriage rides through Saratoga Springs. For contracted private rides, they'll pick you up at your hotel or inn in Saratoga.

3 Albany

The local author William Kennedy famously chronicled the state capital with his cycle of Albany novels, including *Legs* and *Ironweed,* which summoned not only the politics and grime of the city, but also its ghosts. Kennedy's depiction was of a city that has long been a little raw and rough around the edges—a reality Albany struggles to escape. The much-maligned capital of New York State, Albany is a manageable, medium-size city dominated by government and banking—and a firm wish for greater respect. Locals are proud of their city's great history in the Upper Hudson Valley, its culture, and continued efforts at urban renewal, but the city has had a somewhat difficult time convincing many from around the state of its charms. Beyond school groups on civics-class field trips, Albany attracts many more visitors for government and business trips than for leisure travel. The latter, though, are likely to find a fascinating dose of history, a full roster of summer festivals, user-friendly public spaces, and a few surprises that may just win the city some newfound respect.

Two monumental building projects have distinguished the city's physical evolution. The New York State Capitol, a stunning pile of native stone, took more than 30 years and the efforts of five architects to build, finally exhausting the patience of the governor, Theodore Roosevelt, in 1899. In the 1970s another governor, Nelson Rockefeller, left his imprint on the capital by building the dramatic Empire State Plaza and remaking downtown as one of the most starkly modern government headquarters this side of Brasilia. Rockefeller's ambition was to make Albany the country's most beautiful capital city; whether that was accomplished or not is a matter of debate, but the modern-art collection he amassed in the name of the capital is the largest publicly owned and displayed one in the country.

VISITOR INFORMATION

The **Albany Heritage Area Visitors Center,** 25 Quackenbush Sq. (© **800/258-3582** or 518/434-1217; www.albany.org), is open Monday through Friday from 9am to 4pm and weekends from 10am to 4pm. In addition to the tourist information center, there are a small history gallery, a planetarium, and a gift shop. Trolley tours leave from here in summer (see "Organized Tours," below). For pretrip information, consult the website www.albany.org.

CITY LAYOUT

Downtown Albany is relatively small and easy enough to get around, by foot, by bus, or by trolley. However, much of the city's hotel accommodations and dining establishments lie beyond the major highways that ring the city, I-787 and I-90, in suburbs like Colonie (north of Albany). Central Avenue is the main thoroughfare that leads all the way from downtown to Colonie, and is often referred to as "Restaurant Row." The major highways around Albany are notoriously difficult for newcomers to navigate; one frequently circles and circles, unable to determine which way one actually wants to go. Map out destinations in advance if you're staying on the outskirts of town, and ask locals for directions.

GETTING AROUND

BY PUBLIC TRANSPORTATION   The Downtown Albany Circulator (bus nos. 16 and 20; $1) runs between Empire State Plaza and Broadway on weekdays from 6:30am to 6pm; there is also an Albany City Trolley (© **518/462-DUCK**) downtown, which also offers 1-hour tours on the "Albany Aqua Ducks" ($12 adults, $10 seniors, and $6 children ages 4–12). For schedules and additional route information, contact the Capital District Authority (© **518/482-3371;** www.cdta.org).

BY CAR   Car-rental agencies in Albany include **Enterprise Rent-A-Car,** Pepsi Arena, 51 S. Pearl St. (© **518/383-3444**), and **Hertz Rent-A-Car** in the Crowne Plaza Hotel (© **518/434-6911**). You'll find representatives of Avis, Budget, Enterprise, Hertz, National, and Thrifty at Albany International Airport (see "Arriving," p. 257).

BY TAXI   Taxi services include **Yellow Cab,** 137 Lark St. (© **518/426-4609**); **Advantage Limousine & Car Service** (© **518/433-0100**); and **Premiere Transportation,** 456 N. Pearl St. (© **800/515-6123** or 518/459-6123).

BY TRAIN   See "Arriving," p. 257.

Downtown Albany

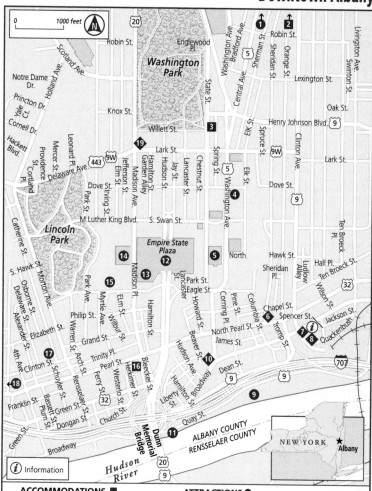

0 1000 feet **N**

Robin St. Englewood Pl.

Washington Park

Notre Dame Dr.

Princton Dr.

Cornell Dr.

Hackett Blvd.

Scotland Ave.

Holland Ave.

Knox St.

Willett St. **3**

19 Lark St.

443 **9W**

Delaware Ave.

Dove St. Stirring St.

M. Luther King Blvd. S. Swan St.

Lincoln Park

Catherine St.

S. Hawk St.

Morton Ave.

Park Ave.

14

15

13

Madison Pl.

Empire State Plaza

12

Lancaster

Park St.

Eagle St.

5

North Hawk St.

Sheridan Pl.

Robin St. **1** **2**

Washington Ave. Bradford Ave.

Sherman St. **5**

Sheridan St.

Orange St.

Central Ave.

Lexington St.

State St.

Oak St.

Henry Johnson Blvd. **9**

Elk St.

Spruce St.

Spring St. **9W**

Clinton Ave.

Lark St.

5

Elk St.

4

Dove St. **9**

Livingston Ave.

Swinton St.

Ten Broeck Pl.

Ludlow Alley

Hall Pl.

Wilson St.

32

Philip Ave.

Myrtle Ave.

Elm St.

Wilbur St.

Hamilton St.

Howard St.

Pine St.

Corning Pl.

Columbia St.

Chapel St. **6**

Spencer St.

Tromp St. **i**

7

8

Jackson St.

Quackenbush

S. Hawk St.

Osborne St.

Delaware Ave.

Alexander St.

Elizabeth St.

Philip St.

Warren St.

Arch St.

Grand St.

Trinity Pl.

Pearl St.

Westerlo St.

Herkimer St.

Bleecker St.

Hamilton St.

Hudson Ave.

Beaver St.

North Pearl St.

James St.

Dean St. **9**

10

Broadway

9

707

4th Ave

Clinton St. **17**

Schuyler St.

Ferry St.

Bassett St.

Plum St.

18

Franklin St.

Green St.

Dongan St.

32

Church St.

16

Liberty St.

Hamilton St.

Broadway

Quay St. **11**

ALBANY COUNTY

RENSSELAER COUNTY

Green St.

Broadway

i Information

Dunn Memorial Bridge

Hudson River 20 9

NEW YORK ★ Albany

BY BUS   Adirondack Trailways, 34 Hamilton St. (© **800/776-7548** or 518/ 527-7060; www.trailways.com), and **Greyhound Bus,** 34 Hamilton St. (© **518/434-8095**), travel to Albany and other destinations in upstate New York.

EXPLORING ALBANY

Albany has just a handful of must-see sights, including two excellent museums and the State Capitol building, almost all conveniently located downtown. The best idea is probably to start at the unmistakable Empire State Plaza, where several of the top sights are located.

THE TOP ATTRACTIONS

Albany Institute of History & Art ★ *Kids*   Albany's best art museum is the second-oldest museum in the United States—older even than the Smithsonian and Louvre. Restored and sensitively expanded in 2001—two turn-of-the-20th-century buildings were linked by a modern glass lobby—the museum presents the history of the Hudson River and Albany through the works of local artists and artisans. The permanent collection includes decorative arts, furniture, and nearly 5 centuries of paintings and sculpture. Among the most important are paintings by artists such as Thomas Cole, from the Hudson River School, the first American school of art. In the Colonial Albany gallery are furnishings, paintings, and artifacts that tell the story of the ancient Dutch settlement in this area 350 years ago. Ancient Egypt galleries feature a pair of mummies, a priest, and a priestess, from 304 B.C. and 966 B.C. The museum presents special exhibits that are among the best in upstate New York, and there are plenty of lectures and activities geared toward children. An hour or two should be sufficient here.

125 Washington Ave. © **518/463-4478.** www.albanyinstitute.org. Admission $8 adults, $6 seniors and students, $4 children 6–12, free for children under 6. Free admission first Fri of every month. Wed–Sat 10am–5pm; Sun noon–5pm.

Empire State Plaza ★ *Kids*   This dramatic public plaza is Albany's most distinctive urban feature. Its official name is Governor Nelson A. Rockefeller State Plaza, after the man who undertook the massive project in 1962 (it wasn't finished until 1978). Rockefeller envisioned a kind of starkly modern Brasilia in upstate New York. Fiercely controversial at the time, for not only its daring aesthetics but the fact that an entire residential neighborhood was wiped out to install it, the plaza and its unique buildings have since grown on most locals and visitors. The centerpiece of the plaza is the spherical Performing Arts Center, known to all as "The Egg." One glance and you'll know why. The plaza is flanked by the New York State Museum, the New York State Capitol (alongside legislative and justice buildings), four tall state agency buildings, and the tallest structure in Albany, the 42-story Corning Tower. War and other memorials share the open air with an important 92-piece collection of large-scale modern sculpture, most by artists associated with the New York School, including Tony Smith, Alexander Calder, David Smith, and Claes Oldenburg. The Empire Plaza might be cold and off-putting, but the city schedules events such as concerts, festivals, ice-skating, fireworks, and other activities that draw Albany residents, rather than keeping them away. Free public 1-hour tours are held Monday through Friday at 11am and 1pm; call for details.

Bordered by State St., South St., and Madison Ave. © **518/474-2418.** www.ogs.state.ny.us/visiting/cultural/default events.html. Free admission (hours vary for individual components).

New York State Capitol ★★   This impressive building, seat of New York State government since the 1880s and a jarring contrast with the starkly modern Empire Plaza and agency buildings that rise around it, was the first massive and problematic

Kids Albany's Highs & Lows

It takes just 28 seconds to reach the 42nd-floor **Corning Tower Observation Deck,** which makes this the tallest building between New York City and Montreal. On a clear day, you can see the Catskills, the Green Mountains of Vermont, and the Hudson River. The observation deck is open Monday through Saturday from 10am to 2:30pm; admission is free. At the other extreme, underground in the Concourse passageway that travels beneath the Empire State Plaza, is a most unexpected art gallery—the largest publicly owned and displayed **art collection** in the U.S., purchased at the behest of Gov. Nelson A. Rockefeller, who strongly believed that art was a fundamental component of a capital city. Mixed in with fast-food shops and government offices are dozens of works by some of the most important artists of the 20th century, almost all of whom were identified with the New York School, including Isamu Noguchi, Robert Motherwell, Ellsworth Kelly, Franz Kline, Mark Rothko, and Donald Judd, among many others. Note that many large sculptures are also placed outside, on and around the plaza. The Concourse is open Monday through Friday from 6am to 11pm and on weekends from 10am to 2:30pm; free admission.

project in the area. It took more than 3 decades (beginning at the end of the 19th c.) and five architects to build, and cost more than $25 million (making it relatively one of the most expensive buildings ever erected in the U.S). One of the last load-bearing structures to be built, with no steel reinforcements until the top floor, and constructed of solid granite masonry, it was to have been crowned by a cupola, but the governor at the time, Theodore Roosevelt, had had enough and proclaimed it finished in 1899. Its grandest features are the Great Western Staircase—the so-called "$1-million staircase," a riot of elaborate stonework that contains more than 1,000 carved small faces (most are anonymous, but there are 77 "famous" visages, such as Andrew Jackson and Henry Hudson)—and the vibrant William de Leftwich Dodge ceiling murals of battle depictions in the Governor's Reception Room. Free walk-in tours last about 45 minutes; it's wise to phone ahead to confirm the schedule.

Plaza Visitor Center, Room 106 Concourse, Empire State Plaza. ℂ **518/474-2418.** www.ogs.state.ny.us. Free admission. Guided tours Mon–Fri 10am, noon, 2pm, and 3pm; weekends 11am, 1pm, and 3pm. No parking (paid parking on the street or next to the New York State Museum).

New York State Museum ★★ Kids   This massive museum, which from the exterior looks like a giant monolith, is the largest museum of its kind in the country. It aims to tell the story of New York State, both natural and cultural. Several new galleries have really enlivened this war horse. The newest permanent gallery, "The World Trade Center: Rescue, Recovery, Response," was the first major museum exhibit of artifacts from the September 11, 2001, terrorist attacks. It documents the 24-hour aftermath of the disaster; on view are giant fragments of the towers, a destroyed fire engine (one of the first on the scene), and the stunning video shot by two French brothers. Elsewhere, New York City is traced from early port to metropolis, with a recent gallery addition devoted to Harlem. A large and accurate depiction of a Mohawk Iroquois village longhouse is a visitor favorite. Of great interest to visitors who can't visit New York City is the hall of rotating great art from the city's major museums (including the Metropolitan, Guggenheim, and MoMA). On the top floor is the new Café Terrace, with great views of the Empire State Plaza and creative regional displays, along with something that kids run screaming toward: a historic, functioning 36-horse carousel, hand-carved in the 1890s in Brooklyn. Allow a couple of hours.

Madison Ave. (between Eagle and Swan sts.). © 518/474-5877. www.nysm.nysed.gov. Free admission (donation suggested). Daily 9:30am–5pm. Paid parking on the street or next to the museum.

MORE TO SEE & DO

Historic Cherry Hill　This stately home, a big yellow clapboard Georgian Colonial that once looked over gentle lands to the edge of the Hudson River, is today in the middle of a bad neighborhood and the din of the highway. But no matter, it still presents an interesting history lesson, told through the story of Catherine Putnam and the Van Rensselaer family, whose descendants occupied the house for 200 years, until 1963. The house is overflowing with original furnishings, documents, and artifacts, and is most interesting for the way organizers present it as a reflection of Albany history.

523½ S. Pearl St. (off I-787). © 518/434-4791. www.historiccherryhill.org. Admission $4 adults, $3 seniors, $2 college students, $1 children 6–17. Apr–June and Oct–Dec Tues–Fri, guided tours on the hour noon–3pm, Sat 10am–3pm, Sun 1–3pm; July–Sept Tues–Sat, guided tours on the hour 10am–3pm, Sun 1–3pm. Closed Jan–Mar.

Hudson River Way _Finds_ _Kids_　This cool pedestrian bridge, opened in 2002, connects downtown to Corning Preserve Park on the banks of the Hudson. It is lined with 30 _trompe l'oeil_ paintings on lampposts that depict the city's history and heritage, from prehistoric times and early Dutch merchants to the present. There are also two large murals on staircase landings.

Maiden Lane/Corning Preserve Park. © 518/434-2032. Free admission.

New York State Executive Mansion　The Governor's Mansion, built in 1856 as a banker's home, was totally remodeled in the 1860s. The first governor to live (and rent) here was in 1875; in 1877 the state purchased it, and it was given its third major makeover in 1885, to its current Queen Anne style. Famous inhabitants include Theodore Roosevelt and Franklin Delano Roosevelt (whose wheelchair you can see in the exhibit space on the second floor). The house, which isn't overly large or grand, is still the official residence of the current governor, Eliot Spitzer, and his family (at least when he's in Albany). Tours last about an hour.

138 Eagle St. © 518/473-7521. www.ogs.state.ny.us. Free admission. Guided tours Sept–June Thurs at noon, 1pm, and 2pm (by appointment). No parking (paid parking on the street or next to the New York State Museum).

Schuyler Mansion State Historic Site　This large, English-style 1762 estate, the home of Philip Schuyler, one of the first four generals under Washington during the first 2 years of the Revolutionary War, is more interesting for what it represents than what there actually is to see. The house is only partially restored, but it was essentially a military outpost during the war, with visits by George Washington, Benedict Arnold, and Alexander Hamilton, who married Schuyler's daughter at the mansion. Incredibly, Schuyler had the British general John Burgoyne and his retinue under house arrest here after their defeat at the Battle of Saratoga, and Loyalists raided the house in an attempt to kidnap Burgoyne in 1781.

32 Catherine St. © 518/434-0834. www.nysparks.com. Admission $4 adults, $3 seniors and students, $1 children 5–12. Mid-Apr to Oct Wed–Sun 11am–5pm; June–Aug also open Tues; Nov–Mar Mon–Fri 11am–4pm (by appointment only); closed early Apr.

Shaker Heritage Society America's first Shaker settlement, the 1776 Watervliet Church Community, retains its 1848 Meeting House and seven other buildings, where modern life has now encroached. The Shakers (the United Society of Believers), the early American religious group, were known for their remarkable craftsmanship as well as their religious devotion. Work was a way of devoting oneself to God, and they sought to create heaven on earth with communitarian social structure and celibacy; they adopted needy children and brought them into the "family," to work on the estate; on Sunday, outsiders came to see their mesmerizing church services. The Shakers, who at their peak numbered about 350 here, abandoned the site in 1924. Mother Ann Lee and more than 400 other Shakers are buried on the grounds. Craft workshops are held on the premises, where there is a small gift shop. Allow about a half-hour.

875 Watervliet-Shaker Rd., Colonie. 𝄞 518/456-7890. Free admission (donations accepted). Guided tours (June–Oct 11:30am and 1:30pm) $3 per person (free for children 12 and under). Feb–Oct Tues–Sat 9:30am–4pm; Nov–Dec Mon–Sat 10am–4pm. Closed Jan.

USS Slater _Kids_ A World War I destroyer escort ship, one of three remaining, sits docked on the banks of the Hudson, open to tours of the crew's quarters, galley, and main guns. The ship is currently being restored.

Snow Dock, adjacent to Dunn Memorial Bridge (off I-787). 𝄞 518/431-1943. www.ussslater.org. Admission $7 adults, $6 students 12–16, $5 children 6–11, free for children under 6. Apr–Nov Wed–Sun 10am–4pm. Closed Dec–Mar.

ESPECIALLY FOR KIDS

Albany, as the state capital, gets tons of school visits, of course, but at first glance it might not appear the best place to travel with kids. Actually, it's got plenty for children of all ages. Starting with the Albany Visitors Center, the **Henry Hudson Planetarium** (𝄞 518/434-0405 for tickets and information) has shows every Saturday at 11:30am and 12:30pm. The **Albany Institute of History & Art** schedules a bevy of special children's programs. The **New York State Museum** has interesting exhibits that will appeal to both younger and older children, including one on 9/11, another on the Adirondacks, and a Native American longhouse that kids can enter and play around with using a nifty interactive feature. But best of all is the antique carousel on the museum's top floor. The **Hudson River Way** is a pedestrian bridge with lampposts marked by paintings that trick the eye and tell the story of Albany's history. And young soldiers will surely find it cool to board a World War I destroyer, the **USS _Slater_**, docked on the Hudson.

ORGANIZED TOURS

The **Albany Area Visitors Center** (𝄞 800/258-3582 or 518/434-1217; www.albany. org) offers a variety of seasonal tours, including Hudson River walking tours, guided horse-drawn carriage tours, mansion garden tours, and guided trolley tours of downtown. Some are free, while others charge a fee of around $10; most are offered from July to the end of August. Guided trolley tours of downtown, historic homes, and historic churches are offered from July to the end of August. They begin at the visitor center at Quackenbush Square (corner of Clinton and Broadway). For more information, call 𝄞 518/434-0405; advance reservations are recommended. **Albany Remembered Tours,** 100 State St. (𝄞 518/427-0401), offers guided walking tours of historic sights. The **Upper Hudson River Railroad,** 3 Railroad Place, North Creek (𝄞 518/251-5334), runs seasonal 2-hour train trips along a gorgeous section of the Upper Hudson River, spring, summer, and fall; $13 adults, $12 seniors, $9 children 3 to 11. **Dutch Apple Cruises,** corner of Quay and Madison avenues (𝄞 518/463-0220;

Fun Fact **Rack 'Em Up**

The modern billiard ball was created in Albany in 1868, using celluloid as a substitute for ivory (of which there was a shortage), by John Wesley Hyatt. The Albany Billiard Ball Company on Delaware Avenue produced billiard balls until it went out of business in 1986.

---

www.dutchapplecruises.com), cruises the Hudson with narrated lunch and dinner trips with entertainment. **Canal Pilot,** Waterford (© **518/928-1863**), does custom boat tours of the Hudson River as well as Lake Erie and Champlain canals. **Hart Tours,** 1 Becker Terrace, Delmar (© **800/724-4225** or 518/439-6095), is a tour operator that has 1-, 2-, and 3-day area itineraries, including tours of the Adirondacks and Capital District.

OUTDOOR PURSUITS

BIKING, IN-LINE SKATING & JOGGING The **Hudson-Mohawk Bikeway** is a 41-mile path along the Hudson and Mohawk rivers, connecting Albany with Schenectady and Troy, with smaller, more manageable paths. It begins in Island Creek Park and continues through Corning Preserve Park (at the end of the Hudson River Way bridge). **State Bike Route 9** runs to Hudson Shores Park, near Watervliet. For more information, call © **518/458-2161** or pick up a copy of *Capital District Regional Bike-Hike Map* at the visitor center.

FESTIVALS Especially in summer, Albany thrives with public outdoor festivals, many held at the Empire State Plaza. Visit www.albanyevents.org and www.albany.org for more information, as dates and specifics change. Here's a sampling:

- The **Tulip Festival** ✦. Washington Park (early to mid-May; © **518/434-2032**). The city and park bloom with tens of thousands of tulips, a 60-year-old tradition and reflection of the city's Dutch ancestry.
- **Albany Alive at Five.** Thursday-night free outdoor summer concerts in Albany Riverfront Park (June–Aug; © **518/434-2032**).
- **Price Chopper Fourth of July.** Empire State Plaza: fireworks, music, and more.
- **Classic Rock, Swing, and Oldies concerts.** Empire State Plaza (Wed July–Aug; © **518/473-0559**; www.ogs.state.ny.us).
- **African-American Family Day.** Empire State Plaza (first week of Aug; © **518/ 473-0559**; www.ogs.state.ny.us).
- **Food Festival.** Empire State Plaza (mid-Aug; © **518/473-0559**; www.ogs. state.ny.us).
- **Albany LatinFest.** Washington Park (late Aug; © **518/434-2032**).
- **Albany Riverfront Jazz Festival.** Albany Riverfront Park: outdoor jazz followed by fireworks (early Sept; © **518/434-2032**).
- **Columbus Parade and Italian Festival.** Albany Riverfront Park (early to mid-Oct; © **518/434-2032**).

GOLF **Orchard Creek Golf Club,** 6700 Dunnsville Rd., Altamont (© **518/861-5000;** www.orchardcreek.com), an 18-hole public course, was rated America's no. 1 Best New Bargain by *Golf Digest* in 2001 (greens fees $26–$40). Family-owned **Stadium Golf Club,** 333 Jackson Ave., Schenectady (© **518/374-9104;** www.stadiumgolfclub. com), is another 18-hole course, just north of Albany. Greens fees are $26 to $32.

PARKS & GARDENS **Washington Park,** at State and Willett streets, is where the annual springtime Tulip Festival is held. **Corning Riverfront Park** is at the west bank of the Hudson, at the end of the **Hudson River Way** pedestrian bridge.

WINTER SPORTS You can **ice-skate** outdoors at Empire State Plaza (© 518/ 474-2418) and Swinburne Rink (© 518/438-2406). The closest downhill skiing is at **Ski Windham,** Windham (© 800/729-7549; www.skiwindham.com), and **Catamount,** Route 23, Hillsdale (© 800/342-1840; www.catamountski.com), on the Massachusetts border in the southern Berkshires.

SPECTATOR SPORTS

The **Albany Conquest** (© 518/487-2000; www.albanyconquest.com) is the local Arena football team, and it plays its eight home games at the Pepsi Arena from April to July. Tickets are $9 to $45. The **Albany River Rats** (© 518/487-2244; www. albanyriverrats.com), an affiliate of the American Hockey League's New Jersey Devils, also plays at Pepsi Arena, October through May. Tickets are $16 adults, $12 seniors and students. They're accompanied by their dance team, the Ice Mice. The Class A minor-league baseball team, the **Tri-City Valley Cats,** an affiliate of the Houston Astros (© 518/629-CATS; www.tcvalleycats.com), plays in a 4,500-capacity stadium on the Hudson Valley Campus in Troy. Tickets are $4.50 to $8.50.

FARMERS' MARKETS

A good farmers' market, south of Albany on Route 9J along the Hudson, is **Goold Orchards,** 1297 Brookview Station Rd., Castleton (© 518/732-7317), which features an apple orchard, farm store, cider mill, and bake shop. It offers pick-your-own apples, strawberries, and pumpkins in season, as well as an apple festival in October and a corn maze. City versions of farmers' markets in town are Wallenberg Park, Clinton Avenue and North Pearl (Mon 10am–1pm); SUNY Plaza, corner of Broadway and State (Thurs 11am–2pm); and Empire State Plaza (Wed and Fri 11am–2pm).

WHERE TO STAY

The supply of good downtown hotels in Albany is woefully limited for a state capital. By far the best choice is one of the small B&B/boutique inns that have cropped up to take the place of larger hotels. Not only is it the best place to stay in Albany, but it's one of the finest inns in upstate New York. Most decent hotels of any size, which tend to be standard hotel and motel chains, are on the outskirts of town, in a suburb called Colonie.

Angels Bed and Breakfast ★ *Finds* An intimate urban B&B in the heart of downtown Albany—within convenient walking distance of major capital sights like the capitol and The Egg performing arts center—this lovingly restored home was the John Stafford House when it began life in 1811. Transformed into a luxurious small inn in 2003, the architecturally significant residence provides just three cleanly decorated and comfortable rooms, all with a private bathroom, on the second floor; on the ground floor is a cute little cafe, and the third floor is where the innkeeper lives. An outdoor roof deck is a fine place to relax.

96 Madison Ave., Albany, NY 12202. © 518/426-4104. www.angelsbedandbreakfast.com. 3 units. $115–$225 double. Rates include full breakfast. AE, DISC, MC, V. Free parking on street. *In room:* A/C.

The Desmond *Value* This large, 30-year-old hotel and conference center is designed to look like a village of sorts, which I guess it does in that faux-Disney way. It looks a little bit more like a food court at the mall. Bellboys are even dressed in faux-Colonial get-ups. But it's actually a pretty good place to stay, with good-size and comfortable

Hotel & Motel Chains in the Albany Area

If none of the recommended hotels are available—and Albany can get crowded during large conventions and when lobbyists are swarming the capital—try one of the following international hotel chains, which are mostly located on the outskirts of downtown, near the airport: **Best Western Albany Airport Inn** (200 Wolf Rd., Albany, NY 12205; ℭ 800/310-6143 or 518/458-100; www.bestwestern.com; $99–$109 double); **Holiday Inn Albany** (205 Wolf Rd., Albany, NY 12205; ℭ 518/458-7250; www.sixcontinentshotels. com; $105–$149 double); **Quality Inn Hotel Albany** (Everett Rd., Albany, NY 12206; ℭ 518/438-8431; www.qualityinn.com; $85–$95 double); **Red Roof Albany Inn** (188 Wolf Rd., Albany, NY 12205; ℭ 518/459-1971; www.red roof.com; $79–$89 double); **Courtyard by Marriott** (168 Wolf Rd., Albany, NY 12205; ℭ 800/321-2211 or 518/482-8800; www.courtyard.com; $89–$159 double); or **Days Inn Wolf Road** (16 Wolf Rd., Albany, NY 12205; ℭ 800/329-7466; www.thedaysinn.com; $70–$90 double).

For additional chain hotels and motels (many are in the greater metro area), see **www.albany.org**.

rooms overlooking the courtyard, which have four-poster canopy beds, 18th-century replica furnishings, and lots of floral prints. The hotel is close to the airport and has all the facilities you're likely to need.

660 Albany-Shaker Rd., Albany, NY 12211 (in Colonie; I-87, exit 4). ℭ **800/448-3500** or 518/869-8100. Fax 518/869-7659. www.desmondhotelsalbany.com. 324 units. $174–$184 double. AE, DC, DISC, MC, V. Free parking. **Amenities:** 2 restaurants; indoor/outdoor pools; fitness center; business center; limited room service. *In room:* A/C, TV, coffeemaker, hair dryer.

The Morgan State House ⭐⭐⭐ *Value*   One of the finest urban B&Bs you're likely to stumble upon, the elegant and professionally run Morgan State House is really a European-style boutique hotel. Its rooms are nothing short of extraordinary: huge and gorgeously (and uniquely) decorated, with great 19th-century period detailing and furnishings, tile bathrooms with claw-foot tubs, and some of the best down and feather bedding and linens you'll ever rest your head on. A couple of rooms even have working fireplaces. The beautiful town house, on "Mansion Row" just a few blocks from the Empire State Plaza and across the street from peaceful Washington Park, was built in 1888 by the same architect who designed the cathedral in Albany. It remained a single-family house until 1975. The B&B's six rooms are in high demand; if none is available, perhaps you can land one of the 10 apartments with kitchenettes at The Washington Park State House, in a condo building a couple of doors down at 399 State St. They have the owner's same unmistakable good taste, though they're a touch more modern, and are ideal for business travelers. Guests at Washington Park also have breakfast at The Morgan State House (on a nice day, sip your coffee in the charming interior garden courtyard). No children under 16 are accepted at either place.

393 State St., Albany, NY 12210. ℭ **888/427-6063** or 518/427-6063. Fax 518/463-1316. www.statehouse.com. 16 units. Morgan State House $135–$200 double; 2-bedroom suite $260. Washington Park State House $135–$165 apt. Rates include full breakfast. AE, DISC, MC, V. Free parking. *In room:* A/C, TV, Wi-Fi, kitchenettes in Washington Park State House rooms.

WHERE TO DINE

Lark Street downtown is home to a number of small neighborhood eateries with cuisine from around the world, while the majority of chain and fast-food restaurants are located on Central Avenue, also known as "Restaurant Row."

EXPENSIVE

Nicole's Bistro ✸✸ *Value* FRENCH BISTRO In what is in all probability the oldest standing home in Albany, an original Quackenbush (early Dutch, ca. 1730) structure, this handsome, upscale two-story French bistro is one of Albany's best. Charming and elegant, it's surely the best place in the heart of Albany for a celebratory or romantic dinner. The seafood cassoulet is a standard in southern France, a hearty fish stew of shellfish, scallops, mussels, crab claws, and seafood sausage in a spicy tomato-fennel broth. Classic meat dishes include rack of lamb with garlic mashed potatoes and steak au poivre. The lunch menu is considerably lighter and cheaper. A truly excellent deal is the three-course prix-fixe dinner special Monday through Friday for $26 (Sat, four-course menu for $35). Bread fanatics take note: The basket of assorted home-baked breads delivered to your table is irresistible. A cute little cocktail bar at the entrance is a good spot for a before- or after-dinner drink (you can also eat there).

Quackenbush House, 633 Broadway (corner of Clinton Ave.). ✆ 518/465-1111. Reservations recommended. Main courses $19–$28. AE, MC, V. Mon–Fri 11:30am–2:30pm and 5–10pm, Sat 5–10pm.

Yono's ✸✸ CONTINENTAL/ASIAN/INDONESIAN Prior to its recent change of location to a downtown hotel, this constituted one of the oddest restaurants anywhere. A white-gloved haute Indonesian dining establishment, it was set in a mini-mall of car dealers and a garage. While the new incarnation is still elegant, in an ostentatious way, but less idiosyncratic, it is also more convenient for diners to sample fine Indonesian cuisine. The acclaimed chef Yono, who appeared on NBC's *Today* show and picked up numerous awards, creates a sophisticated menu focusing on delicious Indonesian specialties, though another page is a full roster of well-prepared Continental dishes "if you're feeling less adventurous." Yono's signature dish is a Balinese specialty, *Babi Kecap Singa Raja,* a mouthful that translates into pork tenderloin in sweet soy, ginger, and orange rind. If you're unfamiliar with Indonesian cuisine, your best bet is the *Nasi Rames,* a tasting menu of five dishes. The wine list is outstanding, with more than 500 bottles (though pairing wines with spicy Indonesian dishes is a bit of an art; try a Riesling or even a Belgian-style beer). For an update, see www.yonos restaurant.com.

25 Chapel St. (in Hampton Inn & Suites). ✆ 518/436-7747. Reservations recommended. Main courses $18–$49. AE, DISC, MC, V. Wed–Sat 5:30–11pm.

MODERATE

Albany Pump Station (Evens Brewing Co.) *Kids* *Value* AMERICAN/PUB FARE Housed in a cavernous 19th-century former pump station, this is part microbrewery and part restaurant. It gets crowded at happy hour with downtown office workers, but then begins to fill up with individual and family diners. The menu is surprisingly diverse, with plenty of salads, pastas, burgers, sandwiches, and other pub grub, but also good entrees such as old-fashioned meatloaf, French Quarter gumbo, and eggplant lasagna. The house beers are quite good; check out the award-winning Kick-Ass Brown Ale and the Quackenbush Blonde, or the cask ales available on Friday. A late-night menu of pub food kicks in after 10pm (11pm Fri–Sat), and there's a special (and cheap) kids' menu, as well as "Sunday Family-Style Dining," a complete meal for just $13.

19 Quackenbush Sq. ℂ **518/447-9000.** Reservations recommended on weekends. Main courses $6.95–$19. AE, DISC, MC, V. Mon–Thurs 11:30am–10pm; Fri–Sat 11:30am–midnight; Sun noon–8pm.

Jack's Oyster House 🏵 CLASSIC AMERICAN   Known locally simply as "Jack's," this Albany classic has been around since 1913, and it still has the kind of clubby insider ambience associated with another era. It's the kind of place where lobbyists and politicos come to hammer out government contracts. Waiters are nattily attired in black jackets and bow ties with white aprons; the restaurant has black-and-white tile floors, dark wood paneling, deep booths, and photos of old Albany. The menu for the most part stubbornly resists trendiness. Classic appetizers include Jack's Famous 1913 Manhattan clam chowder, clams casino, shrimp cocktail, and oysters Rockefeller. Main courses include steak Diane, calves' liver, and jumbo lobster tail. In fact, there's an entire 1913 traditional dinner menu (at current prices, alas). There's little worry about being trendy at Jack's.

42–44 State St. ℂ **518/465-8854.** Reservations recommended. Main courses $17–$40. AE, DISC, MC, V. Daily 11am–3pm and 5–9pm.

Justin's on Lark 🏵 ⓥalue AMERICAN/INTERNATIONAL   This longtime anchor of the Lark Street dining scene received a much-needed makeover a couple of years ago, with menu and chef changes. The result is a pretty hip but relaxed joint that serves up comfort food such as a grilled, center-cut pork chop or something with a Latino, Asian, or Caribbean twist (like the Jamaican jerk chicken) and nightly live jazz, making it an excellent neighborhood hangout. For night owls, the good news is that it's open late (until 1am). For those with a lighter meal in mind, there's a cafe menu of salads and sandwiches.

301 Lark St. ℂ **518/436-7008.** Reservations recommended on weekends. Main courses $8–$24. AE, MC, V. Daily 11:30am–1am.

ALBANY AFTER DARK

The Egg 🏵🏵, Empire State Plaza Concourse Level (ℂ **518/473-1845;** www. theegg.org), is the funky spherical half-egg on the plaza; its two theaters inside are nearly as cool as the exterior. It hosts a diverse range of entertainment, from the modern dance of Mark Morris and classical music to comedy, theater, international performers including Cesaria Evora, and the guitar riffs of rock bands like Cheap Trick. **The Palace Performing Arts Center** 🏵, 19 Clinton Ave. (ℂ **518/465-3664;** www. palacealbany.com), is a gorgeously restored, grand 1931 movie theater that now hosts top-level talent, including pop concerts (such as Billy Joel and Sum 41), comedy (Jerry Seinfeld), and the Albany Symphony Orchestra and the Albany Berkshire Ballet. It also handles a number of children's theater performances during the school year. The **Pepsi Arena,** 51 S. Pearl St. (ℂ **518/487-2000;** www.pepsiarena.com), is the big place in town for large rock and country-music concerts in addition to sporting events. The **Capital Repertory Theatre,** 111 N. Pearl St. (ℂ **518/462-4531;** www. capitalrep.org), features Broadway and Off-Broadway touring musicals and dramatic theater. Outside of town, the **Troy Savings Bank Music Hall** 🏵, 7 State St., Troy (ℂ **518/273-0038;** www.troymusichall.org), a wonderfully preserved concert hall in a former 1823 bank, hosts some of the area's best jazz concerts as well as chamber music and other performances; there's almost always something interesting scheduled, and it's just 8 miles from downtown Albany. Its heritage includes performances by such musical eminences as Ella Fitzgerald and Yo-Yo Ma.

Bars and pubs worth visiting include **Noche,** 895 Broadway (© **518/434-4540**) in North Albany(also known as the Warehouse District, Albany's best impersonation of New York City's Meatpacking District), a cool, industrial lounge and tapas bar that inhabits an old firehouse; **Albany Pump Station,** 19 Quackenbush Sq. (© **518/447-9000**), a brewpub within a historic pump station; **Riverfront Bar & Grill,** Corning Riverfront Park (© **518/426-4738**), which you can access by crossing the Hudson River Way pedestrian bridge; and the **Waterworks Pub,** 76 Central Ave. (© **518/465-9079**), with a large dance floor and DJs spinning tunes. Movie theaters include **Hoyt's** at Crossgates Mall (© **518/452-6440**) and **Spectrum 7 Theaters,** 290 Delaware Ave. (© **518/449-8995**).

10

Central New York

by Rich Beattie

Sandwiched in between the bustling Albany area, the subtle Catskills, the gorgeous Adirondacks, and the pretty Finger Lakes, central New York may not immediately spring to mind as a destination hot spot. To be honest, there are only a few must-sees and -dos here, but those few "musts" warrant passing through.

The area has certainly seen better days—in the 19th century and into the 20th, this region of the state produced more hops than elsewhere in the country. As always, some people profited mightily. But ultimately, the Depression, agricultural disease, and the discovery that hops could be grown cheaper in the Pacific Northwest ruined this economic outlet.

Today, the centerpiece of this region—and the main reason people go—is the amazing village of **Cooperstown,** the former home of legendary author James Fenimore Cooper and current home to the Baseball Hall of Fame. You could easily spend a couple of days here wandering around the charming town, with its gorgeous lake and variety of attractions.

Though Cooperstown is the area's main draw, it doesn't have the only hall of fame in the region, since soccer and boxing each have one as well. Look closer and you'll find that you're in cavern country, and the show cave Howe Caverns makes for an interesting journey underground. The city of Utica has a couple of surprises, and recreation abounds on the beautiful Oneida Lake.

And, of course, once you're done scoping out the scene here, you'll be perfectly positioned on the doorstep to the Adirondacks, the Thousand Islands, the Finger Lakes, and the Catskills.

1 Cooperstown ★★★

77 miles W of Albany; 141 miles E of Rochester; 213 miles NW of New York City

Set on gorgeous (and mostly undeveloped) Lake Otsego, this tiny village feels frozen in an era when gracious mansions lined the streets, folks greeted you by name, and people played a stick-and-ball game that didn't even have a name yet. The town of 2,400 people swells to 50,000 on summer weekends, but despite the crush of visitors, Cooperstown hasn't outgrown its small-town roots. With a couple of exceptions, you won't find chain stores here (the horror! no Starbucks!). Coffeehouses, bookstores, and restaurants are, for the most part, independently run. That personalized, hands-on ownership shows: People are friendly and excited to turn you on to their town.

Though once home to author James Fenimore Cooper—who named Lake Otsego "Glimmerglass" in his *Leatherstocking Tales*—the town was actually named for his father, William Cooper, in 1786. Today most people come to see the **Baseball Hall of Fame,** but that's not the only game in town. There are several worthwhile sites, and

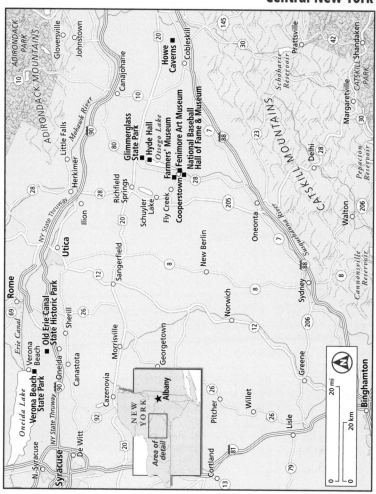

Lake Otsego harbors a magic all its own. ***Warning:*** The town shuts down early—there are no movie theaters, and restaurants close as early as 9pm in the winter.

ESSENTIALS

GETTING THERE   Off on its own, Cooperstown is easiest to get to by car. From the New York State Thruway, take exit 30 at Herkimer and go south on State Highway 28 or State Highway 80—both will take you to Cooperstown. By bus, **Trailways** (© **800/776-7548;** www.trailwaysny.com) provides service between Cooperstown and other towns both big and small. The closest airport, **Albany International Airport** (© **518/242-2200;** www.albanyairport.com), is about 75 miles east. See chapter 9.

VISITOR INFORMATION   The helpful **Cooperstown Chamber of Commerce,** 31 Chestnut St. (© **607/547-9983;** www.cooperstownchamber.org), is open daily

May through October from 9am to 5pm; from November to April, it's open Monday to Saturday from 9am to 5pm. To receive brochures and other promo stuff, call Cooperstown New York Getaway (© **888/875-2969**).

GETTING AROUND   With thousands of people converging on Cooperstown during the summer, you're best off leaving your car outside town and taking the **trolley** (unless you're staying in town, of course). Look for the blue PARK AND TAKE THE TROLLEY signs as you approach Cooperstown. Parking is free in the outer lots, in the following locations: off Route 28 just south of Cooperstown (traveling north from Oneonta); off Route 28 (Glen Ave.) at Maple Street (traveling south on Rte. 28 from Rte. 20); on Route 80 at the upper parking lot of Fenimore House Museum (traveling south on Rte. 80 from Rte. 20). An unlimited daily trolley pass is $3 for adults, $1 for kids. The trolley stops at the museums, Main Street shopping, and other points of interest. From Memorial Day to the last week in June, it runs weekends only, from 8:30am to 9pm; from the last week in June to Labor Day, it runs daily from 8:30am to 9pm; from Labor Day to Columbus Day, weekends only, from 8:30am to 9pm.

EXPLORING COOPERSTOWN

Baseball Hall of Fame 🏀🏀🏀   Yes, you'll find plenty of statistics-spouting baseball fanatics walking around the Hall. But this museum isn't just for passionate lovers of the game or its coveted collectibles. After all, this is America's pastime, and some 30,000 exhibited items demonstrate how important this sport has been to America's past and present. The Hall collected its first artifact in 1937, and now you can find baseballs, bats, uniforms, ballpark artifacts, priceless trading cards, and a microcosm of American history. You'll learn about the Negro Leagues and the integration of baseball, discover the president who established the tradition of throwing out the first pitch on opening day, and, of course, see some of the greatest moments of the greatest players ever. A 3-year, $20-million renovation was completed in 2005, adding 10,000 square feet of exhibit space and new technology, so depending on how big a fan you are, you could spend anywhere from an hour to a full day (or more) browsing, learning, and loving the game.

25 Main St. © **888/HALL-OF-FAME** or 607/547-7200. Admission $15 adults, $9.50 seniors, $5 ages 7–12, free for children under 7. Memorial Day to Labor Day daily 9am–9pm; off-season daily 9am–5pm.

Brewery Ommegang 🏀🏀   Forget microbrews—Belgian beers blow most of them away with their hoppy taste and high alcohol content. And even though this farmland brewery is some 3,600 miles from Belgium, the brewers are absolutely passionate about the very specialized science of creating the European beverage. Using their own strain of yeast, high-temperature open fermentation, and warm cellaring, they've created small batches of award-winning beers that are strong, hoppy, and worth the trip out of town. Tours are interesting, and you'll get some free samples.

656 County Hwy. 33. © **800/544-1809**. 25-min. tours are free and include beer tasting. Memorial Day to Labor Day daily 11am–6pm; Labor Day to Memorial Day daily noon–5pm. From Main St. in Cooperstown, turn onto Pioneer St., continue to the T, and turn right. Then turn left on Susquehanna Ave. Continue ½ mile. Turn right on County Hwy. 33.

Farmers' Museum 🏀   Don't let the name throw you: This walk-through-the-buildings museum is an interesting look at rural village life around 1845. The 25 historic buildings were moved to this site, a working farm since 1790, to re-create a 19th-century village. Workers staff some of the buildings dressed in period costumes and fully acting the part: The blacksmith is banging out horseshoes, the printer is creating a

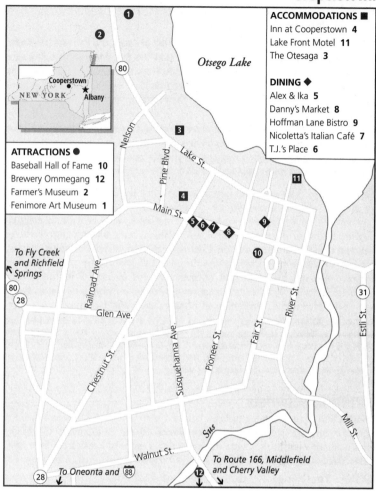

To Fly Creek
and Richfield
Springs

ACCOMMODATIONS ■
Inn at Cooperstown **4**
Lake Front Motel **11**
The Otesaga **3**

DINING ◆
Alex & Ika **5**
Danny's Market **8**
Hoffman Lane Bistro **9**
Nicoletta's Italian Café **7**
T.J.'s Place **6**

ATTRACTIONS ●
Baseball Hall of Fame **10**
Brewery Ommegang **12**
Farmer's Museum **2**
Fenimore Art Museum **1**

Otsego Lake

poster, and the pharmacist is passing out information on the herbal remedies of the time. They bring the museum to life and make it worth spending an hour or so here.

Lake Rd., 1½ miles north of Cooperstown. © **888/547-1450** or 607/547-1450. www.farmersmuseum.org. Admission mid-May to mid-Oct $11 adults, $9.50 seniors, $5 children 7–12; other times $9 adults, $8 seniors, $4 children; always free for children under 7. Apr to mid-May and mid- to late Oct Tues–Sun 10am–4pm; mid-May to mid-Oct daily 10am–5pm.

Fenimore Art Museum ⋆ A visit to this elegant 1930s mansion overlooking Otsego Lake, built on the site of James Fenimore Cooper's home, is a great way to spend an hour. Inside you'll find a revolving collection depicting local life, portraits of Cooper, a great collection of folk art, and examples of Hudson River School paintings. The real treasure is in the collection of Native American art, a section of the museum

---

Tips **Value Pass**

If you're planning on visiting the Baseball **Hall of Fame,** the **Farmers' Museum,** and the **Fenimore Art Museum,** buy a pass at the first one you visit. Entrance to all three costs $29 for adults, $12 for kids. Entry to the Hall of Fame plus one other museum costs $21 for adults, $8 for kids.

---

added in 1995. You'll see masks, sculptures, bows and arrows, headdresses, moccasins, and gorgeous beadwork from tribes all over America.

Lake Rd. © 888/547-1450 or 607/547-1400. Admission $11 adults, $9.50 seniors, $5 children 7–12, free for children under 7. Mid-May to mid-Oct daily 10am–5pm; mid-Oct to Dec and Apr to mid-May Tues–Sun 10am–4pm.

Hyde Hall ⟨ℛ⟩   This enormous neoclassic mansion museum is quite the anomaly here in the land of small towns. Built by George Clarke, the 50-room home was built between 1817 and 1834 to be a showplace at the center of his agricultural empire. It's considered one of the nation's major private architectural undertakings in the years between the Revolutionary and the Civil wars, and it provides a stunning contrast to the Farmers' Museum in showing how the other half lived. Today, you'll explore great rooms, a wine cellar, a chapel, and, of course, servants' quarters. With four structures on the property, 50 rooms, and a gorgeous view of Lake Otsego, you'll want to spend some time beyond the hour-long tour. Bring a picnic lunch!

1 Mill Rd. © 607/547-5098. Tours are either 40 or 70 min.; $7.50–$10 adults, $6.50–$8 seniors, $4–$5 children 5–14. July–Aug Thurs–Tues 10am–5pm, tours on the hour with last tour at 4pm; May to mid-June weekends 10am–5pm (last tour at 4pm), weekdays by appointment; Sept–Oct weekdays 10am–3pm (last tour at 2pm), weekend tours on the hour 10am–5pm (last tour at 4pm). From Cooperstown, go east on Main St. over the bridge and up E. Lake Rd. (Rte. 31) about 8 miles, past Glimmerglass State Park. Turn left on Mill Rd. and follow it for about ½ mile. Turn left.

OUTDOOR ACTIVITIES

BOATING   Take a 1-hour, partially narrated historic tour of gorgeous Lake Otsego aboard the double-decker *Glimmerglass Queen,* 10 Fair St. (© **607/547-9511**). Or do it yourself without the chattering by renting a canoe or kayak from **Sam Smith's Boat Yard,** 6098 State Hwy. 80 (© **607/547-2543**), for $10 to $25 an hour.

GOLF   The Otesaga, 60 Lake St. (© **800/348-6222** or 607/547-9931; www.otesaga. com), has a renowned course that consistently rates among the nation's top resort courses. Even if you're not a duffer, it's worth checking out the intimidating 18th tee, which sits on an island; you have to hit back over the water toward the hotel. Greens fees are $80 for guests, $90 nonguests; save $25 by teeing off after 3pm.

SHOPPING

As you can imagine, baseball memorabilia and all kinds of accessories are the heart of the shopping world here. From autographed baseball cards to inscribed bats and old-time photos, you'll find it all along Main Street. You'll find a good selection at **Pioneer Sports Cards,** 106 Main St. (© **607/547-2323**). Get your wooden bat personalized at **Cooperstown Bat Co.,** 118 Main St. (© **888/547-2415**). Outside of the baseball realm and just outside of town, **Fly Creek Cider Mill & Orchard,** 288 Goose St., Fly Creek (© **607/547-9692;** May–Dec), squeezes out some outstanding cider and is the home of all things apple, even salsa and fudge.

WHERE TO STAY

With a limited supply of rooms and tons of visitors in the summertime, even hotels of dubious quality jack up their rates to near the level of some of the inns in the "expensive" category. In other words, you're better off paying $20 more per night and getting accommodations you can count on. One chain in the city limits is the **Best Western,** 50 Commons Dr. (📞 **607/547-7100**). In Oneonta, 25 miles away, you'll find a **Holiday Inn,** 5206 State Hwy. 23 (📞 **607/433-2250**).

VERY EXPENSIVE

The Otesaga 🏨🏨🏨   Since 1909, The Otesaga has been the grande dame of the area, with luxurious digs on the shores of the gloriously undeveloped Lake Otsego—and today you can experience it only from mid-April to the end of November. Though its infrastructure is thoroughly modern, with voice mail and high-speed Internet, the property has maintained its formal country look. Rooms boast heavy wooden doors, high ceilings, and tons of space. They come luxuriously furnished and very comfortable, not stuffed full of useless amenities; some of them, like no. 245, are huge. Done in creamy tones and floral patterns, there's a refined elegance about the place; step out onto one of the numerous verandas and you'll find serenity as well (along with some great views of the lake and the challenging golf course). ***Drawbacks:*** The service is spotty—some staffers at this old-time hotel are not favorable to special requests. Also, you must stay on the Modified American Plan (MAP), which includes breakfast and dinner.

60 Lake St., Cooperstown, NY 13326. 📞 **800/348-6222** or 607/547-9931. Fax 607/547-9675. www.otesaga.com. 135 units. Late May to mid-Oct $380–$510 double, $510–$550 suite; mid-Apr to late Apr and late Oct to mid-Nov $320–$450 double, $450–$485 suite; May and mid-Oct to late Oct $350–$480 double, $480–$515 suite. Rates include breakfast buffet and 5-course dinner. 2-night minimum on weekends. AE, MC, V. Free valet parking. **Amenities:** 3 restaurants; 2 lounges; heated outdoor pool; 2 tennis courts; exercise room; complimentary canoe and boat use; game room; concierge; small business center; limited room service; babysitting; laundry service; dry cleaning. *In room:* A/C, TV, dataport, hair dryer, iron, safe.

EXPENSIVE

Inn at Cooperstown 🏨🏨   This gorgeous, yellow Victorian inn dates from 1874, and with no TVs or phones in the rooms, it remains a great place to get away from it all. A classic inn without a trace of pretension and amazingly affable innkeepers, it's right off of Main Street and just a short walk from the Hall of Fame. The hotel was the first designed by Henry J. Hardenbergh, who went on to design New York City's Plaza Hotel. The grand dreams he had are more apparent outside of the inn, with the extravagant facade and sweeping veranda. The inside has a very cozy feel: Rooms are by no means enormous but they're comfortable, even though some rooms have quite small showers. Upgrade to the new premium rooms, which have been beautifully redone with four-poster beds and antiques. People congregate downstairs in the sitting room to watch TV, or sit out on the veranda in a rocking chair with a book.

16 Chestnut St., Cooperstown, NY 13326. 📞 **607/547-5756.** Fax 607/547-8779. www.innatcooperstown.com. 17 units. June to Labor Day $203–$253 double, $305 suite; Sept–Nov $189–$209 double, $280 suite; Dec to late Mar midweek $102–$128 double, $175 suite, weekend $118–$148 double, $195 suite; late Mar to May $165–$195 double, $255 suite. Rates include continental breakfast. 2-night minimum on weekends. AE, DISC, MC, V. *In room:* A/C, hair dryer, iron, CD player, no phone.

MODERATE

American Hotel 🏨🏨   Just 25 miles from Cooperstown, the 1847 building that houses the American Hotel was saved from complete ruin by its affable owners and opened in

2002. They've done such an amazing job restoring it that they're actually brave enough to put the "before" photos on their website. Today, the pillars of this inn stand tall outside, while the interior bursts forth with good taste. Though the rooms are on the small side, their simple, subtle colors and eclectic decor keep them bright, airy, and cheery. A couple of rooms have two twin beds, so be sure to specify if you want one bed.

192 Main St., P.O. Box 121, Sharon Springs, NY 13459. © 518/284-2105. www.americanhotelny.com. 9 units. Memorial Day to Columbus Day $108–$190 double; mid-Oct to early Mar and Apr–May $130–$165 double; closed for a month in spring, usually Mar. Rates include full breakfast. 2-night minimum on weekends July–Aug. AE, DC, DISC, MC, V. Between I-88 and I-90 at the crossroads of routes 10 and 20. The hotel is on the east side of Main St./Rte. 10, 3 blocks north of Rte. 20. **Amenities:** Restaurant; lounge. *In room:* A/C, TV, dataport, hair dryer.

INEXPENSIVE

Lake Front Motel and Restaurant   For decent, affordable accommodations that are close to town and come with a view of Lake Otsego, this is your best bet. Yes, rooms are blandly decorated, but still rather spacious considering the price and location. In fact, you get a view of the water from all but a couple of the rooms. Pay a bit more and you can upgrade to a room that sits practically on the water and comes with a private porch.

10 Fair St., Cooperstown, NY 13326. © 607/547-9511. Fax 607/547-2792. www.lakefrontmotelandrestaurant.com. 45 units. July–Aug $125–$190 double; Sept–Oct $85–$150 double; Nov–Apr $70–$150 double; May–June $85–$190 double. 2-night minimum on weekends June–Oct. MC, V. From the traffic light, follow Rte. 80 (Chestnut St.) 1 block north, turn right on Lake St., and continue 2 blocks to Fair St.; turn left. **Amenities:** Restaurant. *In room:* A/C, TV, hair dryer.

CAMPGROUNDS

Cooperstown Shadow Brook Campground, 2149 County Hwy. 31 (© **607/264-8431**), has a pool, playground, stocked fishing pond, and theme weekends and is great for families. **Glimmerglass State Park,** 1527 County Hwy. 31 (© **607/547-8662**), 8 miles outside of Cooperstown, overlooks Lake Otsego.

WHERE TO DINE
EXPENSIVE

Alex & Ika ★★★ CONTINENTAL   This duo recently moved their house of culinary masterpieces from tiny Cherry Valley into the thick of things in Cooperstown, so their inventive dishes are now more accessible when visiting baseball's home. The new restaurant occupies two floors instead of one, but because each floor is roughly the same size as its old location, the cozy feeling hasn't been lost. Fortunately, neither has the quality of the food. Still coming out of the kitchen are spectacular combinations of flavors, like a star anise confit of duck with a lemon grass kaffir-leaf coconut curry. And the changing menu means you'll be able to sample the restaurant's latest creations, which is reason enough to come back to Cooperstown again and again.

149 Main St., Cooperstown. © **607/547-4070.** Reservations suggested. Main courses $30–$32. AE, MC, V. Wed–Sun 5–10pm.

MODERATE

Hoffman Lane Bistro ★★ CONTEMPORARY AMERICAN   Cooperstown's hippest locale sits just off the mayhem of Main Street. People crowd into the lively downstairs bar to hear the occasional musician or just relax. The noise doesn't disrupt a quiet dinner, but for extra privacy, head upstairs. Entrees include tasty pastas, such as mushroom ravioli with toasted almonds, sun-dried tomatoes, and hazelnut cream, as well as inventive home cooking, like the meatloaf made with lamb, pork, and beef, or more complex dishes like pan-seared tuna au poivre in a brandy cream sauce.

2 Hoffman Lane. © 607/547-7055. Reservations recommended. Main courses and pastas $14–$26. AE, MC, V. June–Sept daily 5–9:30pm; Oct–May Wed–Sat 5–9pm.

Nicoletta's Italian Café 🐦 ECLECTIC ITALIAN   Step into this small Main Street restaurant and the delightful aroma of roasted garlic and Italian spices practically knocks you off your feet. You'll find paintings of Italy on the wall and will likely hear Sinatra playing. But even when it gets crowded in this intimate restaurant, it's never too loud for conversation. And once your meal arrives, you may not want to talk anyway. Nicoletta's covers all the basics and does them well—one house favorite is the *frutti di mare,* a full platter of shrimp, scallops, mussels, and clams sautéed in a light roma tomato sauce served over capellini.

96 Main St. © 607/547-7499. Reservations recommended. Main courses and pastas $11–$22. MC, V. Daily 4–9pm.

INEXPENSIVE

Danny's Market 🐦🐦 *Value* DELI   This bustling deli is Main Street's busiest, and there's a good reason: great sandwiches served on excellent homemade fresh-baked bread. The best ones: "Aged in Caves," paper-thin slices of prosciutto with smoked Gouda, tomato, and honey mustard; and the "Chicken Dilemma," which comes with homemade mozzarella and marinated red peppers. Or design your own sandwich. My suggestion? Take it to go and enjoy it lakeside.

92 Main St. © 607/547-4053. Sandwiches $7–$8. MC, V. Mon–Sat 7:30am–7:30pm; Sun 10am–5pm; closes earlier in the winter. Also mid-June to Labor Day Fri–Sat 11pm–3am. Closed Jan.

T.J.'s Place *Kids* AMERICAN   With a life-size hot-dog statue, old Coca-Cola signs, and signed photos of former ballplayers lining the walls—all of it for sale—this is a great place to bring the kids and look for memorabilia. And if you're in the market for lunch or dinner, you'll find all the burger basics, plus down-home cookin' like barbecued spareribs, lasagna, and even liver and onions.

124 Main St. © 800/860-5670 or 607/547-4040. Reservations not accepted. Main courses $10–$17; lunch $6–$10. AE, DISC, MC, V. June–Aug daily 7:30am–10pm; rest of the year daily 7:30am–8pm.

COOPERSTOWN AFTER DARK

PERFORMING ARTS   Glimmerglass Opera, north of Cooperstown on Route 80 (© 607/547-5704), has evolved from performances in the auditorium of Cooperstown High School in 1975 to an internationally acclaimed summer opera house. With four operas in July and August, it produces new, little-known, and familiar operas, among other works of musical theater—all of which are performed in the original language with projected English titles. The 900-seat theater, open since 1987, sits on 43 acres of farmland with unusual sliding walls that allow everyone to enjoy fresh air and views of the countryside before performances and during intermissions. For a fun and easy way to get there, take the Cooperstown Trolley from The Otesaga hotel (round-trip tickets $5).

2 Utica & Environs

96 miles NE of Albany; 203 miles E of Buffalo

Utica had its heyday in the era of the Erie Canal, when manufacturing was booming. It attracted business, travelers, even the founders of a Utopian society—one that went on to create some of the country's finest flatware. The famous Oneida company is still around, and you can buy its gorgeous home products at the **Oneida Outlet Store,** 606 Sherrill Rd., Sherrill (© 315/361-3662), but the Utica/Rome area is hardly the same. Those cities are trying to stage something of a comeback, but it's an uphill struggle: The biggest success story has been the reopening of the gorgeous **Hotel Utica.** Unfortunately, you won't want to spend much time in the cities—there's not much there—but the countryside is very pretty. For nature exploration and outdoor fun, try Howe Caverns and gorgeous Oneida Lake.

ESSENTIALS

GETTING THERE   The New York State Thruway (I-90) passes through the heart of it all. **Amtrak, Greyhound,** and **Adirondack Trailways** all arrive into Utica at Union Station, 321 Main St. (© **315/797-8962**). The major airport in the area is **Syracuse Hancock International** (p. 360).

VISITOR INFORMATION   For the most detailed info, visit or call the **Oneida County Convention & Visitors Bureau,** exit 31 off I-90 (© **800/426-3132**; 9am–7pm daily). For general information, contact the **Central Leatherstocking Region** tourist office (© **800/233-8778**).

GETTING AROUND   This is not the place to be without a car—I-90 will be your quickest (if most boring) way of getting around; just be aware that it's a toll road. If you need a taxi, call **Black & White** (© **315/732-3121**) or **City Comb** (© **315/ 724-5454**).

AREA ATTRACTIONS

Erie Canal Village ★★ *(Kids*   This reconstructed 18th-century settlement makes for a fun and interesting half-day outing for the family. Built on the site where the first shovelful of earth was turned for the Erie Canal on July 4, 1817, there's now an entire village full of Colonial buildings staffed by costumed players. Sound like the Farmers' Museum in Cooperstown? They're very similar, though here you can also take a 40-minute boat ride on the Erie Canal. Walk around at your own pace: you'll see a tavern, ice house, church, blacksmith shop, train station, school, print shop, and three homes. There's also a nice collection of horse-drawn carriages, sleighs, and farm equipment.

5789 New London Rd., Rte. 46 and 49, Rome. © **888/374-3226** or 315/337-3999. Admission $15 adults, $12 seniors and children 13–17, $10 children 5–12, free for children under 5. Memorial Day to Labor Day Wed–Sat 10am–5pm; Sun noon–5pm. Take I-90 to exit 32, turn right on 233N to 49W.

Fort Stanwix ★ *(Kids*   The wooden posts that now guard this 18th-century fort may look out of place today in the middle of downtown Rome, but this fort makes for a fun brief stopover. It's hard to imagine that at one time this area was an essential portage that helped bridge the waterways between the Atlantic Ocean and the Great Lakes, but protecting the strategic position was exactly why this fort was built in 1758. It went on to be an important base of protection during the French and Indian War and the Revolutionary War, and today the fort has been almost completely reconstructed. Take a walk or a guided tour through its grounds and get a glimpse of how fort-bound pioneers once lived.

112 E. Park St., Rome. © **315/338-7730.** Free admission. Fort Apr to late Dec 9am–5pm daily; museum year-round. New York State Thruway to exit 32 to Rte. 233 north to Rte. 365 west, following the signs to downtown Rome.

Howe Caverns ★   Discovered in 1842 when farmer Lester Howe found a passage to central New York's underworld in his field, Howe Caverns has become the area's biggest attraction—you'll see billboards for miles around. And since 1929, when walkways, lighting, and elevators were installed, people have flocked to take the journey.

While it's hardly in the same league as big holes like Mammoth Cave in Kentucky, there's a certain charm to this relatively small underground space, and kids think it's pretty cool. The 80-minute tours are guided and include a quarter-mile boat ride on the underground Lake of Venus.

255 Discovery Dr., Howes Cave. ✆ 518/296-8900. www.howecaverns.com. Admission $18 adults, $15 seniors and children 12–15, $9 children 5–11, free for children under 5. July–Aug 8am–8pm daily; Sept–June 9am–6pm daily. I-90 to exit 25A; I-88 west to exit 22.

Matt Brewing Company 🔍 It has garnered awards for its excellent Saranac Beer, but the Matt Brewing Company, now run by the fourth generation of the Matt family, also produces Saranac and some fun specialty brews, like Three Stooges Ale, out of the Utica headquarters. The 1-hour tour takes you through the entire beer-making process—with tastings, of course.

Brewhouse Sq., Utica. ✆ 800/765-6288 or 315/732-0022. Tours $5 adults, free for children under 14. June–Aug tours are on the hour Mon–Sat 1–4pm, Sun 1–3pm; Sept–May tours Fri–Sat at 1 and 3pm. Tours run 1 hr.; call in advance to make reservations. New York State Thruway exit 31, take Genesee St. south through downtown Utica to Court St. and take a right.

BEACHES & OUTDOOR ACTIVITIES

HITTING THE BEACH On the eastern shore of Oneida Lake lies a nice stretch of sand—**Sylvan Beach.** Lined with restaurants and an amusement park, the slender beach gets absolutely packed with sunbathers in the summertime and parking is tight. If you're planning to soak up the sun, come early or stay here (see below). Farther north on the shores of Lake Ontario, **Sandy Island Beach,** off Route 3 on County Route 15 in Pulaski (✆ 315/387-2657), is part of the Eastern Lake Ontario Dune and Wetland Area, a 17-mile stretch of shoreline. The area is the only significant freshwater dune site in the northeastern U.S., which means not only can you relax on the beach, but you can also go hiking among the dunes to see several species of migratory birds and waterfowl, including sandpipers, plovers, killdeer, gulls, and terns. You may also see foxes, deer, beavers, and turtles moving among the wetland and shore areas.

GOLF In Rome, hit the links at the 9-hole **Delta Knolls Golf Course,** 8388 Elmer Hill Rd. (✆ 315/339-1280; greens fees $7). And in Utica, line up your shots at the **Valley View Golf Course,** 620 Memorial Pkwy., Utica (✆ 315/732-8755; greens fees $33).

ESPECIALLY FOR KIDS

Right on the shores of Oneida Lake is **Sylvan Beach Amusement Park,** on Route 13 in Sylvan Beach (✆ 315/762-5212), which boasts central New York's largest roller coaster. Granted, that's not saying much, but this is a fun little amusement park, especially for younger kids, with bumper cars and boats, a slide, and plenty of games. Best of all, admission is free—you just pay for your activities. A smaller spot for summertime family fun is the **Peterpaul Recreation Park,** Route 49 West, Rome (✆ 315/339-2666). And the **Fort Rickey Children's Discovery Zoo,** 5135 Rome–New London Rd. (✆ 315/336-1930), is a petting zoo where kids can touch a python or a porcupine.

WHERE TO STAY

There are some chains in the area. The nicest is the **Radisson,** 200 Genesee St., Utica (✆ 888/201-1718 or 315/797-8010).

MODERATE

Hotel Utica *★★★ Finds* One of central New York's success stories was the reopening of this grand historic hotel that opened its doors in 1912, shut them in 1972, and reopened in 2001. It's dripping with history: FDR campaigned here in the '20s, jazz great Lionel Hampton played here in 1939, Judy Garland sang here around 1950, and Bobby Kennedy stayed here on a campaign trip. Now it's been totally gutted and redone in grand style, with pillars and chandeliers gracing the elegant lobby. Rooms are huge and outfitted with very comfortable furniture. Decorated in mahogany, royal blues, and deep reds, the rooms have sizable workstations and big bathrooms. In fact, the rooms are big enough that suites aren't worth the extra price unless you need meeting space. Get one on the eighth or ninth floor (future renovations will open floors 10–14) and you'll get a view over the city, which is always nice, even when the city is Utica.

102 Lafayette St., Utica, NY 13502. *©* **877/906-1912** or 315/724-7829. Fax 315/733-7621. www.hotelutica.com. 112 units. Apr–Oct $99–$109 double, $149–$169 suite; Nov–Mar $99–$109 double, $139–$159 suite. AE, DC, DISC, MC, V. **Amenities:** Restaurant; lounge; small exercise room as well as access to nearby health club; 24-hr. small business center; limited room service; same-day dry cleaning. *In room:* A/C, TV w/pay movies (suites have VCRs), dataport, Wi-Fi, fridge (in most rooms), coffeemaker, hair dryer, iron/ironing board.

Sunset Cottages *★* This collection of cottages sits right on the beach at the edge of Lake Oneida. Its location means that there's always a party going on, but inside the rooms it's surprisingly quiet. The cottages themselves are nothing fancy, though they are spacious, with full kitchens, and nicer than any of the lakefront motels. When you book, confirm that linens will be provided, and reserve one of the newer cottages, which are bright and airy.

Park Ave. (P.O. Box 134), Sylvan Beach, NY 13157. *©* **315/762-4093.** www.sylvanbeach.com/sunset.html. 28 units. Apr–Sept $125–$150 double, Oct–Mar $100 double. 2-night minimum stay. MC, V. From I-90 take exit 34 at Canastota. Turn right on Rte. 13 N. for 7 miles. Turn right after crossing the bridge; it loops around to become Park Ave. *In room:* A/C (in the newer units), TV, kitchen.

Turning Stone Resort & Casino *★★* A sprawling, 700-room resort with lots of restaurants, three golf courses, and two spas to complement the ringing slot machines, the Oneida Indian-run Turning Stone has accommodations for every price point and type of traveler. Value seekers can stay down the road in the "inn," a converted Super 8 that has clean, comfortable rooms with a free shuttle to the casino complex. Another option is the casino hotel, where standard rooms are basic, but suites are large and come with upgraded amenities. The "tower" opened in 2004 with dramatic, contemporary rooms and amenities like balconies and fireplaces, not to mention great views of the rolling countryside from the upper floors. Most luxe is the "lodge" that also opened in 2004 and feels like a separate resort. Heavy on wood and modern decor, the spacious suites here boast balconies, and some even have outdoor Jacuzzis. Between the golf and the pools (there are three), you won't get bored here; but you will need to wind down, so book a massage in the new Skaná Spa—it's a soothing environment with several treatment rooms, along with mineral baths and Jacuzzis. *Warning:* At press time, the resort had no liquor license, and was requesting that guests not bring their own, since the policy would help in securing their license for the first time. Call ahead for updates. The excellent restaurant Wildflowers is reviewed below.

5218 Patrick Rd., Verona, NY 13478. *©* **800/771-7711** or 315/361-7711. www.turningstone.com. 713 units. July–Oct doubles $80–$165 midweek, $105–$215 weekend, suites $185 midweek, $235 weekend; Apr–June doubles $69–$149 midweek, $95–$205 weekend, suites $169 midweek, $225 weekend; Nov–Mar doubles $65–$129 midweek, $85–$175 weekend; lodge suites $295 midweek, $395 weekend year-round. Packages available. AE, DC, DISC,

MC, V. Free valet parking. From I-90 take exit 33. **Amenities:** 13 restaurants, from carryout to formal dining; 3 indoor pools; 3 golf courses; 3 indoor tennis courts, 3 outdoor; 2 large exercise rooms; 2 spas; 2 Jacuzzis; game room; courtesy shuttle; small business center; 24-hour room service (in most of hotel); massage (can do in-room); laundry service; same-day dry cleaning. *In room:* A/C, TV w/pay movies, dataport, minibar (in some rooms), coffeemaker (in most rooms), hair dryer, iron, safe (in some rooms).

CAMPGROUNDS

To pitch your tent with a great view of Lake Oneida, set up at **Verona Beach State Park,** 6541 Lake Shore Rd. S., Verona Beach (✆ **315/762-4463**). For another waterview campground, check out **Delta Lake State Park,** 8797 State Rte. 46, Rome (✆ **315/ 337-4670**).

WHERE TO DINE
EXPENSIVE

Wildflowers 𝕳𝕳𝕳 AMERICAN   Turning Stone's signature restaurant in its upscale Lodge is one of the area's best places to eat. The space is contemporary, with wood floors and angled banquettes, but be sure to get a table in the brighter front room; you can also sit outside. Several flambé dishes are prepared tableside by the affable servers, like the Steak Diane in a mushroom red-wine sauce, but even plates presented from the kitchen are dramatic. Fortunately the food delivers, from starters like the Kobe steak and egg to entrees like prosciutto-crusted scallops with seared cantaloupe and orange beurre blanc. *A caveat:* The casino property doesn't have a liquor license and was requesting that guests not bring their own, since it would help in securing a license. Call ahead if this is a concern.

5218 Patrick Rd., Verona (in Turning Stone Resort). ✆ **800/771-7711.** Reservations accepted. Main courses $25–$39. AE, DC, DISC, MC, V. Sun–Thurs 6am–2pm and 5–10pm; Fri–Sat 6am–2pm and 5–11pm.

MODERATE

Savoy 𝕳 AMERICAN   The Savoy is a friendly neighborhood spot that starts filling up fast the moment it opens. Everyone rushes in for the menu that features a good selection of soups, salads, and starters, along with heaping portions of chicken, steak, and fish—along with prime rib on Friday and Saturday nights. You'll also find pastas, like linguine shrimp scampi and a rigatoni with vodka sauce. Or opt for a burger—it's just $6.50.

225 E. Dominick St., Rome. ✆ **315/339-3166.** Main courses $9–$23. AE, DC, DISC, MC, V. Mon–Thurs 11:30am–10pm; Fri 11:30am–11pm; Sat 5–11pm; Sun 4–9pm.

INEXPENSIVE

Harpoon Eddie's 𝕳 AMERICAN   Since this eatery is set right on the beach, there's always a party happening here. In fact, it's the area's best place to sit outside and have a cold drink while checking out all the beach activity. If you want a bite, there are the basic hot dogs, burgers, and wings plus some nice fish dishes like mahimahi, grouper, and haddock sandwiches.

611 Park Ave., Sylvan Beach. ✆ **315/762-5238.** Main courses $5–$12. MC, V. Spring Mon–Thurs 4–10:30pm, Fri–Sat noon–11:30pm, Sun noon–9:30pm; summer Thurs–Sat noon–11:30pm, Sun–Wed noon–10:30pm (the season changes when the owner says it does).

Sea Shell Inn 𝕳 AMERICAN   This is a good alternative to the party-hearty beachfront bars that line Lake Oneida. This laid-back restaurant has knotty pine walls and ceiling fans, while the unique tables are filled with sand and shells and covered with glass. For the most relaxation, head to the tables on the back patio, on a lawn overlooking the lake. Outside of the fried frogs' legs, you won't find anything wildly different on the menu, but it's mostly done well, with emphasis on seafood. Don't fixate on the appetizers: Dinners come with plenty of extras.

Lake Shore Rd., Verona Beach. (© **315/762-4606**. Main courses $9–$16. AE, DISC, MC, V. Apr–Oct Sun from 1pm; Tues–Sat from 4pm.

UTICA & ENVIRONS AFTER DARK

You'll never mistake Utica for New York City, but there's an area called the Brewery District where you can find some decent bars and the occasional live-music show. **The Electric Company,** 700 Varick St., Utica (© **315/792-9271**), displays the work of local artists and hosts local bands while serving up locally (and nationally) brewed suds. To imbibe hipper, more upscale drinks (like martinis) at a hipper, more upscale spot, try **Space 26,** 26 Bank Place, Utica (© **315/735-4407**). And for a homey bar that's been around forever, head to **Griffin's Pub,** 226 Genesee St., Utica (© **315/724-5792**). Gamblers and those in search of name performers should check out **Turning Stone Casino,** just off I-90's exit 33 (© **800/771-7711**). Run by the Oneida Nation, you'll find a wealth of slots and table games, as well as some of the biggest stars that come to this part of New York State. And if you're in the mood for more live entertainment, check out **Beck's Grove Dinner Theater,** 4286 Oswego Rd., Blossvale (© **315/336-7038**), which dates from Prohibition.

11

The Finger Lakes Region

by Neil E. Schlecht

On a map of New York, 11 skinny blue streaks can be seen snaking across the middle of the state. These curious parallel formations are the Finger Lakes, carved by glaciers receding at the end of the last ice age and named for their obvious resemblance to the slender, crooked digits of a human hand. The lakes are deep cobalt, glossy-surfaced, and as narrow as rivers. The vast Finger Lakes region beyond them is a pastoral patchwork of storybook waterfront villages, grand Victorian homes, dairy farms, forests, and wineries amid sloped vineyards. But the lakes run through it all.

The principal "fingers" are the five major lakes that stripe the region. These unique bodies of water, which range in length from 3 to 40 miles and are as narrow as ⅓ of a mile across, are framed by a gentle rise of vineyard-covered banks and rolling hills. The region is one of mesmerizing beauty, like a dream marriage of Scotland and Napa Valley. The lakes have created unique conditions and microclimates that are ideal for grape growing, and this is one of the most notable winemaking regions in the country; an ever-growing roster of nearly 100 wineries dot the banks of the lakes. In contrast to the massive operations of decades past, several are boutique and family-owned wineries that have made great strides in challenging the accepted supremacy of West Coast winemakers. Organized wine trails—comprising the wineries along Cayuga,

Seneca, Keuka, and Canandaigua lakes—make it easy to visit Finger Lakes wineries and taste their wines. Now, chef-driven restaurants are fast taking root to take advantage of the local wines and farm-fresh products.

Quite remarkably, though, the Finger Lakes region remains unknown to many Americans—and even many New Yorkers. Anchored by medium-size upstate cities on either side—Syracuse and Rochester—the Finger Lakes are largely about outdoor recreation and small-town life. Yet the area packs a few surprises, such as the astounding Corning Museum of Glass, in the town made famous by CorningWare; the progressive charms of Ithaca, a quintessential college town; the summer haunts of Mark Twain; the legacy of the Underground Railroad that carried slaves to freedom; and the origins of the women's suffrage and civil rights movements, American aviation, and the modern Mormon Church.

In warm months, the Finger Lakes region comes alive with boaters, cyclists, and wine tourists. Though the area is most often thought of as a summer destination, the ideal time to visit extends from spring to late fall. It can be gorgeous even in winter—which is actually milder than most parts of upstate New York—but perhaps most stunning in autumn, when the brilliant blue lake waters are framed by an earthy palette of reds and yellows and sun-kissed, golden vineyards.

1 Orientation

ARRIVING

BY PLANE   Most visitors traveling by air will fly into either the **Greater Rochester International Airport,** 1200 Brooks Ave., Rochester (© **716/464-6000;** www.roc airport.com), or Syracuse's **Hancock International Airport,** 1000 Colonel Eileen Collins Blvd., Syracuse (© **315/454-4330;** www.syrairport.org); both are serviced by most major airlines. Smaller regional airports are **Elmira/Corning Regional Airport,** 276 Sing Sing Rd., Horseheads (© **607/795-0402;** www.ecairport.com), and small **Ithaca/Tompkins County Airport,** 72 Brown Rd., Ithaca (© **607/257-0456;** www. ithaca-airport.com).

BY CAR   The Finger Lakes region is within a day's drive of most major metropolitan areas in the northeastern U.S. and eastern Canada; Seneca Lake is about 300 miles from New York City, 400 miles from Boston, 230 miles from Toronto, and 275 miles from Philadelphia. The New York State Thruway (**I-90**) travels across the top of the region, from Albany all the way to Rochester and beyond. From Binghamton and Pennsylvania, **I-81** travels north to Syracuse, and **Route 17** west to Corning.

The major car-rental agencies have outlets at the two largest airports.

BY TRAIN   Amtrak (© **800/USA-RAIL;** www.amtrak.com) has service to the Finger Lakes region and heads to Syracuse and Rochester from New York City, Buffalo, Boston, and other cities.

BY BUS   Bus service to the Finger Lakes is available on **Greyhound Bus Lines** (© **800/ 231-2222;** www.greyhound.com), with stations in Ithaca, Syracuse, Geneva, and Rochester, and **Trailways** (© **800/343-9999;** www.trailways.com), which travels to Elmira, Geneva, Rochester, and Syracuse.

VISITOR INFORMATION

For general tourist information before your trip, contact the **Finger Lakes Association,** 309 Lake St., Penn Yan, NY 14527 (© **800/548-4386;** www.fingerlakes.org). Its Web page has contact information and links to each of the region's individual county websites. Another very helpful tourism organization is **Finger Lakes Wine Country** (© **800/813-2958;** www.fingerlakeswinecountry.com), which focuses on the southwestern quadrant of the region, where most of the best wineries are located.

Many good free publications are widely available across the region, at hotels, restaurants, and other sites, with tons of information on wine routes, outdoor activities, accommodations, festivals, and more.

⌐ Fun Fact Say What?

The Finger Lakes take their names from Native American languages of the original inhabitants of the region. Lake and place names can work a real number on your tongue; here's a guide to meanings and pronunciations:

Skaneateles	"long lake"	skinny-atlas
Cayuga	"boat landing"	*kyoo*-gah
Seneca	"place of the stone"	*sen*-uh-kah
Keuka	"canoe landing"	*kyoo*-kah
Canandaigua	"chosen place"	can-uhn-*day*-gwuh

The Finger Lakes Region

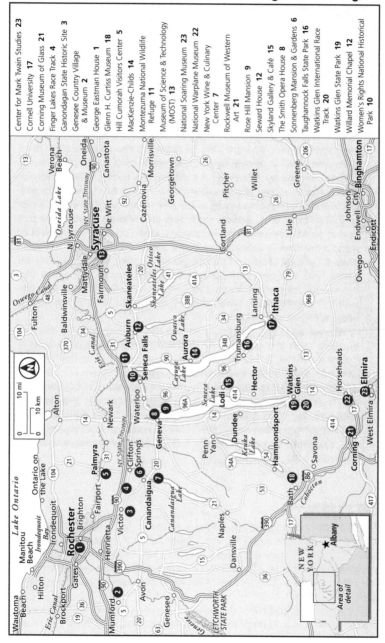

Moments   The Finger Lakes Wine Trails

The Finger Lakes region, with nearly 100 wineries and some 10,000 acres of vineyards, is one of the nation's great wine-producing regions. The region is continually growing in name recognition and estimation among wine aficionados, and many visitors compare it to the Napa Valley of 2 decades ago. A cool-climate viticultural region—comparable to the Burgundy and Champagne regions in France—the Finger Lakes are ideal for growing vinifera, or noble (European), grapes. The region produces excellent Riesling, chardonnay, cabernet franc, and sparkling ice wines. It's also a terrific place to try more unusual wines, such as Gewürztraminer, Rkatsiteli, and rare ice wines.

The wine country is centered around four main lakes: Cayuga, Seneca, Keuka, and, to a lesser degree, Canandaigua. Pick up brochures on the individual trails in the region as well as the *Free Map & Guide* of all the wineries in the Finger Lakes, and see the listings and sidebars on each wine trail below. An indispensable stop for anyone either prior to winery visits or without the time or inclination to attack a wine trail is the new **New York Wine & Culinary Center** in Canandaigua (see p. 334), and while there are events held at wineries throughout the warm months, one of the best times—or at least one of the most hedonistic—is the **Finger Lakes Wine Festival** (*©* **866/461-7223**; www.flwinefest.com), held in late July at the Watkins Glen International racetrack.

You may want to think about someone else doing the driving; limo and bus wine tours are quite popular in season. For organized wine tours in limousines and other multipassenger vehicles, contact one of the following wine transportation and tour specialists: **Finger Lakes Winery Tours & Transportation** (*©* **315/828-6289**; www.fingerlakeswinerytours.com); **Quality Winery Tours** (*©* **877/424-7004**; www.qualitywinetours.com); **VRA Imperial Limousine, Inc.** (*©* **800/303-6100**; www.implimo.com); **Park Place Limousine and Transportation Services** (*©* **585/223-6244**; www.rochesterlimousine.com); and **Grapevine Country Tours** (*©* **800/536-8123**; www.grapevinecountry tours.com).

AREA LAYOUT

Stretching from Lake Ontario in the north almost to the Pennsylvania border, about midway between New York City and Niagara Falls, the Finger Lakes region covers some 9,000 square miles and touches upon 14 counties, occupying a huge chunk of central-western New York. The region is roughly equidistant between Albany and Buffalo and extends from Lake Ontario in the north and almost to the Pennsylvania border in the south.

The region is covered below in a clockwise direction, beginning with the southeast region around Ithaca. Many of the major towns and attractions in the area tend to be clustered at the top or bottom ends of lakes. When you're traveling by car, it's probably easiest to move in one direction from east to west or west to east, rather than circling entire lakes that, though not wide, are certainly long.

GETTING AROUND

BY CAR   A car is virtually indispensable for any kind of traveling in the Finger Lakes region. There is very little public transportation in the area, except between major cities. The major car-rental companies have outlets at both Rochester International Airport and Syracuse's Hancock International Airport.

BY ORGANIZED TOUR   Finger Lakes Tours, Ltd., Drawer 9, Jasper, NY 14855 (© **607/792-3663;** www.finger-lakes-tours.com), offers all-inclusive family, hunting, fishing, biking and hiking, wine festival, and even "women only" organized tours of the region, in a variety of price ranges. **New World Tour Company** (© **607/387-6292**) and **Grapevine Country Tours** (© **877/536-8123;** www.grapevinecountry tours.com) organize Finger Lakes Wine Trail tours.

2 Ithaca ★★ & Southern Cayuga Lake

240 miles NW of New York City; 40 miles E of Corning

Ithaca, home to Cornell University and Ithaca College, may be best known as a laid-back college town, but given its stunning setting on the south shore of 40-mile-long Cayuga Lake, and sandwiched between two incredible gorges, it perhaps deserves to be even better known for its natural beauty. Certainly that's not lost on residents, many of whom cruise around town with T-shirts or bumper stickers that read "Ithaca is Gorges." Ithaca is a cosmopolitan town with many of the amenities of a bigger city, such as good restaurants, bars, and theaters, but few of the hassles—all of which contributed to its once being ranked as the no. 1 "emerging city" in the U.S., by *Cities Ranked & Rated.* The city and surrounding Tompkins County abound in beautiful natural areas ripe for hiking, biking, and other outdoor activities, while wine fans can follow the Cayuga Wine Trail. Some 15 wineries line the southern (and mostly western) section of the lake, where they are easily accessible from Ithaca.

ESSENTIALS
GETTING THERE

BY AIR   The regional **Ithaca/Tompkins County Airport,** 72 Brown Rd., Ithaca (© **607/257-0456;** www.ithaca-airport.com or www.flyithaca.com), is serviced by US Airways and Northwest Airlines. It's less than 10 miles north of town on Route 13.

BY CAR   Ithaca is about a 4-hour drive from New York City. The nearest major highways are I-81, which travels north to Syracuse, and Route 17, which heads west to Corning. Routes 13 and 96B head directly into Ithaca.

BY BUS   Greyhound stops in Ithaca at the Brenda Wallace Bus Terminal, 710 W. State St. (© **800/231-2222** or 607/272-7930); **Shortline Bus** (© **800/631-8405** or 607/277-8800; www.shortlinebus.com) travels to Ithaca, also stopping at 710 W. State St., as well as Elmira, from New York City.

VISITOR INFORMATION   The **Ithaca/Tompkins County Convention & Visitors Bureau** is located at 904 E. Shore Dr., Ithaca (© **800/284-8422** or 607/272-1313; www.visitithaca.com).

EXPLORING ITHACA & SOUTHERN CAYUGA LAKE

The top attraction in town is probably **Cornell University ★★,** a handsome Ivy League school on 745 acres, which sits high on a hill in so-called "Collegetown," from which it surveys the rest of Ithaca and the splendid stripe of Cayuga Lake that stretches

Cayuga Wine Trail

The **Cayuga Wine Trail** ⚐ (© 800/684-5217; www.cayugawinetrail.com) comprises a grouping of 15 small wineries clustered around Cayuga Lake. As the first wine trail in New York State, it has served as the model for the three other Finger Lakes wine trails. A tour of the wineries on the west side of Cayuga (all but two on the trail) could easily be combined with visits to wineries on the east side of Seneca Lake (see p. 316). Among those welcoming visitors for tours and tastings are (listed in order from south to north on each bank of the lake):

East Bank
- **Long Point Winery** ⚐, 1485 Lake Rd., Aurora (© 315/364-6990; www. longpointwinery.com), is one of the few Finger Lakes wineries that might make better dry reds—including merlot, cabernet franc, and Syrah—than whites. The farmhouse tasting room has great long views of Cayuga Lake. (Mon–Thurs 10am–5pm, Fri–Sat 10am–6pm, Sun 11am–5:30pm; closed Jan)

West Bank
- **Lucas Vineyards** ⚐, 3862 County Rd. 150, Interlaken (© 800/682-WINE; www.lucasvineyards.com), Cayuga Lake's oldest winery, is a family-owned operation with a farmhouse tasting room and attractively landscaped gardens with great water views. Don't mind some wines' cutesy names ("Miss Behavin'"; "Miss Chevious—a Nautie white."). (Jan–Apr Mon–Sat 10:30am–5pm, Sun noon–5pm; May–Dec Mon–Sat 10:30am–5:30pm, Sun noon–5:30pm)
- **Sheldrake Point Vineyard & Simply Red Bistro** ⚐⚐, 7448 County Rd. 153, Ovid (off Rte. 89) (© 866/743-5372 or 607/532-9401; www.sheldrakepoint. com), has one of the more appealing compounds on a mid-19th-century

northward. On campus, the top public draw is the **Herbert F. Johnson Museum of Art** ⚐ (University Ave.; © 607/255-6464; www.museum.cornell.edu; Tues–Sun 10am–5pm; free admission), a modern cement structure designed by I. M. Pei (1973). The museum counts more than 30,000 pieces in its collection, with particular strengths in Asian art (ranging from antiquity to contemporary artists from Japan, China, India, and the Himalayas and Middle East), as well as prints and photographs. The museum hosts interesting traveling exhibitions, but even visitors without strong interests in art shouldn't miss the unsurpassed fifth-floor views of Cayuga Lake and the gentle hillsides surrounding Ithaca. Across the street from the museum is a path that leads down to a suspension bridge over **Fall Creek Gorge** ⚐, one of two beautiful and deep gorges that frame the Cornell campus, and Beebe Lake. The trails around the gorge and lake are popular with sunbathing students who make their way down to the water. Find your way to **Ithaca Falls** and stand near the cascading falls that rush down tiers of stone 100 feet high and 175 feet wide. The most visible building on campus, McGraw Tower, is known for the **Cornell Chimes,** an old school tradition played daily by students and alumni (for information about chimes concerts, call © 607/255-5330). **Cornell campus tours** are available by calling © 670/254-INFO.

farmstead, with a nice lakeside restaurant serving lunch and dinner (May–Oct; see p. 311) and outdoor seating, a professionally run tasting shop, and handsomely designed labels. I quite like their dry Riesling and cabernet franc. (Jan–Mar daily noon–5pm; Apr–Dec daily 11am–5:30pm)

- **Hosmer Winery** 🐸🐸, 6999 Rte. 89, Ovid (© **607/869-3393**; www.hosmer winery.com), produces some of the finest dry Rieslings in the region. The tasting room and gift shop are the antithesis of slick, but fans of cool-climate whites are in for a treat. Try the Vintner's reserve Riesling, the award-winning dry and semidry Riesling, and the dry rosé. (Apr–Dec Mon–Sat 10am–5pm, Sun noon–5pm; Jan–Mar Fri–Sun noon–4pm, Mon–Thurs by appointment)

- **Goose Watch Winery** 🐸, 5480 Rte. 89, Romulus (© **315/549-2599**; www.goosewatch.com), has a relaxed tasting room in an old barn and excellent views of the lake, a picnic deck, and boat docking—not to mention an interesting selection of premium wines, including a number of unusual varietals you may never have heard of, like Diamond, Chamcourcin, Lemberger, Villard Blanc, Melody, Rosé of Isabella, and Traminette, as well as pinot gris, viognier, and white port. (Open year-round daily 10am–6pm)

- **Swedish Hill Vineyard**, 4565 Rte. 414, Romulus (© **888/549-WINE** or 315/549-8326; www.swedishhill.com), is a family-owned operation that offers a very large selection of wines, including chardonnay, Riesling, port, and brandy. (Year-round daily 9am–6pm; guided tours May–Oct weekdays 1 and 3pm, weekends noon, 2, and 4pm)

East of Beebe Lake is the university's museum of living plants, **Cornell Plantations** 🐸 (1 Plantations Rd., Cornell University; © **607/255-2400;** www.plantations.cornell.edu; daily 9am–6pm; free admission), a real find and well worth a visit for garden lovers or anyone seeking a bit of solace. The public is welcome to visit the botanical garden, wildflower garden, and Newman Arboretum, which specializes in New York State trees and shrubs, as well as any of the 3,000 acres of natural areas in and around the campus (which contains more than 9 miles of walking trails). Of particular interest are the orderly herb garden with raised theme beds (herbs are grouped according to usage) and a quiet knoll area that contains more than 300 species of rhododendrons. Free "drop-in tours" are offered on Wednesdays and Saturdays, and there are other walks and classes available; check the schedule online for events. Part of the Cornell Lab of Ornithology is the **Sapsucker Woods Bird Sanctuary** 🐸 (159 Sapsucker Woods Rd., off Rte. 13, Ithaca; © **800/843-BIRD;** www.birds.cornell.edu; Mon–Thurs 8am–5pm, Fri 8am–4pm, and Sat 10am–4pm; trails open daily; free admission), housed in a fabulous new building within the Sapsucker Woods Sanctuary, home to many different bird species. An observatory, a bird-feeding garden, trails, and a multimedia theater that allows visitors to hear birds in surround sound will appeal to hard-core birders.

Just 7 miles north of Ithaca, in Trumansburg along the west side of Cayuga Lake, is one of the region's most beautiful sights. Tucked in **Taughannock Falls State Park** ★★ (Taughannock Park Rd./Rte. 89 N.; © 607/387-6739) is the highest free-falling waterfall in the eastern U.S.; at 215 feet, it is higher even than Niagara Falls. You can drive up to a lookout or hike in from the entrance to the park (the hike is an easy, flat 3/4-mile walk). The falls are best viewed in spring and fall; in summer there is often very little water and visitors are inevitably disappointed. Summer concerts are held in the park.

ESPECIALLY FOR KIDS

Families will enjoy a visit to **Sciencenter,** 601 First St. (© 607/272-0600; www. sciencenter.org), a hands-on science museum with a walk-in camera, outdoor playground, "piano stairs," and other exhibits that will entertain children. It's open Tuesday to Saturday from 10am to 5pm, Sunday from noon to 5pm (July and Aug, also open Mon 10am–5pm; admission $6 adults, $5 seniors, $4 children 3–17). The museum's **Sagan Planet Walk** is an outdoor scale model of the sun and nine planets, built as a memorial to Cornell astronomer Carl Sagan. The walk starts at The Commons in downtown, goes along Willow Avenue and Cayuga Street, and ends at Sciencenter, about ¾ mile away; kids can get a passport to the solar system stamped at stations along the way and earn free admission to Sciencenter.

The **Museum of the Earth** (at the Paleontological Research Institution), 1259 Trumansburg Rd. (© 607/273-6623; www.museumoftheearth.org), is an 18,000-square-foot interactive exhibit and education facility dedicated to the 3.5-billion-year history of life on Earth. It displays one of the country's largest fossil collections, including the skeleton of the Hyde Park Mastodon and a 500-foot mural, "The Rock of Ages, Sands of Time." It's open Monday, Wednesday, Friday, and Saturday from 10am to 5pm, Thursday 10am to 7pm, and Sunday from noon to 4pm. Admission is $8 for adults and teens, $5 for seniors, and $3 for children 3 to 12.

Children will enjoy the opportunity to climb high into the forest canopy on the TreeTops observation tower at **The Cayuga Nature Center,** 1420 Taughannock Blvd. (Rte. 89; © 607/273-6260). The falls, trails, and swimming at **Taughannock Falls State Park** are also popular with kids of all ages.

SPORTS & OUTDOOR PURSUITS

Tompkins County, and specifically the area around Ithaca and Cayuga Lake, replete with gorges, glens, and state parks, is one of the best in the Finger Lakes for all manner of outdoor sports, from hiking and biking to golf and sailing. Locals are a very outdoorsy lot, so you'll have plenty of company.

Outdoors outfitters, with backpacking, canoeing, and skiing equipment, include **Cornell Outdoor Education,** Bartels Hall, Campus Road, Cornell University (© 607/255-1807); **The Outdoor Store,** 206 The Commons (© 607/273-3891); and **Eastern Mountain Sports,** 722 Meadow St. (© 607/272-1935).

BOATING & SAILING   Cayuga Lake Cruises' **Dinner Cruise** aboard the 1915 **M/V Manhattan** is a great way to see Cayuga Lake. The boat sets sail mid-April to late October from the waterfront (M/V *Manhattan* Pier), 708 W. Buffalo St. (© 607/256-0898; cayugalakecruises.com). The company offers dinner, lunch, and brunch cruises. Lake charters for sightseeing and fishing on Cayuga Lake are available from **Tiohero Tours** (© 866/846-4376; www.tioherotours.com), which offers 1- and 2-hour narrated lake tours, and from **Loon-A-Sea Charters** (© 607/387-5474; www.loon-a-sea.com).

(Kids) Ithaca Festival

If you're lucky enough to find yourself in Ithaca the first weekend after Memorial Day, you'll stumble upon an event that reveals the community-based soul of this college town, during the lively and friendly annual **Ithaca Festival**, which has been put on in charming low-key fashion since the late 1970s. The opening parade on Friday is a wacky classic, including adults parading as dancing tofu, kids dressed up like compost piles, and the hilarious Volvo Ballet, complete with tutus wrapped around boxy station wagons. Call (C) **607/273-3646** or visit www.ithacafestival.org for information.

Private boat rentals are available from **Taughannock Boat Rentals,** Taughannock Park Road (Rte. 89; (C) **607/387-4439**), and **Puddledockers,** 704 W. Buffalo St. ((C) **607/273-0096;** www.puddledockers.com), for nonmotorized boat rentals.

CAMPING   Taughannock Falls State Park, Taughannock Park Road/Route 89 in Trumansburg, allows camping; call (C) **800/456-CAMP** or 607/387-6739 or visit www.reserveamerica.com for more information. For private campgrounds, check out **Spruce Row Campsite & RV Resort,** 2271 Kraft Rd. ((C) **607/387-9225**), near Taughannock Falls State Park, which has a swimming pool and plenty of family recreation.

HIKING & BIKING   **Excellent trails for hiking and biking exist all over the Ithaca area. On the Cornell University campus, there are more than 9 miles of trails operated by **Cornell Plantations ((C) **607/255-2400**). **Six Mile Creek Gorge,** on Hudson Street across from the South Hill School, is an old Native American trail that passes a former mill and a wildflower preserve. The beautiful **Cascadilla Creek Gorge** (K), at University Avenue and Court Street, is a greenway connecting downtown Ithaca to the colleges on the hills (Cornell and Ithaca College). The gorge walk, past gently cascading waterfalls, is just over a mile long with plenty of stairs for a good workout. The **South Hill Recreation Way,** off Hudson Street, is a gravel trail built on a railroad track and it's very popular with local joggers, cyclists, and cross-country skiers. You can enter near Crescent Place, where there's a self-guided interpretative nature tour. Trails in and around **Ithaca Falls,** off Lake Street, are among the most scenic in the area, as are those that lead to the falls in **Taughannock Falls State Park,** off Route 89 in Trumansburg. The **Cayuga Waterfront Trail,** when completed over the next few years, will be a 6-mile linear park along the southern tip of Cayuga Lake.

The **Cayuga Nature Center,** 1420 Taughannock Blvd. (Rte. 89; (C) **607/273-6260**), has 5 miles of hiking trails and the TreeTops observation tower. The **Circle Greenway,** 108 E. Green St. ((C) **607/272-1313**), is a 10-mile walk that passes the waterfront, gorges, the Cornell campus, and The Commons downtown.

Trail maps for many of these hikes are available at the tourism information office or local sports shops.

Bike rentals are available from **The Outdoor Store,** 206 The Commons ((C) **607/273-3891**), and **Cayuga Mountain Bike Shop,** 138 W. State St. ((C) **607/277-6821**). Check with these outfitters to see which trails allow mountain bikers.

GOLF   **There are half a dozen golf courses in the area; one of the best is **Hillendale Golf Course, 218 N. Applegate Rd. ((C) **607/273-2363;** www.hillendale.com). Greens fees are $16 during the week, $18 on weekends; discounts for seniors and juniors (under 18) are available.

SWIMMING   **Buttermilk Falls State Park,** Route 13 South (© 670/273-5761), has a natural pool at the base of the falls. There is also swimming in **Taughannock Falls State Park,** off Route 89 in Trumansburg, though areas close to the falls are off-limits. **Cass Park,** 701 Taughannock Blvd. (Rte. 89N; © 607/273-9211), has an Olympic-size swimming pool that's open to the public.

WINTER SPORTS   Cross-country skiers should head to **Taughannock Falls State Park** (© 607/387-6739), off Route 89 in Trumansburg, or the terrifically named **Podunk Cross-Country Ski Center,** Podunk Road, Trumansburg (© 607/387-3093), which has 7 miles of trails, with rental and instruction available. Most of the state parks in the area allow Nordic skiing. The closest downhill skiing is in Cortland, at **Greek Peak Mountain,** 200 Rte. 392 (© 800/955-2-SKI; www.greekpeak.net). Ice-skating is found at **Cass Park Rink & Pool,** 701 Taughannock Blvd., Route 89 (© 607/273-9211).

SHOPPING

Downtown Ithaca Commons, or simply "The Commons," at the corner of West State and Cayuga streets, is a pleasant area of shops and restaurants along a wide pedestrian boulevard. It's packed with gift shops, clothing stores, bookstores, and art galleries. If you're interested in touring art studios and galleries, pick up a copy of *Greater Ithaca Art Trail* (www.arttrail.com), a guide to the studios of 49 local artists; open studio weekends are held in October. For a good sense of the region's agricultural and artsy roots, visit the **Ithaca Farmers Market,** Route 13 at Steamboat Landing (Third St.); it's open April through December on Saturday from 9am to 3pm, and June through October, Sunday from 10am to 3pm (© 607/273-7109; www.ithaca market.com). A cooperative with more than 125 local members, the market, in a covered pavilion on the waterfront, delivers a fabulous and entertaining array of produce, food vendors, music, art, and crafts. Cheese heads and others interested in local farm products should make the short trek to **Bronson Hill Cheesery,** 5491 Bergen Rd., Mecklenburg (on the west side of Cayuga Lake; © 607/387-3108), a family farm that specializes in fresh, handcrafted cow-milk cheeses.

WHERE TO STAY

Hotel rooms are at a premium (both impossible to find and expensive) during Cornell and Ithaca College graduations (end of May) and Finger Lakes region festivals and events (including NASCAR); high season lasts from April to November. Rates at inns are generally also higher on weekends. The newest addition to the Ithaca hotel scene is the **Hilton Garden Inn,** 130 E. Seneca St. (© 607/277-8900; www.ithaca.garden inn.com). It has 104 rooms ($164–$229 double) and excellent lake views from the top floors of a new nine-story building. Visitors might also want to consider staying in Aurora at the spectacular **Aurora Inn** (35 min. north along Cayuga Lake's east bank); see the sidebar on p. 312.

EXPENSIVE

The Statler Hotel   On the campus of Cornell, this large and well-run hotel is associated with the university's Hotel Management School and the staff includes part-time student workers. Rooms are good-size, standard modern hotel rooms, though they have Four Seasons pillow-top bedding and nice linens. Bathrooms are small, but have nice marble countertops. Many rooms have excellent views of the campus extending all the way to Cayuga Lake.

11 East Ave., Cornell University, Ithaca, NY 14853. © **800/541-2501** or 607/257-2500. Fax 607/254-2504. www. statlerhotel.cornell.edu. 153 units. $160–$199 double; $175–$475 suite. AE, DC, MC, V. Free parking. **Amenities:** 3 restaurants; limited room service; laundry service. *In room:* A/C, TV w/pay movies, dataport, high-speed Internet access, coffeemaker, hair dryer.

MODERATE

Inn on Columbia 🍴🍴 *Finds*   Less B&B than European-style boutique hotel (albeit with just three rooms), this completely revamped 1832 Greek Revival house on South Hill, near Ithaca College and Cornell, is a swank and stylish place to stay. It's owned by a married couple, the husband an architect (he did the revamping) and the wife a chef who cooks up Asian-fusion dishes and inventive breakfasts "when guests allow her to." Choose the room in the main house, with vaulted ceilings and skylights; the carriage house, with an outdoor deck, full kitchen, and living room; or the hexagonal gazebo room (the last two are detached from the main house, in the pretty gardens out back). No architectural detail has been overlooked, from automatic lights to custom furniture; the overall aesthetic is cool and modern. For longer stays, ask about rooms in several other houses similarly restored by the owners in the same neighborhood. If you're pulling into town with no shelter arranged, check out the "Procrastinator's Special"—any unoccupied room is just $99 if reserved for that night.

228 Columbia St., Ithaca, NY 14850. © **607/272-0204.** www.columbiabb.com. 3 units. $175–$225 main house double; $250-$275 carriage house and gazebo. Rates include full breakfast. DC, MC, V. Free parking. *In room:* A/C, TV, Wi-Fi, hair dryer, stereo.

La Tourelle Resort & Spa 🍴   Another fine country inn in a peaceful location on the outskirts of Ithaca, this small hotel is a good choice for those who like the amenities of large hotels, but some of the intimacies of smaller inns. La Tourelle recently added a full-service "August Moon" day spa as well as 19 new rooms. The lobby is handsomely done in Mexican tiles, and the 70-acre grounds, with four tennis courts, are lovely. Rooms are large and decorated with either light wood furnishings and salmon-colored floral designs or darker Mexican, handcrafted furniture and more masculine decor. The feather beds are plush and the bathrooms quite large. Though their appeal may be limited, two incongruous tower rooms are circular and have kitschy sunken round beds, mirror-paneled ceilings, and even a disco ball—perfect for that retro anniversary weekend! Tennis fans can stay at the tennis cottage near the courts. The John Thomas Steakhouse on the property is a fine country restaurant specializing in dry-aged beef.

1150 Danby Rd. (Rte. 96B), Ithaca, NY 14850. © **607/273-2734.** Fax 607/300-1500. www.latourelleinn.com. 54 units. $125–$299 double. AE, DC, MC, V. Free parking. **Amenities:** Restaurant; cafe; 4 tennis courts (2 lighted for night play). *In room:* A/C, TV w/pay movies, dataport, high-speed Internet access, coffeemaker, hair dryer.

Taughannock Farms Inn 🍴🍴 *Value*   Well known for its restaurant, which has served deluxe four-course meals for more than 60 years, this large inn is really a compound, occupying an exquisite 1873 mansion and three more modern guesthouses. It's on a beautiful location at the edge of Taughannock State Park, overlooking Cayuga Lake. The main house has but five rooms, with either lake or forest views; though guests have to contend with the restaurant's popularity, those rooms have a bit more character than the more private and generally modern guesthouse rooms. Rooms are nicely decorated with some Victorian antiques and bold wallpapers and floral decor. The guesthouses are particularly good for families and friends traveling together; one guesthouse is the former early-1900s icehouse, and a few rooms are in the innkeeper's

Cayuga Lakeside Inns

Ithaca may overlook the southern tip of Cayuga Lake, but if you want a real lakeside room, the **Silver Strand at Sheldrake,** a Victorian B&B on the west bank, is about as close as you can get to being on the lake without sleeping on a boat. Come for the stupendous views; the inn sits on a quiet road on Sheldrake Point, which opens to expansive, distant vistas of the lake. All five of its simply decorated rooms have lake views as well as private decks. The inn, in a large mid-19th-century manse at 7398 Wyers Point Rd., Ovid, NY 14521 (© **800/ 283-5253;** www.silverstrand.net), is about 20 miles north of Ithaca on the west side of Cayuga Lake (and only minutes from about a half-dozen wineries). Silver Strand offers guests the use of bikes, boats, and a private beach and sun deck. Rates are $125 to $205 double, including breakfast. Another great lakeside inn, **Aurora Inn,** is on the east bank of Cayuga Lake, about a half-hour from Ithaca; see more about it in the sidebar on Aurora, on p. 312.

residence. The inn, a member of the Select Registry of Distinguished Inns, is open seasonally only, from May to November. The new 10-room guesthouse across the property has great lake views (in king rooms, you can even survey the lake from your Jacuzzi tub), but the modern decor is a bit lacking in personality.

2030 Gorge Rd. (Rte. 89 at Taughannock State Park), Trumansburg, NY 14886. © **888/387-7711** or 607/387-7711. www.t-farms.com. 22 units. $80–$180 main inn double; $75–$200 guesthouse double. Rates include full breakfast. AE, DC, MC, V. Free parking. **Amenities:** Restaurant; small bar. In room: A/C, TV (in guesthouse rooms only), dataport, high-speed Internet access, coffeemaker, hair dryer.

William Henry Miller Inn ★★★   The top B&B in Ithaca—one of the most beautiful private homes in town—has an enviable downtown location: just paces from The Commons. An 1880 Victorian built by Cornell's first architecture student (he of the inn's name), and owned by just two families before becoming an inn, the house combines rich details like stained-glass windows and custom chestnut woodwork. Seven rooms are in two floors of the main house, and there are a two-room suite and another room in the carriage house. Rooms are very handsomely decorated, with select antiques, but without the clichéd crush of Victoriana one often finds. Bathrooms are uncluttered and modern (several have Jacuzzi tubs), and several are simply huge. It's tough to pick a winner, but my favorite may be the soothing Library guest room. The charming and considerate owner, Lynette, has added ramps and a wheelchair elevator, making a couple of rooms completely accessible, a real rarity at a B&B. She also puts out home-baked dessert items in the evening, and serves a lovely breakfast.

303 N. Aurora St., Ithaca, NY 14850. © **607/256-4553.** Fax 607/256-0092. www.millerinn.com. 9 units. $155–$215 double; $200–$235 suite. Rates include full breakfast and evening dessert. AE, DC, MC, V. Free parking. **Amenities:** Wi-Fi; Wheelchair elevator; rooms for those w/limited mobility. In room: A/C, TV, hair dryer, CD player, Jacuzzi (some rooms).

WHERE TO DINE

Ithaca is quite cosmopolitan for a small city, and its roster of diverse restaurants of various nationalities and persuasions, everything from Greek to barbecue and cutting-edge vegetarian, reflects its widespread tastes and personality. You can choose to dine on the waterfront, at a college hangout, or out in the country at an elegant inn.

EXPENSIVE

Simply Red Lakeside Bistro ★★ *Value* CREATIVE AMERICAN BISTRO   Relocated in 2007, after 4 years in the little village of Trumansburg, to the welcoming arms of Sheldrake Point Winery on the west bank of Cayuga Lake, Simply Red still has the South Africa–born chef Samantha Izzo at the helm, and it's named for her flaming locks. Although this terrific bistro now presents a tidy, uptown look—the original tilted more toward intimate bohemian chic—it's still one of the best restaurants in the Finger Lakes. Its fresh menu, best sampled in the "chef's table" prix-fixe menu that changes every week, is all about fresh, made-from-scratch items based on locally grown produce and regionally raised, free-range, grain-fed meats. Izzo makes a real effort to show off the bounty of the Finger Lakes. Monday nights feature "Mama Red's Comfort Kitchen," featuring Southern standards such as fried green tomatoes, shrimp and grits, and cornmeal-crusted, Cajun-spiced catfish. The three-course prix-fixe dinner on other nights, just $35, is an outstanding deal (and you can pair it with wines for just an extra $10). Lunch is mostly tasty salads, sandwiches, and tartlets, while Sunday brunch features live jazz musicians. The small but select wine list has some of the best vintages from the Finger Lakes and some interesting international selections.

7448 County Rd. 153, Ovid. ℭ **607/532-9401.** Reservations recommended. Main courses $17–$27. DC, MC, V. Daily 11am–3pm; Mon and Fri–Sat 5–9pm.

Taughannock Farms Inn ★ *Value* AMERICAN   This large Victorian inn and estate has an elegant dining room overlooking Cayuga Lake. It has been an inn since 1945, and its four-course meals—for which diners pay a single entree price—are a local favorite. Diners start with an appetizer, which might be roasted almond-and-mushroom pâté; move on to a salad; and then tuck into a timeless entree: New York strip, rack of lamb, prime rib, or the catch of the day. Vegetarians have a single choice: Portobello Wellington. Save room for dessert; the menu lists more than a dozen homemade options.

2030 Gorge Rd., Trumansburg. ℭ **607/387-7711.** Reservations recommended. Main courses $25–$51. AE, MC, V. May–Oct Mon–Sat 5–9pm, Sun 3–8pm; Apr and Nov Thurs–Sat 5–9pm, Sun 3–8pm.

MODERATE

Just a Taste Wine & Tapas Bar ★ SPANISH/TAPAS   The tantalizingly long list of authentic Spanish tapas at night and the casual lunch menu of salads and creative sandwiches at this popular spot take a back seat to its locally nonpareil wine lists. Choose from among 40 wines by the glass (or taste or half-liter) and many more by the bottle, or check out the interesting international wine flights of five to six wines (on my last visit, there were seven different flights and a few very hard-to-find bottles on offer). If you're not sure about a wine, your server will even give you a "sip," just like getting a taste at the local ice-cream parlor. The main restaurant is a little nondescript, but the backyard garden patio is a very pleasant place to dine—or, let's face it, just drink—in warmer months. If tapas aren't your bag, there are usually a couple of pasta dishes and a meat or fish dish featured.

116 N. Aurora St., Ithaca. ℭ **607/277-WINE.** Reservations recommended on weekends. Main courses $9.50–$15; tapas $3–$8. AE, DC, MC, V. Mon–Fri 11:30am–3:30pm; Sat–Sun 10:30am–2:30pm; Sun–Thurs 5:30–10pm; Fri–Sat 5:30–11pm.

Maxie's Supper Club and Oyster Bar ★★ *Value* CAJUN/SEAFOOD   A lively local late-night favorite, this New Orleans–style restaurant in a former Union hall is a taste of Cajun country in upstate New York. It's a great place to kick back and enjoy

Aurora's Amazing Makeover

Until recently, the diminutive but picturesque village of Aurora was just a little-known town speck in the Finger Lakes, albeit one with million-dollar views from the east shore of Cayuga Lake. It basically consisted of a main street, a tiny women's college, and an idiosyncratic ceramics factory. In the past few years, though, it has undergone a startling makeover. For a while, whispers could be heard all over the Finger Lakes: "Did you hear about the town that rich woman bought?" As it turns out, Pleasant Rowland, who attended Wells College in Aurora and made a fortune with her American Girl dolls (which she sold to Mattel), didn't exactly purchase the town. Rather, she decided to direct her philanthropy toward her alma mater, bestowing both the college and the town with a series of gifts, including multimillion-dollar restorations of historic buildings owned by the college. She also bailed out MacKenzie-Childs, a whimsical but previously bankrupt ceramics maker. Rowland's Aurora Foundation gutted and resurrected the **Aurora Inn** ✦✦✦, 391 Main St., Aurora, NY 13026 (© **866/364-8808** or 315/364-8888; fax 315/364-8887; www.aurora-inn.com; $150–$300 double, $225–$350 suite), owned by the college and overlooking the lake. The foundation completely transformed the 1833 inn into a boutique hotel of rich, though restrained, style. It is now one of the most exquisite country inns in the Finger Lakes region, with gorgeously decorated rooms (several with decks overlooking the lake), a luxurious restaurant, and services to match a much larger hotel (the Aurora Inn has just 10 rooms). Check out special packages and summer events (such as a lake wine cruise) online.

Also new to the previously under-endowed town that didn't even have a gas station are a village market, a pizza restaurant, and an ice-cream parlor, while the Victorian **Morgan Opera House** (© **315/364-5437**), on the second floor of the Tudor-style Aurora Free Library, was recently restored with the help of MacKenzie-Childs. Aurora, which has earned a place on the National Register of Historic Places, remains tiny, but its bold transformation has left some historians and preservationists nervous about the remaking of the town's historic buildings. For many others, including many residents of Aurora, it's hard not to see it as a hopeful beacon of revitalization across the Finger Lakes.

some Jambalaya "me-oh-my-ho," po' boy sandwiches, "Jumbo Gumbo," and fresh seafood from the raw bar, as well as good daily specials like fried-fish tacos. The feel-good menu, attentive service, microbrew beers, and superb cocktails make it popular with all sorts of folks, from professors and students to young professionals and families. I'm happy to report that Maxie's now features a healthy roster of Finger Lakes wines among its wide-ranging list of boutique wines, and a semi-dry Riesling or Gewürztraminer goes well with Cajun fare. Sit in the dark and noisy bar area, in the hip Velvet Room, or in warm months on the covered terrace. Oyster junkies should check out the half-priced raw oysters and clams every day from 4 to 6pm. On Sunday there's brunch from 11am to 3pm, and live music at night ranges from jazz, blues, and bluegrass to neo-hippie jams.

A couple of miles north of town, **MacKenzie-Childs** ⊛⊛⊛, 3260 Rte. 90 (© **800/640-0546** or 315/364-7123; www.mackenzie-childs.com), makes uniquely fanciful and brightly colored handmade ceramics, glassware, and furniture that might be called modern baroque. You'll either love it or hate it (my wife absolutely loves the stuff). The headquarters and factory are ensconced in a 65-acre Victorian farm campus that is as stunning as its products. The visitor center presents behind-the-scenes studio tours daily from 9am to 5pm. Visitors can tour the utterly incredible, dreamlike 19th-century **Farmhouse**, done up in high MacKenzie-Childs Victorian style, with four rooms (40 min.; daily 10am–4pm; free admission). For now, the equally spectacular, but even more mind-bending, **Restaurant MacKenzie-Childs** is no longer open for meals or tea. (Hopefully, they'll find a way to make it operational again, because it looks as though it were decorated by someone dreaming of Alice in Wonderland while on acid, and it's not currently visited on the tour.) Also on campus is a full shop of tableware and home furnishings, as well as a uniquely decorated hot-dog cart.

The original creators and owners of MacKenzie-Childs have opened their fanciful homestead in nearby Kings Ferry as a small and decidedly funky inn. If you like the dinnerware, you'll love staying at **Home Again** ⊛, 1671 Rte. 90, King Ferry (© **315/364-8615**; www.stayhomeagain.blogspot.com), decorated in full-on MacKenzie-Childs style. The six idiosyncratic rooms range from $90 for the childlike room to $200 for the master bedroom suite, which occupies the entire third floor of the house. Breakfast is DIY (do-it-yourself). For reservations, e-mail vrhomeagain@earthlink.net.

For breakfast or lunch in Aurora, check out the counter or back deck at **Dorie's**, 283 Main St. (© **315/364-8818**), a nostalgic ice-cream and soda fountain (open Sun–Thurs 7am–8pm, Fri–Sat 7am–9pm), or yummy **Pizza Aurora**, a cute and brightly colored artisanal pie maker across the street in a 1940s garage (it's open Mon–Thurs 11am–8pm, Fri–Sat 11am–10pm, and Sun noon–8pm).

635 W. State St. (corner of State St. and Rte. 13S), Ithaca. © **607/272-4136**. Reservations not accepted. Main courses $10–$22. AE, MC, V. Daily 4pm–1am; Sun 11am–3pm.

INEXPENSIVE

Moosewood Restaurant ⊛ (Value (Kids GOURMET VEGETARIAN/INTERNA-TIONAL   Vegetarians and innovative chefs around the world know the Moosewood cookbooks—and here is where it all began. This informal restaurant—now in its fourth decade—located in a converted school-building-turned-alternative-mall, is run by a cooperative (or "collective," as they call it) that delivers imaginative vegetarian and healthy cooking. *Bon Appétit* magazine named the Moosewood one of the 13 most influential restaurants of the 20th century. The menu is forever changing, but always features fresh, locally grown (and usually organic) produce and whole grains, beans, and soy. The creative soups, salads, and side dishes are enough to make a hearty meal, but the homemade pasta dishes are also excellent and filling. Sunday-night dinners are ethnic menus. Nonvegetarians will be delighted to find fresh fish on the menu, as will parents who can order simple and very cheap kids' plates.

215 N. Cayuga St. (in the DeWitt Mall), Ithaca. ⓒ 607/273-9610. Reservations not accepted. Main courses $9–$15. AE, DISC, MC, V. Lunch Mon–Sat 11:30am–3pm. Dinner summer Sun–Thurs 5:30–9pm, Fri–Sat 6–9:30pm; winter Sun–Thurs 5:30–8:30pm, Fri–Sat 5:30–9pm. Bar and cafe year-round Sun–Thurs 11am–11pm; Fri–Sat 11am–midnight.

ITHACA AFTER DARK

Ithaca has quite a lot of theater and music programs, especially in summer. The **Kitchen Theater,** 116 N. Cayuga St. (ⓒ **607/273-4497**), in the historic Greek Revival Clinton House, is a top spot for year-round classic and contemporary theater. In summer the **Hangar Theatre,** just north of downtown, on Taughannock Boulevard/Route 89 (ⓒ **607/273-8588**), offers professional, children's, and experimental theater in a renovated municipal airport hangar near Lake Cayuga. The **State Theatre** ⓡ, 111 W. State St. (ⓒ **607/277-6633**), a historic theater that had been condemned, is in the process of being fully refurbished; it hosts a wide array of programs from rock (Ani DiFranco) to plays like *The Vagina Monologues*. **Summer outdoor concert series** are held at The Commons, Taughannock Falls State Park, and the Cornell University quad. For more information on music and performing arts, see **www.ithacaevents.com**. The annual 4-day **Ithaca Festival,** held the first weekend after Memorial Day, features several stages and performances by musicians, painters, dance groups, and more. Visit **www.ithaca festival.org** for more information or call ⓒ **607/273-4646.**

Just a Taste Wine & Tapas Bar (see above) is a good stop for flights of wine and appetizers before moving on for dinner or a show. Another restaurant with a great bar and a late-night crowd is **Maxie's Supper Club** (see above). **Chanticleer,** 101 W. State St. (ⓒ **607/272-9678**)—famous for its neon rooster sign on the corner—is a low-key watering hole with a bit of a gritty feel to go with its pool tables and jukebox. Also near The Commons is **Micawber's Tavern,** 118 N. Aurora (ⓒ **607/273-9243**), a lively bar with live pop and rock music and "Happy 15 Minutes" starting at 5:15pm. If it's a more relaxed drink you're after, **The Baggage Room,** 806 W. Buffalo St. (ⓒ **607/ 2721-2609**), a small but atmospheric lounge set in the luggage room of Ithaca's former train station, is a real throwback. Up on the hill in Collegetown near Cornell, **Stella's Martini Bar,** 403 College Ave. (ⓒ **607/277-1490**), is one of the coolest spots, with live music on weekends.

Ten miles north (on Rte. 96) of Ithaca, in Trumansburg ("T-Burg"), is a handful of bars, including the curiously named live-music pub **Rongovian Embassy to the U.S.** (known to local barflies as the Rongo). Find its stage featuring local rock bands and a good selection of beers at 1 Main St. (ⓒ **607/387-3334**). It's open until 1am Tuesday to Sunday.

3 Watkins Glen ⓡ & Southern/Eastern Seneca Lake

28 miles W of Ithaca; 21 miles N of Corning

At the southern tip of Seneca Lake, the deepest and second-longest of the Finger Lakes and the one with the most wineries clustered around it, Watkins Glen is a small town that looms large on the tourism landscape in summer. It is home to Watkins Glen State Park, site of a spectacular gorge and thundering waterfalls—perhaps the single most beautiful natural area in the entire region—as well as the annual NASCAR rally at "The Glen" and Finger Lakes Wine Festival. But even those heavily attended events have a hard time competing with the town's peaceful, picturesque location on the waterfront of Seneca Lake.

The southeast bank of Seneca Lake, which local winemakers only somewhat facetiously call the "Banana Belt," due to its warmer microclimate, is home to several of the Finger Lakes' best wineries and most notable farm-fresh, chef-driven restaurants, as well as a growing number of small inns. In fact, Route 414, which skirts the eastern edge of the lake, is emerging as the restaurant row of the Finger Lakes.

ESSENTIALS

GETTING THERE   From the north, take exit 42 off the New York State Thruway (I-90); from the south, take Route 17 (I-86) to Route 14 North.

VISITOR INFORMATION   The **Schuyler County Chamber of Commerce Visitors Center** is at 100 N. Franklin St. (at First St.) in Watkins Glen (© **800/607-4552;** www.schuylerny.com). It's open Monday to Friday from 9am to 5pm.

EXPLORING WATKINS GLEN & SOUTHERN SENECA LAKE

If you can look past the off-putting old salt factory, cluster of low-end retail shops, and trailer campground that mar the southern end of the lake, otherwise lovely **Seneca Harbor** ⊛ is a perfect picture. It consists of a marina full of bobbing sailboats and fishing boats, a New England–style red schoolhouse at the end of the public fishing pier, and vineyard-laced hillsides rising from the lake. The boardwalk provides some of the most beautiful views of any vantage point in the Finger Lakes. This part of Seneca Lake is the perfect place to get out on the water on a yacht or sailboat. Most chartered boats set sail from May to the end of October. Check out the *Malabar X,* a vintage schooner yacht built in 1930; scheduled cruises are daily at 10am, 1pm, and 5:30pm ($29–$39 adults, $15–$20 children under 12). Call © **607/535-5253** or visit www.senecadaysails.com for more information. The larger *Seneca Legacy,* at Capt. Bill's, offers dinner, lunch, and moonlight cocktail cruises ($25–$38 adults, $15–$24 children). A smaller vintage motor vessel, the *Stroller IV,* is also available. Call © **607/535-4541** or visit www.senecaharborstation.com for reservations and information.

Watkins Glen State Park ⊛⊛⊛, off Route 14 at the south end of the village, is one of the certain highlights of the Finger Lakes. Opened in 1863, the 776-acre park contains a spectacular gorge sculpted in slate, formed more than 12,000 years ago at the end of the last ice age and carved by the flow of Glen Creek ever since, and 19 separate waterfalls. The walking trails in and around the gorge are splendid and accessible to almost all walkers; you can walk right in behind the 60-foot drop of Central Cascade. It takes about an hour to walk the gorge trail, with a steep climb at the end. Shuttle buses ($3) return walkers to the entrance, or you can walk back along the Indian trail, which is parallel to the gorge but flatter. Hikers should wear appropriate hiking shoes, since the trails can be wet and slick. Park entrance is $6 per vehicle. Call © **607/535-4511** or visit www.nysparks.state.ny.us for more information.

The **Watkins Glen International Race Track,** 2790 County Rte. 16 (© **866/461-RACE** or 607/535-2481; www.theglen.com), opens up with car-club events and races in June and July, including the SCCA Glen Nationals, but it really heats up at the end of the first week of August with the NASCAR Nextel Cup series, a race that draws many thousands and fills every hotel and inn and campsite for hundreds of miles in New York State's largest sporting weekend. Other racing events are held in summer, including the Vintage Grand Prix in September, but none comes close to NASCAR.

Seneca Lake Wine Trail

The **Seneca Lake Wine Trail** ★★★ (© 877/536-2717; www.senecalakewine. com) includes 31 wineries dotting the shores of Seneca Lake, producing some of the best wines in the region. Visits to those on the east side of Seneca Lake might easily be combined with a tour of wineries dotting the west bank of Cayuga Lake (p. 304), while those on the west bank of Seneca could be combined with visits to Keuka Lake wineries (p. 330). Among the wineries worth visiting for tastings and/or touring are the following:

East Bank

- **Atwater Estate Vineyards** ★, 5055 Rte. 414, Hector (© 800/331-7323; www.atwatervineyards.com), is a relatively new winery situated among some of the area's oldest vineyards. It has a handsome yellow tasting room and gift shop attached to a barn, and a deck with views of Seneca Lake. The wines, with colorful, distinctive labels, have become among those to contend with in the region; try the Gewürztraminer and dry Riesling. Open Monday to Saturday 10am to 5pm and Sunday from 11am to 5pm.

- **Red Newt Cellars** ★★, 3675 Tichenor Rd., Hector (© 607/546-4100; www. rednewt.com), is as much a winery as a restaurant (p. 320). The winery is directed by David Whiting and the restaurant by his wife, the chef Debra Whiting. Red Newt's wines, including a top Riesling reserve and very nice cabernet franc (and even an unexpectedly good Syrah), are recognized as some of the finest in the region, though the winery produces no estate wines (all fruit is purchased). If you've grown tired of small sips of wine, the restaurant's outdoor terrace overlooking vineyards is a terrific place for a more substantial wine flight, glass or bottle. Open Monday to Saturday 10am to 5pm and Sunday from 11am to 5pm; winter daily noon to 5pm.

- **Damiani Wine Cellars** ★, 5435 Rte. 414, Hector (© 607/546-5557; www. damianiwinecellars.com), is a new and tiny operation crafting some very good wines since its first vintage in 2004. I particularly liked the cabernet franc and meritage (bordeaux-styled blend). Open Friday to Sunday noon to 5pm and by appointment.

- **Hazlitt 1852 Vineyards** ★, 5712 Rte. 414, Hector (© 888/750-0492 or 607/ 546-9463; www.hazlitt1852.com), is best known for its party atmosphere, rock-'n'-roll music, and mass-market "Red Cat" wines. If you just want to have fun and taste some wines, this is the place. No intimidating wine-snob atmosphere here. It's not just grape juice, though; some wines, like the 2004 Riesling, are quite fine indeed. Open November to May, Monday to Saturday from 10am to 5pm and Sunday from noon to 5pm; June through October, Monday to Saturday 10am to 5:30pm and Sunday from 11am to 5:30pm.

- **Shalestone Vineyards** ★★, 9681 Rte. 414, Lodi (© 607/582-6783; www. shalestonevineyards.com), is a real rarity in these parts, known for its Rieslings and chardonnays; winemaker Rob Thomas and his wife make only reds. "Red is all we do" is their slogan. Their small-batch, hand-crafted reds are surprisingly excellent; try the Harmony, a cabernet franc/merlot blend, and the cabernet franc. You'll usually find either Rob or Kate, or both, in the cool little tasting room, and they're fun to engage on wine or any topic. Open May through Sept, Friday to Sunday noon to 5pm.

- **Wagner Vineyards** ⊛, 9322 Rte. 414, Lodi (© **866/924-6378**; www.wagner vineyards.com), operates an unusual octagonal winery producing 30 wines and a full slate of microbrew beers, and a gift shop, and offers nice guided tours and full tastings. Open daily 10am to 5pm. There's a pleasant restaurant, Ginny Lee Café, that serves lunch daily from 11am to 4pm; on Friday nights in the summer, live music plays on the terrace overlooking Seneca Lake, and dinner (fish fry or barbecued chicken) is served from 7 to 9pm. It's one of the best evening spots around, popular with both locals and visitors.

- **Lamoreaux Landing Wine Cellars** ⊛⊛, 9224 Rte. 414, Lodi (© **607/582-6011**; www.lamoreauxwine.com), is housed in a Napa-style building with floor-to-ceiling windows and views of surrounding vineyards. It has won numerous awards for its serious vinifera wines, including its cabernet franc, Gewürztraminer, chardonnay, and a sparkling blanc de blanc. Open year-round for tastings, Monday to Saturday 10am to 5pm and Sunday noon to 5pm.

West Bank

- **Lakewood Vineyards** ⊛, 4024 Rte. 14, Watkins Glen (© **607/535-9252**; www.lakewoodvineyards.com), a family-run and friendly, low-key winery, has beautiful views and good Rieslings and chardonnays, as well as a surprising pinot noir. Open year-round Monday through Saturday from 10am to 5pm and Sunday from noon to 5pm.

- **Glenora Wine Cellars** ⊛, 5435 Rte. 14, Dundee (© **800/243-5513** or 607/243-5511; www.glenora.com), which makes a great variety of wines, has terrific views of Seneca Lake and vineyards as well as a picnic area and large tasting and gift shop. The winery operates a very nice restaurant and inn overlooking vines and the lake. Open year-round Monday through Saturday from 10am to 5pm and Sunday from noon to 5pm (open later in summer).

- **Anthony Road Wine Company** ⊛⊛, 1020 Anthony Rd., Penn Yann (© **800/559-2182** or 607/243-5511; www.anthonyroadwine.com), has quickly become one of Seneca's finest producers. In a large, airy space overlooking the lake, it shows off its wide range of serious wines, including a delicious dry Riesling and rosé. The select, low-production Martini-Reinhardt wines are standouts—especially the Riesling and trocken-beeren. Open year-round Monday through Saturday from 10am to 5pm.

More Top Wineries

Among wineries that are not official members of the Seneca Lake Wine Trail, but are still very much worth visiting, are these:

East Bank

- **Standing Stone** ⚜, 9934 Rte. 414, Hector (📞 800/803-7135; www.standing stonewines.com), is a small, hands-on family winery with a pretty yellow farmhouse, gardens, and a cheese room with gorgeous lake views from the deck. Standing Stone makes nice whites, including the Riesling and reserve chardonnay, and an outstanding vidal ("ice") dessert wine. Open May to mid-October daily 11:30am to 5pm; mid-October to April, Thursday to Monday 11:30am to 5pm (until 6pm on Sat).

- **Silver Thread Vineyard** ⚜, 1401 Caywood Rd., Lodi (📞 607/582-6116; www.silverthreadwine.com), though tiny and easy to overlook, is a winery to watch. The owner is committed to organic, artisanal winemaking, and he produces six very nice wines, including a dry Riesling, Gewürztraminer, and burgundy-style pinot noir. Look for signs indicating the long gravel road that wends toward the lake. Open May through November, Saturday and Sunday from noon to 5pm; other times by appointment only.

West Bank

- **Hermann J. Wiemer Vineyard** ⚜⚜⚜, 3962 Rte. 14, Dundee (📞 607/243-7971; www.wiemer.com), is one of the Finger Lakes' standout wineries, headed by a dedicated German transplant who produces very serious, elegant white wines in the European cool-climate tradition. His dry Johannisberg Riesling, Gewürztraminer, and semi-dry Riesling go toe-to-toe with my other favorite winery, Dr. Frank's (on Keuka). Also not to be missed are the late-harvest Rieslings, which make excellent dessert wines. Tastings here are more intimate, as limos and buses are welcome only by prior appointment. If you're serious about wine, this is a must-stop. Open year-round Monday through Friday 10am to 5pm; April to November, also Saturday 10am to 5pm and Sunday 11am to 5pm.

The new IRL IndyCar Series is held at the end of September. The other huge event in town, also held at the WGI, is the annual **Finger Lakes Wine Festival** ⚜⚜ (📞 866/461-7223 or 607/535-2481; www.flwinefest.com), held in mid-July. Most of the local 70-plus wineries are on hand, along with musicians, craft vendors, exhibits from the Corning Museum of Glass, food and wine seminars, and even a toga party. As you can imagine, plenty of wine is consumed and people get pretty festive. Advance tickets (and accommodations) are a must for most of the events at WGI, so plan ahead (way in advance for NASCAR, as much as a year or more). Tickets ($30; $35 for 2 days) for the wine festival are available at many of the local wineries. The largest concentration of wineries in the region is clustered about Seneca Lake, and many of the wineries on the **Seneca Lake Wine Trail** are just a cork's throw from Watkins Glen; for more on that collective and wine tours, see the sidebar on p. 316.

On the east side of Seneca Lake is **Skyland Gallery & Café** ⟨★⟩, Route 414, Lodi; ✆ **607/546-5050;** www.skylandfarm.net), which owner Barbara Hummel describes as a "fantasy land of high art, exquisite craft, joy, and dessert." The large gallery space shows off the unique works, including pottery, jewelry, and wood toys, of 300 local and regional artisans, all part of a compound that consists of a renovated barn (with a two-story tree soaring through the cafe), gardens, and animal pens. It's the kind of place that will entertain both kids and parents for at least a couple of hours, and the cafe makes an excellent lunch pit stop, with nice sandwiches, salads, and incredible gelatti and other desserts.

WHERE TO STAY

Watkins Glen proper isn't loaded with great lodgings, though it has one outstanding B&B. Other options are to stay at a winery on the west bank, or at one of the growing number of small inns along the east bank of the lake. If you're arriving for NASCAR or the Finger Lakes Wine Festival, you may have to look far and wide for accommodations, so be sure to look at hotels and inns listed in other sections of this chapter; those in and near Geneva, Corning, Elmira, Ithaca, and Hammondsport are all easy drives from Watkins Glen. Call ✆ **800/607-4552** or see www.schuylerny.com for assistance in getting a room. If you want to camp, check out the sites at **Watkins Glen State Park** (✆ **607/535-4511**), **Clute Memorial Park** (✆ **607/535-4438**), or the "kutely" spelled **KOA Kampground & Kabins,** located on Route 414 (✆ **800/ 562-7430;** www.watkinsglenkoa.com), which has a heated pool and good bathrooms.

The Fox and the Grapes ⟨★⟩ ⟨Value⟩   A young and friendly, somewhat improbable innkeeper, James Pellegrini, oversees this very relaxing and spacious B&B. It's ideally located, just up from the east bank of Seneca Lake, near plenty of the area's best wineries and restaurants. The house is a large white 1885 Victorian manor with lake views from the terrace and back room (the deck is the place to be for sunset). James did a fine job restoring the house, and he runs it pretty much as a one-man show. Accommodations are elegant, but not overly fussy, with relatively sedate colors and furnishings, and fine bedding. One room has its own private balcony, and the East Lake suite, with its exposed brick, is particularly masculine (even though the walls are a dusky pink!). Speaking of which, men who might otherwise be disinclined to check into a Victorian B&B will be happy to see the huge-screen TV and collection of DVDs in the massive living room that boasts a fireplace and an entire floor of Persian rugs.

9496 State Rte. 414, Lodi, NY 14860. ✆ 607/582-7528. www.thefoxandthegrapes.com. 5 units. $100–$160 double. Rates include full breakfast. AE, DC, MC, V. Free parking. *In room:* A/C, Wi-Fi.

Idlwilde Inn ⟨★★⟩ ⟨Value⟩   One of the top B&Bs in the area, this sprawling, 18-room, 1892 Victorian mansion features a great veranda, attractive gardens, and stupendous lake views. There's a nice mix of rooms, from the impressively grand to small, affordable, and simply furnished (the cheapest share a bathroom). The master bedroom, no. 6, is stunningly large, like an absolutely palatial New York City apartment, with its own deck, two fireplaces, and two sitting rooms, while no. 10 has a sitting room in a circular turret and a private deck with excellent lake views. Two new rooms have been added upstairs in the carriage house; they've been creatively inserted, with cathedral ceilings. The inn, run by a charming European couple (he's Dutch, she's Italian) and their partners (her in-laws), is open seasonally from the end of April to November.

1 Lakeview Ave., Watkins Glen, NY 14891. ✆ 607/535-3081. www.idlwildeinn.com. 5 units. $95–$250 double. Rates include full breakfast. AE, DC, MC, V. Free parking. *In room:* A/C.

The Inn at Glenora Wine Cellars ✦   At Glenora, perched on the west bank of Seneca Lake and just 8 miles north of Watkins Glen, wine lovers are in for a treat: They can sleep at a winery. This modern hostelry is set amid acres of vineyards and only steps from the tasting room. The location is by far the hotel's biggest selling point: All the comfortable rooms—large and equipped with Stickley furniture—have expansive, unimpeded views of the water from either private terraces or patios. "Vintner's select" rooms have king-size beds, Jacuzzi tubs, and electric fireplaces. The inn also has an excellent restaurant and easy access to other Seneca Lake wineries and major attractions.

5435 Rte. 14, Dundee, NY 14837. ✆ 800/243-5513. www.glenora.com. 30 units. $159–$259 double. Rates include full breakfast. AE, DC, MC, V. Free parking. **Amenities:** Restaurant; bar. *In room:* A/C, TV, coffeemaker, hair dryer.

WHERE TO DINE
EXPENSIVE
The Bistro at Red Newt Cellars ✦✦✦ *Kids* AMERICAN BISTRO   On the premises of one of the region's top wineries, this appetizing bistro restaurant is an excellent place to match food and wine. It's a family affair at Red Newt: the chef and winemaker are a husband-wife team, Debra and David Whiting. The restaurant's covered terrace overlooks vineyards and farmland and is a particularly fine spot for lunch. Debra, a former scientific researcher, is a committed member of the Finger Lakes Culinary Bounty organization (her business card reproduces its "vision statement"). Focusing on the best locally produced ingredients, she makes creative entrees like lamb chops with mint-and-macadamia-nut crust in red-wine sauce, with macadamia-nut risotto; or grilled bacon-wrapped pork tenderloin stuffed with chèvre, pork sausage, and chard. Sample from eight different Finger Lakes wine flights, all available by the glass or small glass, and a comprehensive list of local wines by the bottle. You'll find live acoustic music on Wednesday nights, Thursday is wine lover's night, with any bottle half-price with dinner, and Friday features additional bistro-made pastas. Lunch is casual, but still delicious, featuring incredibly fresh salads and sandwiches. There's even a "Little Newts" menu for the kids.

3675 Tichenor Rd., Hector. ✆ 607/546-4100. Reservations recommended for dinner. Main courses $18–$28. AE, MC, V. Wed–Sun noon–4pm and 5–9pm.

Suzanne Fine Regional Cuisine ✦✦✦ *Finds* UPSCALE AMERICAN   One of the few real fine-dining options outside the cities in the Finger Lakes, this small chef-driven restaurant is a hopeful sign of the region's future. To my mind, it fits the bill for what this wine region cries out for: uncomplicated, fresh, perfectly prepared dishes, in an elegant, even romantic, country atmosphere. Run by chef Suzanne and her husband, Bob, the restaurant inhabits the first floor of a handsome 1903 farmhouse, in a peaceful spot with pristine views of Seneca Lake from the veranda and front tables (it's not uncommon to see guests get up from their tables with glasses of wine in hand to inspect the sunset). Everything is made from scratch (using seasonal local ingredients), the presentation is delightful, and service is exceedingly gracious. The menu is small, with usually just four entrees, but you can't go wrong with items like wild Alaskan king salmon with corn salsa, or a perfectly cooked filet mignon with potato purée and chanterelle ragout. The terrific homemade desserts—or cheese plate—pair perfectly with a Finger Lakes Riesling or ice wine from a winery just down the road (there are 40-odd local wines on the list). Open seasonally, from the end of April to November.

9013 Rte. 414, Hector. © **607/582-7545.** Reservations required. Main courses $19–$26. MC, V. June–Oct Wed–Sun 5–9pm; Apr–May and Nov Fri–Sat 5–9pm.

MODERATE

Dano's Heuriger ★★★ AUSTRIAN   Along the shore of Seneca Lake, the newest addition to the dining scene is this unique restaurant, a modern take on the traditional Viennese wine garden or tavern (known as a *heuriger*). The Austrian chef Dano Hutnik and his wife, Karen Gilman, have created a challenging but relaxed, hip eatery, where patrons can sample small plates of Austrian specialties, such as charcuterie, sausages, smoked and poached fish, and roasted meats, all of which can be easily paired with either Finger Lakes or Austrian wines. The menu is written in large stylized script on a blackboard wall that runs the length of the kitchen, and the modern minimalist architecture of the restaurant—something akin to a contemporary bunker with massive overhead lamps and large windows—is fairly radical in these parts. Though Dano's is a definite departure from the usual, it's an easygoing place where the staff is happy to walk you through the menu setup. Basically the idea is to order a couple of small appetizer spreads and salads, along with a basket of breads, followed by a fish and/or meat (or vegetarian) course and sides, such as braised sauerkraut with bacon or spaetzle. Desserts are emphatically traditional, including strudel, linzer torte and *rigo jansci*—but I'll let the waiter describe the last item.

9564 Rte. 414, Lodi. © **607/582-7555.** Reservations recommended. Main courses $9–$18. MC, V. June–Sept Wed–Mon noon–9pm; call for winter hours.

Seneca Harbor Station AMERICAN/SEAFOOD   This spot, in a former 19th-century train station, has the distinct advantage of fantastic views of the marina at the southern end of Seneca Lake. A casual bar and restaurant, it's a good stop for an informal lunch like chicken Florentine and classic dinner items such as seafood pastas, grilled meats, and fresh-fish dishes and platters (such as rainbow trout Florentine). Nothing fancy, but reliable and with those dockside views, it's a place to linger.

3 N. Franklin St., Watkins Glen. © **607/535-6101.** Reservations not accepted. Main courses $10–$35. AE, MC, V. Daily 11:30am–4:15pm; Sun–Thurs 4–9pm; Fri–Sat 4–10pm.

Stonecat Café ★★ *(Finds* REGIONAL ORGANIC/BISTRO   In a former roadside fruit stand, which preserves some old details and the original coolers, this cool, relaxed restaurant is not only the hippest joint in the area, but also one of the best. The renovated interior has just the right touch of shabby chic, but the deck overlooking vineyards and with distant views toward Seneca Lake is my favorite place to dine and watch early evening turn into night, accompanied by strains of live jazz or blues coming from inside and a bottle of the Finger Lakes' finest on the table. The menu features organic local produce and meats, and items are casually presented but tasty and well prepared, with a specialty of house-smoked meats and fish. I'm a fan of the pulled-pork barbecue, slow-cooked for 8 hours on grape and apple wood, and the cornmeal-crusted catfish. However, diners should steer clear of the puttanesca pasta, made from a family recipe, or anything with ramps (wild leeks) in it. Lunch might also include those items, as well as gourmet sandwiches and organic salads (with some vegan options). The wine and beer lists are exclusively from New York State. Sunday is jazz brunch, a great time to linger over the views of the vineyards. Open seasonally, from the end of April to October.

5315 Rte. 414, Hector. © **607/546-5000.** Reservations recommended. Main courses $11–$23. AE, MC, V. Apr–Oct Wed 5–9pm; Thurs–Sat noon–4:30pm and 5–9pm; Sun 10:30am–3pm and 5–9pm.

Veraisons Restaurant 🍯 CONTINENTAL   On-site at the Glenora winery (and inn), this handsome, modern space is not only in the midst of vineyards, it boasts cathedral ceilings, a large stone fireplace, and panoramic views of Seneca Lake. If the weather is good, dining on the outdoor terrace is essential. The menu combines traditional French cooking with regional ingredients. On one visit, I had a very nice roasted pork roulade, stuffed with mushrooms and served with roasted garlic-cheddar mashed potatoes. Many of the dishes are, appropriately, prepared with wine, and the wine list focuses on the house and other Finger Lakes wines. But on Friday nights, it's time for a fish fry and microbrews.

5435 Rte. 14, Dundee. Ⓒ 607/243-9500. Reservations recommended. Main courses $17–$27. AE, MC, V. Daily 11:30am–3:30pm; Mon–Thurs 5–9pm; Fri–Sat 5–10pm; Sun 4–9pm.

WATKINS GLEN & SENECA LAKE AFTER DARK

Perhaps the best option in Watkins Glen is to hang with locals at **The Crooked Rooster BrewPub** 🍯, 29 N. Franklin St. (Ⓒ 607/535-9797), which serves up its own Rooster Fish craft ales, plus a good list of Finger Lakes wines, live music, and pub grub. Around the bend of the east bank of Seneca Lake, though, there are three surprising options about 10 miles from town. One is the live music on Friday and Saturday nights (from jazz and blues to folk) at **Stonecat Café,** a restaurant near Hector (recommended above). Another is **Big Johnsons,** 800 Rte. 414, Hector (Ⓒ 607/ 546-5800), a congenial roadside bar that's not so far removed from a Texas honky-tonk or roadhouse blues bar. It's got stuffed moose heads and other taxidermy, and a large and rocking bar, with tables out front where the regulars tend to gather. Big Johnsons is the big draw for locals, who come to knock back beers and listen to live rock and country bands on weekends. The crowd isn't just kids—there are plenty of older "friendly folks," as the sign outside says. Wagner Vineyards features live music outdoors on Friday evenings at **Ginny Lee Café,** 9322 Rte. 414, Lodi (Ⓒ 866/924-6378), a fun spot that's a big draw for locals and visitors alike.

4 Corning ★★★ & Elmira

250 miles NW of New York City; 150 miles E of Niagara Falls; 90 miles SE of Rochester.

Two towns just south of the Finger Lakes proper give travelers a taste of something different in this region known for its unique bodies of water and pastoral charms. Corning is a small town of just 12,000 people, but as the headquarters of the Fortune 500 company Corning Inc., it's a very big deal in the Finger Lakes region. Quite literally, it's the town that Corning built; the company, the original makers of Corning-Ware, Pyrex, and now high-tech materials like fiber optics, has employed as much as half the town's population. Corning was once known as "crystal city" for its concentration of glassworks, and today glass remains the town's calling card. One of the Finger Lakes' biggest attractions is the world-renowned Corning Museum of Glass.

Elmira, just to the east, is a largely blue-collar town, and though it serves as a southern gateway to the Finger Lakes, it doesn't figure as a stop on many itineraries. However, it offers a handful of nice surprises. Home to Elmira College, the town is known in select circles as the "soaring capital of the United States," a reference to its important place in aviation history. It also makes much of its association with the legendary writer and humorist Mark Twain, who wrote many of his most famous works while summering in Elmira. Fans of late-19th-century architecture will also delight in the surprising concentration of Victorian homes; Elmira is said to have more per capita than any other area in North America.

ESSENTIALS
GETTING THERE
BY AIR   Elmira-Corning Regional Airport, 276 Sing Sing Rd., Horseheads (© 607/795-0402; www.ecairport.com), serviced by Northwest and US Airways, is 12 miles from downtown Corning.

BY CAR   Corning is directly off Route 17/I-86 and a straight shot along Route 414 south of Watkins Glen; from the south, take Route 15. Elmira is off Route 17/I-86, just 20 minutes east of Corning.

BY BUS   Trailways (© 607/734-2001; www.trailways.com) travels to Elmira and its terminal at 100 E. Church St.

VISITOR INFORMATION   The **Steuben County Conference & Visitors Bureau** is located at 1 W. Market St., Corning (© 866/946-3386 or 607/936-6544; www.corning fingerlakes.com). The **Chemung County Chamber of Commerce** is located at 400 E. Church St., Elmira (© 800/MARK-TWAIN; www.chemungchamber.org).

GETTING AROUND   The Corning Museum of Glass operates a **free shuttle service** daily from 8am to 6pm, from the museum along Cedar Street to Market Street and the Rockwell Museum, and back, allowing visitors to park for free at either museum.

EXPLORING CORNING
Corning Inc.'s major gift to the city, the **Corning Museum of Glass** ★★★ (I-86, exit 46; © 800/732-6845 or 607/937-5371; www.cmog.org) is the premier and most comprehensive collection of historic and art glass in the world. Anyone with an interest in glass (even if that doesn't describe you, you're almost certain to be surprised and engaged) could spend many hours or even days here; it is quite literally dazzling. On view are 35,000 glass pieces representing 35 centuries of glass craftsmanship, beginning with a piece dating from 1411 B.C. There is also a gallery of glass sculpture and a glass innovation center, with ingeniously designed interactive exhibits that depict the use of glass in technology. The museum, now entering its sixth decade, is anything but static: It offers indoor and outdoor hot-glass demonstrations, glassmaking workshops, and some of the best shopping to be found, with a sprawling array of shops dealing in glass, crystal, and jewelry. Crystal fans familiar with Steuben glass (which originated in Corning), and particularly the work of glass artist Frederick Carder, will delight in finding a huge gallery of his works.

The museum is especially well designed for children, who usually can't get enough of the interactive science exhibits and opportunities to handle telescopes and peer through a periscope that "sees" out the roof of the building. A walk-in glass workshop allows visitors to make their very own glass souvenirs. The museum is open daily from 9am to 5pm; July through Labor Day it's open daily until 8pm. Admission is $13 for adults, $11 for seniors and students, and free for children under 17. Audio guides are $3. With one paid admission, you are allowed to visit again one time in the same calendar year for free. A $17 combination ticket for adults ($16 for seniors and students) includes admission to CMoG and the Rockwell Museum (see below). The museum also operates a free shuttle service from the museum to Market Street, downtown. Plan on spending about 3 hours at the Corning Museum of Glass, and more if you plan to take part in workshops.

The **Rockwell Museum of Western Art** 𝒢𝒢, 111 Cedar St. (𝒞 607/937-5386; www.rockwellmuseum.org), which occupies the former City Hall, maintains an excellent collection of both historic and contemporary western and Native American art, as well as one of the best-designed small museums in the Northeast. An inviting design of bold colors and gorgeous woods inside the shell of a neo-Romanesque building, the museum features daring juxtapositions that work surprisingly well, including a number of fantastic pieces by Native Americans. The second floor has a lodge room with a fireplace, couches, and chairs, and feels like it's been ripped from a classic western lodge. A neat idea for children: the color-coded "art backpacks" that come equipped with games and lesson and drawing books, making the museum an especially interactive place. Museum hours are as follows: July through Labor Day daily from 9am to 8pm; September through June, Monday to Saturday 9am to 5pm and Sunday 11am to 5pm. Admission is $6.50 for adults, $5.50 for seniors and students, $4.50 for children 6 to 17, and free for children under 6. Allow an hour or two.

Those hungry to get outdoors south of the lakes can get up in the air. **Balloons Over Corning,** 352 Brewster St., Painted Post (𝒞 607/937-3910), has organized hot-air balloons with beautiful views over Corning and the Finger Lakes area for the past 15 years. Flights take off 2 hours before sunset in summer. And spectacular **glider flights** are available at the Harris Hill Soaring Center in Elmira; see the sidebar on p. 327.

SHOPPING

Corning, devastated by floods in 1972, rebuilt the picturesque centerpiece of its downtown, Market Street, which today retains a 19th-century appearance and is alive with glass galleries, gift shops, and restaurants and bars. **Vitrix Hot Glass Studio,** 77 W. Market St. (𝒞 607/936-2488); **Lost Angel Glass,** 79 W. Market St. (𝒞 607/937-3578); and **West End Gallery,** 12 W. Market St. (𝒞 607/936-2011), are three of the best galleries representing the American studio glass movement, though a number of others are easily discovered as you walk about town. The two major museums in town, the Rockwell Museum of Western Art and Corning Museum of Glass, both have excellent on-site shops. The latter is a must for anyone with the slightest interest in glass; items range from inexpensive glass souvenirs to one-of-a-kind glass art and Steuben crystal pieces.

WHERE TO STAY

Corning can get pretty crowded, both with business travelers and when big events occur, such as the Corning Classic LPGA golf tournament, the NASCAR race, the Finger Lakes Wine Festival in nearby Watkins Glen, and even Cornell University's graduation. In addition to the chain motels below, you might check out one of these in town: **Comfort Inn** (66 W. Pulteney St.; 𝒞 607/962-1515), **Days Inn** (23 Riverside Dr.; 𝒞 607/936-9370), and **Staybridge Suites** (201 Townley Ave; 𝒞 607/936-7800; www.staybridge.com/sbscorningny). For campers, there is the **Hickory Hill Family Camping Resort,** Route 17/I-86, exit 38 (𝒞 800/760-0947; www.hickory hillcampresort.com).

Hillcrest Manor 𝒢𝒢𝒢 𝒱𝒶𝓁𝓊𝑒   One of the finest B&Bs in the Finger Lakes, this impressively grand, 1890 Greek Revival mansion, with massive pillars, porches, and terraces, sits in a quiet residential neighborhood up the hill from downtown Corning. Rooms are huge and impeccably decorated with great, luxurious taste by two gentlemen, art-glass and antiques collectors who moved to Corning from Seattle. The house has stately parlors, an elegant candlelit dining room, and a palatial cedar stairway. Two of the rooms, the Master Bedroom and the Honeymoon Suite, are almost ridiculously large; they, as well as the normal rooms, are excellent values given the level of quality exhibited throughout the house. I can envision myself relaxing here for days on end. The inn's website, unfortunately, offers but a glimpse of the house's true elegance and sophistication. Prices are rather moderate given the surroundings and service.

227 Cedar St., Corning, NY 14830. © **607/936-4548.** www.corninghillcrestmanor.com. 5 units. $145 double; $175 suite. Rates include full breakfast. MC, V. Free parking. *In room:* A/C, TV, dataport, hair dryer.

Radisson Hotel Corning *Value*   This large and well-run hotel has an excellent location: tucked into a small campus of sorts at the east end of Market Street, just steps from all the restaurants, bars, and shops. It is the only full-service hotel in downtown Corning, a reason for its popularity with business travelers, though with its pool and on-site restaurant, it's also a good place for families and other leisure travelers. Rooms are spacious and attractively appointed, with nice bedding, large work desks, and high-speed Internet access.

125 Denison Pkwy. E., Corning, NY 14830. © **888/201-1718** or 607/962-5000. Fax 607/962-4166. www.radisson.com/corningny. 173 units. $118–$174 double, $235 suite. AE, DC, DISC, MC, V. Free parking. **Amenities:** Restaurant; bar; indoor heated pool; fitness center; outdoor Jacuzzi. *In room:* A/C, TV, Wi-Fi, high-speed Internet access, minibar, coffeemaker, hair dryer.

WHERE TO DINE

Virtually all the places to eat out in town are on Market Street, which makes it easy to stroll up and down the blocks while shopping and choose one of about a half-dozen restaurants.

The Gaffer Grille and Taproom INTERNATIONAL/GRILLED MEATS   This casual eatery and bar, with some nice, cozy booths set against exposed-brick walls, is one of the most popular among Corning residents. It features a pretty standard menu, with lots of steaks, ribs, and chicken, along with other items like crushed peppercorn yellowfin tuna and cheese tortellini with vodka sauce, but dishes are consistently well prepared, and the ambience is very agreeable. The tap room, with a more casual menu, serves dinner until 11pm.

58 W. Market St. © **607/962-4649.** Reservations recommended on weekends. Main courses $11–$24. AE, DISC, MC, V. Mon–Fri 11:30am–4:30pm; Mon–Sat 4:30–10pm; tap room Mon–Sat 11:30am–11pm.

London Underground ♠ AMERICAN   For fine dining in Corning, this three-level, family-owned restaurant on Market Street is your best bet. Elegant but not stuffy, it provides a sophisticated menu and very attentive service, with a pianist on Saturday evenings. Dishes are classic, like roasted rack of lamb; prime pork loin stuffed with cranberry, apple, and raisin chutney; and filet mignon finished with a Finger Lakes red-wine reduction. More casual dishes include fish and chips with peas (served every Fri) and a daily pasta. Desserts are all homemade, and the pies (pecan, deep-dish apple) are to die for. For lunch, there are plenty of fine salads and nicely prepared sandwiches. If you're in the mood for a late-afternoon snack, stop in for tea and scones or soup and salad from 3 to 5pm.

69 E. Market St. © **607/962-2345.** Reservations recommended. Main courses $12–$26. AE, DISC, MC, V. Daily 11:30am–3pm and 5–9pm; tap room Mon–Sat 11:30am–11pm.

Three Birds Restaurant ♠♠ AMERICAN BISTRO   This upscale restaurant, run by a husband-wife team on Corning's historic Market Street, is tops for dining in this agreeable town and is popular with locals for a special night out. On its creative American menu, signature dishes include excellent salads, crispy Chesapeake crab and corn cakes, and honey-roasted, pecan-crusted pork tenderloin. Lots of Finger Lakes wines make the nice but manageable list. Gourmands will be interested in the Chef's Table, a specially prepared five- or seven-course dinner paired with wines (for groups of four to eight people only, at $60–$75 per person). One side of the high-ceilinged restaurant is a lively bar known for its excellent martinis, with a special bar menu (and free Mediterranean olive bar on Thurs evenings).

73 E. Market St. (℃ 607/936-8862. Reservations recommended. Main courses $14–$31. Chef's table prix-fixe $60–$75. AE, DISC, MC, V. Mon–Thurs 5–9pm; Fri–Sat 5–10pm.

CORNING AFTER DARK

There's not a whole lot going on in Corning after dark, though a couple of bars on Market Street—once a long lineup of bars in the blue-collar, pre–great flood of 1972—draw locals and visitors alike. **Market Street Brewing Co.,** 63 Market St. (℃ **607/936-2337**), and **Glory Hole Pub,** 74 Market St. (℃ **607/962-1474**), are both watering-hole-cum-restaurants. **Palace Theatre,** 17 W. Market St. (℃ **607/936-3844**); www.corningpalacetheatre.com), is a historic movie theater showing current and occasional art-house releases.

EXPLORING ELMIRA

Although Elmira's most famous son currently is Tommy Hilfiger, the designer who co-opted red, white, and blue from Ralph Lauren and successfully marketed his clothing to the hip-hop and rock-'n'-roll communities, the city was once home to a more important cultural figure. Mark Twain, born Samuel Clemens, met and married his wife, Olivia Langdon, in Elmira, and he spent 20 summers in the area. From his study at Quarry Farm, he composed some of his most famous works, including *The Adventures of Huckleberry Finn* and *The Adventures of Tom Sawyer.* On the pretty campus of **Elmira College,** 1 Park Place (between Fifth St. and Washington Ave.), is the Center for Mark Twain Studies (closed to the public) as well as **Twain's original study** from 1874, now a literary landmark, with several original artifacts, including his chair, photographs taken at the farm, and some documents. The study, located next to the pond, is open to visitors mid-June through August, Monday to Saturday from 9am to 5pm (℃ **607/735-1941;** free admission). Twain, his wife, and their children are buried at Elmira's **Woodlawn Cemetery** (Walnut St.; ℃ **607/732-0151;** daily 8am–9pm). Twain himself wrote many of the epitaphs on the tombstones. Nearby, **Woodlawn National Cemetery** hides a little-known secret: the graves of some 3,000 Confederate soldiers, making it the northernmost Confederate grave site (at one time, there were about 12,000 POWs in Elmira, which earned it the sobriquet "Hellmira," at least down south).

Architecture buffs may be amazed by the collection of Victorian, Greek, Tudor, and Georgian Revival houses, built in the mid-to-late 19th and early 20th centuries. Pick up a copy of *A Walking Tour of the History Near Westside* (available at the Tourism Information Office and several inns and hotels), which spotlights and describes a few

---

(Fun Fact **Women Make the Grade**

Founded in 1855, **Elmira College,** off exit 56 of Route 17/I-86, was the first exclusive women's college and the first institution of higher learning to grant women degrees that were equal in stature to those awarded men.

Soaring over the Finger Lakes

Taking to the sky in a motorless glider plane, or sailplane, is a singular experience, especially in a region as pretty as the Finger Lakes. Flights are available to visitors (Apr–Oct, weather permitting) at the **Harris Hill Soaring Center** (© 607/734-0641), located between Elmira and Corning, just south of Interstate 86. I recently took to the air with a young pilot who'd been flying since he was 13 (er, yes, don't expect to fly it yourself!). While it's a thrill to glide silently above the patchwork quilt of farms and small towns along the Chemung River, it's really a trip if your pilot decides to "pull some Gs" and do some fancy maneuvers, suddenly plummeting the sailplane toward the earth and then pulling up, yanking the bottom out of your stomach. Moves like that aren't for those with a fear of flying or heights, but anyone with a predilection for roller coasters will be in heaven. Visitors can opt for either relatively clunky Schweizer 2-33 trainers or ultrasleek Schleicher ASK-21 high-performance sailplanes. I highly recommend the latter, which can sail higher and more silently (and are only $10 more, $75 for a 40-min. ride). You can sit either up front or in back, and a tow plane tows the glider down the runway and to a height of about 4,000 feet, at which point the pilot releases and begins to soar on his own. Warm weather and cumulus clouds provide the best conditions for flight, so if you can, try to go on a sunny day, and preferably in the afternoon. Top speed in a high-performance sailplane is 140 knots, or 180 mph. Quietly flying that speed without the aid of a motor, with the world below, is a rush. See soaring details below.

dozen homes along West Church and West Water streets, and to a lesser degree, Gray, Walnut, and Grove streets, all just north of the Chemung River.

About 5 miles north of Elmira, the **National Warplane Museum** ✦, 17 Aviation Dr., Horseheads (© 607/739-8200; www.warplane.org), is the place to see 37 original military flying machines from World War I to the Gulf War. Even better than seeing the planes up close, though, is the opportunity to go up in one—whether a PT-17 or a B-17 bomber, known as "Fuddy Duddy." Flights aren't cheap (ranging $150–$400 per person; Apr–Nov only; reservations required), but they can be the thrill of a lifetime. The museum is open Monday through Friday from 10am to 4pm, Saturday from 9am to 5pm, and Sunday from 11am to 5pm; admission is $7 for adults, $5.50 for seniors, and $4 for children 6–17.

The **National Soaring Museum** ✦, Harris Hill, 51 Soaring Hill Dr. (just south of Rte. 17, exit 49, 50, or 51; © 607/734-3128; www.soaringmuseum.org), has the country's largest collection of gliders and sailplanes, which takes visitors through the history of motorless flight. Next door, the **Harris Hill Soaring Center** offers graceful **sailplane rides** ✦✦✦ in either a Schweizer 2-33 trainer or a Schleicher ASK-21 high-performance sailplane ($65–$75; spring through fall; reservations recommended), a unique and mesmerizing experience (see above). Flights soar after takeoff from Harris Hill, providing stunning views of the valley. The Soaring Center has one of the most active youth clubs in the country, and several of the pilots are teenagers and college kids. The museum is open daily from 10am to 5pm. Admission is $6.50 for adults, $5.50 for seniors, and $4 for children 5 to 17.

Tip: One of the best ways to see a lot of Elmira in a short time is to hop aboard **The Elmiran,** a green trolley car that makes daily runs July and August, with a narrated history of the town, Mark Twain, and more. Catch it at the Holiday Inn Riverview, 760 E. Water St. (© **607/734-4211;** $2 adults, free for children under 12).

WHERE TO STAY & DINE

By far the best place to stay in Elmira is **The Painted Lady B&B** ★★, 520 W. Water St., Elmira, NY 14905 (© **607/732-7515;** fax 607/732-7515; www.thepaintedlady.net), a very large and meticulously decorated Victorian mansion in the heart of the historic district. Accommodations are massive and have luxurious bedding and bathrooms for $125 to $195 for a double or $170 to $225 for a two-bedroom suite. Breakfasts are home-cooked and delicious, and there's a fantastic billiards room.

The finest restaurant in town, and one of the best in the southeast region, is **Pierce's 1894 Restaurant** ★★, 228 Oakwood Ave., at West 14th Street (© **607/734-2022**). This family-run AAA four-diamond restaurant is fairly nondescript from the outside, but the four unique, supper club–like rooms inside are elegant and understated. The wine list is outstanding, with a nice selection of wines from the Finger Lakes. Service, led by the owner himself, is impeccable. The American and Continental menu features standouts like pan-seared salmon, chateaubriand, and rack of lamb (main courses $12–$26), and the dessert cart overflows with terrific homemade desserts. Pierce's recently added a new bar and casual bistro menu in the lounge. Reservations recommended.

5 Keuka Lake ★★★

30 miles NW of Corning; 40 miles SW of Geneva

The far southwest quadrant of the Finger Lakes region contains but a single Finger Lake, the small and curiously Y-shaped Keuka Lake. To many locals, Keuka is the most beautiful of all the Finger Lakes—an assessment I'd have to agree with. It's something about the deep blue of the water, the way the narrow lake splits in two, and how vineyards blanket the gentle rise of the banks. Two of the more charming small villages in the Finger Lakes, Hammondsport and Naples, are located near the lake, and the Keuka Lake Wine Trail includes some of the most interesting and best-sited wineries in the Finger Lakes region.

ESSENTIALS

GETTING THERE

BY CAR Hammondsport, at the southern end of Keuka Lake, is off Route 54, which intersects with Route 17/I-86. Routes 54 and 54A travel north along the east and west sides of Keuka Lake toward Geneva.

VISITOR INFORMATION The **Finger Lakes Association,** which oversees promotion for the entire region, is located at 309 Lake St. in Penn Yan (© **800/530-7488;** www.fingerlakes.org). There are also tourist information offices relatively nearby in Watkins Glen and Corning (see above).

THE FAIREST OF THE FINGER LAKES?

Uniquely shaped **Keuka Lake** may be the prettiest and most pristine of all the Finger Lakes—though you'll undoubtedly get arguments from natives with preferences for Skaneateles, Seneca, or Cayuga. The name "keuka" in the original Native American language is thought to have meant "crooked"—a quality reflected in the lake's Y shape. **Keuka Lake State Park** has a nice public beach for swimming, a boat launch, fishing, picnic facilities, and a children's playground. The park is located along the north shore of the West Branch of Keuka Lake, 6 miles south of Penn Yan on Route 54A.

For further exploration of the lake, **North Country Kayak & Canoe,** 16878 W. Lake Rd., Hammondsport (© **607/868-7456;** amsailing02@yahoo.com), offers kayak and canoe rentals from June to September. If fishing is your thing, serene Keuka Lake has rainbow trout, lake trout, largemouth bass, and more. Check **www.fishsteubencounty. com** for details on fishing and lodging packages and equipment and tackle shops.

Another way to enjoy the water is to take a cruise aboard the massive *Keuka Maid,* Route 54 (Champlin Beach), Hammondsport (© **607/569-2628;** www.keukamaid. com). Known for its evening dinner cruises, it also offers lunch and Sunday brunch cruises (Apr–Nov), as well as moonlight cruises most Saturday nights and special day-long cruises in August and September. Esperanza Mansion (see below) operates the *Esperanza Rose,* a 65-foot vintage wooden sailing vessel (© **866/927-4400;** www. esperanzaboat.com). It offers lunch, sightseeing, and dinner cruises Tuesday through Sunday, Memorial Day to October.

Another spectacular way to see Keuka Lake is to drive (or cycle) around its 20-mile perimeter. **Route 54A** ⍟, which travels south of Penn Yan between the two upper prongs of the lake and then traverses its western length, is a mesmerizing scenic drive, hands-down one of the prettiest in the entire state. If you're planning to visit some wineries, you can take Route 54A to High Road.

EXPLORING HAMMONDSPORT

Tiny **Hammondsport** ⍟, at the southern end of Keuka Lake, is a postcard-perfect small town built around an attractive village square. Though tiny, it bustles with a disproportionate number of antiques and gifts shops, an ice-cream parlor, and a couple of restaurants and inns. If you'd like a bit of small-town life to complement your Finger Lakes experience, it makes a good base.

Besides the lake and wineries (see the "Keuka Lake Wine Trail" box, below), the biggest attraction in the immediate area is the **Glenn H. Curtiss Museum** ⍟, 8419 Rte. 54, Hammondsport (© **607/569-2160;** www.glennhcurtissmuseum.org; May–Oct Mon–Sat 9am–5pm, Sun 11am–5pm; Nov–Dec Mon–Sat 10am–4pm, Sun noon–5pm; Jan–Apr Thurs–Sat 10am–4pm, Sun noon–5pm; $7 adults, $5 seniors, $4 students 7–18, free for children under 7), devoted to one of the true pioneers of American aviation, who was also a Hammondsport native. In the early 20th century, Curtiss began designing motorcycles and moved on to dirigibles, airplanes, and hydroaeroplanes ("flying boats"). His first flight, in 1908, was the first advertised public flight of aircraft (the Wright Brothers had already been aloft, but in total secrecy). The museum displays a fine collection of historical aircraft and antique Curtiss motorcycles (including a reproduction of the one he used to achieve the world speed record of 136 mph). The museum also presents dioramas on turn-of-the-20th-century life and winemaking, as well as an interactive children's gallery.

Shoppers in Hammondsport should check out **Opera House Antiques,** 61–63 Shethar St. (© **607/569-3525**), a multidealer shop featuring silver, linens, and period furniture. Across the street is **Scandia House,** 64 Shethar St. (© **607/569-2667**), a shop specializing in women's clothing, Scandinavian sweaters, and housewares. **Mud Lust Pottery,** 59 Shethar St. (© **607/569-3068**), features locally crafted fine pottery. Chocoholics should check out **The Chocolatier of Hammondsport,** 69 Shethar St. (© **607-569-2157**), a new shop that deals in high-end chocolates and confections.

Keuka Lake Wine Trail

Fifteen wineries are within easy reach of the banks of beautiful Keuka Lake. The **Keuka Lake Wine Trail** *&&* (© **800/440-4898**; www.keukawinetrail.com; brochure widely available in the area) comprises eight independent wineries located on or near the lake. Check the trail's website for special scheduled events throughout the year. Visits to Keuka Lake wineries can easily be combined with a tour of those along the west (and even east) bank of nearby Seneca Lake; see p. 316 for details on the Seneca Lake Wine Trail. **Heron Hill Winery** *&&*, 9249 County Rte. 76, Hammondsport (© **800/441-4241**; www.heronhill.com), has a gorgeous setting high above Keuka Lake, and very nice wines, among which the owner's single-vineyard Ingle wines are standouts, as well as frequent music events, a cafe with an outdoor terrace, and a good gift shop. It's open year-round Monday through Saturday from 10am to 5pm and Sunday from noon to 5pm.

The most distinguished winery in the entire region and a favorite of connoisseurs is **Dr. Konstantin Frank's Vinifera Wine Cellars** *&&&*, 9749 Middle Rd., Hammondsport (© **800/320-0735**; www.drfrankwines.com). Dr. Frank, as it's known, produces outstanding perennial, international award-winning wines, including a splendid dry Riesling and Gewürztraminer. Though the Finger Lakes aren't yet well known for their reds, Dr. Frank's cabernet sauvignon, cabernet franc, and pinot noir are quite excellent, and the rare Rkatsiteli and Chateau Frank sparkling wines are surprisingly good. Dr. Frank's Salmon Run wines are the winery's second label, and they use both estate grapes as well as grapes grown at other Finger Lakes vineyards. No winery tours are offered, but the setting on the slopes of Keuka Lake is lovely (a large new tasting pavilion was just added in 2007, as the previous one in Dr. Frank's original ranch-style home was getting a bit overwhelmed), and the full tasting, while serious about the wines, is conducted by a lively group of folks who make it educational but not stuffy. Dr. Frank was a Ukrainian viticulturist who almost single-handedly brought noble European varietals (vinifera grapes) to the Finger Lakes when he began making wine in 1962; he became the iconic figure in the region, emulated by many up-and-coming winemakers. Dr. Frank's remains a family-owned operation, now run by Frank's grandson. It's open year-round Monday through Saturday from 9am to 5pm and Sunday from noon to 5pm.

Not officially part of the Keuka Lake Wine Trail, but very near those that are, **Bully Hill Vineyards**, 8843 Greyton H. Taylor Memorial Dr., Hammondsport (© **607/868-3610**; www.bullyhill.com), has a reputation as one of the

If you're sore from driving around the lakes or boating or cycling, pay a visit to the family-run **Finger Lakes Wellness Center & Health Spa,** 7531 County Rte. 13, Bath (© **607/776-3737;** www.fingerlakeswellness.com), just south of Hammondsport, for a massage.

zaniest wineries in the region, a reflection of its original owner, a gadfly who left the Taylor winery and repeatedly battled Coca-Cola (for the rights to use the Taylor name) after it purchased his family's business. Tours and tastings aim to inject fun into the sometimes formal wine world. Also on the premises are a restaurant and the **Greyton H. Taylor Wine Museum,** with antique winemaking implements and artwork (much of which found its way onto Bully Hill labels) of the owner. Open Monday to Saturday from 9am to 5pm and Sunday from 11am to 5pm; restaurant and wine museum open daily mid-May through October (restaurant for lunch daily, dinner Fri–Sat).

On the east side of Keuka Lake, **Ravines Wine Cellars,** 14630 Rte. 54, Hammondsport (© **607/292-7007;** www.ravineswinecellars.com), is a boutique winery with a tasting bar inside an attractive new Tuscan-style villa (a drawing of which appears on the wine labels). Ravines makes quality, European-style vinifera wines, including Riesling, pinot noir, and meritage, a bordeaux-style blend. Open Monday to Saturday from 10am to 5pm and Sunday from noon to 5pm, from April through November (plus weekends in Mar and Dec). Tucked away on a quiet country road a mile or so from Keuka is **McGregor Vineyard** ⓡ, 5503 Dutch St., Dundee (© **800/272-0192;** www. mcgregorwinery.com). The family-run winery, in a cool space that looks more like a beer hall than a tasting room, has developed a cult following for its oddball varietals from eastern Europe. Chief among them is the coveted, powerful, and age-worthy Black Russian, a blend of Saperavi and Sereksiya Charni. It sells out quickly every year, though, so it may be tough to get a taste of it. Open year-round daily 10am to 6pm (until 5pm Dec-Mar), but July and August, until 8pm on Friday and Saturday.

For a taste of old-school Finger Lakes wineries and a time when the region concentrated more on jugs of sweet wine than on low-yield noble grapes, visit **Pleasant Valley Wine Company** ⓡ, Route 88, Hammondsport (© **607/569-6111;** www.pleasantvalleywine.com). Established in 1860, it's the oldest bonded winery in the Finger Lakes region, holder of U.S. Bond No. 1, in fact. Physically, it is the most atmospheric winery in the entire region—it retains original buildings carved out of the rocky hillside. Closed for a couple of years, it's being worked on by the new ownership to restore it to its former stature. Full tours include an introductory film. It's open year-round: April to December daily from 10am to 5pm, and January to March, Tuesday through Saturday from 10am to 4pm.

WHERE TO STAY

If you're looking to explore Keuka Lake and its wineries, or even nearby attractions in Watkins Glen and Corning, Hammondsport makes an excellent base, and its small-town attributes are attracting more and more travelers. But it remains strictly a place for small inns rather than hotels.

Black Sheep Inn ★★★ *Value* One of the newest inns to open in the Finger Lakes has immediately vaulted to a place among the small number of top-tier inns in the region. In a historic and immaculate 1859 octagon house—one of only about 100 that remain in New York State—owners Debbie Meritsky and Marc Rotman have created a handsome and stately, but completely relaxing, inn. The enthusiastic couple restored the house virtually by themselves over a period of more than 6 years, and while commuting from Cleveland! Debbie is a chef and Marc an interior designer, and their attention to detail is showcased throughout the house. The five rooms are built around a formal spiral staircase and are wonderful oases, with top-quality linens and bedding, well-chosen antique furnishings, period-specific wallpapers, and luxurious bathrooms. Debbie's breakfasts, cooked in a restaurant-worthy kitchen, are suitably gourmet: I recently tasted an organic waffle with local sausage and a compote of baked apples, apricots, and flat or donut peaches. The inn is progressive-minded, promoting organic foods and environmentally conscious policies; Debbie makes all her own cleaning products and soaps, which make great souvenirs.

8329 Pleasant Valley Rd., Hammondsport, NY 14840. (© 607/569-3767. www.stayblacksheepinn.com. 5 units. $109–$259 double. Rates include full breakfast. AE, DC, MC, V. Free parking. *In room:* A/C.

Elm Croft Manor Bed & Breakfast ★★ This elegant 1832 Greek Revival mansion, walking distance from the Hammondsport Village Square and Keuka Lake, has been handsomely restored with period antiques and equipped with an outdoor pool and a canopied deck. The four units, curiously named for star destinations in Italy, are exquisitely decorated with four-poster or wrought-iron beds and lovely fabrics and quality linens and bedding. The Florence room is perhaps the standout; it has its own private screened-in porch.

8361 Pleasant Valley Rd., Hammondsport, NY 14840. (© **607/569-3071.** Fax 607/569-2399. www.elmcroftmanor. com. 4 units. $200–$250 double. Rates include full breakfast. AE, DC, MC, V. Free parking. *In room:* A/C, TV, dataport, hair dryer.

Esperanza Mansion ★ Spectacularly sited high on a bluff overlooking one of the upper prongs of Keuka Lake, this property is an imposing, completely restored 1838 Greek Revival manse with rooms in the main house and simpler, motel-style rooms attached, in addition to two restaurants. The setting is absolutely stunning; at a minimum, it merits a visit for lunch or a glass of wine on the terrace for the dreamy distant views of the lake—perhaps the finest in all the Finger Lakes. The nine upscale mansion rooms are spacious and appointed with nouveau antiques; about half of the rooms have stunning lake views. The 21 inn rooms, which are a good value, also have lake views, though they're not quite as spectacular; still, I like their less self-conscious cottage feel better than the more expensive mansion rooms. The inn would rate even higher, were it not for the fact that it seems rather overly restored; though it was in a disastrous state prior to 2003, it now retains little of the original building. The formal dining room (fine-dining menu for dinner only) will impress some visitors as elegant and strike others as pretentious. I much prefer to order the Jack Daniels BBQ Flat Iron steak or cognac-and-mushroom potpie from The Grill Menu and sit on the deck with a glass of local wine, absorbing the scenery. The same menu is available in the informal, rustic Grill.

3465 Rte. 54A, Bluff Point, NY 14478. (© **866/927-4400** or 315/536-4400. www.esperanzamansion.com. 30 units. Mansion rooms $180–$260 double; inn rooms $160–$185. Rates include full breakfast. AE, DC, MC, V. Free parking. **Amenities:** 2 restaurants; bar. *In room:* A/C, TV, dataport, hair dryer.

Village Tavern Inn *(Value*   Above one of the most distinguished restaurants in this section of the Finger Lakes, and right on the Village Square and just a block from Keuka Lake, this good-value small inn has four simple but nicely equipped and comfortable rooms. Staying here is like having a nice dinner, or perhaps too many glasses of wine, and stumbling upstairs to crash. The owners have added another seven rooms in renovated old houses (the Champagne and Gulf Stream houses) a couple of blocks away. The latter units are larger, quieter, and more private; they all have fireplaces, private entrances, and sparkling hardwood floors.

30 Mechanic St., Hammondsport, NY 14840. (© **607/569-2528.** www.villagetaverninn.com. 11 units. $99–$290 double. Rates include full breakfast. AE, DC, MC, V. Free parking. *In room:* A/C, TV, dataport, hair dryer.

WHERE TO DINE

In addition to Hammondsport's one very good restaurant, **Union Block Café,** on the village square at 31 Shethar St. (© **607/569-2244**), is a good spot for coffee, paninis, wraps, and pizzas, as well as Wi-Fi access.

Village Tavern Restaurant *(★★ (Kids*   SEAFOOD/INTERNATIONAL   Though it is virtually the only place in town to dine, that hardly matters: This cozy, family-owned restaurant would be a winner even with plenty of competition. It looks more like a comfortable neighborhood joint than a haven for gastronomes, so its encyclopedic wine and beer lists are completely unexpected. (Surprising for such a small village, the tavern boasts one of the most extensive selections of Finger Lakes wines anywhere, including many by the glass and library wines, and 130 beers, including some Belgian and English rarities.) While one might be tempted by drinks alone, the wines and beers are perfect complements to well-prepared American and Continental fare. The menu features many good seafood specialties, such as crayfish étouffée, catfish Creole, and fried seafood platters; there are also homemade soups, nice salads, and roast prime rib and the "famous Friday fish fry." Although the menu may seem all over the map—the house specialty is seafood paella—the kitchen does most everything very well, and the restaurant, which has a small kids' menu, is popular with local families. The long bar is a popular and friendly regional hangout and occasionally features live music. In fact, the tavern is much cooler, with a hip staff and hip music, than the dated wood paneling and pink tablecloths under glass would lead any reasonable person to expect—which makes it a village charmer.

30 Mechanic St., Hammondsport. (© **607/569-2528.** Reservations recommended. Main courses $11–$40. AE, DISC, MC, V. Memorial Day to Oct daily 11:30am–9:30pm (Sun brunch 10am–3pm); Nov–Dec and Feb–Mar Thurs–Sun 11:30am–9:30pm; Apr to Memorial Day Wed–Sun 11:30am–9:30pm; tap room open same days as restaurant 11:30am to 1am. Closed Jan.

6 Canandaigua Lake

30 miles SE of Rochester; 19 miles W of Geneva

Canandaigua, which lies at the northern end of the lake of the same name, is the kind of laid-back small town that epitomizes the Finger Lakes region. Canandaigua Lake, the birthplace of the Seneca Nation that ruled this area in pre-Colonial days, is the area's principal attraction, but there are a number of unique sights and experiences in this part of what is rather redundantly called Lake Country. (Ontario County is home to 5 of the 11 Finger Lakes.) With the addition of the splendid new **New York Wine & Culinary Center,** Canandaigua is looking to become an important gateway to the Finger Lakes.

ESSENTIALS
GETTING THERE
BY CAR Canandaigua is reached along either Route 21 or 332 south from I-90.

VISITOR INFORMATION The **Finger Lakes Visitors Connection** (© 877-FUN-IN-NY or 585/394-3915; www.visitfingerlakes.com) is located at 25 Gorham St.

EXPLORING CANANDAIGUA LAKE
The Finger Lakes region is increasingly focused on its fast-improving wineries and the local gastronomy tied to the wines. And there is no better expression of this newfound interest than the massive **New York Wine & Culinary Center** ✶✶✶, 800 S. Main St. (© **585/394-7070**; www.nywcc.com). Built just removed from the north shore of Canandaigua Lake in 2006, with important funding from local businesses, including Wegmans and Constellation Brands wines, this sparkling center offers a window onto the best local food and wine products. Of greatest interest to most visitors will be the wine-tasting room, where tasting flights of New York State wines change frequently. It's a great place to learn about the wines before embarking on your own wine trail—or, if you don't have time for that, a decent substitute. The wine pourers are knowledgeable and friendly, so if you have any reticence about being over your head at wineries, this is the perfect place to begin your education. The center also has a great hands-on kitchen, where short-term cooking classes are offered (look for CIA-type boot camps in the future). Finally, head upstairs to the excellent Taste of New York Lounge for lunch or dinner. The menu, naturally, focuses on local products and New York wines and craft beers. There's live music and a terrific wraparound deck. The restaurant is open Memorial Day to October 31, Monday to Saturday, 11:30am to 9pm and Sunday noon to 9pm; November 1 to Memorial Day, Tuesday to Thursday 11:30am to 6pm, Friday and Saturday 11:30am to 9pm, and Sunday noon to 6pm. For a special treat, check out the schedule of winemaker dinners, held in the sumptuous, medieval-styled wine and spirits room.

Naturalists and garden enthusiasts should not miss the **Sonnenberg Mansion & Gardens** ✶✶, 151 Charlotte St. (© **585/394-4922**; www.sonnenberg.org). The 50-acre estate and 1887 Queen Anne Victorian mansion, which once belonged to the founder of what is today Citibank, possesses some of the loveliest formal gardens and landscaping you're likely to encounter, including Italian, Japanese, and rock gardens. The grounds also maintain an impressive conservatory and Finger Lakes Wine Center, which conducts tastings on the premises. Special events, such as the "Haunted Gardens" in October and "Festival of Lights" in November and December, are truly special. The Sonnenberg is open daily May 7 to May 29 and September 6 to October 9 from 9:30am to 4pm; May 30 to September 5 from 9:30am to 5:30pm. Admission is $10 for adults, $9 for seniors, and $5 for children 5 to 14.

CANANDAIGUA WINE TRAIL The small vineyards and wineries clustered around Canandaigua Lake have joined forces to form the Canandaigua Wine Trail (© **800/554-7553**; www.canandaiguawinetrailonline.com), making it easy for visitors to group them together for tours and tastings. They include **Casa Larga Vineyards** ✶, an impressive facility producing a collection of very nice wines, including ice wines, just outside Rochester, 2287 Turk Hill Rd., Fairport (© **585/223-4210**; www.casalarga.com; open year-round Mon–Sat 10am–6pm, Sun noon–6pm); **Arbor Hill Grapery,** 6461 Rte. 64, Bristol Springs, Naples (© **800/554-2406**; www.thegrapery.com; open May–Dec Mon–Sat 10am–5pm, Sun 11am–5pm; Jan–Apr Sat–Sun 11am–5pm), which features a shop selling a large selection of wine, food, and gift items (including grape pies), and a great little bakery/cafe—excellent for breakfast or lunch; and **Widmer Wine Cellars,** 1 Lake Niagara Lane, Naples (✆ **800/836-LAKE;** www.widmerwine.com; open year-round daily 10am–4pm), a massive, old-school Finger Lakes winery that's more than a century old. Part of the winery is the Manischewitz Winery, the largest producer of kosher wines in the world. Also of interest is the **Finger Lakes Wine Center** at Sonnenberg Gardens, 151 Charlotte St., Canandaigua (✆ **585/394-9016;** open daily mid-May to mid-Oct noon–5pm), which offers samples and the sales of more than 30 Finger Lakes wineries.

NEARBY ATTRACTIONS   The Church of Jesus Christ of Latter-day Saints, better known to the rest of the world as the Mormon religion, got its start in the northwest region of the Finger Lakes before moving out west to Utah. Near Palmyra (17 miles northeast of Canandaigua), according to Mormon texts, Joseph Smith received golden plates, later translated into the Book of Mormon, from an angel in 1827. North of Canandaigua, along Route 21, is the **Hill Cumorah Visitors Center** (603 State Rte. 21, Palmyra; ✆ **315/597-5851;** www.hillcumorah.org); anyone who wants to learn more about the Mormon faith can drop in for some low-pressure information about the church and find out about Mormon-related sights in the area, such as Smith's log cabin. However, the big event in these parts is the annual **Hill Cumorah Pageant,** an incredible spectacle and the largest outdoor theatrical production in the U.S., with a costumed cast of 700, a nine-level stage, and music by the Mormon Tabernacle Choir. Every July its seven productions draw many thousands of believers and the curious. For more information, call ✆ **315/597-5851** or visit **www.hill cumorah.com**. Performances are free.

Not far from the Mormons, but on an altogether different spiritual plane, is the **Finger Lakes Race Track** (✆ **585/935-5252;** www.fingerlakesracetrack.com), in Farmington, also north of Canandaigua (1 mile south of I-90, exit 44 on Rte. 332). Thoroughbred horses race here from April to November.

Visitors interested in the region's Native American roots should head to the **Ganondagan State Historic Site** (★, 1488 State Rte. 444, Victor (✆ **585/924-5848;** www.ganondagan.org), a real find located northwest of Canandaigua. A former center of the democratically inclined Seneca people, one of the six nations composing the Iroquois Confederacy, the site today features a replica 17th-century Seneca bark longhouse, as well as marked ethnobotanical, Native American–themed trails that aim to teach visitors about Seneca customs and beliefs. Trails are open year-round from 8am to sunset; the visitor center is open mid-May through October, Tuesday to Sunday from 9am to 5pm. Interpreted trail walks are offered year-round Saturday at 10am and 2pm, Sunday at noon and 2pm. Visits are $3 for adults, $2 for children, though self-guided walks along the trails are free.

SPORTS & OUTDOOR ACTIVITIES

Public-access beaches on Canandaigua Lake include **Butler Beach,** West Lake Road (✆ **585/396-2752;** free admission), on the west side of the lake; **Deep Run Park,** East Lake Road (✆ **585/396-4000**), on the east side of the lake; and **Kershaw Park,** Lakeshore Drive (✆ **585/396-5060;** fee charged), which has a sand beach and an 8-acre park.

If you'd rather see the lake from a boat, the *Canandaigua Lady* (✆ **585/ 396-7350;** www.steamboatlandingonline.com) is a replica 19th-century paddle-wheel steamboat, available for lake excursions and lunch and dinner cruises. From May to mid-September, it departs from Steamboat Landing, 205 Lakeshore Dr. (at the north end of Canandaigua Lake). Fall foliage cruises (mid-Sept to Oct) board at Woodville dock, Route 21 South (south end of Canandaigua Lake). Cruise prices range from $17 to $43. Scuba diving, windsurfing, kayaking, and sailboarding rentals and instruction are available from **Canandaigua Sailboarding,** 11 Lakeshore Dr. (✆ **585/394-8150**).

Golfers will not want to miss the **Bristol Harbour Resort Golf Course** (✆ **800/288-8248;** www.bristolharbour.com), a beautiful 18-hole Robert Trent Jones–designed course right on Lake Canandaigua. Greens fees are $49 to $79.

Good hiking and cycling are available on **Ontario Pathways,** 200 Ontario St., Canandaigua (✆ **585/394-7968;** www.ontariopathways.org), 23 miles of rails-to-trails. In winter months, you can ski at **Bristol Mountain Winter Resort,** 5662 Rte. 64, Canandaigua (✆ **585/374-6000;** www.bristolmountain.com).

SHOPPING

Along Canandaigua's Main Street, an "artwalk" takes you to **Gallery on Main Street** (131 S. Main St.; ✆ **585/394-2780**), **The Christopher Wheat Gallery** (92 S. Main St.; ✆ **585/399-1180**), and **Nadal Glass** (20 Phoenix St.; ✆ **585/374-7850**), which features handblown glass in an old firehouse. The top shopping destination in the area, however, is the **Bloomfield Antique Country Mile,** a cluster of seven antiques dealers along routes 5 and 20 in Bloomfield (just west of Canandaigua). Several are multidealer shops, such as **Alan's Antique Alley,** 6925 routes 5 and 20 (✆ **585/657-6776**). **Wizard of Clay,** 7851 Rte. 20A, Bristol (✆ **585/229-2980**), is a cool stoneware pottery shop. A couple of very large antiques malls are located in Farmington (Rochester Rd., or Rte. 332): **Ontario Mall Antiques** (1740 Rochester Rd.; ✆ **585/398-3030**), with more than 600 dealers, and **Antique Emporium of Farmington** (1780 Rochester Rd.; ✆ **585/398-3997**), with some 60 dealers.

WHERE TO STAY

Low-key Canandaigua, with three of the loveliest inns in the state and some lower-priced hotels along the lake, makes an excellent base for exploring the western section of the Finger Lakes.

Acorn Inn 🖈🖈🖈　A charming, meticulously kept B&B—enough to earn a four-diamond rating from AAA—this 1795 Federal Stagecoach Inn west of Canandaigua Lake is one of the most distinguished small country inns in New York State. The entire place is meticulously designed and maintained. The common room is cozy and lined with several thousand books and warmed by a roaring fire in cold months. In addition to the large and very handsomely appointed rooms on the second floor, all with romantic canopied beds and a couple with fireplaces, guests can luxuriate under the stars in a splendid outdoor hot tub set among the gardens near the carriage house. Among the guest rooms, the Bristol has a large sitting area, and all the rooms are equipped with spacious modern bathrooms. The candlelit breakfast is a lovely affair, served on antique English china with heirloom silver.

4508 Rte. 64 S., Bristol Center, Canandaigua, NY 14424. ✆ **888/665-3747** or 585/229-2834. www.acorninnbb.com. 4 units. $148–$240 double; $198–$260 suite. Rates include full breakfast. 2-night minimum weekends June–Oct, also for holidays and special events. AE, MC, V. Free parking. **Amenities:** Outdoor Jacuzzi. *In room:* A/C, TV/VCR, CD player.

The Chalet of Canandaigua 🖈🖈🖈 *(Finds)*　Ordinarily, I wouldn't find myself seduced by a log cabin, but this extraordinary luxury B&B is leagues removed from expectations of a rustic, Adirondack-style cabin. It is secluded, tucked at the end of a long approach past a pond of ducks and tall trees, and technically it is constructed of logs. But it's as if the Four Seasons hotel chain decided to do a three-room inn as an alpine cottage. It's a luxury lodge, where the rustic elements of this unique 1960s abode combine with inviting furnishings, high-tech features, and stunning attention to detail. The two innkeepers, Pattie and Margaret, have turned the notion of frumpy B&B on its head. The accommodations are almost impossibly large and enveloping, with fireplaces (I can imagine being here on a snowy night!). The top-of-the-line bathrooms, with massive claw-foot soaking tubs, showers with multiple rain heads, and heated towel racks, put many New York City apartments to shame. You could probably argue for hours over your favorite room, but for me it's the peak-ceilinged Balcony Suite. Then, there's the expansive deck; the friendly dog; the savvy, open-minded owners; and those hour-long, three-course gourmet breakfasts (bananas Foster? Belgian waffles? Kiss the waistline goodbye!). A retreat to this chalet, which has both feminine warmth and masculine rusticity in spades, is like getting invited to the woodsy dacha of a Russian official. It may be tough to leave.

3770 State Rte. 21, Canandaigua, NY 14424. © **585/394-9080.** Fax 585/394-9088. www.chaletbandb.com. 3 units. $195–$295 suite. Check online for specials and packages. Rates include full breakfast. AE, DC, MC, V. Free parking. *In room:* A/C, flat-screen cable TV/DVD player, Wi-Fi, minibar, coffeemaker.

The Inn at Bristol Harbour ★ *(Kids)*   This small resort hotel, right on the west bank of Canandaigua Lake, features some excellent outdoors amenities, such as a great golf course (ask about special golf packages), a private beach, and an outdoor swimming pool. The 31 cozy Adirondack-style rooms aren't merely an afterthought: They all have fireplaces and balconies, many with superb panoramic views of the lake. The Lodge restaurant, recommended below, is quite good, and the Tavern is a great place to unwind after a round of golf or touring the area.

5410 Seneca Point Rd., Canandaigua, NY 14424. © **800/288-8248** or 585-396-2200. Fax 585-394-9254. www.bristol harbour.com. 31 units. $129–$199 double; $209–$249 suite. AE, DISC, MC, V. Free parking. **Amenities:** Restaurant; bar; outdoor pool; outdoor 18-hole golf course; Jacuzzi; private beach. *In room:* A/C, TV/VCR, CD player.

Morgan Samuels B&B Inn ★★ *(Finds)*   On 46 sylvan acres, this private and rather prim and proper inn occupying an 1810 English-style mansion is a nice retreat if you're looking for tranquillity. Guest rooms are pretty and romantic, and each is uniquely decorated, with such touches as Oriental rugs and antiques, French doors, and fireplaces (there are an incredible 11 in the house). A lot of care is taken with the inn's ambience, especially at breakfast, which is served fireside by candlelight in the formal dining room. The enclosed garden porch is a lovely spot to sip afternoon tea, and the library is a private nook in which to plunge into a good book. The emphasis on elegance and old-world refinement will not suit everyone, though many visitors will be in heaven.

2920 Smith Rd., Canandaigua, NY 14424. © **585/394-9232.** Fax 585/394-8044. www.morgansamuelsinn.com. 5 units. $119–$225 double; $209–$295 suite. Rates include full breakfast. AE, MC, V. Free parking. **Amenities:** Tennis court. *In room:* A/C.

WHERE TO DINE

The New York Wine & Culinary Center (see p. 334) has an excellent restaurant and bar, the **Taste of New York Lounge** ★★, with a continually changing menu using the finest local ingredients. It is very much worth a visit for lunch, dinner, or predinner wine tasting. In addition to the restaurant below, the Canandaigua Inn on the Lake has a nice restaurant, **Nicole's Lakeside,** with good views and an outdoor terrace. Restaurants in nearby Naples, particularly **Brown Hound Bistro** (see p. 339) are also worth the drive.

Bristol Harbour's Lodge Restaurant *G* GRILL   With gorgeous views of southern Lake Canandaigua, this woodsy, Adirondack-style restaurant on the grounds of an upscale golf resort is a fine place to linger over a cocktail and ease into dinner. It's the kind of mas-culine-looking place that cries out for an order of grilled meat, such as the filet medley with crab cake rémoulade sauce, or New York strip steak with a brandy peppercorn sauce. There are plenty of less macho entrees, however, including grilled sea bass and grilled veg-etables wrapped in phyllo. Even if you're not staying here, the lodge is perfect to drop in for a hearty breakfast or lunch before hitting the links or getting out on the lake. Eat in the main restaurant or the tavern; in nice weather, there's seating on one of two outdoor patios. A grill menu is also offered daily in the Tavern from 11am to 10pm.

5410 Seneca Point Rd., Bristol Harbor. ⓒ 585/396-2200. Reservations recommended. Main courses $12–$24. AE, DISC, MC, V. Daily 7:30–10:30am and 11am–2pm; Sun–Thurs 5–9pm; Fri–Sat 5–10pm.

CANANDAIGUA AFTER DARK

The **Finger Lakes Performing Arts Center,** 4355 Lakeshore Dr., Lincoln Hill, Canandaigua (on the campus of Finger Lakes Community College), a very attractive open-air theater, hosts the Rochester Philharmonic Orchestra and popular musical events throughout the summer. For more information, visit www.rbtl.org or call ⓒ **716/325-7760;** tickets are available through **Ticket Express** (ⓒ **716/222-500**). The Rochester Broadway Theatre League hosts the annual summertime **Finger Lakes Elegant Picnic** in Canandaigua, with concerts at the shell featuring such big-name acts as Diana Krall and Tony Bennett.

NAPLES *G*

At the southern end of Canandaigua Lake, the picturesque village of **Naples** *G* is a quintessential small Finger Lakes town with a number of well-preserved 18th-century buildings. It's a peaceful place primarily known for its arts community from summer to autumn and for the last weekend in September, when the unique **Naples Grape Festival** takes over.

EXPLORING NAPLES

Area wineries worth a visit include **Widmer Wine Cellars** and **Arbor Hill Grapery & Winery;** see "Canandaigua Wine Trail," p. 334, for details.

Trout **fishing** is good on Canandaigua Lake, and small and shallow Honeoye Lake is known for walleye and largemouth and smallmouth bass. **Reel Magic Charters,** 8 Cohocton St., Naples (ⓒ 585/374-5197), runs fishing charters on Canandaigua Lake.

Duffers should check out the scenic **Reservoir Creek Golf Club,** 8613 Cohocton St. (ⓒ 585/374-6828; www.rcgolf.com). Greens fees are $39 Monday to Thursday, $43 weekends and holidays; reduced rates for seniors, juniors, "sunset" play (after 2pm), and fall season (after Oct 10).

The **Bristol Valley Theater,** 151 S. Main St. (ⓒ 585/374-6318; www.bvtnaples.org), schedules professional summer theater in a handsome outdoor amphitheater.

The **Naples Grape Festival** *G* (last weekend of Sept) is a fun-filled weekend built around the town's tradition of making grape pies. The festival has been held in Naples for more than 40 years and draws bumper-to-bumper traffic along routes 64 and 21; as many as 50,000 grape pies are sold in that single weekend. For more information, call ⓒ 585/374-2240 or visit www.naplesvalleyny.com. Grape pies, of course, are notori-ously labor-intensive to make (you have to peel the grapes first), perhaps the reason why they haven't exactly taken off outside of Naples. They are available, however, year-round at the Arbor Hill Grapery & Winery.

WHERE TO STAY & DINE

The top inn in the area is **Monier Manor** *★★*, 54 N. Main St., Naples, NY 14512 (© **585/374-6719;** www.moniermanor.com; $145–$175 double; 2-night weekend stay required, June 15–Oct 31), an elegant B&B. The rooms in this nicely conserved, mid-19th-century, red Federal-style mansion are very spacious and well decorated, with handsome fabrics and luxurious period furnishings. The room names, while a bit precious, pretty much describe the ambience and decor: Opulence, Serenity, Elegance, and Indulgence. Amenities range from fireplaces and Persian rugs to a Greek soaking tub. The lovely grounds are a great place to relax. Check out specials and packages (such as the wine tour package) online, which make Monier Manor an even better value. Another good B&B, and a great value for the money, is **Bristol Views Bed & Breakfast**, 6932 County Rd. no. 12, Naples, NY 14512 (© **585/374-8875;** www.bristolviews.com; $95–$150 double), a renovated old farmhouse with four attractive, clean, and nicely appointed rooms. There's high-speed Internet access, a large deck with a hot tub, and beautiful distant lake views.

For dining, the top spot is **Brown Hound Bistro** *★★*, 6459 State Rte. 64 (© **585/374-9771;** main courses $19–$33), a big regional draw in an intimate 100-year-old house not far from downtown Naples in Bristol Springs. The menu is committed to creative application of the best local culinary ingredients. Try the chicken almond amaretto, or the spicy seafood sauté. Vegetarians will be pleased with dishes like aubergine pouches, eggplant wrapped around basil, fresh mozzarella, and roasted tomatoes. The Brown Hound is open for dinner, Tuesday to Thursday and Sunday 4:30 to 9pm, Friday and Saturday until 10pm. Breakfast and brunch are served Saturday and Sunday from 8am to 1pm. For more casual dining, check out the **Naples Diner,** a longtime fixture at 139 S. Main St. (© **585/374-5420**), or the **Naples Hotel,** 111 S. Main St. (© **585/374-5630**), an 1895 Federal-style hotel with a great old lounge bar.

7 Rochester *★*

85 miles W of Niagara Falls; 45 miles W of Geneva; 105 miles NW of Corning; 330 miles NW of New York City

Rochester, at the southern edge of Lake Ontario, is where the Finger Lakes meet the Great Lakes. Though cities are perhaps not what most visitors associate with the Finger Lakes region, Rochester, one of the northern gateways to the lakes, is a surprisingly agreeable and historic city that's well worth a visit for its trio of excellent museums, fine restaurants, and enjoyable festivals. The third-largest city in New York State, Rochester was an early boomtown and industrial giant in the early 19th century when it ranked as the flour-milling epicenter of the U.S. and the Erie Canal permitted the large-scale shipping of grain and flour to New York City. The city today is perhaps best known for the modern corporate success stories that got their start here, including Eastman Kodak, Xerox, and Bausch & Lomb. An extremely livable, family-friendly, and attractive small city, which many locals and visitors contend feels more Midwestern than East Coast, Rochester has an enviable surfeit of gardens and parks, but is predominantly characterized by its residents' modesty and industry.

ESSENTIALS
GETTING THERE

BY AIR **Greater Rochester International Airport,** 1200 Brooks Ave. (© **716/464-6000;** www.rocairport.com), is 4 miles southwest of Rochester. The airport is serviced by American, AirTran, Continental, Delta, JetBlue, Northwest, United, and US Airways.

BY CAR   Rochester is about 10 miles north of I-90 (New York State Thruway), reached by either Route 390 or 490.

BY BUS   Greyhound and **Trailways** travel to the terminal at 187 Midtown Plaza (© **585/232-5121**).

VISITOR INFORMATION   The **Downtown Visitor Information Center** is located at 45 East Ave. (© **800/677-7282** or 585/546-3070; www.visitrochester.com). The Events line (© **585/546-6810**) is a 24-hour recorded message highlighting current events and activities in the Rochester area. You will also find tourism information centers on the first floor of the Greater Rochester International Airport and at the rest stop of the New York State Thruway (westbound lane) near exit 45.

GETTING AROUND   Regional Transit System (RTS) buses traverse the major routes downtown. An All-Day City Pass ($4) is good for unlimited rides and can be purchased on buses. Call © **888/288-3777** for information.

EXPLORING ROCHESTER

Start your visit in the **High Falls Historic District,** the one-time mill area at the edge of the Genesee River and a 96-foot urban waterfall. The **High Falls Heritage Area Visitors Center,** 60 Browns Race (© **585/325-3020**), has a small museum on the history of Rochester and some great views of the falls.

Genesee Country Village & Museum 𝒜𝒜 *Kids*   About 20 miles southwest of Rochester, this assembly of 58 historic buildings gathered from around upstate New York re-creates a working 19th-century village, a living museum on more than 600 acres of rural land. Interpreters in period costume bring the 1800s to life with demonstrations of pottery making, blacksmithing, basket and cheese making, quilting, spinning, and cooking over an open hearth. Buildings include a tavern, a general store, an Italianate villa mansion, an octagon-shaped home, and the boyhood home of George Eastman (of Kodak fame). The buildings are further enlivened by period gardens, roaming animals, and even a baseball diamond, where New York State's vintage teams in period dress play games according to 19th-century rules. Year-round, there is a full calendar of activities, such as a Civil War candlelight tour or country yuletide celebrations; check the website for the schedule. Finally, there's an extensive gallery of wildlife art, plus a 175-acre nature center with walking trails. Allow at least a full morning or afternoon here.

1410 Flint Hill Rd., Mumford. © 585/538-6822. www.gcv.org. Admission $13 adults, $9.95 seniors and students, $7.50 children 4–16, free for children under 4. May and Oct Sat–Sun and holidays 10am–5pm; June and Sept Tues–Fri 10am–4pm, Sat–Sun 10am–5pm; July to Labor Day Tues–Sun 10am–5pm.

George Eastman House 𝒜𝒜 *Kids*   George Eastman, the founder of the legendary company Kodak and known as the father of popular photography, was born in upstate New York and reared in Rochester. An innovator, philanthropist, and consummate businessman, Eastman endowed the Eastman School of Music at the University of Rochester—just one of many civic-minded projects—and he left his magnificent mansion, now a National Historic Landmark and the oldest photography museum in the world, to the university (in fact, for a time, university presidents lived there). Visitors can tour several rooms and the wonderful formal gardens of his magnificent 1905 Colonial Revival mansion. Every bit as interesting, if not more so, are the extraordinary itinerant exhibitions (such as 2007's Ansel Adams show) and permanent photography collections

Downtown Rochester

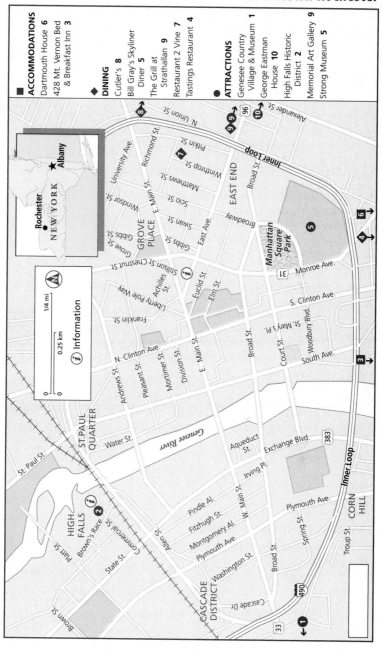

ALBANY
Rochester
NEW YORK

ⓘ Information

¼ mi
0.25 km

ST. PAUL
QUARTER

HIGH
FALLS

GROVE
PLACE

EAST END

Manhattan
Square
Park

CASCADE
DISTRICT

CORN
HILL

Genesee River

that include more than 400,000 prints and negatives. Most children love the "Discovery Room" (open Tues–Sun 1–4pm) that allows them to inspect antique cameras and make filmstrips and sun prints. On-site are a terrific gift shop and a nice cafe.

900 East Ave. ☎ 585/271-3361. www.eastmanhouse.org. Admission $8 adults, $6 seniors, $5 students, $3 children 5–12, free for children under 5; special exhibitions extra. June–Apr Tues–Sat 10am–5pm (Thurs until 8pm), Sun 1–5pm; May daily 10am–5pm. Free (with paid admission) house (Tues–Sat 10:30am and 2pm; Sun 2pm) and garden (Tues–Sat 11:30am and 3pm; Sun 3pm) tours and gallery talks (Tues–Sun 1:15pm).

Memorial Art Gallery ✦   One of the country's best regional museums, the Memorial Art Gallery (MAG), part of the University of Rochester, covers the gamut from medieval to contemporary art, and occasionally hosts excellent traveling shows. Very good galleries of 17th- to 19th-century European art have paintings by Rubens, Rembrandt, Monet, Cézanne, and Matisse. The beautiful central gallery with a skylight over the museum's collection of 20th-century sculpture is a pleasant place to relax among works by Henry Moore and others. The gallery's restaurant, **Cutler's,** is a nice place for lunch (Tues–Sun) or dinner (Thurs–Sat).

500 University Ave. ☎ 585/473-7720. http://mag.rochester.edu. Admission $7 adults, $5 seniors and college students, $2 children 6–18, free for children under 6; Thurs evening (5–9pm) admission $2 for everyone. Director's audio tour free with admission. Fri–Wed 10am–5pm; Thurs 10am–9pm. Docent-led tours (free with admission) Thurs 6:30pm, Fri and Sun 2pm.

Strong Museum ✦✦✦ *Kids*   This imaginative place—a "national museum of play"— is a splendid interactive museum for children and almost certain to entertain adults, too. It is simply one of the finest children's museums in the country. There's a re-creation of Sesame Street, a miniature grocery store where kids can shop and even scan their own groceries, and a fantastic dance lab and radio station where kids make their own sound effects—a real wonderland. Plenty of local families buy annual passes to make it their own personal playground and theme park. The museum even operates its own mini-branch of the local library system, and there are books at every turn. The museum began as an outgrowth of a local woman's 20,000-strong collection of dolls, dollhouses, and toys (one of the largest collections in the world, it is impressive but comparatively static given all the activity going on elsewhere in the building). Adults will surely feel a tinge of nostalgia viewing the National Toy Hall of Fame. Plan on a visit of several hours if you're in the presence of curious children. Also on-site are a great gift shop and an actual 1950s Skyliner Diner, a great place to take a break and refuel for more playing.

1 Manhattan Sq. ☎ 585/263-2700. www.strongmuseum.org. Admission $9 adults, $8 seniors and students, $7 children 2–17, free for children under 2. Mon–Thurs and Sat 10am–5pm; Fri 10am–8pm; Sun noon–5pm (July–Sept open 1 hr. later except for Fri).

SPORTS & OUTDOOR PURSUITS

Beaches on the Lake Ontario shoreline, north of the city, are very popular with locals. **Ontario Beach Park,** often called "the Port of Rochester," at the mouth of the Genesee River, has piers, a boardwalk, and an antique carousel in addition to a pleasant lake beach.

Where the Dead Outnumber the Living

More people are buried in sprawling Victorian **Mt. Hope Cemetery,** Mt. Hope and Elmwood avenues ((☎ 585/428-7999), than currently live in the entire city of Rochester, including a handful of its most notable citizens, such as Frederick Douglass and Susan B. Anthony.

The Erie Canal

Lauded as the most important engineering feat of its day, the **Erie Canal,** completed in 1825, created an international highway from the Great Lakes to the Atlantic Ocean. Shipping costs of flour and other raw materials and manufactured goods were reduced by as much as 90%. The canal stretched 360 miles from the Niagara River and Lake Erie in the west to the Hudson River in the east. It turned Rochester into a boomtown and was instrumental in transforming New York City into a major port, in the process opening up parts of the West for commercial expansion.

The canal diminished in importance as railroads quickly began to crisscross the country, but it is being rediscovered as a tourism waterway. In addition to boating and cruises on the canal, the New York State Erie Canal Heritage trail follows the original towpath along the canal and is ideal for walking, biking, and skiing in winter. Anyone interested in following the canal, by either boat or car, and seeing sights along it should request a copy of *Canal Connections* from any of the country tourism offices. See also www.canals.state.ny.us.

The farm team of baseball's Minnesota Twins, the **Rochester Red Wings** (✆ **800/447-2623** or 585/454-1001; www.redwingsbaseball.com), play at Frontier Field, downtown, across from High Falls. Tickets are $6 to $10. The PGA Championship and the Ryder Cup have been held at Oak Hill Country Club, and the women play the LPGA Wegmans Rochester International at Locust Hill Country Club (www.rochesterlpga.com).

Since 1892, the annual **Lilac Festival** ✿, held in early May at 150-acre Highland Park, has been a magnet for nature lovers: Some 1,200 lilac bushes burst with spring color. The festival also draws musical entertainment and a commercial, carnival-like atmosphere (✆ **585/256-4960;** www.lilacfestival.com). Highland Park, designed in 1888 by Frederick Law Olmsted (who also created New York City's Central Park) and full of beautiful gardens and plantings, is a lovely place for a stroll.

Erie Canal and Genesee River cruises are offered aboard the *Sam Patch,* a 19th-century replica packet boat, daily from May to October. Call ✆ **585/262-5661** for schedules.

ESPECIALLY FOR KIDS

The outstanding Strong Museum and the 19th-century Genesee Country Village & Museum (see above) are musts for kids visiting Rochester. Also of interest is the **Seneca Park Zoo,** 222 St. Paul Blvd. (✆ **585/467-WILD;** www.senecaparkzoo.org), which has polar bears, rare African elephants, and Eurasian Arctic wolves. **High Falls** is also a good place for families. Kids will enjoy the urban waterfall and laser-light show, shown there on weekend nights in the summer; the High Falls Visitors Center also has an educational exhibit aimed at youngsters. Lake Ontario's beaches and the nearby **Seabreeze Amusement Park,** 4600 Culver Rd. (✆ **800/395-2500;** www.seabreeze.com), open mid-June to Labor Day, are great spots in the heat of summer.

SHOPPING

The biggest mall in the area is **EastView Mall,** 7979 Pittsford-Victor Rd., Victor (© 585/223-3693), about 20 minutes south of Rochester. **Craft Antique Co-op,** 3200 W. Ridge Rd. (© **888/711-3463** or 585/368-0670), is one of the state's largest craft-and-antiques co-ops, with 210 shops. Antiques hounds will want to visit the **Bloomfield Antique Country Mile** corridor along routes 5 and 20 in Bloomfield, on the way to Canandaigua, where a few dozen antiques shops are located. **Craft Company No. 6,** 785 University Ave. (© 585/473-3413), which deals in all manner of contemporary American crafts, including jewelry, art glass, and home decor, occupies a Victorian firehouse 1 block from the George Eastman House. One of the best strolling and shopping areas downtown is along **Park Avenue and Alexander Street,** with lots of food and drink pit stops along the way. Don't forget the excellent gift shops at the Strong Museum and George Eastman House.

WHERE TO STAY

Rochester has two very nice B&Bs in residential neighborhoods as well as a handful of large chain hotels downtown, including the **Hyatt Regency Rochester,** 125 E. Main St. (© **585/546-1234;** fax 585/546-6777; www.rochester.hyatt.com; $150–$200 double), probably the best of the lot; the **Crowne Plaza,** 70 State St. (© **585/ 546-3450;** www.crowneplaza.com; $119–$179 double); and the massive **Clarion,** 120 Main St. E. (© **585/546-6400;** www2.choicehotels.com; $139–$169 double). The large but independent **Strathallan Hotel,** 550 East Ave. (© **800/678-7284;** www.strathallan.com; $159–$199 double), in a former apartment building, is worth a look; it's very well located, it has a swanky restaurant with an excellent wine list (p. 345), and most rooms, recently updated, have kitchenettes.

Dartmouth House ⊛   This ideally located 1905 English Tudor inn, nestled in a residential area near the East Avenue entertainment district and Park Avenue, is a fine place to stay. It claims to be the only B&B in Rochester with central air-conditioning. Rooms are elegantly decorated, with nicely chosen period antiques. The public rooms in this 15-year-old inn feature a grand piano, a fireplace, and window seats, as well as handsome Arts and Crafts details.

215 Dartmouth St., Rochester, NY 14607. © 800/724-6298 or 585/271-7872. www.dartmouthhouse.com. 7 units. $125–$150 double. Rates include full breakfast. AE, MC, V. Free parking. *In room:* A/C, TV/VCR, Wi-Fi.

428 Mt. Vernon Bed & Breakfast Inn ⊛ *(Value*   A stately 1917 home on a nice wooded lot just off Highland Park, south of downtown, this relaxed and comfortable place, popular with visiting professors and business travelers, is one of the best places to stay in town. The house has Victorian-style furnishings, but is understated and not fussy. Its biggest advantage is a countrylike atmosphere along with a location that provides travelers a peaceful sanctuary in the midst of the city. Breakfasts are hearty.

428 Mt. Vernon, Rochester, NY 14620. © 800/836-3159 or 585/271-0792. www.428mtvernon.com. 7 units. $125 double. Rates include full breakfast. AE, MC, V. Free parking. *In room:* A/C, TV, Wi-Fi.

WHERE TO DINE

Rochester has a surprisingly lively dining scene. Much of it is clustered around two areas, East Avenue, or the so-called East End "entertainment district," and Park Avenue and Alexander Street. Two restaurants worth visiting, especially when you're out sightseeing, are actually located in museums: **Cutler's** (© 585/473-6380) is an upscale option just off the modern sculpture gallery at the Memorial Art Gallery

(p. 342), serving lunch Tuesday through Sunday, 11:30am to 2pm; and **Bill Gray's Skyliner Diner** (© **585/232-5284**) is the Strong Museum's authentic 1950s diner, with food that kids will love (p. 342).

The Grill at Strathallan ☆☆ AMERICAN   The only Mobil four-diamond restaurant in the state west of New York City, this is the place in Rochester for haute cuisine and fine wine. Entrees are classic, like dry-aged strip steak, veal chop, and slow-roasted salmon, with just a few twists (such as the peach-lacquered duck breast with squash gnocchi, seared spinach, and foie gras). Gourmands and oenophiles should check into the periodic six-course wine dinners, with pairings for each course. The newly remodeled restaurant features live jazz until late Thursday through Saturday nights.

550 East Ave.(in Strathallan Hotel) © **585/454-1880**. Reservations required. Main courses $24–$34. AE, DISC, MC, V. Daily 5:30–10pm.

Restaurant 2 Vine ☆☆ *Value* BISTRO/SEAFOOD   In a renovated 1890s ambulance garage, this cheery and casual, often-crowded restaurant and lively bar—a consistent local award winner—is a great place for dinner before or after a show at Little Theatre, behind which the restaurant is located. The space is large, handsome, and warm, with subdued lighting and a beautiful long bar. The menu features fresh seasonal ingredients, organic produce, and fresh seafood delivered daily from Boston. Choose from elegant entrees like roasted halibut with mushroom-watercress risotto or classic bistro dishes such as mussels steamed in white wine with *pommes frites*. Big appetites and wallets can be steered toward towering iced platters of seafood. Service is good, if occasionally a bit harried. In keeping with its name, 2 Vine has an excellent wine list, even though it features only a handful of Finger Lakes wines.

4 Winthrop St. © **585/454-6020**. Reservations recommended. Main courses $17–$26. AE, DISC, MC, V. Mon–Fri 11:30am–2pm and 5–9pm; Sat–Sun 5–8pm.

Tastings Restaurant ☆ *Finds* AMERICAN   Next to, but more properly a part of, the Wegmans grocery store—surely an odd place to find a good restaurant—this hopping, dimly lit place with brick vaulted ceilings and crowded tables has been a huge hit with locals, who know well the fresh ingredients and meats and fish that Wegmans supplies. Entrees include Australian lamb loin with sweet potato purée, and coriander-crusted rare tuna. A great option is the seasonal four- or five-course tasting menu ($39 or $50), which you can choose to pair with wine if you wish. For dessert, cheese lovers will faint at the sight of the cheese flights, served with a baguette, sourdough bread, and fruit.

3195 Monroe Ave. © **585/381-1881**. Reservations recommended. Main courses $18–$35; tasting menu $39–$50 (wine pairing extra). AE, DISC, MC, V. Tues–Sat 11:30am–2:30pm and 5:30–10pm.

ROCHESTER AFTER DARK

The **Eastman School of Music** ☆ presents more than 700 concerts a year, including jazz, classical, chamber, and opera, among others, at the Eastman Theatre and other venues in Rochester. For concert information, call © **585/274-1100** or visit www.rochester.edu/Eastman. The **Rochester Philharmonic Orchestra** also plays at the Eastman Theatre. Call the box office at © **585/454-2100** or see the schedule at www.rpo.org. The **Rochester International Jazz Festival** (first 2 weeks of June), one of the city's biggest festival and music draws, features more than 50 concerts by major players at 15 venues. Contact the hotline at © **585/234-2002** or visit www.rochesterjazz.com.

The **Geva Theatre Center,** 75 Woodbury Blvd. (© **585/232-4382;** www.geva theatre.org), is the major venue in town for theater productions, and the most-attended regional theater in New York State.

Free laser light shows are projected in the gorge at High Falls on Friday and Saturday nights beginning at 9:30pm from Memorial Day to Labor Day; families and couples on dates hang out on the Rennes bridge that spans the river. The High Falls district is on the way up, with a number of new pubs and restaurants moving in. Expect more on the way. The **East End "entertainment district"** (★), along East Avenue, is one of the best spots to hang out on weekends. The cool Art Deco **Little Theatre,** 240 East Ave. ((C) **585/232-3906**), shows independent and foreign art-house films and often has live music in its cafe. The **St. Paul Quarter,** along St. Paul and Main streets, is also replete with lively bars and restaurants. Among its hot nightspots is **Club Industry,** 155 St. Paul St. ((C) **585/262-4570**). **Dinosaur Bar-B-Que,** 99 Court St. ((C) **585/325-7090**), a biker bar and lively ribs joint in the old Lehigh Valley Train Station downtown, has live blues bands on weekends and can get pretty raucous.

8 Geneva (★)(★) & Northern Seneca Lake

10 miles W of Seneca Falls; 54 miles W of Syracuse; 19 miles E of Canandaigua; 45 miles SE of Rochester

Geneva, tucked midway between the region's two largest cities, Rochester and Syracuse, is a gracious and historic small city hugging the north end of Seneca Lake. With about 15,000 residents, it's one of the larger towns in the region, an eminently livable small city and classic college town (it's home to Hobart and William Smith colleges). During the 19th century, Geneva was the major commercial hub of central New York; today, its revitalized downtown boasts an architecture fan's cornucopia of restored and stately century-old row houses and Victorian mansions with stunning backyards fronting the lake. The deepest of the Finger Lakes at 632 feet and more than 200 feet below sea level, Seneca Lake is a huge draw for outdoor activities.

ESSENTIALS
GETTING THERE
BY CAR   Geneva is south of I-90 along Route 14 and right on routes 5 and 20, coming either west from Seneca Falls or east from Canandaigua.

BY BUS   **Greyhound** and **Trailways** deposit and pick up passengers at the Chalet Coffee Pot, 48 Lake St., Geneva ((C) **315/789-2582**).

VISITOR INFORMATION   The **Finger Lakes Visitors Connection** can be contacted at (C) **585/394-3915** or www.visitfingerlakes.com. The nearest walk-in information center is in Seneca Falls at the **Seneca Falls Heritage Area Visitor Center,** 115 Fall St. ((C) **315/568-2703**); it's open Monday to Saturday from 10am to 4pm and Sunday from noon to 4pm.

EXPLORING GENEVA
Geneva, which grew up at the end of the 18th century on the banks of Seneca Lake, has an unexpected, eclectic collection of well-preserved **mansions** (★)(★) of historic and architectural significance, including examples of Greek Revival, Federal, Victorian Gothic, and Jeffersonian styles, most from the first 3 decades of the 19th century. **South Main Street** is lined with row houses, resembling those of Georgetown in Washington, D.C., and grand mansions overlooking Seneca Lake. Besides the "South Main Street" walking tour brochure, pick up another one called "Architectural Landmarks" (available at the Prouty-Chew House & Museum; see below). Have a look at **Pulteney Park,** the original village green, and Washington, Genesee, Castle, and Jay streets to survey Geneva's architectural feast.

⌜Tips **All Aboard!**

The **Finger Lakes Railway,** with trains operated by the central New York chapter of the National Railway Historical Society, offers occasional scenic trips through Cayuga and Seneca counties, including nine different Memorial Day Weekend excursions (for example, between Cayuga and Waterloo, and between Skaneateles and Solvay). Round-trips generally range between $15 and $30. For more information, call ℂ **315/488-8208** or visit the "unofficial" website at http://fglk.railfan.net.

The **Rose Hill Mansion** ✷, Route 96A, 1 mile south of routes 5 and 20 (ℂ **315/ 789-3848;** www.genevahistoricalsociety.com/Rose_Hill.htm), just east of Geneva and Seneca Lake, is an architectural landmark and excellent example of the Greek Revival style. Built in 1839, it reflects the grandeur of Geneva's early development. Once part of a sprawling lakefront farm, today it is a handsomely restored mansion with Empire furnishings; note the historically accurate and bold wallpaper. On the premises are a good information center, a short film about the house, and two antiques dealers in old carriage houses. The museum is open May through October, Monday to Saturday from 10am to 4pm, and Sunday from 1 to 5pm. Admission is $6 for adults, $4 for seniors and students ages 10 to 18, and $15 for families.

The **Prouty-Chew House & Museum,** 543 S. Main St. (ℂ **315/789-5151;** www. genevahistoricalsociety.com/PC_House.htm), is run by, and the headquarters of, the Geneva Historical Society. The building is an 1829 Federal-style home with significant late-19th-century modifications. Visitors are welcome to have a look around the house's two floors. You can also pick up **a self-guided architectural walking tour** map with details on about 50 buildings in Geneva. The Prouty-Chew House is open Tuesday to Friday from 9:30am to 4:30pm and Saturday (and Sun in July–Aug) from 1:30 to 4:30pm. Admission is free, but donations are expected.

A $2-million renovation has returned **The Smith Opera House** ✷✷✷, 82 Seneca St. (ℂ **315/781-5483;** www.thesmith.org), to its original glory as a grand movie palace. Built in 1894 but given a whimsical Deco-baroque makeover in the 1930s, with fantastic murals and Moorish touches, the 1,400-seat theater was first an opera house and later a vaudeville theater. Today, it has carved out a niche showing independent and foreign art films and hosting rock and other concerts. Try to take in a movie or show; otherwise, if the box office is open and nothing is going on, ask for a peek inside.

Many of the two dozen wineries on the **Seneca Lake Wine Trail** are within easy reach of Geneva; see the sidebar on p. 316.

SPORTS & OUTDOOR ACTIVITIES

Seneca Lake is one of the two largest of the 11 Finger Lakes. Pontoon and fishing-boat rentals are available from **Roy's Marina,** West Lake Road (Rte. 14; ℂ **315/789-3094**). **Seneca Lake State Park,** routes 5 and 20, is on the north end of the lake; it's a good spot for strolls, and small kids will love the new playground and water sprays for cooling off in the summer heat. Seneca Lake is known for its **lake trout fishing,** and catches at the annual National Lake Trout Derby sometimes almost top the 100-pound mark.

SHOPPING

Waterloo Premium Outlets, 655 Rte. 318, Waterloo (℗ **315/539-1100**), near I-90, has dozens of outlet stores, including Polo Ralph Lauren, Coach, and Mikasa. Two antiques shops operate on the premises of the **Rose Hill Mansion** (see above), selling furniture and antique collectibles on consignment. There are several antiques dealers downtown, including **Geneva Antique Co-op,** 473 Exchange St. (℗ **315/789-5100**). **Red Jacket Orchards,** 957 routes 5 and 20 (℗ **315/781-2749**), has a nice array of fresh-picked apples and food items, including salsas, Amish cheeses, and cider from Mennonite farmers. There are several pick-your-own orchards along routes 5 and 20. The **Amish Country Store at Weaver-View Farms,** 1190 Earls Hill Rd. (℗ **315/781-2571**), about 7 miles south of Geneva along Seneca Lake, stocks a good selection of quilts, homemade food items, and oak and pine Amish-made furnishings.

WHERE TO STAY

Geneva has some of the grandest places to stay in the Finger Lakes, making it a good place to splurge. Although I'm not a fan of its bulky, suburban yellow-and-blue presence right on the north end of Seneca Lake, marring the beauty of the lakefront, the **Ramada Geneva Lakefront,** 41 Lakeshore Blvd., Geneva, NY 14456 (℗ **800/990-0907;** www.ramada.com; 148 units; $99–$169 double), does have good views, an indoor pool, and more affordable prices than some of the chic, historic inns in town.

Belhurst Castle ★★ 𝘝𝘢𝘭𝘶𝘦   A late-19th-century castle facing Seneca Lake, this is one of the most extraordinary places to stay in the Finger Lakes region. It truly is a castle, with incredible old-world style and massive proportions. Some of the rooms—especially the Tower and Dwyer suites—are among the largest hotel accommodations I've ever seen. All of the rooms are very different, so it's worthwhile taking a look at the website before deciding. Rooms that are more private and modern, yet not nearly as nice, are available in the Ice, Carriage, and Dwyer houses apart from the main building. A couple of years ago, Belhurst added a new, modern $6-million wing called **Vinifera Inn,** and a wine-themed gift shop. The addition's 20 rooms are large and comfortable; but the design is a tad uninspired, and some of the decorating choices (a Jacuzzi tub in the middle of the room) are questionable. Within the old castle is a sumptuous restaurant—the site of many a wedding—and complimentary wine is always available from a second-floor spigot. Off-season rates are a true bargain.

Rte. 14 S., Geneva, NY 14456. ℗ 315/781-0201. www.belhurst.com. 36 units (16 castle and 20 Vinifera Inn). Belhurst Castle $70–$255 double, $225–$365 suite; Vinifera Inn $110–$355 double. Rates include buffet breakfast. AE, DISC, MC, V. Free parking. **Amenities:** Restaurant; bar; private beach. *In room:* A/C, TV.

Geneva on the Lake ★   This exclusive, elegant, and historic lakeside hotel, a long-time AAA four-diamond property, is one of the most distinguished in the Finger Lakes. It's awfully pricey, though, especially in high season (when some suites cost near a grand), and it feels a bit out of place in the mostly low-key Finger Lakes region. Still, that may be a selling point for some, and plenty of well-heeled folks don't seem to mind shelling out what it takes to stay at a phenomenal mansion with perfectly manicured gardens and views of Seneca Lake. Accommodations are handsomely appointed with Stickley or Chippendale furnishings, if a tad fussy, and all have kitchenettes. Oddly, some of the rooms have Murphy beds. The 70-foot pool perched at the end of the gardens and with lake views is positively Gatsby-like. To me it seems more like a place to attend an over-the-top wedding than a place to sleep on vacation, and judging from the roster of fancy nuptials held here, plenty of people agree. The restaurant dining room is particularly romantic, with wall tapestries and candlelight. Check the website for package deals.

1001 Lochland Rd., Rte. 14, Geneva, NY 14456. © **800/3-GENEVA** or 315/789-7190. Fax 315/789-0322. www. genevaonthelake.com. 30 units. $215–$890 double (as part of package with dinner). Rates include full breakfast. AE, DISC, MC, V. Free parking. **Amenities:** Restaurant; bar; large outdoor pool; formal gardens; fishing dock; sailboats; paddle boats; canoes; Windsurfer. *In room:* A/C, TV.

White Springs Manor 🌟🌟 *(Value)*   Owned by the same people behind Belhurst Castle, this grand Greek Revival farm mansion, a mile or so up the road away from the lake, has incredibly large rooms, like its sister inn. It may not have the lake, but it has plenty of character and splendid distant views of the Geneva area. Rooms are equipped with antiques and many have Jacuzzis. The Lewis Suite is almost ridiculously spacious, and the Dining Room, also giant, has gorgeous views. For privacy, rent the Playhouse, a freestanding little house with a stone fireplace and Jacuzzi in the front sitting room for those romantic evenings (you might want to close the curtains on the front door); it's a very good value. Breakfast is served down at Belhurst Castle (where you'll also check in).

White Springs Lane, Geneva, NY 14456. © **315/781-0201.** www.belhurstcastle.com/whitesprings.html. 16 units. $65–$225 double; $175–$255 suite. Rates include continental breakfast. AE, DISC, MC, V. Free parking. *In room:* A/C, TV, minibar.

Yale Manor Bed & Breakfast 🌟 *(Finds)*   A peaceful B&B on the east side of Seneca Lake (7 miles south of Geneva), this early 1900s manor house on 10 acres with lake views is a very nice place to stay. Visitors can trek down to the lakefront, where there's a little A-frame house with a deck, a nice spot to relax or swim. Rooms are elegant and understated; particularly nice is the Monticello Room. The two simplest rooms share a bathroom (good for families). From May to October, there is a 2-night minimum stay on weekends.

563 Yale Farm Rd., Romulus, NY 14541. © **315/585-2208.** Fax 315/585-6438. www.yalemanor.com. 6 units, 4 with private bathrooms. $90–$160 double, $175–$210 family suite. Rates include full breakfast. AE, MC, V. Free parking. **Amenities:** Lakefront swimming area. *In room:* A/C.

WHERE TO DINE

In addition to the restaurants below, **Belhurst Castle** (see "Where to Stay," above) has a sumptuous formal restaurant, Edgar's, and a more casual grill, Stonecutter's, overlooking the lake. The latter's outdoor terrace can't be beat for lake views.

Cobblestone Restaurant 🌟 NORTHERN ITALIAN/CONTINENTAL   An elegant restaurant in an attractive Greek Revival house (inhabiting a former stagecoach stop and the original tavern of a 1790 gentleman's farm), this is the top dining spot in town. There's an atmospheric small dining room downstairs and several others upstairs, where there's a deck with nice long views over Geneva. The menu focuses on classic dishes, such as wood-grilled steaks and chops, chicken parmigiana, fresh lobster, and veal scaloppine. The small and affordably priced wine list includes a number of the Finger Lakes' best. Note that locals may still refer to the restaurant by its former moniker, "Pasta Only's."

Hamilton St. at Pre-Emption Rd. (routes 5 and 20, west of downtown). © **315/789-4656.** Reservations recommended. Main courses $16–$29. AE, DISC, MC, V. Tues–Fri 11:30am–3pm; daily 5–10pm.

Kyo Asian Bistro ASIAN FUSION 🌟   A funky little spot with a sushi bar and an interesting Eurasian menu, this is the place to go in Geneva if you're in the mood for something different. Choose from a large selection of "small plates and hand bowls"—such as chicken satay, calamari salad, or shrimp salad—perfect for cobbling together a meal or to share. The few "big plates" include curried linguine with shiitake mushrooms and miso sea bass, but also Kobe beef with stir-fry. And, of course, it does the expected, offering good sushi and sashimi.

486 Exchange St. ✆ 315/719-0333. Reservations recommended. Main courses $13–$28. AE, MC, V. Mon–Thurs 5–9pm; Fri–Sat 5–10pm.

Parker's Grille & Tap House GRILL/PUB FARE   Down the street from the Smith Opera House, this is a good, casual place for a meal before or after the show, and it's also a fine spot for a drink. The pub fare of burgers, finger foods, hot sandwiches, and Tex-Mex isn't surprising, but it's inexpensive and solidly prepared. The baby back ribs are a local favorite. A nice selection of beers and a number of local wines are good accompaniment for anything on the menu.

100 Seneca St. ✆ 315/789-4656. Reservations recommended. Main courses $11–$21. AE, DISC, MC, V. Tues–Sun 11:30am–midnight.

GENEVA AFTER DARK

The Smith Opera House★★★, 82 Seneca St. (✆ **866/355-LIVE** or 315/781-5483; www.thesmith.org), is the coolest after-dark spot in town. Whether you catch a concert, such as Blues Traveler or the Dave Matthews Band, or see a movie on its huge screen, this 1930s gem is just a fantastic place to be. There's a neat little bar downstairs, but it doesn't serve alcohol during film sessions. The **Geneva Summer Arts Festival** (July–Aug) features dance, theater, music, and art exhibits. Among the performances, held at several venues including the Smith Opera House, are Lakefront Gazebo concerts, featuring everything from jazz to choral music. For a schedule of events, ask at the Visitor Information Center or contact ✆ **866/355-LIVE** or www.genevarts.com. The restaurant **Hamilton 258,** 258 Hamilton St. (✆ **315/781-5323**), has a cool martini bar.

9 Seneca Falls ★★ & Northern Cayuga Lake

10 miles E of Geneva; 48 miles E of Syracuse; 42 miles N of Ithaca

Perched on the falls of the Seneca River and a section of the legendary Erie Canal, and cradled between the two largest of the Finger Lakes, Seneca Falls was such a quintessential American small town that Frank Capra apparently used it as the model for Bedford Falls in his classic movie *It's a Wonderful Life.* Yet the town is more significantly known for its rabble-rousing past. In the mid–19th century, Seneca Falls was home to political activists who fought for women's suffrage and civil rights for African Americans. The town is considered the birthplace of women's rights, and some women enamored of that history have moved to Seneca Falls to make it their home.

Cayuga Lake is the longest of the Finger Lakes, 42 miles from end to end.

ESSENTIALS
GETTING THERE
BY CAR   Seneca Falls is south of I-90 along Route 414 and equidistant on routes 5 and 20 between Geneva and Auburn.

VISITOR INFORMATION   **Seneca Falls Heritage Area Visitor Center,** 115 Fall St. (✆ **315/568-2703**), is open Monday to Saturday from 10am to 4pm and Sunday from noon to 4pm. **Cayuga County Office of Tourism,** 131 Genesee St., Auburn

(© 800/499-9615 or 315/255-1658; www.tourcayuga.com), is open Monday to Friday from 9am to 5pm, Saturday 9am to 2pm.

EXPLORING SENECA FALLS

The first Women's Rights Convention, the foundation for the modern struggle for civil rights, was held at the Wesleyan Methodist Chapel in Seneca Falls in 1848. The **Women's Rights National Historical Park** ☆☆, 136 Fall St. (© **315/568-2991;** www.nps.gov/wori), which is run by the National Park Service, commemorates the struggle initiated by Elizabeth Cady Stanton, Lucretia Mott, Susan B. Anthony, Frederick Douglass, and others (the abolitionist and women's rights movements were linked from early on); such happenings at Seneca Falls expanded the definition of liberty in the United States. The extant remains of the original chapel, where 300 people gathered on July 19, 1848, and the landmark "Declaration of Sentiments" was drafted, is next to a museum that's jam-packed with information about women's and civil rights history. The museum does an excellent job raising issues to think about for visitors of both genders and all ages, which is why it's also a great place for kids, who can also be made "Junior Rangers." The museum is open daily from 9am to 5pm; admission is free.

Seneca Falls has, quite understandably, become a place of pilgrimage for people with a specific interest in women's and civil rights. A host of related sights, including the **Elizabeth Cady Stanton House,** 32 Washington St. (© **315/568-2991;** guided tours $1; sign up at Park Visitor Center), are located in and around Seneca Falls; pick up the booklet *Women's Rights Trail,* at the museum gift shop. Down the street from the Historical Park is the **National Women's Hall of Fame,** 76 Fall St. (© **315/ 568-8060;** www.greatwomen.org), which is a good place to see, in name and achievement, how far women have come since the days of that legendary convention. It honors the achievements of American women in diverse fields. Worth a brief look, especially for those with an interest in the upstate canal system, across the street, is the **Seneca Museum of Waterways and Industry,** 89 Fall St. (© **315/568-1510**), which tells the story of transportation and industrialization in the region.

Today, Seneca Falls is relatively quiet and unassuming as compared to its tumultuous past. **Van Cleef Lake,** forged as an expansion of the New York State Barge Canal, is one of the prettiest (and most photographed) spots in the Finger Lakes. The banks of the Cayuga-Seneca Canal are being prettified with benches and paths. The downtown area, essentially a main street with two bridges over the canal (one of which distinctly recalls that pivotal scene in *It's a Wonderful Life*), is charming, and Fall Street is lined with nice shops, including the very appropriate **WomanMade Products** (91 Fall St.; © **315/568-9364**), a very enjoyable place to while away an afternoon.

At the north end of Cayuga Lake and 5 miles east of Seneca Falls, **Montezuma National Wildlife Refuge** ☆☆, 395 routes 5 and 20 east, Seneca Falls (© **315/ 568-5987;** www.fws.gov/r5mnwr; daily 8am–5pm; visitor center Apr–Oct, Mon–Fri 10am–3pm, Sat–Sun 10am–4pm; Nov, weekends only 10am–3pm; closed Dec–Mar), established in 1938, is a magnificent spot for birding and a fantastic spot for families to get up close and personal with wildlife. The marshes in this part of the Finger Lakes are a preferred rest stop along the Atlantic Migratory Flyway, and the 7,000 acres of wetlands attract thousands of waterfowl and other water birds—including Canada geese, blue herons, egrets, and wood ducks—on their long journeys from nesting areas in Canada (at the height of migration, as many as two million birds occupy the area). During the fall migration, the peak for geese and ducks is mid- to late November; for shorebirds and wading birds, mid-August to mid-September. During the spring migration that is less flashy than fall, waterfowl peak in late February through April, while the peak of warbler migration is mid-May. In addition to walking trails, there's a self-guided Wildlife Drive (in winter, there's cross-country skiing and snowshoeing). Ask in the visitor center for the location of the bald eagle's nest.

For more information on visiting the area's wineries, particularly those around Cayuga Lake, see the sidebar on the **Cayuga Wine Trail,** on p. 304.

SPORTS & OUTDOOR ACTIVITIES

The Cayuga branch of the Erie Canal system leads directly to Cayuga Lake and flows directly through Seneca Falls. Outdoors enthusiasts could hardly have a better or more historic place to hike or bike than the **Erie Canal Trail,** which runs along the historic canal towpath from the village of Jordan to Montezuma and the Seneca River. For more information, call © **315/252-2791. Liberty Boat Tours** (© **877/472-6688**) in Seneca Falls does canal and lake tours, and the **River Otter Boat Tour,** Riverforest Park, 9439 Riverforest Rd., off Route 34 in Weedsport, operates 2-hour tours (Mon and Sat at 10am and 2pm) of the Seneca River and Erie Canal (for reservations call © **315/252-4171). Cayuga Lake State Park** (© **315/568-5163**), 2678 Lower Lake Rd., on the west side of the lake, has campgrounds (© **315/568-0919**), nature trails, playgrounds, a launch site, and docking. Cayuga Lake is known for its bass fishing, while Seneca Lake has superb trout fishing. On the shores of the two lakes are four state parks and numerous sites for swimming, boating, and picnicking. For fishing charters on Cayuga Lake, try **Eagle Rock Charters** (© **315/889-5925;** www.ctbw.com/eaglerock). *Note:* If you want to sail your own boat along the Erie Canal, get a brochure with more information about docking and attractions from Rochester to Syracuse by calling © **800/499-9615.**

For bird-watching, don't miss the spectacular **Montezuma National Wildlife Refuge** (see above). And if you want to fly like a bird, check out **Sunset Adventures Balloon Rides,** Beach Tree Road, Auburn (© **315/252-9474;** www.fingerlakesballooning.com).

WHERE TO STAY

There are a couple of good B&Bs in Seneca Falls, as well as a large and clean, inexpensive chain motel (the Microtel) on the outskirts of town.

Barrister's B&B ⟨★ This cozy and attractive small inn on one of Seneca Falls' loveliest streets (within walking distance of downtown and the canal) is an 1888 Colonial Revival that has been very nicely restored and converted into a B&B. The house, run by a local couple, retains handsome details like carved fireplaces and original stained-glass windows, and the comfortable rooms, many of which get great light, have been attractively decorated. Grandmother's Room has a very large bathroom, the Grace Yawger room is nice and quiet, and Erin's Retreat is a large suite with an adjoining sitting room.

56 Cayuga St., Seneca Falls, NY 13148. © **800/914-0145** or 315/568-0145. www.sleepbarristers.com. 5 units. $120–$185 double. Rates include full breakfast. AE, MC, V. Free parking. *In room:* A/C, Wi-Fi.

Hubbell House ⟨★ A charming 1855 Gothic Revival meticulously decorated and chock-full of Victorian goodies, including dolls, pictures, and books, this professionally run inn is a very nice place to stay, partly due to its location on Van Cleef Lake. The house has a walkway down to gardens and a sweet little pier on the lake; some rooms, as well as the dining room and screened porch, have picturesque lake views.

Breakfast is excellent, served on china with fresh-squeezed orange juice and items like "Victorian French toast." The Laura Hoskins Hubbell room is over-the-top Victoriana, while other rooms are more sedate and very cozy.

42 Cayuga St., Seneca Falls, NY 13148. (C) 315/568-9690. www.hubbellhousebb.com. 4 units. $130–$145 double. Rates include full breakfast. No credit cards. Free parking. *In room:* A/C.

John Morrison Manor (R) (*Value*) About 3 miles from downtown Seneca Falls, and enjoying nearly 6 acres of pretty hilltop grounds, this 1838 Greek Revival manor is a fine place to decamp. The five rooms are quite different in size and decor, ranging from country elegant to understated cool (the "pool room" is the most sedate, while others feature more decorative flourishes). The house features several parlors, a fireside den, and an in-ground pool. A rarity—no doubt because the two gentleman innkeepers are enamored of their own dogs—the inn has two rooms that are designated pet-friendly.

2138 Rte. 89, Seneca Falls, NY 13148. (C) **866/484-4218** or 315/568-9057. www.johnmorrismanor.com. 5 units. $165 double. Rate includes full breakfast. AE, DISC, MC, V. Free parking. Pets accepted in 2 units. **Amenities:** Outdoor pool. *In room:* A/C.

WHERE TO DINE
Downtown Deli, 53 Fall St. ((C) **315/568-9943**), sporting a deck facing the canal, is a good stop for New York–style sandwiches, salads, and soups. **Bailey's,** 95 Fall St. ((C) **315/568-0929**), is an ice-cream parlor and sandwich shop named, of course, for the character of the same name in *It's a Wonderful Life.*

Henry B's (R) ITALIAN Henry B's is a clubby, upscale restaurant with exposed-brick walls and subdued lighting; it looks something like a New York supper club. It features a good wine list and tempting desserts. Food is family-style, meaning huge portions meant to be shared (a typical main course feeds two). Salads and antipasti are great; for entrees, choose from "Pasta Unica" (one-dish meals of fettuccine rustica or pappardelle with hot Italian sausage, for example), or traditional Florentine T-bone steak or grilled prime veal chops. Henry B's may not be the cheapest spot in town, but it's easily the best.

84 Falls St. (C) **315/568-1600.** Reservations recommended. Main courses $22–$29. AE, DISC, MC, V. Tues–Sat 4:30–10pm.

SENECA FALLS AFTER DARK
Seneca Falls has a surprisingly bustling little cluster of bars on Fall Street. The liveliest is usually **Tavern on the Flats,** 6–8 Bulls Run ((C) **315/568-6755**). With its canalside entrance, it can get very crowded with college students and folks who've pulled up in their boats along the canal. Part of a dying breed, the **Finger Lakes Drive-In,** routes 5 and 20, Auburn ((C) **315/252-3969**), shows first-run movies from April to October, and is a popular spot in summer months.

AUBURN
East of Montezuma and midway to Skaneateles, the town of **Auburn,** though larger than Seneca Falls, doesn't have quite the charms of its neighbor, though it does possess a handful of historic sights. Chief among them is the **Willard Memorial Chapel,** 17 Nelson St. ((C) **315/252-0339**), the surviving piece of the once-grand Auburn Theological Seminary, built in 1818. But this Romanesque chapel holds a treasure: an interior designed by Louis Comfort Tiffany, apparently the only existing example of a complete and unaltered Tiffany interior. The series of stained-glass windows, including a nine-paneled Rose Window, and leaded-glass chandeliers are stunning. The chapel is open Tuesday to Friday from 10am to 4pm; admission is $3.

The Underground Railroad

After passages of the Fugitive Slave Law in 1850, even the free states of the North were considered unsafe for runaway slaves. The Underground Railroad, the secretive lines of communication and safe houses that carried many slaves along a very dangerous path from the South to freedom in Canada, was active throughout central New York State. Many stops were in the Finger Lakes region. Auburn was home of Harriet Tubman, a former slave who conducted more than 300 people to freedom. The Seward House in Auburn was also an important stop on the Underground Railroad. Frederick Douglass, abolitionist and publisher of the newspaper *The North Star,* lived in Rochester and is buried in Mt. Hope Cemetery there. For more information on the Underground Railroad in New York and principal abolitionist activists, see **www.nyhistory.com/ugrr/links.htm**.

The **Seward House** ⊛, 33 South St. (© **315/252-1283;** www.sewardhouse.org), is a National Historic Landmark and former home of the 19th-century statesman who served as U.S. secretary of state, U.S. senator, and New York governor. The handsome 19th-century home is very nearly a national library, so extensive is its collection of family artifacts, historical documents, and items collected from the life and travels of William H. Seward. Seward was known principally for negotiating the purchase of Alaska, derided in the press at the time as "Seward's Folly," and as Abraham Lincoln's Secretary of State, attacked and seriously stabbed by a would-be murderer as part of the conspiracy that felled Lincoln. The museum is open mid-October to December 31 and February through June, Tuesday to Saturday from 11am to 4pm; from July to mid-October, it's open Tuesday to Saturday from 10am to 4pm and Sunday from 1 to 4pm. Admission is $6 adults, $5 seniors, and $2 students 12 to 17.

10 Skaneateles Lake ⊛⊛⊛

23 miles W of Syracuse; 32 miles E of Geneva

Hard to pronounce and harder to spell, Skaneateles is perhaps the most beautiful and photogenic town in the Finger Lakes region, the only one whose main street backs right up to the curved shore of a sinewy Finger Lake. A small village surprisingly well endowed with creature comforts for visitors, it is deservedly one of the most popular stops in the region. With a moneyed past and long favored by those in the know, it gained a considerable amount of attention several years ago when President Clinton and his wife vacationed here at the home of a wealthy friend. Skaneateles comes as close to emitting a chic Hamptons vibe as you'll find in upstate New York, though it's much more relaxed and personable. At Christmastime, the village defines quaint, becoming a Dickensian postcard with costumed carolers parading around the streets.

ESSENTIALS
GETTING THERE
BY CAR Skaneateles is on Route 20 west of Syracuse; from the south, take Route 41 North, which traces the east side of Skaneateles Lake, off I-81.

VISITOR INFORMATION   The **Skaneateles Chamber of Commerce** is located at 22 Jordan St. (© **315/685-0552;** www.skaneateles.com).

EXPLORING SKANEATELES

Skaneateles's charming and **historic downtown** ⟨⟨⟨, which lovingly cradles the northern shore of Skaneateles Lake, is the prettiest in the Finger Lakes region. A graceful collection of 19th-century Greek Revival and Victorian homes and charming independent shops, it looks and feels more like a classic New England village than one in upstate New York. But Skaneateles is endowed with incredible natural gifts as well: transparent Skaneateles Lake—one of the cleanest lakes in North America—cuts a gorgeous, 16-mile-long, gently curved swath through low hills and dense green forest. Former New York State governor and Secretary of State William Seward called it "the most beautiful body of water in the world." On the lakefront are a picturesque gazebo and a long pier that juts out over the water. Elegant homes line the east and west banks of the lake leading south from Skaneateles. The best way to enjoy the lake is to do as locals do: plunge into it. Lake activities abound, from swimming and boating to fishing.

East Genesee Street, which in any other town would be called Main Street, is lined with quaint boutiques and antiques shops, as well as restaurants and inns. Inside the impressive gray-stone town library, at 49 E. Genesee St., is the **John D. Barrow Art Gallery** (© **315/685-5135;** open mid-June to mid-Sept Mon–Sat 1–4pm; mid-Sept to Dec Sat 2–4pm; free admission), where you'll find a nice collection of paintings by the library's namesake, a Skaneateles-born artist and painter of Hudson Valley landscapes. **The Creamery,** 28 Hannum St., off West Genesee Street (© **315/685-1360;** June–Sept Thurs–Sat 1–4pm, Oct–May Fri 10am–4pm; free admission), is a restored creamery dating from 1899 and home to the Skaneateles Historical Society and Museum and its small collection of town historical artifacts. **Walking tours** of Skaneateles are conducted by Historical Society members during summer months; call © **315/685-1360** or 315/485-6841 for information.

Skaneateles's emphasis on culture and the arts is disproportionate to its small size. The town hosts festivals throughout the summer, including free band concerts at the gazebo in Clift Park on Skaneateles Lake during Friday and Saturday evenings in summer; the Finger Lakes **Antique and Classic Boat Show** the last week of July; and the widely attended **Skaneateles Festival** ⟨, 97 Genesee St. (© **315/685-7418;** www.skanfest.org), which features chamber music as many as 5 nights a week at several venues throughout August and early September. However, the biggest event in Skaneateles doesn't take place in summer. The **Dickens Christmas** ⟨⟨ celebration revels in old-world Victoriana, with costumed Dickens characters parading about the streets, interacting with visitors and singing Christmas carols. There are free carriage rides around Skaneateles and free roasted chestnuts and hot chocolate. The celebration, a great family event, begins the day after Thanksgiving and is held every Saturday and Sunday from noon to 4pm through December 22.

SPORTS & OUTDOOR ACTIVITIES

Clift Park on Skaneateles Lake has open public swimming. **Thayer Park,** east of the downtown shops, is a quiet, beautiful park for relaxing and enjoying the view. **Austin Park,** 1 Austin St. (between Jordan and State sts.), has a playground, basketball and tennis courts, and a track for walking, biking, or skating. The **Charlie Major Nature Trail,** along the Old Short line, between Old Seneca Turnpike and Crow Hill Road, is good for hiking. **Biking** the 32-mile perimeter around the Skaneateles Lake is big with cycling clubs (and, of course, with motorcyclists).

However, the best outdoor activity in Skaneateles is getting out on the lake, and a great way to do so is by cruise boat. **Mid-Lakes Navigation Co.** ✪, 11 Jordan St. (© **800/ 545-4318** or 315/685-8500; www.midlakesnav.com), a longtime local, family-run business, organizes cruises on Skaneateles Lake, including 1-hour sightseeing, Sunday brunch, champagne dinner, and luncheon cruises. If that's too typical, try boarding a U.S. mail boat as it delivers mail to old-fashioned camps on the lake. Call for more information. They also do cruises along the Erie Canal. Most cruises are in July and August. For kayaking instruction and rentals, try **Northwind Expedition Kayaks,** 2825 W. Lake Rd. (© **315/685-4808;** www.northwindkayaks.com); for pontoon, sailboat, canoe, and kayak rentals, see **The Sailboat Shop,** 1322 E. Genesee St. (© **315/685-7558**).

The Sherwood Inn owns an antique Chris Craft, *The Stephanie,* on which it offers sunset cruises and sightseeing tours; call © **800/3-SHERWOOD** for more information. For fishing charters and sunset cruises on the lake, contact **Lakeview Charters,** 2478 E. Lake Rd. (© **315/685-8176**). If you'd rather see the lake from a distance, **Fingerlakes Aeroplane Tours,** Skaneateles Aerodome (© **315/685-6382;** skybanky@ aol.com), takes people up over the lakes in a vintage 1942 open-cockpit biplane, from mid-May to October.

SHOPPING

Skaneateles is, with the exception of the two largest cities, Rochester and Syracuse, the top shopping destination in the Finger Lakes. The compact downtown area of the village, with just a couple of streets intersecting Genesee Street, is full of unique shops. **Skaneateles Antique Center,** 12 E. Genesee St. (© 315/685-0752), has several dealers and lots of china, mission furniture, and pottery. Another nice antiques shop 12 miles south of town, on the west side of the lake, is **New Hope Antiques,** 5963 New Hope Rd., in—you guessed it—New Hope (© **315/497-2688**). It's housed in a 1920s farmhouse and has a good selection of furnishings and collectibles; it's open from the end of May until October, but closed Tuesday and Wednesday. **Cate & Sally,** 58 E. Genesee St. (© **315/685-1105**), is a very chic clothing store for women's fashions; I had to usher my wife out of there in a hurry on a recent trip. **Pomodoro,** 61 E. Genesee St. (© **315/685-8658**), is a very feminine, sweet little shop in an adorable house that's packed to the rafters with home furnishings, candles, and all manner of gift items. **Rhubarb Kitchen & Garden Shop,** 59 E. Genesee St. (© **315/685- 5803**), carries an excellent selection of cookbooks, kitchen and garden items, and even gourmet foods. Quilters will be in heaven at **Patchwork Plus Quilt Shop,** 36 Jordan St. (© **315/685-6979**), which stocks more than 5,000 bolts of fabric and has quilting classes.

WHERE TO STAY

Skaneateles has a superb supply of B&Bs, inns, and small hotels clustered around the lake and downtown, including a couple of the best inns in the entire region. Among the many (predominantly Victorian in style) B&Bs—apart from the real standouts, reviewed below—in Skaneateles are **The Benjamin Porter House** ✪✪, 10 State St. (© **315/685-8611;** www.benjaminporterhouse.com; $225 double), a very elegantly decorated, comfortable, and sophisticated 1805 Federal building in the heart of the village; **Lady of the Lake,** 2 W. Lake St. (© **888/685-7997;** www.ladyofthelake.net; $124–$165 double), a large (and pet-friendly) lavender Queen Anne Victorian just off the main drag and facing the lake; **Gray House,** 47 Jordan St. (© **800/891-7118;** www.gray-house.com; $99–$160 double), 1 block from the lake; and **Frog Pond Bed & Breakfast,** 680 Sheldon Rd. (© **315/685-0146;** www.frogpondbandb.com; $150 double), a 180-year-old stone house 2 miles north of Skaneateles on 125 acres.

More inexpensive lodging is available in motels on the outskirts of town on the way to either Syracuse or Auburn, such as **Whispering Winds Motel,** Route 20 (© **800/ 396-7719;** www.skaneateles.com/whisperingwinds; $59–$99 double), open May through October; and the recently renovated but simple **Colonial Motel,** Route 20 (© **315/685-5751;** $79–$89 double), both of which have outdoor pools.

EXPENSIVE

Hobbit Hollow Farm B&B ✿✿✿   One of the most exquisite small inns in the Finger Lakes, this serene and princely estate with luxuriously appointed rooms is a place to pamper yourself. The house, a 100-year-old Colonial Revival, sits on 400 acres about 3 miles from town, next to a large horse barn, with panoramic lake views. The house is first-class in every detail, from the antique furnishings to the crisp linens and beautiful bathrooms. Breakfast is served with silver and Waterford crystal. All the accommodations are different in decor and size; my favorite is the Lake View room, with a four-poster bed and a massive bathroom and Jacuzzi. The Master Suite has a private veranda and fireplace, while the Chanticleer room is sunny and charming, with a funky "pencil" bed. Less expensive rooms are smaller, but cozy and also quite charming; if you're looking for a bargain stay in a rarified place, check out the Twin Room, which ranks as a steal.

3061 W. Lake Rd., Skaneateles, NY 13152. © 800/3SHERWOOD or 315/685-2791. Fax 315/685-3426. www.hobbit hollow.com. 5 units. $100–$230 double; $250–$270 suite. Rates include full breakfast. AE, DISC, MC, V. Free parking. *In room:* A/C, TV, Wi-Fi.

Mirbeau Inn & Spa ✿✿   This new addition to Skaneateles, about 2 blocks west of downtown, strikes out in a bold direction all its own. Designed to echo a French country château retreat, it is a stylish, full-service spa and small hotel. Rooms are decorated in a modern French country style with rich fabrics, fireplaces, and huge bathrooms, and are set around a Monet-like garden and pond and 12 acres of woodlands. The spa facilities, with a sumptuous palazzo of a relaxation room, are extraordinary; the massage rooms are some of the most inviting I've seen. The inn's restaurant stands very much on its own merits; though not inexpensive, it provides one of the finest dining experiences in the region. For a splurge for both body and soul, Mirbeau is among the best. A number of packages, with spa treatments and dinner included, are available; check the website for current offers. The 12,000-square-foot spa is also open to the public as a day spa, though advance booking is essential.

851 W. Genesee St., Skaneateles, NY 13152. © 877/647-2328 or 315/685-5006. Fax 315/685-5150. www.mirbeau. com. 34 units. $189–$399 double. AE, DISC, MC, V. Free parking. **Amenities:** Restaurant; bar; spa w/exercise room; steam room; sauna. *In room:* A/C, TV/DVD, Wi-Fi, CD player.

MODERATE

Sherwood Inn ✿✿ *Value*   This is the best value in the area, right in the heart of Skaneateles. Once a stagecoach stop in the early 1800s, this cozy inn on the main drag, with wide-open lake views from its porch, has been sensitively restored. You'll find hardwood floors in the hallways, four-poster and canopy beds in rooms, and a genteel, lived-in, old-money feel. Accommodations, many with lake views, are all spacious, uniquely decorated, and delightful; some are very feminine in toile, some are

English country, while others are library-like and masculine. My favorite is the swank and romantic Red Room (no. 31), with a fireplace, a Jacuzzi, and a funky light fixture. The elegant restaurant has a beautiful porch with unequaled lake views, and a clubby tavern, a Euro-style pub with wooden booths and green leather chairs. If it's full, you may want to inquire about the nearby Packwood House (www.packwood house.com; $125–$195 double), which the Sherwood manages but which feels decidedly more corporate.

26 W. Genesee St., Skaneateles, NY 13152. (©) **800/374-3796** or 315/685-3405. Fax 315/685-8983. www.thesherwood inn.com. 24 units. $130–$225 double. AE, DISC, MC, V. Free parking. **Amenities:** Restaurant; bar. *In room:* A/C, TV, Wi-Fi.

The Village Inn of Skaneateles (✿)   Just a block off Genesee Street, this tiny inn, like a cross between a European boutique hotel and a B&B, is a smart place to stay. Wholly renovated, it is very well equipped and has a modern feel, though the building dates from 1830. All rooms have gas fireplaces, whirlpool bathtubs, and Stickley furniture. The Cottage Room has exposed-brick walls, while the Terrace Room has a private balcony overlooking Skaneateles Lake. If you choose, you can take breakfast on the porch at the Sherwood Inn.

25 Jordan St., Skaneateles, NY 13152. (©) **800/374-3796** or 315/685-3405. www.villageinn-ny.com. 4 units. $99– $210 double. Rates include continental breakfast. AE, DISC, MC, V. Free parking. *In room:* A/C, TV, high-speed Internet access.

WHERE TO DINE

In addition to the restaurants listed below, **Sherwood Inn** (see above), which has a large formal dining room and inexpensive tavern, offers a large and varied menu and is a popular dining spot—so popular, in fact, that in high season you'll definitely have to wait. For fantastic artisanal breads and pastries, don't miss **Pâtisserie,** 4 Hannum St. ((©) **315/685-2433**), located just behind the Sherwood Inn.

EXPENSIVE

Giverny (Mirbeau Inn & Spa) (✿✿✿) HAUTE COUNTRY   At an innovative small spa hotel, young chef Ed Moro has created an equally inventive and inviting menu. The restaurant has quickly garnered quite a bit of attention, with a number of national magazines calling it one of the top new places in the country. The dining room is elegant French Provincial, with a serene terrace overlooking the pond for outdoor dining. Though refined and sophisticated, patrons are as likely to wear jeans as jackets. Fresh, exquisitely prepared menu items include goat-cheese terrine, Hudson Valley foie gras with caramelized pears and huckleberries, and potato-crusted halibut. You can order a la carte, but few patrons do. Portions aren't terribly large, so you're unlikely to feel bloated; and you can choose a cheese course for dessert if you wish. The lunch tasting menu ($35) is a good way to experience the restaurant if dinner seems like too big a splurge. The wine list is extensive and superbly chosen.

851 W. Genesee St. (©) **877/MIRBEAU** or 315/685-5006. Reservations required. Main courses $30; tasting menus $63–$68 (with wine pairing $113–$123). AE, DISC, MC, V. Daily 11:30am–2pm and 5–10pm.

The Krebs 1899 (✿✿) (*Value*) TRADITIONAL AMERICAN   At this seasonal restaurant, open May to Halloween, every dinner is like Thanksgiving. The Krebs has been serving "traditional meals," or seven-course "soup-to-nuts" dinners, for 108 years. In an old house a long block from the waterfront, the restaurant defines classic fine dining in Skaneateles. The downstairs dining room (dinner only) is formal, with crisp white linen tablecloths and fresh-cut flowers, but not stuffy. The seven-course dinner, for just over

$40, is an excellent value for a meal with their "world-famous" lobster Newburgh and English prime rib, family-style vegetables and sides, dessert, and homemade breads. Sunday brunch is also a huge affair. Upstairs in the classic low-ceiling cocktail lounge, you can order a la carte from the dining menu. A fine wine list is available.

53 W. Genesee St. ℂ 315/685-5714. Reservations recommended. Fixed-price dinner $44; a la carte main courses $14–$21. MC, V. Mon–Sat 6–10pm; Sun brunch 10:30am–2pm.

Rosalie's Cucina ✿✿ TUSCAN   A friendly, family-run, and vibrant Tuscan restaurant, a few blocks west of the center of town, Rosalie's is a local favorite with very loyal customers. The casually attractive Tuscan-style dining room and kitchen are inviting, service is outstanding, and the food is hearty and deliciously authentic. The antipasto is a perfect way to start, and though there are a few choices of homemade pastas, the main courses concentrate on very substantial, country-style meat dishes, such as *vitello Marsala* (veal in Marsala wine), braciola (prime sirloin scaloppine stuffed with prosciutto), and *arrosto di maiale* (slow-roasted pork). Bill Clinton once dined here (though, one should note, that was before his heart surgery). The wine list is composed largely of well-chosen Italian reds, though there is a handful of Finger Lakes wines and good California selections. Out back is an excellent bakery, with hand-rolled pastries and specialty breads, and the desserts are terrific.

841 W. Genesee St. ℂ 315/685-2200. Reservations recommended. Main courses $22–$37. AE, MC, V. Sun–Thurs 5–9pm; Fri–Sat 5–10pm.

MODERATE

KaBuki ✿ SUSHI/ASIAN   The newest hot spot in town, this cute, hip, and colorful sushi and Asian restaurant isn't a typical restaurant in this traditional town, but locals have come around to embrace it. Start with Thai lettuce wraps and move on to a Szechuan tangerine stir-fry or sake-steamed salmon. Or sit at the bar and down sushi and cut rolls to your heart's content.

12 W. Genesee St. ℂ 315/685-7234. Reservations recommended. Main courses $10–$19. No credit cards. Daily 5:30–10pm.

SKANEATELES AFTER DARK

Morris's Grill, 6 W. Genesee St. (ℂ **315/685-7761**), a laid-back bar next to KaBuki, is the local hangout. The tavern at the **Sherwood Inn** (see above), which has a cozy bar and a fireplace, as well as fantastic lake views, is also a popular spot for a drink. In summer, evening activities tend to center around the music festivals in town; on Friday and Saturday nights, there's live music at the gazebo in **Clift Park** on the north shore of Skaneateles Lake.

11 Syracuse

145 miles W of Albany; 245 miles NW of New York City; 58 miles NE of Ithaca

It may not have the romantic ring to it as do many villages in the Finger Lakes, and as a modern, rather industrial upstate city, Syracuse isn't vitally connected to the natural beauty of the region; however, the second-largest city in the area is the principal eastern gateway to the Finger Lakes. Syracuse is perhaps best known as the home of the NCAA National Champion Orangemen, but this city grew up on the Erie Canal and was once known as "Salt City," when its role was to supply the U.S. with salt. Today, Syracuse is staking its future on the largest mall in the U.S., DestiNY USA, the current Carousel Center that developers are remaking into a resortlike shopping experience.

Beyond those outsized shopping opportunities—I mean, experiences—Syracuse is a city that appeals mostly to passersby and business travelers. However, it is also a good, brief gateway stop for families.

ESSENTIALS
GETTING THERE
BY AIR   **Syracuse Hancock International Airport,** 2001 Airport Blvd., Syracuse (© 315/454-4330; www.syrairport.org), 10 minutes from downtown, is serviced by American, Air Canada, Continental, Delta, JetBlue, Northwest, United, and US Airways. **Century Transportation** (© 315/455-5151) provides taxi and van service at Syracuse Hancock International Airport. There are five major car-rental agencies at the airport.

BY CAR   Syracuse is located at the intersection of two major highways: Interstate 81, running north–south, and the New York State Thruway, I-90, running east–west.

BY BUS   **Greyhound** and **Trailways** stop in Syracuse at the Regional Transportation Center, 130 P and C Pkwy., Syracuse (© 315/472-4421 or 315/472-5338).

BY TRAIN   **Amtrak** (© 800/USA-RAIL; www.amtrak.com) travels to Syracuse from New York City, Buffalo, Boston, and other cities. The Regional Transportation Center is located at 130 P and C Pkwy.

VISITOR INFORMATION   The principal font of tourism information is the **Syracuse Convention and Visitors Bureau,** 572 S. Salina St. (© 800/234-4797 or 315/470-1910; www.visitsyracuse.org). The **Syracuse Urban Cultural Park Visitor Center,** 318 Erie Blvd. E (within Erie Canal Museum; © 315/471-0593), offers guided tours of downtown for $2.

GETTING AROUND
OnTrack City Express trains (© 315/424-1212) run from Syracuse University to the main station at Armory Square, 269 W. Jefferson St., and Carousel Center mall. Trains operate Wednesday to Sunday, 11:25am to 6:20pm (in summer Fri–Sun); tickets are $1.50 one-way (pay as you board).

   CENTRO buses (© 315/685-7075; www.centro.org; $1) travel to Skaneateles and Auburn.

EXPLORING SYRACUSE
Principal among Syracuse's attractions is the **Museum of Science & Technology (MOST)** ⚓, 500 S. Franklin St. (© 315/425-0747; www.most.org), which is located in an old armory and filled on three levels with terrific interactive science exhibits, science demonstrations, simulator rides that will entertain both youngsters and their parents, a cool domed IMAX theater, and a planetarium. It's open Wednesday to Sunday from 11am to 5pm. Museum-only admission is $4 adults, $3.50 seniors and children under 12; planetarium admission $2 extra; combination IMAX/museum ticket, $9.50 adults, $7.50 seniors and children under 12. For IMAX showtimes and tickets, call © 315/473-IMAX.

   The **Erie Canal Museum,** 318 Erie Blvd. E. (Rte. 5) at Montgomery Street (© 315/471-0593; www.eriecanalmuseum.org; Tues–Sat 10am–5pm, Sun 10am–3pm; free admission), is in the original 1850 weigh-lock building designed to determine tolls for boats on the canal. It may not be the most exciting museum you've ever visited, but it makes for an interesting historical stop, depicting as it does six vignettes of 19th-century life along the canal. The **Everson Museum of Art,** 401 Harrison St. (© **315/474-6064;** www.everson.org; Tues–Fri noon–5pm, Sat–Sun 10am–5pm; free admission), was the first building designed by noted architect I. M. Pei. It contains a superb collection of American ceramics. Architecture buffs may want to go from Everson to one of the finest Art Deco buildings in Syracuse, the **Niagara-Mohawk building** on North Franklin Street, a miniature Chrysler Building that's illuminated at night.

Finally, while visiting a bakery might not seem like much of an attraction, the **Columbus Baking Company,** 502 Pearl St. (© **315/422-2913**), is an old-style, family-owned and -operated Italian bakery that continues to make only four types of artisanal, traditional Italian bread (with no preservatives), as it has for over a century. The deep, old-school ovens are right out of *Moonstruck.*

WHERE TO STAY

Bed & Breakfast Wellington 🪶   This large and very lovely house, a 1914 brick-and-stucco Tudor named for its architect, is a National Historic Landmark. It is embellished with fine Arts and Crafts details, such as rich woods and fireplaces with Mercer tiles. The guest rooms are spacious and pleasant, if not overly fancy (that may be a good thing), though they are decorated with nice antiques and Stickley furniture and carpets. For a small B&B, it's equipped with lots of amenities, such as high-speed Internet access and central air-conditioning. Downstairs is a huge apartment with a dining room and an efficiency kitchen. The sunny Stickley and Lakeview rooms are my favorites.

707 Danforth St., Syracuse, NY 13208. © **800/724-5006** or 315/474-3641. Fax 315/472-4976. www.bbwellington. com. 5 units. $99–$150 double. Rates include continental breakfast on weekdays, full gourmet breakfast on weekends. AE, DC, DISC, MC, V. Free parking. *In room:* A/C, TV/VCR/DVD, dataport, high-speed Internet access.

The Craftsman Inn *(Value)*   This Arts and Crafts hotel, just a few miles east of downtown Syracuse, has the amenities of a large hotel, but some of the intimacy of a smaller inn. Rooms are spacious and nicely decorated, with understated color schemes and full sets of handsome Stickley furniture (in mission, Colonial, or Shaker style)—a pretty extraordinary look. The Frank Baum room, named for the author of the *Wizard of Oz,* who was born nearby, has nice Oz artwork on the walls. About a quarter of the rooms are in the new, adjoining Craftsman Lodge. The Craftsman House restaurant, next door, is also decorated with the same wonderful Stickley furniture.

7300 E. Genesee St., Syracuse, NY 13266. © **800/797-4464** or 315/637-8000. Fax 315/637-2440. www.craftsmaninn. com. 90 units. $93–$109 double; $135–$150 suite. Rates include continental breakfast. AE, DC, DISC, MC, V. Free parking. **Amenities:** Restaurant; bar; business center. *In room:* A/C, TV/VCR, dataport, high-speed Internet access, kitchen.

Hawthorn Suites 🪶   Across from the MOST museum, in the historic center of Syracuse, this new hotel in a nicely renovated historic building has a great location and large, comfortable suites (some are one-bedrooms and others studios, all with fully equipped kitchens) that are perfect for business travelers and other visitors who want to be in the midst of the restaurant and bar action of Armory Square.

416 S. Clinton St., Syracuse, NY 13202. © **800/527-1133** or 315/425-0500. Fax 315/472-4976. www.hawthorn.com. 60 units. $129–$149 studio; $169–$199 1-bedroom suite. AE, DISC, MC, V. Free parking. **Amenities:** Bar; 24-hr. fitness center. *In room:* A/C, TV/DVD, dataport, high-speed Internet access, kitchen.

WHERE TO DINE

The Craftsman Inn (see above) operates a nice restaurant called **The Craftsman House** (© **315/637-9999**), which serves items like New York strip steak, prime rib, and brook trout. Like the hotel, it is decorated with Stickley furniture.

Coleman's IRISH/PUB FARE   A sprawling, handsome Irish pub and restaurant in the heart of the very Irish neighborhood Tipperary, Coleman's has been around since 1933. The menu is a comfortable mix of simple bar food and Irish specialties, such as Guinness beef stew, Irish roast chicken, and homemade chili, as well as pastas and fresh seafood. For dessert, if you want to stick with the Irish theme, try Bailey's cheesecake or the Irish crème bash. There's live music, from pop to traditional Irish tunes and Celtic rock, from Thursday to Saturday.

110 S. Lowell Ave. ℂ **315/476-1933.** Reservations recommended on weekends. Main courses $12–$21. AE, MC, V. Mon–Sat 11:30am–3pm; Mon–Thurs 5–10pm; Fri–Sat 5–11pm; Sun noon–9pm.

Dinosaur Bar-B-Que *★★* *(Kids* BARBECUE   A ribs-and-juke joint/biker bar, Dinosaur Bar-B-Que is a local legend that looks ripped straight out of Memphis. Don't let the tough-girl waitresses and Harley fanatics intimidate you; at mealtimes the place is a pretty even mix of suits, families, and leather-clad bikers. On weekends when there's live blues until late, the environment is rowdy and fun. The best menu items are classic barbecue: the "Big Ass" pulled-pork plate, pit platters of ribs, and "ass-kickin'" chili, as well as the ⅓-pound barbecued burgers and spicy mojito chicken. Live music rocks every night but Sunday. Older kids will get a kick out of the place.

246 Willow St. ℂ **315/476-4937.** Reservations not accepted. Main courses $5.50–$21. AE, DC, DISC, MC, V. Mon–Thurs 11am–midnight; Fri–Sat 11am–1am; Sun 2–9pm.

SYRACUSE AFTER DARK

The **Landmark Theatre,** 362 S. Salina St. (ℂ **315/475-7979;** www.landmarktheatre. org), the last-remaining Depression-era movie palace in central New York and listed on the National Register of Historic Places, is a great place to take in a concert. The streets in **Armory Square** are lined with hopping bars, and nearby the **IMAX Theater** at the MOST has Friday- and Saturday-evening showings until 9pm. **Coleman's,** 110 S. Lowell Ave. (ℂ **315/476-1933**), is a classic Irish pub.

Syracuse is host to the **New York State Fair** *(★* at the 375-acre Empire Expo Center, 581 State Fair Blvd. (ℂ **800/475-FAIR;** www.nysfair.org; adjacent to Rte. 690 just west of downtown), the last 2 weeks of August. The fair, which hosts all kinds of big-name musical acts and other exhibitions and entertainment, draws more than a million visitors annually. If you're in town during basketball season, try to catch a game of the **Syracuse Orangemen** (national champions in 2003 and a perennial Big East contender) at the Carrier Dome; call ℂ **315/443-2121** or see www.suathletics. com for schedules and information.

12

The North Country

by Rich Beattie

The Adirondack Park and Thousand Islands together make up New York's largest playground. Covering a full 20% of the state, the North Country's mountains, forests, lakes, rivers, and islands afford endless opportunities to get out in the wilderness, explore, and have fun, whether it's hiking, skiing, canoeing, or just kicking back in an Adirondack chair overlooking a glassy lake.

Drive into the Adirondack Park from almost any road and chances are you'll pass a rustic, wooden sign that welcomes you. When you cross that boundary, the smell of fresh air and pine envelops you and won't let you go. It's a distinctive scent, one that can only be described as very, well, Adirondack.

I've been coming here since I was a kid, mostly on summertime getaways with my family, and I can't imagine a more beautiful place to visit. The 'dacks, specifically, is an area you simply can't ignore. Its 600 million acres hold some 2,000 peaks, 100 of them taller than 3,000 feet. Nearly half of the park is forest preserve, vast forests of pine, maple, and birch. The park supports 500,000 acres of old-growth forest, 200,000 acres of which have never been logged. And water? You'll find some 2,500 lakes and ponds, along with more than 30,000 miles of rivers and streams.

Ralph Waldo Emerson and other thinkers found refuge here in the mid–19th century, forming philosophers' camps and using the woods for inspiration. And the park inspired the exploratory dreams of Theodore Roosevelt, who canoed in the St. Regis Wilderness Canoe Area at the age of 12 and often returned to seek refuge.

Make no mistake: Though the peaks of the Adirondacks don't have the rugged, jagged look of, say, the Rockies, this can be harsh territory. But if you prepare well, it can be some of the most beautiful land to explore. It's well stocked with hotels, restaurants, and campsites, so you can get as much or as little civilization as you please.

Drive west of the park and you'll run right into Canada—but you'll have to hop over the Thousand Islands first. A collection of tiny plots of land that sit in the middle of the St. Lawrence River, this is some of New York State's most scenic territory, which makes for terrific boating and some of the country's best fishing. You won't find as many active pursuits as in the 'dacks, though. Since there are no mountains and most of the islands are privately owned, you'll have to enjoy it all either from the deck of a boat or from the shoreline. Unfortunately, this area falls into the once-great category that is the fate of places like Buffalo and the Adirondack Great Camps. When New York's wealthy industrialists vacationed here 100 years ago, there were impressive hotels and more impressive architecture. Much of that is gone now, and what's left is a hodgepodge of motels and only decent resorts that draw mostly boaters and fishermen.

1 Southern Adirondacks ★★★

From Lake George to Old Forge

The southern 'dacks landscape is mostly characterized by lakes. At the center of it all is Lake George, both the 32-mile-long lake and the village. The area is hopping with tourists in the summer and fall foliage season, but most everything shuts down for the winter. Route 28, the only east–west road in the region, takes you past tiny villages, the Gore Mountain ski resort (New York's second-largest), the magnificent Fulton Chain of Lakes, and over into Inlet and Old Forge, which also bustle with activity. It's about 90 miles from Lake George to Old Forge; but it's a beautiful drive (as are all the drives in the park) and it's worth spending some time cruising west from Lake George. The southwestern section of the park stays partially open in the winter to accommodate the thousands of snowmobilers who power through here each year. Enter the park via Route 30 and you'll pass the huge Great Sacandaga Lake, along with even more tiny villages and lakes.

ESSENTIALS
GETTING THERE

BY CAR   You'll likely drive here; I-87 becomes the Northway north of Albany and speeds you south to north along the eastern edge of the park. **Enterprise** (© 800/325-8007) and **Hertz** (© 800/654-3131) operate out of Glens Falls and Utica. Enterprise's Glens Falls location will pick you up and deliver you to the office in Lake George or Warrensburg without charge. Hertz has a rental desk at the Adirondack Regional Airport (see below) with limited hours.

BY AIR   **Continental Airlines** (© 800/523-3273) flies into the **Adirondack Regional Airport** in Saranac Lake (© 518/891-4600), in the northern part of the park, and into **Oneida County Airport** (© 315/736-9404), a 45-minute drive from Old Forge. Other nearby airports include Burlington, Vermont (1 hr. from the eastern section of the region), Albany (1 hr. from the southern border), and Montreal (1 hr. from Plattsburg).

BY BUS   **Adirondack Trailways** (© 800/776-7548; www.trailwaysny.com) serves Lake George, Saranac Lake, Lake Placid, Keene, Keene Valley, Schroon Lake, Pottersville, Chestertown, Warrensburg, Malone, Hogansburg, Massena, Potsdam, and Canton. The daily service from Albany to Lake Placid takes 4 hours.

BY TRAIN   **Amtrak** (© 800/872-7245; www.amtrak.com) stops in Glens Falls, Whitehall, Ticonderoga, Port Henry, Westport, Port Kent, Plattsburgh, and Rouses Point.

BY FERRY   **Lake Champlain ferries** (© 802/864-9804) go from Grand Isle, Vermont, to Plattsburgh, New York; Burlington, Vermont, to Port Kent, New York; and Charlotte, Vermont, to Essex, New York. Schedule depends on season.

VISITOR INFORMATION   The **Adirondack Regional Tourism Council** (© 518/846-8016; www.adk.org) has an information center on I-87 southbound between exits 41 and 40, which is open daily year-round, from 8am to 5pm; from Memorial Day to Labor Day, it's open until 8pm. For information on Lake George, you can also contact **Warren County Tourism,** Municipal Center, 1340 State Rte. 9, Lake George (© 800/95-VISIT; www.visitlakegeorge.com). Farther west, contact **Inlet Information** (© 866/GO-INLET; www.inletny.com) or **Old Forge Tourism** (© 315/369-6983; www.oldforgeny.com).

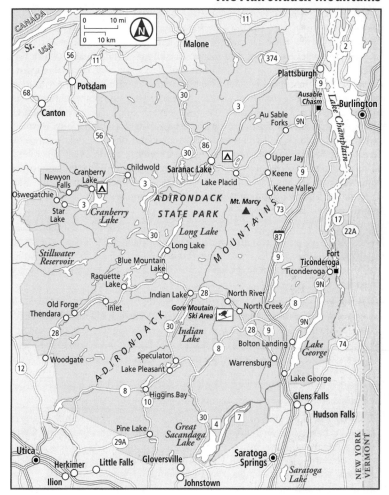

The Adirondack Mountains

SPORTS & OUTDOOR PURSUITS

BOAT TOURS   Explore Lake George on one of the **sightseeing cruises** that ply the lake, generally from May to October. With the **Lake George Steamboat Company,** Steel Pier Beach Road, Lake George (℅ **800/553-BOAT** or 518/668-5777; www. lakegeorgesteamboat.com), you can choose from 1- to 4-hour narrated cruises with or without a meal on the steamship paddle-wheeler or one of the other old-time ships. Or cruise the lake on **The Sagamore** hotel's 72-foot replica of a 19th-century wooden vessel from June to October (℅ **518/644-9400**). To cruise the Fulton Chain of Lakes, take a sightseeing cruise with **Old Forge Lake Cruises** (℅ **315/369-6473;** www. oldforgecruises.com/cruises.htm), or ply Raquette Lake's waters with the **Raquette Lake Navigation Co.** (℅ **315/354-5532;** www.raquettelakenavigation.com).

CANOEING With lakes at every turn, canoeing is the logical method of transportation—a quiet way to explore the waters that are such an essential part of this park. Keep an eye out for white-tailed deer, red fox, beaver, and numerous bird species. More reclusive are the black bear, coyote, and moose. The Fulton Chain of Lakes (which begins east of Old Forge) is a popular and heavily trafficked route, with eight lakes spanning 16 miles. From First through Fifth lakes, you'll find a continuous waterway lined with summer cottages. But you'll have to carry your boat to reach the remaining lakes, which are less developed. Lake George is also a gorgeous place to paddle, with crystal-clear spring-fed waters and a wealth of islands and small bays. It's 32 miles long, so you'll be better off in a sea kayak if you want to do some serious exploring. Get your canoe or kayak from **Mountainman Outdoor Supply Company,** Route 28 in both Inlet and Old Forge (© **877/226-6369,** 315/357-6672, or 315/369-6672; www.mountainman outdoors.com). In the Lake George area, try **Lake George Kayak,** Main Street, Bolton Landing (© **518/644-9366;** www.lakegeorgekayak.com).

DOWNHILL SKIING Whiteface (Lake Placid) it ain't, but **Gore Mountain** (© **518/251-2411;** www.goremountain.com) isn't exactly the ugly stepsister, either. It boasts some serious expert trails and a gondola of its own, making for a fun day on a 3,600-foot summit and 75 alpine trails. *Bonus:* Since the folks up in Whiteface run this place, too, multiday tickets of at least 3 days are good at both mountains if you must get your Olympic fix.

GOLF The Sagamore (© **866/385-6221**) has the area's most renowned course: It dates to 1929 and was designed by the famous course designer Donald Ross. The first tee starts off with a spectacular view of Lake George, but the lake disappears after that, as did most of my golf balls. Greens fees for the visiting public are $125–$135 for 18 holes, or $70–$80 after 2pm. Over on the western side, **Thendara Golf Course** (© **315/369-3136**) is also well known and also a Donald Ross creation from 1921 (the back 9 were added in 1959). Greens fees are $35, or $20 if you tee off after 3pm; just beware—the course can get mosquito-ridden at dusk.

HIKING **Bald Mountain,** east of Old Forge, is a steep but short (2-mile round-trip) climb that nabs you several open vistas and a fantastic open rocky summit. **Cascade Lake,** just north of Eagle Bay, is a 5.5-mile easy loop that takes you to a scenic lake with a beautiful narrow waterfall at its eastern end. Around Lake George, the climb up **Black Mountain** is 8.5 miles round-trip with a 1,100-foot vertical rise. The payoff? A rocky summit and amazing views. For more hikes, check out Barbara McMartin's *50 Hikes in the Adirondacks: Short Walks, Day Trips, and Backpacks Throughout the Park,* 4th edition (Countryman Press). For more hiking info (and other general outdoors info), contact the **Adirondack Mountain Club,** 814 Goggins

---

Fun Fact **The Adirondack Chair**

Those ubiquitous wooden chairs with wide armrests were first designed in Westport, New York, by Thomas Lee, who simply wanted a comfortable lawn chair for his summer home. He called it the "Westport plank chair" and offered the design to carpenter friend Harry Bunnell, who patented it in 1904 and made them for the next 20 years. Originally, they cost less than $4, but originals today can fetch more than $1,250.

Moments **Bowling with the Vanderbilts**

"Roughing it" means different things to different people. To the Vanderbilts and their contemporaries, it meant staying in the woods . . . in luxurious Great Camps. These sprawling camps—many built in the late 19th and early 20th centuries—covered acres of prime forest real estate, with lots of beautifully crafted buildings to accommodate them (hot water and indoor plumbing included, of course!). Several still stand today, and there are remnants of others.

One Great Camp you can visit is the rustic, deserted **Camp Santanoni** in Newcomb, just north of Route 28N (© 518/834-9328). Its 45 buildings are spread out over 12,900 acres. There are no furnishings anymore, and the buildings are closed to the public, but you come here to enjoy the beautiful architecture from the outside in this serene, mysterious setting. The camp is open year-round, but there's a catch: You have to hike or ski 5 miles to get here. Guided tours are seldom offered, but interpreters are on-site from late June through August.

Great Camp Sagamore ★★, 4 miles south of Raquette Lake (© 315/354-5311; www.sagamore.org), lets you see how the Vanderbilts went camping. Their 27-building summer retreat for more than 50 years even included a bowling alley. Tours are offered daily from late June to Labor Day at 10am or 1:30pm, daily from Labor Day to mid-October at 1:30pm, and weekends from Memorial Day to late June at 1:30pm.

The two camps are about 40 miles apart; on these winding roads, that could take some time to drive, so don't expect to see both in the same day, especially with the hiking involved to see Santanoni. Great Camp Sagamore is about 17 miles west of the Adirondack Museum in Blue Mountain Lake, and Santanoni about 25 miles east.

Rd., Lake George (© **800/395-8080** or 518/668-4447; www.adk.org). The club also does group outings several times a year. For maps and supplies, try **Mountainman Outdoor Supply Company,** Route 28 in both Inlet and Old Forge (© **877/226-6369,** 315/357-6672, or 315/369-6672).

RAFTING   The **Lower Moose River,** near Old Forge, is serious white water—April and early May bring Class IV and V rapids (on a scale of 1–5). The **Middle Moose River** is more mellow, perfect for families and inexperienced rafters, from May to October. You can do either with **Whitewater Challengers** in Old Forge (© **800/443-RAFT**).

SNOWMOBILING   With some 15 feet of snow each year, the **Old Forge** area often makes national news. When that happens, adventurers race up here to plow through it in the backwoods of the Inlet/Old Forge area. The most popular snowmobile route connects Old Forge and Inlet to the Sargent Ponds area, the Moose River Recreation area, and the Jessup River Wild Forest. For a trail map, check out www.hamiltoncounty.com. For trail conditions and a downloadable permit application, go to www.inletny.com or call the **Town of Inlet Information Office** (© **866/GOINLET**).

⸨Fun Fact⸩ Parking Space

You could add the acreage from Yellowstone, Grand Canyon, Yosemite, the Everglades, and Great Smoky Mountains National Park and it still wouldn't equal the acreage in the Adirondack Park.

ESPECIALLY FOR KIDS

Lake George provides indoor and outdoor amusement for kids. As a child, I loved Old Forge's **Enchanted Forest,** 3183 Rte. 28 (© 315/369-6145), and now it's even bigger, with amusement park rides as well as New York's largest water theme park (open daily May to Labor Day and weekends mid-Mar to Apr and in Sept). In Lake George, there's **Dr. Morbid's Haunted House,** 115 Canada St. (© 518/668-3077), open from spring to Halloween, and the **House of Frankenstein Wax Museum,** 213 Canada St. (© 518/668-3377). Lovers of kitschy minigolf shouldn't miss **Around the World Golf,** Beach Road (© 518/668-3223), where you can choose to putt around the U.S. (complete with the Empire State Building) or the world (with the Egyptian pyramids and a Japanese garden).

SEEING THE SIGHTS

Adirondack Museum ⸨★★⸩   Having just celebrated its 50th anniversary in 2007, this great museum is looking toward the next 50 years. History buffs can still devour the extensive collection that traces the transportation, tourism, and personal past of this massive park, as well as a rundown of its flora and fauna. But the "Great Out-doors" exhibit offers interactivity, which is fun for the kids as well. They'll love trying out different backpacks, snowshoes, and fishing rods, and everyone will get into the new virtual reality rides: flying in a helicopter over the high peaks, rafting Hudson River white water, and bobsledding down the Olympic track. The museum's setting, overlooking the lovely **Blue Mountain Lake,** is spectacular. Allow 3 hours to see the exhibits and grounds, and bring a picnic lunch to enjoy the view. Can't get enough? Admission is good for 2 consecutive days.

Rte. 30 on Blue Mountain Lake. © 518/352-7311. www.adirondackmuseum.org. Admission $15 adults, $8 children 6–12, free for children under 6. Late May to mid-Oct only, daily 10am–5pm. From I-87, take exit 23, turn left and then right onto Rte. 9 N. Drive through Warrensburg to Rte. 28 and drive west for an hour until Blue Mountain Lake. At the T-intersection, follow Rte. 30 N for 1 mile.

Fort Ticonderoga ⸨★★⸩   Military-history buffs will be in heaven at this fort set right on Lake Champlain. Built by the French beginning in 1755, the fort protected this narrow strip of water from its high perch, and since 1909 it's been open to the pub-lic, detailing the military history of the Lake Champlain and Lake George valleys. The collection is anything but dry: On view are nearly 1,000 muskets, bayonets, pistols, and swords from the 18th century, as well as a unique collection of uniforms. Not interested in the military stuff? There are gorgeous gardens for wandering.

On Lake Champlain, Ticonderoga. © 518/585-2821. Admission $12 adults, $11 seniors, $6 children 7–12, free for children under 7. Mid-May to mid-Oct only, daily 9am–5pm. King's Garden early June to mid-Oct only, daily 10am–4pm. From I-87, take exit 28, then Rte. 74 east 18 miles to Ticonderoga. Continue straight on Rte. 74 for 1½ miles. Turn left continuing on Rte. 74. Proceed straight ⅖ mile to fort entrance.

WHERE TO STAY

Back in the 1950s and 1960s, many of the lakeside retreats were grand inns and lodges, complete resorts that offered everything. Unfortunately, many of them have disappeared, the beautiful old buildings knocked down in favor of sterile condos. But it's still possible to find wide-ranging lodgings, from full resorts to quiet retreats.

You'll find many chains, especially in and around Lake George. The **Quality Inn,** 57 Canada St. (© **800/4-CHOICE**), offers decent rooms, and the **Super 8,** 2159 Canada St. (© **518/668-2470**), provides a microwave in some rooms. The **Holiday Inn,** 2223 Canada St. (© **518/668-5781**), has a beautiful outdoor pool and is a short walk from downtown.

Farther east, the **Best Western Sunset Inn,** Route 28, Old Forge (© **315/369-6836**), has 52 basic rooms.

EXPENSIVE

The Sagamore ★★★ (Kids)   Drive onto The Sagamore's personal 72-acre island and up to its Colonial-style main building and you'll immediately see what has drawn well-heeled vacationers here since 1883: peace, quiet, and luxury. Jutting out into Lake George, this private getaway serves up a wealth of water activities or just lakeside lounging. It's mostly vacationers here—who come for the great golf course and the newly renovated spa, as well as the water activities—though a convention center means plenty of name-tag-wearing guests as well. The common-area decor is more formal than comfy; luckily, that stuffiness doesn't carry over to the helpful staff. The restored main-building rooms—done in flowery patterns and muted tones—have the same formal furniture, but bathrooms give you plenty of room to navigate. Suites, with two full rooms and some with views in two directions, are well worth the extra money. There are several buildings and price options. The contemporary "lodge" rooms are not actually in the lodge, but with balconies and fireplaces, offer the best bang for the buck. An eye-popping, privately owned castle is also for rent. In addition to taking full advantage of its gorgeous lakeside setting, the Sagamore offers a broad array of kid-friendly activities and amenities, including wall climbing, rope courses, and babysitting services.

110 Sagamore Rd., Bolton Landing, NY 12814. © **800/358-3585** or 518/644-9400. Fax 518/743-6036. www.the sagamore.com. 324 units. Late June to Labor Day $229–$410 double, $499 and way up suite; rest of the year $129–$289 double, $295 and way up suite. Packages available. AE, DC, DISC, MC, V. Free valet parking. From I-87, get off at exit 22 and take Rte. 9N north for 10 miles to the town of Bolton Landing. At the 2nd traffic light, turn right onto Sagamore Rd. **Amenities:** 6 restaurants; large indoor pool; off-premises golf course; indoor tennis court, 5 lighted outdoor tennis courts; large exercise room; spa; Jacuzzi; watersports rentals; bike rental; children's programs; game room; courtesy van; small business center; 24-hr. room service July–Aug; limited rest of the year; in-room massage; babysitting; laundry service; same-day dry cleaning in summer. *In room:* A/C, TV/VCR w/pay movies, dataport, kitchenette and coffeemaker (in some rooms), hair dryer, iron.

MODERATE

The Georgian Resort ★ (Kids)   Busy, colorful, and right smack in the heart of the Lake George madness, The Georgian is the kind of place where you'd expect to find dinner theater—and you'd be right. Set right beside the lake with 400 feet of private beach, the resort has some rooms with gorgeous views. However, the standard rooms are without a trace of charm. You'll find two rows of motel-style rooms, many of which face the oh-so-lovely parking lot. Of course, you'll want to stay in the *other* building, closer to the lake, and preferably in room nos. 191 to 198, where nothing will be in front of you but shimmering water. Suites have slightly nicer furniture and generally lots more space. Some suites are huge and have *(ack!)* heart-shaped Jacuzzis. And you thought you had escaped the Poconos.

384 Canada St., Lake George, NY 12845. © **800/525-3436** or 518/668-5401. www.georgianresort.com. 164 units. Late May to early Oct $99-$350 double, $199–$389 suite; Early Oct to late May $69–$199 double, $139–$299 suite.

Some weekends have 2- or 3-night minimums. AE, DC, DISC, MC, V. **Amenities:** Restaurant; outdoor heated pool; limited room service. *In room:* A/C, TV, fridge (suites only), coffeemaker, hair dryer, iron.

North Woods Inn and Resort 🐾   Don't expect a sprawling resort like The Sagamore, but this smallish hotel is still recommended in its price range. Some rooms are in the main building, and others are motel-style along the shores of gorgeous Fourth Lake. All of them are a good size and adequately comfortable, but decked out in unfortunately drab colors. Your best bet is to stay in the lakefront rooms, preferably one on the end, so you actually have a lake view. Jacuzzi suites have the same sad decor, but offer the incentive of more space, a Jacuzzi tucked into a corner, and even a wood-burning fireplace in one.

4920 Rte. 28 and Fourth Lake, Old Forge, NY 13420. ✆ **315/369-6777.** Fax 315/369-2575. www.northwoodsinnresort. com. 28 units. $120–$225 double. 3-night minimum on holiday weekends. AE, DISC, MC, V. **Amenities:** 2 restaurants; lounge; outdoor heated pool; game room; limited room service to suites; complimentary use of 1 canoe. *In room:* A/C, TV (suites have VCR or DVD), fridge (in some units), coffeemaker, CD player (in suites), Jacuzzi in some suites.

INEXPENSIVE

Green Harbor Motel   This small motel with cottages boasts a terrific setting, off in the woods and right on Long Lake. You'll find a beach, hiking trails, and plenty of serenity. Rooms and cottages are nothing amazing, but for the price and location, they're okay. Some cottages are decked out with more of an Adirondacky feel, while others are more sterile. And for those who don't want to wait for that morning dip, a couple of cottages are right on the water.

Rte. 30, Long Lake, NY 12847. ✆ **518/624-4133.** www.greenharbormotel.com. 15 units. Mid-May to mid-Oct $75–$130 double for motel rooms; mid-June to mid-Sept cottages rent by the week only, $750 and up; mid-May to mid-June and mid-Sept to mid-Oct cottages $100 less per week. Motel rooms 3-night weekend minimum in high season; off-season cottages 3-night minimum. MC, V. Cottages are cash or check only. Closed mid-Oct to mid-May. **Amenities:** Public tennis courts nearby. *In room:* A/C (in some units), TV, full kitchens (in cottages), fridge (in some units), no phone.

The Lake Champlain Inn 🐾🐾 *Finds*   This gorgeous 1870 Victorian home has a prime location right on Lake Champlain, and its rooms have views of the lake, the Adirondacks, and even Vermont's Green Mountains. While rooms aren't the biggest, their views are among the best in the park. They boast nice touches like wrought-iron beds, claw-foot tubs, and original woodwork. The one suite gives you two adjoining rooms. You'll also find a house with two rooms, called the Schoolhouse, a large, Victorian-style house that's very modern inside and sits on 130 acres. The adjacent state land is perfect for hiking or cross-country skiing.

428 County Rte. 3, Ticonderoga, NY 12861. ✆ **518/547-9942.** www.tlcinn.com. 6 units. $95–$135 double. Rates include full breakfast. 2-night weekend minimums apply in high season. AE, MC, V. Take I-87 to exit 20, turn left onto Rte. 9. At light, turn right onto Rte. 149 for 12 miles, left on Rte. 4 for 10 miles. Go straight through intersection on Rte. 22 for 15 miles. Turn right (there will be a TLC road sign) onto Lake Rd., go 2 miles, bear right, go ½ mile. **Amenities:** Free use of bikes. *In room:* A/C, hair dryer, iron, no phone.

CAMPGROUNDS

Glen Hudson Campsite in Warrensburg (✆ **518/623-9871**) is a nice riverside campground with wooded river or open sites and it's close to Lake George; it's open mid-May through mid-October. Get away—far away—from the crowds and the RVs on **Lake George Islands** (✆ **518/623-1200**). Accessible by boat only, the 387 isolated shoreline campsites are on 44 state-owned islands. It's an amazing back-to-nature experience. The camping fee is $18 and is available mid-May through Columbus Day. **Golden Beach Campground** (✆ **315/354-4230**) has a prime perch on the southeast shore of Raquette Lake, and its 205 tent and trailer sites accommodate everyone from backpackers to 40-foot RVs. The fee is $16 and it's open mid-May to Labor Day.

WHERE TO DINE

You can walk through the village of Lake George and find all sorts of eateries, many of dubious quality. Fortunately, you have plenty of options.

EXPENSIVE

Seventh Lake House *(Finds* CONTEMPORARY AMERICAN   You might drive right by this unassuming house sitting between Inlet and Raquette Lake. But don't, for inside is probably the best food in the southern Adirondacks. The quiet dining room faces a lake and is decorated in warm tones and has a stone fireplace; you could also choose to sit out on the screened-in deck. The ever-changing seasonal menu combines "comfortable old favorites" with more cutting-edge "contemporary creations." You might start with paper-wrapped shrimp served with mango marmalade sauce and follow up with something similarly inventive, like the triple meatloaf—veal, beef, and pork baked with herbs and spices, wrapped in pastry, and served with an onion sherry sauce.

Rte. 28, Inlet (between Inlet and Raquette Lake). © 315/357-6028. Reservations recommended. Main courses $15–$25. AE, DISC, MC, V. June–Sept daily 5–10pm; Oct–May Thurs–Sun 5–9pm.

Trillium bis CONTEMPORARY AMERICAN   This restaurant has long been the region's standard for culinary excellence, and a renovation several years ago gave it a fresh look to match its fresh take on food. It now has contemporary blue-and-chocolate decor, modern lighting, and fireplaces, and attentive servers decked out in hip, all-black outfits scurry about. The bolder flavors that came with the renovation are still drawing raves: Dig into a grilled Maine lobster with a spicy grapefruit salsa, or try the Syrah-braised short ribs with creamy mascarpone grits. Complement your entrees with a bottle or glass of wine from the large selection of vintages.

In The Sagamore, 110 Sagamore Rd., Bolton Landing. © 800/358-3585 or 518/644-9400, ext. 6110. Reservations required. No denim or sneakers allowed. Main courses $21–$36. AE, DC, DISC, MC, V. Summer season Mon–Sun 6–9pm; variable hours in the off season.

MODERATE

East Cove AMERICAN   This local favorite is thankfully off Lake George's beaten path. Like many area restaurants, it's a small Adirondack-style log cabin, but the interior is fairly charming, with exposed posts and beams and historic photos lining the walls. The food, though, is what keeps diners coming back. The menu spans the meat/fish/pasta realms, and includes center-cut pork chops and the delicious sea scallops casino, baked with green and red peppers in garlic butter with crumb topping. On the lighter side, burgers, fish and chips, and chicken sandwiches are also available.

Rte. 9L and Beach Rd., Lake George. © 518/668-5265. Main courses $12–$30. AE, DC, DISC, MC, V. May–Oct daily 5–10pm; rest of the year Tues–Sun only.

Lanzi's on the Lake AMERICAN   Yes, the lake lives up to its boast of a name, and this great restaurant—run by the five Lanzi brothers—takes full advantage of its lakefront setting (a rarity on Sacandaga) with floor-to-ceiling windows in the restaurant, and a massive outdoor deck. Not only is there a great view outside, but usually a big party as well: Crowds of up to 4,000 have been known to gather for themed parties, such as reggae festivals or chili cook-offs. The kitchen turns out homemade everything, from the salad dressing to the pasta. The portions are huge and very rich.

Consider the Lake Chicken, grilled breast topped with sautéed lobster meat, baked under smoked mozzarella and topped with hollandaise sauce. You may need to join the dance party to work it all off.

Rte. 30, Mayfield. ✆ **518/661-7711.** Main courses $15–$24. AE, MC, V. May–Oct daily 11:30am–10pm (or later, depending on the crowd); Nov–Apr Mon and Wed–Fri 4–10pm, Sat–Sun 11:30am–10pm.

INEXPENSIVE

Keyes Pancake House & Restaurant AMERICAN   Pancakes that live up to their name and the all-day breakfast menu keep people coming back to this Old Forge mainstay. With nine different flavors of pancakes and four different kinds of syrup to choose from, it may just take all day to decide. Though breakfasts of pancakes and omelets are what this place does best, you can still come in for a lunchtime sandwich.

Main St., Old Forge. ✆ **315/369-6752.** Pancakes $4; sandwiches $3.50–$6. MC, V. Summer Mon–Thurs 7am–2pm, Fri–Sun 7am–8pm; off season closed Thurs. Closed Nov and Apr.

2 Northern Adirondacks ⟨⟨⟨

Keene Valley and Plattsburgh to Cranberry Lake

Separated from the southern Adirondacks by a range of mountains known as the **High Peaks,** the northern area of this park is a different entity, where life operates at full speed 365 days a year. Summer brings hikers, bikers, and paddlers, while wintertime beckons skiers and snowboarders to the state's best mountains.

Cut west from I-87 along Route 73 and you'll come to the center of activity: the village of **Lake Placid,** home to two winter Olympics and the birthplace of winter sports in America. Call it one of the ironies of geography that this town actually sits on **Mirror Lake**—the actual Lake Placid is a few miles outside of town. There's some kitsch to the town as it clings to its Olympic heritage—sure, it's cool to ski and skate where the athletes did, but 1980 was a long time ago, and 1932 a *really* long time ago. Nevertheless, the town is a beehive of activity all year-round, as it has been since the Games put the Adirondacks on America's recreation map.

West of Lake Placid, Route 73 becomes Route 86. Along Route 86, you'll pass through the village of **Saranac Lake,** which may not have the quality of restaurants that Placid does, but doesn't have the crowds, either. Cut north up Route 30 and you'll be in one of the most remote and gorgeous canoeing areas in America: the **St. Regis Canoe Wilderness Area.** Back on 86, the road takes you past two more huge lakes with countless opportunities for fishing, hiking, camping, and canoeing. Head east from Lake Placid and you'll run right into Lake Champlain; though not heavily developed for recreation or tourism, it's a gorgeous sight.

ESSENTIALS

GETTING THERE   I-87 cuts right through the forest, making it easily accessible. Cut over Route 73 and you'll be headed toward Lake Placid. **Amtrak** stops in Westport and Plattsburgh, both 50 miles from Saranac Lake. Westport is the closest stop to Lake Placid; book your transfer with Amtrak when you buy your ticket and **Majestic Limousine & Transportation,** 2 Main St., Lake Placid (✆ **866/226-1152** or 518/523-0294), will shuttle you back and forth for $15 each way. For bus and plane information, see section 1, "Southern Adirondacks," earlier in this chapter.

GETTING AROUND   You'll need a car. **Rent-A-Wreck** (✆ **800/698-1777** or 518/523-4804; www.rentawreck.com) in Lake Placid offers free pickup/drop-off service to

Value **Savings Passport**

You can get a discount on most Lake Placid attractions (and other money-saving coupons) for $29 by purchasing the **Olympic Sites Passport,** available from the Olympic Regional Development Authority (© **518/523-1655;** www.orda. org). Different options are available seasonally.

customers in the local vicinity. **Enterprise** has an office in Saranac Lake (© **800/325-8007** or 518/891-9216; www.enterprise.com). From late December through March, a **free shuttle** links Whiteface with Lake Placid. The shuttle runs every 2 hours during the week and hourly on the weekend and picks up at a few hotels in town—Howard Johnson, Mirror Lake Inn, Best Western, and Art Devlin's—but if you flag them down on Main Street, they'll stop. From town, the shuttle runs direct to Whiteface.

VISITOR INFORMATION   The **Adirondack Regional Tourism Council** (© **518/846-8016;** www.adirondacks.org) operates an information center on I-87 southbound between exits 41 and 40. It's open daily year-round, from 8am to 5pm; from Memorial Day to Labor Day, it's open until 8pm. The **Lake Placid/Essex County Visitors Bureau,** Olympic Center, 2610 Main St., Lake Placid (© **800/447-5224** or 518/523-2445; www.lakeplacid.com), is open year-round Monday to Friday from 8am to 5pm and Saturday and Sunday from 9am to 4pm. The office is closed on Sunday in April and November.

SEEING THE OLYMPIC SIGHTS

The 1932 Winter Olympics put Lake Placid in the international spotlight; hosting the Games again in 1980 cemented its legacy. You can see some of the sites where legends were made, including the "Miracle on Ice" hockey victory of the Americans over the Russians. **The Olympic Regional Development Authority** (© **518/523-1655;** www.orda.org) handles it all.

Skip the Olympic Training Center (421 Old Military Rd.); there's not much open to the public. For downhill skiing on **Whiteface,** see "Sports & Outdoor Pursuits," below. You can see all of the following in 1 day. Start off at the **Olympic Sports Complex** ൴൴, Route 73 (© **518/523-2811**), 20 minutes west of Lake Placid, for cross-country skiing (see "Sports & Outdoor Pursuits," below). In the same complex—and definitely something you should not miss—is the **bobsled/luge/skeleton track,** where you'll watch athletes bomb down on crazy machinery. You can even strap yourself into a bobsled and race down the half-mile track with a guide and brakeman ($55 summer, $65 winter)—you'll never watch the Olympics the same way again. The sleds are on wheels in summer, but they go much faster on the winter ice. Then, drive 10 minutes back toward town and you'll see the towering presence of the ski jump towers at the **MacKenzie-Intervale Ski Jumping Complex** ൴, Route 73 (© **518/523-2202**). From December to March and May through October, watch athletes soar off these ramps. Ride the lift alongside it and take the 26-story elevator to the top of the 394-foot tower to get the skiers' terrifying perspective ($10). From May to October, you can watch them jump, too—into a 750,000-gallon pool at the adjacent **Freestyle Sports Park.** Drive back into town and spend a half-hour in the **Winter Olympic Museum** ൴ (© **518/523-1655**) at the **Olympic Center;** it's $4 to check out a good history of the Games in Lake Placid and tons of memorabilia. While there, go skating on the rinks where legends like Sonja Henie and Eric Heiden made history (see below).

SPORTS & OUTDOOR PURSUITS

CANOEING   It's rare to find a stretch of water reserved solely for nonmotorized boats, but the St. Regis Canoe Wilderness beckons with the promise of quiet. In fact, the only sounds you'll hear in this remote part of the park are birdcalls and the sound of your paddle as it slices through the glassy water. Just be prepared to carry your canoe: There are lots of portages here. But whether you're just interested in a 1-day outing or a weeklong trip, you can get outfitted, with or without a guide. **St. Regis Canoe Outfitters,** 73 Dorsey St., Saranac Lake (© **888/SRKAYAK** or 518/891-1838; www.canoe outfitters.com), can set you up with canoe and kayak rentals, guided trips, and camping-gear rentals. **Adirondack Lakes and Trails Outfitters,** 541 Lake Flower Ave., Saranac Lake (© **800/491-0414** or 518/891-7450; www.adirondackoutfitters.com), is another great place for canoeing advice and/or rentals; it offers a wealth of self-guided and guided trips.

CROSS-COUNTRY SKIING   Just outside Lake Placid, **Mount Van Hoevenberg X-C Center** at the Olympic Sports Complex, Route 73 (© **518/523-2811**), is where Olympic athletes train; trail fees are $14 per day and equipment rental is available. **Dewey Mountain Ski Center,** Route 3, Saranac Lake (© **518/891-2697**), is another fun place to explore. Hard-core skiers up for a challenge can head into the backcountry and take on the **Jackrabbit Trail.** Pick up the trail (and any equipment you need) at the **Cascade Cross Country Center,** on Route 73, 5 miles from Lake Placid (© **518/523-9605**). This is also a great place to come on nights of a full moon from January to March, when the trails are set with bonfires, and hot chocolate, beer, and hot dogs are served.

DOWNHILL SKIING   **Whiteface,** Route 86, Wilmington (© **518/946-2223;** www.whiteface.com), is the East's only Olympic mountain (elevation 4,400 ft.) and has the best skiing in the state. With the greatest vertical drop in the East (3,430 ft.), it has a variety of terrain that will appeal to all levels. In fact, 35% of the trails are rated for novices. There are 77 trails and 10 lifts in all. A 1-day lift ticket costs $65 to $67. **Mount Pisgah,** Mt. Pisgah Road, Saranac Lake (© **518/891-4150;** www.saranac lake.com/pisgah.shtml), is decidedly less Olympic, and good skiers will get bored here; but with only five trails, it's a good hill for beginners and families. It also boasts a fun tubing hill. Lift tickets cost just $15 to $20.

FLY-FISHING   The Ausable River offers tumbles and flows, twists and turns, and a pristine environment to cast your line. The village of Wilmington, about a 20-minute drive northeast from Lake Placid, is your headquarters. World-renowned fisherman Fran Betters and the guides at his **Adirondack Sport Shop,** Route 86, Wilmington (© **518/946-2605;** www.adirondackflyfishing.com), know the waters as well as anyone. A day out with the guides will run you $195 per day, including lunch and a box of flies.

FLYING   Soar high over the treetops and look down on the mountaintops during a scenic flight any time of year with **Adirondack Flying Service,** Lake Placid Airport, Route 73, Lake Placid (© **518/523-2473;** www.flyanywhere.com). A 20-minute flight is $30 per person (two-person minimum), with family discounts available.

GOLF   There are lots of places to tee up in this part of the park. The **Whiteface Club & Resort,** Whiteface Inn Road, Lake Placid (© 800/422-6757 or 518/523-2551; www.whitefaceclubresort.com), was rated four stars (out of five) by *Golf Digest;* greens fees are $70 and club rental is available. Or hit the links at a municipal par-72 course, the **Craig Wood Golf and Country Club,** Route 73, Lake Placid (© 877/999-9473 or 518/523-9811; www.craigwoodgolfclub.com). Greens fees May to June, $28; July to November $34; add $32 for a cart.

HIKING   Everyone wants to climb the Adirondacks' highest peak, Mount Marcy, and its 5,344 feet of rock. On summer weekends, the paths can seem more like mid-town Manhattan than wilderness. The most popular (and crowded) approach is from the north, but the most scenic and less-crowded trail (don't tell) is the **Range Trail.** You use your feet only to scramble the last bit to the top of Whiteface; it's actually accessed by a highway that costs $9 to drive up (car and driver; additional passengers are $5 each) and is open only from mid-May to mid-October (weather permitting). Then it's a short climb via a nature trail in the rocky ridge of a glacial cirque. **High Falls Gorge,** 8 miles east of Lake Placid on Route 86 (© 518/946-2278), affords a beautiful stroll along the Ausable River, past 700 feet of waterfalls in summer or winter. You'll cross bridges and follow trails as the water spills over ancient granite cliffs. Admission in winter is $12 for adults, $10 for kids 4 to 12; summer is $10 for adults, $7.25 for kids. To take a guided hiking tour, talk to the folks at **High Peaks Mountain Adventures Guide Service,** 331 Main St., Lake Placid (© 518/523-3764).

ICE-SKATING   Skate on the same rink where Eric Heiden won his record five gold medals in 1980. Lake Placid's Olympic Center on Main Street (© 518/523-1655) gets you onto the outdoor rink in winter nightly from 7 to 9pm for $6. On summer weeknights, you can skate indoors at the 1932 arena where Sonja Henie won Olympic Gold ($5). Rentals are $3.

RAFTING   Nothing quite beats the rush of white-water rafting, especially when the water is high from snow runoff in the spring. **Adirondack Rafting Company** (© 800/510-RAFT or 518/523-1635; www.lakeplacidrafting.com) provides everything you need for a guided run of the Hudson River Gorge. The water is Class IV and V in April and May, when trips run on weekends only, and Class III June through August, when trips run Tuesday, Thursday, Saturday, and Sunday. Fall foliage runs are on the weekends in September and October. For a low-key raft ride, plus a walk along nature trails through primeval Adirondack forest, check out **Ausable Chasm** on Route 9, 12 miles south of Plattsburgh (© 518/834-7454; www.ausablechasm.com). It expanded the "Rim Walk" by 2 miles in 2006; walking the entire rim and peering down into the chasm is pretty spectacular. The entrance fee is $16 for adults, $9 for kids 5 to 12, and free for children under 5; the raft ride (weather permitting) is $9 for everyone.

TOURING LAKE CHAMPLAIN   Unfortunately, the tour boat that left from Plattsburgh is no more, so you'd have to leave from the Vermont side on the *Spirit of Ethan Allen III* (© 802/862-8300; www.soea.com). Fortunately, you can still paddle the lake yourself in search of eagles. Rent kayaks (and powerboats) from **Westport Marina,** 20 Washington St., Westport (© 800/626-0342; www.westportmarina.com).

TRAIN   Climb aboard for a 45-minute rail journey through the forest (between Lake Placid and Saranac Lake) on the **Adirondack Scenic Railroad** (© 518/891-3238; www.adirondackrr.com). Trains depart weekends and summer weekdays from the end of May to mid-October from Saranac Lake (19 Depot St.) or Lake Placid (20 Averyville Rd.); themed rides take place throughout the summer. Round-trip tickets are $16 adults, $15 seniors, and $8 for kids 3 to 12.

ESPECIALLY FOR KIDS

In winter, nothing in town is as much fun as screaming down onto the ice of Mirror Lake, holding onto your toboggan for dear life. Right in Lake Placid, you'll slide down a converted ski jump (✆ **518/523-2591**); get a four-person toboggan and a 40-mph rush ($5 per toboggan, $5 per adult, $3 per child). The slide is near the Olympic Center and the Best Western. Go mushing around the lake with **Thunder Mountain Dog Sled Tours** (✆ **518/891-6239**), located across from the Lake Placid Hilton ($10 per person). For a true Christmas experience (for part of the year, anyway), take the kids to **Santa's Workshop,** 324 Whiteface Mountain Memorial Hwy. (Rte. 431), 1½ miles northwest of Route 86 in Wilmington (✆ **800/806-0215**), where they can hop on rides, pet reindeer, and see Santa's house. The place is geared toward the wee ones; older kids will get bored quickly. Open daily 9:30am to 4:30pm from the end of June to Labor Day; weekends only (9:30am–4pm) Labor Day to Columbus Day and 5 weekends prior to Christmas (10am–3pm). Admission is $19 adults, $17 for seniors and for kids 2 to 16.

SHOPPING

For outdoor gear, try **EMS,** 2453 Main St., Lake Placid (✆ **518/523-2505**). For unique Adirondack crafts, visit the **Adirondack Craft Center,** 2114 Saranac Ave., Lake Placid (✆ **518/523-2062**), where you'll find works from more than 300 artisans. Another good bet is **Adirondack Reflections,** Main Street (Rte. 73), Keene (✆ **518/576-9549**).

WHERE TO STAY

Accommodations range from tiny lakeside motels of varying quality to chains to exclusive getaways and secluded campsites. In Lake Placid, room rates are not set in stone. The village hosts many events, such as major hockey tournaments, so even in the off season, you could find rates on some days that rival those of the summer season. Chains offer good value for families. The **Best Western Mountain Lake Inn,** 487 Lake Flower Ave., Saranac Lake (✆ **800/780-7234** or 518/891-1970), provides clean, spacious rooms and has an indoor pool.

VERY EXPENSIVE

Lake Placid Lodge ✦✦✦   This exclusive inn, a Relais & Châteaux member, is set right on Lake Placid outside of town, with an upscale rustic look (*very* Adirondack) and lots of privacy. Sadly, a fire destroyed the main lodge in December 2005, but the lodge stayed open and made clever use of its lakeside cabins. Best of all, a rebuilding effort is forging ahead, to be completed in 2008, so when the lodge's three rooms, eight suites, eight additional cabins, and expanded deck open, you can expect the place to be back in its finest form. Cabins will still afford the ultimate in luxury and privacy—most are set right on the lake's shore, with stone fireplaces, giant beds, and picture windows. They're the perfect place to sit in an overstuffed sofa and watch the moon as it rises and reflects off the lake.

Whiteface Inn Rd., P.O. Box 550, Lake Placid, NY 12946. ✆ **877/523-2700** or 518/523-2700. www.lakeplacidlodge.com. 30 units upon full reopening in 2008. $550 double; $700–$1,200 suite; $1,000–$1,800 cabin. Rates include breakfast. Packages available. AE, DISC, MC, V. From Main St. Lake Placid, turn left on Rte. 86, turn right at the Lake Placid Lodge sign (Whiteface Inn Rd.). Dogs allowed. No children under 14. **Amenities:** Restaurant; lounge; access to health club; complimentary watersports and bike rentals; courtesy car; 24-hr. room service; laundry; dry cleaning. *In room:* A/C, dataport, fridge, coffeemaker, hair dryer, iron, safe.

The Point ✸✸✸   This secluded Great Camp on the banks of Saranac Lake was built as an exclusive retreat for the very wealthy by William Avery Rockefeller. It remains so secluded that there are no signs; you don't even get directions until you've paid in full. Once you're there, the ultraluxurious, all-inclusive, 11-room property emulates the glory days of the Great Camps, with the very affable general manager serving as host of the party. Huge rooms are sumptuously decked out with amazingly comfortable furniture, huge stone fireplaces, and some with original pieces (my bathroom's slate sinks were Rockefeller's darkroom sinks). But the experience of staying here is just as important as the rooms. Any whim, no matter how large or small, can be satisfied at any time of day or night; the excellent staff doesn't know the word "no." Fantastic gourmet meals are served at communal tables with new-found friends (and unlimited wine), though you can also choose to dine aboard a boat, at a remote cabin, or in your room. Love water-skiing? Go all day long. Take out an electric boat or kayak. Hike the resort's trails (stocked with water), then pour yourself a drink from one of the lodge's many open liquor cabinets and gaze out over the lake. Watch the chefs at work, request changes to your dinner menu, and finish off each night around the bonfire with a drink and something tasty like s'mores or truffle popcorn.

P.O. Box 1327, Saranac Lake, NY 12983. ✆ **800/255-3530** or 518/891-5674. Fax 518/891-1152. www.thepointresort. com. 11 units. $1,350–$1,750 double; $1,950–$2,100 suite; $2,600 boathouse. Rates include all meals, drinks, and activities. AE, DC, DISC, MC, V. Directions given upon receipt of payment. No children under 18. **Amenities** (all are included in the rate): Restaurant; lounge; tennis court; watersports; winter sports equipment; bikes; 24-hr. room service; in-room massage (extra charge); laundry service. *In room:* A/C, hair dryer, iron.

EXPENSIVE

Mirror Lake Inn ✸✸✸   Just beyond Lake Placid's busy Main Street, on a hill overlooking Mirror Lake, sits this classy and gorgeous inn. Dating from 1883, it maintains a very traditional upscale feel—rustic it's not. Mahogany walls, walnut floors, and chandeliers fill the lobby and its cozy nooks. With the exception of the smallish "Cobble Hill" accommodations, standard rooms are extremely comfortable and very spacious, with an understated luxury—there's nothing overly grand or unique about them. Many, however, boast gorgeous views of the lake and mountains—some even have balconies. Suites are huge with graceful furnishings and touches like four-poster beds in some; they're the most elegant rooms in the town. Best of all, a renovation and expansion have given this excellent inn even more suites in buildings across the street, right on the lake. Two major pluses: The View (reviewed below) is outstanding, as is the state-of-the-art spa.

77 Mirror Lake Dr., Lake Placid, NY 12946. ✆ **518/523-2544.** Fax 518/523-2871. www.mirrorlakeinn.com. 131 units. Mid-June to mid-Oct, some holiday weeks, and some off-season weekends $290–$380 double, $425 and way up suite; Jan–June, excluding some holiday weeks, and mid-Oct to mid-Dec $195–$290 double, $375 and way up suite. Modified American Plan available as well as many packages. 2-night weekend minimum. AE, DC, DISC, MC, V. **Amenities:** 3 restaurants; lounge; 2 pools (1 indoor, 1 heated outdoor); tennis court; exercise room; spa; Jacuzzi; sauna; free use of canoes, kayaks, rowboats, and paddle boats; concierge; salon; limited room service; laundry service. *In room:* A/C, TV w/DVD, dataport, fridge, hair dryer, iron, safe.

MODERATE

Golden Arrow Lakeside Resort ✸✸ *Kids*   This former Best Western sits right in the heart of Lake Placid and directly on the shore of Mirror Lake, and the views are a major reason to stay here (if you stay on the lake-facing side, of course). Most rooms even have balconies to take full advantage of the scene. You can even grab a complimentary canoe or kayak and go paddling on the lake, right outside your door. Rooms are comfortable, if a little bland—look for them to get a makeover soon. Suites aren't worth the extra money, though they have nice extras like fireplaces and fridges or whirlpool tubs; in some, a wall creates two cramped rooms instead of a single large one.

2559 Main St., Lake Placid, NY 12946. © 800/582-5540 or 518/523-3353. www.golden-arrow.com. 153 units. Mid-June to Columbus Day $129–$249 double, $249–$459 suite; Columbus Day to mid-June weekdays $79–$209 double, $109–$359 suite; weekends high-season rates apply. Packages available. AE, DC, DISC, MC, V. **Amenities:** Restaurant; indoor pool; elaborate health club; Jacuzzi; sauna; complimentary watersports equipment; game room; salon; limited room service; in-room massage; laundry service. In room: A/C, TV w/pay movies, dataport, kitchenette (in some units), fridge, coffeemaker, hair dryer, iron, safe (in some units).

Hilton Lake Placid Resort ☆☆ (Kids) Located right in the village, this resort sprawls across two streets in three different buildings, one of which is right on the water. It has loads of amenities, from four(!) pools to complimentary boats for use on the lake, so you'll never be lacking for activity on the hotel grounds. Since about half the guests are here with a group, the place constantly buzzes. Rooms are uniformly outfitted in what the hotel calls Modern Adirondack style, one that bears a striking resemblance to standard Hilton style. That's okay, though, since they have lots of space, are comfortable, and will all be renovated by April 2008. My suggestion: Upgrade to the Lakeview Building for great lake views. For superhuge rooms that look straight down on the water, grab a room in the Waterfront Building. These had been renovated at press time and are modern and extremely comfortable. Just be aware that they can book up a year in advance.

1 Mirror Lake Dr., Lake Placid, NY 12946. © 800/755-5598 or 518/523-4411. Fax 518/523-1120. www.lphilton.com. 178 units. Mid-June to Aug $169–$369; Sept–Dec $109–$289; Jan to mid-June $79–$269, unless there's an event or holiday, when high-season rates apply. Packages available. AE, DC, DISC, MC, V. Pets allowed with $25 fee. **Amenities:** Restaurant; lounge; 4 pools (2 indoor, 2 heated outdoor); small exercise room; Jacuzzi; complimentary boat use; children's programs; game room; concierge; tour desk; small business center; salon; limited room service; laundry service; dry-cleaning. In room: A/C, TV w/pay movies, dataport, fridge, coffeemaker, hair dryer, iron.

INEXPENSIVE

Adirondack Motel ☆ (Value) This small lakeside motel offers a way to get a place right on the water at a great value. Rooms, as you might expect, are nothing unique; but they are spacious and comfortable, and even the most inexpensive have views of the water. If you're staying for a while, consider a boathouse room or cottage, both of which have kitchen facilities and are right on the water. Cottages even have fireplaces. The property definitely takes advantage of the water; you can take a dip in the lake or grab one of the canoes and go out for a spin.

248 Lake Flower Ave., Saranac Lake, NY 12983. © 800/416-0117 or 518/891-2116. www.adirondackmotel.com. 14 units. July–Oct $109–$160 double; Dec–Feb and May–June $65–$135; Mar–Apr and Nov $60–$99. Rates include continental breakfast. AE, DISC, MC, V. From Lake Placid, take Rte. 86 north; Lake Flower and the inn will be on your left. Dogs allowed with $10 charge. **Amenities:** Free use of paddle boats and canoes. In room: A/C, TV, dataport, kitchenettes in boathouse, full kitchens in cottages, fridge, hair dryer.

Art Devlin's Olympic Motor Inn ☆ (Value) If you enjoy the kitsch value of Lake Placid, you'll adore this small hotel just 3 blocks from the Olympic Center—in the lobby, you'll find some 450 trophies and medals from ski jumper extraordinaire Art Devlin. Now run by Art's son (also Art), this hotel is a little less than extraordinary, but a good-value option. Rooms are simple, but spacious and painted in nice bright colors. Some give you a glimpse of high peaks, even from a balcony, while others look out onto the less-romantic parking lot. Rooms in the back building are bigger, but you should splurge on one of the deluxe rooms, added in 2007. The best ones have plasma TVs, 180-degree-view balconies, huge showers, Jacuzzi tubs, and lots of space—one of the best values in town.

2764 Main St., Lake Placid, NY 12946. ② 518/523-3700. Fax 518/523-3893. www.artdevlins.com. 41 units. Mid-June to mid-Sept midweek $68–$128 double, weekend $88–$198 double; rest of year midweek $64–$104 double, weekend $78–$198 double. Rates include continental breakfast. 2-night minimum some weekends. AE, DC, DISC, MC, V. Dogs allowed. **Amenities:** Heated outdoor pool (summer only). *In room:* A/C, TV, fridge, hair dryer.

CAMPGROUNDS

For a truly unique experience, canoe out to one of the solitary sites on **Saranac Lake Islands,** Saranac Lake (② **518/891-3170;** www.dec.ny.gov/outdoor/24496.html), and pitch your tent away from the crush of car campers. Sites cost $18. Open mid-May to Columbus Day. **Whispering Pines Campground,** Route 73, Lake Placid (② **518/523-9322),** is a sprawling campground right on the outskirts of Lake Placid. You can set up deep inside the woods, but be prepared for loud partyers in RVs. If you're one of them, you'll love it here. Tent campers in search of a back-to-nature experience will want to look elsewhere. Tent sites are $19; water and electric hookups are $25 to $29. **Ausable Point Campground** (② **518/561-7080;** www.dec.ny.gov/outdoor/24452.html) sits on a stunning patch of land overlooking Lake Champlain with 123 sites. There's a shore-line of natural sand, and the campground borders a wildlife management area with a hiking trail. Open mid-May to mid-October, **Cranberry Lake Campground,** off Route 30 in Lake Cranberry (② **315/848-2315;** www.dec.ny.gov/outdoor/24460.html), sits on a lake in one of the most undeveloped parts of the park, yet the campground is eas-ily accessible.

WHERE TO DINE

Dining options range from romantic lakeside hideaways to busy food feasts in Lake Placid. In these parts, dining after dark isn't chic, it's just silly—with all this lakefront property, you'll want to make the most of the daylight views.

EXPENSIVE

The View ✦✦✦ AMERICAN   Like the Mirror Lake Inn to which it's attached, this restaurant (formerly the Averil Conwell Dining Room) is upscale, traditional, classic, and unfailingly excellent. The change from black-tie servers to a more casually attired staff better reflects the lake view out the picture windows. However, the less formal atmosphere doesn't mean a more casual kitchen—if anything, the food has improved with a change in chefs. With the spa just downstairs, a whole section of the menu is devoted to spa dining—healthy items like five-spice tofu with Oriental noodles. This is fine, but to really experience the cuisine, dig into the meat such as venison loin or filet mignon, which are fall-off-the-bone tender. You'll also find an excellent wine list.

77 Mirror Lake Dr. (inside the Mirror Lake Inn), Lake Placid. ② **518/523-2544.** Reservations recommended. Casual dress. Main courses $20–$36. AE, DC, DISC, MC, V. Daily 5:30–9pm.

MODERATE

Ere's ITALIAN   Not enough restaurants in Lake Placid take advantage of the lake view, but this small, charming place offers views through the picture window as well as some tables out on the deck. It serves basic Italian fare, from linguine to stuffed shells to chicken cutlet parmigiana, but dishes are done well. Or dig into one of the

Backcountry Blunders: Do's & Don'ts

- Don't camp within 150 feet of roads, trails, or bodies of water.
- Lean-tos are for everyone; yes, you must share!
- No outhouse? No problem: Dig a hole 6 to 8 inches deep and at least 150 feet from water or campsites. Cover with leaves and soil.
- We like you smelling fresh, but no soap within 150 feet of water.
- Giardia is one bug you can avoid: Boil, filter, or treat water.
- Use only dead and down wood for fires.
- Carry out what you carry in.
- Leave wildlife and plants undisturbed—doing otherwise is not nice *and* it's illegal.

pizzas, either red or white and with a variety of toppings. Lunches—salami or meatball subs with a view—are an even better bargain.

2439 Main St., Lake Placid. ✆ **518/523-2997.** Main courses $13–$19. Lunch sandwiches $7–$8. MC, V. Daily 11am–10pm.

Great Adirondack Steak & Seafood Company ★★ STEAKHOUSE   A steakhouse and microbrewery in one—a winning combination. Right on Main Street in Lake Placid, this recently renovated restaurant comes complete with Adirondack antiques, a fireplace, large bay windows overlooking Mirror Lake, and some of the best food in town. There's nothing shocking or inventive on the menu, just very good pastas, meat, and fish. Try the rack of ribs basted with the house amber-ale barbecue sauce, or the shrimp and scallops simmered in a garlic cream sauce with mushrooms and shallots, topped with puff pastry. You won't be able to ignore the wonderful ales: Each dish is matched with one of the house brews. The Ausable Wulff Red Ale is great.

2442 Main St., Lake Placid. ✆ **518/523-1629.** Reservations not accepted. Main courses $15–$31. AE, DC, DISC, MC, V. July 4 to late Aug 8am–10pm; Sept to early July 11am–10pm.

INEXPENSIVE

Blue Moon Cafe ★★ *Finds* DINER   This small cafe has a loyal following that borders on a cult. The Blue Moon is a gathering spot and breakfast place in one, patronized by locals and out-of-towners alike, who return here every time they visit the 'dacks. The reason? It may not hit you until you start digging into the big, fluffy omelets or huge stacks of moist pancakes. Oh yes, and the coffee is amazing. Just be warned: It's easy to get hooked on this place.

46 Main St., Saranac Lake. ✆ **518/891-1310.** Omelets and sandwiches $4–$8. AE, DISC, MC, V. Mon–Fri 7am–3pm; Sat–Sun 8am–2pm.

Players Sports Bar & Grill ★ *Kids* AMERICAN   This is very simply the cheapest eats-with-a-view place in Lake Placid. Set downstairs from Main Street right at water level, Players is a simply decorated place that serves up the basics as you gaze out at the water. Come here to chow on burgers, ribs, sandwiches, and salads. You'll find everything from barbecued chicken to pulled pork to hot wings and nachos.

2405 Main St., Lake Placid. ✆ **518/523-9902.** Sandwiches $6–$8. AE, MC, V. Daily 11am–11pm in summer; closes earlier in the off season.

LAKE PLACID AFTER DARK

There are a few fun places to grab a drink in Lake Placid. **Dancing Bears Lounge** in the Lake Placid Hilton (© **518/523-4411**) offers live music on Friday and Saturday nights from 8pm to midnight. The **Lake Placid Pub and Brewery,** 14 Mirror Lake Dr. (© **518/523-3813**), brews up some good ales (try the Ubu Ale) and offers two floors of partying. *Hint:* It's quieter downstairs. **Zig Zags,** 130 Main St., Lake Placid (© **518/523-8221**), is a fun place to drink for the under-30 crowd. And **Roomers,** 137 Main St. (© **518/523-3611**), is the town's nightclub, where dancing lasts till the wee hours. But if your idea of a good time consists of cozying up to a fire with a nice glass of wine or fine liqueur, your place is **The Cottage,** 5 Mirror Lake Dr. (© **518/523-2544**), part of the Mirror Lake Inn, set on the water across the street from the hotel. Inside it's quaint, and there's also an outdoor patio—perfect in summer.

3 Thousand Islands

30 miles NW from Watertown; 90 miles N from Syracuse

While everyone has heard of the 'dacks, even longtime Empire State dwellers may stare blankly at mention of the Thousand Islands and ask "Is that where the salad dressing came from?" (The answer is yes; see "The Skinny on Salad Dressing," below.)

Salad dressing notwithstanding, there's also another group of folks who are absolutely passionate about the region. At first glance, it's easy to see why: With hundreds of islands dotting the miles-wide St. Lawrence River, it makes for one of the most beautiful backdrops in the state. How many islands are there? It depends on who you ask and how they define "island." Is an island a rocky outcropping that sticks out of the water? Is it visible 365 days a year? Does there have to be vegetation on it? There's some debate: Everyone agrees there are at least 1,000 islands and some say as many as 1,800. However, everyone agrees that two-thirds of these land masses belong to Canada, so there shouldn't be any international incidents. Should you cross the border to enjoy the islands? You can, but it's not necessary as it is at Niagara Falls—you'll find essentially the same things on either side.

The islands were carved out some 10,000 years ago, when an ancient river was forced to change course and a new channel was formed, allowing water into areas where mounds of granite had been left by a retreating glacier. Ancient people called it "The Garden of the Great Spirit," but it was those extraordinary explorers, the French, who called it the Thousand Islands.

While the region is beautiful, frankly it's not as much fun as its park neighbor to the east. First, most of the islands are privately owned—so look, but don't touch. Also, the river completely freezes over in winter as temperatures drop to below zero, making this area essentially a summertime-only destination; most hotels and restaurants don't fully open until Memorial Day, and the season lasts just through mid-October. After that, most places close their doors and locals head to Watertown or Syracuse to work—one village on the Canadian side drops to a population of three.

You won't find mountains to climb or many trails to hike; there are no natural beaches, and few swim in the river. But the boating and fishing are unbeatable; in fact, this area offers some of the country's best fishing, with record-size salmon and muskie just waiting to be caught.

Like the Great Camps of the Adirondacks and the heyday of Buffalo, the Thousand Islands saw its most glamorous time 100 years ago, when the Industrial Revolution created New York State millionaires who discovered the concept of leisure travel.

Wealthy city dwellers would come by private rail car and be swept off by private water taxi to large, glamorous hotels. Europeans called it the Venice of the New World: People named Kellogg and Dodge owned islands, as did the founders of Neiman-Marcus and the inventor of Lifesavers candy. They left behind gorgeous mansions, oddly referred to as "cottages." Unfortunately, all of the classic grand hotels burned to the ground years ago and the area is now dominated by motels. The Thousand Islands' current claim to fame is being the busiest freshwater shipping lane in the world.

While the Seaway Trail stretches all the way up the St. Lawrence, the heart of the Thousand Islands region is in the "tri-cities": the small towns of Cape Vincent, Clayton, and Alexandria Bay, with Alex Bay being the heart of it all.

ESSENTIALS
GETTING THERE

BY CAR   I-81 shoots you north from the New York State Thruway very quickly, passing through Watertown straight up to the Thousand Islands Bridge, which crosses to Canada. Watertown, 30 miles south, is the closest city to the region but is served only by **Greyhound** (© 800/231-2222). The terminal is at 540 State St. Otherwise, Syracuse is the closest big city, so the major airport in the area is **Syracuse Hancock International** (© 315/454-4330), about 90 miles south, and serviced by **American Eagle** (© 800/433-7300), **Continental** (© 800/525-0280), **Delta** (© 800/221-1212), **JetBlue** (© 800/538-2583), **Northwest** (© 800/225-2525), **United Express** (© 800/241-6522), and **US Airways** (© 800/428-4322). Grab a rental car from **Avis** (© 800/331-1212), **Budget** (© 800/527-0700), **Dollar** (© 800/800-3665), **Enterprise** (© 800/325-8007), **Hertz** (© 800/654-3131), **National** (© 800/227-7368), or **Thrifty** (© 800/847-4389).

VISITOR INFORMATION   The **1000 Islands Welcome Center,** 43373 Collins Landing, Alexandria Bay (© **800/847-5263** or 315/482-2520; www.visit1000islands.com), is your informational hub, conveniently located next to the Thousand Islands Bridge. It's open from May to mid-October daily from 8am to 6pm, and mid-October to April, Monday to Friday from 8am to 4:30pm.

GETTING AROUND   I-81 passes right through the heart of the region and is the road to take to cross into Canada over the Thousand Islands Bridge. Otherwise, cut off on Route 12, the road that passes through the Alexandria Bay and Clayton, becoming 12E as it follows the water down to Cape Vincent.

⌒ Fun Fact   The Skinny on Salad Dressing

Yes, Thousand Island dressing did indeed originate in these here parts—to be specific, in the town of Clayton. A fishing guide named George LaLonde offered this new and unusual dressing as part of his shore dinners served after a long day of fishing. The dressing went public at the hotel that's now called the 1000 Islands Inn, and the recipe ended up in the hands of George Boldt, Thousand Islands resident and owner of New York City's Waldorf=Astoria Hotel, who put it on his hotel's menu. You can still get "original recipe" dressing at the 1000 Islands Inn: Only 5,000 bottles are produced each season and are sold between mid-May and mid-September for $6.95 each.

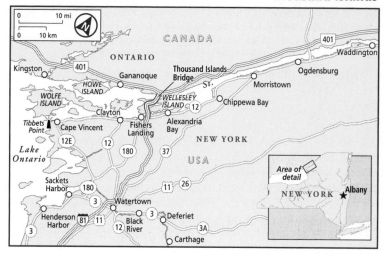

Thousand Islands

MUSEUMS & OTHER ATTRACTIONS

Antique Boat Museum ✪✪✪   Boating enthusiasts simply cannot skip this museum, which contains the largest collection of inland freshwater boats in the U.S. Even people with just a passing interest in boats, or those who appreciate gorgeous woodwork, will like this place. More than 250 boats grace the property, including a Chippewa dugout canoe dating from 1860 and the world's largest runabout, along with old rowboats and sailboats. There are Chris Crafts and Gar Woods, 1920s racing boats, and other rare breeds, like a 100-year-old, 110-foot houseboat owned by Andrew McNally (of Rand McNally fame). Try your hand at rowing a St. Lawrence skiff or (for an extra charge) take a speedboat ride. Show up in August and you can catch the antique-boat show, the town's biggest event and the oldest wooden-boat show in the U.S.

750 Mary St., Clayton. ✆ 315/686-4104. Admission $12 adults, $11 seniors, $6 children 7–12, free for children under 7. Mid-May to mid-Oct daily 9am–5pm.

Boldt Castle ✪   One of the last remaining symbols of true American grandeur in the Thousand Islands, this sprawling stone mansion built by Waldorf=Astoria Hotel owner George C. Boldt casts a regal presence over Heart Island and the shoreline of Alexandria Bay. With turrets, 365 windows, a Gaudí-like kid's playhouse, its own power house, and formal gardens, the castle and all its pieces are gorgeous—and look entirely out of place today. The home comes with a sad tale: Boldt had the castle built over the course of 4 years to give to his wife on her birthday in 1904—Valentine's Day—but she died a month before and the castle, 80% complete, was never occupied. After falling into disrepair, it's been slowly restored, but by design will never be more than 80% complete. The few restored areas are gorgeous: There's an oval stained-glass window in the foyer ceiling, a formal dining room, and an impressive billiards room. But most of the house is still gutted, so you won't spend as much time as expected during your self-guided tour. Still, bring a picnic lunch and spend some time on the 5-acre island's grounds. Then take a shuttle from Heart Island to the Yacht House and check out Boldt's amazing collection of antique wooden boats.

Heart Island. ✆ **800/847-5263**. Admission $5.75 adults, $3.50 children 6–12. Mid-May to end of June and Sept to mid-Oct daily 10am–6:30pm; July–Aug daily 10am–7:30pm. Yacht House admission is $3 adults, $2 children; mid-May to end Sept daily 10:30am–6:30pm. Uncle Sam Boat Tours, on the water in Alexandria Bay (✆ 315/482-2611), runs a shuttle for the 10-min. trip to the castle, with frequent departures mid-May to mid-Oct for $7.

Frederick Remington Art Museum ✪

You'd expect to find an impressive collection of Remington's Western-themed paintings and bronzes in the town he called home for many years, and fans of that genre won't be disappointed. Cowboys, Indians, and the horses they rode on are depicted in lifelike grandeur, cast in action poses for eternity. But what makes this museum interesting is its treasure-trove of work that only die-hard fans know about: Remington's later-in-life Impressionist landscape paintings of his beloved New York State North Country. You'll also get a look at some of the tools, furniture, and artifacts from his studio.

303 Washington St., Ogdensburg. ✆ **315/393-2425**. Admission $8 adults, $7 seniors and students, free for children under 6. May–Oct Mon–Sat 10am–5pm, Sun 1–5pm; Nov–Apr Wed–Sat 11am–5pm, Sun 1–5pm.

Singer Castle ✪✪

Opened to the public only since 2003, this dramatic medieval castle is worth going out of your way to see. It's a stunning creation, made of the same granite used for Boldt Castle and erected at the same time in the first years of the 20th century. Unlike its sister castle, however, Singer was actually occupied, and it's still furnished with period pieces. Its builder and owner, Frederick Gilbert Bourne, was a self-made millionaire who became the director and president of the Singer Sewing Company at age 36. He bought the island and built this four-story, 28-room gem with a four-story tower as a retreat for himself and his family. It's a sprawling, beautiful creation, with plenty of parking space for his boats and oddities like underground passageways and dungeons. You have to take a tour, but it's an interesting one: Guides point out Bourne's secret passageways and peepholes used to spy on guests.

Dark Island. ✆ **315/324-3275**. Admission $12 adults, $11 seniors, $6 children 4–12, free for children under 4. No strollers allowed. Mid-May to mid-June and early Sept to mid-Oct Sat–Sun only 10am–5pm; mid-June to early Sept 10am–5pm daily. Private boaters can land anytime; Uncle Sam Boat Tours, on the water in Alexandria Bay (✆ 315/482-2611), runs a 3½-hr. 2-castle tour with a 1-hr. stop at Singer ($28 adults, $14 kids), including admission to Singer. Boat departs at 10am and 2pm Sat–Sun from end of May to end of June and early Sept to mid-Oct. Departs daily early July to early Sept.

Thousand Islands Museum

This tiny museum is only worth a half-hour of time, but to anyone with an interest in the area's history, it does have some interesting displays and artifacts. You'll find remnants of the grand old Frontenac Hotel, lots of duck decoys (a tribute to the importance of hunting in the area), and an old skiff used for waterfowl hunting and fishing, as well as old lures and hooks.

312 James St., Clayton. ✆ **315/686-5794**. Suggested admission $2 adults, $1 seniors and students, free for children under 6. Early May to Columbus Day daily 9am–5pm; mid-Oct to late Dec daily 10am–4pm.

1000 Islands Skydeck ✪ *Kids*

Every place with a view must have an observation tower, right? Even the relatively undeveloped Thousand Islands have a candy-cane-looking deck hovering high in the sky. Take the elevator up 400 feet and on a good day you'll get a 25-mile view over the St. Lawrence River. Three decks (one of them is enclosed) let you take in the scattered islands sitting in the river. You do have to cross the Canadian border to get here, so bring your passport.

Hill Island, Lansdowne, Ontario. ✆ **613/659-2335**. Admission C$8.95 ($7.90) adults, C$4.95 ($4.40) children 6–12, free for children under 6. Daily mid-Apr to late Oct 9am–dusk.

SPORTS & OUTDOOR PURSUITS

BOAT TOURS   Lots of tour ships run the island circuit all summer, offering close-up views of the islands and occasionally interesting narration peppered with the standard bad jokes. You can stop at newly opened Singer Castle, as well as Boldt Castle (with an unlimited stop to jump off and check out the grounds), Millionaire's Row (with amazing mansions, called "cottages"), and interesting points like **Tom Thumb Island**—the region's smallest at 3 square feet. You'll cross over into Canadian waters, pass under the international bridges, and see that some islands are just big enough for a shack, while others are a whopping 45 square miles in area. Go with **Uncle Sam Boat Tours** ♠♠, 45 James St., Alexandria Bay (② **315/482-2611**), and those 12 and under will get to drive the boat for a few seconds and get a captain's license. The two-nation, 2-hour tour is $16; a 1-hour tour is $12. Uncle Sam also offers lunch and dinner cruises ($27–$35).

FISHING   To say that the St. Lawrence is a haven for fishermen would be an understatement. The creatures that ply these waters are the main reason many people venture up this way during the season (which generally runs Apr–Nov)—it's truly a world-class area for fishing. Why? Because of areas like Henderson Trench, a glacier-cut area west of Henderson Harbor between Stony Island and Stony Point, which averages 120 feet in depth. In late summer, the waters attract mature king salmon; as they wait for their ancient call to head up the Black River to spawn and die, they gorge themselves and grow to some 30 pounds or more. What other beasts will you encounter? In eastern Lake Ontario, you'll hook salmon, lake trout, steelhead, and walleye. On the St. Lawrence, there's walleye, pike, perch, muskellunge (get your muscles ready—these grow up to 35 lb.), and bass. In the inland waters, expect trout, walleye, muskellunge, and pike. Some of the less expensive fishing charters are out of Clayton: **Ferguson Fishing Charters** (② 315/686-3100), **St. Lawrence Charters** (② 315/686-1216), and **1000 Islands Fishing Charters** (② 877/544-4241).

GOLF   The flat, lush riverside terrain makes for some nice golf courses. Play in the middle of the river out on Wellesley Island at the **Thousand Islands Country Club,** 21496 Clubhouse Dr. (② **800/928-TICC;** www.ticountryclub.com), which boasts two 18-hole courses. Greens fees are $21 to $31 weekdays, $27 to $37 weekends. Or try the par-71 **C-Way Golf Club,** Route 12, Clayton (② **315/686-4562;** www.cway resort.com), where greens fee are $17 to $19.

KAYAKING   Get an up-close-and-personal tour of the islands as you skim along the surface in a kayak. With all the water traffic out here, especially the enormous tankers, it's good to go with a guide. Besides, it's easy to get lost among all the islands! Kayak past **Grass Point Marsh** and keep an eye out for wildlife as you work your way toward historic **Rock Island,** with some of the area's most beautiful cottages. Paddle through the **French Creek Wildlife Preserve** and look for birds. Or take on something seriously adventuresome and spend the day circumnavigating the region's third-largest land plot, **Grindstone Island.** Go with **T.I. Adventures,** 1011 State St., Clayton (② **315/686-2000**).

RAFTING   The Thousand Islands are home to some of the nation's most renowned white water, namely the **Black River Canyon.** From May to October, the Black gushes with pounding white water, and scores of paddlers fly down it on rafts. It's Class III and IV, which means there's some serious rollicking going on (and you must be at least 14 years old to go). As you cruise through Rocket Ride and Knife's Edge, you'll see fabulous waterfalls cascade from the canyon walls. Go with **Whitewater Challengers** (© **800/443-RAFT** or 315/639-6100); it's $56–$69 for a day trip. You can also go with **ARO Adventures** (© **800/525-RAFT**).

ESPECIALLY FOR KIDS

Check out the **Family Fun Park at Colonial Village** (578 State Hwy. 11B, east of Potsdam; © **315/265-PARK**), with its go-karts, laser tag, and a virtual roller coaster. In the winter, there's ice-skating. You can get your speed-on at **Alex Bay Go-Karts** on Route 12, ¼ mile north of the Thousand Islands Bridge (© **315/482-2021**). Or get lost in the 7-foot-high hedges of **Mazeland,** also on Route 12, ¾ mile north of the bridge (© **315/482-2186**).

WHERE TO STAY

The old Frontenac Hotel was a 300-room grande dame patronized by Vanderbilts and President U.S. Grant at the turn of the 20th century. Unfortunately, the Frontenac and other grand hotels were all claimed by fire, so you won't find any old classics like the Adirondacks' Sagamore. The historic properties were replaced by motels and two-story resorts, which have the benefit of being on the water, but generally promise little else. Fortunately, there are a couple of gems (reviewed below). Few spots are open year-round, and virtually all hotels require a 2-night minimum stay on summer weekends.

For chain options, you'll have to stay near Watertown, a 30-minute drive from the Thousand Islands, where you'll find a **Microtel,** 8000 Virginia Smith Dr. (© **800/ 771-7171** or 315/629-5000). Farther north in Ogdensburg, there's a **Quality Inn,** 6765 State Hwy. 37 (© **877/424-6423** or 315/393-4550).

EXPENSIVE

Hart House 🌟🌟🌟 *(Finds)*   Overlooking the 1000 Islands Golf Course on huge Welles-ley Island, this wood-shingled inn is a luxurious getaway off the beaten track. The inn is actually what remains of a mansion where Waldorf=Astoria owner George Boldt lived while his Heart Island castle was being built. In the small, nonsmoking rooms, you'll find nice touches like Tiffany-style lamps, propane fireplaces, and old-time radios. Opt for one of the rooms in the "luxury area," which are nicer and larger, with added ameni-ties like sleigh or canopy beds, whirlpools, skylights, and sitting areas. The Hart Room has a deck overlooking the golf course, while the Kashmir Garden Suite is one of the most romantic rooms I've seen. Dramatic without being cheesy, it has an elaborate canopy bed and huge bathroom with gorgeous hand-painted walls, a whirlpool, and a propane fireplace that can be seen from both bedroom and bathroom.

P.O. Box 70, Wellesley Island, NY 13640. © 888/481-LOVE. Fax 315/482-LOVE. www.harthouseinn.com. 8 units. May–Oct $155–$325 double; Nov–Apr rates may be lower depending on area activities. Rates include full breakfast. Packages available. 2- to 3-night minimum summer weekends. AE, DISC, MC, V. From I-81, take exit 51 on Wellesley Island to the stop sign and turn right. Turn left at the next stop sign. Turn right on Club Rd. **Amenities:** Restaurant; free use of bikes. *In room:* A/C, TV/VCR or DVD (in some units), hair dryer, no phone.

Riveredge 🌟🌟🌟   Sitting on the water in the heart of Alexandria Bay, these are the area's most luxurious accommodations, boasting two pools and a great restaurant. The very comfortable (though cookie-cutter standard) rooms, with decent-size bathrooms, are in the middle of a face-lift, as the Florida pinks and blues of the previous owners give way to creams and earthen tones of its current Kentucky owners. All are fitted with elegant blonde wood furniture and comfortable beds and balconies with water views (request one with a view of Boldt Castle). Even the Jacuzzi rooms feel elegant and not at all tacky. Standard rooms have a desk and sitting chairs; the concierge-level floors have a cool circular staircase and loft, but no desk.

17 Holland St., Alexandria Bay, NY 13607. © 800/ENJOY-US or 315/482-9917. Fax 315/482-5010. www.riveredge.com. 129 units. Late June to early Sept $175–$215 double, $209–$259 suite; early Sept to late Oct $139–$179 double, $169–$259 suite; late Oct to late Apr $79–$119 double, $99–$129 suite; late Apr to late June $139–$179 double, $169–$259 suite. Packages available. 2-night holiday weekend minimums. AE, DC, DISC, MC, V. Free valet parking. At Rte. 12 and Church St. turn left, turn right onto Walton St. and left onto Holland St. Pets allowed with a $20 fee. **Amenities:** Restaurant; lounge; small indoor and heated outdoor pools; tiny fitness area; 2 Jacuzzis; concierge; small business center; limited room service; massage; concierge-level floor. *In room:* A/C, TV w/pay movies, dataport, coffeemaker, hair dryer, iron, safe.

MODERATE

Edgewood *kids* Recently purchased out of bankruptcy, this 40-acre waterfront property is being completely renovated, with exciting results. Set back from the road, the grounds are nice and quiet. All rooms have balconies or porches, and many look directly over the water—some people even fish from their balconies! Some rooms boast mahogany decks and cedar posts, giving an upscale, woodsy touch to the roomy but otherwise basic sleeping areas. Done in earthy greens and browns, the guest rooms are simply furnished with industrial carpeting, scratchy sofas, and wildlife stencils on the walls. But the rooms have a fine deck, so you'll hardly want to sit indoors. The Edgewood also has a great lounge and snack bar with a huge deck overlooking the water.

Edgewood Park Rd., Alexandria Bay, NY 13607. © 888/EDGEWOOD or 315/482-9923. www.1000islands.com/edgewood. 101 units. July–Aug Sun–Thurs $89–$229 double, $259 suite, Fri–Sat $119–$249 double, $299 suite; May–June and Sept–Oct Sun–Thurs $69–$179 double, $209 suite, Fri–Sat $89–$209 double, $249 suite. July–Aug 2-night weekend minimum. AE, DISC, MC, V. **Amenities:** 2 restaurants; 2 lounges; large outdoor pool. *In room:* A/C, TV, hair dryer, iron.

Pine Tree Point Resort This sprawling resort feels a bit rusty at the hinges, with heavy antique velvet furnishing and a dark atmosphere, but its location just outside of town and among the pine trees is key. Fortunately, the dining room and patio don't feel so dark, and some rooms have balconies for enjoying the view. Each room is slightly different, but all have a motel feel to them (some with worn vinyl furnishings, some with old TVs). Try to score a room with great outdoor space: No. 201 has a huge balcony with an amazing castle view and no. 311 has an enormous split-level deck. In general, go for a room in the newer "Chateau" or "Cliff" buildings. Cottages have knotty pine walls and kitchenettes, but surprisingly not that much more space, so they don't end up being a great investment.

P.O. Box 99, 70 Anthony St., Alexandria Bay, NY 13607. © 888/PINE-BAY or 315/482-9911. Fax 315/482-6420. www.pinetreepointresort.com. 99 units. Mid-June to Labor Day $119–$209 double, $139 and way up cottage; mid-May to mid-June and Labor Day to Columbus Day $99–$189 double, $119 and way up cottage. Packages available. 2-night summer weekend minimum. AE, DC, DISC, MC, V. Closed mid-Oct to Mother's Day. Pets allowed in some rooms. **Amenities:** Restaurant; lounge; outdoor heated pool; small exercise room; Jacuzzi; sauna; video arcade; limited room service. *In room:* A/C, TV, dataport, kitchenette (in some units), coffeemaker, hair dryer (in most units).

INEXPENSIVE

Capt. Thomson's Resort Occupying the prime waterview grounds of the historic Frontenac Hotel, this two-story motel is decidedly less glamorous but has an equally grand view. Rooms are nothing more than standard motel-type accommodations—industrial carpeting, IKEA-ish furniture, cramped bathrooms—but with historic photos on the walls. The payoff is in the views: Those rooms not facing the parking lot offer picture-perfect scenes of the river and islands.

Moments **A Fishin' Tradition**

In this hugely popular fishing destination, it only makes sense to find tradi-tions surrounding the consumption of fish. One that began in the early 1900s is that of the shore dinner: River guides would set out in their skiffs, fish all morning, and set up on one of the islands to prepare and eat the feast. Thankfully, this tradition continues today.

Here's how it works: After a full morning of fishing, you'll stop on a deserted or nearly deserted island and relax around picnic tables as the guide sets up, starting with a fire. Traditional shore dinners begin with the guide putting sliced fatback in the skillet—100% fat from the back of a pig. Why all fat? The grease that's rendered from the fatback is used to fry the fish and dessert. As the fat fries, slices of bread are loaded up with sliced onion and pieces of fat and folded into a sandwich. There's your appetizer. You may also enjoy a salad (with Thousand Island dressing, of course). Meanwhile, the guide is frying up the just-caught fish, as well as cooking potatoes and corn on the cob.

As you chow on the fish, dessert preparations begin. Eggs, sugar, and cream go into a dish, along with bread that has been drying in the sun. When the mixture is thrown into the hot fatback grease, the batter puffs up, making the French toast–like concoction resemble a puff pastry. Top it with butter, maple syrup, cream, and brandy. *Mmmm.*

Note: Most of the fishing companies mentioned in "Fishing," above, offer a traditional shore dinner for an extra charge.

47 James St., P.O. Box 160, Alexandria Bay, NY 13607. ℂ **315/482-9961.** Fax 315/482-5013. www.captthomsons.com. 68 units. Late June to early Sept $75–$198 double; May to late June and early Sept to mid-Oct Sun–Thurs $49–$128 double, Fri–Sat $64–$158 double. Packages available. 2-night minimum weekends. AE, DC, DISC, MC, V. Closed mid-Oct to May. **Amenities:** Restaurant; outdoor heated pool; limited room service. *In room:* A/C, TV, 2 units with kitchenettes, coffeemaker.

Channelsyde Motel   This small motel takes advantage of its riverside location without breaking the bank. It's set on a large lawn with a small beach, and you can go swimming in the river or just relax on one of the lawn chairs. Rooms are done in light colors and floral patterns. They're hardly huge and are set up motel-style, but are not uncomfortable. Still, the big benefit to the Channelsyde is its location, 3 miles from downtown Alex Bay and just steps from the water.

21061 Pt. Vivian Rd., Alexandria Bay, NY 13607. ℂ **315/482-2281.** www.channelsyde.com. 14 units. Mid-June to Labor Day $72–$105 double; early Sept to mid-June $52–$72 double. 2-night minimum on summer weekends. DISC, MC, V. **Amenities:** Restaurant. *In room:* A/C, TV, fridge.

CAMPGROUNDS

Fortunately, some very choice properties in this region are state parklands, making for fantastic campsites with great views. One of the best options is **Long Point State Park,** 7495 State Park Rd., Three Mile Bay (ℂ **315/649-5258**), on a long narrow peninsula facing one of Lake Ontario's bays. With 87 campsites, only 16 of them are electric, assuring a relatively peaceful experience. **Cedar Point State Park,** 36661

Cedar Point State Park Dr., Clayton (© **315/654-2522**), also offers some tent sites right on the water. Off by itself is **Association Island RV Resort and Marina,** 15530 Snowshoe Rd., Henderson (© **800/393-4189** or 315/955-6522), which juts out into Lake Ontario. The entire island is devoted to camping, but with 305 RV sites, along with cottages and a marina, you'll hardly be alone.

WHERE TO DINE

With few exceptions, restaurants here follow the hotel trend—decent and reliable without being anything fancy. Only a few are located right on the water. But these places do have personality: They're local hangouts where menus give inside jokes about residents and where most meals come with a loaf of bread for carving and a presentation of relishes that you may or may not want to spoon onto your plate. But try to at least nab one dinner on the river as the sun sets—it makes for a magical moment.

EXPENSIVE

Clipper Inn ☆☆ AMERICAN   Ask most locals where they go for a "night out" and they'll direct you to this building on Route 12. The nicest place not on the water, the Clipper definitely caters to a hometown crowd, with references to locals and inside jokes typed on the menu specials page. A recent expansion has added to the once-small dining room: Get a table in back, where fans and a huge skiff hang from the ceiling. It's the type of place that calls its own appetizers unnecessary, and they are, since food comes with salad, a loaf of warm bread, and the de rigueur relishes (which are better than average). The menu is standard American but has some dashes of brilliance, like the Chicken Alaska, with crabmeat, broccoli, and béarnaise sauce. There's also scrod prepared several different ways. Homemade desserts are good; the white-chocolate raspberry bread pudding with white-chocolate sauce is not to be missed. One drawback: The service, while friendly, is frustratingly slow.

126 State St., Clayton. © **315/686-3842**. Reservations suggested. Main courses $18–$35. AE, DC, DISC, MC, V. Early Apr to late Oct daily 5–10pm.

MODERATE

Captain Thomson's ☆ *Kids* AMERICAN   To reach this fun floating restaurant, you have to step across the creaking docks. Inside it's dark and candlelit, but the wide-open space makes it less romantic and more family-friendly. Go with the chicken tenders or order a Cajun prime rib, the crab legs, or sea scallops. There's no need for appetizers, since dinners come with bread, vegetable, baked or mashed potatoes, rice, or fries, and a tossed salad. In fact, after all that, you may not have room for the entree! But for the huge appetite or for sharing, choose some nice appetizers such as baked brie topped with strawberry sauce and crab-stuffed mushroom caps topped with a cheese sauce.

45 James St., Alexandria Bay. © **315/482-9961**. Main courses $11–$24; lunch $6–$9. AE, DC, DISC, MC, V. Mid-May to mid-Oct daily 7am–9pm (1 hr. later in high season).

Cavallario's Steak House ☆ AMERICAN   While steaks are the specialty in this large restaurant with a faux castle facade, the menu actually features only a few red-meat options; the rest focuses on fish, chicken, and veal. You can even get an entire "shore dinner" brought to your table. While the standard menu offers no surprises, the well-prepared food gets high marks. You'll find sautéed honey-mustard chicken breast topped with macadamia nuts, along with fish dishes like broiled salmon with a home-made mustard sauce.

26 Church St., Alexandria Bay. ℂ **315/482-9867.** Main courses $13–$25. AE, DC, DISC, MC, V. May–Oct daily 5–9pm (1 hr. later in high season).

Foxy's (Finds) (Kids) AMERICAN   Another local favorite that's tucked between Clayton and Alexandria, Foxy's is the best midrange restaurant on the water, and those lucky enough to find it come back year after year. Unfortunately, there's very little outdoor seating, but come for the sunset outside the many windows. The food is better than the plastic tablecloths and paper napkins would suggest. Lobster bisque comes creamy, spicy, and chock-full of lobster chunks. Entrees include the predictable mix of lasagna, steak, scallops, and haddock. Dishes come simply presented but tasty. Ask about the specials, which tend to be more inventive, like a chicken breast stuffed with cheese, apples, and cranberries. Desserts are generously sized and good, like fried ice cream or turtle cheesecake.

Fishers Landing. ℂ **315/686-1191.** Main courses $10–$20. AE, MC, V. Mother's Day to late Sept daily 4–9pm; open 1 hr. later July–Aug. From Rte. 12, turn west on Rte. 195, at the blinking light between Clayton and Alexandria Bay.

Sackets Harbor Brewing Company BREWPUB   Located in a refurbished railway station of the now-extinct New York Central Railroad and right on the shore of Lake Ontario, this brewpub serves up great views and good food that's complemented by fantastic home-brewed beers. Dine outside on the patio or in the dining room that's decked out in deep reds with lots of wood, brass, and ceiling fans. Sample the signature 1812 amber ale and tuck into homey pub food like a filet mignon over mashed potatoes, a vegetable-crusted halibut, or an angel-hair pasta served scampi style with scallops or shrimp.

212 W. Main St., Sackets Harbor. ℂ **315/646-2739.** Main courses $11–$25. AE, DISC, MC, V. June–Sept daily noon–10pm; rest of year 4:30–10pm daily, open at noon Oct–Nov and Apr–May.

INEXPENSIVE
Aubrey's Inn (Kids) AMERICAN   This homey place with the lumpy booth seat cushions is a local fave that's hopping anytime it's open. Why? Very simple: mammoth portions of good food at an unbelievable price and friendly service to boot. The only water views are of the murals on the walls, but you don't come for the ambience. You're here for the $6 heaping plate of spaghetti or the enormous pork chops or pancakes the size of manhole covers.

550 Broadway, Cape Vincent. ℂ **315/654-3754.** Main courses $6–$14. AE, DISC, MC, V. Winter daily 7am–8pm; summer daily 7am–9pm.

JReck's DELI   The Thousand Islands area's answer to Subway subs. Get 'em piled high with ham, corned beef, or Italian sausage and your favorite toppings, or order up a burger with sides of onion rings or macaroni salad.

29 Market St., Alexandria Bay. ℂ **315/482-3403.** Sandwiches $2.50–$6. MC, V. Summer daily 10am–9pm; winter daily 10am–8pm.

THOUSAND ISLANDS AFTER DARK

There's not much to do here after dark, though some of the bars in Alexandria Bay hop till the wee hours. Check out the **Dockside Pub,** 17 Market St. (ℂ **315/482-9849**), and **Rum Runner Wharf Bar & Grill,** 219 Holland St. (ℂ **315/482-4511**). Or head across the river to Canada, where the **Thousand Islands Playhouse** in Gananoque, Ontario, boasts two theaters: the Springer Theatre, at 690 Charles St. S., and the Firehall Theatre, 185 South St. (ℂ **866/382-7020** or 613/382-7020). They present dramas, musicals, and comedies from May to October. Or try your luck at the **Thousand Islands Charity Casino,** 380 Hwy. 2, Gananoque, Ontario (ℂ **866/266-8422**).

13

Western New York

by Rich Beattie

For most travelers, the main draw to this swatch of New York State is tucked up in its northwest corner: world-famous Niagara Falls. The cascading cataracts draw millions of people every year, and it's a pretty cool sight, whether you're 775 feet above them in the Skylon Tower or down below in the *Maid of the Mist.*

There's long been much to do on the Canadian side of the falls, and a gorgeous new hotel on the American side is breathing life back into Niagara Falls, NY. But the pummeling water isn't the only thing this part of the state has to offer. Buffalo, the area's commercial center, is also its only major city. You may know it simply as the home of the Buffalo chicken wing, but it harbors all kinds of surprises. In the early 20th century, Buffalo was one of the richest cities in America, and it still has a wealth of architectural treasures that warrant a couple days' stay. Frank Lloyd Wright was just one architect who left his mark on the area; fans will definitely want to check out the Prairie-style Darwin D. Martin House and Graycliff in nearby Derby. The city is also trying to forge a renaissance during economically hard times by recovering the glory days of its downtown area. Results are mixed, but there's a lot going on, from renovated hotels to excellent restaurants.

As for the rest of the area, maybe it's the hefty snowfall, the long winters, or something in the water, but western New York is home to some unique characters, unusual museums, and strange foods that are fun to check out.

The legacies don't end there, though. Religious pioneers and other groups have been a major factor shaping the land as well, providing more to explore. Drawn by a rural landscape and gorgeous lake, Methodists arrived in southern New York's Chautauqua in the 1860s and created what is now one of the nation's most preeminent arts retreats, Chautauqua Institution. Elbert Hubbard started a movement of craftsmen in East Aurora, just outside Buffalo, bequeathing a treasure-trove of gorgeous furniture and a tradition of craftsmanship. Mediums flocked to teeny Lily Dale, and now that area is the epicenter for communication with spirits of the deceased. The Amish have set up camp in a small area of the state as well, so it all makes for an interesting drive.

1 Buffalo

70 miles W of Rochester; 398 miles NW of New York City

It's the eighth-largest city for population in America, with more millionaires per capita than any other American city. It's an industrial hub that hosted a world's fair. The country's top architects are flocking here to design and construct landmark buildings, including the world's largest office building.

At least, this could have been said about Buffalo at the turn of the 20th century. It's no secret that this city has seen better days, but the legacy of its past—one that's being renovated with some modern quirks thrown in for good measure—makes Buffalo a worthwhile stop for a couple of days' stay.

I grew up in nearby Rochester, and all I knew about Buffalo was that it was home to the invention of the chicken wing and it got more snow than anywhere else in the universe. My loss. When industrialists realized that the Great Lakes/Erie Canal/Hudson River route was the way to get things from America's heartland to Europe, it inspired a boom. And those businessmen put their money back into the city: They brought Frederick Law Olmsted, fresh off his creation of Central Park in New York City, to design Buffalo's park system. They summoned architects Frank Lloyd Wright, H. H. Sullivan, and E. B. Green to fulfill their every architectural whim for business and personal space, and many of their treasures still stand downtown.

The economy is still struggling, but Buffalo is forging ahead anyway. The Burchfield-Penney Art Center collection is slated to move into a new museum in 2008; the Westside Rowing Club is building a new boathouse based on Frank Lloyd Wright plans (scheduled to open late 2007); and city officials are hoping a museum built around the original terminus of the Erie Canal will open around the same time. In the meantime, you can satisfy yourself architecturally with a walk downtown, and there are a couple of cool hotels and a growing number of very good restaurants. Oh, and just for the record: Chicken wings aren't the only quirky food this city created; and though the city does indeed get some 90 inches of snow each year, it also averages 85 days with temperatures over 75.

ESSENTIALS

GETTING THERE   The **Buffalo Niagara International Airport** (✆ 716/630-6000; www.buffaloairport.com), 10 miles east of downtown, is served by a number of airlines including **JetBlue** (✆ 800/538-2583), which has lots of cheap one-way flights from other parts of New York; **AirTran Airways** (✆ 800/AIRTRAN); **American** (✆ 800/433-7300); **Continental** (✆ 800/525-0280); **Northwest** (✆ 800/225-2525); **Southwest** (✆ 800/435-9792); **United** (✆ 800/241-6522); and **US Airways** (✆ 800/428-4322).

The **ITA Shuttle** (✆ 800/551-9369 or 716/633-8294) can take you from the airport to the downtown hotels. It's $15 per person one-way and shuttles leave every hour on the hour from 6:30am to 10pm. If you'd prefer to rent a car—and you'll need one if you want to get beyond the downtown Buffalo attractions—**Alamo** (✆ 800/327-9633), **Avis** (✆ 800/331-1212), **Budget** (✆ 800/527-0700), **Enterprise** (✆ 800/325-8007), **Hertz** (✆ 800/654-3131), and **National** (✆ 800/227-7368) all have rental counters at the airport.

By car, Buffalo is reachable via the New York State Thruway (I-90).

Amtrak (✆ 800/USA-RAIL) rolls into Buffalo's tiny train station at 75 Exchange St. (at Washington St.).

Greyhound (✆ 800/231-2222) and **New York Trailways** (✆ 800/295-5555) make their way to the station at 181 Ellicott St. (at N. Division).

VISITOR INFORMATION   The **Buffalo Niagara Convention & Visitors Bureau,** 617 Main St. (✆ 800/BUFFALO; www.buffalocvb.org), is located in the Market Arcade downtown. It's open Monday to Thursday 9am to 5pm, Friday 9am to 4pm, and Saturday 10am to 2pm. Drop by and pick up brochures.

GETTING AROUND While Buffalo has a rail and bus system, driving is still recommended. The **Metro Rail** runs along Main Street from HSBC Arena to the South Campus of the University at Buffalo (a SUNY school), with several stops in between. Along Main Street, aboveground, it's free; once it goes underground at the Theater stop, it's $1.50 per ride (exact change not necessary). If you want a taxi, it's best to call, since they're hard to find on the street. Try **Broadway Taxi** (© 716/896-4600).

EXPLORING THE AREA

WALK DOWNTOWN Don't just drive by Buffalo's architectural gems. Take a couple of hours and hoof it downtown to check out the sights—they are truly beautiful. Start at the E. B. Green and William S. Wicks–designed **Market Arcade** at 617 Main St., just north of Chippewa Street. Built in 1922, the arcade now houses shops, cafes,

---

Fun Fact **Where the Buffalo Roam?**

The bushy beasts never even lived in the area. Most think the city's name comes from French explorers, who called the Niagara River *"Beau Fleuve"* (or "beautiful river"). Another possibility? A mistranslation of the Indian word for "beaver," since the words are similar.

---

and the visitor center. Continue south on Main; just south of Chippewa is Green's neoclassical, Beaux Arts **Buffalo Savings Bank** (1901), now the M&T Center. Continue down Main Street past **Lafayette Square** and imagine the great 19th-century orators Daniel Webster and Henry Clay speaking there. Now, on summer Thursdays, there's live music here from 5 to 8:30pm. On your right is the 352-foot **Liberty Building,** adorned with two reduced-scale replicas of the Statue of Liberty. At Church Street, on your right, is the gorgeous **St. Paul's Episcopal Cathedral.** And on your left is the **Ellicott Square** building; with 500,000 square feet, it was the world's largest office building for 16 years after it opened in 1896. Step inside to see the majestic interior courtyard with its glass roof and Italian marble mosaic floor. It's also a good place to stop and try Buffalo's take on the roast beef sandwich, called Beef on Weck, from Charlie the Butcher Express, right in the lobby. Cut over Swan Street to Pearl Street, and on your left is E. B. Green's **Dun Building,** named for Robert Dun, who founded the nation's largest credit-reporting agency, Dun & Bradstreet. Walk north on Pearl Street, and just before Church Street on your left is Louis Sullivan's stunning **Guaranty Building** from 1895, with its terra-cotta tiles. Make a left onto Eagle Street and then an immediate right on Niagara Street, down to the **Buffalo City Hall,** an Art Deco gem with a brightly colored crown. Go up to the 28th-floor observation deck (free) for a great panoramic view of the city (© **716/851-5891;** Mon–Fri 8am–3pm). Continue up Court Street, make a left on to Pearl, and finish with a coffee at **Spot,** 227 Delaware Ave. (© **716/332-2299**), at the corner of Chippewa, where people flock at all times of day and night.

OUTDOOR PURSUITS

BOATING   Unfortunately, Buffalo doesn't have much in the way of a developed waterfront, but you can find out what Lake Erie is all about on a trip aboard the *Miss Buffalo II* sightseeing cruises. Narrated tours and lunch cruises, which provide views of Buffalo's unique architecture, depart from the Erie Basin Marina downtown from July to Labor Day (Tues–Sun). Call © **800/244-8684** or 716/856-6696 (www.miss buffalo.com).

PLAYING IN THE PARKS   In Buffalo's heyday, the city hired New York Central Park designer Frederick Law Olmsted to create a parks system unrivaled at the time. That's exactly what he did. If you only have time for one, **Delaware Park** is a 350-acre gem with wide-open spaces and quiet walkways. On some summer evenings, you can enjoy Shakespearean plays performed alfresco. The other parks are Martin Luther King, Jr., Front, South, Cazenovia, and Riverside.

SPECTATOR SPORTS

Buffalo residents are incredibly passionate about their football and hockey teams, and when the NHL's **Sabres** went deep into the playoffs in 2007, games would fill the stadium and streets with screaming fans. The Sabres play downtown at the HSBC

Downtown Buffalo

NEW YORK • Buffalo ★ Albany

ACCOMMODATIONS ■

Adam's Mark **19**
Comfort Suites
  Downtown **12**
Doubletree by Hilton **7**
Hyatt Regency **15**
The Mansion on
  Delaware **9**

DINING ◆

Anchor Bar **3**
Bacchus **10**
Charlie the Butcher's Kitchen **22**
Cozumel Grill **4**
Louie's Texas Red Hots **2**
Mother's Restaurant **8**
Pearl St. Grill & Brewery **24**
Spot **13**
Tempo **6**

ATTRACTIONS ●

Albright-Knox Art Gallery **1**
Buffalo Transportation/Pierce-Arrow Museum **25**
City Hall **16**
Dun Building **23**
Ellicott Square **22**
Guaranty Building **20**
M&T Center (former Buffalo Savings Bank) **14**
Market Arcade **11**
Lafayette Square **18**
Liberty Building **17**
St. Paul's Episcopal Cathedral **21**
Theodore Roosevelt Inaugural National Historic Site **5**

Fun Fact Sears Model Homes

Between 1908 and 1940, Sears, Roebuck and Co. sold as many as 100,000 build-it-yourself kit homes: Order one up and a full 30,000 pieces, including 750 pounds of nails and 27 gallons of paint and varnish, were sent to your plot of land. A 75-page instruction book showed you how to assemble it. One of them still stands at the corner of Jewett and Parkside, across from Delaware Park.

Center, 1 Seymour H. Knox III Plaza (© **888/GO-SABRES;** www.sabres.com), while the NFL's **Buffalo Bills** play just outside the city in Ralph Wilson Stadium in Orchard Park, 1 Bills Dr., Orchard Park (© **716/649-0015;** www.buffalobills.com).

MUSEUMS

Albright-Knox Art Gallery 🎯🎯🎯   The gorgeous Albright-Knox is one of Buffalo's can't-miss attractions, a treasure-trove of 5,000 works that should attract more attention than it does. This Greek Revival building, with 18 dramatic marble columns on its facade, dates to 1905 and nabs some exhibits that don't even make it to New York City. The Albright has recently intensified its efforts to sell older works and buy more contemporary art, which fit in well at the museum's newer wing that opened in 1962. Gauguin, Picasso, Pollock, de Kooning, and Warhol are all represented in the permanent collection, while some artists of the moment and cutting-edge photographers are shown here as well. The collection is well organized and not overwhelming, but plan on at least a half-day here—and lunch in the excellent cafe.

1285 Elmwood Ave. © 716/882-8700. www.albrightknox.org. Admission $10 adults, $8 seniors and students, free for children under 14, free to all Fri 3–10pm. Wed–Thurs and Sat–Sun 10am–5pm; Fri 10am–10pm.

Buffalo Transportation/Pierce-Arrow Museum 🎯🎯   In the early 20th century, the Pierce-Arrow Company was manufacturing some of America's best high-end cars. It supplied wheels to the White House, the royal families of Japan and Saudi Arabia, and some of the wealthy local industrialists. Now this museum pulls together some of these behemoth autos in its huge open space, along with the bikes and motorcycles the company also made before the Depression sent it spiraling downward. The museum is still trying valiantly to raise enough money to build the only gas station designed by Frank Lloyd Wright. Built to Wright's specs, it's a filling station he designed but never realized in his lifetime.

263 Michigan Ave. (at Seneca St.). © 716/853-0084. www.pierce-arrow.com. Admission $7 adults, $6 seniors, $3 ages 6–17, free for children under 6. Usually Sat noon–5pm; tours at other times may be possible; always call first.

Darwin D. Martin House 🎯🎯🎯   A must for any lover of Frank Lloyd Wright architecture. One of Wright's greatest works, this Prairie-style home was designed and constructed between 1903 and 1906. Wright imagined the 10,000-square-foot residence for Martin, who was one of Buffalo's wealthy industrialists and one of Wright's biggest boosters. Its low-slung profile with an emphasis on the horizontal was—and remains—an amazing piece of architecture. A tour of the inside reveals the architect's genius for expanding spaces and hiding bookcases. A painstaking, masterful restoration has re-created parts of this house from scratch; walking through it truly gives you an appreciation for Wright's genius. With more re-creation (and a new visitor center) on the way, this site will become even more breathtaking.

118 Summit Ave. ✆ **716/856-3858.** www.darwinmartinhouse.org. Admission $15. Reservations strongly recommended. Apr–Nov Wed–Mon 4–6 tours a day; Jan–Mar closed Tues and Thurs, 1–3 tours a day. From downtown, take Rte. 33 east to NY 198 west to Parkside Ave. exit, bear right off Rte. 198 onto Parkside Ave., go 2 lights to Jewett Pkwy., and turn right. Martin House is 2 blocks up at Jewett and Summit.

Pedaling History Bicycling Museum ★★ *Kids*   You don't have to be a two-wheeling fanatic for the world's largest bicycle museum to grab your attention. Amid the crammed collection of historic frames and spokes, you'll find army bikes mounted with machine guns, and unique tandem bikes with side-by-side seating. You'll see folding paratrooper bikes from World War II, the only surviving floating marine bike from the 1880s, and a bicycle built for five. Families can easily spend an hour here perusing the collection and picking the brains of the bike fanatics who run the place.

3943 N. Buffalo Rd. (Rte. 277), Orchard Park. ✆ **716/662-3853.** www.pedalinghistory.com. Admission $7.50 adults, $6.75 seniors, $4.65 children ages 7–15. Apr to mid-Jan Mon–Sat 11am–5pm, Sun 1:30–5pm; mid-Jan to Mar Fri–Sat and Mon 11am–5pm, Sun 1:30–5pm. Closed major holidays. From I-90, take exit 56, go east on Mile Strip Rd., turn right on Rte. 277, go ⅕ mile.

Theodore Roosevelt Inaugural National Historic Site ★   This mansion, the home of Roosevelt's friend Ansley Wilcox, became famous on September 14, 1901, when T. R. was sworn in as the 26th president of the United States in the home's library. Hours earlier, President William McKinley had died by an assassin's bullet, taken at the Pan-American Exposition, and Roosevelt had been summoned to Buffalo. Now the library has been re-created to reflect what it looked like on the inaugural day, and the rest of the home is an interesting glimpse into how Buffalo's wealthiest families lived.

641 Delaware Ave. (between North and Allen). ✆ **716/884-0095.** Admission $5 adults; $3 seniors and students; $1 children 6–14; free for children under 6. Mon–Fri 9am–5pm; Sat–Sun noon–5pm.

WHERE TO STAY

The downtown hotel scene in Buffalo is dominated by a couple of large chain hotels that serve both the convention and visitor populations. However, they're by no means your only options.

Situated in a great locale, right on Millionaire's Row and close to downtown, you'll find **Best Western Inn on the Avenue,** 510 Delaware Ave. (✆ **888/868-3033** or 716/886-8333); **Hampton Inn,** 220 Delaware Ave. (✆ **800/HAMPTON** or 716/855-2223); and **Holiday Inn Buffalo Downtown,** 620 Delaware Ave. (✆ **800/HOLIDAY** or 716/886-2121). A little farther out, you'll find more options, such as **Courtyard by Marriott Buffalo/Amherst,** 4100 Sheridan Dr. (✆ **800/321-2211** or 716/626-2300); **Holiday Inn Express & Suites,** Rossler at Dingens St. (✆ **800/HOLIDAY** or 716/896-2900); and the **Boulevard Inn and Suites,** 3612 Main St. (✆ **716/837-3344**).

EXPENSIVE

Hyatt Regency ★★★   With a prime downtown location right on Main Street, the dramatic 395-room Hyatt soars into the sky and above its competition as the most elegant of the downtown chains. A former office building, it's now a French Renaissance–style structure—with its spectacular glass-topped lobby and sizable rooms. Since it's connected to the convention center, it attracts a business-focused clientele, but its location makes it a great option for the leisure traveler, too. Rooms, though uniformly decorated, aren't cookie-cutter at all, since designers had to transform them from variously shaped offices. Comfy and spacious, the bedrooms have a brand-new feel to them, and at press time the hotel had just begun a $6-million renovation. Grab one above the eighth floor facing Lake Erie and you'll get the added bonus of a fantastic view.

2 Fountain Plaza, Buffalo, NY 14202. ℂ **716/856-1234.** Fax 716/852-6157. www.buffalo.hyatt.com. 395 units. $165–$180 double; $229–$629 suite. Packages available. AE, DC, DISC, MC, V. Self-parking $6. **Amenities:** 2 restaurants; access to nearby health club; small exercise room; small business center; salon; limited room service; laundry service; same-day dry cleaning; executive-level rooms. *In room:* A/C, TV w/pay movies, dataport, coffeemaker, hair dryer, iron.

The Mansion on Delaware ★★★ *(Finds* Buffalo's most luxurious hotel blends right in with the elegant homes on Millionaire's Row; without its tiny—and I mean tiny—sign, you'd never expect to be allowed in the door. It's also one of Buffalo's recent success stories: The 1860s building was brought back from the brink of complete collapse to become the city's swankiest place to stay. The service is excellent, and the sleekly designed (and completely nonsmoking) rooms with their very modern furniture, workstations, and amenities have attracted everyone from Hillary Clinton to Kiefer Sutherland. Big bathrooms are fitted with multihead showers and whirlpool tubs; personalized stationery and business cards make for memorable touches. The "grand" rooms are larger and worth the extra money, and though suites are a little too small for two separate rooms, they come decked out with fireplaces and plasma TVs. My favorites: no. 202, a "premium grand" room with high ceilings and huge floor-to-ceiling bay windows; and no. 212, cozy and quietly situated in the back with a fireplace.

414 Delaware Ave., Buffalo, NY 14202. ℂ **716/886-3300.** Fax 716/883-3923. www.mansionondelaware.com. 28 units. $180–$300 double. AE, DC, DISC, MC, V. Rates include continental breakfast. Free valet parking. **Amenities:** Exercise room; concierge; courtesy car within 3 miles; 24-hr. room service; laundry; same-day dry cleaning. *In room:* A/C, TV/DVD, dataport, coffeemaker, hair dryer.

MODERATE

Adam's Mark ★★ You may think you've died and gone to Las Vegas when you enter the sprawling, 486-room Adam's Mark. This enormous member of the chain clearly caters to the convention crowd, with huge ballrooms and meeting spaces filled with everyone from bridge players to motivational speakers. What's the benefit to you? Since conventioneers rarely leave the hotel, it offers lots of amenities, like a nice pool and exercise area. From the outside, the place looks like an East German bunker, but inside, rooms are comfortable and spacious (if bland and cookie-cutter). And though the Hyatt and Radisson occupy the best locales, this one is also central and downtown.

120 Church St., Buffalo, NY 14202. ℂ **716/845-5100.** Fax 716/845-0310. www.adamsmark.com. 486 units. $79–$209 double; $199–$399 suite. AE, DC, DISC, MC, V. Valet parking $15 per day. **Amenities:** Restaurant; 2 lounges; indoor pool; exercise room; sauna; tour desk; courtesy car; small business center; 24-hr. room service; laundry; same-day dry cleaning; executive-level rooms. *In room:* A/C, TV w/pay movies, dataport, coffeemaker, hair dryer, iron, safe (in some rooms).

Doubletree by Hilton ★ Located across the street from a hospital, the hotel caters to hospital visitors and a corporate crowd, which tend to be longer-term residents. That works out perfectly for leisure travelers, since you'll get added amenities. The decor is simple and plain (think corporate monotone), but rooms are generally quite spacious. All of them have fridges and microwaves, while some have full kitchenettes. You'll also find comfy public areas, like a library where you can sit and read or play board games.

125 High St., Buffalo, NY 14203. ℂ **716/845-0112.** Fax 716/845-0125. $129–$159 double. AE, DC, DISC, MC, V. **Amenities:** Restaurant; small exercise room; game room; concierge; courtesy car; small business center; limited room service; coin-op washers and dryers; same-day dry cleaning. *In room:* A/C, TV w/pay movies, dataport, kitchenette (in some units), fridge, microwave, coffeemaker, hair dryer, iron.

INEXPENSIVE

Comfort Suites Downtown ✦✦   Formerly the Radisson, this hotel gives you plenty of living space in a superb downtown location, right on Main Street, for less than the former owners were charging. While you won't find the same amenities as, say, the Hyatt, the Comfort Suites gives you some of the best bang for your buck in Buffalo. The all-suite hotel offers lots of square footage, and French doors that divide the living room from the bedroom. While you're not paying for exquisite furniture or huge bathrooms, you'll still find plenty of breathing space.

601 Main St., Buffalo, NY 14203. ✆ **800/424-6423** or 716/854-5500. Fax 716/854-4836. www.choicehotels.com. 146 suites. $109–$159 suite. Rates include continental breakfast. AE, DC, DISC, MC, V. Free self-parking. **Amenities:** Restaurant; exercise room; limited room service; laundry service; same-day dry cleaning. *In room:* A/C, TV, dataport, fridge, microwave, coffeemaker, hair dryer, iron.

Holiday Inn, Buffalo International Airport   It's the nicest of the airport hotels, and a location east of the city makes it ideal for those early-morning flights or for spending the night if you're heading east. In true airport-hotel style, it's pretty bland on the outside, but the rooms, though dressed in chain-quality furnishings, are spacious and quiet.

4600 Genesee St., Cheektowaga, NY. ✆ **716/634-6969.** Fax 716/634-0920. www.hibuffaloairport.com. 207 units. $120–$149 double; $149–$189 suite. Packages available. AE, DC, DISC, MC, V. **Amenities:** Restaurant; outdoor heated pool; exercise room; Jacuzzi; sauna; courtesy car; limited room service; coin-op washers and dryers; laundry service; same-day dry cleaning; business-class rooms. *In room:* A/C, TV w/pay movies, dataport, coffeemaker, hair dryer, iron.

WHERE TO DINE

The home of the Buffalo wing, Buffalo is renowned for creating or passionately embracing somewhat suspect food items (watch for a popular homegrown concoction called Beef on Weck, roast beef on a salty *kummelweck* roll). Fortunately, amid the unhealthy oddities, you'll also find that some of the renovations downtown have brought about some excellent, upscale restaurants.

VERY EXPENSIVE

Tempo ✦✦✦ ITALIAN   This newcomer has made a splash on the Buffalo dining scene with its inventive Italian menu and contemporary setting. Exposed brick, modern art, and dark wood floors lend classic touches, while candlelight and jazz strains offer a dash of romance. Start with the homemade ravioli in a tomato vodka cream sauce filled with shrimp and scallops, or two towers of beef carpaccio with arugula and shaved Parmesan. Then continue on to the prosciutto-wrapped filet topped with warm Gorgonzola, served with a homemade gnocchi just slightly fried so that it melts in your mouth. The long wine list (mostly from Italy and California) complements the meal, and desserts are equally well done. This young restaurant has already hit its stride, and people are flocking: Even a Monday night was bustling.

581 Delaware Ave. ✆ **716/885-1594.** Reservations recommended. Main courses $24–$49. AE, DC, MC, V. Closed Sun, open other days at 5pm.

EXPENSIVE

Bacchus ✦✦✦ INTERNATIONAL TAPAS   A hip restaurant in downtown's busiest area, Bacchus is indeed a wine mecca, offering more than 200 bottles, all available by the glass. It's a crowded, sometimes noisy space that combines a bar with a chic candlelit dining room. You can order delicious larger plates of lamb chops and filet or ahi tuna, but the culinary ingenuity is best found in the small plates. They're larger than traditional tapas plates (two per person will do) and trade the typical Spanish flair for innovations like a carpaccio of sirloin with egg crostini, arugula, reggiano cheese, and truffle oil. Crowds form early, but a wait at the classy bar is hardly a bore.

56 W. Chippewa St. ✆ 716/854-WINE. Reservations recommended. Small plates $9–$15; large plates $19–$32. AE, DISC, MC, V. Tues–Sat 5–11pm.

Mothers Restaurant ★★★ *Finds* AMERICAN   Step inside from the alleyway and you'll find a quiet, brick-wall-lined, candlelit hideaway that every local will recommended as historic Buffalo's finest. The handwritten menu boasts a suffusion of flavors and a wealth of ingredients. The grilled lamb rib chops, for example, come with an orzo, toasted almond, and caramelized onion salad and apple-pear compote. The equally complex appetizers shine, too, with offerings like potato gnocchi topped with fresh tomato sauce with mushrooms, peas, hot peppers, and fresh mozzarella. Full dinners served until 3am every night make it ideal for late-night gourmet diners. *Bonus:* There's an outdoor patio.

33 Virginia Place (between Virginia and Allen sts.). ✆ 716/882-2989. Reservations accepted. Main courses $15–$25. AE, MC, V. Mon–Sat 5pm–3am; Sun 2pm–3am.

MODERATE

Cozumel Grill MEXICAN-AMERICAN   While you won't find anything earth-shatteringly amazing on the menu, Cozumel does an above-average job with its basic burritos/taco/fajita menu. You'll often find red and blue corn tortillas, and the salsa is excellent. You can get basic steaks and burgers, but why? The best entrees have a healthy dose of south-of-the-border flair, like the Drunken Chicken, which comes sautéed with Sauza Hornitos tequila, red and green peppers, onions, mushrooms, and sausage.

153 Elmwood Ave., between Allen and North. ✆ 716/884-3866. Reservations accepted. Main courses $8–$22. AE, DC, DISC, MC, V. Sun–Thurs 11am–11pm; Fri–Sat 11am–4am.

Pearl Street Grill & Brewery ★ AMERICAN BREWPUB   One of downtown's most happening scenes, Pearl Street attracts college kids and families alike. Set in an old warehouse with leaded windows, exposed brick, wood beams, and low-level lights, Pearl Street is two floors of nonstop beer-pouring, food-running, and pool playing. The warehouse-cum-microbrewery is a stereotype by now, but Pearl Street pulls it off well. The menu offers basic burgers and salads, and upgrades with tasty pasta and pizza, excellent kielbasa, and more upscale options like grilled Atlantic salmon with lemon dill butter. Definitely sample the beer: The Lake Effect Pale Ale and Trainwreck are both excellent.

76 Pearl St. (at Seneca). ✆ 716/856-BEER. Reservations accepted. Main courses $9–$20. AE, DC, DISC, MC, V. Kitchen opens Mon–Fri at 11am, Sat at noon, and Sun at 3pm and is open until at least 9pm.

INEXPENSIVE

Anchor Bar *Overrated* CHICKEN WINGS   Okay, it's kinda cool to eat chicken wings in the restaurant where they were accidentally discovered in 1964, but the wings are nothing exceptional—after all, there's not much you can do with chicken wings but deep-fry 'em and serve 'em with hot sauce, blue cheese, and celery—and there are certainly nicer places to eat them than in this divey bar. Come only if you want to pay tribute to an American culinary tradition.

1047 Main St. (at North St.). ✆ 716/886-8920. Reservations not accepted. Wings are 20 for $12, 50 for $25; other entrees $11–$18. AE, DISC, MC, V. Mon–Thurs 11am–11pm; Fri 11am–1am; Sat–Sun noon–1am.

Charlie the Butcher's Kitchen ★ DELI   Beef on Weck is one of those "only in Buffalo" creations, and Charlie has made the sandwich into a science—and an experience. What the heck is weck? It's short for *kummelweck,* a German kaiser roll sprinkled with caraway seeds and pretzel salt and baked again for several minutes until crusty. Add sliced, rare roast beef and you'll have the basic sandwich, but Charlie insists on dipping the top of the roll in au jus and adding horseradish. He's set up in the food court of the gorgeous Ellicott building downtown; grab a sandwich and enjoy the Italian mosaic floors and the skylight.

295 Main St. (in the Ellicott Sq. building). 🕐 **716/855-8646.** Beef on Weck $5.50; other sandwiches $4.50–$7.50. AE, MC, V. Mon–Fri 10am–5pm.

Louie's Texas Red Hots HOT DOGS   No, the hot dog wasn't invented here, but Buffalonians have embraced it with an unequaled passion. So forget the Texas reference—this is a Buffalo institution. The dogs do taste better here (all that practice cooking 'em); at Louie's they come nicely seared with mustard, onions, and Louie's special Greek sauce. Best of all, you can "getcha hot dogs" 24 hours a day.

2350 Delaware Ave. 🕐 **716/877-6618.** Hot dogs $1.69. No credit cards. 24 hr.

BUFFALO AFTER DARK
PERFORMING ARTS

Shea's Performing Arts Center, 646 Main St. (🕐 **716/847-1410**), is a gorgeous former movie palace dating from 1926 and built in the style of a European opera house. It now hosts touring shows, concerts, opera, and dance performances. The **Buffalo Philharmonic Orchestra** performs at the acoustically perfect Kleinhans Music Hall, 3 Symphony Circle (🕐 **800/318-9404**), most every week from mid-September to the end of July. For theater, head to **Studio Arena,** 710 Main St. (🕐 **800/77-STAGE** or 716/856-5650), one of the finest regional theaters in the country. Each season (Sept–May) features several productions.

NIGHTCLUBS & LIVE MUSIC

The bar scene is centered around two streets: The most happening is Chippewa Street, downtown, where you'll find loud bars pouring local brew Genesee and others. Try the down-home **Big Shotz,** 45 W. Chippewa St. (🕐 **716/852-7230**), and the more upscale **La Luna,** 52 W. Chippewa St. (🕐 **716/855-1292**). **Crocodile Bar,** 88 W. Chippewa St. (🕐 **716/853-CROC**), is a favorite with the well-dressed, over-25 crowd, due partly to its extensive martini menu. Allen Street is a bit quieter, but you can also find some good bars like **Gabriels Gate,** 145 Allen St. (🕐 **716/886-0602**), and **Colter Bay,** at Delaware and Allen (🕐 **716/882-1330**). This is also where you'll find Buffalo's gay scene, in bars like **Cathode Ray,** 26 Allen St. (🕐 **716/884-3615**). Another good bet for gays: **Club Marcella,** 622 Main St. (🕐 **716/847-6850**), which features drag shows and underwear contests, along with DJs spinning tunes till the wee hours. For live music, join the slightly older set at the **Tralf,** 622 Main St. (🕐 **716/852-2860**), which hosts all sorts of music, comedy, and theater performances. Many acts are local, but sometimes you'll get a national name, like Roomful of Blues or Lisa Loeb, or touring shows, like Shear Madness. The **Lafayette Tap Room,** 391 Washington St. (🕐 **716/854-2466**), is committed to the blues and offers a full schedule of local and national acts in its small space.

2 Day Trips from Buffalo

Since it's only 70 miles or so from Buffalo to the Pennsylvania border, consider making Buffalo your base to explore the area if you don't want to stay in small towns. Niagara Falls, of course, should be one of your destinations and is discussed later, in section 5. Another thing you'll likely want to do is to take a drive either south along Lake Erie or northeast along Lake Ontario—the views over both of these Great Lakes are spectacular. Inland, however, is a different story. Outside the city, the landscape quickly changes into rural farmland and it's not such an exciting drive—you probably won't want to do much random exploring through the back roads. However, there's plenty worth seeing. You'll find quirky museums celebrating everything from the kazoo to Lucille Ball, along with one of the nation's premier educational vacation spots and one of the state's best parks.

ESSENTIALS

GETTING AROUND A car is absolutely essential in this rural part of the state. See "Getting There," in section 1, for car-rental options.

VISITOR INFORMATION **Cattaraugus County Tourism,** 303 Court St., Little Valley (✆ **800/242-4569**), is open Monday to Friday from 8am to 5pm.

MUSEUMS & ATTRACTIONS

Graycliff ★★★ Any worshiper of Frank Lloyd Wright will want to make the pilgrimage to Graycliff. On a 70-foot cliff overlooking Lake Erie, this 1927 home that Wright built for his most generous patron, industrialist Darwin D. Martin, is set on more than 8 acres. The two-story, 6,500-square-foot house was Martin's summer home through the mid-1940s. Full of sunlight and air, with many windows, and long and narrow in plan, the home captures summer light and cool lake breezes. The house also blends into the natural landscape. It's a transitional point from Wright's earlier Prairie style—found in Buffalo's Martin House (p. 396)—to his late concrete designs like Fallingwater in Pennsylvania. It's a fascinating tour, even for those not familiar with Wright's work, and ongoing renovations mean it's just going to keep getting better.

6472 Old Lake Shore Rd., Derby. ✆ **716/947-9217.** www.graycliff.bfn.org. Admission $14 for adults, $10 for students under 23. 1-hr. tours mid-Apr to early Dec daily except Wed. Reservations required. I-90 to exit 57, Rte. 75 north to Rte. 20W, go 7 miles, turn right on S. Creek Rd. to end, turn left on Old Lake Shore Rd.

Herschell Carrousel Factory Museum ★ Lovers of old carousels, bygone ages, or just exquisite woodworking shouldn't miss this museum. The world's only museum housed in an original carousel factory building, this one opened in 1915 to carve wood into fanciful carousel horses. You'll see some 20 hand-carved carousel animals and music-roll production equipment from the Wurlitzer Company. There are also two historic carousels to ride, one dating from 1916.

180 Thompson St., North Tonawanda. ✆ **716/693-1885.** www.carrouselmuseum.org. Admission $5 adults, $4 seniors, $2.50 ages 2–12. Apr to mid-June and early Sept–Dec Wed–Sun noon–4pm; mid-June to early Sept Mon–Sat 10am–4pm, Sun noon–4pm. I-290 to exit 2. Rte. 425 north for 2 miles, left on Christiana, right on Payne, left on Thompson.

Kazoo Museum ★ This museum is one of those upstate quirks that makes the area an interesting exploration. Unless you're a kazoo fanatic—or lover of the offbeat—you probably shouldn't drive out of your way for this museum, but lovers of the unusual will be in heaven. You'll find kazoos of all shapes and sizes: wooden kazoos, liquor-bottle-shaped kazoos that celebrated the end of Prohibition, silver and

No Séances, Please

That's the sign you'll find in the **Maplewood Hotel** in **Lily Dale** ⭐⭐, a tiny Victorian enclave where some 40 registered mediums reside. How did it happen that this small corner of the state became the centerpiece of the spiritualist movement? Was it the isolation of the frontier or just something in the water? Whatever the explanation, the three Fox sisters of sleepy Hydesville in Wayne County created an international stir in 1848 with public exhibitions of their communication with the dead. From these small beginnings, the modern role of a medium evolved.

These days you can visit anytime; the town isn't much to look at, so most of the year you shouldn't bother coming unless you're getting a reading. Summer is the exception, though: From the end of June to early September, travelers descend on the place for daily events that include meditation and healing services, clairvoyant demonstrations, and workshops.

Workshops and speakers cost up to $350 (most are in the $25–$50 range), but you can watch the basic activities just by paying the gate fee of $10. A very basic hotel (occupied by spirits, of course) and private homes can put you up for the night, and there's camping as well. Lily Dale is 1 hour south of Buffalo. For more information, call © **716/595-8721** or visit www.lilydale assembly.com.

gold kazoos, and many more. You can watch them make kazoos on the original equipment (Wed–Fri) and even make your own.

8703 S. Main St., Eden. © 716/992-3960. www.edenkazoo.com/museum.php. Free admission. Tues–Sat 10am–5pm. Take I-90 west to exit 57A, turn left to Rte. 62, turn right.

Lucy-Desi Museum   Yes, tiny Jamestown gave birth to the famous actress and comedienne Lucille Ball, and now this tiny museum celebrates her with video tributes and memorabilia. Learn how Lucy and Desi met and how they collaborated on what the museum calls "the most famous comedy series of all time." Hmm. Still, if you're a fan of *I Love Lucy*, you'll love the collection of Lucy's clothes and the volumes of merchandise produced in connection with the show. If you're not a fan, skip it.

212 Pine St., Jamestown. © 877/LUCY-FAN or 716/484-0800. www.lucy-desi.com. Admission $10 adults, $9 seniors, $7 children 6–18. Mon–Sat 10am–5:30pm; Sun 1–5pm. Take I-90 to exit 59, toward Dunkirk/Fredonia, turn left onto Rte. 60/Bennett Rd., turn right onto Rte. 60N, which turns into N. Main St.; turn left onto E. 2nd St.

Toy Town Museum ⭐⭐ (Kids)   The tiny town of East Aurora is where toy gurus Fisher and Price started their company. Now this small museum preserves some of America's earliest dolls and playthings, as well as some of the latest toy crazes. There's a great play space for the kids, with lots of interactive toys. But adults also love this place: Since the museum exhibits toys by decade from the early 1900s, it's easy to find trinkets from your formative years, an adventure that leads to lots of reminiscing about the toys you had . . . and the ones you always wanted.

636 Girard Ave., East Aurora. © 716/687-5151. www.toytownusa.com. Free admission. Mon–Sat 10am–4pm. From I-90 take exit 54, take Rte. 400 to Maple St. exit, make a right to Girard Ave., and turn left at the blinking signal.

Fun Fact **Watching It Wiggle**

Jell-O was discovered long before Bill Cosby was born, and the world-famous dessert can trace its roots to this area—in particular, the town of LeRoy. A local carpenter stumbled upon the gelatinous stuff in 1897, then sold the patent for just $450; by 1909 Jell-O was a million-dollar industry. For the entire history— likely more than you ever wanted to know—visit the **Jell-O Gallery,** 23 E. Main St. in LeRoy (55 miles from Buffalo; © 585/768-7433). The museum is open April through December, Monday to Saturday from 10am to 4pm, Sunday 1 to 4pm; January to March, Monday to Friday 10am to 4pm. Admission is $4 adults, $1.50 children 6 to 11, free for 5 and under.

SHOPPING

Elbert Hubbard started his furniture-building movement and founded the Roycroft Arts and Crafts Community more than 100 years ago in the tiny town of East Aurora. Now, craftspeople carry on the fine workmanship of the Roycrofters and have made it a big business here. Browse their galleries and shops; with any luck you'll see them at work. Go to **Schoolhouse Gallery & Cabinet Shops,** 1054 Olean Rd. (© 716/655-4080), for some of the most beautiful works. Other craftspeople sell their work at **West End Gallery,** 48 Douglas Lane (© 716/652-5860).

For a step back in time of a different kind, visit **Vidler's 5 & 10,** 676–694 Main St., East Aurora (© 877/VIDLERS). Since 1930, this quaint store has been selling candies, confections, dry goods, and knickknacks. There's even a section of the store with the original wood floors and brass cash register.

The **Amish** maintain a small enclave on the eastern border of Chautauqua County and the western border of Cattaraugus County, bisected by Route 62 in the Conewango Valley area. Drive along Route 62 and you'll run across numerous shops selling cheese, crafts, and baked goods. Shops aren't open on Sunday and the Amish request that you not take photographs.

OUTDOOR PURSUITS

ERIE CANAL EXPERIENCES   Take a ride on the man-made water route that transformed upstate New York. Get on a boat with **Lockport Locks and Erie Canal Cruises,** 210 Market St., Lockport (© 800/378-0352 or 716/433-6155), for the 2-hour experience of being raised through the 49-foot elevation of the Niagara Escarpment in the only double set of locks on the canal (open mid-May to mid-Oct; $14 adults, $8 kids 4–10). Pass under bridges, see water cascade over locks, and travel through the solid walls of the "rock cut." No, it's no speedboat ride, but for anyone who hasn't experienced going through a lock, it's pretty cool. Or go through the **Lockport Cave and Underground Boat Ride,** 2 Pine St. (© 716/438-0174). You'll walk through a 1,600-foot tunnel, blasted out of solid rock in the 1800s, then ride a boat to see the start of geologic cave formations and miner artifacts (open early May weekends only, end of May to mid-Oct daily; $9 adults, $6 kids 4–12).

PARKS   You can explore cliffs, crevices, cavernous dens, and caves of quartz in two parks with tons of the hardened rock. **Rock City Park,** Route 16 South, Olean (© 866/404-ROCK or 716/372-7790), open early May to the end of October, is the world's largest exposure to quartz conglomerate, with gigantic rocks that climb stories high. Admission is $4.50. Native Americans used the rocks as a fortress for protection; now the narrow alleys of rock harbor wildflowers and mountain laurel. **Panama Rocks,** Route 10, Panama (© 716/782-2845), open mid-May to mid-October (admission $6), is the world's most extensive outcrop of glacially cut ocean quartz conglomerate—a technical distinction, as both parks are pretty much the same. Take an hour for either. Or get out among the trees in **Allegany State Park** (© 716/354-9121): Its 65,000 acres, most of it primitive woodland, make it the largest state park in the system, with sand beaches as well as hiking and nature trails.

SKIING   It's not exactly Colorado, or Vermont, or even, well, the Adirondacks. But here's where to go when you absolutely must get your schuss on. At **Kissing Bridge,** in Glenwood (© 716/592-4963; www.kissing-bridge.com), you'll find 36 snow-covered slopes, encompassing 700 acres of terrain and served by nine lifts. And **Holiday Valley,** in Ellicottville (© 716/699-2345; www.holidayvalley.com), has 12 lifts, 53 slopes spread over 1,400 acres, and a 750-foot vertical drop—so you'll get good variety no matter what kind of skiing or riding you like.

WINERIES   It's not just in the Finger Lakes region that you'll find nice upstate New York State wines. The southern shore of Lake Erie, with just a thin strip of soil suitable for grape production, has its own grape-and-wine heritage; the wineries make for a fun stop-off. Check out **Johnson Estate Winery,** 8419 W. Main Rd., Westfield (© 800/374-6569); **Woodbury Vineyards,** 3215 S. Roberts Rd., Fredonia (© 716/679-9463); and **Merritt Estate Winery,** 2264 King Rd., Forestville (© 888/965-4800).

WHERE TO STAY
EXPENSIVE
The Roycroft Inn 🖈🖈🖈 *(Finds*   Get a touch of history and a dash of artistry in your hotel stay. The small country inn in its current form was opened in 1995, but the property dates from 1895, when the Roycroft Arts and Crafts Community was founded by Elbert Hubbard. Hubbard's self-contained community supported hundreds of craftspeople, and he opened his door to those journeying to this craftsman's mecca. Common areas are intimately rustic, with lots of Roycroft originals that you're actually allowed to sit on. Though guest rooms aren't huge, they're hardly cramped. A touch of history is in all of them—they're outfitted with at least one original Roycroft piece, plus some reproductions: heavy, solid wooden pieces that lend a distinguished air to your stay. But there's nothing stuffy about the place—it's comfy and thoroughly modern, as are the sizable bathrooms. The restaurant is fantastic and listed separately, below.

40 S. Grove St., East Aurora, NY 14052. © 716/652-5552. Fax 716/655-5345. www.roycroftinn.com. 29 units. $130–$240 double. Rates include continental breakfast. Packages available. AE, DC, DISC, MC, V. I-90 to Rte. 400 to Maple St. exit, turn right, turn left on Main and make your 1st right onto S. Grove St. **Amenities:** Restaurant; access to nearby health club; limited room service. *In room:* A/C, TV/VCR, dataport, hair dryer, iron.

MODERATE
Old Library 🖈   Right next door to The Old Library Restaurant, a former Carnegie home, this pink house looks decidedly un-Carnegie, as it's more frilly than stately. A historic home dating from 1895, it's been hosting guests only since 1988. Beautifully decorated inside with a rich woodwork of oak, blistered maple, mahogany, and parquet floors, you'll also find stained-glass windows and tons of antiques. None of the units, however, can boast the charm of the public spaces; they are unfortunately carpeted and done in pastel colors, and the standard rooms are quite cramped. Upgrade to one of the huge suites if you can.

120 S. Union St., Olean, NY 14760. ℂ 877/241-4347 or 716/373-9804. Fax 716/373-2462. www.oldlibraryrestaurant. com. 9 units. $75–$85 double; $125–$135 suite. Rates include breakfast. Packages available. AE, DC, DISC, MC, V. I-86 to exit 26, which leads you right onto S. Union St. **Amenities:** Restaurant; lounge; nonsmoking hotel. *In room:* A/C, TV, dataport, hair dryer.

CAMPING

Lake Erie State Park 🏕🏕   Set on high bluffs overlooking Lake Erie, this campground is all about the view. Open daily from May to October, the park has a shoreline of over ¾ mile bordering the shallowest of the Great Lakes. Full of great hiking (and in the winter cross-country skiing) trails, the park is also a prime place to birdwatch: It's a natural stopping place for birds before they fly across the lake. Cabins are primitive, with bunk beds and no hot water, and you must bring your own bedding. If you can get one, grab one of the "prime" sites that line the lake.

5905 Lake Rd., Brockton, NY 14716. ℂ **716/792-9214.** 97 campsites, $13 for nonelectric hookups, $19–$25 for electric. 10 cabins, $63; 1 week minimum cabin rental ($250 late June to late Aug). AE, DISC, MC, V. New York State Thruway W. (I-90) to exit 59 to Rte. 60 north. Left on Rte. 5. Park is located 5 miles west of Dunkirk.

WHERE TO DINE
EXPENSIVE

Roycroft Inn 🏵🏵 AMERICAN   Like the Roycrofters who flocked to the area to make the distinctive furniture that fills the inn, the dishes are simple but well crafted. Get a table in the Larkin Room, which overlooks the serene courtyard garden. The fish is excellent; you can't go wrong whether you choose the seared ahi tuna or applesmoke bacon-wrapped salmon with a maple-and-black-pepper glaze. But landlubbers are hardly out of luck: The lamb chops with a sweet and spicy dark-rum glaze finished with black cherries is a winner. And whatever you do, don't miss desserts. You can order by the sliver, so get a sampling of the amazing cheesecake, pie, and cobbler.

40 S. Grove St., East Aurora. ℂ 716/652-5552. Reservations requested. Main courses $17–$30; lunch $7–$12. AE, DC, DISC, MC, V. Mon–Sat 11:30am–3pm; Sun–Thurs 5–9pm; Fri–Sat 5–10pm; Sun 10am–3pm. Take I-90 to Rte. 400 to Maple St. exit, turn right, turn left on Main and make your 1st right onto S. Grove St.

MODERATE

The Old Library 🏵🏵 AMERICAN   A Carnegie library from 1910 to 1974 in tiny Olean, this gorgeous brick building now houses an excellent restaurant. Fortunately, it has held onto its book-loving roots without getting old and musty. The interior is decorated with ornate woodwork and friezes and laden with antiques. The menu, presented as—what else?—a chapter in a book, offers more than 550 wines and a wealth of food choices, everything from pastas to jumbo lobster tail or a rack of lamb with a Dijon-mustard-and-garlic glaze.

116 S. Union St., Olean. ℂ **877/241-4348** or 716/372-2226. Main courses $11–$30; lunch $6.50–$13. AE, DC, DISC, MC, V. Mon–Fri 11am–3pm; Mon–Sat 4–10pm; Sun 11am–9pm.

Root Five 🏵 AMERICAN   There's nothing like waterfront noshing as the sun sets over Lake Erie. Set on a magical plot of land that's perfect for sunsets, this lakeside joint jumps, especially in summer, when live blues bands rock the place. The large covered patio area provides tons of room to enjoy the water view. With plenty of nachos and potato skins, the menu may seem like typical bar food, and much of it is, but there are upscale choices as well, like a pecan chicken breast with Japanese bread crumbs and raspberry demi-glace, and seafood (the specialty), including excellent crab cakes.

4914 Lakeshore Rd., Hamburg. ℂ **716/627-5551.** Reservations accepted. Main courses $14–$27; lunch $5.25–$8. AE, DISC, MC, V. Daily noon–11pm. Take Rte. 5 south from downtown Buffalo.

INEXPENSIVE

The Silo *(Kids)* AMERICAN   There's more than just kitsch value in this cylindrical coal silo that was transformed into a restaurant in 1998—it's set right on the Niagara River, making for great views. Order up your food inside—choose from burgers, salads, chicken sandwiches, hot dogs, and more—then take it out to the picnic tables that ring the restaurant and chow down overlooking the shimmering water.

115 N. Water St., Lewiston. © **716/754-9680.** Sandwiches $2.20–$5.49. DISC, MC, V. May–Sept 10am–10pm. From the Robert Moses State Pkwy., take Center St. all the way to the water.

Ted's Jumbo Red Hots *(Kids)* HOT DOGS   For more than 75 years, Ted and his local chain have been perfecting the hot dog—and now his delectable dogs come regular-size and foot-long, and are served plain, with cheese and/or chili. Buffalo knows hot dogs, and they flock here to get 'em hot off the charcoal grill, often with an old-fashioned milkshake. Not into hot dogs? You can also order a burger or chicken sandwich. And with eight locations around the Buffalo area, you'll never be too far from one.

All locations open daily for lunch and dinner. Hot dogs $2–$3.50. No credit cards. 2351 Niagara Falls Blvd., Amherst; © **716/691-7883.** 1 Galleria Dr., Cheektowaga; © **716/683-7713.** 4878 Transit Rd., Depew; © **716/668-7533.** 6230 Shimer Rd., Lockport; © **716/439-4386.** 333 Meadow Dr., North Tonawanda; © **716/693-1960.** 3193 Orchard Park Rd., Orchard Park; © **716/675-4662.** 2312 Sheridan Dr., Tonawanda; © **716/834-6287.** 7018 Transit Rd., Williamsville; © **716/633-1700.**

3 Letchworth State Park

60 miles E from Buffalo; 35 miles S of Rochester

Of all the places that call themselves the "Grand Canyon of the East," Letchworth comes closest in living up to that claim. Stretched along a thin strip of the Genesee River, this park is one of the state's best and a destination unto itself as one of the most scenically magnificent areas in the eastern U.S. Lush woodlands sprawl over the park's 14,350 acres, bisected by the roaring Genesee River, which cuts a gorge through it, creating all sorts of waterfalls along the way. You can get up close and personal with the falls just by driving through the park; for an even closer view, go hiking along some of the 66 miles of trails. Stick to the southern end; as the park moves north, the land flattens out and isn't that interesting or dramatic. But down south, cliffs climb as high as 600 feet; there's also wonderfully dense forest. Keep an eye out for the park's beavers, deer, eagles, hawks, river otters, and tons of birds.

ESSENTIALS

GETTING THERE   From Buffalo, take the New York State Thruway (I-90) west to Route 400 south and take the East Aurora exit. Turn left onto Route 20A east. Follow 20A to Warsaw. Make a right onto Route 19 south to Route 19A, to Denton Corners Road. Turn left on Denton Corners Road and into the park. From Rochester, take I-390 to exit 7.

VISITOR INFORMATION   The grounds at Letchworth State Park, Castile (© **585/493-3600**), are open daily from 6am to 11pm year-round.

OUTDOOR PURSUITS

BALLOONING   One of the more unique ways to see this gorgeous split in the earth is from overhead in a hot-air balloon with **Balloons Over Letchworth** (© **585/493-3340;** www.balloonsoverletchworth.com). Float over the canyon in a seven-story hot-air balloon and look down on the many waterfalls and 600-foot cliffs. End the flight with a champagne celebration. Flights take place from April to October at a price of $200 per person, $210 in October when the leaves are gorgeous. Plan on 3 hours; you'll be in the air 45 minutes to an hour. Flights depart from the Middle/Upper Falls picnic area.

HIKING   The park's most scenic hike is the Gorge Trail, which follows the river as it meanders through the park, creating deep cuts in the earth. It's a 7-mile trail one-way and moderately difficult, so don't do the whole thing unless you're feeling adventuresome. For an easy .75-mile hike, and one you can do with the kids, the Pond Trail takes you out to a small pond stocked with fish (no fishing unless you have a license).

RAFTING   See the park from the bottom up, screaming as you course through the rollicking white water. Take a 5½-mile trip along the Genesee River through Class II white water with **Adventure Calls Outfitters** (© **888/270-2410** or 585/343-4710; www.adventure-calls.com). The trip is perfect for novices and families. You can even get out of the rafts and go bodysurfing at the New Wave Rapids or get soaking wet at the Leap of Faith. Open April to mid-November, Saturday, Sunday, and holidays ($30); from the end of June to the end of August also open Tuesday to Friday ($28).

WHERE TO STAY
EXPENSIVE
Glen Iris Inn 🅰🅰🅰 *Finds*   This historic former home of William Pryor Letchworth is the only inn inside the park. Rustic yet formal, it's been a hotel since 1914; today it's a yellow-and-green wooden home that's been restored to its roots. Rooms are on the small side, but tastefully decorated in antiques, floral prints, and lacy table coverings. Public spaces are done with dark woods in formal Victorian style, but are very cozy and comfortable. Step out onto the porch and take in the view of the Middle Falls and the rush of water, surrounded by the dense woodlands of the park. Though "lodge rooms" are more spacious, they're also more modern and bland; stay at the inn. There, the Cherry Suite is spacious and exquisite with gorgeous floors, but the real prize is the huge balcony with a view of the Middle Falls. Three separate homes, Caroline's Cottage, the Stone House, and the Chalet, offer lots of space and your own swath of land in the park. *Warning:* Rooms book up quickly and up to a year in advance. The restaurant is reviewed below.

7 Letchworth State Park, Castile, NY 14427. © 585/493-2622. Fax 585-493-5803. www.glenirisinn.com. 25 units. $85–$185 double; $195–$310 cottage. AE, DISC, MC, V. Closed mid-Nov to Good Friday (usually mid-Apr). **Amenities:** Restaurant; lounge; limited room service. *In room:* A/C, TV/VCR in lodge rooms and cottages, fridge and coffeemaker in lodge rooms and cottages.

CAMPING
Letchworth has camping and cabins set deep in the woods. Unfortunately, the 270 tent and trailer sites are located at the northern end of the park, far from the falls, and are open only May to October. The 82 cabins, though, are spread throughout the park. Don't expect anything fancy from those cabins—they're simple and rustic, with bunk beds, fridges, stoves, and (in some) cold-water-only sinks ($38–$99 a night, 2-night minimum with reservation). Call © **800/456-2267** to reserve.

WHERE TO DINE
EXPENSIVE
Glen Iris Inn 🅰🅰 *Finds* AMERICAN   Serving a small menu of classic American dishes, the Glen Iris is the area's best dining experience. Set in a formal Victorian dining

room, you'll tuck into dishes like a grilled New York strip steak with roasted pearl onions and baby mushrooms. Fish dishes are also delicious: Sample jumbo shrimp stuffed with feta cheese, wrapped in bacon, and served over sautéed spinach in a light cream sauce.

7 Letchworth State Park, Castile. ℂ **585/493-2622.** Reservations recommended. Lunch entrees $8.75–$11; dinner entrees $19–$23. AE, DISC, MC, V. Daily 8–10am and noon–4pm; Sun–Thurs 5–8pm; Fri–Sat 5–9pm.

4 Chautauqua Institution ✶✶

77 miles S of Buffalo; 142 miles SW of Rochester; 406 miles NW of New York City

Chautauqua Lake is more than just a gorgeous, 18-mile-long body of water surrounded by woods. Every summer, thousands of people flock to this tiny section of southwestern New York State for a learning vacation at one of the nation's most renowned arts institutes: Chautauqua Institution. A learning vacation is certainly more palatable when it's set among Victorian mansions on a stunning lake amid 750 acres of beautiful wooded grounds. This is no mere school: During its 9-week summer season, some 7,500 people are in residence daily, taking courses in art, music, dance, theater, and foreign languages. Others flock here for lectures by leading intellectuals, and for operas and concerts. You can choose from more than 2,000 events every summer, and some 150,000 people come here to do just that. Though many guests are on the far side of 70 years, there are extensive programs, from sailing to dancing, for kids of all ages. Even recreational day camp is offered at the Children's School (for kids ages 3–5) and the Boys & Girls Club (for kids 6–15).

All this began in 1874 when two Methodists founded the institution as an educational experiment in vacation learning. It grew quickly to include academic subjects, music, art, and physical education. The institution now boasts its own symphony; has operatic, theater, and ballet companies; and has popular entertainers perform in its 5,000-seat amphitheater.

Recreation and relaxation are an important part of the mix: Sand beaches, swimming, fishing, sailing, watersports, tennis, and 36 holes of golf are all on premises, as well as a gorgeous Victorian hotel with a first-class restaurant.

The 9-week summer season runs from the end of June to the end of August. Each week has a theme, which might be about governance, the Middle East, or science and ethics. Not much happens in the off season, though the library and archives are open.

ESSENTIALS

GETTING THERE You'll need to drive here. Chautauqua is 70 miles from Buffalo. From the New York State Thruway (I-90), take exit 60, then Route 394 west. From the Southern Tier Expressway (I-86/Rte. 17) if eastbound, take exit 7, then Route 33 north, and Route 394 east. If westbound, take exit 8, then Route 394 west.

VISITOR INFORMATION The **Chautauqua County Tourism Bureau** is located at the gates of Chautauqua Institution, Route 394 (ℂ **800/242-4569**). For information on the institution, call ℂ **800/836-ARTS** or visit www.chautauqua-inst.org.

ADMISSION TO THE INSTITUTION To get through the gates of the institution costs $15 for a daytime pass, $33 for day/evening, and $48 to be on the grounds from 7am to midnight, plus another $5 if you're spending the night. (That's in addition to any hotel charges.) Your gate fee gets you into all the lectures and entertainment (with the exception of opera and theater) that you can squeeze in. You can also take a dip in the lake. Additional sporting options, of which there are many, all cost extra.

OUTDOOR PURSUITS

The grounds of the institution have a wealth of activities, all of which cost extra beyond the gate fee. Activities include a state-of-the-art fitness center ($7 a day), a swimming pool ($2 per swim session), weeklong sailing instruction (call for rates), bike rental ($45 per week), tennis ($12–$16 per hour), and golf (greens fees $36 weekdays, $46 weekends), or you could always go swimming in the lake for free.

WHERE TO STAY

Thousands of Chautauqua guests choose to stay right on the institution's grounds in privately owned accommodations that range from quaint rooming houses and inns to luxury homes and condominiums. Some recommended properties include **Ashland Guest House,** 10 Vincent Ave. (© **888/598-5969** or 716/357-2257 [in season] or 716/837-3711 [off season]; ashlandguesthouse@yahoo.com); **Vera Guesthouse,** 25 S. Terrace (same contact info as the Ashland); **The Cambridge Inn,** 9 Roberts Ave. (© **716/357-3292** [in season] or 727/866-7965 [off season]; info@thecambridgeinn.com); **The Gleason,** 12 N. Lake Dr. (© **716/357-2595;** gleasonhotel@netzero.com); and the **Tally Ho Hotel,** 16 Morris Ave. (© **716/357-3325** [in season] or 954/920-2088 [off season]). Rooms may be available by the day, week, and/or season, and amenities run the gamut from a single bed with shared bathroom to gorgeous, fully loaded lakefront condos that go for a few thousand a week. For a complete list of accommodations, try the institution's online "Webervations" system that can help match your needs with appropriate lodgings.

A few chains in the area provide basic accommodations, including **Days Inn,** 10455 Bennett Rd., Fredonia (© **716/673-1351**); **Holiday Inn Express,** 3025 Rte. 426, Findley Lake (© **716/769-7900**); and **Best Western,** 3912 Vineyard Dr., Dunkirk (© **716/366-7100**).

Athenaeum Hotel ★★★   A step back in time, this Victorian grande dame sits on a tree-shaded hill overlooking Chautauqua Lake on the grounds of the institution. It's only open regularly during the Chautauqua Institution's season (end of June to end of Aug) and may be open at scattered times after that until October. It's unfortunate that such a gorgeous place has such a short season: Around since 1881 (and the first hotel in the world to have electric lights), the hotel retains its grandiose lobby with soaring ceilings and old woodwork. It feels very presidential, and indeed, no fewer than nine U.S. presidents have stayed here, from Grant to Clinton. Rooms have been renovated and, though quite comfortable, the basic structure hasn't been changed since it was built—so don't count on tons of space, and be prepared for cramped bathrooms. But you'll want to spend your time outdoors anyway, enjoying the grounds and the lake, or just lounging on the deck under the soaring arches and pillars of the outdoor space.

On S. Lake Dr. P.O. Box 66, Chautauqua, NY 14722. © **800/821-1881** or 716/357-4444. Fax 716/357-4175. 156 units. $299–$499 double. Rates include 3 meals daily. AE, DISC, MC, V. Parking $6 per day, valet $5 in, $5 out. **Amenities:** Restaurant; limited room service; laundry service; dry cleaning. *In room:* A/C, TV, hair dryer, iron.

CAMPGROUNDS

Right on Chautauqua Lake, you'll find 250 campsites with 2,000 feet of lakefront at the sprawling **Camp Chautauqua,** Route 394 (© **800/578-4849** or 716/789-3435). Count on lots of RV traffic. Still, you'll be able to find a spot for yourself to pop a tent. You'll also get tons of amenities like a teen center, coin-op laundry, heated pools, and tennis.

WHERE TO DINE

In addition to meals at the glorious Athenaeum (see below), casual dining for breakfast, lunch, or dinner is available on the institution's grounds at the **Refectory.** In Mayville, 4 miles away, there's **The Watermark,** 188 S. Erie St. (© **716/753-2900**); **Webb's Captain's Table,** 115 W. Lake Rd., Route 394 (© **716/753-2161**), overlooking Chautauqua Lake; and **Olive's at the Country Grill,** 43 S. Erie St. (© **716/753-2331**).

Athenaeum Hotel 👌👌 AMERICAN   Though most people who dine here are guests of the hotel, you can still enjoy a meal in this gorgeous grand hotel with a reservation and proper attire. Look out onto the lake as you enjoy the restaurant's formal elegance. Like the hotel, meals are very traditional, with classic American dishes. From the five-course menu, choose from a couple of different appetizers, soups, and salads. You may start off with a smoked salmon or tortellini Bolognese, then move through soup and salad, and onto a choice of four or five entrees, like a roast half duck or crab cakes a la Newport.

On S. Lake Dr. P.O. Box 66, Chautauqua. © 800/821-1881 or 716/357-4444. Jacket and tie required for men at dinner. Reservations required. Breakfast $16, lunch $23, dinner $36. AE, DISC, MC, V. Summer season daily 8am–9:30am, noon–1:30pm, and 5–7:30pm.

5 Niagara Falls 👌👌👌

21 miles NW of Buffalo; 165 miles NW of Ithaca

Okay, let's ignore the wedding and honeymoon thing for a minute and just focus on the water. It flows down the Niagara River, picking up speed as it courses along its ancient migratory pathway, reaching speeds of up to 30 mph before tumbling, hundreds of thousands of gallons at a time, over the craggy rocks of Niagara Falls. You can get the view with your toes just inches from both sets of falls, the American Falls and the Horseshoe Falls; you can also check them out from way up high, from your hotel room, or from down below, with the mist spraying up in your face.

That's the cool part of the falls. And since we share the attraction with Canada, you can take in the view from the New York side or the Ontario side. On the American side you can see the pre-falls rapids and get varied views of the water. Across the border is a gorgeous panorama of both the American Falls and Horseshoe Falls. The Canadian side is much better set up for travelers, with a wealth of hotels, restaurants, and activities that you won't find on the American side.

Now let's get to the kitsch. Ever since two American aristocrats honeymooned here in 1801, followed by Jerome Bonaparte (Napoleon's younger brother) and his bride 3 years later, the area surrounding the falls has been a draw for elopers and honeymooners, complete with heart-shaped whirlpool tubs and mirrored ceilings, along with wax museums and souvenir shops.

That Niagara Falls still exists, though it's changing; hotels with heart-shaped tubs are slowly disappearing, being replaced by standard chains and more deluxe options. The contest on the Canadian side is to see who can build the tallest hotel; right now it's the Embassy Suites (42 floors), but in January 2007, the Hilton broke ground to build up to 50 floors, and there are reports of an even taller hotel in the works.

The American side of the falls is still economically depressed, but it has taken a huge leap forward with one of the best hotels on either side of the falls, the 26-floor, 600-room **Seneca Niagara Casino Hotel & Spa** (310 Fourth St.; © **877/8-SENECA;** www.senecaniagaracasino.com), which fully opened in 2006. While it lacks the full-on view of the falls that you'll find in Canada, it's a luxury hotel in every sense of the word, with great restaurants, shows, and an ever-expanding casino.

Still, overall, the Canadian side is where the most fun is, especially for the kids. Bring your passport.

ESSENTIALS

GETTING THERE   Niagara Falls International Airport is mostly for charter and cargo planes (the one passenger option is Myrtle Beach Direct Air, with twice-weekly service to Myrtle Beach), so plan to fly into **Buffalo Niagara International Airport** (4200 Genesee St.; © **716/630-6000;** www.buffaloairport.com). See section 1, earlier in this chapter, for all airline listings. **ITA Shuttle** runs from Buffalo Niagara International Airport to both the American and the Canadian sides of the falls (© **800/ 551-9369** or 716/633-8294) five times a day. The cost is $30 per person one-way to the American side, $40 to the Canadian side.

When driving from I-90, take Route 290 to Route 190 to the Robert Moses Parkway—this will put you in downtown Niagara Falls, New York, and you'll see signs for the Rainbow Bridge to Canada. The **Greyhound station** (© 800/231-2222) is at 303 Rainbow Blvd.; **Amtrak** (© 800/USA-RAIL) comes right into the Niagara Falls station at 27th Street and Lockport Road.

VISITOR INFORMATION   On the American side, the **Niagara Tourism and Convention Corporation** is at 345 Third St., Suite 605, Niagara Falls (© 877/ **FALLS-US** or 716/282-8992; www.niagara-usa.com). Office hours are Monday to Friday from 8:30am to 5pm. In Canada, **Niagara Falls Tourism,** 5400 Robinson St., Niagara Falls, Ontario (© **800/563-2557;** www.niagarafallstourism.com), is open June to August, Monday to Friday from 8am to 5pm, Saturday and Sunday from 10am to 5pm; rest of the year 9am to 5pm daily.

Note: At press time, US$1=C$1.13.

WHEN TO GO   While hotels and restaurants stay open here year-round, several of the top falls attractions, like *Maid of the Mist* and Cave of the Winds, operate only when the ice has melted, which could be in April or as late as May. The season usually runs through October.

GETTING AROUND   A car is not essential for getting around on either side of the falls; in fact, if you're just planning on seeing the in-town attractions on either side, you'd be better off without one—traffic and parking in the summer are nightmarish, and parking at the attractions is expensive year-round. Though most attractions are fairly close to each other, you don't even have to walk: Shuttles on both sides of the falls will take you to the major hotels and the major attractions.

CROSSING THE BORDER   You can get to Canada by either driving or walking. I recommend hoofing it. The walk across the river is only a couple of city blocks long and you'll get great views along the way. More importantly, you'll avoid the lineup of cars—the wait can be an hour or more in summer. Either way, be sure you have proper documentation of citizenship: U.S. citizens will need a passport when arriving by land or sea. Customs folks on both sides will ask why you're going, how long you'll be, and,

---

Fun Fact **Niagara Falls for Marilyn**

Marilyn Monroe strutted her stuff at the falls in the 1953 flick *Niagara*. The following year, visitations to the falls skyrocketed.

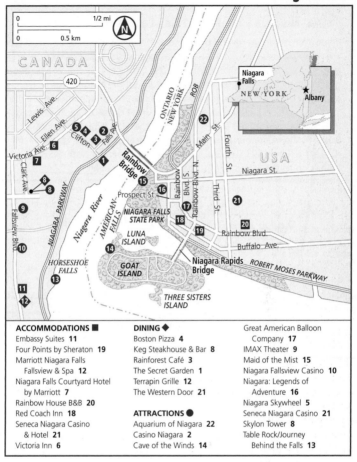

ACCOMMODATIONS ■

Embassy Suites **11**
Four Points by Sheraton **19**
Marriott Niagara Falls
 Fallsview & Spa **12**
Niagara Falls Courtyard Hotel
 by Marriott **7**
Rainbow House B&B **20**
Red Coach Inn **18**
Seneca Niagara Casino
 & Hotel **21**
Victoria Inn **6**

DINING ◆

Boston Pizza **4**
Keg Steakhouse & Bar **8**
Rainforest Café **3**
The Secret Garden **1**
Terrapin Grille **12**
The Western Door **21**

ATTRACTIONS ●

Aquarium of Niagara **22**
Casino Niagara **2**
Cave of the Winds **14**

Great American Balloon
 Company **17**
IMAX Theater **9**
Maid of the Mist **15**
Niagara Fallsview Casino **10**
Niagara: Legends of
 Adventure **16**
Niagara Skywheel **5**
Seneca Niagara Casino **21**
Skylon Tower **8**
Table Rock/Journey
 Behind the Falls **13**

upon your return, if you're bringing anything back with you. If you're in a car, be prepared to pop the trunk.

SEEING THE FALLS

Start off in the **Niagara Falls State Park** (① **716/278-1796;** www.niagarafallsstate park.com), the oldest state park in the United States. Designed by Frederick Law Olmsted, it's also the best thing about the American side of the falls. In winter it's quiet and serene; the summer brings a crush of people. You can either walk or ride the trolley ($2 adults, $1 kids 6–12; operates year-round) along its 3-mile route. Parking is $10. Walk out onto the newly renovated **Observation Tower,** which stretches into the river ($1; open late Mar–Dec).

In the park, visit **Cave of the Winds** ⁂ ($10 adults, $7 kids), where you'll take an elevator down 175 feet and emerge onto boardwalks to walk around the base of the American falls. They'll give you a raincoat and sandals.

Value **Niagara Falls Attractions Passes**

If you plan on doing several of the falls attractions, consider buying a pass. On the American side, the Park Service's **Passport to the Falls** (© 716/278-1796) will gain you up to 35% off the *Maid of the Mist,* Cave of the Winds, and other nearby attractions, plus unlimited free rides on the Niagara Scenic Trolley ($28 adults, $21 for ages 6–12). Pick up your pass at the visitor center inside the park. On the Canadian side, the **Niagara Falls & Great Gorge Adventure Pass** gets you into the Journey Behind the Falls, *Maid of the Mist,* White Water Walk, and the Butterfly Conservatory (plus transportation and discount coupons) for C$43 (US$38) adults, C$27 (US$24) for children 6 to 12. On both sides of the falls, admission to the attractions is free for kids 5 and under.

Accessible from the New York Observation Tower and from the Canadian side is the famous *Maid of the Mist* boat ride ★★★ (© 716/284-8897; www.maidofthemist.com; Apr or May–Oct, $13 adults, $7.30 kids). Hands down, this is the coolest way to see the falls. From up top, the water can look like a painting in slow motion. But board this famous boat and chug upriver toward the deafening roar of both the American and the Horseshoe Falls. You'll sail right up the base of both, with the mist spraying up in your face. Don't worry, they'll provide the slicker to keep you dry. The downside: The trip is only 30 minutes, and the boat will be packed.

Over on the Canadian side, the view is pure panorama and absolutely stunning. A walkway stretches along the Niagara River, offering a picture-perfect view with every step. When you get out to Table Rock, take the **Journey Behind the Falls** (© 905/354-1551). An elevator takes you down to tunnels, where you'll get to view the blur of water right behind Horseshoe Falls through little portholes cut in the rock. There's also a midfalls platform that gets you a dramatic midfalls view of Horseshoe, just off to its side. Admission is C$12 (US$11) for adults, C$7.50 (US$6.65) for kids 6 to 12, and free for children 5 and under.

On the Canadian side of the falls, every Friday and Sunday from May to September, there's a concert from 8 to 10pm, followed by a fireworks show. The falls are lit up every night of the year.

BIRD'S-EYE VIEWS

Creating Niagara Falls' distinctive skyline is **Skylon Tower,** 5200 Robinson St., Niagara Falls, Ontario (© 905/356-2651; www.skylontower.com), which rises 775 feet above the Maid of the Mist pool. It's been shooting people up above the falls since 1965, and it's a pretty cool view, though its restaurant is overrated. Take one of the yellow elevators up the outside of the tower (C$11/US$9.70 adults, C$9.95/US$8.80 seniors, C$6.45/US$5.70 children 12 and under). Helicopter tours are more expensive but clearly provide for the most dramatic views. Go with **Niagara Helicopters,** 3731 Victoria Blvd., Niagara Falls, Ontario (© 905/357-5672; www.niagarahelicopters.com), or **Rainbow Air,** 454 Main St., Niagara Falls, New York (© 716/284-2800). It's around $70 per person for a quick 10-minute ride. If you prefer to stay in touch with the earth, but still get an aerial view, you can go up 400 feet in a balloon that's still tethered to the ground with the **Great American Balloon Company,** 310 Rainbow Boulevard S., Niagara Falls, New York (© 716/278-0824). Take a 15-minute "ride over the falls" from May to

October. It's $20 for adults, $10 for kids. Or check out the new **Niagara Skywheel,** 4946 Clifton Hill (© **905/358-4793**), which circles up to 175 feet in the air. It's C$10 (US$8.85) for adults, C$6 (US$5.30) for kids.

OTHER ATTRACTIONS

The **Whirlpool Aero Car,** 3 miles north of the falls, at 3850 Niagara Pkwy. (© **905/ 354-5711**), is a cable car that takes you high above the churning white water of the **Niagara Whirlpool,** created by an abrupt change in the river's direction. Admission is C$11 (US$9.75) for adults, C$6.50 (US$5.75) for children 6 to 12, and free for children 5 and under. The **White Water Walk,** 2 miles north of the falls, at 4330 Niagara Pkwy. (© **905/374-1221**), is just a walk down by the white-water rapids on a boardwalk. If you're going to skip an attraction, this would be it. Admission is C$8.50 (US$7.50) for adults, C$5 (US$4.40) for children 6 to 12, and free for children 5 and under. Both of these close down in the heart of winter. The **Botanical Gardens,** 9 miles north of the falls, 2565 Niagara Pkwy. (© **905/358-0025**), boasts 100 acres of formal and informal gardens. Admission is free. On the grounds you'll also find a **Butterfly Conservatory,** which has more than 2,000 free-flying tropical butterflies in a rainforest-like setting. Admission is C$11 (US$9.75) adults, C$6.50 (US$5.75) children 6 to 12, and free for children 5 and under. Both of these are open year-round.

On the American side, the small, year-round **Aquarium of Niagara,** 701 Whirlpool St., Niagara Falls (© **800/500-4609** or 716/285-3575; www.aquariumof niagara.org), lets you get up close and personal with penguins, sea lions, and sharks, as well as rare species of fish. The best time to come is just before 2:30pm; that's when they feed the penguins (quite a sight). Then stay for the sea lion demonstration at 3pm. Admission is $8 for adults, $5.50 for kids 4 to 12. On the Canadian side, **Marineland,** 7657 Portage Rd. (© **905/356-9565**; www.marinelandcanada.com), is a lot more like SeaWorld (with prices to match)—a huge, summertime-only park with killer and beluga whales jumping out of the water, a petting zoo, and amusement park rides. Admission is C$39 (US$34) for adults, C$32 (US$28) for kids.

Then catch **"Niagara: Legends of Adventure,"** a dramatic 40-minute action film, on the new 45×25-foot screen on the American side, 1 Prospect Park (© **866/750-4629**). Admission is $10, $6 for kids 6 to 12. Or see it on the Canadian side at the IMAX theater at 6170 Fallsview Blvd. (© **866/405-IMAX**), where it costs C$14 (US$12) and C$9.85 (US$8.75) for kids 4 to 12.

On the American side, **Old Fort Niagara,** in Youngstown (© **716/745-7611;** www.oldfortniagara.org), is a 17th-century fort on one of the most scenic (and strategic, of course) pieces of land in upstate New York—right on Lake Ontario at the mouth of the Niagara River. The carefully arranged buildings form what's believed to be the longest continuously operating fort in North America. Used by the French, British, and Americans, it has cannons, living quarters decked out in the time period, and underground gunpowder-holding rooms. There's also a new $5-million visitor center to explain it all, featuring a preserved 24×28-foot 1812 flag that once flew over the fort. Open year-round; admission is $10 adults, $6 children 6 to 12. Over in Canada, **Old Fort Erie,** 50 Lakeshore Rd., Fort Erie, Ontario (© **905/871-0540;** www.oldforterie.com), is a series of flint-stone buildings 17 miles south of the falls, which saw action only during the War of 1812. Interiors are reconstructed similar to Fort Niagara, with gunpowder storage, officers' quarters, and soldiers' living areas giving insight into the living conditions at the time. Open mid-May to mid-October. Admission is C$9 adults (US$7.95) and C$5 (US$4.40) kids 6 to 12.

Kids **Kid Stuff in Canada's Clifton Hill**

Set up to keep kids entertained all day and night, the Clifton Hill area on the Canadian side (www.cliftonhill.com) abounds with haunted houses, Disney-esque rides, and nonstop video game action. Walk down the strip and duck into whatever grabs your attention. Stop in at the **Ripley's 4D Moving Theater,** 4983 Clifton Hill (© 905/356-2261), and ride the virtual roller coaster (buckle up—your seat heaves and pitches in sync with the roller coaster movie). You can skip the Ripley's Believe It or Not! Museum; the **Guinness World Records Museum,** 4943 Clifton Hill (© 905/356-2299), is more interesting—you'll learn useless trivia like the largest collection of naval fluff (.54 oz.).

For a boat ride you won't soon forget, climb aboard a 48-person craft with **Whirlpool Jet Boat Tours** (© **905/468-4800;** www.whirlpooljet.com). Tours leave from 115 S. Water St., Lewiston, and 61 Melville St., Niagara-on-the-Lake, Ontario. Crashing along at speeds up to 65 mph, you splash along the Niagara River through the Niagara Gorge and into the Whirlpool on this 1-hour, 18-mile ride. With all the white-water splash, you'll get wet—soaking wet, actually. (Bring a complete change of clothes.) You won't see the falls on this trip, but you do get to see what happens after the water goes over the brink and through the river canyon.

SHOPPING

Yes, there are tons of souvenir shops here selling everything from commemorative spoons to snow globes. But there are a couple of things you can get only on the Canadian side, such as a Cuban cigar (which, of course, you're not supposed to bring back over the border). Lots of places sell them (you'll see the signs): One of the better places is **Gordon's Cigars and Pipes,** 5860 Ferry St., Niagara Falls, Ontario (© **905/358-7425**). His best cigars are in the back room. And for something emblazoned with the red coats of the Canadian Mounties, head to the **Mounted Police Trading Post,** 5685 Falls Ave. (© **800/372-0472** or 905/374-2288). If outlet malls are your thing, you have a couple of options: **Fashion Outlets,** 1900 Military Rd. (© **800/414-0475**), has Calvin Klein, Gap, and Nine West, among others, while on the other side, head to **Canada One Factory Outlets,** 7500 Lundy's Lane, Niagara Falls, Ontario (© **866/284-5781** or 905/356-8989), with Esprit, Nike, and the Rocky Mountain Chocolate Factory—*mmmm.*

WHERE TO STAY

Accommodations range from huge chains to quaint B&Bs to disgusting motels. In general, hotels are much nicer on the Canadian side. Rates from June to August are decidedly higher than the rest of the year and fluctuate wildly depending on the particular week, whether any events are in town, and, of course, availability. So if you call to book and the rates are astronomical, try the following week.

Both sides abound in chain hotels. On the American side, good choices include **Comfort Inn,** 1 Prospect Pointe (© **800/28-HOTEL** or 716/284-6835), which is superclose to the water; **Crowne Plaza,** 300 Third St. (© **877/227-6963** or 716/285-3361); and the **Hampton Inn,** 501 Rainbow Blvd. (© **800/426-7866** or 716/285-6666).

On the Canadian side, the **Quality Inn,** 4946 Clifton Hill (© **800/263-7137** or 905/358-3601), puts you in the middle of all the Disney-like action, as does the **Super 8,** 5706 Ferry St. (© **888/442-6095**). You'll also find a **Best Western,** 6289 Fallsview Ave. (© **866/475-0004** or 905/356-0551).

EXPENSIVE

Marriott Niagara Falls Fallsview & Spa ✮✮✮ For the most up-close and personal view of the falls, combined with luxury accommodations, this is the place to stay. Closer to the falls than anyone (just 300 ft.) and built in a curving design that allows virtually every room an unobstructed view of the falls, the hotel also boasts loads of amenities and excellent service, along with a recently expanded spa. Even standard rooms are big with large bathrooms; upgraded rooms let you take a whirlpool bath with the falls just a glance away. With comfy beds, a spa, a great restaurant (reviewed below), a pool, and the best hotel falls view in town, you may never want to leave the place. One annoyance: As with the Embassy Suites, valet parking is mandatory.

6740 Fallsview Blvd., Niagara Falls, Ontario, Canada L2G 3W6. © **888/501-8916** or 905/357-7300. Fax 905/357-0490. www.niagarafallsmarriott.com. 432 units. C$119–C$599 double (US$105–US$530). Packages available. AE, DC, DISC, MC, V. Valet parking C$20 (US$18). **Amenities:** Restaurant; lounge; large indoor pool; small exercise room; spa; 2 Jacuzzis; sauna; children's programs; game room; concierge; tour desk; small business center; limited room service; massage; laundry service; same-day dry cleaning; executive-level rooms. *In room:* A/C, TV w/pay movies, dataport, minibar, coffeemaker, hair dryer, iron, safe.

Red Coach Inn ✮✮ *(Finds)* Just across the street from the rapids, this 1920s-era Tudor-style hotel with a distinctive gabled roof is one of the only luxury properties on the American side, and the most comfortably intimate hotel on either side. Skip the tiny standard rooms and go with a suite; these are more like apartments, with full kitchens, dining tables, comfy chairs and sofas, and tons of amenities. The guest rooms at the nonsmoking hotel are carpeted and decked out in antiques, but you won't find them stuffy or musty at all; staying here feels just like relaxing at home. In fact, there's not even a formal front desk—you just check in at the restaurant. All suites have a view of the rapids, a separate bedroom, and spacious bathrooms.

2 Buffalo Ave., Niagara Falls, NY 14303. © **866/719-2070** or 716/282-1459. www.redcoach.com. 19 units. July–Aug $139–$179 double, $189–$339 suite; Jan–Mar $89–$129 double, $129–$249 suite. Rates change monthly in spring and fall and are in between low and high. Packages available. AE, DISC, MC, V. **Amenities:** Restaurant; lounge. *In room:* A/C, TV/VCR, dataport, kitchens (in some units), fridge, microwave, coffeemaker, hair dryer, CD player.

Seneca Niagara Casino & Hotel ✮✮✮ Rising 26 stories above the low-slung landscape, this newcomer (which opened fully in 2006) has quickly become the luxury standard-bearer for the area. No, you won't get a view of the falls—the hotel is a few blocks away—but for a combination of modern amenities and comfort, it's hard to do better on either side of the falls. Rooms are decked out in subdued tones and plump furniture, along with Native American design touches, in honor of the Seneca Indian owners. Even the standards are large, but upgrade to a corner suite and you'll get an enormous space, two full walls of floor-to-ceiling windows, and a Jacuzzi tub with a dramatic view (on one side of the hotel, anyway) of the river and the Canadian skyline. Flat-screen TVs and great sound systems make it hard to leave the rooms, but you'll want to explore the several fine restaurants (their steakhouse is reviewed below), spa, shows, and of course lots of gambling space.

310 Fourth St., Niagara Falls, NY 14303. ✆ **877/873-6322.** www.senecaniagaracasino.com. 604 units. May–Oct $129–$199 double, $299 suite; Nov–Apr $99 double, $199 suite. Packages available. AE, DC, DISC, MC, V. **Amenities:** 5 restaurants; 2 delis; 3 lounges; large indoor pool; exercise room; spa; Jacuzzi; concierge; tour desk; business center; salon; 24-hour room service; massage; laundry service; same-day dry cleaning; high-roller rooms. *In room:* A/C, TV/DVD w/pay movies, dataport, minibar, fridge (in suites), coffeemaker, hair dryer, iron, safe.

MODERATE

Embassy Suites ⭑⭑   With spacious suites that rise 42 stories directly above the falls, the Embassy Suites doesn't disappoint with its square footage or its views. At press time, it is the tallest hotel in town, and the rooms on the highest floor are very dramatic (the best ones have fireplaces, Jacuzzis, and curving windows with views of both falls). There's also the bonus of the Embassy Suites–standard extensive breakfast each morning and a happy hour each evening, plus a large indoor pool. Still, this is no Ritz-Carlton, so while the furniture is comfy and serviceable, it's not exactly high-end. Also, be prepared: Some of the living rooms are windowless and dark.

6700 Fallsview Blvd., Niagara Falls, Ontario, Canada L2G 3W6. ✆ **800/420-6980** or 905/356-3600. Fax 905/356-0472. www.embassysuitesniagara.com. 512 units. End of May to Labor Day C$99–C$299 double (US$88–US$265) mid-week, C$199–C$399 double (US$176–US$353) weekend; Labor Day to end of May C$199–C$399 double (US$176–US$353); full breakfast and evening happy hour included. Packages available. AE, DC, DISC, MC, V. Valet parking: $C20 (US$18) **Amenities:** 2 restaurants; deli; lounge; indoor pool; small exercise room; Jacuzzi; game room; concierge; tour desk; small business center; limited room service; coin-op laundry; laundry service; same-day dry-cleaning. *In room:* A/C, TV w/pay movies, dataport, kitchenette, minibar, coffeemaker, hair dryer, iron, safe.

Four Points by Sheraton ⭑⭑   This first-rate property on the New York side of the falls saw a $2-million renovation in 2006, and it shows. Wood floors, Sealy pillow-top mattresses, airy spaces, and comfy furniture give these rooms the feel of being more expensive than they are, and the hotel overall has a good mix of amenities. You'll also find a view of the rapids from some rooms—about as good as the views get on this side. The only downside: Bathrooms are a bit cramped.

114 Buffalo Ave., Niagara Falls, NY 14303. ✆ **800/368-7764** or 716-285-2521. Fax 716-285-0963. www.fourpoints.com/niagarafalls. 189 units. July–Sept $140 double; May–June and Oct–Nov $110 double; Dec–Apr $80 double; suites $60 more. Packages available. AE, DC, DISC, MC, V. **Amenities:** Restaurant; deli; indoor pool; exercise room; Jacuzzi; sauna; arcade; concierge; limited room service; coin-op washers and dryers; laundry service; same-day dry-cleaning; executive-level rooms. *In room:* A/C, TV w/pay movies, dataport, kitchenette (in suites), coffeemaker, hair dryer, iron.

Niagara Falls Courtyard Hotel by Marriott ⭑⭑   Right across the street from the HoJo, the Courtyard offers rooms that are a little larger in a hotel that's decidedly newer and less kitschy. You'll find an upscale restaurant and a large pool area, and all in the same great location—close to everything without being in the middle of the Clifton Hill mayhem. Rooms are spacious and simply furnished. It's a great option for families, but with fireplace and Jacuzzi rooms available, it's also an affordable option for couples.

5950 Victoria Ave., Niagara Falls, Ontario, Canada L2G 3L7. ✆ **800/321-2211** or 905/358-3083. Fax 905/358-8720. www.nfcourtyard.com. 258 units. July–Aug C$139–C$349 (US$123–US$309) double; Sept–June C$79–C$299 (US$70–US$265) double. Packages available. AE, DC, DISC, MC, V. Self-parking C$10 (US$8.85). **Amenities:** Indoor-outdoor pool; small exercise room; Jacuzzi; sauna; children's programs; game room; tour desk; coin-op laundry. *In room:* A/C, TV w/pay movies, dataport, coffeemaker, hair dryer, iron, safe.

INEXPENSIVE

Rainbow House B&B   Staying at this small inn is like visiting your favorite grandmother's house. Owner Laura Lee's home is charmingly cluttered and extremely cheery and welcoming. The nonsmoking rooms are decked out in wicker and wood furnishings and filled with knickknacks; though they aren't huge, they all have private bathrooms. Stick with one of the standard rooms—the suite isn't worth the extra dough. ***Bonus:*** The place has a wedding chapel if you get the itch to tie the knot.

423 Rainbow Blvd. S., Niagara Falls, NY 14303. ℭ 800/724-3536 or 716/282-1135. www.rainbowchapel.com. 4 units. Mid-Mar–mid-Nov $80–$150 double; mid-Nov–mid-Mar weekdays $65–$95 double, weekends $75–$110 double. Rates include breakfast. MC, V. Take Robert Moses Pkwy. to Fourth St., turn right onto Rainbow Blvd. *In room:* A/C, no phone.

Victoria Inn   Even the budget chains in the heart of Clifton Hill push their rates through the roof in summer, but this family-run inn is holding fast to its menu of decent accommodations at good prices. No, the digs are nothing fancy, but they are clean, and some even have balconies overlooking the street. And cheap prices aren't the only thing holding fast; this is one of the few places left to still offer heart-shaped Jacuzzi tubs in some rooms.

5869 Victoria Ave., Niagara Falls, Ontario, Canada L2G 3L3. ℭ 905/374-6522. Fax 905/374-3038. www.victoriamotor inn.com. 33 units. Memorial Day to Labor Day midweek C$70–C$100 (US$62–US$88), weekend C$129–C$150 (US$114–US$133) double, C$10 ($US$8.85) more for suite; early Sept to late May midweek C$40–C$65 (US$35–US$58), weekend C$70–C$90 (US$62–US$80) double. DISC, MC, V. **Amenities:** Restaurant; outdoor pool. *In room:* A/C, TV, no phone.

CAMPGROUNDS

Set right on the shore of Lake Ontario, **Four Mile Creek State Park,** Lake Road, Youngstown (ℭ 716/745-3802), is a huge expanse of park with 266 campsites and great views—on a clear day you can see Toronto. Be sure to pay the few bucks extra for a prime site, which puts you right on the water. There's lots of exploring to do around here: The marsh at the mouth of Four Mile Creek is home to many varieties of wildlife, like great blue herons, along with hiking trails along densely wooded bluffs.

WHERE TO DINE
EXPENSIVE

Terrapin Grille ✵✵✵ AMERICAN   Combining one of the best restaurants in town with the best unobstructed falls view, the Marriott Hotel's restaurant is an ideal—if pricey—fine-dining experience. Yes, every table has a view of the falls, but with just one wall of floor-to-ceiling windows, some tables are better than others—try to get one as close as possible to the windows. The restaurant, done in classic deep reds with low lighting, makes for a romantic experience. And the cuisine is some of the city's best, incorporating local fruits wherever possible and fusing traditional Italian, French, and Asian cuisines. There are pastas on the menu, but you'll want to come for steak and/or seafood, the specialties. Consider delicious entrees such as rack of lamb with a red-wine reduction, or the signature dish: sea bass with cilantro chili and a raspberry reduction. There's also an extensive wine list featuring area wines.

At the Marriott Fallsview, 6740 Fallsview Blvd., Niagara Falls, Ontario. ℭ 905/357-7300, ext. 4220. Reservations suggested. Lunch C$14–C$45 (US$12–US$40); dinner main courses C$26–C$69 (US$23–US$61). AE, DC, DISC, MC, V. Daily 6am–11pm.

The Western Door ✵✵✵ STEAKHOUSE   The new standard of luxury on the American side—the Seneca Niagara Hotel—has some pretty serious restaurant firepower to complement its fancy digs, and the Western Door is the nicest of several great places inside. Walk up the stairs, away from the clanging machines, and you enter a hide-out full of dark woods, romantic candlelight, swirling carpets, and top-quality meats (which you can inspect at the meat counter in the back). Appetizers like the blackened shrimp are worth sampling, but meat is fittingly the real star here: Filets and rib-eyes come perfectly marbled and cooked exactly how you like; the huge slab of prime rib is excellent as well. The usual steakhouse sides are just average, but that's okay, since you'll want to save room for the wonderful and huge desserts, like sweet-potato-glazed cheesecake. The only annoyance is a lack of communication between the two servers who wait on each table, so you may end up repeating every order and request. Still, reserve a table in one of the nooks overlooking the casino floor and you'll truly feel like a high roller.

At the Seneca Niagara Casino & Hotel, 310 Fourth St., Niagara Falls, NY 14303. ℭ 877/873-6322. www.seneca niagaracasino.com. Reservations suggested. Main courses $21–$58. AE, DC, DISC, MC, V. Wed–Thurs 5–10pm; Fri–Sat 5–11pm; Sun 4–9pm.

MODERATE

Keg Steakhouse & Bar ℛ STEAKHOUSE   This Canadian steakhouse chain feels more expensive than it is, with its classic wood decor, relaxed setting, and stone fire-place. You might be fooled into believing it's not a chain; the food, too, is a cut above chain-restaurant cuisine. Excellent steaks are the specialty, but don't overlook the chicken and ribs. Everything comes keg-size (in America we say "supersized") so there's no need to order appetizers. Do grab a side dish: The steamed asparagus, gar-lic cheese toast, and other dishes are big enough to share.

5950 Victoria Ave., Niagara Falls, Ontario. ℭ 905/353-4022. Main courses C$20–C$30 (US$18–US$27). AE, DC, DISC, MC, V. Mid-June to Labor Day noon–11pm weekday, noon–1am weekend; Labor Day to mid-June noon–10pm weekday, noon–1am weekend.

Rainforest Café ℛ *Kids* AMERICAN   Family fun in a place straight out of Disney. Predictably set in the kid-centered Clifton Hill neighborhood, this outlet of the Rain-forest Café chain boasts faux rain and trees with comical touches like bar stools painted to resemble animal tail-ends (complete with tails). There are endless distrac-tions: With an 80-foot erupting volcano and a shark exhibit, it's every kid's dream come true. The food is fine and comes humorously named, like the Planet Earth Pasta and the Rumble in the Jungle turkey wrap, and it spans the range from chicken-fried steak to coconut shrimp, burgers, and pizza.

5785 Falls Ave., Niagara Falls, Ontario. ℭ 905/374-4444. Reservations recommended. Main courses C$13–C$23 (US$12–US$20). AE, DC, DISC, MC, V. June to Labor Day daily 11am–1am; early Sept to May Sun–Thurs 11am–11pm, Fri–Sat 11am–midnight.

INEXPENSIVE

Boston Pizza ℛ *Kids* PIZZA   Games, games, and more games. Oh yeah, and food. Boston Pizza combines every video game on earth with a restaurant under the same roof. Right in the heart of the Clifton Hill action, the place runs on its own pace, which is usually fast forward. Kids pour into the video game area nonstop, returning to their tables for a bite of burger. Adults crowd around the noisy bar to watch sports on the many TVs. Food-wise, folks come for the pizza, with more than 20 specialties.

4950 Clifton Hill, Niagara Falls, Ontario. ℭ 905/358-2750. Main courses C$13–C$21 (US$12–US$19). AE, DC, DISC, MC, V. Daily 11am–2am.

The Secret Garden ITALIAN AMERICAN   Hardly a secret, this restaurant, often frequented by large tour groups, is front and center on River Road, overlooking the falls. There is a beautiful garden outside; unfortunately, you can't see it from inside the restaurant. In fact, one wall of windows just gives you a view of the gift shop. The other windows do give you a good view of the falls, but come here only during the summer months, when you can sit outside and take in the view of the falls from the patio. The view almost makes up for the bland menu of salads, sandwiches, and pastas.

5827 River Rd., Niagara Falls, Ontario. © 905/358-4588. Reservations suggested. Lunch C$9–C$18 (US$7.95–US$16); dinner main courses C$9–C$30 (US$7.95–US$27). AE, DC, DISC, MC, V. May–Oct daily 8am–11pm; Nov–Apr daily 8am–8pm.

NIAGARA FALLS AFTER DARK

GAMBLING   In 2002, **Seneca Niagara Casino,** 310 Fourth St., Niagara Falls (© 877/8-SENECA or 716/299-1100), opened on the American side, and this Seneca Indian–operated casino just keeps growing. Over the river, the **Niagara Fallsview Casino Resort,** 6380 Fallsview Blvd., Niagara Falls, Ontario (© 888/ FALLSVU), is a sprawling complex of 180,000 square feet with more than 3,000 slot machines and 150 gaming tables. **Casino Niagara,** 5705 Falls Ave., Niagara Falls, Ontario (© 888/946-3255), has had to take a back seat to the newer Fallsview, but this gambling standby is good to hit if the new casino is overly crowded. Both the Americans and the Canadians have ubiquitous slots, as well as blackjack, craps, roulette, music, bars, restaurants, and nonstop action.

NIGHTCLUBS   The drinking age in Canada is 19, and most clubs there cater to the younger (read: much younger) set. **Pumps Nightclub & Patio,** 5815 Victoria Ave. (© 905/371-8646), offers a great outdoor space for those hot summer nights. **Rumours Night Club,** 4960 Clifton Hill (© 905/358-6152), is smack in the middle of the tourist district and regularly sees lines out the door. **Club Rialto,** 5875 Victoria Ave. (© 905/356-5646), is the one place in town that caters to an over-30 crowd, with music that's a little less hip-hop and a little more Billy Joel. If Vegas-like shows are your thing, you'll be in heaven in the **Seneca Events Center** (at the **Seneca Niagara Casino**), 310 Fourth St., Niagara Falls (tickets © 716/852-5000), where you'll find big names like Bill Cosby and Aretha Franklin, or hit the other bars in this huge complex. Performers like Don Henley and Jay Leno take the stage at the **Avalon Ballroom** (at the **Niagara Fallsview Casino Resort**), 6380 Fallsview Blvd., Niagara Falls, Ontario (tickets © 888/836-8118). There you can also catch music and comedy acts in the **365 Club** or listen to live music at the **Splash Bar.** Call the resort's main number (© 888/FALLSVU) for information on performances.

Index

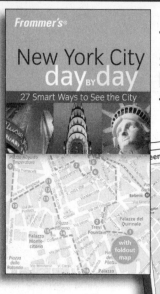

CLOSED
due to
accidental demolition

WEGEN BISSIGEN
EICHHÖRNCHEN GESCHLOSSEN

CERRADO
CABRAS

Κλειστό
Μετεωρίτες

プール も

POOL CLOSED

ELECTRIC EELS

閉鎖中

Hotel
closed for
facelifting

FERMÉ POUR
RAISON
DE GRÈVE
DES BONNES

FECHADO!
POR CAUSA DE
ATAQUES DOS CROCODILOS

I don't speak sign language.

A hotel can close for all kinds of reasons.
Our Guarantee ensures that if your hotel's undergoing construction, we'll
let you know in advance. In fact, we cover your entire travel experience.
See www.travelocity.com/guarantee for details.

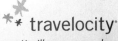

travelocity
You'll never roam alone.

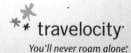